Advance Praise for Anne ᵤₚ...

"A remarkable well-written, wholly unique and seminal study combining a deep understanding of the academic literature on terrorism with an extraordinary number of sensitive and revealing interviews with terrorists. Everyone interested in terrorism will find this study fascinating and rewarding." —*David C. Rapoport, Founding and CoEditor, Journal of Terrorism and Political Violence*

"The embarrassing truth about Terrorism Studies is that most writers on the subject have never met a terrorist. Dr. Anne Speckhardis an exception; in the last ten years she conducted more than 400 interviews with terrorists and other members of the radical milieu they come from, making her work highly original and, indeed, unique. With her empathetic approach, she makes clear that most terrorists are both shockingly normal and human—but also tormented souls. Nobody has gotten closer to the 'heart of darkness' than she has. An amazing achievement." —*Alex P. Schmid, Director, Terrorism Research Initiative*

"A daring woman with an open heart." —*Farhana Qazi, Counter-Terrorism Expert*

"Anne's passport is filled with stamps from obscure and far-flung corners of the earth. All these countries have something in common: terrorism. Other researchers may interview terrorists in a controlled setting. Anne is one of a handful who goes alone and without security into the lion's den to interview her subjects who most often have blood on their hands. This is a first-hand account from an internationally recognized terrorism expert and it's sensational!" —*Peter S. Probst, Former Assistant for Terrorism Intelligence, Office of the Assistant Secretary of Defense for Special Operations and Low-Intensity Conflict (OASD/SO/LIC), Former Special Assistant for Concept Development - Office of Special Planning - Office of the Secretary of Defense and Former CIA Officer (Directorate of Operations and Directorate of Intelligence)*

"Invaluable to those in the field of terrorism studies, as well as to the general public." —*Yoram Schweitzer, Director of the Low Intensity Warfare and Terrorism Project and Senior Research Fellow at Israel's Institute for National Security Studies*

"Anne Speckhard is one of the rare psychologists who studies terrorism objectively without preconceived notions. She insisted to go to the Middle East, and at times to take serious risks, to meet with suicide bombers, to visit them in prisons, and to interview their families and friends in their homes. She tried to understand, not only the specific mind of the potential terrorist, but also his environment, motives and misrepresentations. As a result, Dr. Speckhard treats the phenomenon of terrorism as one that arises within a socio-political and cultural context as well as within the individual psyche. She wisely understands the clear distinction between personal faith and belief tradition, and the possible perverted and brutal acts of a terrorist. Her condemnation of this type of violence is carefully nuanced and has nothing to do with the incorrect and misguided conclusions of many other western experts who broadly and incorrectly condemn Islam as a religion, and Islamic civilization in totality. I highly recommend reading Talking to Terrorists."—*Mokhtar Benabdallaoui: Professor of Islamology, Hassan II University, Casablanca – Morocco*

"Anne has made seminal contributions to the field of terrorism research, particularly in highlighting the importance of geography and trauma. Her ability to extract critical information related to motivations is absolutely uncanny, as is her ability to get access to radicalized individuals and their victims. One of the best in this area."—*Laurie Fenstermacher, U.S. Air Force Research Laboratory*

"Talking To Terrorists is an important contribution to the literature. Written by a psychologist with extensive field experience interviewing terrorists from a wide variety of backgrounds, countries and contexts, the book provides critical new insights into the contemporary terrorist mindset." —*Professor Bruce Hoffman, Director, Center for Security Studies, Georgetown University*

TALKING TO TERRORISTS

UNDERSTANDING THE PSYCHO-SOCIAL MOTIVATIONS OF MILITANT JIHADI TERRORISTS, MASS HOSTAGE TAKERS, SUICIDE BOMBERS & "MARTYRS"

ANNE SPECKHARD, PH.D.

First published 2012
by Advances Press
McLean, VA

Book Design by Nikki Hensley (www.hensleygraphics.com)
Editing by Jayne Carapezzi Pillemer
Cover Design by Jessica Speckhard

Library of Congress Control Number: 2012917370

ISBN 9781935866510 – Talking to Terrorists Hardcover
ISBN 9781935866527 – Talking to Terrorists E Pub
ISBN 9781935866534 – Talking to Terrorists Paperback

DEDICATION

To Daniel, my husband, my children Leah, Jessica and Danny who taught me what love is really all about, and Katarina who keeps us all laughing.

TABLE OF CONTENTS

FOREWORD

by Reuven Paz, Israel

In the first weeks of my work in the Israeli security service, I was just 21-years-old. An older veteran member of the service, who was born in Palestine/Eretz Israel and who had grown up with Arabs, took me on a tour among the Arabs of the Galilee. On the way, in nowhere, he suddenly stopped the car and asked me to follow him. We went to the side of the road and he pointed at an old Arab man, one of those we used to call Israeli Arabs as if they belonged to us Israelis.

"What do you see?" he asked me. I carefully looked at the old Arab man but could not see in him anything special. "Look what he is doing," said my companion who acted as my trainer. I looked again and suddenly I realized that the man, dressed in a traditional Arab costume, wearing a Kuffiyyah on his head, standing in the middle of an uncultivated field, leaning on a rough wooden stick, was checking the soil. He slowly bent down, collected a handful of land, hardly straightened his back, and rubbed the land in his hand, with closed eyes, as if he was touching a beloved woman. He repeated it several times, each time with sighs probably from back pains. The somewhat surrealist view fascinated me, in addition to the fragrant land, which was a bit wet from the last rain, a few weeks earlier.

My trainer than looked at me and said: "Whatever we think of them, this bond to the land is something we shall never take from them. It is part of their genes, even if they move to the city and live in modern apart- ments. No war, fighting, arrests, or prison, will ever change it. Therefore, we should first study their minds and genes and RESPECT them, even though we bitterly fight some of them. This is the foundation of what we call counter-terrorism".

His words reminded me of my late mother, who was born in a Jewish settlement on the border of Lebanon and grew up with Arab neighbors, spoke Arabic fluently, and knew very well themes of Arab culture. I grew up on her stories about the South Lebanese who used to work for the Jewish farmers until 1948. One of her favorite stories was how as a little girl she loved sitting close to the female workers while they ate their poor lunch. However poor it was, she envied them for eating a piece of homemade

Arab bread, dipping it in fresh and aromatic olive oil, with some scallion they had picked in their small garden on the way to work. They did not stop talking, mainly telling each other the latest gossip in the villages of the region. They knew everything. Nothing skipped their ears or eyes. The half an hour they sat there, laughing with no men around, was their hour of freedom.

This story, and many others I heard from my mother, bore the "perfume" of a fascinating culture, even though it was also the culture of our enemy. It planted within me two elements. One was the drive to study Arabic, which I started at the age of 13. Since that age and until today, for 48 years, there has not been one day of my life that I was not engaged in Arabic, and Islam, and with Arabs and Muslims, both with sworn enemies or good friends. When I studied for my B.A. degree in the department of Arabic language and literature, we, the Jewish students, were in the minority. I befriended very quickly the Arab students, almost all of them, including those who were radicalized by the rise of Palestinian nationalism in the early 1970s, in response to the revived connections between the Arabs in Israel and their brothers in the Palestinian occupied territories in the wake of the 1967 war. Once I was sick for a few days and did not show up at the university. One of these days there was a knock on the door of my parents, where I was still living, and an Arab student came to visit me and see how I was doing. He held in his hands a big carton box with a huge typical Arab cake, decorated with lots of whipped cream colored in many colors. It was a gesture he did almost automatically as part of his culture, and it was very touching. Even this gesture was part of the manners and customs we ought to learn about the societies we fight with.

The second element is not just the need to study the culture of our foes, with whom we might be allies one day, but to carefully understand the significance of culture and state of mind in the emergence and behavior of terrorists and political violence. We Israelis, who have lived with Arab, Palestinian, and or Lebanese terrorism for over a century, should understand that this terrorism, violence, wrath, wish for revenge grows on a certain background—whether right, wrong, twisted, false, or a result of poisoning agitation—and this is something we have to acknowledge as part of countering it.

I wrote all the above said, which may surprise some of the readers since it comes from an Israeli, an ex-agent of the Israeli security service, and an expert for the Jihadi most evil terrorism of modern times. However, I demand from the Arabs, Muslims, and above all the Palestinians, to study and primarily understand the effects of two millenniums of anti-Semitism and persecution of Jews, and the significance and centrality of the Holocaust in the Israeli life and norms of behavior, that is so suspicious towards the others, the Goyim/gentiles, and tends not to trust anyone but rely only on ourselves, and above all and under the slogan of NEVER AGAIN, create a powerful military force and consider it an integral part of our society, culture, and pride. And in the same way, I also demand from my Israeli colleagues to study and understand the suffering and tragedy of the Palestinians, whether they brought it upon themselves or not. One of the best Israeli intellectuals, Mr. Aba Even (Abe Evan) who served in the 1970s as Minister of foreign affairs, coined a famous term, saying that "the Palestinians have never missed an opportunity to miss an opportunity". Whether he was right or wrong, Israelis and Palestinians, Sunnis and Shi'as, Chechens and Russians, or minorities of immigrants and the majority societies should talk to each other, during the fight or following it.

Dr. Speckhard takes us in her book and presents a very accurate and realistic photo for the better or worse. She comes from a very comfortable background, of a skilled and experienced psychologist, the wife of a U.S. ambassador, and involved in workshops all over the world, and navigates during an entire decade in the dirtiest, darkest, and most problematic places of the world, looking not just for terrorists but for the people and human beings inside them. This is a journey that can be achieved only by talking to plain people, seeing them in their homes, poor neighborhoods, refugee camps, seeing them in their slippers. For me, the most important sentence is in her conclusion: **"What I learned above all else is that no one is born a terrorist. Something has got to put them on the terrorist trajectory, and if we are clever in our approaches to dealing with terrorists, we can also take them off of it ."**

The terrorists we know and the manner they, their friends and family members are presented in the book, shows that they are mostly peons or players in a theatre that is much bigger than them, and they do not necessarily control their roles in it. If people are not born terrorists, even though some societies for various reasons are more willing, ready, or prepared to produce terrorism and terrorists, countering this violent phenomenon should include not only drones, machine guns, or sophisticated bombs, but also the thorough understanding of the roots of terrorism, Islamist or not.

As you can find in Anne's book, we know each other. The book opens with a surprising question Daniel, Anne's husband was asked on the whereabouts of his adventurous wife in Gaza. Twice during Anne's journeys I was surprised to receive night phone calls, one from Ben-Gurion airport and the second from Erez check-point between Israel and Gaza, being asked whether I knew her. Twice, I "rescued" her from the Israeli security officials who could not manage too well with an American lady, and an Ambassador's wife at that, who was running in the curved alleys of Gaza, Nablus, or Ramallah. Twice I smiled to myself visioning Anne and her students in their adventures in Gaza or Jenin, sleeping in small poor houses of Palestinians, chasing people to talk to.

However, beyond the smiles, I cannot but admire her spirit, courage, and understanding of the material she deals with. Her warmness towards anyone—enemy or friend, terrorist or his small child, brother, or mother—rises from every line here. Some will say she is naïve, others may criticize her attitude, but no reader can remain indifferent to this important book and to the so human spirit that comes from it and from Anne's personality.

Reuven Paz
Herzliya, ISRAEL
September 2012

INTRODUCTION

"Excuse me, Mr. Ambassador, but do you know where your wife is?"

It was seven a.m., and my husband of twenty-four years, Daniel Speck-hard, a diplomat posted to NATO's International Staff in Belgium, was standing at the door of our home in Brussels, barely awake. One of the plainclothes agents handed him an FBI calling card.

Daniel rubbed his eyes and asked, "Excuse me, what?"

"We're sorry, Ambassador Speckhard, to disturb you like this, but your wife has been running around in Gaza meeting with terrorists. Is she pull-ing a Patty Hearst or something?"

My husband, now wide-awake, said, "No. Wait a minute."

He invited them to come in and take a seat while he ran up to my office and returned with papers in hand. "My wife is a university professor, a psychologist. She's an expert on terrorism. She studies this type of thing, does interviews. Here's her latest paper… and her business card," he said handing them a thick document.

"She's a professor?"

"Yes," Daniel said.

"Well, Sir, we received a very angry phone call from the Israelis last night, accusing us of running an undisclosed CIA agent in Gaza. They thought your wife was undercover."

At this, Daniel laughed. "She's got nothing to do with CIA! At least not that *I* know of!"

"Okay, sorry for disturbing you. But could you please ask her to come in and talk to us when she gets back. It might be a good idea to discuss security issues with her, how to stay safe…"

He nodded. Yes, he thought. That would be a good idea.

• • •

A couple of months earlier in January 2006, I am seated on a cold metal office chair in a sparsely furnished safe house, facing Zakaria Zubeidi, leader of the al Aqsa Martyrs Brigade in Jenin, Palestine. Zubeidi has sent dozens of suicide operatives to date into Israeli settlements and check-points; their mission: to kill Israeli soldiers as well as many hundreds of unarmed civilians. Now, dressed in casual western clothes, he leans back in his chair, his legs sprawled out in from of him and an M-16 assault rifle in his lap, and brazenly regards me. Fifteen of his young cadres, also armed with assault rifles, dressed guerilla style, mill about the room. One of them peers through the blinds to the street outside. I hear vehicles rumbling by and know at any point there could be an Israeli raid. The Mossad, Israel's equivalent of the CIA, has Zubeidi on their "hit list." If they know he's here, they won't hesitate to kill him.

The Israeli army uses cell phones to help capture and kill enemies; they zone in on the whereabouts of a killer, phone him to confirm his voice and location by GPS signal, and then fire missiles that can destroy the target within seconds of the call. And they have gotten so good at minimizing collateral damage, they can aim their hits within fourteen centimeters of accuracy.

The guard looks out the window again and quickly lets the blinds slap shut. I try not to get caught up in their fear. The Israelis may know he's here, but my cell phone also has GPS. While I am unsure if the Israeli army is tracking my movements and I want them to know I'm here too, I also know my phone can be used as a listening device and that doesn't seem fair, so I reach into my bag to switch it off.

Zubeidi immediately challenges me, his tone rough. "What are you doing?"

"If the Mossad wants your interview, they can come get it themselves," I say. "My telephone won't be acting in their service."

He laughs derisively and tosses his phone on a small coffee table between us, leaving it switched on - a theatrically bold move on his part. I wonder again if the IDF will strike knowing that Westerners are with him.

I'm here to learn Zubeidi's thoughts about the young men and women that he sends into Israel to bomb themselves. The Palestinians have just declared a "hudna," a temporary laying down of arms while they assess the situation with Israel and look for avenues to peace. But prior to this he has been actively sending suicide bombers under the banner of the al Aqsa Martyrs Brigade.

Looking at his rifle and his armed cadres I say, "It must be hard to suddenly lay down arms, to stop the struggle."

Zubeidi jerks up in his chair and looks at me angrily.

"It's not hard at all," he answers, a cold edge to his voice. "We do what the people want us to do. If they want us to struggle, we struggle; if they want us to lay down arms, we lay down arms."

I feel badly that I've started with a wrong assumption about him, so I ask, "How do you know what the people want?"

He spits out his answer definitively, "They tell me."

I can tell that the interview is about to falter and that my opportunity to build rapport is waning.

I soften my voice so that he knows I don't mean to offend him. "How do they tell you? How can you know what they really want? Do you have some way of talking to them, to get a good indication of what they want from you?"

He softens a bit in turn and answers more thoughtfully, "I sleep in a different house each night. I stay with many families and every night we talk about the situation so I have a pretty good idea of how they feel."

"Can you tell me what the feelings are right now?" I ask, hoping that we are starting to make that essential connection.

He leans forward tapping his rifle hard as he talks, "Right now the people are tired. There has been too much fighting, too many deaths. They are fatigued. They need peace right now."

I can see his growing frustration with my questions, and I struggle to recover, struggle with how to proceed to regain my footing. And then his phone rings.

Zubeidi answers, "Hello?" He's silent, waiting, but there is no reply.

"Hello?" He says once more.

I eye the table between us, mentally measuring the distance. Fourteen centimeters. It can't be much more than that. I feel a strong urge to back my chair away from him, panicked that a missile may be coming any second now.

"Hello?" He says once more.

The room is completely silent, bodies tense. There is no answer. It seems it can mean only one thing. I resolve to stay in place. I don't move my chair. If a missile is coming, we will be killed together. Curiously, I feel ready, unafraid.

Zubeidi repeats again, this time angrily, "Hello?"

Silence. He switches off his phone and slams it down on the table, cursing. At once he looks up, his flashing black eyes lock with mine. I don't move - just hold his gaze. The moments tick by. No missile. Zubeidi has noticed that I haven't flinched, haven't backed away, that I am still here with him. I see the sudden respect in his eyes. He curses at the phone and at the Israelis, and then I proceed.

"What is it like to be a hunted animal?"

• • •

My life was not always like this. Growing up in small town Wisconsin pre-feminism, as a young girl I pictured my future as an involved mother and never thought a career would be possible simultaneously. I never expected to be a high-powered professional *and* a mother. Little did I know that events in my life would unfold in such a way that I would catapult myself into a fast paced and exciting career as a researcher and family psychologist.

I was no stranger to academia. My father was a university professor and mathematics whiz who wrote calculus and linear algebra textbooks. My mother had been a chemist. When she died, my stepmother who had worked up to the executive ranks in an insurance company at a time when few women worked as professionals, raised me. But both she and my mother had given up their intellectual and professional pursuits to raise our family. So, while I was expected to be educated, I was taught that raising a family was to be my most important life aspiration. But when I married my high school sweetheart, smart, blond, ambitious Daniel, he threw that plan off course by virtue of being a year younger than me. I needed to find something to keep me busy after college, while he finished his final year. I opted to earn a master's degree, and then when he also went for his master's, I pursued my doctorate—completely changing my small town girl's conception of what my life would hold.

My husband and I moved to the northern Virginia suburbs of Washington, D.C. where he took a job in the federal government as a Presidential Management Intern, and I followed in step, working in the US Department of Health and Human Services, as a Public Health Service Fellow until I finished my doctoral research. Then I had children, earning my doctorate in the same month that I gave birth to our eldest daughter. And the kids were certainly my priority. I turned down further government work and an offer to a tenure-track university position and established my career by working primarily in a private clinical research and forensic psychology practice that I ran from a home office.

Apart from that, I was like the other Moms on the street. I took the kids to the swimming pool in the summer, watched them race around on their Big Wheels and taught them to ride bikes. When they got old enough, I rollerbladed with them around our cul de sac in suburban Alexandria, usually with the smallest one in the stroller helping me keep my balance. We built snow castles in the front yard in the winter. We lived like most other middle class suburban families, peacefully unaware of a bigger world "out there".

My husband was the one that upended our tranquil life. At that time, he was working at the U.S. State Department and surprised us all when he came home excitedly announcing, "Guess what? They want to make me Ambassador to one of the former Soviet republics!"

My reaction was immediate. "We can't do that—we have a family!" I said.

He persisted.

"It will mess up the kids," I argued. "They need stability, not to be dragged around from foreign country to foreign country." I had seen too many Foreign Service kids as patients and had seen the effects of the migrant lifestyle on them. But my husband saw a bigger picture of the world and his place in it. Eventually I conceded, though it meant giving up my private practice, something that was hard for me.

"It's going to change the power balance in our marriage," I complained. "I've never not had my own income. I won't know what to do with myself!"

He laughed, his blue eyes sparkling as he held me by the shoulders, and answered confidently. "You will find something meaningful, I am sure. You are not one to be held down."

Nine months later, in 1998, we were sent to Minsk, Belarus. Having grown up during the Cold War, I was strangely anxious when our plane landed on the other side of the former Iron Curtain and we had to walk our children past armed soldiers in the Soviet airport, quietly aware that KGB agents were prowling around. While the nature there looked familiar to the northern climate we had been raised in, the people did not. The tall blonde women wore long fur coats and hats, the men looked rough, all the signs were in Cyrillic Russian lettering and practically no one spoke English. As we set up home in the official residence of the U.S. Ambassador in Minsk, it gave me the shivers to think that if there were a nuclear war with Russia, we had relocated our young children to a city where U.S. missiles would strike. It was also strange to experience the world from this other point of view; our former ideological enemies were now teaching us to speak their language and showing us how they lived and saw the world. But we also found many commonalities: my hockey-playing husband quickly found a team to join and we rediscovered the snow sports we had enjoyed in our native state of Wisconsin.

For three years, we learned Russian, traveled around the former Soviet Union and made many friends. And my husband had been right. Almost immediately upon arrival in Belarus, I started new research. First, the Chernobyl liquidators (the clean-up workers) came and asked me to work with them on a study of their posttraumatic stress responses. I did, in addition to interviewing hundreds of Chernobyl survivors about the psychosocial fallout of the 1986 nuclear disaster.

Then, after a year of living in Minsk, we were taken to visit Trostinetz, one of the largest Nazi killing centers for European Jews. As I stood on the edge of a killing pit, a voice of a survivor next to me spoke:

"There is a man still alive who crawled out of this pit as a young boy. His whole family was shot but he was overlooked and climbed out at night."

I turned to the man in horror and said, "I hope someone is recording these histories." No one was. So, the job became mine. I ended up starting the Holocaust Oral History Project - Belarus, interviewing every remaining Holocaust survivor in Minsk who was still capable of giving an interview and writing several books and a screenplay about them.[1]

After leaving Belarus, and then living in Belgium where Dan was serving at NATO, I heard that Chechen terrorists had overtaken the Dubrovka Theater in Moscow. They were holding eight hundred people hostage. I e-mailed my friend in Moscow, Nadya Tarabrina, a fellow psychologist well known for her work on posttraumatic stress disorder (PTSD). That e-mail resulted in travel to Moscow, where Nadya and I worked together with some of the surviving hostages to help them overcome the psychological aftermath of the ordeal.

Interviews with these hostages opened a door to studying terrorists in a way that I had never contemplated. They had sat side by side with their captors, conversing with and observing these terrorists with suicide bomb belts strapped around their waists. They had information no sane interviewer could ever attempt to collect, which helped us gain access into the minds of activated suicide terrorists. That experience led to my meeting a Chechen colleague with whom I worked over the next two years to collect histories of the Chechen suicide bombers, interviewing their family members and close acquaintances to learn what had put them on the terrorist trajectory.

While doing research, I was also teaching at Vesalius College, then part of the Free University of Brussels. A year earlier while on a study abroad year, one of my students, Ken, had walked out of the Hebrew University cafeteria minutes before it was blown up. Still struggling with posttraumatic responses, he deeply wanted to understand what motivated the Palestinians to become suicide terrorists. Ken talked me into returning to Israel with him; we ended up traveling through the West Bank and Gaza, interviewing family members and close associates of former suicide bombers.

By then, I was hooked. And I was just getting started. I was surprisingly good at finding terrorists and getting them to talk. Maybe it was the naïve, small-town girl inside me who still wanted to find the good in everyone. Maybe it was the strong maternal presence I've carried with me since becoming a mother. Maybe it was my deep curiosity, coupled with twenty-two years of training as a clinical psychologist, which allowed me to enter another person's inner world while suspending judgment and putting my own feelings (including terror) on hold. Whatever it was, the terrorists were talking, and I was completely fascinated by their answers.

My curiosity led me to the slums of Casablanca, Morocco to find the friends of the 2003 Casablanca bombers, twelve suicide terrorists who killed thirty-three innocents in four separate attacks. I also went to Lebanon to interview one of the leaders of Hezbollah about their longstanding cadre of suicide bombers, to Uzbekistan to try and find the families of recently activated female suicide bombers there. After September 2004 when Chechen suicide terrorists held more than three hundred children and mothers hostage in Beslan for three days, I traveled there to interview survivors. And when I realized I was living inside a worldwide terrorist hub right in Brussels, I began to interview extremists and terrorist supporters inside Belgium, the Netherlands, France and the UK.

As a result of my work, in Fall 2006, I was invited by the U.S. military to design and pilot test a deradicalization program for the more than 20,000 detainees that U.S. forces then held in Iraq. This meant traveling into a war zone to work inside Camp Cropper and Camp Bucca prisons. The effort became one of the largest detainee rehabilitation programs in the world. During the same time frame I also traveled to London and frequently consulted with the UK Home Office and many nongovernment groups as well about their beginning efforts to try to prevent, disengage, deradicalize, and rehabilitate terrorists.

Somehow over the years I managed to both raise a family and have a career far beyond what I ever thought it would be. I always worried about the effect my work and our life abroad would have on our children, and they used to tease me that they would have to go to therapy to deal with my "adventurous" research career. But in reality, they became sensitive and thoughtful young adults likewise committed to having a broader perspective of the world and working for the greater good.

• • •

In all, I conducted more than four hundred interviews with terrorists, extremists, hostages, their family members and close associates, trying to understand and get at the roots of their motivations for committing terrorist acts. When I began my journey I thought terrorists were incomprehensible evil figures that I would never have dreamed of trying to interview. I fell into this work mostly by being the kind of person that readily offers to help others. I ultimately found that my small-town girl's heart had led me forward down a path that had opened my small-town girl's eyes wide.

As I ventured into field research in Israel, Palestine, Iraq, Morocco, Uzbekistan, Lebanon, Jordan, Russia, Belarus, France, the Netherlands, the UK and Belgium, I found that I had to find a way to approach and connect with the terrorists I wished to interview to create an empathy, which would encourage them to open up to me and share their inner thoughts and feelings and allow me to get inside their heads. This required that I approach them as people rather than monsters and understand that they probably did not enter this life endorsing violence. I needed to find what had changed them: what had put them on the terrorist trajectory and if they had gotten off, what took them off. Likewise, when I went to Iraq we worked actively to do just this: designing and putting together a program to "deradicalize" and rehabilitate terrorists, and this too required approaching them with a great deal of empathy. And in Palestine the logistical difficulties of crossing checkpoints dictated that if I wanted to collect multiple interviews I had to be willing to meet them in their homes, safe houses and community centers, often stay overnight in their communities and I even ended up staying at times in the homes of several terrorists.

Sometimes when I present my results, I've found that the understanding I used to get terrorists to talk can be misunderstood as sympathy for their tactics, and that of course is a misperception. While certainly I found, just as highly renowned counter-terrorism expert Bruce Hoffman found, that terrorists are surprisingly normal in many ways and surprisingly human[2], I do *not* harbor any sympathy for or endorse their violent methods. I simply had to suspend all judgments as I listened in order to get them to talk, which thereby allowed me to "get into their heads" and learn about a lot about the emotional pain, psychological trauma, desperation and complete sense of powerlessness that many of them feel: emotions that drove them to endorse terrorism. And I must admit that in spending time with them I did feel sympathy for their suffering and deep emotional pain caused by the traumas, traumatic bereavements and disturbing experiences many had undergone. So certainly in these pages my care for them as humans who suffered will come through, but it's important to me that my natural human compassion for other humans is not mistaken in any way as sympathy for the violent methods they embrace to express and address their pain. There is *never* any excuse for or acceptable rationale for terrorism.

Now after interviewing so many and working to rehabilitate terrorists, I am certain there are no simple answers. In my ten years of researching this subject, I learned above all else that there is a lethal cocktail of terrorism that relies on a combination of four things: a terrorist group, vulnerable individuals, social support and a terrorist ideology. With terrorism there is always (by definition) an individual (in the case of lone-wolf terrorism) or terrorist group working toward a *political* goal for which it is willing to use terrorist violence. The group adheres to or develops an ideology that it then uses to convince its adherents that terrorism is justified. In the case of the "martyrdom" ideology used by al Qaeda, militant jihadis[3], the Chechens and many of the Palestinian terrorist groups written about in this book, an individual is recruited and convinced by the group and its ideology to become a "cosmic warrior" (as Mark Juergensmeyer coined the term), fighting a demonized enemy according to what the recruit comes to believe are the dictates of God. And because it's a cosmic struggle usually pitched as necessary to defend God and religion, extreme measures, including targeting civilians, are allowed.[4] And of course the more persons in one's reference group that adhere to this ideology, the more easily a vulnerable individual will be to embrace it and act out its virulent message.

But we must always remember, no one is born a terrorist. Some may, as Jerrold Post[5] states in reference especially to the Palestinians who grow up amidst a cult of martyrdom, have terrorism "bred into the bone" from a very young age, learning to hate, being fed a daily diet of fanaticism teaching that it is heroic to sacrifice themselves to strike at their political enemies. But we must remember that even for these persons, individuals who become terrorists are always seduced into and move along a terrorist trajectory that takes advantage of their individual vulnerabilities and receptiveness to the terrorist ideology and group. These susceptibilities become motivations for terrorism, I learned from my extensive studies, and can and often do include personal traumatization, deep traumatic bereavement, anger, a desire for revenge, heightened sensitivity to the suffering of others, humiliation, frustrated aspirations, social alienation, marginalization, secondary trauma, a desire to prove one's manhood, to belong, to protect others, to have an adventure or to be a hero. And these vulnerabilities or motivations tend to be very clearly delineated between active conflict zones (where trauma, loss and a desire for revenge tend to be more active) and non-conflict zones (where social marginalization, alienation, secondary trauma, sensitivity to the suffering of others, a desire to prove one's manhood, to belong, to protect others, to have an adventure or to be a hero) are more active. Humiliation and frustrated aspirations tend to cross both areas and neither are *completely* delineated, as I found when interviewing gangs in London: mini-conflict zones can be embedded and exist within peaceful countries, cities and even exist within the context of a family environment. And certainly I found that the experience of violence in one's home and community eases the passage into embracing violence as a political answer. Likewise when individuals felt their sacred values were trampled upon it was much easier to cross over into violent responses. And as I studied those who went as "martyrs", I found that just as with normal suicide, one of the best indicators of their willingness to die, especially in conflict zones, was a depth of pain, "psychache" as suicidologist Edwin Shneidman would term it, that tipped them into a desperation to exit this life in the hopes of passing quickly into a better one.[6] And when psychache is present, and suiciding on behalf of the group while targeting others is both venerated and encouraged, this type of terrorism can quickly explode into being.

Lastly, while I studied groups who made use of the "martyrdom" ideology by twisting Islam and its teachings to take advantage of those who willingly trade in their suffering lives for entry into a better world, I learned that Islam alone is not the problem. Indeed perhaps because of my Catholic upbringing and the fact that as a young child I read all the "martyrs" books (or lives of the saints as some would refer to them) in my elementary school library, probably some six hundred or so volumes while also being fed a steady Catholic diet that to die for God and religion is the most honorable death[7] and also being told that one's salvation while in a state of sin is not guaranteed, I did not find it hard to understand how another religion could be manipulated to make young adherents willing to sacrifice their lives for what they believed was for God and religion. While dying for one's religion is very different than targeting others, we have seen Christianity and Judaism also manipulated to create fanatics and terrorists who have shot abortion clinic doctors, bombed abortion clinics or attacked Muslims bending in prayer. Fanaticism is not limited to only one religion and terrorist groups that are clever enough to twist and make use of religion are powerful indeed.[8]

It should also be noted that while some of the chapters contain the actual names of those interviewed, many of my subjects, as indicated in the text, were given pseudonyms to protect their identities and thereby allow them to speak more openly.[9] As I ventured into their territories, homes, community centers and in some cases prison cells, I took verbatim notes while they spoke; their words, recorded here, give the reader a rare glimpse of how terrorists live, act, feel, think, and speak. Of the over four hundred interviews I conducted, only a sampling could be presented here to demonstrate what I learned: that terrorism[10] is a complex phenomenon and while there are patterns and categories of terrorist behaviors, no two terrorists are alike. While the ideology a group uses to convince its members to enact political violence may be the same across regions, what motivates an individual into terrorism inside a conflict zone may be very different than what may activate another outside a conflict zone. Likewise, groups in different areas vie for and recruit members differently, and social support for terrorism also varies considerably. But no matter where and how terrorism arises, we as Americans are targets. And while these interviews concern actors outside the U.S. we have now had our fair share of terrorists following the same ideology and following some of the same groups addressed in this book moving along the terrorist path just as described herein. We need insight to understand where, when, why and how the terrorist's trajectory can and does begin. We need to learn about the opportunities we have to change this course and perhaps save thousands of lives. Hopefully this book and additional material that I maintain on my website (www.AnneSpeckhard.com) will begin to provide answers.

CHAPTER 1

"We Came to Die"

It's October 23, 2002. I turn on the news and hear that forty Chechen rebels have stormed the Dubrovka Theater in Moscow and taken approximately eight hundred theatergoers hostage. My thoughts and heart race at the prospect that my friend, Professor Nadya Tarabrina, who lives there with her family is in danger. Are they, by chance, among the captives?

Nadya e-mails, assuring me that they are safe, and says she is watching the events unfold in preparation for the psychological blowback when the hostages are released. Nadya is the director of the Posttraumatic Stress Disorder Laboratory at the Institute for Psychology of the Russian Academy of Sciences and Russia's premier expert on posttraumatic stress disorder (PTSD).

Russian reporters ask her to comment on how the hostages are likely to fare psychologically when they are released. I know there will be trauma.

"Will the Institute run some sort of psychological program for them?" I ask.

"They will do nothing, Anne," Nadya answers cynically. "This is Russia."

I can't let that prevent the hostages from getting help. They will need it—desperately. "Is it 'too American' to suggest you do something similar to the psychological triage we did after September 11th?" I ask, referring to the programs like one that I ran for the American ex-pats in Brussels who had watched their homeland attacked from afar and found their workplaces turned into overseas military outposts overnight.

Nadya pauses. "Come to Moscow and we'll see what we can do."

In the meantime we keep our televisions on, watch and wait for the siege to play out. And it turns out to be quite a show.

The Chechen terrorists have carefully considered the theatrical value of their attack and how it will play in the world media, as well as to potential Middle Eastern allies and future sponsors. Half of the forty terrorists are young women, all dressed in long black fundamentalist Muslim robes that look like funeral garb to the western eye. The women have bomb belts strapped to their bodies and carry pistols in their hands. Tied around their foreheads are strips of fabric inscribed with the last cry of Islamic suicide bombers: "Allahu Akbar," which translates to "God is Great!" And in a nod to the practice of suicide bombers in Palestine, the group has created "martyrs'" last statements on a pre-recorded videotape that has now been released to al Jazeera television. The women's pretty young faces and sad almond eyes stare plaintively at the camera as they proclaim that they have come to Moscow to die with their prisoners if their demands for Russian military and security forces to immediately withdraw from Chechnya are not met.

"Even if we are killed, thousands of our brothers and sisters will come after us ready to sacrifice themselves," they say on tape.[11]

Viewers recoil in horror at the realization that these terrorists may kill not only their hostages but themselves by self-detonation. Around the globe spectators wonder what could possibly have brought such pretty, young, vulnerable looking women to Moscow to carry out an event like this.

It's soon discovered that some of them are widows whose husbands died in Chechnya's brutal battles for independence from Russia. The Chechens had lost nearly half of their population from death and displacement in their 1994 and 1999 fights for freedom.[12] Russian journalists immediately dub the sorrowful female suicide bombers inside the theater as "black widows", a title when translated into English becomes even more sensationalist as it equates them to comic book anti-heroes – some kind of female super-killers. And the black widows captivate world attention.

This is part of the Chechens' plan. In recent years Putin had managed to close off journalists from reporting on the situation inside Chechnya, and the terrorists know they have to take their cause outside of Chechnya to get worldwide attention and swing Russian public opinion. Their female bombers and the theater spectacle dominate the television, Internet and print media as the world watches, riveted. The Moscow mass hostage-taking event at the theater is a coup de force, and the Chechen terrorists have won the first round. They have - with the words of their leader, Barayev, echoing: "We came to die,"put the Chechen political situation and their dire human rights issues back on the world journalistic map.[13]

"But how did these women turn from widows into terrorists?" Viewers ask. Later I would learn that it occurred between the two wars of independence and when the Russians carpet-bombed the Chechen capital of Grozny. At this time the Chechen rebels transitioned from freedom fighters to adopting the militant jihadi ideology .[14] They unleashed a campaign of suicide bombings on the Russians, sending many of their traumatized and despairing left-behind wives, sisters and daughters along with Chechen men to carry out their messages of death and revenge against the Russians.[15]

As the Nord Ost siege unfolds, I prepare to go to Russia to help the hostages, and try to imagine what the terrorists will do and what it will be like when I get there. Then the unthinkable happens: instead of the terrorists negotiating to get some of what they want, or worse—killing themselves and their hostages—the Russian Special Forces gas and storm the theater without making adequate preparations for reviving the unconscious hostages. The gas knocks everyone in the theater out, and the female terrorists with bombs strapped on either do not realize they are being gassed or do not detonate without an order from the men. The Russian Special Forces enter to briefly battle the male terrorists who patrol the anterooms, and then entering the theater shoot all the unconscious female suicide bombers at point blank with a bullet to the head.

The unconscious hostages are unceremoniously hauled to waiting buses and ambulances and taken to hospital where the medical staff is unprepared and uninformed about what they have inhaled and how to treat them. Many die. The surviving hostages, stunned and weary from their ordeal, emerge deeply traumatized.

Nadya and I soon begin our work. First, we inquire about the events that went on inside the theater, so that we can best understand how to help.

"People in camouflage military uniforms appeared on the stage. It was a musical about World War II so that was expected," one hostage recounts. "They were carrying automatic rifles and shot in the air, yelling 'You are hostages!' and announcing who they were. I thought it was a special effect.

"But then, another camouflaged terrorist appeared in the door of the balcony, where we were seated just four or five seats in. He, too, shot in the air and shouted, 'You are hostages! Put your hands up behind your heads!'

"At that moment, my wife looked at me and said, 'It's not a joke.' But a man nearby had not yet realized and stood up from his seat and started to smile. The Chechen beat him on the shoulder and bloodied his face with the butt of his automatic rifle. The lights were on, the music was still playing and the actors were still on the stage. He didn't understand, but we understood."

From the hostage accounts, I learn the terrorists had rushed the stage and staked out the aisles in lightening speed, securing the theater. The older males wore camouflage, while the younger men wearing black sweaters were responsible for placing bombs about the theater. The women with suicide bombs strapped around their waists held a detonator in one hand and a pistol in the other and awaited commands to set themselves off.

From the stage, Barayev made his announcement. " You will be held here until the Russian government withdraws all its forces from Chechnya. Anyone who does not cooperate will be shot."

The theatergoers knew that this was *not* an empty threat.

"Everyone knew what he or she must do," describes one hostage. "They demanded we pass our mobile phones and bags to the aisles and then put our hands back up behind our heads. Men and women were separated. They placed a big bomb in the balcony in front of the first row of seats. Down below, on stage, they put explosives on the backs of plastic chairs. I was afraid they would put people in these chairs."

Though we don't yet know the details, this information is expected from the hostages.

What we don't anticipate is that the first hostage we work with begins to tell us about her conversations with the terrorists over the three-day ordeal. I suddenly realize that in trying to help the hostages overcome their psychological fallout, Nadya and I have stumbled into something much deeper – these hostages can give us secondary interviews of conversations with activated suicide terrorists who had bombs strapped on. No researcher would be brave or crazy enough ever to try and interview an activated suicide terrorist, but here these hostages have spent three days together with them, observing, conversing and interacting with them— learning what they think, say and do in their last moments of life.

After the first hostage leaves, I turn to Nadya in amazement. "We have two studies," I say. "One about helping hostages after a suicide terrorist hostage-taking and another completely new study of secondary interviews and observations of suicide terrorists in action."[16]

We immediately decide we must expand our study beyond simply helping the hostages and attempt to also learn more indirectly about the suicide terrorists through the hostages. These interviews mark the beginning of my terrorism research and a worldwide journey of interviewing hostages, close friends and family members of terrorists, and performing a kind of "psychological autopsy" on those who are willing to kill themselves in order to kill others.

Like that, Talking to Terrorists has begun.

CHAPTER 2

Wild Chechen People

It's a snowy January night in Moscow in 2002. Nadya and I are tucked away in the corner of a large wood-paneled room inside Dom Literatura (the Writer's Guild) having dinner with Victor Olshansky, one of the premier Russian authors on the psychology of terrorism. Victor has the hardened look of a former Soviet Union man who has drunk a lot of vodka and smoked all his life. He chain smokes now as we talk and wait for our dinner to be served, inhaling each cigarette down to its filter-less tip. Victor doesn't admit it, but it's obvious he's a former KGB[17] agent—he traveled as a military psychologist in nearly all the proxy war countries of the former Soviet Union including North Korea, Afghanistan, and Africa at a time when travel was prohibited. He tells the stories of being there from a hardened vantage point, talking about paying Afghan insurgents to bomb empty Soviet buildings. But Nadya and I are here to talk about one thing and we turn the conversation to the Moscow theater hostage-taking event.

"Victor, what I want to understand is what could possibly make forty men and *women* come all the way to Moscow, intent on taking eight hundred innocent civilians hostage and willing to explode themselves with their victims?" I ask.

"Chechens are wild, violent people; they have been attacking Russians for centuries. There is no logical explanation for what they did."

Although I don't know any Chechens, I recoil as he explains his views and I don't accept this explanation. I've lived in Belarus (when my husband served as U.S. Ambassador there from 1997-2000), and I know the common Russian view of Chechens as uncontrollable people. But Victor is a psychologist and should know better. There has to be a deeper, more compelling reason.

A string quartet plays close by as we eat, filling the hushed room with unbearable beauty. Victor's words seem violent and out of place here. I also know that his explanation is not historically correct. Russia has been the overlord of the Chechen people who have sought their independence for centuries but never won it. During Stalin's reign of terror the Chechen people were accused during World War II of being Nazi collaborators and were deported in mass out of their country, many dying in route and others starved once they'd reached their destination. With the fall of the Soviet Union, Chechens (like the other Soviet bloc and former USSR countries) followed Yeltsin's advice of "Grab as much freedom as you can." They declared independence. Two lost wars ensued (in 1994 and 1999) and now in 2002 the Chechen freedom fighters have changed tactics.

I want specific answers about how the Chechens who came to Moscow were convinced to use terrorism. Victor may be willing to accept crude stereotypes of an entire population, but I am not.

"Victor, wouldn't it be possible to ask the families or friends of the Chechens who came to the theater what motivated them to do it?" I ask.

Victor laughs as if I've said something both hilarious and stupid, and then sips his Georgian red wine. "You can't get into Chechnya unless you're willing to risk having your fingers chopped off or worse yet, getting decapitated! Anyway it's all political, and probably orchestrated by Berezovsky[18] in London to embarrass Putin."

The thought that Chechen terrorists are just pawns in a bigger fight between an oligarch and Putin gives me a chill, especially when I hear a former KGB agent put it forth as the explanation, but I don't accept that either. Not everything in this world is a KGB plot, and I believe there is a way to get answers from the Chechen people themselves about what motivated their men and women to come to Moscow to die and to kill. I just have to find it.

"What about a university professor? Wouldn't it be possible to collaborate with a Chechen academic and ask these questions?"

"You have no idea what Chechnya is like," Victor answers chidingly. "All the universities have been bombed, all of Grozny is rubble."

"What about the Internet, couldn't you ask these questions of someone by Internet?"

"Impossible! There is no Internet in Chechnya," Victor claims.

I'm distracted by the exquisite music of the string quartet as Victor goes on telling us that there is no understanding the terrible Chechen people. It seems such a juxtaposition of beauty and evil and part of me just wants to block him out because I feel that what he's saying isn't true.

That night, Nadya and I walk home along the snowy sidewalk to her small apartment and compare our impressions of Victor.

"He's KGB, Anne, and sees the whole world through that lens," Nadya says shaking her head. As a young child Nadya's father and hence her entire family was exiled to an island near Japan and she knows the price honest Soviet citizens pay when their government decides they are enemies.

The next day Nadya wakes me with excitement. "Anne, a Chechen psychologist has come to Moscow for supervision on her doctoral studies. She telephoned and asked to meet me today. Would you like to come?"

I can't believe our luck. We will be meeting a real Chechen, a psychologist and academic—a person that Victor said couldn't possibly exist—and will be able to ask her opinion of how Chechen people are motivated to become terrorists! We go together to Nadya's Posttraumatic Stress Disorders Laboratory at the Russian Academy of Sciences.

There we meet Dr. Khapta Akhmedova. She arrives in posh flat leather boots and a stylish coat that she takes off to reveal a long slim skirt topped by a high-necked blouse. Khapta is petite, elegant and beautiful, with big doe eyes and shoulder length brown hair. When I struggle in Russian to ask if there is a still a functioning university in Grozny and if she has Internet, she smiles gently and answers in Russian, "Our university was heavily bombed but we still function among the ruins. I have Internet if I go to neighboring Ingushetia." I smile back glad to see Victor proved wrong on nearly all counts.

Khapta and I sit in chairs gathered around Nadya's desk. Nadya leans forward across her desk chain smoking and smiling warmly as she asks Khapta what she thinks were the motivations of the Chechen terrorists. From time to time, when I cannot grasp the Russian, Nadya translates for me.

"We have suffered two wars now in only a few years. Grozny was heavily carpet bombed and many civilians were killed. Nearly half our population fled and those who stayed are devastated. There are still many Chechen refugees living in tent camps in Ingushetia. Young people have spent nearly their whole lives in war and witnessed too much trauma. They are too young to remember how we co-existed peacefully with Russians under the former Soviet rule. Some of them go easily to extremist groups."

Khapta spends the next hours explaining how life changed with the two wars, how devastated Chechnya has become. She tells us that her family doesn't have running water at home anymore, that her university is in rubble, and that countless young men – innocent students and neighbors

- simply disappeared only to have their families find their tortured bodies months later. As she speaks I notice how fragile she is and how her large brown eyes have a haunted look. As she continues, my heart goes out to her and I feel a desire to protect her.

Khapta explains to us that the extremists—wahhabists[19] as she calls them—who fought against the Russians and won in Afghanistan, came from Arab countries and taught the people that Chechen Sufi Islam is not the true Islam.[20]

"They took over many mosques in Grozny, and until recently you could find their extremist book claiming that their version of Islam is correct anywhere in Grozny.[21] That was until the Russians finally realized what was happening and cracked down on them.

"The wahhabists say they are a brotherhood and that the bonds between them are stronger than blood or family ties. They are willing to die for each other. This is very appealing after the people have suffered and lost family members."

Khapta tells us about a woman in her neighborhood who tried to protect her son from being hauled away by Russian soldiers tasked with rounding up terrorists. The soldiers were less concerned with the crimes of the young men they arrested than with meeting their quota and making money from those they let slip through their fingers. Khapta's neighbor had screamed to the soldiers to leave her son alone and when they'd demanded gold she cried that she had none. When she realized they would take her son she fell to her knees begging them to take the gold fillings from her teeth. And they did.

Listening to Khapta relate all the traumas she's personally witnessed during the wars, I am able to better understand how people can be brought to such a high state of anxiety that they desire a sense of protection and need to believe in their ability to fight back, no matter the cost.

Khapta explains how the wahhabist converts withdraw from society, mentally preparing to fight back. Physically they reveal their psychological withdrawal from mainstream society by changing their appearance. Women dress in abayas and cover their heads like Arab women even though this form of dress was never a part of Chechen Islamic practices, and the men wear short pants and grow beards.

"The wahhabists live apart and teach their followers that they must take part in a militant jihad against the Russians. They teach them to use suicide terrorism and that becoming a martyr is the highest goal in life."

I am horrified as Khapta explains that those who lose a family member, who are victims of torture, who are outraged and in need of revenge, or who are in such despair that they want to die, are the most vulnerable. Regardless, they all know where to find the rebels and how to join.

"Until recently their mosques were active in Grozny. Now you just have to go to the mountains to find them. Everyone knows this," Khapta explains.

As Khapta speaks I notice how thin she is and how delicate her hands are. I soon learn that Khapta's response to the overwhelming stress she has endured has often been anorexia.

But for now, we are just meeting and I marvel at how much work Khapta has accomplished amidst the ruins of war, as she details her research of traumatized people in Chechnya, including more than four hundred clinical case studies.

"In every case those who have suffered traumas and have posttraumatic stress disorder also have an increase in fanaticism," Khapta says.

"We've had so much violence. Sometimes the federals come and arrest anyone just to say they made an arrest of a terrorist. It can be a young man of fighting age that hasn't done anything, but they take him to the filtration camps and torture him. If they get released these young men come back changed. Some of them go immediately to join the wahhabists."

We've been speaking for two hours by now, and it's been difficult for me to follow in Russian. Suddenly Khapta notices I am tiring.

"I can speak in English if you like," she offers. Amazingly this gentle, sensitive woman is fluent not only in Chechen and Russian, but English as well. I am ecstatic that she has appeared here to puzzle with us over what Victor could only explain by make ethnic slurs.

Nadya and I exchange smiles—both of us so impressed by Khapta. I tell her that we are just beginning and want to seek funding to do a larger research study with the hostages.

"Khapta, I know you cannot help us in Moscow with our hostage interviews," I say, "but maybe you could be part of our team working from Chechnya—interviewing the families and close associates of the suicide bombers to try to understand what put them on the terrorists' trajectory and what could be done to prevent others from joining? Would you be interested?"

"Yes of course, but I don't think you could come there, Anna," Khapta answers, calling me by my Russified name. "It's too dangerous, everyone would realize you are a foreigner and you would end up kidnapped for ransom—unless we pretended you were mentally ill and could not speak but that would make it impossible to do interviews."

I nod. "Would you be willing to do the interviews yourself?" I ask.

"Yes," she says. "The people there trust me because I have been working with them through both wars, and they know I am not on any one side of the issues. Yes, I think it's a good idea."

Nadya and I return to our interviewing hostages, while Khapta goes back to Grozny to find the family members and close associates of the terrorists. Together we begin our research to uncover the cause for their terrorist trajectory and explore the ways to prevent or reverse it.

CHAPTER 3

"To Die in Jihad is the Highest Happiness"

On her return to Chechnya, Khapta quickly sets out. While we start out quite sure that fear and psychological trauma are likely high in the list of motivators to terrorism, we also know that these alone can not be the only causes because the majority of Chechens share the same horrific wartime experiences as the extremists and *do not* join terrorist groups.

Surely, we realize, the Chechen population feels defiant in the face of Russian troops controlling their territory and angered over the multitude of human rights offenses, and they may even quietly cheer the rebels on, but largely, as Khapta knows from living there, the Chechens do not relate to the imported militant jihadi ideology and do not support "martyrdom" missions, nor do they approve of targeting civilians. So what is different for or about the terrorists that leads them to this fate? Trauma and fear may be necessary but they are not sufficient, and Khapta and I are determined to find out which other things put some on the terrorist trajectory and leaves others off. No one is born a terrorist, and perhaps our findings will help us put together a prevention program to keep others from joining and staying on the terrorist path.

Khapta is well known and trusted by the local Chechen population for her work as a psychologist with Medecins Sans Frontieres in Grozny and in the refugee camps that house over two hundred thousand Chechen refugees from the second war (in 2000) with Russia.[22] We decide that the best way to learn is to find the family members or close friends and associates of Chechen suicide bombers and ask for an interview.

Khapta and I both know that her work on this project is sensitive and that if she garners undue attention from the Russian authorities or conversely, the Chechen rebels, she will be putting her life at risk. During this time period ordinary people in Chechnya disappear for any reason and she too can easily become a causality of either side—murdered, taken into custody and tortured or suddenly disappearing with no trace. She also knows that it is only because of the trust she has already earned with family members and close associates that allows them to even dare talk to her about what has potentially motivated the terrorists. She will ask about how the "martyrs" got involved and the steps that led them to the Moscow theater or other venues where they carried out a suicide mission.

Khapta has to tread carefully, but her courageous yet light touch proves to be natural for her. Khapta belies her looks as a wispy-figured, wide-eyed, quiet woman because as I soon learn, she is a dynamo—smart, sensitive, deeply caring and able to walk through fears that would stop most from ever daring to enter.

Khapta and I develop our interview questions and she begins approaching family members—literally going to their homes and asking for an interview. I wait anxiously in Brussels where my family and I live at the time, researching everything I can find in the media and scholarly sources about the bombers. Khapta and I communicate by e-mail, and as her first interviews appear in my inbox, I feel a small clutch of terror seeing them, wondering if her computer files are being read by the Russian FSB and if their existence and her sending them to me over the Internet endangers her life. Likewise when I become bolder in our e-mail correspondence and begin peppering her with questions about Russian propaganda and the black widows, I worry that my questions and her honest answers are being read by the FSB and also putting her in danger.

My fears are not unfounded. Anna Politkovskaya, a Russian journalist who travels throughout Chechnya interviewing civilians, has just published a book critical of the Russian forces in Chechnya, and the people she interviewed in Chechnya have been tracked down one by one and murdered. Anna herself is also targeted, suspiciously poisoned while on a flight home from North Ossetia, and some years later, she is brutally gunned down in Moscow. No one can prove that it is the Russian government that has targeted her, but it's clear that her critical and honest reporting of the situation in Chechnya led to her and some of her informants' final demise.

So Khapta's interviews make me nervous, and daily I worry that maybe it's not worth it. But Khapta is persistent. With no funding, she and I begin collecting and analyzing our data, developing theories and publishing scholarly papers as we begin to get to the heart of what turns ordinary Chechens into terrorists willing to kill themselves while killing others.[23]

We are only at the beginning, but each time I sit down to my computer screen in Brussels I scan my inbox for an e-mail from Khapta and when I see her icon, I feel such relief knowing she's still alive, still interviewing and we are still learning about an entirely new form of terrorism and the militant jihadist ideology that fuels it.

One of the boys that Khapta interviews is fifteen-year-old Omar who may be on his way to becoming one of the next Chechen "martyrs". Omar's school psychologist brings him to Khapta's attention because Omar has replaced his own passport picture with that of Osama bin Ladin, a highly risky move at that time in 2003 when it's possible to encounter as many as seventeen military checkpoints crossing Grozny. At each of these, Chechens must produce their passport—whole busses are even disembarked so that every individual is reviewed. So far, none of the Russian Forces have noticed Omar's photo, but if they do, it will result in his arrest, likely torture and possible death sentence.

Khapta asks him, "Aren't you afraid when the soldiers look inside your passport?"

"No. Let them look," Omar answers, his chin thrust defiantly forward. "Bin Laden is a hero. Even America is afraid of him! Let the Russians know that he will reach them too."

Khapta smiles and gently chides him. "And the Chechens, they aren't also heroes?" She hopes to remind him of his proud Chechen ancestry, but Omar has lost his faith. He clenches his fists, as he answers dejectedly, "Of course not! The Chechens couldn't win the war against the Russians."

Omar is like many "macho" boys in conflict zones who saw the men of his country, including his father—who he believed were strong—humiliated and made powerless in the face of their enemy. And this has devastated him. He tells Khapta that he has joined a "jamaat", a Muslim brotherhood of believers, who have ties as strong as blood and stand ready to die for each other.

"What is most important to you now?" Khapta asks peering into his eyes, trying to get a sense of where his young life is directed.

"Jihad. To be killed in war is the highest happiness, because you will be in paradise," Omar says proudly puffing his chest out as he explains. Now that the rebels have transitioned to fighting "jihad", Omar believes that to die fighting along with them is to win a martyr's death.

"And you aren't afraid of death?" Khapta asks, her eyebrows rising in concern.

"No," Omar answers, pursing his lips and shaking his head as he looks down at his hands. "I'm not. I already saw the face of death."

Indeed Omar has seen death—too much of it. As he opens up about his history, it is not difficult to see why the militant jihadi ideology resonates with him and why he identifies with the brotherhood of believers who have taken him in as a young traumatized boy. Omar tells Khapta his story; as he paints horrific pictures of violence that no child should ever have witnessed, he explains that these are images he cannot stop himself from remembering. Like full sensory movies they play unrelentingly, over and over again in his mind.

"It was in Zakan-Yurt," he recalls as his face contorts in pain, "a morning in January of 2000. Russian soldiers brought two Chechen guys to the village. Their hands were in handcuffs behind their backs and grenades were taped to their legs. The soldiers exploded them in front of everyone! Their bodies were scattered into pieces. All the people stood and looked, but everyone was afraid to approach them. Only my friend and I came and started to collect their remains. I shouted to the adult men that they should help. But they waited for the soldiers to leave. Then some women came and helped us. Their remains were placed in the mosque so that their relatives could bury them."

Khapta is hardened to hearing war stories; she lives them daily, but I am not and reading this story makes me want to vomit. And I understand, as does Khapta, that this trauma confirmed for Omar that Chechen men are failures—a sentiment that grew from his father's inability to protect their home from the Russian onslaught.

Omar continues speaking of his violent childhood, making clear to us that his sense of safety and normalcy were torn apart by the experiences of war as literally as the buildings were ripped from their girders by the Russian bombing of Grozny. "In the first war Papa drove us to our relatives in the village and returned to Grozny to guard our house," Omar says, his eyes taking on a faraway look. "When he went to get water for us, the Russian soldiers shot at him from a helicopter. He lay there for a long time and bled profusely. Nobody came to help him. Then our neighbor saw him [lying] there and brought him home. Nobody could transport him to a hospital for a long time because of the bombardments. His wounded leg began to decay and then was amputated." Omar winces with the pain of recall.

In the second war, Omar recalls another event similarly burned into his mind. "Once, before we left Grozny," Omar tells Khapta, "we were fired on from all sides, so we sat in a cellar. Russian soldiers came to us and accused us of staying in Grozny to help the Chechen fighters. They shouted and talked dirty. My father told them not to speak so because women and children were in our cellar. They became angry and removed my father, our neighbor and me from the cellar. They said that they will shoot us. Mama began to cry and screamed that Papa is an invalid and not to shoot him because he can't participate in war. But they didn't listen to her and led us into a courtyard. They ordered us to stand with our faces to a wall. I closed my eyes and started to pray silently. They shot at this moment. Then it seemed to me that I became deaf and I thought to myself, *I have died. Where is my father?* Then I looked to him. He also looked to me and I understood that we are still alive! It was strange that they didn't kill us. They shot above our heads. Maybe they wanted to frighten us."

In this and many other incidents, Omar felt completely powerless. His father couldn't protect him and his mother fought only for his father's life, resigning herself to the idea that they might take and shoot her son. Of course for a teenage boy the horrifying realization that your parents cannot protect you and witnessing his mother trying to shelter only her husband and not her son from harm was terrifying. One by one these events, and many more like them, turned the innocent and trusting child that Omar had been into a young boy that realizes he has to find others who might offer him protection when his family cannot. And like all Chechens he knew where to find them: in the mountains of Chechnya, among the rebels.

Soon after this near-death experience Omar found other stronger role models among the militant jihadi converts who welcomed Omar, invited him to join their "jamaat" and called him "brother." The extremists offered a belief that there was someone who could protect him. "Fictive kinship," as such non-familial bonding is called, is very powerful and appealing to those in conflict zones who are young and vulnerable and have lost immediate family members – a mother, father, brother or sister and who still seek protection.

And as Omar fell under the Chechen militant jihadis influence he began to exalt them and their movement and came to falsely believe that they were all powerful, unlike his parents who had failed him. He lived under the delusion that with Osama bin Ladin pasted into his passport and his "Muslim brothers" standing alongside him in the "jamaat" he could stand up to the Russians. What he didn't want to face and therefore pushed out of his consciousness by clinging to his new "brothers" was his horrifying reality: that he lived in total and utter chaos, there was no real protection from anyone, and his life could end or take a bad turn at anytime. As a youth of fighting age, he was an easy target to be arrested and thrown into the filtration camps for torture or death; he could be bombed or strafed at and lose his limbs just like his father, or be killed in countless other meaningless ways. This was just too much horror for a young boy to be able to face without help, so until he met Khapta he had sworn his allegiance to and believed in the almighty power of Osama bin Ladin and his cadres.

Omar's dreams of dying as a martyr in war and going straight to paradise are also a powerful diversion from his real fears. "I am afraid to be a cripple like my father. I don't want to die a victim. I would like to die a worthy and heroic death," he tells Khapta, showing the trapped and religiously delusional mentality of a victim of war suffering from posttraumatic stress disorder.

"Do you have any dreams of a future life without war?" Khapta asks, hoping to activate some recall of a past that promised a future of productivity.

Omar blankly answers, "No, I don't. While the enemy is in our homeland, I cannot think about it."

The "jamaat" has become Omar's new empowered family, and if the group he belongs to wants to activate him as a suicide bomber, he will be an easy candidate.

We can't let that happen. So Khapta arranges for Omar to have therapy with her sister, also a psychologist, who intervenes and begins to help him face his horrifying past and present through painful but healing conversations about his posttraumatic stress and bereavement. He is able to make psychological adjustments that do not involve clinging to aggressive men and trading his life for a violent death and is put back on the path of a normal childhood. As is often the case, when trauma survivors get the chance to sit in a safe environment and talk to someone who can help them face their posttraumatic recall, they can begin to overcome their traumas. And the stories they cannot stop remembering—the ones that drive them to escape with alcohol, drugs, or taking their own lives in suicide terrorism—can lose their power to propel them into self-destructive behaviors.

Another boy named Yacoub[1] was not so lucky, becoming one of the young men who died as a terrorist in the Moscow theater siege. Khapta learns about him when she goes to speak to his cousin who decides to trust Khapta and speak to her anonymously, explaining that Yacoub's father

---

1 This is a pseudonym for a real person who was involved in the siege.

and elder brother had been killed in the first war in 1995. Yacoub's cousin recalls the effects of war and the deaths of his family members on Yacoub.

"He was an adolescent (fifteen years old) when his father and brother were killed," Yacoub's cousin says. "He became closed and gloomy saying that he should avenge his family members, that he hates the Russians who have killed them. All his interests became reduced only to the weapon, war and revenge. Then he began to be interested in religion although before he didn't even know how to pray.

"His mother was very much afraid of these changes that occurred in him so quickly. But she no longer had any influence over him. She asked me to talk with him because we had good relations. But when I tried to talk with him about his new beliefs he told me that if I criticize him, he will quarrel with me. In general, the conversation failed.

"After his father's death, our extremist uncle was the biggest authority for my cousin. He started to read the wahhabists' books that he took from this uncle. He changed externally, grew his hair long and grew a beard. Then he went to Khattab [a Saudi born rebel leader in the terrorists' camps] in the Jamaat, a group where our uncle was included. He trained in Khattab's base and remained in Grozny to fight in the second war. After, he went into hiding because he was listed as fugitive."

"How do you view your cousin after his involvement with the Moscow theater hostage-taking?" Khapta asks.

Yacoub's cousin wrings his hands and answers with sad eyes. "I understand him and I don't condemn him. It had to happen. He told me that he dreams to die in jihad and that life is a burden, that happiness can be only in paradise."

As Khapta sends these interviews through the Internet for me to read, we both see a theme repeated again and again in conflict zones: fear of facing a violent and senseless death, especially among the young, while also becoming empowered by the militant jihadi ideology" is a powerful force propelling the young into terrorism. We see the sense of control joining a terrorist group can give its supporters, as well as the alluring promises "martyrdom" offers. When death is looming anyway—especially for fugitives or those who feel they will be killed—immediate delivery into paradise for the "martyr" along with the promise of paradise extended to seventy of his or her relatives doesn't look so bad. It's the call of Loreli for traumatized Chechens—too sweet to ignore, too dangerous to follow. Indeed after some time I begin to understand the militant jihadi ideology offers short-term psychological first aid—temporarily attending to the psychological needs of the person following it,but short-lived because it ends in death.

CHAPTER 4

"Do You Remember Me?"

Unlike Omar and Yacoub who replaced lost or humiliated family members with the militant jihadis groups, Elza followed another road to radicalization. She married into it.

Elza's mother and sisters tell Khapta that Elza's husband, while not a rebel himself, joined the Wahhabi sect as a supporter. Before her marriage, Elza followed the Sufi path like most Chechens but after her wedding began to follow in her husband's footsteps and converted to the more conservative Wahhabi practice of dressing in a long black abaya and covering her hair with a headscarf (hidjab). After her marriage, Elza also began to take on the more extremist views of the Wahhabi sect in Chechnya, believing that she was following the "true Islam" and that fighting the infidel Russians was a holy calling.

Though Elza knew her husband's rebel friends and supported them, her family says it's unlikely she would have ever become a terrorist herself if not for what happened one evening when her brother came to visit. She'd only been married two months and was so happy to see him that they exceeded the curfew imposed by the Russians. After six p.m. it was dangerous for him to return home—young men his age found on the streets at night were routinely picked up and accused of being rebel fighters. "Stay the night with us," Elza cajoled and her brother agreed.

It was a fateful decision because that night, Chief of the Commandant's office General Geidar Gadzhie, who was well known for personally heading up and participating in the torture of many civilians, showed up at her house with his henchmen. The soldiers accused her husband and brother of being rebel fighters, even though Elza's relatives claim that neither had participated directly in any rebel activity. The soldiers harshly beat them in front of Elza. Then they bound their arms, arrested them and took them away.

The next morning Elza's sisters came to her home and went frantically with Elza to the Commandant's office, begging for information about their brother and Elza's husband. Everyone they spoke to denied knowing anything. Hysterical, Elza then went from one "filtration" camp, where rebel and terrorism suspects are frequently held and tortured, to the next with bribe money in hand. Elza knew that it had become big business within the corrupt Russian Federal Forces to arrest innocent Chechens and hold them for large bribes and that it was typical to bring a whole year's salary to win the freedom of a loved one. Prepared to hand over her money, Elza was devastated when every soldier she begged to free her loved ones said they had not seen her husband and brother and that no one knew their fate.

Elza collapsed when she learned after two weeks of searching, that her husband and brother were found dead on the outskirts of town, their mutilated bodies thrown in a ditch. Elza, like many deeply traumatized persons, especially those who survive a murder, reacted in despair and wanted to erase the horror, pain and grief from her mind by dying. She wished suicide wasn't forbidden in Islam. But she did know from her exposure to wahhabism that "martyrdom" or suicide terrorism is the loop-hole for people like her, that going as a suicide bomber is not included in the Islamic definition of suicide among extremists. In her grief, she searched for someone to make it possible for her to die honorably while avenging her family members' deaths. She didn't have to search far; the militant jihadis who had been her husband's friends agreed to equip her for a suicide mission. Within three months, Elza went with a bomb strapped to her body to the commandant's office to kill the man who had arrested and presumably ordered the torture, mutilation and death of her family.

At his office Elza told the guards, "I have very important information for the chief." Not expecting a woman to do them any harm they allowed her to pass. And as she approached the commandant, she pointedly asked him, "Do you remember me?"

No one knows if he did or if he even had time to answer, because after asking her question Elza exploded herself, killing him and the guards around him.

While revenge for the death of family members is a cultural norm in Chechnya, until the second war of independence when foreign ideologues promulgated the militant jihadi ideology, women never carried out such missions. But with terrorist groups growing and now more than willing to equip females for revenge, Chechen women suddenly became avengers. In fact, the first suicide bombers in Chechnya, Khava Barayeva and Luiza Magomadova were women, and as the number of Chechen "martyrs" mounted, female suicide bombers nearly equaled their male counterparts (as was the case in the Moscow theater hostage). This statistic, however, is still not borne out among Arab terrorist groups whose sponsors send female bombers on missions far less often. Palestinians and Iraqis held off in their inclusion of women until the male terrorists were blocked from crossing checkpoints. Perhaps the overwhelming despair in Chechnya led women immediately into the fray or perhaps Chechen woman were more used to functioning professionally outside of their homes before the wars equalized things, but in either case Chechen women participated from the start.[24]

The case of Elza brings up a number of important points that I would later find repeatedly present in conflict zones. The first is the quick radicalization of a person previously described as gentle and kind that can occur following the traumatic death(s), injury or torture of a loved one. The second is that exposure to an extremist ideology and group that is eager to equip traumatized persons for suicide missions is necessary to make use of motivations of trauma and revenge inside a conflict zone. If Elza had only been traumatized but never exposed to an ideology and group that glorified taking one's own life in order to kill others and that stood ready and willing to equip her, she would never have been able to carry out her suicide act. Instead, she would have mourned and struggled her way through the posttraumatic stress and traumatic bereavement of her husband's and brother's deaths and possibly become a psychologically damaged person but eventually would have likely made a livable adjustment to her grief, as most war and murder survivors do without becoming violent. It took a terrorist group and an extreme ideology to take advantage of her in her most vulnerable moments of posttraumatic grief to turn her into a bomber who was willing to kill and be killed. And as we soon learn in Palestine, the more social support there is for terrorism, the easier the decision becomes.

Khapta finished her interview with Elza's mother, who pulling at her hair complains that it has gone immediately gray and her teeth have fallen out since she lost both her daughter and son. And like other parents who see their son's or daughter's overwhelming emotional pain taken advantage of by a terrorist group, Elza's mother knows that her daughter could never have done it alone.

"Where would she find the explosives, how could she know what to do with it, how to make herself into a bomb?" she asks."She was only seventeen years old!"

CHAPTER 5

Short-term Psychological First Aid

"Retribution will occur. Evil should be punished," nineteen year old Fatima told her cousin, who now recounts Fatima's story to Khapta a year after Fatima dressed herself in black and participated in the Moscow theater siege with a suicide bomb wrapped around her waist.

It's hard for most people to watch evil flourish unchecked, and Fatima[1] was no exception. Her cousin recalls that while flipping through a photo album Fatima stopped at a picture of her brother and murmured, "It is a dirty world in which evil reigns" as she stared at all that remained of him: his sweet face enclosed in a plastic envelope. The Russians had killed him a few months earlier.

"It's difficult to live in this world, remaining pure," she continued, tapping gently at the page as tears welled in her eyes and she explained to her cousin. "For those reasons my brother left this world." But even as she said the words Fatima didn't seem to feel those reasons for her brother being killed were enough—her eyes searched for meaning, any meaning, in his senseless death at the hands of the Russians.

"I see him frequently in my dreams and he calls me to him, in paradise. But I still have not yet done anything to deserve paradise," she told her cousin.

But unbeknownst to her cousin, Fatima was already preparing to earn her way into paradise. The plan: to leave for Moscow donning a black burka and suicide belt and die in the siege with the Moscow hostages, hoping to reunite with her brother in doing so.

This longing to reunite with a dead loved one, even if it means dying to do so, and receiving visits from the deceased in vivid dreams or daydreams are frequent attributes of traumatic bereavement, even in normal but traumatically bereaved persons. It can be very confusing, making the traumatized individual much more susceptible to suicide during the unresolved period of grief. Coupled with a desire for revenge, it's probably what compelled Elza Gazueva to seek out her husband's militant jihadi

1 Fatima is a pseudonym for a real participant in the Moscow hostage-taking event.

comrades to equip her to go on a suicide mission. It was also what pushed Fatima to take part in the Nord Ost hostage taking.

• • •

"Sometimes I feel such strong hatred to Russians for this war," another of our respondents, Laila[1], tells Khapta. Laila is thirty-nine years old and she, too, fights with the urge to suicide in order to revenge on the Russians.

"My brother was killed in the last year, exploded on a mine," she explains, her voice quivering with grief. "He was only seventeen years old." Laila's grief and inclination to express her outrage in an act of revenge like Fatima's makes her vulnerable to being recruited to join the militant jihadis. The thing that stops her now is that she has not yet been convinced of the militant jihadis' claims of the righteousness of attacking civilians or the glory in dying to kill others.

"I will never go to kill civilians who are not guilty in anything," she says, her eyes widening at the thought. "But after the death of my brother, I have thoughts about blowing myself up in some checkpoint with *military* men," she says. "When I pray, I ask Allah to give me reason and patience not to do it."

Laila needs patience. Only a month before speaking to Khapta she found herself on the bus from Grozny into neighboring Ingushetia where she had to get out at all of the numerous checkpoints and in doing so she was unable to deaden her feelings of rage against the Russian soldiers. Like Elza and Fatima, Laila confesses to Khapta that she has been finding it increasingly difficult to carry on in the face of daily humiliations and dangers and remain passive.

"At the last checkpoint, our bus was stopped by Russian service men," Laila recalls, her voice laced with anger. "They ordered all of us to leave the bus and to show our passports. We got off and the servicemen with their dogs began to check the bus."

This checkpoint is particularly well known and feared by Chechens because at the time it had a "pit" into which Chechens were sometimes thrown for many days, their stories usually ending badly.

Laila's anger had already been bubbling inside, and as all the riders were hauled off of the bus, the terror of knowing any one of them could be hauled off to the pit to be tortured and perhaps eventually killed lit the fuse of a bomb ticking inside her. Like anyone faced with overwhelming threat

---

1 Laila is a pseudonym for a Chechen informant.

to life, Laila had three instinctual choices: to fight, take flight or freeze. Without even thinking it over, her brain chose to fight.

"After checking my passport I moved a little to the side and waited for the check to end," she tells Khapta as her eyes widen in terror. "I saw nearby two soldiers drinking beer, and their automatics lay near them. I don't know how I did it or what for—during that moment there were not any thoughts in my head," she says as her voice raises in fear. "I approached them and snatched up an automatic and pointed it at these two soldiers and told them, 'Hands up!'"

What Laila is describing is a severe dissociative moment in which her posttraumatic rage took over. Common in extreme trauma survivors, it occurs when overwhelming fear, anger or other strong emotions are triggered by reminders of past trauma(s), severely altering their normal state of consciousness and battling helpless terror they move to cold anger in order to be able to cope. In these moments of rage the individual may feel nothing, stop thinking rationally, feel outside of their own bodies or fail to record memories. Laila describes having no thoughts that drove her actions—that she acted automatically in choosing senseless aggression as the involuntary defense to her consuming fear and powerlessness.

"They turned pale, absolutely white - such fear was in their eyes!" Laila smiles grimly, remembering her short moment of power. "I don't remember how long I held them under the barrel."

"Some women from our bus ran up to me and took the gun away and put it back in its place and put me into the bus quickly. Then all the people in the bus screamed at me, that I am not a normal person and so on. They were very frightened, but I didn't feel anything." Laila looks confused by how she could have acted so out of character. To a trauma psychologist, she acted normally in very abnormal circumstances of extreme threat: her amygdala and hippocampus took over, her normal cognitive functions dropped out and her brain judged for itself in its altered state how to save her.

It took some time for Laila to return to her normal self, she recalls with a blank look on her face. "Now I understand that I could have been arrested or killed in that place, but I don't know how I did it."

Although Laila prayed to Allah to stop her from taking violent actions, when her posttraumatic stress disorder (PTSD) was severely triggered, she succumbed into a trance-like state and re-enacted what had been done to her many times—this time with her in the empowered position. Interestingly, her reaction appears both non-volitional and irresistible. Given her posttraumatic grief and rage coupled with her posttraumatic dissociative tendencies, Laila can also fall prey to the militant jihadi ideology enacting terrorism as a means of restoring her sense of empowered self under threat.

Alarmed, Khapta responds to Laila telling that she must find a way to grieve her brother and protect herself from falling into the hands of the militant jihadis, who would tell her that her prayers to Allah to restrain her posttraumatic rage are unnecessary and that Allah wants her to take up arms, kill her enemies and if need be "martyr" herself in doing so. Khapta warns Laila how easily her psychological vulnerability could be manipulated by a group that tells her that to suicide is a sin, but to "martyr" oneself is to honor God and family. They would tell her that "martyrdom" will take her out of her overwhelming emotional pain and bring her to a good end—but in reality that end is death.

CHAPTER 6

"Why Did You Want to Kill Me?"

"I think I have this . . . this PTSD thing," my student Ken confesses anxiously. We are at Vesalius College, the English speaking school within the Free University of Brussels where I teach Psychology classes alongside my research duties, including working on the Chechen suicide terrorism research. The class today is Psychological Testing and we are studying tests that determine posttraumatic stress disorder (PTSD). Ken is leaning in across the desks we've assembled into a small square to hold our small five-student class. His blue eyes stare plaintively into mine as he rubs his hand through his tousled hair. He's an attractive young man and I find it a bit unnerving how he does that from time to time—getting in my space and staring me down, challenging me with his deep blue eyes and sassy smile. I often feel intimidated that he is a young man playing with me and I have to consciously stop myself from blushing in response to his flirtatious male challenges and retain my professorial self with him. But this time it's different. He looks pained and serious. The other students turn to me inquisitively.

"Why do you think you have PTSD, Ken? Did you survive some trauma?" I ask, expecting a story about some childhood experience.

"I was in a suicide bombing. It was in Jerusalem. Some Palestinians blew up the cafeteria at Hebrew University. I had just walked out of the cafeteria when it exploded."

All eyes turn from me to Ken, riveted. My breath catches.

"Can you give us more detail?" I ask.

"It was the second day after I arrived in Jerusalem for my year abroad experience, and I went to have lunch in the Hebrew U cafeteria. During lunch I argued with an Israeli soldier about their treatment of the Palestinians. He told me that it was easy for me to feel that way because I didn't live there, that I was just passing through, and I might feel differently if I lived there. I finished my lunch and left on friendly terms. When I walked out of the cafeteria it exploded. I wasn't far from the door when it went off."

I note that Ken has a look of shock on his face, as though he is reliving the moment.

"What happened to the solider?" I ask.

"He's dead."

"And the others?" I prompt, looking into his eyes.

"The place was completely destroyed," he answers. "There were dead and dying people and body parts scattered all around. And I just stood there like a dumbass staring at them. I didn't do a thing. I didn't help anyone. I stood there like that even when the police and rescue workers came. They put up the security tape and asked me to step back. I didn't help anyone."

"You were shocked," I explain, sensing his deep survivor's guilt and shame at not having offered assistance to the victims. "It's normal Ken. You didn't know what to make of it."

"Yeah, but I just stood there frozen, like an idiot. I watched the ambulances come; I watched them put up the emergency barriers and I did nothing. I feel like a real asshole now."

"It's normal Ken," I repeat, "to freeze in a trauma. It's called peritraumatic dissociation and it actually protects you from being totally and completely overwhelmed. You have flashbacks from this?"

"Yes, but I don't feel like I'm back there in it. It's detached, unreal. You see, I chose to go to Israel because I was watching the Palestinian Intifada [the uprising] on the television every day, and I thought 'I'll go there and see it for real, not on the television, and make up my mind what I think about things, when I see them for myself.' But when the bomb went off I suddenly saw everything back like it was on the TV screen. That's how I see it now too. It's in a television box and it's not real."

I nod. Like many trauma survivors Ken dissociates whenever posttraumatic flashbacks occur. They are so real, so sensory that just like in the real event, his mind can't cope with the overwhelming sights, sounds and sensory data and automatically finds a way to distance himself from it. In some survivors this can go so far as to include amnesia. For Ken, posttraumatic recall is kept at bay by feeling as if he's watching it on television and that it never really happened to him. As Ken begins to understand his peritraumatic dissociation and work through his shame over having frozen, he will begin to own the events as part of his narrative, and no longer have to keep them at a distance.

On the first day of the semester, I told my students, "No matter what you admit here in class, I will think you are completely messed up and incurable." The students looked at me in fear, and I laughed heartily. They picked up on my joke and chuckled: I had just given them permission to admit anything without fear of judgment. Throughout the semester, the students had opened up to me, whether it be in class or in private one-on-one meetings as they lingered after to talk. One had grown up in a seriously violent home and talked about what he had endured as a child. One described surviving a massacre while camping in the former Soviet Union with her father.

In the class, I had all the students take the psychological tests we studied, and we discussed them in detail, deciding if the items really measured what they were supposed to and if they felt the test results gave a fair assessment. I never made them share their results, yet just undergoing the testing made them all incredibly anxious. I was constantly bombarded with questions of, "Do you think I'm abnormal?" which just made me laugh more. I always tried to convey that anyone can be healthy if they want to be, and our lack of mental health is usually only because we got stuck by some experience, thought, belief or emotion that still needs sorting out.

Ken pauses and looks at me afraid, as if I might tell him that, yes, this time, he *is* abnormal. But he reads compassion without judgment in my eyes and continues, "It's like a movie, I can see it all again exactly like it was. But it's not real, not me there in that scene. It's like watching the news."

"This happens to many trauma victims—that sense of it not being real," I explain. "But it shouldn't last so long."

I already know from previous classes that Ken had a bizarre and chaotic childhood. His mother grew up as the oldest child of deaf parents, and his father was a businessman who came from a rough upbringing. According to Ken, he and his brother were left unsupervised a lot; he ended up in a Jesuit reform school after crashing the family car at age thirteen, and his brother went in and out of prison for petty crimes. Ken is always emotionless when describing his childhood, a blank look on his face and a matter-of-fact tone as though growing up somewhat neglected is normal. And his early childhood behaviors sound a bit on the autistic spectrum to me. He says as a toddler he loved to watch the clothes flying around in the washer while he would do rhythmic motions with his hands, hypnotized watching them. Likewise he describes going on dissociative flights of fantasy in classes that bore him, pretending that he is sky-diving out of an airplane or on some other fantasy adventure that completely absorbs his imagination while he "escapes" for five to ten minute spurts of time. While it's normal to block the emotions of a trauma and Ken has certainly done that, he blocks a lot of things, so maybe this is a lifelong pattern for him, not just a response to a trauma.

After class, I ask Ken if he might like to talk privately with me about the suicide bombing rather than in class, but he declines. Instead every chance he gets, he brings it up in the classroom and we discuss it at length for the remainder of the semester. I feel this is fine, as it will help him come to terms with this horrible experience and his informal classroom "psychotherapy" is a strong case for the others to learn from. Indeed, his peers are relentlessly engaged by his full-blown case of PTSD.

As the weeks progress, we learn that Ken had responded to his shame over freezing in the face of the terrorist attack by instituting a series of compensation and preparation measures.

"After the attack, whenever I got on the bus in Jerusalem I picked out the person that was going to die if we got attacked," he admits.

"What do you mean, Ken?" I ask, confused.

"Well there were suicide attacks nearly every week and most of them were on the buses," he explains. "I was ready. If a guy came on the bus and shouted 'Allahu Akbar', I had already picked out the person I was going to throw at him to knock them both out the door of the bus."

The whole class recoils in horror making audible gasps in response to his disclosure, followed by silence.

"That's awful, Ken." I answer, shocked. "I can see saving the rest of the bus by fighting him yourself, but you picked someone else to throw at him?"

Ken is resolute. "Listen it was either we would all die, or because I was ready and watching I could save us and only one person would die. I wanted to live, so I picked out the person that would have to die, to save the rest of us. It was usually somebody old that had already lived a long life."

The whole class is intrigued that his desire to save himself is greater than his desire to be truly heroic.

"Don't you feel bad for the one you are throwing off the bus?" Beatrice asks, her voice rising with concern.

"Hell no!" Ken says. "The way I see it only one of us dies this way, instead of all of us."

"Why wouldn't you throw yourself on the bomber versus pick someone else to die instead of you?" I ask surprised by Ken's callous admission that he is not a hero.

"I want to stay alive," he says laughing cynically. "At least I save the rest of the bus." Ken shrugs his shoulders.

Ken has no shame about his decision to sacrifice one of the bus riders to save the rest, and yet his deep shame over his inability to act following the suicide attack persists. For me, it's a bit of a contradiction—I wouldn't morally feel right selecting and sacrificing another person to die so that I and others could live. Although, in practical terms, he has made a rational and humanistic decision that likely would save the entire bus if no one else was ready or willing to sacrifice themselves. My discomfort is likely a product of my Christian upbringing where Ken was raised as a modern European and has no such deeply ingrained beliefs. Yet the other students, also agnostic Europeans, side with me in giving Ken a hard time over what he's just admitted, and this remains a topic of discussion for weeks to come.

Ken's determination to be ready in the event of another attack also led him to take martial arts and emergency medical response training. During the year he spent in Jerusalem at the height of the second Intifada, he assisted as a volunteer medic in the ambulances that served the areas of Jerusalem frequently hit by suicide bombers.

Despite this training, he describes changes in behavior that suggest his ongoing fear of a similar occurrence.

"I never linger in a restaurant anymore. I always eat fast and bolt out of there," he explains.

Ken's experience turns the class into an unusual learning experience for all of us. He asks to circumvent the class assignment of designing his own psychological test and instead wants to develop an interview for Palestinians in jail in Israel on the subject of suicide bombing. He knows that it is a subject I am researching, and he pulls out all the plugs arguing for why it is an appropriate substitution. I give in, believing it will help him grapple with some of his issues.

Ken brings his first attempt at the interview to class to circulate and test it out on his peers, but it turns out to be no more than an angry rant. Instead of asking them about themselves, his questions include angry challenges such as, "So do you really believe this seventy-two virgins crap?" (He is referring to the Islamic belief that a "martyr" meets seventy-two virgins in Paradise.) I send him home pointing out that he needs to formulate serious questions, and that angry accusations are not research and will not get at any real answers. But repeatedly, Ken returns to class with similar rants at the Palestinians who represent those who almost killed him, and repeatedly I send him home to work on it some more. Finally I get exasperated and ask Al, another student, to team up with him and develop it into a real interview. When they do, I put them through the paces.

"Try it out here in class, Ken," I instruct. "Al, you be the imprisoned Palestinian, Ken you be the interviewer coming to prison."

They fall into their roles immediately.

Ken who has an angry chip on his shoulder when it comes to suicide bombers is surprisingly charming.

"I can't just start the interview without some offering of hospitality—this is the Middle East!" he explains to us as he turns to Al asking, "Would you like some tea? And have some dates," he offers, pushing an imaginary plate of dates over to Al.

Al goes along as they move through the interview questions: How long has he been in prison? What is his crime? (He was arrested for being involved in a suicide attack). Did he have family members? I focus on Al, coaching him to make sure he gives answers realistic for a suicide bomber, and so I don't notice how upset Ken is becoming as Al moves deeper into his role. As Al justifies his actions, explaining what it is like to live under the blockades in a militarized Israeli occupied zone and that his suicide mission was for revenge, Ken suddenly leaps up, his chair crashing to its side behind him, and lunges for Al, grabbing him by the throat.

Everyone in the class gasps and pushes their chairs back from the sudden action happening in front of us.

"Why did you want to kill ME you bastard?" Ken screams. "Why ME? I'm Irish. I'm not even fucking Israeli! Why did you try to kill ME?"

Al is fast and he pushes Ken back off himself, and they both tumble to the ground. "It's a role play, man," Al says. "Get a grip!"

They rise from the floor, both laughing and shaking off the dust from their clothes. Ken picks up his chair and Al his, and they sit down, Ken dazed by his sudden outburst but still finding it humorous.

In a way it's a breakthrough. Ken is there finally feeling everything, feeling his anger, working through it and healing. By keeping his poise in response, Al has given Ken the opportunity to see how much emotion he has still locked inside.

They keep at the mock interviews for a few more weeks, Ken settling in and asking his questions calmly as Al first acts the part of the suicide bomber, then Beatrice. During that time, we notice a very strange phenomenon among the people playing the terrorist. Each begins by following basic suggestions about what it is to be a Palestinian in the occupied territories, but then they fall deeply into character and seem to get dissociative as they discuss their role as a suicide bomber. Their faces go slack, they seem to enter a trancelike state and it looks like they need to separate, or clinically speaking "dissociate", their own emotions to be able to "remember" putting on a suicide vest, even in role-play. This discovery gives rise to yet another adventure from this class. I ask the students if they would like to develop this concept into a "thought experiment" and they agree immediately.[25]

We develop a project in which nineteen students of varied nationalities are invited one by one into our laboratory to take part in a role-play in which, after a safety screening and informed consent process, they are asked to play the part of a failed suicide bomber. Each student is told that they should pretend to be a Palestinian who has been arrested and prevented from carrying out a suicide bombing at the very last moment, and that now, at the time of the interview, they are being visited by researchers in prison. We give them context about the difficult circumstances of Palestinian life and some basic constraints as to how they were brought into terrorism: they are sometimes confined to their homes for days on end and cannot get to university or work, they were self-recruited (i.e. volunteered) for their suicide mission, and that one of the tipping points for them in becoming a suicide bomber was that they saw *on television* an Israeli soldier kill two Palestinian boys. The students are then free to construct their own story for the role-play and to even pick their own target for the "would-be" suicide bombing.

We have several goals in giving the role players the particular set-up of suggesting that they have watched an Israeli soldier kill two young

Palestinian boys on TV. We are first curious to see if they imagine signs of secondary traumatization[26] from witnessing a soldier killing innocents on the television and if they will identify with the victim. Secondly we wonder how far their identification will go—if they will create a sense of "fictive kinship" with these two imaginary boys.

Khapta and I had already learned in our Chechen research that *witnessing* injustices in a conflict zone is enough to be an individual motivator for terrorist activity, and from what we know, television and Internet images are an amazing medium when it comes to the potential to traumatize. Even when one witnesses from a distance over this medium, the psychological impact can be immense and the memory of it can be confused with having had the experience in reality. The same is true for victims of terrorism, some who have strong acute stress responses from viewing televised images of events they were not even close to experiencing.[27]

Nichole Argo, a colleague I was corresponding with at the time in 2006, was conducting research interviews in Palestine and reports the response of a leader of the Popular Front for the Liberation of Palestine (PFLP) from Khan Yunis (June 2004) on the impact of television:

"The difference between the first Intifada and the second is television. Before I knew when we were attacked here or in a nearby camp, but the reality of the attacks everywhere else was not so clear. Now, I cannot get away from Israeli attacks—the TV brings them into my living room. When they are not in my camp, they are in Rafah, Gaza City, Ramallah, Jenin... And you can't turn the TV off. How could you live with yourself? At the same time, you can't ignore the problem—what are you doing to protect your people? We live in an internal struggle. Whether you choose to fight or not, every day is this internal struggle."[28]

Incarcerated Palestinian "failed" suicide terrorists also recounted their posttraumatic stress responses after viewing televised images of violence to journalist Amira Hass: "The things we see on television are nauseating and make us lose our taste for life…", One such respondent even goes so far as to credit what he saw on television as the main motivation for his thwarted act of suicide terrorism, " The pictures we saw on television are what influenced me and pushed me to make the decision to do the operation."[29]

As I would learn as I went along, terror-sponsoring organizations understand this psychological effect and make use of video, televised and Internet images to motivate and capture impressionistic youth outside of conflict zones into joining jihadi groups. Indeed, some of the images found on the Internet used to promote al Qaeda-type terrorist ideologies urging violent responses to the West have become iconic. When one delves deeper into the images and stories behind them, the truth is often much different than what is portrayed, but like all iconic images, the truth is often of much less importance than what they have come to represent: a rallying call to action in behalf of the downtrodden and victimized.

But while we now suggest to our subjects that seeing the Israeli soldier kill the Palestinian boys on TV was a type of "galvanizing event", something that we know actually pushed the "failed" suicide terrorists into action, we are curious to see if the role players, unfamiliar with such media propagation and methods of indirect traumatization, will be able to accept the suggestions of an event witnessed on television as a strong and rational motivator for and justification of suicide terrorism, rather than being told they personally experienced a trauma or injustice, and if they will successfully submerge themselves in their character.

All of the students who arrive at the role-play are surprised at the request to act the part of a suicide bomber, often dropping their jaws or opening their eyes wide at the suggestion before agreeing, but when they realize we are serious they shrug their shoulders or laugh and calmly agree.

I do the interviewing and we always start with Ken's technique of pretending to offer a sweet. I ask first about the subject's imagined family and life as a Palestinian, and soon we get to the motivations for becoming a bomber.

The students quickly and strongly identify with the story, so much so that many construct stories that include two boys either as brothers or as sons that need to be protected or revenged for, or they change the suggestion to say that they had actually viewed the killing in person, even though the initial direction had emphatically said it was *viewed on the television*.

Seventy-nine percent of the students identify immediately with the shooting of the two small children by fantasizing themselves as either the parent of small children or the older sibling of younger siblings.

For instance in role-play, one student says he has two younger brothers and tells us, "I was thinking of the kids at home the whole time, it made me stronger … it could have happened to them. It could have been my brothers. As I went toward the target I didn't look to the soldiers. I was thinking of those two boys. I felt conscious of what I was going to do, to help stop massacres. Everyday kids die from Israelis soldiers."

These answers also strike another concept: the idea of fictive kin, which we defined as present in the role-play if our subjects create some sense of family ties with the two boys that we told them they had seen killed on TV by an Israeli soldier. For example, if the subject told us that he or she had a family member of the same age as the boys and/or directly named a relationship to the boys (i.e. stating they could have been my sons or brothers and therefore I was willing to die in their behalf), fictive kinship is considered present. Scott Atran writes that current terrorist ideologies, particularly those of an Islamic nature and their sponsoring units, often promote this concept within their ideology and practices by referring to other Muslims undergoing traumas, even in other cultures and nationalities, as "brothers" invoking the widely held Islamic conviction that all Muslim believers belong to a worldwide "ummah" or family of Muslim brothers and sisters.[30] On the home front, terrorist ideologues also encourage terrorist members to identify with their terror cell mates as fictive kin, inspiring loyalty and a willingness to die for them as they would for mother, father, brother or sister—a phenomena we have found in our research as well.[31]

In our study seventy-nine percent of the students identify immediately with the shooting of the two small children by fantasizing themselves as either their parent or older sibling, making the shootings both personal and "real.

With their motivations set in place, we ask the students about their imagined targets. About a quarter of the students limit their choice to a strictly military or government target (i.e. military checkpoint, government house, etc.).

One young man explains, "I was going to the government building, because I wanted the people in charge with some authority to die." One young woman explains, "I chose the Western Wall because it is where I'd inflict the most pain, hit them where it hurts."Another young woman states, "I went on a crowded bus full of civilians. Because they pick civilians to kill." Another young man states that his target was a school because, "They kill our children all the time. If you want to hurt them you have to hurt their future."

The remainder of the students chose civilian targets but don't mention specifically targeting children, teenagers or extremely sensitive locations (i.e. cafes, buses, busy markets, etc.). Hence the majority of the students (seventy-four percent) display the concept of generalized revenge and the willingness to target civilian populations.

Regarding targeting civilians a female states, "I had a quick flash of pity, but I didn't let it overtake me."

It's interesting to me to listen to this mix of international students because some of them I know from other classes I've taught and I know they are generally mild-mannered, nice kids. Yet in role-play they become ruthless in their decisions about who they would kill. One girl who chose an elementary school as her target bursts into tears when she "returns" to herself, shocked that she was so cold hearted in choosing to target children.

As we proceed with the interviews, we notice the same phenomena that we found amongst ourselves in class.

"How did you get the bomb?" I ask. "And how did you feel when you put it on?"

More than half of the subjects go "dissociative" at this point. They describe how putting on a bomb made them feel powerful, invincible, and how they felt like were floating, or outside of their own body, once it was strapped on. Some describe euphoria. Others describe emotional numbing.

For example, a young female student states, "[The bomb] felt heavy, not only physically but emotionally heavy, because there was no turning back once it's on. I had no fear, more of a tranquility. Committing so strongly—it is like your medicine, your remedy that this will solve everything. . . The journey wearing the belt was like a dream, I floated along. I interacted with people but my mind was not there. I was not totally unconscious, but it was a muted scene, my senses were dulled. It felt euphoric, everything at ease."

"How did you feel about being caught?" I ask.

"Like being woken up from a dream."

Another female role player tells us, "I was in a kind of euphoria. I was afraid it wouldn't last. I had to hurry."

Another female describes how she felt strapping on the imaginary bomb: "I started getting adrenalin, a good feeling. I was not scared. I thought of my mission that I was going to fulfill."

A male student explains his imagined mental state with the bomb strapped on, "I felt a very peaceful moment. I'd made everything let go, I'd been cleansed of all doubt, all big burdens lifted from me. There were very vivid, very bright colors, and I could smell the air. My adrenaline was pumping and I noticed everything, like in sports."

"It's like being in control of your own destiny," one young man explains. "I felt confidence and knowledge that my destiny is already sealed. You lose that insecurity of the future… I felt calmness and security."

A female student explains using a dissociative defense to shut out her fear and recognition of the finality of death. "I was very focused," she explains. "I shut everything out."

"You were in your own world?" I ask.

"Yes.…You just see the plan in the future, getting to that goal. I don't know why I wasn't terrified. I knew everything would be better afterward."

Listening to these students in role-play, I am amazed. A professional colleague, Bruce Bongar, who studied normal suicide years earlier told me that surprisingly many people audio or video tape their suicide. As a graduate student, he had reviewed countless videos and audio tape recordings of normal suicides that were carried to completion. In nearly every case he reviewed, the suicidal person generally went "dissociative" as he came closer to doing the act.[32] It makes sense. How else could someone kick the chair, pull the trigger, or in the case of a suicide bomber, pull the strap that would detonate himself along with all his victims? Without dissociation, it's too horrible of a death to contemplate.

And here are ordinary students with no knowledge of suicide bombing—some don't even know where Israel is—who, after strapping on imaginary bombs, describe experiencing the same dissociative effects as real bombers, floating outside of their bodies, feeling emotionally numb, euphoric or all powerful. I realize if this response shows up even in a role-play with normal students, we as humans must have some internal mechanism to detach from ourselves and our emotions to be able to kill ourselves. Dissociation in suicide is therefore innate.

Some students also mix statements of religious beliefs with descriptions of their dissociated mental state. A male student says in his role-play, "When one is dying for one's religion, it is the most noble death one can experience. I felt a certain peace of mind. I was dying for my religion. I felt a little high on myself. In that state of mind, you have to understand, everything stops around you. You're in your own little world. It's strange."

"Is it a good feeling?" I ask.

"Yes definitely."

"You still have it?" I ask, knowing as I watch him slack-jawed and relaxed that he has entered that euphoric state as he describes it in his role-play "memory".

"Yes," he answers.

"Could it be stronger?" I ask, curious what would strengthen it for him.

Chillingly he answers, "Yes, by completing my mission. I felt untouchable and a sense of awe." Interestingly I will later meet a real Palestinian bomber [Omaia Damaj – written about in Chapter Twenty-three] who was stopped from carrying out her task and she will say almost the same things.

Likewise when we ask about what their mental and emotional state was with the bomb strapped on, eighty-four percent of the students imagine experiencing positive feelings going forward to explode themselves. Nearly half state that they suddenly felt empowered as they strapped on the bomb.

One male states, "It felt like I had extra power. Knowing I could take someone's life with the press of a button. It felt really good—like I could do anything." Another male says, "I felt powerful, very powerful, full of courage, full of might. It was the first time I felt that way."

A young woman states, "Yes, it has power to kill and to take lives without them having any say, like a surprise. I had never taken another's life in my hands before. I had to be strong and couldn't back down. I couldn't let fear interrupt my mission. I didn't feel joy but pride."

We ask all the students about their feelings facing death, and well over half state that they are peaceful. A very bright young man explains, perhaps not comprehending the finality of death, "I'd be at peace, no longer frustrated and no longer see others frustrated. It would be good for my own state of mind."

Perhaps this can be compared to the real thwarted Palestinian student bomber, reported to me by a research colleague, who agreed to be a bomber but told his sender he would have to wait for his mission until the day after he completed his exams—as though having completed his exams would make any difference after his death.

As we conduct our study watching ordinary students fall so easily into these roles, unknowingly spouting many of the same words that terrorists do, it suddenly becomes abundantly clear: it is not hard to push even an ordinary person into the mindset of justifying killing for revenge.[33] If a terrorist leader knows how to emotionally manipulate others by making a relation to age (in that we all feel some sense of protection to children) or to religion (in that we often name each other as brothers and sisters within the same faith group) and creating a sense of fictive kin, by taking advantage of secondary traumatization and making use of dissociative behaviors, he can motivate an ordinary person along a trajectory to become a terrorist. If he's dealing with a traumatized population inside a conflict zone, he can engender the dissociative response without too much difficulty, enabling recruits to go emotionally numb, or, even more chillingly, feel power and euphoria, both of which can lead to the birth of a suicide bomber. And, as I learned already from the Chechen interviews, if a recruit has personally experienced a traumatic event, they may seek out a terrorist group to equip them for revenge and to help them exit life in a way they come to believe is glorious.

As I watch it with the students, the various pieces of the terrorist's trajectory begin to come together, preparing me for Palestine.

CHAPTER 7

Entering Palestine

It's early morning, November 1, 2004. Amar Rahim Ahmed Ali, a sixteen-year-old Palestinian, is on his way into Israel, traveling through the checkpoints on the West Bank along with his handlers. Meanwhile, Ken, Al and I are in Brussels, boarding a plane, also headed for Israel. After the thought experiment, Ken has finally talked me into going to Israel, promising me has good contacts with a Palestinian translator and places for us to stay. He wants me to try to study the Palestinian suicide bombers, and Al, another student, is in for the ride as well.

Amar has been waiting for his suicide mission for more than a month. Originally, he was to go on a double suicide attack, but the killing of a senior member of the Popular Front for the Liberation of Palestine (PFLP) and the arrest of several co-conspirators has delayed the mission and now reassigned him as the sole attacker. While our plane is soaring over the Alps, Amar walks into the crowded outdoor Carmel Market in Tel Aviv and blows himself up. I check my Blackberry as our plane taxis to the gate and read the horrific news: the Israeli papers are already reporting that three Israeli citizens have been murdered and forty injured as a result of the bombing. Amar and his two handlers, I read, came from Nablus, a hotbed for suicide bombers and a city that will be on our itinerary.[34]

As we exit the plane, Al is singled out on the tarmac by a tall, tanned, dark haired, and shapely female border agent sporting reflective sunglasses.

"Why are you traveling on a brand new passport?" she asks aggressively.

Flustered, Al spouts, "Terrorism."

Though we are there to interview Palestinians who support and are involved in terrorism, that is not what we are supposed to say.

Al corrects himself with a quick, "Tourism."

The woman nods, looking at him quizzically for a moment and then smiles and lets him through.

As we present ourselves at passport control, I go over once again the advice that I've received so many times from more experienced colleagues. "Don't admit your plans to go to the West Bank. Say that you came to sightsee in Jerusalem." You don't need to speak behind closed doors to get this kind of advice—even the U.S. State Department, one of Israel's staunchest allies, states in its travel advisories that visitors who admit to plans to travel to the West Bank or Gaza may well be turned back at the border. I breathe deeply as I slide my passport into the entry officer's hands.

After a careful study of my passport the young female officer looks up and asks, "What are your reasons for coming to Israel?"

I smile into her pretty face and tell her, "I'm the Director of the Holo-caust Oral Histories Project—Belarus and I am here to work on my research as well as hopefully to do some sightseeing." This begins a conversation with the officer, who is clearly impressed that I have interviewed all the Holocaust survivors still living in Minsk. "These are my students," I say nodding toward Ken and Al. "Ken studied in Israel for a year abroad and speaks Hebrew, so I brought him along to help translate. Al is here more for the tourist experience." She looks at their passports and questions them as well. For the most part they defer to me, but we all smile genu-inely when we tell her that we hope to enjoy Jerusalem. That I am a Holo-caust researcher is true and if I get time I will go to the museum on this trip to look up Belarusian Holocaust histories to compare to the many I've already collected in Minsk. Our passports get stamped and we pass into a massive sunny limestone hall to recover our bags.

With some relief we congratulate ourselves on having passed border control and begin excitedly discussing the experience. Ken and Al laugh recalling how good-looking the woman who stopped Al on the tarmac was. Perhaps it was Al's shy smile that made her let him pass? Reliv-ing the tense moment, Ken chides, "Geez, Al with your shaved head and brand new Belgian passport they probably thought you were a skinhead!" I glance over at Al and think he could fit the type, although I know he's far from it.

We pick up our bags, head toward the exit, and pass a glimmering foun-tain, the bright yellow sun glinting through the open doors of the terminal. Then a plain-clothes guard suddenly steps out in front of us and blocks our way, as he asks to see our passports.

"Why have you come to Israel?" he asks. "And why," he turns to Al, "do you have a new passport?"

"We were so close," I think as I read the serious look on his face. I suddenly realize the airport is surely crawling with hidden cameras, listening devices, and undercover agents.

"Look," I intervene, "these are my students. They are traveling with me and helping me with my Holocaust research project."

The mention of anything related to the Holocaust once more brings respect. He asks a few more questions and then backs off. We walk through the sunlit exit and disappear into the crowds of people hailing taxis.

Ken leads the way to the minibus that will take us from Tel Aviv to Jerusalem and into the heart of the old city, where we are expecting to meet Dara, one of Ken's Arab Israeli friends. She has agreed to house me while Ken and Al stay with other friends from his study year abroad and serve as our translator inside the West Bank. Evening falls as we approach the limestone walls encircling the inner city. They are lit up like candelabra, the battlements at the tops of the ancient walls conjuring images of fight scenes in old movies. Inside the old city we pass by the Western or Wailing Wall of the ancient Jewish temple, the last remnant of the temple built by Herod in the first century, which rose out of the ruins of the original temple built by Solomon. For Jews the place is sacred, thought to be the closest site to the Holy of Holies, the original gateway to heaven. Now the al Aqsa Mosque, one of the holiest places for Muslims, towers over the wall, its gold dome gleaming in the last rays of sunlight. The clash of cultures is evident in these iconic sites, one rising over the ruins of the other in the heart of Jerusalem.

"Maybe we should stop to pray?" I suggest given how anxious we've all been about coming to Israel. Ken and Al don't take God very seriously, but Al says he would like to see the Wall so we pass through the heavily guarded checkpoint. Hundreds of devout Jews stand and kneel in two gender segregated areas, the men dressed in long black suits and wool hats that emulate the 16th century Hassidic dress of Eastern Europe, the women wearing long skirts, long sleeves, and head coverings. They all pray while rocking back and forth, bending to touch their heads to the Wall as they cry out their lamentations over the destruction of the temple.

I've been to the Wall before and I believe in the holiness of the site, hoping a bit like a naïve child, that my prayer written on a small folded paper wedged between the rocks of the Wall won't simply fall down unnoticed but will catch the attention of the Almighty. Ken and Al poke fun at me for praying, though I think Al left a prayer in the Wall as well.

We continue along into the arched stone walkways between the holy sites of Jerusalem, entering corridors of colorful markets where vendors hawk their candles, crosses, commemorative plates, headscarves, menorahs, evil eyes, prayer rugs, shawls, spices, and countless other sparkling items that tourists stop to buy as they make their pilgrimages through the inner city. Ken leads us to the Damascus Gate in East Jerusalem, where the Arab Israelis live. As we approach I note the dwindling number of Westerners. Women wearing long colorful abayas and head coverings and men in Arabic thobes (robes) sandals and short circular caps soon surrounded us.

It's Ramadan, the ninth month of the Islamic calendar—a month of daytime fasting and evening gathering for Muslims. Ramadan is considered a holy month because Muslims believe this is when the first verses of the Koran were revealed to their Prophet, Muhammad. During the month of Ramadan, participating Muslims abstain from food, drink and sexual relations from dawn to sunset. It's a time for reflection, prayers, self-purification and giving charity to the poor. In the evenings Muslims break the Ramadan fasts together with an Iftar meal, and it is traditional in some settings for guests to bring small presents for the children. In many places festive lanterns are lit and hung in the evenings and many people are out late at night.

Here at the Damascus Gate under the setting sun, many Arab Israelis have come out to gather in a celebratory mood. Vendors hawk hot food and bread, entertainers juggle fire sticks, children run chasing each other, the crowds mill about festively. We emerge from the inner city into the cool evening air, and the crenellated walls surrounding the old city look as though they reach up to touch the stars. Suddenly we hear gunfire and stop in our tracks. It's a couple of Arab Israeli teenagers shooting a pistol into the sky, laughing and hooting as they fire. They look far too young to have a pistol in their hands, and I wonder what happens when the bullets fall back to earth. Two policeman come running and the boys take off. No one seems alarmed, though my feet suddenly begin to feel wooden as we move deeper into the Arab side of town. Ken leads us through the crowds and into a youth hostel aptly named "The Palms."

It isn't until we reached the Damascus Gate that Ken admits his plans for our stay have fallen through. Now he announces we will stay in the youth hostel. I'm shocked by the news and feel concerned about his dependability as we check in.

The nice Palestinian man at the desk asks, "Would you like the only room that has an actual lock on the door, or will you be fine with the communal bunkrooms?" I have no idea how to answer. I like the idea of a private room, but the man explains that this would mean sharing one large bed with my two male students—an awkward proposal, to say the least. My mind is already reeling at the fact that I've ended up in a hostel on the Arab side of Jerusalem so I defer to Ken when he opts for the communal bunks.

My communal room, it turns out, is already filled with middle-aged Christian evangelical women who have each come alone to Jerusalem on a holy mission to preach repentance to the Jews of Jerusalem. The apocalypse, in their minds, is imminent. They talk quietly, a few moving rosary beads through their fingers, and I can't help but think that they look a bit mentally deranged, though kind. I find an empty bunk against the wall. I'll have to drag the only chair in the room over to the bunk to climb up to sleep. As I store my wheelie bag under the bottom bed, I laugh softly, thinking, "My things should be safe with this crowd." Then I go out to rejoin Ken and Al.

We have a good dinner together and later meet up with Ken's friends who tell us, as I have been telling Ken all along, that Dara will not be able to come with us as a translator when we go to the West Bank. Ken didn't listen when I told him Israelis, even those with Palestinian heritage, are prohibited from traveling to the West Bank and Gaza. One of the Arab students suggests we instead travel to Birzeit University in Ramallah (in the West Bank) to try to pick up a translator.

The evening brings the disquiet of sleeping with a community of women who appear schizophrenic; the morning, the further indignity of appearing in the communal bathroom in the one and only nightie I brought—a skimpy little thing that would have looked fine in a private apartment but that reveals far too much for a youth hostel, let alone one filled with Arabs and half-crazed evangelical Christians.

Lounging on a low wall, I later sit alone under the bright Middle Eastern sun, munching the fresh bread sold by a nearby vendor and looking over at the ancient battlements of old Jerusalem. I watch the buzz of

Arab men selling and delivering goods while the women in bright abayas bustle along the streets laden with grocery bags full of fresh produce. In Belgium we live under nearly permanent grey skies so I feel like a sponge soaking up the sunlight. I can't stay mad at Ken—despite the failures, it's not a bad adventure we're on. I just won't be letting Ken make any more important arrangements.

It's a short walk from our hostel to the lot of white minibuses that travel into the West Bank. Ken runs from bus to bus trying to decipher the Arabic labels. I don't want any more misadventures, so I also begin asking the many Palestinians which bus goes to Ramallah. No one speaks English, but they understand when I say Ramallah, and point shyly to the stop where we should line up for the bus. Ken returns to tell us that the small minibus I've found is indeed headed for Ramallah and laughs when he sees I've lost trust in him. We board and find we're the only western-ers and English speakers on the bus. We are the obvious subject of a lot of staring and conversation. My students, both handsome young men, laugh flirtatiously as some of the girls make furtive glances and smile in our direction.

After traveling a half hour up a winding olive tree-lined road our mini-bus stops to let us off in an unpaved and dusty car park. We follow the streams of Palestinians walking to the Kalandia checkpoint, where we will officially pass out of Israel and into the occupied West Bank. Our greet-ing: a high, cyclone-fenced dirt corridor and a gigantic sign that reads "Mortal danger—Passing this fence you are entering into a Military Zone. Any person who passes this fence endangers his life."

I look around at the Israeli soldiers that line the other side of the fence. All wear helmets and flak jackets and carry automatic rifles. We move like herded animals into a pen. I notice a high, round cement lookout tower with small slots at the top. More soldiers lounge near it under a camou-flage mesh tent, watching through their mirrored sunglasses as the crowds of Palestinians make their way through the long column up to the check-point. The soldiers look aggressive with a dangerous mix of boredom and alarm, ready for anything to erupt at anytime.

I feel intimidated and humiliated trudging beneath these men with guns. Looking around me I notice that many more men than women are passing. Everyone looks tired, worn and poor. The men appear to be day laborers; they are heavily tanned and dressed in casual work clothes. The women are either young stylish students in body hugging jeans and knit shirts, many of them wearing headscarves, or older heavier women with traditional abayas, headscarves and shawls that cover them from head to foot.

My colleagues advised me how to dress: flat shoes, dress pants, and a suit-coat long enough to covers my backside, with a scarf wrapped around my neck and my hair drawn up into a clip. As I look around I realize I could easily pass for one of the Palestinian women. My hair is long and brown, my brown eyes are large almond shaped, and I'm dressed close enough to the style to pass. Only my students stand out—they look European next to the dark hair, dark eyes, and sun-darkened Palestinians—and they are dressed much more stylishly in modern jeans and college style t-shirts.

Our passports are not checked on the way in. We freely pass soldiers holding back the long lines of men and women waiting to head the other way, into East Jerusalem. On our side of the checkpoint, lines of taxis and white minibuses wait for customers as crowds of Palestinians pick their way across the rocky and rutted car-park. We hear one of the minibus drivers calling out "Ramallah! Ramallah! Ramallah!" We double-check with a young girl who smiles shyly and answers, "Yes, this is the correct bus," as she boards in front of us. As we take our seats, we ask if she can help us find Birzeit University. She agrees to show us to the city center and point out the next minibus, but that's as far as she will go.

Our minibus leaves the dusty lot behind and begins climbing a winding road through the hills around Ramallah. In another half hour we arrive, and the girl signals to us to follow.

The Ramallah city center is made up of mostly two and three story limestone buildings similar to those in East Jerusalem; the boulevards are lined with short trees. As we pass by the smooth stone buildings we see hundreds of "martyr posters" plastered to the windows and the walls of the buildings. The posters depict young men, old men, women, even children—all "martyrs", many posing with automatics who either went to kill themselves while killing Israelis or were gunned down in street demonstrations.

Near the city center we see a crowd of young men gathered around a small monument of bronze lions and a steel structure with more posters and writings hanging from the beams. They yell out slogans. Suddenly we hear repeated gunfire. The girl looks alarmed and tells us, "I don't want to walk any further." She points out where we need to go to catch the bus to Birzeit, but we stand frozen in our tracks.

"It's okay," she says. "Just stay away from the shooting." Some comfort. We hesitate, take courage from her words, and then continue on toward the gunshots and the next bus.

The Birzeit university campus is another twenty minutes out of town, uphill all the way. It's an impressive sight: a modern university with multiple buildings, well groomed grounds full of colorful plantings and new facilities—rivaling many a U.S. campus. We go to speak to the administration, where we are warmly welcomed and directed to the English faculty to explain our project. After some discussion about how difficult it may be to carry out our interviews, they agree to help find a student translator the next day.

On our way out, we approach some students lounging around the campus. They laugh and act shy at first, but one girl in jeans and a headscarf, Nadia, speaks up and begins to translate for us. She asks who we are and what we are doing and I decide to answer with total honesty. I tell her, "I'm a university professor in Belgium and these are my two students. I study terrorism and we want to interview people involved in suicide missions." Nadia gasps and her eyes widen. "That's impossible!" she says. "No one will agree to talk to you about that!"

I explain my hope that people will trust me enough to speak about it. Nadia turns to the group of students and they have an animated discussion. Then she translates, "No one here knows anyone involved but they say you can come back tomorrow and try to interview some of the other students who have served time as political prisoners in Israeli prisons. We are having a meeting tomorrow to protest the 'wall' and you can come for that." We agree and arrange to meet again in the morning—with Nadia now as our translator.

The next morning we gather at a tent with students protesting against the construction of what the Israelis call the "security fence" and what Palestinians call the "wall." Made up of twenty-four foot high semi-moveable barriers, the security wall is a huge, continuous cement barrier separating Palestinian and Israeli territory that will ultimately be close to five hundred miles (eight hundred kilometers) long. There is also a hundred-and-eighty-foot (sixty meter) exclusion area alongside the wall, which is equipped with sensors to prevent prospective suicide bombers from climbing over in unpatrolled areas.

During the second Intifada, or Palestinian uprising, which began in September 2000, Israel suffered far more suicide attacks than the country ever had before. According to Israeli security statistics, seventy-three mass attacks, killing two hundred ninety three Israelis and wounding one thousand nine hundred and fifty, occurred between September 2000 and August 2003. After the completion of the wall in 2003 the number of attacks dropped from seventy-three to twelve, with far fewer Israelis killed and wounded. There is, in other words, clear evidence that the wall works.

But, opponents of the wall argue that it is placed well inside the Green Line (the Israel–Palestine border established prior to the Six-Day War of 1967), constituting an illegal attempt to annex Palestinian land under the guise of security. Palestinians also argue that the wall preempts any final negotiations over the status of their country, severely restricts access to work in Israel and free movement within the West Bank.

International law has so far been on the side of the Palestinians. In 2004, the International Court of Justice, in response to a request by the United Nations General Assembly, issued an opinion against the wall, calling for its removal and for the Arab residents to be compensated for any damage done. The Court stated, "Israel cannot rely on a right of self-defense or on a state of necessity in order to preclude the wrongfulness of the construction of the wall." In other words, though it's cut down on suicide attacks, the wall is considered illegal by the International Court. As we traveled in the minibus into Ramallah we passed by sections of the wall, much of it heavily graffitied with pictures showing caged animals and people.

Now in Birzeit University, surrounded by angry young Palestinians, we meet Jamilah, a student who created a life-size silkscreen picture of the sad face of a Palestinian woman, cut in half by the Wall. We chat with Jamilah and some of the English-speaking students gathered inside the tent while Nadia, our translator, assembles the young men who have been in Israeli prisons. Together we move to a room that Nadia has arranged and we set up chairs to begin the interviews.

Ken and Al, I learn as the day goes on, left the hostel and spent the night before partying while I slept unawares surrounded by the middle-aged female prophets of the "end times". Ken collapses, lying down on the top of a garden wall and falls asleep for a bit while we get organized, but when we begin the interviews, they are both ready. I can see that the students like them a lot and from time to time some of the young men take them aside and they talk, smoke cigarettes, and laugh together. Likewise

I can see that I have been accepted, perhaps because they see me watching over my students, which is a feminine role that f

its with their cultural stereotypes.

I'm glad to see we are fitting in now that our first serious interviews are about to begin. As we sit down I have no inkling that we have already hit the research jackpot: that the young man we are about to interview will admit that he is seriously contemplating becoming a suicide bomber and that he is in fact waiting for a mission.

CHAPTER 8

A "Martyr" in Ramallah - Mustafa

The first young man that Nadia has arranged for us to interview is an eighteen-year-old boy of medium height and slim build who served time as political prisoner in Israel. He is dressed in black pants, a striped, western-style collared shirt and worn shoes and he is dark and handsome. He is seated across from me and leans forward in his metal folding chair, eager to tell his story of being arrested by the Israelis, but first I explain to him my study—the risks that exist for participating, the ways I intend to protect his confidentiality and that Ken and Al will listen as research interns but are bound to confidentiality. Nadia is translating and I see that she is easy to work with, as the young man and I, speaking through Nadia, have already created a good rapport. He nods his informed consent, and I begin by asking him to give me a false name to prevent anything appearing in my notes that could incriminate him later.

"Mustafa," he says just as a few of his friends gather round, circling their chairs nearby, curiously listening in. I discuss this briefly with Nadia, concerned for his confidentiality, but when she speaks with Mustafa, neither he nor Nadia see any problem. I then realize that with their communal culture it may be impossible to do separate interviews in complete privacy, one by one. I confirm that Mustafa is comfortable with this diminished level of confidentiality and then decide given that they are his friends, to just go with the flow.

I don't have a rigidly prepared list of questions, as I want to create an engaging conversational atmosphere, and after doing the Chechen research I know already the variables I want to cover and the areas I hope to explore. I've learned that even when a question doesn't receive an open answer the first time around, if one interviews in a conversational manner it's often possible to circle back to it a second and even third time once more trust has been established or when another topic tangentially touches it. This will be my technique throughout, and I start the interview.

"How were you arrested?" I ask.

"I was in the 12th grade at the time, seventeen. I was at home, and it was three a.m. when they pulled up in jeeps and came into the house with guns. My mother couldn't do anything but cry. They demanded that everyone leave the house and go outside. It was winter, and my brother was only two years old and sleeping, so my father asked if we could leave him inside. The [Israeli] soldier said, 'If you don't go and get him now, I will go and kill him.'

"Outside, with my brother crying, they asked for IDs of our whole family. One of the soldiers had a file. He looked at all the IDs and compared the picture in the file with me.

"He asked me, 'Are you Mustafa?'

I said, 'Yes.'

'Are you sure you are Mustafa?'

'Yes.'

'Step aside from your family,' he told me. And I did. Once we were separated, the solider asked me, 'Why are we here?'

'You tell me, why are we here?' I answered.

'Soon you will know,' he said, threateningly.

"The soldier then went to my father and told him, 'Your son is in big trouble. He is putting you in danger too.'

"My father was silent at first, and then when he tried to answer, the soldier stopped him.

'Don't say anything,' he said. 'I know every detail about your family.'

"The soldier turned to me and said, 'Say goodbye to your family.' He ordered me to lie down on my stomach and then tightly cuffed my hands behind my back. I tried to move but the plastic cut my wrists."

'Does it hurt?' the soldier asked.

'Yes,' I answered. Then he tightened it even more.

"There were four arrests that night in the same village. They put two of us in each jeep, blindfolded. It took three hours from my house to the detention center [this trip should have taken no longer than an hour at most], and the soldiers hit and punched me, kicked and rifle-butted me on my face, everywhere, the whole way.[35]

"The first soldier at home spoke Arabic, the others spoke only Hebrew, and I couldn't understand. I was transferred from investigation center to investigation center throughout the whole day. So what began at three a.m. ended at ten p.m. the next night. Once we got to the final one, we were very tired and went to sleep in cells. After three days, they started their investigation."

Though surprised and sickened to hear of the alleged brutality of the Israeli soldiers, I don't comment, asking instead, "Did you know why were you arrested?"

"No idea," Mustafa answers. "I tried at first to talk to them in English—to speak in a language they will know. But they answered me, 'Don't even try. We know Arabic very well.'

"So, I stayed in the interrogation center for thirty-six days. There were interrogations two times a week that could last from two to nine hours. Physically, they did me no harm. Psychologically, they hurt me by threats. They told me, 'We will sentence you for years. You'll have no future. You're putting your parents in trouble.' Sometimes we used to have very big arguments, and I'd say bad words back to them. Then the guards would hit me. But other prisoners were hurt far worse than me."

When Mustafa contradicts himself by saying physically the guards did him no harm, but then saying the guards did hit him, I don't ask him to clarify as it seems he is being macho and means to make the point that their beatings were not serious and were of no real consequence to him. It seems the psychological threats were much harder for him to deal with. Indeed, later as I continue in my research in the Arab world, I find that corporal punishment is still the norm in their culture and that many young men were beaten by their own parents while growing up—so perhaps to get beaten in prison was not registered as abnormal or extremely traumatizing to Mustafa.

Mustafa continues his story, "I was supposed to stay for eighteen days but they kept extending the days. My cell was three by two meters, and there were eight men[36] in it. Our breakfast was one cup of yogurt, one cucumber, one tomato, and some bread—this was for eight men. Lunch was beans, burned potatoes, one cup of rice. We were given one piece of meat a week. On Saturdays they don't even bring bread because it's their holiday. I was hungry all the time, but not starving. It was just enough to survive.

"No contact [with family or outsiders] was allowed. An institute got me a lawyer, but I was allowed to see him just two times in thirty-six days and just for ten minutes each time. It was a very horrifying phase with a very big effect on my life. I became more aware of others, more mature and more aware of the Palestinian struggle."

His response fits with what researcher Nichole Argo has already pointed out to me from her research in the West Bank: that Palestinian young people are arrested so often that imprisonment as young men has become a rite of passage for many of them.

Mustafa wears a leather necklace with a pendant bearing the photograph of what he calls a "shaheed", which is the Arabic word meaning a martyr for his faith. When we ask him about that particular martyr, he says, "He was the leader in our cell. They murdered him during interrogations, beat him to death." Mustafa looks down while fingering the pendant and continues, "I wish to be like him. I consider him a hero. He is a person to look up to. I have the idea in my mind to survive and to have hope, but I would like to die shaheed. Any Palestinian will want that."

I'm shocked by his statement and don't think that all Palestinians will agree so I am even more surprised when Nadia, our very mild looking and polite interpreter senses my doubt and turns to explain to me that she agrees wholeheartedly with what he has just said.

"It's true, we are all ready to die," she explains. Looking into Nadia's young and peaceful face, I decide to hide my horrified feelings for now and just listen.

I turn to Mustafa and ask somewhat provocatively, "It sounds like you are really upset about the young man in your cell who was killed in interrogation by the Israelis and that you want to die shaheed. Do you ever think of revenge, that you might want to become a suicide bomber?"

Mustafa draws himself up suddenly and answers solemnly, "I can't say." I see that I have breached an area he wishes to keep hidden, but his tone answers everything, and I immediately say without even thinking, "But you just did!"

There is a long moment of silence while everyone in the room stares at us, waiting to hear what Mustafa will say next. We are locked on each other's faces, trying to gauge the other person's honesty and how much trust there is. I see he is serious because unlike those who brag about wanting to die as "martyrs", he doesn't want to open up on the subject.

But I decide to go with my heart—to be in my natural role of nurturer, psychotherapist, healer—and to go the whole way with this. I keep my face and voice soft speaking just barely over a whisper, "Mustafa, this is why I came. I want to understand why people like you become suicide bombers. Please, I see that you are serious about this. Please teach me." Everyone is leaning forward in their chairs to hear what I am saying and to see how he will answer. I point to my paper and say, "Remember I don't know your real name, I'm not recording anything about your personal details."

Mustafa has had a long look into my eyes, and he decides to trust. The rest of the room is riveted on him as he continues.

"I want to have my freedom, my rights. I want to live like a human. I want to live like anyone else. I want to go back to my land." He pauses and then adds, "Definitely I will die for it."

The room is suddenly abuzz. The boys become excited and begin discussing among themselves, and Nadia has a hard time keeping up.

Mustafa continues explaining himself, "Our struggle is not religious. It's about them taking our land. There is nothing left after life. I'm a communist."

Hamid, one of the boys listening disagrees, "Every person who dies as a shaheed has religion to do with it. Religion has to be in the picture."

But Mustafa explains, "I do it for myself and for Palestinians. After death I can't do more." He pauses, "For me it's right. Others may disagree."

The boys discuss that it takes even more courage to die for others in this way, out of a political motive rather than a religious directive.

"Life is unfair," Mustafa says. "They took my human rights. Every moment when you pass the line of death, you are already dead." At first I don't understand what he means by this, but another one of the boys— someone whom I will record as Jamal later explains, "He has a line drawn inside himself and it's already crossed. It's too much pain. He will do anything to make it stop. Every Palestinian has this line and many have crossed over it."

Jamal without realizing it put into words the central thesis of world-renowned psychologist and suicide researcher Ed Shneidman, who wrote that the common psychological stimulus for suicide is intolerable psychological pain—psychache as he called it—and the best predictor of suicidal behavior is overwhelming psychic pain.[37] Thus even a normally healthy person who is pushed past his limit of psychic pain is very vulnerable to suicide.

These boys are growing up in a conflict zone, seeing their family and friends arrested, beaten, detained, and even killed. They are subjected to daily humiliations and frustrations: unemployment, checkpoints, curfews, and so on. And they can expect to be imprisoned in Israeli prisons at any moment during their young adult years. It takes me some time to grasp it, but they are explaining the same thing as what Ed Shneidman observed with normal suicides – too many of them have been pushed into a psychic zone where the emotional pain in their lives is so strong that they are driven to act in a way that ends the pain – the psychache - that makes suicide missions a very viable option for them.

The others don't feel in as much pain as Mustafa is and are horrified when he announces his decision. Hamid speaks up, "I don't agree to die as a shaheed! The whole struggle is to live your life as normal."

Mustafa answers him sadly, "I will give my life to have a normal life – for others."

"You mean you will die for others to live normally? You will sacrifice yourself for their good?" I ask.

Mustafa nods solemnly and turns the conversation to describe another young inmate who had a tremendous effect on him. "When I was in prison there was another young man there who had volunteered as shaheed (to be a suicide bomber). He was arrested before being able to complete his mission as a suicide bomber. I can't describe my emotions," Mustafa says with awe filling his face, "to know this person who went to bomb himself. It's an honor for me just to talk to him! He was a sixteen-year-old from Nablus." Mustafa's eyes shine as he continues. "The person willing to die as a shaheed for paradise knows that there will be a better day for Palestine."

Mustafa is explaining that he would not take a suicide mission only to go to paradise; his motivation lies in his firm belief that such actions can further the Palestinian cause.

"How would your parents feel if they knew this?" I ask.

"My parents raised me this way," he says. "They are the ones who suffered."

It now registers that Mustafa has been hugging his book bag to his chest for the entire second half of the interview. He looks so young and like he wants to be comforted.

Hamid steps in again. "There is not a mother willing to let her son go to sacrifice himself. Well, there is only one mother who did this—she introduced her son to it," he says referencing the one case among Palestinian suicide bombers in which a mother pushed her son into doing it.[38] Later when I interview the parents of other bombers I will see Hamid is generally right. The parents may state pat phrases about being proud of their children's actions but when pushed it's clear that they are devastated that their son or daughter decided to go on a suicide mission.

Nadia suddenly interrupts our discussion to tell us that she has to leave—if she doesn't cross the checkpoint on her way home before it closes, she will be stranded. I want to know if Mustafa already has a concrete plan of action to suicide bomb or if it's just thoughts at this point, but without a translator I cannot ask him more, so I finish for today, telling Mustafa with as much empathy as I can that I hope he never does it. He looks resolute though appreciative of the caring words for his life. Then we turn to Nadia to discuss leaving with her and to ask if she can translate again the next day.

At that point, one of the boys, Yousef, who has been listening all along speaks up in pretty good English, "You don't have to return to Jerusalem for the night. There's no point in going all the way back through the checkpoints to stay in a hotel, and then travel all the way here again in the morning. You'll lose time. It's better to stay here in Ramallah."

I turn to Nadia to ask if we can get a hotel in Ramallah, but Yousef continues, "You don't need a hotel. You will stay here with us." Turning to me he says, "You are a woman so you will come to my house and stay with me, my mother and sister. These two will stay in the student housing with the others."

Everyone is standing now, and Nadia needs to rush off. It's true we will lose a lot of time in transit, but I'm not sure I want to accept his offer. I look to Nadia for advice but she simply smiles and shrugs, leaving it to me. I turn to my students and they also say, "It's up to you."

Yousef continues, "You came to learn about us right? If you want to learn about us, come and stay in our homes, see how we live."

I am shocked by the suggestion, but at the same time I feel the warmth of his invitation, and I'm really curious. I look to Ken and Al for some hint of their thoughts and they say, "He's right, we came to learn."

I protest, "Yes but you'll be going together. I'm going alone."

Yousef starts to laugh and says, "Don't worry you'll be safe." And for some reason I trust him. Yousef picks up his book bag, I take my brief-case, and our group suddenly disbands. Nadia leaves for the checkpoint, and Yousef leads me away as I say hurried goodbyes to Ken and Al asking one more time, "You're sure you're okay?"

Ken waves his cigarette in his macho I've-got-everything-under-control manner and tells me, "Don't worry we're fine!"

I leave with Yousef, glancing back over my shoulder to see them laughing and smoking with the other students. As I head out for my first night staying in the home of a Palestinian living in the West Bank, I wonder, "What have I gotten myself in for?"

CHAPTER 9

At Home in Ramallah with Yousef & Fatima

At five-foot-nine with thick black hair cut fashionably short and a small well-trimmed beard that frames his chin and mouth, Yousef is handsome and has a warm smile. We talk quietly as he sits beside me on the minibus traveling from Birzeit University back into Ramallah.

"Do you think he will really go and bomb himself?" I ask, still musing over Mustafa.

"No. If it was a few months ago I would say 'Yes,' but now I don't think he has anyone to send him. The operatives that originally were going to send him were killed and arrested. It will take him some time to establish new contacts that trust him enough to put him on a new mission."

I'm relieved to hear that.

Mustafa, like most Palestinian young men, pick their political factions, including the terrorist wings that they identify with in the same manner as other boys in other cultures pick their sports teams—unfortunately with deadly results.[39] The Popular Front for the Liberation of Palestine (PFLP), a Marxist group that Mustafa is affiliated with, only recently joined the fray of sending suicide bombers into Israel. Eager as they are to dispatch suicide bombers, it will take some time to for Mustafa's new contacts to ensure that he is serious and not a security risk—that he won't compromise the entire group if he is somehow caught or decides to brag before going on his mission.

My counter-terrorism colleague Mia Bloom theorizes that a strong motivator for groups to begin sending suicide bombers, or to increase the numbers they send, is a result of competition between the groups, what she calls "outbidding." When there are multiple terrorist groups competing for followers and funding, as there are in Palestine, the groups may have to convince their potential supporters that they are as self-sacrificial and serious as the other groups sending bombers.[40] That may be what has happened now that the PFLP is also sending bombers.

I silently reflect on the sadness in Mustafa's story and hope that he will have to wait forever: that he will never find others that trust him enough to equip him for a suicide mission.

"You think he'll find new ones to send him?" I ask. Yousef shrugs, he doesn't know.

Yousef tells me that he aligns himself with the political faction "Fatah" which also has an armed wing, but he tells me that he has no inclinations to bomb himself. However, he adds, "I agree with the struggle. We need to free Palestine." I wonder how much terrorist violence he endorses and where his moral lines are drawn, but I decide I've listened to enough horror for today.

We arrive in the city center and walk past the traffic circle with the bronze lions and then another half mile along a busy tree lined boulevard into an area where new four-story limestone apartment blocks have been built. Yousef's building is in the back. We enter, walk up the stairs to his apartment and are standing at the door when I ask him, "Have you told your mother that you are bringing an American professor—a woman— home to stay the night?" He turns to me laughing and says, "Yes, she doesn't believe me!" He rings the doorbell and we wait, while I wonder what is in store for me beyond the closed door.

Yousef's mother, Latifa, greets me enthusiastically, pulling me into their foyer as she speaks excitedly in Arabic. Yousef translates.

"She cannot believe that it's really true. She thought I was pulling her leg," Yousef says, laughing. His mother ushers us into the apartment and offers us tea as she asks in Arabic about my research.

Yousef's sister, Fatima, comes to greet us as well. She is a slender girl, two years older than Yousef. Dressed in rose-colored velour leggings and a sleek turtleneck sweater, she throws her long shiny dark hair back over her shoulders, dark eyes flashing as she says "Marhaba!" and then smiles as she explains, "That means welcome in Arabic."

The apartment is spacious and beautiful with a large living room and kitchen in the center and three large bedrooms off to the sides: one for Yousef and his younger brother, Bashar, a smaller one for Fatima and another for their mother. The kitchen has a wide arched entryway and is bright and modern with a ceramic tiled floor. As is customary of the kitchens and bathrooms in Palestine, there is one tile that lifts to expose a drain, which makes for easily scrubbing the floors as the soiled water conveniently drains away when that tile is lifted.

Yousef explains that his mother is a widow and works in a store. Everyone in the family works and pitches into the family expenses, he says, although he and his mother carry the heaviest shares, and it was only after saving all of their money that they were able to buy the apartment they are now in. I can see he is very proud of it.

"You can stay in my bedroom," Fatima offers and she and Yousef take my things in, ignoring my protests about not wanting to displace her. Instead, they suggest I take a shower before dinner. I don't realize this yet, but many Palestinians heat their water overhead in tanks mounted on the rooftops, using sunlight as their heating source. This means that an evening shower provides hot water and waiting until morning can mean a freezing cold one! Uninformed, I defer to morning and we go back out to the kitchen.

It's Ramadan and they have been fasting all day. Now that the sun is setting they are anxious to eat. Bashar arrives home, and Fatima and her mother finish preparing the food. I offer in English to help, but they get embarrassed. I join in anyway, doing little things here and there until gradually they realize I'm genuine and accept my help.

Fatima lays newspapers out on the carpeted floor in the dining area. There is no dining table, so she places the meal—grilled chicken, hummus, baba ghanoush, steamed greens, pita bread, some spices I don't recognize and glasses of juice—onto the newspaper and we sit on the carpeted floor to eat together. Yousef offers me a glass of Coca Cola, but I say the apricot juice is perfect. Though boxed, it tastes fresh and delicious, and I smile to myself thinking about how ubiquitous some iconic American products are—even Coca Cola is here, although bearing an Arabic label. We eat in a communal style using the bread and our hands as utensils and sharing food from common plates. No one is using their left hand of course, since this is the hand reserved for bathroom duties and considered unclean for eating. Everyone is hungry so it becomes quiet as we eat, though I offer many compliments to the cook.

When we are finished, Fatima and her mother take the things to the kitchen while the boys retire to their room for homework. I try to help with the dishes, but Fatima tells me that her mother is tired and has a bad back and that I am to sit with Latifa in the living room to drink tea while Fatima finishes the clean up. I join Latifa in their living area and Fatima serves us tea. We watch together a large television, and as I sip my tea, Latifa flips through the multiple Arabic satellite channels and stops momentarily to show me a scene of Mecca at Ramadan. Hundreds of thousands of pilgrims all dressed in immaculate white robes are circling the holy site of Kaaba, which is lit festively for the Ramadan services. I smile appreciatively at the beauty of the masses of pilgrims moving hypnotically together in a circle under the soft lights reflecting off the heavily engraved Arabic arches that frame the Kaaba. Even though I am not Muslim, the muezzin's call to worship is so soulful it tugs at my heart and makes me feel as though I too would like to join in their prayers. Latifa waves her hand over the television screen as if to touch it and smiles at me. Despite our language barrier, I try to communicate to her that I too appreciate the beauty of it.

Then she turns on a video of a wedding the family recently attended, and Fatima joins us with a steaming mug of tea. As we watch, I get my education on how young women in Palestine get engaged and married. Fatima's cousin, it turns out, was introduced to a wealthy Palestinian ex-pat from the U.S. through their parents who arranged their marriage. The video shows their engagement party, the young groom bringing the bride-to-be gold necklaces, some of which are traditional with hundreds of gold coins, and placing them over her head one after another. Fatima excitedly tells me that if the man is very wealthy and wants to impress her family, he may put so much gold around her neck that it's heavy and hard for the girl to stand up straight.

Fatima tells me that arranged marriages are normal in their society, and for her, it's only natural that the family will be involved in making introductions. She doesn't expect to marry someone she meets on her own.

"The families should know each other and really check the guy out well," she explains, saying that it's especially important to her that her mother and eldest brother agree with the choice of whoever she will marry. Later however, I learn she has a big crush on a guy she saw in public while working, but she doesn't have a clue how to speak with him, even though she's sure he's noticed her as well. It's a completely different world than the one we Westerners are used to when it comes to dating in Palestine.

The wedding itself is actually a contract that is signed between the families before hand and the party is what we are watching on video. I notice that all of the guests are women—the Palestinians, like many Arabs, segregate by gender for wedding parties and other gatherings. The only time on the video that we see a man is when the bride and groom enter the reception, causing the women to break into joyful dancing.

"It's often at weddings that introductions come," Fatima explains. "All the women are there together and the older women see who are the beautiful and smart young girls. Then they go home and discuss it with their families and later we get introductions made."

She goes on to tell me about relatives of suitors who have tried to meet her.

"The boys come with their mothers to see me and I wonder, 'Am I box of candy bars or something?' No. They are looking for a girl who is polite. Some girls find boys they love on the street, in university, but not me. I am a good girl. I told my mom, 'Okay let them come.' The first one that came was a doctor. I wanted him to be older. To be close in age is not good, he should be six or seven years older. There was no chemistry. The second one was too shy and his grandmother was checking me, touching my arms and she told my mother I'm too skinny! 'I'm not a chicken!' I told my mom afterwards. Also he let the women speak for him. He was so rich, but I told my mother 'No more'."

I look at Fatima and smile. She is lounging on the sofa with me in tight velour pants and a body-hugging, ribbed knit top. She has a curvy, young figure and glossy long black hair that she glides her fingers through. Her face lights up when she smiles, and she has a brightness in her eyes. I cannot imagine any young man not thinking she's beautiful.

When the video ends, I am getting sleepy. Fatima's mother goes to bed, but Fatima is talkative so I decide to stay up and listen to her. Bashar joins us for a few minutes, and I ask them about why they think Palestinians become terrorists and suicide bombers.

"We are desperate," Fatima says plainly. "People don't understand our lives."

Bashar elaborates by explaining some of the politically motivated traumas in their lives.

"Our home was destroyed [by the Israeli soldiers]. I didn't see it when it happened, but I went back with my father to try to find some of our things, our clothes..." his voice trails off.

"It was so hard because our dad saved a lot to make the house," Fatima continues. "The U.N. gave us a tent to live in at first, and after we moved from house to house. Then, our father was killed at work ten years ago. It's better he died then to live and see this life."

Bashar looks upset and gets up and goes to his room, perhaps because he has trouble keeping up with the English or perhaps because remembering troubles him.

I haven't seen a destroyed home yet, but I have been told that it's Israeli practice to destroy extended family, communal homes in retribution if one of the members is active in a terror cell.

"Do you know why the Israelis did it?" I ask.

Fatima searches her mind, "I don't know why. Maybe because my uncle threw a stone at a van carrying religious Jews. At that time, my two uncles and aunts lived with us, but then they were killed in a road accident by a military truck. Though I don't think it was an accident."

It seems there are many "accidents" in Fatima's family. I know that all through the West Bank, there are Israeli-sponsored communities of Jewish settlers, many of them American Jews who have decided to relocate to Israel and claim the monetary benefits of subsidized housing and income by living in settlements in the West Bank and Gaza. It seems likely to me that the people Fatima's uncle threw the stone at were settlers in the West Bank and knowing that usually the Israelis feel they have good cause for destroying a family home, I conclude that it's likely her uncle was more involved in anti-settler activity rather than simply throwing stones. However, I don't challenge her story. I want to listen open-mindedly and hope that she will continue to open up.

"Tell me about the settlers," I prompt.

Fatima is wide-eyed and says, "I am so scared of them; they'll do anything to you." She recalls how her friends were at a checkpoint when a settler began shooting at Palestinians randomly until an Israeli soldier disarmed him. "There is a road now in their area that is restricted only to settlers. No Palestinians can use it."

"I am also scared to go to Jerusalem," Fatima continues. "Israeli soldiers in street clothes carry guns. They will use them. After age eighteen, all Israelis are allowed to carry guns. Sharon [the Israeli Prime Minister at the time] said he won't allow the people of Palestine to carry guns. We have only pistols and we are not allowed to shoot them."

With all the terror attacks by Palestinians, the borders between Israel and Palestine have become so strict that it's hard for Palestinians to cross for work into Israel like they used to. Israelis now encourage immigrants from the Philippines, the former Soviet Union and elsewhere to come for domestic, menial and factory jobs in order to avoid hiring Palestinians. I ask Fatima how life is for normal Palestinians at this time and whether or not these current circumstances radicalize them into terrorist groups.

"Most men haven't been able to find or keep their jobs," she explains. "The women still can get work, but men here like to be in charge, and if she's working and buying his clothes, his cigarettes, everyone judges them and he feels awful inside." Still, Fatima says most Palestinians agree with women becoming educated and working and denounce the propaganda of al Qaeda and the veiling of women in burkas.

"You are a psychologist, right?" Fatima asks.

"Yes," I say.

"I have always wanted to talk to a psychologist," she says, shyly. "My friends worry about me. I talk a lot, I smile a lot, but sometimes I don't want to go to work. Everything is black. I feel so terrible. My big concern is finishing school. I want to be someone. But I feel I'm half a person. Most of my friends finished university and even do their Masters. But I wasted two years going through checkpoints to university in Jerusalem and coming home late hours. I was so scared that I finally dropped out of university. Now I worry about my future."

"Yes, you must finish university," I say. "There must be a way to do it."

"I don't like people to see me weak," Fatima continues. "I don't cry in front of others. I don't like my mom to cry either. I want her to be strong."

"You've had a lot of losses. It sounds like you keep so much inside, try to keep on going even when you are stressed, but you can't always do it?" I prompt gently.

"Yes," Fatima says and she tells me about the time her purse was stolen. It had a picture of her when she was little and a coin, both things her father had carried with him before he died, as well as her father's Koran.

"Every night when I check my memory, I remember all the things taken from me," she says. "I try to soothe myself."

"How did your father die?" I ask.

"I remember it really clearly," she says. "I told my mother I wanted to buy an eraser for school. I took Yousef along. We were out and a woman came screaming, 'He died! He died! There was an accident!' My mother began screaming too, and soon everyone in the store as well. No one paid attention to me, but I'm shocked and don't want to believe what's happened. I tell myself, 'He left in the morning and he'll come back at night. He'll be okay.' I never cried actually."

Fatima tells part of this story in the present tense as though it's still happening, and I see how alive the traumatic memory still is for her. She also never explains exactly what happened to her father other than to imply that it was a work accident. Maybe she doesn't know or cannot stand to remember. It's not important for me to know, so I decide not to ask.

Fatima says, "I wanted to go to a psychologist for so long. I think all people here need to go to a psychologist. They are angry and upset, but everyone is afraid to go. We think psychiatrists are for crazy people. We go to movies, for drugs, anything else."

Later in Spring 2005 when I consult with the psychology faculty at Birzeit University they tell me that the lack of mental health care and resources is a huge problem in Palestine. In the West Bank there is only one practicing psychologist, and she closed down after the blockades in Bethlehem made it impossible for her to work. In Gaza there is an excellent mental health clinic run by premier psychiatrist Eyad Sarraj with a staff of forty, but it only serves Gaza and still cannot possibly meet all the needs of the entire population given twenty percent are estimated to have posttraumatic stress disorder. Fatima is right—they will turn to other remedies like drugs, fantasies, and ideologies and actions that promise what seems to be an honorable exit from life – taking their own lives while killing their enemies.

Fatima begins to explain her fears to me, "I hate loud voices. My ears tingle. If anyone yells, I'm scared and angry. I'm afraid of big knives. I imagine it's going to cut someone, hurt someone."

"You are describing what often occurs in trauma survivors," I tell her trying to normalize her generalized fears and calm her.

She pauses. "I'm really strong. How can a person be so strong and then be so weak?"

"This is always the confusion of trauma survivors," I explain to Fatima, trying to gently help her see how posttraumatic stress plays itself out.

"People who have lived through traumas can be feeling so solid, and then suddenly a posttraumatic reminder occurs and triggers them into a flashback. They may feel the terror again as though it's here in the present, or they may be thrust into a dissociative fog where they can't think and feel caught between the pain of the past and the present-day trigger, which they can't decode accurately because it's so mixed with the traumatic flashback."

Fatima understands and describes this dissociative fog exactly. "You should see me when a soldier comes beside me and demands, 'Where are you going? Give me your ID.' My hands are shaking. My brain stops. I think, *They are going to take me to jail! Shoot me now!* I hear the bullet coming."

"This is normal after trauma," I reiterate gently.

Fatima continues to out pour. "I saw the soldiers once taking my father from the house. They put him on the front of a jeep then drove it fast and braked hard. He went flying. They did this many times in front of me and my mom. He was hurt of course. Then much later the soldiers came again for my father, and one of his friends told them that he died. If my father had still been alive they would have arrested him!

"My two uncles went in and out of jail. The one in the car accident I told you about, he drinks now. His head was split open in that accident, and when he was arrested, they beat him on his injury. He was also tortured and beaten in his testicles. He wants to get married and have children, but he has to take medicine now because he cannot."

"Why are the soldiers so violent?" I ask wondering what provokes them. Fatima tries to explain.

"If a child throws a rock at them, they stop and pick him up." I realize she cannot explain why the soldiers act as they do, only how terrified they make her feel. I learn as I go along that many of the young Israeli men and women who serve their military duty in the occupied territories and on the checkpoints don't want to be there and are also terrified. They are young and afraid, knowing that at any moment they can be killed in a senseless act of terrorism. It makes some of them angry and trigger-happy. But Fatima cannot empathize well with their terror, she is too caught up in her own.

"You think it can happen to you?" I ask referring to how the Israeli soldiers shoot at and arrest the young kids that throw rocks at them.

"Yes," Fatima answers. "Since the (second) Intifada, I know I can be killed anytime. Before it started, when I was in high school I wanted to be a Spice Girl. All my friends decided which one we were, and I was Baby Spice. I wanted to be modern and wore my veil only after school. Then when the [second] Intifada started, I was in a minibus with a group of girls when gunshots fired in our direction. If the bus was not moving so fast, one of us would have been shot dead. At that moment, I became so afraid of dying!"

Fatima explains that she became more religious with the threat of imminent death and couldn't stand to think of dying without her veil (hidjab) on, fearing that failing to follow the traditions of her faith at the moment of her death might compromise her eternal soul.

I told my mom, 'Buy me one now! I will wear hidjab for my life!' I see how pretty the girls are without veils, but I am not comfortable anymore to go out without it. I wear it now for four years."

Her story makes me reflect upon how religion and extremism often gain in importance in cultures when people feel threatened. A research survey repeated among West Bank Palestinians at various times asked how much they supported suicide terrorism and their responses correlated with actual threat events, such as Israeli incursions into Palestinian towns and targeted assassinations going on at those times. In his analysis, the author, Khahil Shikaki, found that Palestinians endorsed suicide terrorism far more when they felt threatened by the Israelis, and less so when they felt safe.[41] Fatima, not particularly observant of her religious traditions, became more so overnight when she felt her life was endangered. We saw the same in Chechnya, a great increase in religious fanaticism with those who had been highly traumatized. I wonder how much it takes for people with traumatic pasts who re-encounter a serious life threat to gravitate to extremist religious messages that endorse terrorist violence as the answer to calm their fears of death and dying.

Eventually I tire listening and say, "Fatima I was up so early and it's late now. I love talking to you, but I really need to sleep." I have the feeling that she is so glad to have found someone who will listen and can understand and help her and that she could go on all night. She's polite though and takes me to her room to get settled for the evening.

Fatima's room surprises me. Even though she is a conservative Palestinian her room looks nearly identical to my own teenage daughters' rooms—except perhaps neater! It's a mix of stuffed animals left over from girlhood and all the trappings of an adolescent. She has Spice Girls posters on the wall, cosmetics, perfumes, and costume jewelry lined up neatly across her chest of drawers. The only thing different about her room from my girls' is that her wardrobe by the bedside is filled with Arabic style pastel below-the-waist tops and matching pants for wearing outside the home.

I tell Fatima I need a bit of soap to wash my underwear so I can wear them again in the morning, and she shows me a drawer full of sexy panties and offers me to take any I need. I suppress surprised laughter and give her a sweet kiss goodnight.

"Are you sure you don't mind giving up your room?" I ask.

"No," she says. "I love to sleep in my mother's bed. Ever since my Dad died I almost always join her sometime during the night."

With that thought, I lay down in her pink-sheeted twin bed and fall peacefully to sleep.

It doesn't last though. After maybe four hours of sleep, I wake up to hear a pounding drum outside the windows. At first it's so loud that I think it's in the next room, but as I wake up I realize there are people outside, banging the drum to wake us all up. I look at the clock and it's six a.m.—three hours before we have agreed to leave the house to go back to Birzeit University. I roll over and put a pillow over my head to drown out the drumming, but it continues loudly for at least another half hour at least and I don't get back to sleep for a long time.

When I finally pull myself from bed later that morning, I wake up thankfully to a still-warm shower. When I emerge from my room I see a completely new Fatima about to leave home. Her hair is pulled back into a tight ponytail high on her head, and she has expertly wrapped a powder blue scarf to completely cover her hair and neck. She's put a lot of makeup on that softens her scarf wrapped face, and she wears a long billowy jacket covering her hips and pants, both also powder blue. It's hard to make out her figure beneath her street clothes or to imagine how glossy and beautiful her hair is hidden under her scarf. That must be how the matchmaking works. The other women who see her exposed at the weddings can tell their young male relatives, "Trust me, she's gorgeous underneath all those clothes!"

I ask the others about the drumming and they laugh and say, "Oh that's a religious guy who comes along the streets to wake everyone up well before sun-up so we can get in a meal before the fasting begins." I realize I've missed breakfast because the sun has long been up and it's Ramadan. They insist I eat since I'm not a Muslim, but not wanting to eat when they can't, I decide to try out fasting with them. Yousef and I head back out to Birzeit with me curious to see how it went for Ken and Al.

CHAPTER 10

The Palestinian 'Princess' and other Prisoners of PTSD

Yousef and I walk from his apartment back through Ramallah's center, past the brass lions where we heard shooting the first day we arrived in town. Already it feels familiar and I enjoy the sun shining warmly on my shoulders as we walk. The town is bustling with older women in bright abayas buying their produce and young men and women in western clothes on their way to the minibuses that take them to their various universities. We board the one for Birzeit, pay a few coins for riding it and sit back as it climbs the steep hill up to the campus. When we arrive, Ken and Al are nowhere to be seen. Yousef calls his friends to find out how they are and reassures me that everything is fine.

"They drank a lot last night and didn't wake up early," he says, smirking as he puts his phone back into his pocket. "They'll be here soon." I'm surprised to hear that the students in Palestine drink and I'm intensely interested to see how Ken and Al fared the night.

Meanwhile we make our way into the crowded cafeteria to meet Nadia, our translator from the day before. She has agreed to continue translating and has invited a group of students who have all been held as political prisoners in Israel to be interviewed. I smile when I see Nadia. She's dressed in blue jeans, an ivory high-necked, long-sleeved blouse, a soft pink headscarf that hides all her hair and matching lipstick.

"How are you today?" I ask and she replies that things are good. I scan the cafeteria and notice that most of the students are eating even though it's Ramadan. Even Yousef goes and gets a plate of food, despite appearing observant at home in front of his mother. He lights up a cigarette as he sits to eat, another prohibited activity during the Ramadan fast.

"You don't keep Ramadan?" I ask.

"No not here. It's too hard at university," he says, waving his cigarette to indicate the rest of the students who are also violating the fast. "You see most everyone eats here. How else can we study without eating all day?"

I decide if that's the case then I can get some food too, though I feel ashamed for eating in front of those in the room who are struggling to keep the fast. Later I will learn that this actually enhances their blessings—the more hardship the greater the blessings promised.

As we prepare for our interviews Nadia invites the first of our subjects, a veiled woman with creamy white skin who appears too young and innocent to be speaking about being imprisoned, to sit down. This time the interview is going to be one-on-one, except for Nadia translating and Yousef listening in to help when Nadia gets stuck on a word. Ken and Al are nowhere to be seen. Again I explain the study to the interviewee, making sure she understands the risks and the limits of confidentiality and consents to be interviewed. She does and asks us to give her the pseudonym of "Princess".

For many young Palestinians, arrest and imprisonment are like a ritual initiation of coming of age, events that marks the onset of posttraumatic stress disorder (PTSD) and set the stage for the rest of their sometimes brief, but violent lives. Though probably pre-disposed to PTSD already by all they have witnessed and lived through, their terrorism-related activities and the stress of being jailed at a young age exacerbates the problem. Human rights organizations report that from the beginning of the second Intifada in 2000 through April 2003 more than 28,000 Palestinians were incarcerated,[42] the majority of them youth. In April 2003 alone, there were more than 5,500 arrests.

The incarceration of Palestinian minors is a terrorism-related phenomenon that has not been extensively studied. According to Defense for Children International, a human rights organization, during the second Intifada (between 2000 and 2009), the Israeli authorities arrested approximately 6,700 Palestinian minors between the ages of twelve to eighteen. And at the beginning of 2009, there were 423 Palestinian minors being held in detention, interrogation centers and prisons in the West Bank and Israel.[43] Princess was one of them.

"I was going to Sharml Sheik [from Eilat airport in the south of Israel] with my sister," Princess begins. "At the checkpoint they took my passport and asked, 'Are you Princess?' I said, 'Yes.' The officers left for some minutes and came back with the military. They blindfolded and handcuffed me with my hands behind and took me away. The first hour they didn't say anything. Then the captain of the [Eilat] airport came and said, 'From now on, you are under arrest.' I was seventeen and a half at the time.

"After an hour and half, I was no longer blindfolded and I saw my sister through an open door. I pushed the soldier aside and screamed to her, 'I am under arrest.' She was on the telephone and told my parents what was going on. Then they arrested her too and made her sign [a paper saying] that nothing happened to me. During the next three hours they checked all our bags and bodies.

"Next, they took me to a station in Eilat. All the rooms there are open, and you can see the other Israeli prisoners. There were six Russian women in a small room, in for drugs. I stayed overnight, and the next day the captain came and took us all to Masamia.[44] They took us to court and told me that I was forbidden to speak to my mother, father or to a lawyer. After one week the interrogations began. It was eighteen hours per day, from 6:30 a.m. to 12:30 at night for two months. I was under a bad situation."

"Did they hit you?" I ask.

"They didn't beat me," Princess says, "but they burned a cigarette into my leg."

"Can you show me?" I ask.

Princess carefully lifts her skirt to show me the scar from a cigarette burn. "It was very painful," she continues, "but I didn't scream. They asked, 'It didn't hurt?' I said, 'No.' Then they made another one.

"They put me in a cell with a woman who was taking drugs. She scratched herself like a crazy woman and made herself bleed, then she began sucking and licking this blood. I was screaming so hard. The guard came and said, 'Shut up!' and beat me on my face, arm and shoulder until I was black and blue. That was in the first two weeks. I showed the interrogators what the guard did to me, 'Look what happened to my face, my upper arm!' They transferred me to Beit Shemesh, a small city within Jerusalem, where there were many cockroaches as big as twelve centimeters and black. I spent four to five days there.

"In interrogation they wanted me to admit that I planned to kidnap a soldier and kill him. It wasn't true."

Looking at Princess with her gentle face and childlike demeanor, it does seem difficult to believe, although I know that one Palestinian young woman, Muna Amneh, had an Internet "affair" with an Israeli soldier, lured him over to the West Bank with the insinuation of a sexual tryst and had him killed when he came to her.[45] Perhaps Princess *is* a serious criminal or was talked into taking part in a similar kidnapping plot. It seems the Israeli soldiers thought so.

Princess describes the challenges and humiliations of being a female prisoner. "I got my period [in Beit Shemesh]. I asked for [sanitary] napkins. The guards said, 'Where the hell do you think you are? This is prison.' I had a sponge for cleaning that they gave me, so I covered it with my socks and washed them everyday.

"During the interrogations, they gave me a dress that had small skinny straps and that came only to my knees. They also took my bra away and left me with just two pairs of underpants. At court they gave me trousers and a shirt, but this dress without a bra in front of the soldiers was very immodest for me." Indeed for a veiled Palestinian girl to be forced to show her legs, bare arms and have her chest exposed with no bra is deeply humiliating and would be an outrage in her culture.

"After two months of eighteen-hour daily interrogations, I still did not admit to plans of kidnapping a soldier. They put me in handcuffs, sometimes fastened behind and other times in front, holding me in different positions for stress. They put me in pressure positions on the chair so that I had to arch my back."

I nod. This treatment of being handcuffed into stressful bodily contortions is referred to as "soft" torture, and she claims it caused vertebral disc damage in her back.

"After two months they took me to isolation. For two and a half months I had nothing to read, listen to or see. I always asked for books so I could continue to study, to continue my life, but got nothing. If they allowed me, I got one hour outside my cell alone—well, with six soldiers around me holding sticks to beat me if I did anything, despite the cuffs on my hands and my legs."

Princess continues, "I had a bed there, very close to the floor, made from metal, and it had barely any mattress. Sometimes they cuffed me to this bed with my arms and legs spread open."

"Were you molested?" I ask, horrified to imagine a young girl handcuffed to her bed in this position. "Did you feel sexually threatened in this position?"

"No. At that point I had clothes," she answers.

"How did you cope?" I ask.

"For two months I thought of the past: days of my family, when I was small, of my dreams, of what I can do when I can go out. After the first month of isolation they allowed my parents to visit every two weeks for thirty minutes."

Princess explains the time line of her imprisonment: Two months of interrogation eighteen hours per day, followed by two months of isolation interrogations, followed by five months of security isolation which she says was not as bad as the first isolation, then three to four months with other girls in prison, and then release.

"In security isolation there were Israeli prisoners who take drugs or kill and lesbian girls. They tried to come to me and did profane things in front of me. I was afraid to walk in front of them." Princess is not likely exaggerating. In one Israeli prison where my colleague Yoram Schweitzer made interviews, one of the female prisoners dominated the others; when they did not comply, she punished them, one time tossing hot oil into another girl's face, scarring her forever.

Suddenly Princess flushes very deeply, her whole face red.

"What is happening to your face?" I ask. "Is it fear?"

Woodenly, she responds. "I don't have fear anymore."

It's chilling to realize that after this traumatizing imprisonment she has learned to dissociate the normal and very useful emotion of fear and claims she no longer feels it.

"Then what is it that you feel now? What is showing on your face?"

Princess is confused. She answers, "It's hot, really hot. It's like really hot—something exploding. I feel like I'm ... it's coming out."

"What is 'it'?" I inquire. "Anger? Rage?"

"Rage," she answers, "Not fear. I just saw the things I have been through. I succeeded. I stayed Princess. I stayed the person that I am. There is nothing I can be afraid of."

I realize that this is probably the first time she has processed her prison experience. There are no psychologists here to help her with the traumas she's endured, and I may have just offered her for the first time the safe space that allows her to recall and speak about her experiences in a coherent way without going so far into a posttraumatic flashback that she loses that coherence. And in speaking to me, she also hasn't had to deal with the angry or hysterical reactions of others such as her parents and family members when she tries to tell them. It's why she can now make the realization that she survived and remained the same person, though the experience has also touched her profoundly and made deep and lasting changes within.

"I gave a lot to be strong to handle it. I don't feel that I am twenty now. I feel much older," she says with great sadness.

Princess shakes herself out of her self-pity saying, "If you want the truth, what happened to me is nothing compared to what is happening to other girls in the prison. Two women were pregnant and gave birth there, and now two years later, the baby is being taken from one of the girls. When she was pregnant, they didn't feed her well and during labor she was handcuffed with her hands and legs open on the bed." Princess speaks a bit more about how her overwhelming fear upon being arrested and imprisoned turned overtime to a numb acceptance.

"Do you feel guilty?" I ask curious to learn if she has the survivor guilt typical of those who survive harsh traumas when others did not.

"No. If I am guilty in anything it's that I didn't give the other girls in prison all the love in my heart."

I nod and smile thinking she seems still so innocent. Yet I wonder how she feels about those who go as suicide bombers to revenge for experiences like her own.

"How do you feel about 'martyrs'?" I ask.

"I used to believe in them, but now I see, with courage, we can use them in another way. I also think a lot of explosions happen, but we still have prisons, "martyrs", buildings and children destroyed."

"So, how can you fight against what's happened to you?" I ask.

"With my studies," she says. "I should study and learn and give understanding to people who don't know about us. I can fight them with this. Not stones, not bombs."

• • •

When she finishes, Princess is reluctant to leave. Hamid, a tall, strongly built twenty-six year old Palestinian, joins to speak about his prison experience and invites her to stay, saying they share a similar story of imprisonment, although Hamid says he was arrested and imprisoned on what he calls an "open check," meaning that the length of his prison term was indeterminate and he can be rearrested at any point.

"The first time they came to take me, I was not home," Hamid begins. "They took my father instead. After three days, I returned to my house, and the Special Forces came and surrounded it. They checked me to be sure I was the right person, and the soldier who handcuffed and blindfolded me was so happy. He said, 'No one else touch him.' They took me to Ofra prison in the northern West Bank.

"On the way there, the soldiers took me to an Israeli settlement. When they saw me, the settlers started screaming and clapping. I was still blind-folded. From where they arrested me to the Beit El detention center (located in the settlement by the same name in the hills north of Jerusalem east of the Palestinian city of alBireh) took four hours. Normally, it's a short journey, ten minutes."

Hamid doesn't mention it, but the others who later tell me similar stories all say that the soldiers beat them throughout the whole, slow drive. He does, however, describe their brutality once they were on site.

"At Beit El in the interrogation room, I was beaten by their hands on my face, chest and stomach. I began laughing. The first soldier asked me 'Why are you laughing?' I was laughing because the soldiers are so small and I saw them trying to be powerful men." Hamid, who was twenty-three and two hundred forty-two pounds[1] at the time, continues, "I knew who is really a man.

"[In Ofra prison] they put me in a small isolation cell: three meters by two meters and said, 'You will stay here. From now until four days if I hear your voice you will curse the gods.' There was only a bottle of water and something like a blanket, one for placing on the bare floor and one for on top. The smell of them was disgusting. There was no bed, no mattress. It was the end of summer so it was not cold, but there were many mosquitoes eating me. There was no window except for on the door of the cell, which they kept closed. I asked the man at night, 'Why do you close this window?'

'For security,' he answered.

"In the next cell, there were security prisoners thirteen and fourteen years of age, and the soldiers told them that no one could talk to me. My self-confidence was already really down. I hadn't energy to continue. I was in really bad condition. A prisoner child opened the window and said, 'Don't be afraid, they just try to make you feel bad.' At that moment I felt that God sent me light. Another prisoner child also came and opened the window and gave me a towel and said, 'Keep this with you.'

"I stayed one year in Ofra and then in a prison called Naqab for six months. I don't know my crime. When the soldiers know something, they don't say. It is psychological play."

"Were you afraid?" I ask.

---

1 Two hundred forty-two pounds is approximately one hundred ten kilograms

"Yes," he answers, 'but when you see the rest of the prisoners in the same situation, you begin to feel it's normal and you can handle it."

But, Hamid begins to describe symptoms of PTSD, including racing thoughts and feeling nervous all the time.

He recalls, "[In prison] my thinking can't stop. *When will I get out? Why do they accuse me?* It was really difficult."

Hamid tells me he lost sixty-six pounds in prison.

"Prison is a challenge to the person to mature and a challenge to the sense of self," he says. "It is a playground for war. Everyday they were beating us; they threw tear gas on us when we were protesting for food. They use isolation, where I stayed for one and a half years. I didn't know when it would end."

Hamid returns to this point—that he was an "open check" prisoner— many times. In legal terms, Hamid's imprisonment is referred to as administrative detention, which generally lasts for prolonged periods of time, ranging from several months to several years. Under this system the prisoners are not prosecuted or informed of the charges against them, making it impossible for them (or their attorneys) to study the evidence and mount an effective defense.[46] According to B'tselem, an Israeli human rights organization, the highest number of administrative detainees was documented during the first Intifada. During the height of the second Intifada in 2005-2007, administrative detentions averaged about seven hundred fifty at any given time,[47] and in October 2008, Haaretz, Israel's newspaper, reported that six hundred Palestinians were being held in administrative detention in Israel, including fifteen minors.[48]

According to Hamid, it is much harder to cope with imprisonment when one has no idea when, or if, it will end.

"When I left prison it was the twenty-ninth of January. The first day I was very happy thinking of my future. On the second day I heard the news: they arrested again five of us who were freed. They put them back in prison. At that moment, my feeling of safety was completely finished, and to this day, I always feel fear. I don't know what will happen to me. In prison you dream of your future, but it is all dreams. When you get out, it's nothing."

When Hamid speaks this way I think how easy it would be for a group to take advantage of his constant fear of being imprisoned again and feeling that his life is already a type of "living death"; given his psychological state, he could easily be manipulated by terrorists into giving his life for the Palestinian cause.

Hamid was finally freed in a prisoner exchange arranged with Hezbollah, or the Party of God, a powerful political and military organization operating in Lebanon made up of mostly Shia Muslims. Hezbollah was formed with financial backing from Iran in the early 1980's to drive out Israeli troops that had invaded Lebanon. They continue to this day perpetrating terror acts against Israel, and from time to time many of their prisoners along with Palestinian political prisoners have been released in exchange for Israeli military prisoners held by them.

"Will you fight back after what happened to you?" I ask.

"The Palestinians are under occupation and we have the right to self-defense," he says, "but I don't need to be shaheed."

I can see that Hamid is frustrated by my question. "If you want to understand the Palestinians, why they do this, don't go and ask them," he chokes angrily. "Just put your American passport in your drawer at home and go to any Israeli checkpoint, and you will feel it in a very small way. Come and live like us for awhile and you will understand." Hamid continues, "Just feel this: when you lose your child in front of your eyes, when you see him killed.

"Not only are [the Israelis] practicing killing with us, they let us feel how we will die. I'm sure after awhile if you come back, you will see more awful things that will happen, like building a wall. This makes us [feel] more like monsters. We are not monsters. Just imagine a cat in a cage."

I notice that Hamid's hands, which have been trembling all the while, are now shaking violently as he continues, "Go to Gaza if you want to see who wants to do explosions. Thousands say, 'I want to.' Here [after the wall] it will be the same."

I decide to address the violent trembling that he seems unaware of by asking, "Hamid, do you have a feeling of fear in your body sometimes?"

"Yes," he answers. "For example, last week around four a.m., a car came in front of our house; it braked loudly. Without thinking I jumped out of bed and put on my clothes, my shoes and my hat and sat waiting for them."

Princess, who has been listening, agrees. "Everyone feels it," she says. "If I see a[n Israeli] jeep, I think, okay it's now. I expect [another arrest] always, and I think '*Here it is.*'"

Hamid and Princess both have a sense of a foreshortened future, a symptom of posttraumatic stress disorder that occurs when the trauma survivor has had his foundations and beliefs about life so shaken that normal life expectations are lost and replaced with the expectation of having one's life cut off early or that significant normal expectations, like getting married or having a family, won't occur.

Also typical to PTSD are frequent nightmares, and both Hamid and Princess say they get them often.

"The worst dreams were not when I was in prison, because in prison there is no more fear of arrest," Hamid explains. "There I always dreamed that I am strong and we are the ones beating them in a good challenge. Now that I am out, it's the reverse. Now I dream we are the victims. The worst dream I had was the soldiers start to knock in a bad way loudly at the door. My mother opens the door and two soldiers come in and say, 'You are Hamid?' 'Yes.' They pull their pistols and shoot me in the head and the stomach. I wake up terrified."

Princess tells us, "My nightmare is always the fear of them taking me from my mother." After such dreams, Princess goes to her mother who holds her and soothes her back to sleep.

Hamid admits that he drinks to calm himself, though alcohol is forbidden in strict Islamic households. He tells me that he has two to three drinks, but I go by the standard practice in alcohol abuse counseling and double that number.

I ask him kindly, "You really mean six?"

He nods. He's obviously deeply ashamed. "When I used to drink before prison, I drank for fun, but now I drink so that the pressure becomes less."

Many of the Palestinians refer to "pressure" and I think it is what I would clinically call bodily arousal: heart pounding, sweaty palms, physiological responses in the body due to fear. I ask Hamid to clarify what he means by this word and he explains, "I know the life I have is not right. I am abnormal. I hope to change."

Hamid also describes psychic numbing, where he tries not to or is actually unable to feel his emotions. He says this happens when there are reminders of prison: "A car in the night. When I see people are dying or arrested in a bad way. I can't do anything for them. I keep on seeing and seeing and then suddenly I am numb. It happens from time to time."

Hamid tells me that he is not psychologically well after prison and that he cannot marry and take care of a family in his state. We end the interview with one of the others giving him a cigarette and he accepts it by mocking the Israelis who in prison also gave them cigarettes to try to trick him into talking.

• • •

A nineteen-year-old girl, Sharina, joins us next. She is the daughter of Ahmed Sa'adat, the current leader of the PFLP, and a liberal arts student.

"I lived in a difficult situation," she says. "My father wasn't there. All the time he's in jail, out of jail. Prison is like his home since I can remember. We felt like we didn't have a father. My mother played a great role in my life. She was father, sister, friend, everything. We had some money from my father, from the movement, but mother had to work with the Union of Palestinian women. Mother was educated.

"When the Palestinian Authority (PA) came in 1969, we expected that life would become normal again, that our father will come back. But this that we hoped for we didn't get. He was working to give ideas to the people about the Palestinian case and to struggle for it. The PA collaborated [with the Israelis] and took him too."

"I want my father to come back," Sharina says sadly. "Father raised us to struggle this way and we will continue the struggle for Palestine."

Sharina's family has also experienced the pain of the Israeli's violence.

"My uncle was murdered in the Intifada in Ramallah," Sharina states. "Some prisoners told about him, so the Israelis came to arrest him."

Sharina recalls that he was determined not to be imprisoned and tortured. "He said, 'I won't surrender, I'd rather die than surrender.' So when they came he ran away. They shot out his legs. He shot back once. And another soldier came out and shot him with five bullets to make sure he died."

"How do you feel about "martyrdom" and "martyrdom" missions?" I ask.

"The minute I took the idea of defending my country, this idea came with it," Sharina says. "I am not against it and at a certain point I will go too," she explains. "I will use my body if it is necessary. But, I don't feel it is necessary now."

"You would ask to carry a bomb?" I ask, surprised. "You seem like you have way too much life in your eyes."

"Yes, I am ready to die for my country, but I'm not with the idea of martyrdom [by suicide]. Why should I go and die when I can make a bigger difference with my life?"

I nod and understand that she is not interested to volunteer herself as a suicide bomber; she feels there are many other ways to fight and that she can be effective in those ways, although if things got desperate enough, she would—a sentiment that I am finding is shared by many Palestinians.

"Do you fear prison?" I ask.

"No, but I expect it in my life," she says. "My mother in the last half year was arrested at a conference in Birzeit University and kept for forty-five days. The goal was to pressure my father to talk."

Sharina feels the pursuit of the Israelis is relentless.

"They come to our university everyday," Sharina says. "They come to our town every night. We don't consider ourselves in our own country. They come and go as they like anytime. They take anyone. Even right now, there is nothing and no one who can stop them."

"Are you constantly alert because of this?" I ask.

"There is fear," she admits. "I keep struggling inside with it but I never show it. Because if I do, [the Israelis] will see it as a sign of weakness and exploit it. If I show it, he will beat me. I don't feel fear always. I have some violence in my personality and I saw death since, so there is fear inside, but even to me it is not always obvious."

Sharina is describing being dissociative. Her feelings of fear have dropped out of conscious awareness and have been replaced by a type of posttraumatic bodily arousal coupled with psychic numbing.

"Does it go so far that, at times, you feel you are not in her own body?" I inquire, and she confirms.

"When does it happen?" I ask.

"When I lose someone, when someone is arrested, shot or killed. I reach a point when I cannot concentrate on anything. I feel I am lost, too."

Sharina is describing exactly the hyperaroused and dissociative state of a trauma victim: the loss of concentration, loss of self, *and* she says that anger helps her persevere through these feelings.

"Do you need your anger to keep yourself together?" I ask.

"Yes," she answers, "Anger pushes me further. It gives me hope."

"Do you expect to see a free Palestine?"

"It will be," Sharina says. "It will be magnificent."

"And will Jews be present?"

"They won't be here. Anywhere but here. The most important thing is to resist and keep on resisting until they are out. Even using small things we can do to push them out."

"By small things, do you mean "martyrdom" missions?" I ask checking once more for her thoughts on this subject.

"Our group works to make political awareness, but in everyone's mind is this last choice."

"How would you feel if your brother or a close friend went as a bomber?"

"I would be sad," she answers, "but the one who is dead chose to do it. It's an honor. It doesn't mean our sadness will control us."

• • •

We interview Majid[1], another student, next. He passed through a checkpoint on his way to university, and when the guards checked his ID, they arrested and beat him as they took him to jail. Of the three years Majid spent in Israeli prison, three months of it were in isolation, and he would still be there if the prisoner exchange agreement with Hezbollah had not resulted in his freedom. Majid reminds us that imprisonment is a rite of passage for young males in his culture.

"Most Palestinian [men] pass through prison sometime between the ages of seventeen and thirty."

Majid spent his time thinking about his family, but says only women could visit, and only in his last year of imprisonment was he allowed to receive visits from his mother and little sister. When he wasn't missing his family, he was dreaming of the future—it is all that prisoners can do, he says, when they are deprived of their present.

Majid recalls violence by the Israeli guards; when the prisoners protested over the food or other prison issues, the soldiers responded by shooting tear gas into the cells. He wants to fight back but not as a suicide bomber.

"I want to live and fight," he explains. "Not die. Not martyrdom." On the other hand he sounds conflicted and open to "martyring" himself saying, "It's hard *not* to be a shaheed, but it depends on the situation. If something happens I will be shaheed, but I will not join an organization first."

Majid doesn't explain what could push him over the edge to suicide in a "martyrdom" mission but his words give a clue to how quickly Palestinian youth can activate into suicide missions. He doesn't need a long prep-

1 A psuedonym

aration time or months of indoctrination; his experiences and the social milieu have already prepared him to go as a "shaheed". He also doesn't see it as necessary that he already be part of a terrorist group as he knows he could quickly join and nearly instantly activate to become a "martyr". Whereas Mustafa, who we interviewed days earlier, was tied to the PFLP and waiting to be sent when his group's operatives were arrested and now waits to build trust with new ones, Majid knows that there *are* other terrorist groups that he could go to that would likely take him and activate him nearly immediately.

The speed with which suicide bombers are activated to their missions is a theme that I will explore not only in Palestine, but in other places as well. In the first Intifada there was some evidence of suicide bombers being coerced into missions with groups playing upon discovery of an individual's homosexuality, an illicit affair, or financial need and the desire to leave their family with a monetary reward during those years when some "martyrs" families received large monetary payouts from Saddam Hussein (which was up until 2003). Those that weren't coerced in the first Intifada were indoctrinated for a fairly long period of time to ensure they would carry their mission to completion.

Now in the second Intifada, the "cult of martyrdom" has so inundated Palestinian society with posters, videos, songs, parades and other societal glorifications of those willing to become suicide bombers that there is no longer a need to coerce youth. And while Saddam Hussein issued payments of up to $25,000 to some "martyr's" families in the years up to 2003,[49] money for these youth does not appear as an important incentive, other than to leave one's family with a way to rebuild their destroyed home or to survive the loss of a breadwinner. Now during the second Intifada, suicide missions are accepted on a society-wide level as a legitimate part of the struggle, thereby cutting the lengthy ideological indoctrination period previously needed to launch a bomber. An individual can approach a group and if accepted, activate to become a bomber in a matter of weeks or days. The only things a bomber needs after acceptance is the group's technical expertise, instructions on how to pass checkpoints to reach the target and help in making a "martyr's" video, testimony and posters for glorification after death. And the groups claim they have too many volunteers for suicide missions and turn many away.

Majid is definitely vulnerable to suicide. He admits that his biggest fear in life is to become depressed and give up on living. Perhaps he knows he would be vulnerable to act self destructively in this state, and with all the groups sending suicide bombers he has plenty of support for exiting life as a "martyr". To avoid this path, Majid tells us that one of his ways of coping is writing, that it helps him withstand the fear. "Marriage also helps to take the mind away from prison," he adds although he is still waiting to get married and will need a good job in order to marry. He also studies psychology and wants to help people who come out of prisons.

"I wish someone would have done that for me," he explains. "To help others with psychology is another way of avoiding struggle.

"Martyrdom is not the aim. We love life and the future—not to die. There are thousands of ways to fight. With love and learning we can over-come this. And even if you are depressed, it does not mean that you will join an organization." As I listen I wish to believe him, but I know there are plenty of terrorist groups that would gladly take advantage of him in a depressed and suicidal state.

"I would love to travel," he adds, "but [the Israelis] want us to leave, so we stay. We are a people who love life and we want people to help us, to trust us."

At night Ken and Al speak with the other students and learn that Israe-li prisons are not the only incubators where young Palestinians develop PTSD. Palestinian jails are as well. One of them tells Al about his brother who was arrested by the Palestinian Authority for writing political graffiti on the walls, jailed for nine months, and released with extreme psycho-logical problems.

"His hands would shake after he came out of prison and he began to believe he was the greatest man in the world," the student recalls. Grandi-osity is a psychic defense to having been made totally powerless in prison, particularly during a crucial developmental stage in addition to all the other posttraumatic stressors of being raised in a conflict zone. Grandios-ity can also be a symptom of schizophrenia, which can be triggered by extreme stress as well.

Al's informant describes his brother's prison experience: "The prison cell was two meters by three meters, and he was held in solitary confine-ment. He was beaten so much, even our parents could not recognize him. He became used to being alone so when he was freed, he couldn't handle being around others. After nine months of solitary confinement, he didn't care about anything around him. He became crazy. He burned a mosque because he felt like God and didn't want others worshipping another God.

He does not want to take medication for his condition. His condition varies from days of normal behavior to crazy. He talks about prison, but only to me. The guards hit him with the butt of the guns. Maybe they caused brain damage?"

"If he reads the newspaper he gets excited and angry," the student tells Al. Amazingly, this informant has seven brothers and five of them are held in Israeli jails and the sixth, who became mentally ill, was held in the PA jail.

Another Birzeit student, Abu Thaer , tells Al that he was also imprisoned at age seventeen in the Palestinian Authority (PA) prison after the PFLP killed the Israeli tourism minister Rehavam Zeevi. He was arrested when he, like others, went to the streets shouting support for the assassination of Zeevi and for the release of the jailed PFLP leader Ahmed Sa'adat. Abu Thaer spent two months in a constantly lit cell in the PA prison and describes being woken at three a.m. for interrogations. "There was no hitting," he explains, "but other humiliations. I was not put in stress positions, but others were for between two to twelve days."

He becomes extremely nervous speaking about the "soft torture" he and his inmates endured and concludes by saying, "The Intifada is not just about Israel coming and taking land, but also about the Palestinian Authority."

Abu Thaer is indicating that many Palestinians are outraged that the Palestinian Authority, in an effort to win back their own self-determination, made a cooperative agreement with Israel to imprison and even mistreat their own militants who are fighting against Israel for Palestinian freedom.[50]

As we listen to these stories of arrest and imprisonment I begin to see how deeply the Palestinian youth are affected. They are already raised in a conflict environment, frustrated by checkpoints complicating or restricting their access to school and travel, and facing the unlikelihood of finding employment. Then being arrested while in high school or university severely disrupts their education. But much more importantly, the separation from close-knit family and community and enduring prison and "soft" torture at such a vulnerable age poses a serious challenge to the long-term emotional health of these Palestinian youth. Additionally, the arrests of some make *all* of the youth fear and contemplate the possibility of their own arrest.

Our interviews with Palestinians who had been jailed as minors, or even later in their twenties, made it clear to us that the experience left all of them with posttraumatic symptoms and some with full-blown PTSD. In many ways, the complete powerlessness, helplessness and stress of imprisonment returned them to a childlike state, and they needed their parents or someone capable to calm them from the psychological trauma upon their release. However, even parents cannot protect their children in situations such as this, and often times, the parents are also traumatized by their child's sudden arrest. And the youth are exposed to terrorists groups and leaders who indoctrinate them inside the prisons.

As the second Intifada wore on and the number of Palestinian suicide bombers increased, Israel hardened its defenses by tightening checkpoints and initiating Operation Defensive Shield in the West Bank, which enclosed whole communities suspected of harboring militants. These measures resulted in the arrest and deaths of many militants who were planning suicide missions, and terrorist organizations increasingly found themselves blocked from sending male suicide bombers across the Israeli border. As a result, they turned to women and children, who were unexpected in the region.

From September 2000 through 2003 the IDF reported forty plans for suicide attacks to be carried out by minors, twenty-nine of these carried to completion. Many of these involved fourteen- and fifteen-year-olds, leading to an alarming escalation of arrests of Palestinian children. Ten children between the ages of twelve and thirteen were arrested in the first two months of 2009, compared to three children for the whole of 2008. While the Israelis claim to handle the arrests of young children as compassionately as possible, no thirteen-year-old is ready to face imprisonment. This is a dilemma for the Israelis—if the senders are willing to use child suicide bombers, they are forced to arrest and hold potential child suspects.

• • •

As we continue our research, I learn by doing. I find that I don't want our subjects to tell us about crimes they are planning to commit because it puts us in the difficult ethical dilemma of doing nothing or reporting them to the police in the interest of protecting human lives. For instance, when Mustafa said he was waiting to go on a suicide mission we had to seriously consider if we should try to stop him by letting the Israeli authorities know. Since his militant cell had been decimated and our informants didn't think he could be sent anytime soon we decided to let it be, yet it deeply haunted me and for the year afterward I kept asking about him and how he was doing. I would have hated to know he was contemplating murdering innocent civilians and I did nothing, yet I also did not want to betray the trust he confided in me sharing his pain. Finally, a year later I was saddened to learn that Mustafa had been arrested but also greatly relieved that he was no longer available to go on his suicide mission.

Thus, I learn to tell our informants to please refrain from telling us about *active* plots and stop them if they do stray into those descriptions, explaining that I came to their countries, spent time in their homes, shared meals with them and interviewed them in order to learn and do not want those experiences to end by me becoming their betrayer. Also, informing on those I interviewed could place me, my guides, and others following in my footsteps in danger when returning for more interviews. This request for discretion undoubtedly helped me gain the subjects' confidence.

The only thing my subjects did not appear totally forthcoming about before I instituted this policy was the serious crimes they may have committed in the past or had under immediate consideration. I learned both in Palestine and later in Iraq that prisoners especially are rarely willing to admit guilt of crimes for which they haven't been prosecuted. Given what could happen to them if they were caught, it is probably a wise and self-protective stance to be reticent about such subjects.

In many cases, it seemed our interview subjects had been incarcerated for minor crimes—for being in the wrong place at the wrong time or for responding with aggression to soldiers when in tumultuous circumstances. Sweeping up these kinds of suspects is always a serious difficulty in conflict zones, as soldiers are under threat of life and often respond quickly with aggression to those they feel could harm them. They are not in a position to have the time or luxury to decipher immediately who are the serious threats and who happens to be in the wrong place at the wrong time. Once someone is arrested, it's easy for the judicial system to bring an accusation about their criminal intent or activities. In Israel there is unfortunately an advantage to retaining many low-threat political prisoners, as they can later be released en masse in prisoner trades with little concern about their recidivism. But even in the best of systems, it takes time for the bureaucracy to sift through who has committed serious crimes and who simply sprayed graffiti on a wall, threw a stone or shouted in a demonstration.

As we listened to these stories of arrest and imprisonment we take what the students report at face value, hoping they are telling us the truth, but also realizing that they may want to mislead or influence us to their way of thinking. We listen carefully for contradictions and things that don't ring true. As an experienced trauma psychologist, it's very clear to me that *all* of the young people we have interviewed are genuinely traumatized by their arrest and imprisonment experiences and have a very difficult time speaking about it. In many cases, I am not sure that without me to hold their emotions and pace the material that they could even have told a coherent account of what happened to them.

I am impressed that all of the young people we interviewed don't seem to want to exaggerate Israeli cruelties. Most even go out of their way to say they were not beaten if that was the case. It's clear that while they want us to understand what happened to them, their posttraumatic recall is so painful that they tell us only enough to make sure we understand and are reticent to enter fully into their posttraumatic memories.

Listening to their accounts, I am horrified to think that Israelis, so many of whom come from families with Holocaust histories, could infringe upon the human rights of others in the ways we are hearing. Yet I know that Israelis also live under constant threat and that the civilian death and injury toll of innocent Israeli men, women and children from suicide bombers during the second Intifada has become intolerable and unbearable. The question is, does what they are doing make them safer or guarantee that yet another generation will grow up to hate and want to annihilate them?

CHAPTER 11

Palestinian Student Center: Birzeit

It's now nightfall, and we have taken a taxi outside of Ramallah to a student center where a slim, dark-haired college student agrees to an interview. Yousef has already told me a bit about him: He is from Beit Fourik, an infamous village just outside Nablus that has had the highest number of suicide bombers from any one location in this Intifada.

As we take our seats at a table, introduce ourselves and my study and begin, I ask what pseudonym he would like.

"Shakespeare," he answers. "I'm a writer." Then acknowledging the grandiosity of his choice, he chuckles bitterly, "Jokes, you know. We have to laugh at our pain. To let the tensions out."

I'm beginning to understand that the whole Palestinian population is in pain, carrying bottled up anger, frustration, grief, trauma and loss inside themselves.

When I explain to Shakespeare that I came to understand the suicide bombers, he tells me, "I studied them myself. I went and read all their last testaments. I wanted to know, 'Do those people try to get a solution for just themselves, or for the whole?'"

It's a good question and interesting that a college student seeks a methodical way to study it. Indeed, one American researcher of Palestinian descent, Professor Mohammed Hafez, made much of his academic career as a counter-terrorism expert by studying the last wills and testaments of suicide bombers, which he found consisted mostly of propaganda messages organized and choreographed by the sending group. He also found, however, that a brief personal message was often included, usually telling the family not to grieve or giving specific instructions about how to cope after the bomber's death.[51]

"I'm impressed!" I respond to Shakespeare about his study. "What did you find when you studied their last wills and testaments?"

"I learned that all of them tried to get a solution for the whole; they are not looking out only for the individual," Shakespeare explains. "They also say, 'Don't cry, I'm not alone. I'm with the best army of shaheeds.'"

When I ask him about himself, he tells me that he is from Beit Fourik, the village near Nablus with a shockingly high statistic of suicide bombers.

"We were thirty-one [male] students in my high school class," Shakespeare says, rubbing his forehead. "Twenty-seven of them exploded themselves." He stares down at the table in grief.

Stunned, I try to imagine being college-age and having only four classmates left out of my high school class—the rest having died as suicide bombers.

"Why are there are so many 'shaheeds' from your village?" I ask.

"Our village is on a road that connects two [Israeli] settlements," he explains. "There are many problems with the settlers. Two of our old men were killed when they went near the settler's road to collect olives. You know we pray five times a day at specific times. One was killed in the olive grove when he stopped to pray. His head was to the ground and a settler took a rock and smashed his head. They let their dogs bite his body. Another old man was walking on the road, and a settler came with his huge four-by-four Mitsubishi jeep and ran into him. He flew on this jeep and was killed."

Shakespeare goes on to explain how it feels for young Palestinians who can only find work inside Israel. They are treated poorly by the Israelis and simultaneously see the better Israeli standard of living. The Palestinians then return home and compare their lives to those of the Israelis who constrict them.

"The [Palestinian] students who go to work inside the green line [in Israel][52] see that the Israelis think the Palestinian is his donkey. The Israeli attitude is 'You have to pee over him [the Palestinian donkey] and take him to water—not for *him* to drink but for *you* to drink. And then you can kill him. You can see this mentality in their school.

"When these Palestinian students return to my village, they want to know why do we have a different life? It is our right to eat and drink just like the Israelis do. They have rights, but we lose everything."

But the thing that brings out the most anger in the young men, Shakespeare explains, is being essentially locked inside their village of Beit

Fourik. They are only able to cross out of it at the Hawara checkpoint into the Palestinian city of Nablus, where the university and the jobs are.

"When the Israelis built their settlement here, they built the settler's road as well and destroyed everything surrounding the road and settlement—any home, any tree—for their security. And they created checkpoints for our people: large hills of soil with tanks and Israelis on top. To get from Nablus to the village, there is the Hawara checkpoint, which is very difficult to pass. We have to leave our cars and walk to the checkpoint."

Shakespeare's voice cracks and his fists clench as he describes it. "Let me tell you how it is. When you climb the hill of muddy soil to the tank, you sink into it up to your thighs. Many women have to lift their skirts to get up. It's so disgusting. When we get there we stand in line for hours waiting to cross. I have stood for hours at the Hawara checkpoint: the Israelis take my ID, always keep me for at least five hours and then free me. Every time, I thought, 'Come on get out of your tank, I want to kill you. Come on, come out of your tank, give me your hand, I want to kill you.'"

These feelings are not Shakespeare's alone as he explains, "It's not only me that felt this anger—this checkpoint is what has created 'shaheeds' in my village. The line 'Come, give me your hand–from mine to yours ...' that was written in so many wills of the martyrs before they exploded themselves." They all felt the anger inside, just like I did. But unlike me they decided to do something about it."

As Shakespeare describes it, I can imagine the anger rising within the young Arab men after being detained for hours at the checkpoints and witnessing their women immodestly having to lift their skirts while sinking into thigh-high mud. There must be such an overwhelming feeling of powerlessness,anguish and frustration over being unable to do anything about it. I begin to see why so many young men from his village responded to the call to become bombers, trying to fight the Israeli incursions into their land.

But Shakespeare is one of the few in his class who did not heed the call, and he reflects with sadness.

"My father called me each time they went and said, 'Your friend has become shaheed...'." Caught in the memory, Shakespeare momentarily stares into space, mute as he must have been on the phone with his father.

Then he says in a barely audible voice, laced with pain, "Okay dad, thank you."

He continues, anguish choking his voice, "I begin to think 'What am I? Why am I here?' I have to stop them [the Israelis] with their jeeps in the street."

I shudder following his mental process, watching him wonder if he also should become a bomber.

He asks himself softly, "Where is my friend Anin?" and answers in a staccato voice, "He is dead." He pauses and vocalizes his internal debate, "I will go with him. . . . . How?. . .Explode myself. . . . Why?. . . To get another solution. . . . For you or for the whole?. . . I want to go to be with him, to be in his army [of shaheeds]."

Shakespeare shakes himself out of his memory and looks up at me to explain how their collective society works.

"Some martyrs who exploded themselves have left behind wives and children. They don't feel that they abandoned them and tell themselves, 'My comrades will help them, and my sons will understand and continue the struggle.' That is because inside our village there is a history of strong relations between people; we are very loyal to each other and to our village."

As I listen, I feel overwhelmed by his obvious confusion.

"How do you deal with your pain?" I ask.

"Maybe I can cover it," he says. "I have acted in the theater. I can express myself and be someone else there. I can act out a different life. I can be the problem and the solution in the theater. There was a play I wrote. I was two personalities: Shaheed and Palestinian." I see that this was the dialogue he just went through—the internal argument to join his classmates in death or struggle to stay alive and find another non-violent way to fight.

Shakespeare goes on to tell me that in this play, one actor plays both parts and the shaheed does not win out. I'm heartened to hear that despite what he has experienced, he hasn't yet crossed that line of too much pain.

I tell him, "You know I am a psychologist, and it seems to me that you have a lot of pain and confusion about what to do with the situation in Palestine and in your village, but I don't think you will join your classmates as a 'shaheed'. It seems to me that you still have hope and have found creative ways, apart from violent action, to vent and transform your emotions. Am I right?" I ask.

"You are a psychologist!" Shakespeare exclaims joyfully. "You know there is no place to go to get help here, no psychological services. My friends and I discuss this often." I try to imagine the dearth of psychologists being a normal topic of conversation of nineteen-year-old males anywhere else.

"But," Shakespeare continues, "there is a place to escape if you want to have a relationship with the Israeli cultural center." He describes programs that invite Palestinian youth to come to Israel, to see the beach. "They show them 'This is life! Life is beautiful! You can have it! This is peace!'" Then he darkens, "But it is the peace based on no (Palestinian) right of return,[53] no Jerusalem, no government for us, Israel as it is. It is called Seeds of Peace and this program is very dangerous and disgusting. I went many times."

I imagine him soaking up the sun, beach, good food and good times inside Israel, maybe even making some temporary friends, replenishing himself and then going home to Palestine; returning to helplessness, hate and despair. At least rejuvenating himself through this program, even with his mixed feelings about his hosts, is a better answer than staying trapped in pain and finally becoming a shaheed.

"Keep going to this camp even if you don't agree with the Israeli politics they wish you to accept, it recharges you." I tell him. "And keep writing. You have found the ways to stay alive and fight without violence. That's good."

I thank him and move on to the next interviewee.

• • •

The next student is a tall, lanky young man who has joined us midway during talking with Shakespeare. As Shakespeare leaves, we are introduced and I begin by explaining to him my project, tell him about keeping interviews anonymous and ask, "What name would you like me to call you by?"

"Che Guevara," he answers with no hesitation. "I respect him so much."

Indeed, all through the West Bank I've noticed the communist revolutionary Guevara's face printed on t-shirts, posters, stenciled on walls and adorning backpacks. For Palestinians, the former physician and Cuban guerilla warrior of the 1950s is an icon of revolution and freedom fighting, and for many years, Palestinian revolutionaries followed Marxist revolutionary ideologies that he and his ilk promoted. It was only in recent decades with the birth and growth of Hamas, that Islamist ideologies entered into Palestinian culture (mirroring the ideological shift that swept across Arab societies as a whole). These ideologies are adept at mixing widely held Islamic beliefs into nonviolent, as well as violent, political movements.

It is also recent, and mainly in the second Intifada, that the idea of self-sacrifice, i.e., killing oneself in order to kill others through suicide terror-ism became widely popularized and accepted as a form of Islamic martyr-dom among Palestinians. The Palestinian factions that have propagated this ideology take Islamism one step further, making use of respected Islamic beliefs like martyrdom in this case, claiming that suicide bombers are Islamic "martyrs" for their faith. Che may believe this as well, but from his choice of pseudonym, it's obvious he follows the popular non-religious Marxist ideologies that are still espoused by the PFLP and other factions in Palestine.

"I graduate at the end of the semester in finance," Che says. "I hope there will be a job for me. I seriously need money, but I am sure there will be many difficulties. I hear from my friends who have graduated that there are no jobs. Why? It's all because Israel closed everything, attacked everything, destroyed everything."

I find it interesting that he puts no blame on the wave of suicide terror-ism and violence unleashed by Palestinians in the second Intifada that forced Israel to tighten its border and made many Israelis loathe to hire Palestinians—but I decide to keep silent on that point and simply listen.

Perhaps Che reads my doubt about his opinion by the look on my face. Suddenly irritated he asks me, "Why did you come here? Why don't you study in Abu Ghraib in Iraq with all the terrorists? Why here?"

He probably means to taunt me on the scandal of some American soldiers who were court-martialed for abusing prisoners in Abu Ghraib in recent months and blames me for coming to study terrorists here in Pales-tine when the Iraqis also have a resistance—in their case to the American-led coalition—but I don't take the bait.

"Yes, what happened there was no good," I answer. "But I came here to learn from you," I say staying calm, watching him and listening for when he's ready to resume.

Agitated, Che takes a cigarette and lights up. Then he looks up at a poster on the wall of a crying Palestinian child who lost his mother. He gestures to it, waving his lit cigarette, and tells me, "This is our life."

Che is tall and seated at the corner of the table diagonally to me, his knees nearly touching mine. All the while that Shakespeare has been describing the situation in Beit Fourik and now while he speaks, I have felt his legs going crazy with nervous energy, literally jumping up and down. From time to time, his knee hits my leg and he rests his leg next to mine momentarily. I feel as if he is yearning for contact, for someone to calm him emotionally and physically, and I intentionally force myself not to flinch or pull away when his jumping knee touches mine. I want him to know I'm here for him, solid and calm, listening and ready to hold his emotions.

Che holds his open hands out over the table, examining them before he asks, "You are a psychologist. When you look at my hands, can you tell anything about me?"

I find this touchingly naïve, as though I could somehow read his mind or character from the shape of his hands. Yet his legs jumping next to me, and his knee stopping to rest on mine, drawing comfort, give me a lot of information. I shake my head smiling, "No, but your jumping legs tell me a lot."

Confused, Che stares at me. I realize suddenly that he is completely unaware. "Your legs have been jumping the entire time we have been talking," I explain gently. I push my chair back from the table, taking his knee and showing him how his leg has been moving up and down, not just trembling, but bobbing four inches into the air at least.

Surprised Che says, "I didn't know."

I slide my chair back in place and we begin talking again. In a few moments, his leg starts jumping again. Che is still unaware, so I put my hand gently on his knee, careful not to startle him, showing him how it is moving in response to his emotions.

"Wow, I didn't know that," he says, frightened. I watch as he shuts down, overwhelmed by his acknowledgement of this bodily response and his inability to track or control his emotions.

I let him rest briefly, respecting his needs, and soon I feel his knee, resting on mine again, drawing strength. I know that it's strange in his culture for me as a woman, to allow him to rest his knee on my leg and I wonder if I should let him do it, but I also know he needs comfort, something solid to hold him, so he can open up and tell me what's happening inside.

We rest together, his knee on my leg, as I breathe deeply and quietly, willing my calm and presence into his agitated body. Soon, Che finds strength and begins again.

He points at the poster, stares sadly at it, and takes a long drag on his cigarette. "I am like that child. I lost my father and my mother. My home is destroyed. I feel so sad. And I felt so bad when Shakespeare talked, but he told only small things about one village, one checkpoint. It's a disaster. There are many checkpoints."

Che's leg is bobbing up and down again. When he pauses, I show him again, gently. I want to help him and to take this small opportunity to help him become more conscious of his behaviors. I know from years of experience as a trauma psychologist that even a tiny intervention can make a huge difference in a trauma victim's life. "I am not aware," he repeats. "It's spontaneous."

Che seems to be taking strength from me and begins to open up. "Look, last week I didn't go to two classes. I searched for a beautiful girl to sit with, to tell her about myself. I feel so bad." He may be making a reference to my letting him rest his leg on my knee, but I don't think so. I think he really was searching for someone specific in his own age group to talk to and help him make sense of his posttraumatic experiences.

Trauma survivors who have been overwhelmed with violent and life threatening experiences are forced into re-living these posttraumatic memories until they find meaning and a way to fit what has happened into their life narrative. At the time of a traumatic event, the human brain literally cannot process something so unreal, terrifying and horrific, and therefore, their experience remains in their brains as a "live" memory, full of the original sensory impact. Then triggered memories of it will keep firing (from the amygdalya section of the brain) in posttraumatic flashbacks that inescapably invade their present-day space until they find a way to piece the experience into their life meanings and narrative, which is not an easy task. It's the mind's way of trying to heal itself and to make sense of what happened and is likely an in built neural mechanism to help process past trauma and make useful decisions about what is dangerous, what is not and what needs to be avoided to stay safe. And while most ordinary tragedies can be more simply processed, allowing the individual to achieve full closure soon afterward, survivors of severe trauma frequently spend years oscillating between reexperiencing horrific memories with high bodily arousal (fear) states, to shutting them down with posttraumatic avoidance and psychic numbing and back again.

This oscillation is what describes a full-blown case of posttraumatic stress disorder (PTSD), which is what I am beginning to see too often among the young Palestinians I am meeting. Indeed Palestinian psychiatrist, Eyad Sarraj who runs the Gaza Community Mental Health Programme, the only mental health clinic in Gaza, writes that with the ubiquity of trauma among the youth of Palestine, it is a wonder that only a few, versus all, Palestinian youth chose to exit life as suicide bombers.[54]

I see that Che needs to rest again. Likely, this interview is causing his brain to fire posttraumatic recall of terror, inescapability and other feelings of overwhelming emotional pain, which is hard to distinguish as a past, versus present, experience. I know from my own personal experience with traumas and from years of treating trauma victims, that safety is needed to effectively process posttraumatic recall. A safe place and safe personal attachments, whether it be a relationship to a therapist, a beautiful girl, a friend, loving family members, or anyone who can stand to listen, will help a trauma victim make it through the chaotic and agitated thoughts and emotions that spill out incoherently when trying to make sense of what happened—and what should not have.

Che needs to rest again, so I take the opportunity to give him some space and understanding. I explain to our Palestinian translator and Che how posttraumatic stress disorder often looks as it manifests among young men: what it is, and how to deal with it. They listen to my explanations about PTSD and the various ways to cope. When Che regains his composure, we resume and he comments on why it has been difficult for him to cope.

"Islam – it's a strict society," he says. "There are no open relationships between men and women here. I would like to live in an open society. We have limited relationships here. There are barriers. So,when I feel so sad, I go to the mountains. I love olive trees, I take a beer, and I sit and think about the situation in Palestine, the situation in our university [with the blockades and Israeli incursions] and sometimes about God. *Where is He? Why does He allow this?* Sometimes I feel peace after this picnic. I return back home, maybe I sleep."

Che is trying to calm his mind and body with these behaviors, and his searching questions are typical of all trauma victims. I heard the same from the Holocaust survivors I interviewed: "Where was God? How could

He allow it?" Childhood incest survivors, rape and torture victims, or anyone who has suffered as a victim of serious injustice also ask the same.

I know that these are questions that eat away at one's soul until they are answered satisfactorily, and if I get into a philosophical discussion about this with a therapy patient, my only answer is this: If there is a God that created us, were we created with free will or not? If God wanted creatures that would come into relationship with him freely, not as automatons, then he voluntarily tied his hands, allowing many to choose goodness, love and truth, while others were equally free to chose evil, hatred, and doing harm to others. It's a hard thing to accept, but I have been the agent of healing in many lives that have been touched by evil, and I've watched trauma survivors heal their anger and hurt at God by working through these thoughts and understanding that in the free will scenario, evil does not necessarily come from God; he just allows it. This opens to them the possibility that there may be a loving God who is also available to grant comfort and peace to help undo the effects of those who chose to enact evil.

But I don't share any of these thoughts with Che. It's too much to discuss in one sitting, and I am not doing therapy for him—I'm here to listen and learn and to help, if I can, in the small things I say that may make a difference.

Che continues, telling me how he sometimes finds a woman to sleep with or drinks alcohol to dull the pain. Both are forbidden for a devout Muslim and it's obvious he feels ashamed, yet I'm impressed he is able to be open about it here with me. Despite being forbidden both responses to trauma do work—temporarily, anyway: an orgasm releases oxytocin, a neuro-hormone that psycho-biologically creates an antagonistic response to posttraumatic arousal in the body. The oxytocin damps down the cortisol released by posttraumatic flashbacks and brings the body back to a state of calm. Alcohol works by suppressing the amygdala, therefore stifling its ability to bring about posttraumatic recall. Sex and booze have long been coping choices of war veterans and other trauma survivors for self-medication.

Che's turning to sex as a way of coping reminds me of well-known counter-terrorism expert who admitted to me a similar coping response. He had been called in to interrogate a group of villagers to determine those who had been involved in terrorism. During the course of interrogations he learned that many of the villagers were involved, but most only peripherally. He tried to shield the most innocent from full retribution of the security services he was working with. It didn't work. The next morning, after having completed his report, he learned that many of those whom he had identified as mostly innocent, i.e. only peripherally involved, including a young girl, had been hacked to pieces by the security services, their body parts stuffed into old tires, doused with gasoline and burned. Stunned and sickened by the role he had played and his failure to protect the many "mostly innocent" victims, this tormented man told me, "I left my country immediately and spent a year in the U.S. trying to recover. During this time I either had to rent a movie every night or find a woman to have sex with. It was the only way I could sleep - otherwise I was awake the whole night with horrific memories."

"Che," I say, "these things will work to deal with your posttraumatic stress disorder, but they are short-term remedies only, and probably not very good for you. It would be much better to find someone, a psychologist if possible, to talk through the traumas you have been through and to put them behind you, to free yourself from this painful posttraumatic recall."

But as we know from Shakespeare, the problem is that these services basically don't exist in the West Bank. And there are plenty of groups that will be happy to play upon Che's posttraumatic pain and enlist him for a fast and easy exit out of this life. I know from experience treating trauma victims that just learning that their trauma response is normal, and understanding PTSD can help a great deal, but I have so little time. It feels awful to wonder what will happen to these young men and knowing if I had longer, I could help.

I leave Shakespeare believing he will continue creatively vent his pain with writing and hopefully his encounters at the beach in Israel will also rejuvenate him somewhat and remind him that Israelis are people too.

Che, however, has a serious case of PTSD, or at least repeated flashbacks that occur with very high bodily arousal states of terror. He successfully but temporarily controls them by drinking and sleeping with women. But this is no way to live, especially in his society, with all the secrecy these choices require and the shame they engender.

As I thank Che for his interview I try to pump him up with genuine care and hope for the future. Sometimes just knowing that someone else took the time to listen and actually cares can make the difference. In his case, I hope it does.

CHAPTER 12

Beit Fourik

After our interviews in the evening at the student center, I am intrigued by the story Shakespeare told us about Beit Fourik, the village outside of Nablus where many of his classmates have already died as suicide bombers, and tell Yousef I would like to go there if possible and interview the bombers' friends and families. Yousef calls and asks Shakespeare if he'd like to accompany us there the next day, but he cannot, so they arrange for another friend, Belal, to be our guide.

We set out early in the morning and our traveling party consists of me, Ken, Al, Yousef, and Belal and a new female friend that Ken and Al have picked up at the university: Jamilah, the pretty young girl who had made the silk painting of the weeping woman's face drawn on the wall. She appears excited to be hanging around with Ken and Al, on whom she seems to have a crush.

It is already hot when we meet in the city center in the morning, and we sit under the bright sun on the curbs where the minibuses congregate to discuss our plan. My colleague Nichole Argo, who has also conducted research in the West Bank, has already told me that many of the suicide bombers come from Nablus, and while it's worth a visit, it can also be dangerous. Nablus is a hotbed of militant activities and sometimes the entire city is encircled and shut down by the Israelis. Nichole advised that I carefully assess the situation before going there.

Our new guide, Belal, is an American of Palestinian ancestry going to Birzeit University. He wears blue jeans and a nicely pressed cotton collared shirt and if that doesn't suggest he's an American, something in the way he stands makes it clear. He smiles through his braces as he excitedly responds to our questions about getting to Nablus. He's young, smart, and energetic with perfect English, but he carries himself with a certain swagger, like he wants to prove he is as macho as the Palestinians born here, that he fits in.

"Listen Belal," I say, "I want to make these interviews but I want you to understand something. I'm a mother, I have three children at home that need me to return, and these are my two students. I know there is some risk in going to Nablus, but I don't want to place any of us in any unnecessary danger, okay? I don't want to get into a situation where anyone gets hurt."

Belal nods his understanding as he sucks a fresh orange and carrot juice from the corner vendor through a straw. He explains to us that the only way to Beit Fourik is to take the mountain road that bypasses the Israeli settlements. What he doesn't explain is that there is technically no road, that we will essentially being going off road for the last part of the journey and traveling in that area and in that manner is strictly forbidden by the Israelis.

Once we agree on a plan, Belal and Yousef speak to some of the drivers for hire and negotiate a price for the day. Once they have found a driver, Yousef calls me and Ken over and translates that this driver agrees to take us to Beit Fourik. Once there we will have to decide if we will return with him within a few hours of arriving in order to avoid driving at night, or if we will spend the night in Beit Fourik and he'll return for us in the morning. "Okay," we say assuming we can find somewhere to stay if necessary. We agree on his price and leave our return plans open.

We pack into the oversize car and head out.. Ken, Al and Jamilah smoke cigarettes, crack jokes, and Ken and I try to learn some Arabic from Belal, while Al flirts with Jamilah to pass the time. Belal leans over the front seat and tells us a bit about the village of Beit Fourik and the city of Nablus. After about an hour on the main roads the driver turns off onto a gravel lane. Belal tells us this is the road leading to the mountains that we will traverse to get to Nablus. It's a picturesque climb, and I enjoy taking in the hills covered with low sage-colored bushes and big boulders.

After about a half hour we get to a fork in the road. The driver takes one branch of the gravel road leading steeply uphill to the left. When he gets to a certain point on the overlook he gets out, takes a look, and then gets back into the car, and inexplicably begins reversing it back down the road until he gets again to the fork. He takes the other branch.

"The Israelis have a checkpoint on that part of the road," Belal explains, "so we'll go this way instead." We all nod, having no idea we are already on an illegal road.

After awhile we come to another overlook, and the driver gets out to have another look. This time he gets back into the car and takes the car further down the gravel road we've been on and then turns off the road completely, starting to make his way through the sage brush and boulders. He steers around the large boulders, but drives over the smaller ones as well as the low shrubbery. I am astounded to see the abuse to which he is subjecting his car.

"Belal, what's going on?" I ask as we jostle back and forth across the seats.

"He's got to go off road now because the Israelis don't allow any cars to travel to Beit Fourik," Belal answers. "They only let one or two cars pass on this road in the mornings and in the evenings to carry supplies into the village, and other than that no one is supposed to be going in and out. That's why he's going off road."

I knew I needed to be careful when visiting Beit Fourik, but I hadn't realized entry was forbidden. I still don't comprehend the danger until Belal suddenly blurts out, "It's really dangerous actually. The Israelis get angry when they discover cars going around the mountain. They'll shoot out our tires if they see us, and as you know, the Israelis don't really care if they hit your tires or your car."

I am dumbfounded. "What are you saying Belal? We could be shot at?"

Belal nods, surprised at the intensity of my reaction. Ken, Al and I exchange looks. At this point we have been driving off road, among the boulders, for at least a half hour and its only another half hour to Beit Fourik. So it's probably just as dangerous to turn back, given the driver spotted Israeli soldiers blocking the two roads we didn't take. "Don't worry," Belal says, the driver checked and he knows where all the Israelis are. They won't find us."

Small comfort I think. Yet there is no point in getting upset at this point, and I'm also a bit in denial. I cannot really believe that Israeli soldiers would simply open fire on a car full of civilians. Surely they have binoculars and excellent marksmen capable of taking out the tires in the worst-case scenario. And I hope they have better training and intelligence than to fire on innocents. But on the other hand they could think we are transporting militants or guns or that we are militants ourselves.

At this point we are high up in the low mountains. The driver pulls over and we all get out of the car and walk to the edge of the mountain to look down into the valley. It's a beautiful vista of rocky blue hills in the distance with a green and brown valley stretching out below. It's completely unblemished, no villages or roads to be seen anywhere below us. We all smile, drinking in the natural beauty, and take a few photos posing on the edge of the mountain before we carry on.

Belal has called ahead, and when we arrive in Beit Fourik, we are welcomed by the village elders and as well as some younger men. We are brought into a small one-story cement block community center that we learn was built by Belgians. Al is from Belgium and the villagers treat him handsomely, like it is his own personal money invested in their community. We enter the two-room facility and sit down in a circle on metal chairs. The village men offer us a sweet fruit juice from the Nablus area and surround us, eager to see foreigners and hear why we came.

I explain my research, and the men begin to tell me about life trapped in the village, the hardships since the second Intifada began, and the impossibility of crossing the Hawara checkpoint into Nablus, the only legal exit out of Beit Fourik.

"The Israelis see males under the age of thirty as security threats," one of the village elders explains. "With the exception of university students, who are also often barred, adult males under age thirty are not allowed to cross out of Beit Fourik."

Belal turns to me and explains that consequently, these men are virtually imprisoned in the village, and with no employment for them there, they have nothing to do, no future.

"My father died at the checkpoint of a heart attack," one of the men tells us. "They wouldn't let him pass out of the village for medical care."

"They build their settlements here on our land," the elder who spoke before continues. "And they built their road and settlements close by, destroying many of our local olive groves and limiting local travel. The settlers are aggressive to the villagers. They killed two elderly men when they went to tend to the surviving olive trees."

"Can you tell me about the young men of the village that have gone off as bombers?" I ask.

"The Israeli military incursions into the village are frequent," the elder continues, "and the young grow up watching their elders humiliated. When the Israeli soldiers drive through the town, the young kids get angry and throw rocks at the military jeeps and are fired upon in response."

The man whose father died at the checkpoint says, "Sometimes, they use rubber bullets, but even these can have razor sharp edges and cut the skin, or if they hit an eye or delicate part of the body they can do real damage. Many of the villagers have been hurt. And it isn't always just rubber bullets that they use, they use live ammunition as well."

"I would like to understand the mentality of the young men who went as 'martyrs,'" I explain.

"It's really hard to describe, but it's a type of greatness," the man whose father died of a heart attack answers. "He is an abnormal person. He throws his fears away. There are many people who put on a suicide belt and then return. They couldn't do it."

"Even after he makes his 'martyr' video he can turn back?" I ask curious to learn if making a video locks him in to carry out an attack.

"Yes, of course. There are many people who returned back who could not do it," another of the men answers, his young son on his lap. This man, Belal explains to me, is the father of a bomber. His view that there is no problem in turning back from a suicide mission seriously contradicts one of the top Israeli expert's theory on suicide terrorists; Ariel Merari contends that the groups entrap their young recruits by filming them in heroic 'martyrs' videos that then lock them into a rock solid commitment to suicide for the groups violent goals.[55]

"If they return are they then viewed as cowards?" I ask.

"No, he has the right. It's his decision," the father of the 'martyr' answers. This again disputes Merari's position that backing out would be too humiliating. "Think of the prisoner who stays fifty days and another who in four days breaks under torture," the father of the bomber continues. "They are each the same. Each has his limit, his abilities. There is a weakness in the period of time. Either he passes it or his fears are his own prison. My son reached that point."

"So the one who reaches his limit will become a 'martyr'?" I ask.

"Yes," the father of the bomber answers. "It depends on the beliefs of the people who do the operation. Take a bomb and that's it. If I grab my weapon and shoot as many as I can, maybe I might return back alive, and I can go and do it again."

"My brother died as a martyr," one of the younger men says. "I went to jail for four years. There is a difference in people, how much they can take."

"I was not afraid in prison," the man whose father died at the check-point adds. I went to jail four times."

"I expect at any moment to get caught at the checkpoint for no reason," the father of the bomber explains, reflecting on the Israeli practice of frequently rounding up family members of suicide bombers for interroga-tion and imprisonment.

"How do you feel about the organizations that send the boys?" I ask.

"It's their work," this same elder continues. "They don't send them, the boys come to them. The boys tell them, 'If you don't send me, I'll go to another group.' So they send him."

"But this wouldn't be possible if there were no one to send?" I argue.

"We also don't like to kill others," the elder says. "But we are under occupation. In every revolution in the world, some die. They take over our land. We tried peace. We have pride for those who die."

I ask if any of the families of the kids who went as bombers might be willing to speak to me. The men tell me they will try to arrange it.

As we leave the community center Belal tells me that we have an invi-tation from one of the village leaders to stay at his house that night and that he thinks we should take it because the driver is anxious to head back. Ken, Al and I discuss it, and since we have already had a good experience staying with Palestinians, we decide it's a good idea. Plus, if we spend the night, we will learn even more about the people we came to study and have a chance to see Nablus as well.

The community leaders are anxious to take us to see two homes that they say were destroyed by Israelis in the last few days: the extended-family houses of the men suspected of planning and sending Amar Rahim Ahmed Ali, the sixteen-year-old suicide bomber who detonated in Tel Aviv on the day of our arrival. We set out in cars that take us up a hill to the outskirts of the village.

First, we visit a poured cement three-story house that has had its exteri-or and interior walls blasted with explosives, leaving a fragmented, empty shell. An elderly Palestinian man dressed in a western style shirt, faded brown pants and a white keffiyeh stands barefoot in the driveway, accom-panied by his wife dressed in an abaya and head scarf and their two young grandchildren, ready to greet us. The man takes us inside what he says used to be his home. He explains that each floor of the house was assigned for the various segments of his extended family. Later I will understand that this is how Palestinians and most Mediterranean people live, with nuclear families housed in floors built one on top of the other, often with a new floor added each time a son marries. One of this man's sons lived with his wife and children above him and the other—the fugitive suspected of involvement in the recent suicide attack—below.

The room we stand in now is just an empty cement shell—no furniture, no carpets, no belongings. The grey cement walls have holes blasted into them. Strands of rebar overhang one huge hole that overlooks a two-story drop. I am aghast and begin taking photographs. The elderly man is now holding his two-year old granddaughter in his arms. She's wearing plaid flannel pants with a embroidered little red sweater and has curly black hair drawn back into pigtails and big dark eyes that watch our every move. He tells us that the Israelis came and ordered them to get out of their home. The elderly couple along with their extended family members and the children stood powerless in their yard watching as the soldiers began placing explosives inside. His eyes fill with tears.

I've read complaints about Israelis and collective punishment, but I now grasp what is really meant by the phrase. What crime has this child committed, and did her grandparents even know what their son was up to? This substantial home that this elderly man probably spent his life building is now in ruins. I know there must be many facets to the story, but looking at him now, I feel extreme sorrow.

The next home we visit is built close to the street and abuts the other homes on either side. The door opens as we arrive and a heavy set, middle-aged woman in a blue abaya and black headscarf stands waiting to greet us. Her six-year-old daughter, barefoot and in blue pants and a cute red shirt, hides behind her partially inside the doorway, peering out occasionally to have a look.

The house doesn't look too damaged from the outside but when enter, we see it is totally destroyed on the inside. Explosives have destroyed all the walls and ceilings, and there is nothing left except debris and one chair. The village men rush to bring me the sole surviving chair and insist I sit to write my notes, as they want their story recorded. I ask what happened and the woman begins to wail as she tells us that the Israelis came to her home late at night, surrounded it and demanded they leave. She explains that the other villagers came quickly and removed their furniture and belongings as the family members vacated their home, and within an hour of that the Israelis wired the place with explosives and then detonated the bombs that destroyed her home.

"I didn't see it," she explains. "I had to take my daughter away, because it was too cold to stand outside with her late at night and too awful to watch." The men explain that her house was not totally destroyed because to do so, the Israelis would have had to ruin the adjacent homes.

Seeing the way everyone is gathered around me, the little girl approaches and touches my hands. I put my arm around her waist and pull her onto my lap. I melt looking down at her head of curls and feeling how easily she trusts me, melding against my body.

"What do you remember?" I ask.

In a small sweet voice she tells me, "I was sleeping and the soldiers came banging on the door. There were so many of them."

"Were you scared?"

She nods. "They told us to get out of the house. I didn't have time to get my homework before they made us go. They destroyed our home and all my school books too." I feel her nestling closer to me as she remembers her terror. I hug her gently.

I ask the woman about her son, the one who is accused of involvement in the recent suicide attack. His apartment was inside the common home, but it is the entire extended family home that has been destroyed. His mother is agitated and begins to cry.

"I didn't know he was involved in such things," she says. "I don't know where he is." I see that she doesn't protest his innocence, but she sounds shocked by his participation and scared about what will happen to him.

As we wrap up our interview, I hug her daughter one last time and thank her as we leave what is left of her home. Ken, Al and I are shocked and upset after seeing two homes totally devastated by the Israeli policy of home destruction, although there appears to be guilt by one family member in both instances. It brings up the issue of collective punishment and engenders a heated debate as we return in the taxi back to the village where we will have two more interviews. Belal, Jamilah and Yousef seem heartened by our upset feelings—glad to know someone else cares, but even more so, they seem emotionally numbed by what is an ordinary experience in their lives. We carry on to the village to meet two of the families of recent suicide operatives.

CHAPTER 13

Habash Hanani

Our next interview is with the family of Habash Hanani, a seventeen-year-old who infiltrated the nearby Itamar settlement and killed three students at the Hitzim Yeshiva High School with a rifle before he himself was gunned down. The Itamar settlement, like the majority of settlements in the West Bank, has been constructed by annexing up to a third of private Palestinian land (vs. using state-owned land as often claimed), an illegal act according to international and Israeli law.[56] Some organizations claim that up to forty percent of the Palestinian land in the West Bank has been subject to such annexations and now falls under control of the Israelis. The hatred toward this settlement by the surrounding Palestinians is so strong because Itamar and its outposts partly encircle the nearby village of Yanan and the Itamar settlement inhibits the development of the Palestinian village of Beit Fourik as well.[57] The Palestinians near Itamar resent having their lands infringed upon and their movements restricted. Relations between the settlers and neighboring villagers have been violent, including attacks against young children from both sides. As we have already heard, the IDF prohibits Palestinian farmers from working at their fields close to the settlement but during the olive harvest the IDF are also supposed to protect the Palestinian farmers. However, there are reports of settlers preventing Palestinians from reaching their trees during the harvest and even being shot at if they try. While Palestinian offenders are quickly apprehended and strictly punished, it appears that Israeli settlers are not controlled in the same manner. B'Tselem, an Israeli human rights organization, has criticized Israeli authorities for being lax on the offenses committed by the Israeli settlers.

Yousef, Belal, Ken, Al, Jamilah and I arrive at the Hanani home and are ushered inside where the family and some other relatives are assembled, ready to share Habash's story with us.

"Thank you for welcoming us into your home," I say as we are seated, looking around at the curious children of various ages gathered around.

"How many children do you have?" I ask after explaining my study and gaining his permission to participate.

"Six," Habash's father answers. "And this is not my house. The Israelis destroyed my house. My relatives let me live here."

I nod. " Can you tell us about your son," I begin.

"Habash was seventeen years old and clever," his father recalls. "He studied industrial electronics engineering at Nablus University. At times he had to live in Nablus because after he managed to cross the checkpoint from here [the village of Beit Fourik], he reached university at ten o' clock, which was too late [for classes]. So he often stayed there with close friends."

"What do you think were his motivations?" I ask. "Do you know how he made his decision to go on his 'martyrdom' mission."

"It's hard to tell how he took his decision," Habash's father says, casting his eyes down to muse on it. "I think he went because of the Israelis' behavior against his friends. An Israeli Apache rocket in the refugee camp struck one of his best friends. Some were killed. And the Israeli soldiers at the checkpoint were abusive to him. His uncle's home was also destroyed by the Israelis."

His father reflects on the violent events of the two Intifadas during which Habash grew up. "He had no childhood really. A kid gets raised up within this mentality—he gets a certain consciousness. And he wanted what's been stolen from him. This is another thing, we have lands and olive trees but because of the settlers we cannot go to them. The Israelis killed an old man from our village who went to harvest his olives and they used a heavy rock to break the arms of many of the children of our relatives. Those children stayed in the hospital many days."

"These son of bitches settlers here. The settlement is not far away, one kilometer," he gestures with his hand to indicate it's nearby presence and becomes agitated. "The settlers killed youngsters just like him. They were playing and four of them were killed, one injured."

"How did he carry out his mission?" I ask.

"Habash climbed up the hill and entered the settlement. There was no fence around it. They don't define their territory so they can expand whenever they want," Habash's father explains, referencing the continued incursion through the process of annexing Palestinian lands.

"What happened when he didn't come home?" I ask.

"I was like a crazy man. It's a regular routine. At eight p.m. [the kids] are home. He wasn't there. I was asking his brother where he is and I called all of his friends repeatedly, expecting to find him at their places. After fifteen minutes [of calling], the soldiers took over our town and no one was allowed out of their homes. No one has seen him. It was not until the second or third day that it gets clarified [that it was Habash that carried out the mission]. He did it on a Tuesday, but I didn't learn until Thursday. I was like a crazy man."

"Did you suspect anything?" I ask.

"Yes," Habash's father says, "from the first shot [at the settlement] I knew it was him. Parents feel their kids. I knew. It's a funny feeling that hits you as a parent," he says and tries to fight back tears.

"Did Habash leave a note?" I ask.

"Yes," his father says, his voice choking with emotion. "It said, 'Don't be upset with me.'" Habash's father stares vacuously, silent. Then he reaches for the baby and kisses him tenderly as he tries to recompose himself. Unable to, he stands up and leaves the room momentarily.

Habash's cousin takes over. "When the Israeli soldiers came and destroyed his house, they took him and all his [adult male] children. He stayed for eighteen days in the investigation department [under interrogation]."

Habash's father returns and takes his seat again. I begin again gently.

"How did you learn of your son's action?"

"From the radio," he explains of the news report that aired two days after Habash carried out his mission. "They announced the group and the people who organized it and gave his name. I couldn't believe it at first. Is it my son or not my son? It took a long time to believe it. I had ambitions for him. He was very clever. I wanted ...," he falters and then continues, "I was shocked. Astonished. It was May 28th, 2002."

He explains that the sending group, al Asqa Martyrs Brigade, arranged the obituary, our mourning gathering, for the family the day the radio announced Habash's death, but that the Israelis did not give over Habash's body, so they held a funeral procession without his corpse.

"How did you feel at that time?" I ask.

"Proud, but you feel bad too," he explains.

"So often we see in the press 'martyr's' parents saying they are happy their sons or daughters went to kill themselves in an operation," I say, "and in the West we find it confusing why a parent would celebrate the death of their child. Can you explain that for me?"

"It's not a celebration," Habash's father answers. "It's an event that honors my son and brings comfort. Anyone can die now or later, and for believers, one who dies this way [as a 'martyr'] is more honorable. We did not organize the obituary; the [sending] group did it all and they held my hand, supporting me at that time," Habash's father recalls adding, "Since the moment my son went on his operation, people give me respect. Anyone who resists the occupation, they are proud of him."

"You grieve over your son?" I ask, wanting to clarify the difference between the public statements made by parents of suicide operatives and their true feelings.

"Living here we know that death can occur at any moment. But we are not ready. No one is ever ready to accept death. I knew he could die by car. I never imagined like this," his father states. "This Western point of view that parents encourage their children to do these operations is completely wrong. I supported him in [his life in] all ways. I bought him a computer as a little kid. I liked him to reach high levels in education. He was my second oldest. We don't encourage them to die."

"No one encourages them in this path?" I ask.

"Well, actually, if you take in the general point of view by the mosques and the Koran and by the speeches and also by the Israelis' actions against us, there is encouragement," his father admits.

I nod. "What happened after the funeral?" I ask, curious to learn how fast the Israelis came to arrest him—how much time a Palestinian father gets to take in the shock of his son's suicide operation before he faces his own arrest and the destruction of his home.

"On Saturday, nine days after I learned it, the Israelis arrested me and my family and took us for investigation," he recalls. "They also brought me from prison to make me see my home get destroyed. I was tied in cuffs."

"'You don't get ashamed when people see you [in handcuffs]?' the Israeli asked to humiliate me.

"'No I get proud,' I answered him. The whole village saw them arrest me.

"After they arrested me and my sons [as well as some of his friends], they opened the [IDF] investigation center. They brought most of our relatives and tied them to trees, giving an order not to talk to each other. They separated all of us from each other and on each person there was an Israeli with a gun. We were under the trees from three p.m. to twelve a.m."

"How do you feel about the people who sent your son on this mission?" I ask.

"Those sons of bitches, they should send themselves!" he answers angrily. "Some should go and others should not. Everyone gets the urge." Evidently he feels everyone in his village at times feels enough despair and anger to be willing to die trying to drive the settlers away but that the group that sent his son preyed upon these feelings.

"What would you have done if you had known?" I ask.

"If I couldn't stop him from doing it," he answers shaking his head sadly, "I would have went with him at least to protect his back. I would go in order to die instead of him."

Then he adds a curious fact. "There was another [infiltration suicide] operation carried out in the same place twenty days after my son did his operation. This boy went with a gun and killed as many settlers as he could. He killed the one who killed my son. It comforted me," he explains.

• • •

The tensions between the settlers and Palestinians living in the area continues to this day. And Habash's legacy lives on, used most recently by the Palestinian Authority in television productions in which his 'martyrdom' is honored, subtly encouraging others to follow in his footsteps. While there are many reasons the Palestinians of Beit Fourik legitimately resent the settlers, official incitement sponsored by the PA also appears to play a role in the continued attacks. After the PA repeatedly aired a show honoring Habash's act along with the acts of other "martyrs" in February 2011, yet another attack on the Itamar settlement occurred a month later, this time carried out by three young Palestinians wielding knives. The Fogel family and three of their six children, one of them only a two-month-old infant, were murdered in cold blood—their throats slashed by the angry Palestinians.[58]

In response to the murders, Prime Minister Netanyahu accused the Palestinian Authority of inciting these murders by honoring, on their television programs and elsewhere, those Palestinians who attack Israeli civilians. Prime Minister Netanyahu made the following statement: "This requires sharp and unequivocal condemnation . . . The time has come to stop this double-talk in which the Palestinian Authority outwardly talks peace, and allows—and sometimes leads—incitement at home. The time has come to stop the incitement and begin educating their people for peace."[59]

His comments however correct, fail to acknowledge the other side of the story—that Palestinians living near Itamar are also incited to acts of terrorism from their anger over their lands being infringed upon and being boxed into their villages by abusive checkpoints and violent harassment from the settlers who continually encroach into Palestinian territory. And that doesn't seem likely to end anytime soon. After the Fogel family massacre, government officials pledged that "an iron fist will land on the murderers" and that hundreds of new homes will be built in West Bank settlements in response to the killings.[60] It seems if both sides continue in this manner, young men like Habash will continue to live in anger and despair and his terror act is doomed to be repeated in the future.

CHAPTER 14

Yousef Ahmed Hanani — the Gunman of Beit Fourik

Next we walk down the village streets to the family home of Yousef Ahmed Hanani, who followed in the footsteps of Habash Hanani by enacting a suicide attack in 2004 on the Itamar settlement under the direction of the al Aqsa Martrys. We knock on the door and are invited inside by his Yousef's brother. Once inside Yousef's mother, a slim and still attractive middle-aged woman, greets us. She gestures for us to take seats in her living room, the upholstered chairs and sofas arranged in a circle with small tables set out between them. One of the girls brings in a tray of small glasses of hot sweet tea and Yousef's brother also joins us.

As I sip my tea, I begin by asking, "Can you tell me about Yousef? What he was like?"

"He was in Najah University," Yousef's brother begins. "He studied social studies and psychology. After he graduated he was an employee of the PLO [Palestinian Liberation Organization]. He was a very polite and honorable guy. He was also religious —prayed and fasted. He stayed away from problems, but once he was locked in jail."

"He was really quiet," his brother adds. "He always had a sense of humor, told lots of jokes. There was nothing strange about him. He loved his country. He was always upset about the occupation and all the humiliations."

"What was he arrested for?" I ask.

"Some [militant] activities," his brother explains. "He was sentenced for three years but released after only one year in a prisoner exchange. At that time it was the first Intifada. Israeli soldiers made patrols and arrested people at random."

"Did you notice any psychological or behavioral changes in Yousef after being imprisoned" I ask.

His mother shakes her head. "No changes," she says. His brother agrees adding, "He continued studying and graduated."

"Later, did you have any reason to believe he would go to 'martyr' himself?" I ask.

"When we heard the news, we couldn't believe it!" his mother says. "We had no idea he can do this—until the Israelis came to the door. We couldn't even believe it until his father went to the Israeli base to see his body."

"Did you see any changes in his behavior or did he say anything strange before going?" I ask.

"We didn't have one clue," his mother answers. "Two days before the operation he said to us, 'I want you to go and get me a fiancé.' We took it seriously. We thought he wanted a bride."

"How old was he?" I ask.

"Twenty-nine years old," his brother answers.

"How did he carry out his attack?" I ask.

"He went with a weapon to the Itamar settlement," Yousef's brother answers. "We got worried about him when he didn't call and didn't come back home. The next day we learned about it through the media and the television. Before that we were just worried about him, but we never expected him to do such a thing."

"He never spoke of it before," his mother adds. "We never thought he would do it. He used to joke a lot. He said things like, 'I want to paint my home,' and 'I want to get married.'"

"What exactly did he do?" I ask.

"We only know the story from the Israelis," Yousef's brother answers. "He entered the settlement before sunrise and he stayed inside until ten a.m. He was waiting for four to five hours for the security lieutenant who had killed an old man and hurt a boy—to shoot him dead. It finally happened at ten a.m."

"Can you tell me more about the security lieutenant?" I ask.

"This security lieutenant [one of the settlers]—after he killed the old [Palestinian] man—was arrested for two days," Yousef's brother explains. "The Israelis then let him free with no prosecution. Even the Israelis admit this person was making trouble. And [besides what he did] the settlers [from Itamar] took rocks and broke the arms of the boys."

"Yousef killed other settlers as well," his brother adds. This contradicts the news reports I later read that list only one settler death from his mission.[61] "He took his weapon and got in crossfire with the settlers. He killed two and then was killed."

"How was it for you to learn such news from the television?" I ask.

"To know," his mother answers. "It's terrible. We got shocked. To this day I cannot take it in."

"What happened after you learned of it on the news?" I ask.

"I had one hour alone, with this news," Yousef's mother recalls. "I got really upset, really sad and astonished. No one imagined it could happen. Then people started arriving to support us. From the shock I did not know where I was. I had a nervous breakdown and cried a lot."

One of the girls enters carrying a tray of small cups of strongly brewed sweet coffee. Yousef (our translator) tells us this is roasted coffee, a certain type that is served either for happy or sad occasions. I sip it appreciatively honoring the sadness of what we are discussing.

"She didn't lose control," Yousef's brother explains of his mother's breakdown, "but she cried like any mother losing her son."

"Did it help, the people coming to the house?" I ask.

"Yes," Yousef's mother answers. "They helped us move our furniture out."

"How soon did the Israeli soldiers arrive?" I ask.

"They were here in less than two hours after his operation," she answers. They came and surrounded the village and forbade people to leave their homes."

Confused by the Israeli's speed, I ask the family to explain the time-line again to me. "Yousef failed to return home on Thursday night. His operation was at ten a.m. on Friday," Yousef's brother answers. "It was on the news immediately and within the same day the Israelis came and destroyed our home."

"How did they do it?" I ask.

"The Israelis came first to surround the village. It took them another forty-five minutes to an hour to locate our house. They used loudspeakers and told us, 'Come out!'" Yousef's brother recalls. "We refused. Then they used a gas grenade. It was a serious level of gas. Some of the neighbors were overcome by it and went in ambulances and stayed there for one day. Any others with injuries and my mother, also overcome with the gas, were not allowed to go in the ambulances for care."

Evidently the Israelis did not want to send any of the family members away in ambulances, as they were intent on interrogating them once they were "gassed" out of their home.

"The baby was two months old and shocked by the gas," Yousef's mother explains. "Thank God she lived. Her name is Palestine," she adds proudly, telling me that Yousef requested her name in his "martyr" letter.

I nod understanding that she had either held off naming the baby until at that point, which is common in some Mediterranean cultures since so many children in old times did not survive early childhood, or she renamed the baby at Yousef's request.

Once everyone was out of the house the Israelis used dynamite to demolish it.

"They surrounded the house and rigged it up with explosives and destroyed it around one or two p.m.," Yousef's brother explains. "There were demonstrations against them with people throwing rocks. There were many arrests and injuries happening that day."

"You said the people helped you move your possessions. Did you have any time to take things out?" I ask.

"We took only our most necessary things," Yousef's brother answers.

"Where did you go?" I ask.

"Some of the neighbors took us in," Yousef's mother explains. "This is a rented house.

"We are waiting for Yousef's corpse until now," Yousef's mother adds. "The Israelis still keep it."

Indeed, the Israeli official policy until 2012 is to bury the bodies of suicide operatives in unmarked graves inside Israel or to keep their bodies under refrigeration in morgues.[62]

"Did you hold a funeral for him?" I ask.

"We tried to, but the Israelis arrested thirty people and closed the house to prevent us holding an obituary. We processed through the streets, but they stopped us."

"Two to three weeks after his act, the Israelis gave us permission to receive his body," Yousef's brother continues. "But it was just a ploy by the intelligence units of the Israelis to get us to come. When we arrived, there is nothing over there. The whole village is waiting for the body, but we came back with empty hands."

He tells me the Israelis pulled the same trick again several weeks ago.

"Why do you think he did it?" I ask.

"When he was a university student," Yousef's brother answers, "the Israelis used to lock him at the checkpoints for one to two hours daily.

Even though he had a student card they would take it away—for good. Three times he reapplied [for] student cards, but they just took it from him repeatedly and didn't let him pass. At that period of time only students with student cards can pass from Beit Fourik, no others."

"He was turned away from the checkpoint for the last week or ten days of his life. He had no other activities," Yousef's brother continues. "This drove him to go, it was one of the reasons. But the occupation is the main reason: the settlers, humiliations, their killing of the little children."

"In his letter," his mother explains that Yousef wrote, "The thing that made me do it is the killing of old people, old women, children, and the assassinations that the Israelis do."

I am curious if the group filmed a video and used his mission for propaganda and recruitment of other potential "martyrs", but his family doesn't know. They do know that with the help of his sending group he made two "martyr's" posters.

"How do you feel about the organization that equipped and sent him?" I ask.

"Yousef was a well-educated person," his brother answers. "It's the way he chooses. If we had suspicions we would have stopped him, of course. First of all we love him, but also because we will lose our house and our family will be separated."

"Some families of 'martyrs' have told me they think the senders should send their own family members, not others. Do you resent them for sending Yousef?" I ask.

"Some senders send themselves," Yousef's brother answers, shaking his head. "We even read that one of them said, 'I prefer to die than go to prison.'"

As he recounts this I think back to the fugitive Chechens also volunteering for suicide operations, opting for a "martyr's" death rather than to fall into the hands of the Russians where they expected to be tortured and killed. The Israelis do not infringe on human rights on the level of Russians, but for some Palestinians, the preference to death over imprisonment is the same.

"And all the people of the village read the Koran," Yousef's brother adds, "and know that it says, 'Fight them, Allah will make them suffer. Deceive them, make yourself victorious.'"

"Did Yousef leave a last will and testament?" I ask.

"Yes," his brother answers. "It said, 'First I say for all who read this paper: Peace on you and Allah's mercy on you and his benefits. Peace and praise on the most honorable creature, our leader Muhammad; Allah's prayer upon him and peace. Days and years pass, and all the [Israeli] systems fall, collapsing, giving the people and the Palestinian [space so their] dream grows and grows until it gets its perfect shape and order. For this to happen we have to make some sacrifices and to give up money and souls. And as this dream grows up, there are groups of people we cannot mention that collapse because they are trying to take this holiest right away from us.'"

The room is silent.

I turn to Yousef's mother and gently ask, "You miss him?"

Throwing her hands up she answers, "Who else can I miss?" We smile in understanding. Then she adds, "For all that has happened we still believe in peace and settlement between Palestinians and Israelis. It's the occupation. When the occupation ends we can live in peace."

On that note, we end the interview, thank the family and depart.

CHAPTER 15

Said Hanani

Next we visit the family of Said Hanani, an eighteen year old who exploded himself in December of 2003 at the Geha bridge bus stop near Tel Aviv—a bus stop often used by members of the military. When Said detonated, he blew up a bus, killing four Israelis (three of whom were soldiers) and wounding fifteen others. According to news reports, Said was sent by the Popular Front for the Liberation of Palestine (PFLP). A leaflet distributed after the attack pointed out that Said Hanani was a close relative to Fadi Hanani, a PFLP activist killed by Israeli soldiers in the Balata refugee camp two days before. A PFLP spokesman said of the retaliation attack, "We cannot stay silent as Israel continues with its crimes."

Now we are here at his home to learn from his family who he was and what possibly motivated him to become a suicide bomber.

After we are introduced and seated with Said's siblings also present, I ask his father, "Can you tell us about Said? What he was like, who he was?"

His father nods sadly. "He lived at home. He used to love playing volleyball and soccer. He used to volunteer. He did many kinds of good works. He helped in many centers. He helped build the community center."

"How old was he when he went on his mission?" I ask.

"He was eighteen," his father answers, "The oldest with two younger brothers and sisters. He stopped studying at sixteen because of expenses. We couldn't afford to have him in school. In one month I had only five days of work. I do construction—I am a rock cutter."

"Do you know what may have led him to do this?"

"Yes," his father answers. "At the Hawara checkpoint he suffered humiliation. They don't let him cross. They always kept him until dark. They arrested him there and they beat him. They shot him five times. One time they made he and two of his friends lay in the street while they took a jeep to run over him. They were about to do it when a General stopped them. It was really sick, yes?"

I nod. "Can you tell me about the times when he was shot?" I ask.

"It was always rubber bullets," his father says, "but each time it was bad enough that we took him to the hospital to see a doctor. He was fourteen years old the first time—they shot him in the knee. He went one week without working. The next time he was fifteen or sixteen. They shot him on the side of his abdomen. The third time it was two bullets in the chest. They bruised his ribs. The fourth time they hit his right shoulder from behind. The fifth time he got shot coming back from school."

"Was he throwing rocks or doing anything to provoke them?" I ask, marveling at the idea of a teenager being shot five different times before reaching adulthood!

Said's father shakes his head. "The patrol just started shooting at the kids."

"Was there anything else that could have put him on this path?" I ask.

"Said lived during the times of destroying the houses of martyrs," his father explains. "Everyone goes to support the family [whose home is being destroyed]. He saw nine destructions. Said was also a member of a football [soccer] team. Two of the members were shot dead by the Israelis, two became martyrs [they made operations], and four were arrested and imprisoned." He shakes his head sadly. "When the teams are playing on the fields, they arrest most of them and others they beat. So one of them applies for an operation because of what he sees everyday and for the humiliations of himself and his friends. You cannot enter any house in this village where you won't find one person either in prison or a martyr."

"After all of these things do you know how Said finally made this decision to go as a 'martyr'?" I ask.

"I don't know," his father says running his hand back through his hair, seemingly still puzzled by it all. "He was completely normal. We were sitting at home at night together. If we knew he was going to do it, we would have stopped him."

"Can you tell me what happened on the day of his action?" I ask.

"He went early in the morning and did not return back," his father says sadly.

"How did you find out about it?" I ask.

"We learned about it on the television, Said's father says. "It happened at seven p.m. on the 26th of December, 2003. It was nearly live on the news. The story on the television said, from an Israeli broadcast, that a soldier girl discovered a bomber and she was about to shoot him [when] he jumped on her and hugged her and bombed himself. He got shot by her bullet [as well]."

"And after two hours they said his name—at nine p.m."

"What did you do upon learning?" I ask.

"I fell on the ground and went into a coma! I had a nervous breakdown. His mother went to the local doctor with a nervous breakdown as well. People started coming to the house immediately to collect all the furniture and get it out. After five hours, the Israelis surrounded the house and said, 'We want to destroy the house.' They came at two a.m. and put us out of the house. It was raining outside. We stood three hours under the cold rain. Our youngest was eight years old."

"Did you manage to get your belongings out?" I ask.

"No not everything out," he answers. "Just the simple things like televisions, clothes. Our cupboards and sofas we could not get out."

"Do you know his senders?" I ask.

"The PFLP announced his operation the next day," Said's father says, "But I don't know who sent him. It's a secret thing who sent him.

"There was no funeral," he continues. "They still have the corpse. [The PFLP] made the obituary for him."

"How did you feel at the obituary?" I ask.

"How else would it feel?" he asks. "Like losing a child."

"In the obituary parents often seem to be celebrating their son or daughter's death," I say.

Said's father nods smiling and explains, "As an Arab society we have our own customs, our own traditions. We share sadness, food, hold the family members' hands."

As Said's father speaks I begin to grasp the celebratory aspects of the Palestinian "martyr's" obituary. It wasn't so long ago that I attended the funeral of a very dear aunt who died in her sixties of cancer. She had been healthy and then suddenly got sick and died quickly.

"At my aunt's funeral," I reflect to him, "the family sang Christian songs that claimed that she had gone to paradise and that we expected to see her again—and we sang them loudly and jubilantly. A stranger might have claimed we were rejoicing, but of course we were all devastated that she had died. But, all the same, we sang joyfully of our hope to see her again in the next life. Perhaps it's not so different from your traditions?"

"Yes, it's the same concept for us," Said's father says. "We sing in very loud voices and they are happy songs. The women ulate [an Arabic form of joyous expression often made by women at weddings]. It is some way of letting what is inside out and to bring comfort. The [celebratory] sounds are like medicine. Maybe we should say the martyr has a special funeral."

Perhaps it is the dawning comprehension of how similar we are despite my previous horror in hearing Palestinian parents of "martyrs" say things like they are glad their son or daughter is in paradise after an operation, but I feel suddenly as if I can understand Said's father before the translator speaks and that he can understand me as well. I have been watching him closely and looking in his eyes. Even this thought he senses. "I feel you know what I am saying even before it's translated and I feel the same, even though I know no English," he says.

I nod and smile warmly, my eyes still connected to his, wondering how we have made this bond.

"Did Said leave a 'martyrs' letter?" I ask.

"Yes," his father answers. "He wrote about his father and mother, brothers and sister. He encouraged them to be good in school. He said, 'I want to sacrifice myself for Palestine and my family to live better.' It was his handwriting."

"Can you think of any reason right at that time about why he went?" I ask.

"It's something that Allah has written," Said's father answers.

We end the interview and drink tea together as I pack up my things and bid this father of a "martyr" goodbye, thanking him for helping us to understand.

CHAPTER 16

Entering Nablus

In the afternoon after our interviews in the village, we return again to the community center where we once again meet the village elders to thank them for their hospitality. They offer us more sweets and drinks and tell us we are welcome anytime, inviting us to come back in the summer to teach English. They promise to feed and house us if we return. Ken and Al think it's a good offer and say that they could learn Arabic that way. Everyone disbands, agreeing that we will continue our interviews with community members later in the day and the next morning.

I take a restroom break and get a little education about Arab toilets. The toilet is normal but there is no toilet paper, just a sprayer connected to the side of the toilet that looks like what many American homes have inside the kitchen sink to rinse their dishes. I give it a try, finding that I am clumsy and spray water all over the floor, the toilet, and myself. There is no towel or paper to dry myself or to clean the wet floor, so mortified, I try to shake myself dry and then pull my pants up over my dripping, but clean backside and laugh as I emerge. Ken is waiting for me and seeing the wet floor he guffaws, "I see you've learned how to use the Arab toilet!" It turns out he's had the same problem in the men's room.

Jamilah and Belal are outside having a smoke with Yousef and Al. Although the community center is nothing much to see, the dusty crushed rock paths surrounding it are adorned with tall hibiscus plants, in full bloom and covered with large orange flowers. The sky is also clear blue above us and the sun creates a yellow glow that is almost too bright. It's beautiful despite the poverty.

Belal divulges our plan for the rest of the day. "We can make interviews here in Beit Fourik this evening and tomorrow morning. The guys are setting it up for you, but I think right now if you want to see Nablus, we should go because it's hard to cross the checkpoint, and then we can return before dark." It sounds reasonable, so we agree. We catch a taxi to the Hawara checkpoint that crosses into Nablus to see if we will be allowed in.

Belal has been talking on his phone and stops me as we walk across crushed stones to get to the checkpoint. "Listen," he says in a low voice, "I've been calling some of my friends and they tell me that the two fugitives that sent the bomber into Tel Aviv are in Nablus. They agree to meet us in a safe house and give us an interview. Do you want to meet them?"

It is an amazing research opportunity, but given they are fugitives, it also seems we would be placing ourselves in a great deal of danger to meet them.

"What do you know about the safe house?" I ask. Belal tells me it's a place that's often used by fugitives and that the Israelis don't know anything about it.

"I think we will be safe there, and they may or may not come, depending on how dangerous it is for them to move. Right now the Israelis don't know where they are so they think they can get there safely. I think we should do it."

I turn to Ken and Al, and they shrug agreement. "Okay," I say tentatively, "But Belal, we want to be safe. I don't want to go there if you think it's really dangerous."

Belal nods and says, "Let's wait and see. I'll keep calling my friends and we can judge it closer to the time when we are there. Let's see if we can even get across the checkpoint."

We enter the checkpoint area and walk along one of two long stalls of cement barricades, the type that often line the sides of highways under construction, in this case set up for long lines of Palestinians to stand for hours waiting to cross the checkpoint. Overhead there is a corrugated roof to block out the sun. At this time of day there are no lines. As we near the group of young Israeli soldiers manning the checkpoint, we reach for our identity documents. I gather our IDs and approach the young male soldier holding out his hand. He looks them over and passes them back to me saying, "These three can pass, but the others no." I see they are divided between foreign passports and Palestinian ID cards.

Some Israeli men dressed in khaki military greens and carrying automatic rifles gather near us. Ken whispers to me, "Settlers. I bet they're Americans." They begin to ask questions and comment on our group. It's confusing because they are armed, and I'm not sure if they have authority at the checkpoint or are just harassing us. I think it's the latter.

One, a hefty thirty-year-old with long curls that fall beneath his shoulders, speaks in a scornful voice: "Why do you want to go over there anyway? To see animals walking on two legs?" He and his friends laugh, mocking the Palestinians we are with. I place myself strategically between him and my students and emit the body language of "better not approach closer."

I turn back to the Israeli soldier manning the station. "I'm a university professor and all of these," I wave to the group standing behind me, "are my students. I'd like to cross over into Nablus, but I can't go there by myself because I don't speak Arabic. I need my Palestinian students as interpreters. It doesn't help to take only these two," I say indicating Ken and Al.

The soldier looks like he wants to be helpful and to steer clear of a confrontation with the settlers. He avoids the settlers' eyes and the provocations they are making both in English and Hebrew. I can see by Ken's nervousness watching them that he understands what they are saying, but he doesn't let on. The soldier tells me to wait and goes to confer with the other soldiers, two men and a young woman standing nearby.

I turn back to my students and see Jamilah is wide-eyed and scared, Yousef is upset and Belal is furious. Al and Ken are also angry.

"Don't listen to them," I say trying to calm them.

The young soldier returns with his superior and says, "I'm sorry. I can't let any of the Palestinians pass." I ask his superior if there is anyway to get an exception. I tell him I have just this one day to see Nablus and it's important to me, stressing that I'm an American social science researcher. He shakes his head no. They are basically kind, but firm.

We turn and leave the checkpoint, walking back along the stone drive to the taxis that are waiting. Jamilah is crying now, and Belal is beside himself with anger.

"I wish I had a knife. I'd cut them to pieces. Just give me a knife and I'll do it now," he rages as we walk across the crushed stone parking lot.

"Belal," I say, "you can't really mean that!"

His eyes flash and he says, "Oh, but I do! If I had a knife, I'd kill as many of them as I could right now."

Al understands and comments about the Israeli settler. "How could he say such a racist remark? Right in front of everyone?"

"I've seen that before," Ken answers. "They're fucking arrogant pigs, the settlers. They think they can do and say whatever they want," Ken answers.

We get into one of the waiting cars and Belal says, "Listen, there is another way to cross. Let's go there."

We agree, assuming he means there is another checkpoint, although we should have known better after the village elders told us how the young men are trapped in Beit Fourik because the Hawara checkpoint is the only legal outlet from Beit Fourik. The taxi driver takes us through the village roads away from the checkpoint out to a sandy path that leads up to a small grove of young trees and a pretty meadow.

Ken, Al and I all think we are approaching another checkpoint, and we get out of the car and pay the driver. He leaves as we begin walking toward the small grove of trees. When we get amongst the trees, a car on a modern road far away on the other side of the meadow approaches. It's very far from where we are, but seeing it Belal points to it and alarmed calls out in a lowered voice.

"Get down," he hisses. "Get down!! There's a car! Hide! Hide behind the trees!"

I don't really get it, and I don't think Ken and Al do either. We crouch behind young trees that are so slim they can hardly hide us and begin giggling.

Belal hisses again, "Get down! Now! They can shoot at us! It's not a joke!"

His words seem surreal, but we all suddenly fall silent and crouch in the low grass and brush. The road is probably a quarter mile away and the vehicle passes without noticing us.

Belal waits a few minutes after it's gone and says, "It's okay now. Let's go. We have to run. Now! Head for the culvert over there!" And he takes off with Yousef, Jamilah and Al running behind him across the meadow toward an overpass in the modern far off road that has a ten-foot high culvert running underneath it. Evidently we are going to cross the road through the culvert laid beneath it.

I realize I have no alternative but to follow, as our taxi is long gone, but I decide not to run. If the meadow is a forbidden area and guarded by Israelis, I am most certainly not going to run across it. Again I put my trust in their training and equipment. Certainly if anyone is looking with a good pair of binoculars, they can make out that I'm an adult white woman dressed in a business suit, carrying an alligator brown briefcase walking in slip-on shoes peacefully, and in open view, across their meadow. I don't believe they will shoot me. If it is forbidden, I think running is the stupidest choice I could make.

Ken has taken off running too but seeing that I am walking he doubles back and informs me of Belal's instruction, "You know Belal said we need to run, that they could shoot us walking out here in the open. I think that's the road to the settlements and Palestinians are not allowed on it. I think we should start running."

"I'm sorry, Ken, but I'm not going to run like a rabbit and risk being shot. It may be the best choice for them, being Palestinians and crossing where we are not supposed to be, but I don't want to run. You can do as you like, but I'm going to walk slowly and purposefully across this meadow with my head held high and carrying my briefcase. If any Israeli sees me in his binoculars or in his rifle scope, I hope he sees that I'm a white, female, American university professor!" I say smiling and walking with dignity.

Ken slows down and walks beside me, talking about how it will be if some Israeli decides to blow our heads off. Ken, I've noticed is attached to me in a protective manner, and probably relates to me much like he does to his own mother.

He is also a bit competitive with the other students that he knows I like, and he often puts them down. He takes this opportunity now to mock Al.

"Look at Al running like a rabbit," he jokes. "He's probably shitting his pants. He left you without even looking back once." I realize it's true and I smile appreciatively at Ken. It was very gallant of him to turn back and now to take his chances walking slowly with me across the field. But truthfully, I didn't expect Ken or Al to protect me. I feel my responsibility is to protect them, not the other way around.

We walk on and Ken, nervous, urges me to walk a bit faster. "What do you say, we pick up the pace a bit? No sense getting shot for nothing." I agree and we walk briskly toward the culvert where the others are hiding, waiting for us.

Belal and Al remonstrate when we get there asking, "Why are you so stupid? Why did you walk? Can't you see the danger?" I explain my point of view and just get raised eyebrows.

"It's okay," Belal says explaining that the worst danger has passed. "We cross through this culvert now," he directs, "and that gets us across the settlers' road. On the other side, there is a small village. We can catch a taxi from there into Nablus."

I take Belal aside and tell him, "Listen, Belal the next time you are going to pull a stunt like that please let's talk about it ahead of time. You remember what I told you—I'm a mother and my kids need me to come home safely, okay? And these are my students. I would have never chosen to cross the settlers' road this way if I had known what you set us up to do. Please don't do that again." Belal nods agreement.

We make our way through the culvert and walk along a wide expanse of muddy piled up dirt and rocks on the other side that finally leads into the tiny village Belal has mentioned. I remember Shakespeare's story about the violence that occurs in the olive groves,and as we walk across the bull-dozed hills of mud, I see all the olive trees in the area have been bulldozed , leaving behind huge swathes of razed hills and mounds of fresh muddy soil.

As we walk along these muddy mounds and put distance between the settlers' road and us, we are all relieved. It's a good mile before we approach the village, a tiny hamlet with goats grazing near the poured cement homes, many of them still partially under construction. Elder-ly men and women putter outside and some children gather around us. We are firmly back in Palestinian territory. I feel such relief. I don't even consider how we are going to return.

Belal asks where we can get a car to go into Nablus and one of the men shows us where to catch a minibus. Night begins to fall, and the stars hanging above us in the velvet blue sky shimmer brightly. Ken and Al smoke as they pepper Belal with questions about how dangerous cross-ing the meadow really was. Belal explains that the settlers will shoot at anyone coming near their road.

I get tears in my eyes thinking about it. Back home my husband has been distant, and the night before I left it felt like he didn't care much if I might be endangered on this trip. I know he's struggling with a midlife crisis that has little to do with me and our relationship, but his aloofness affects me deeply all the same. I wipe away a few tears that trickle down my cheek. Despite the darkness, Al notices and sensitively asks if I'm okay. From the many times when we have sat after class sharing a beer or talking even on this trip, both students know Dan's having a hard time and I'm trying to hang in there, so I don't have to explain much. He pats my back awkwardly and says, "Don't cry, it will all be fine." He tells me he's thinking of Amy too, his girlfriend back home. I guess it's natural for the heart to reach out to loved ones in times when we think our lives could be taken.

It's about a half hour drive into Nablus city center where we are dropped off. The tall grey buildings cast dreary shadows over the deserted streets. The only light is from the glowing orbs of streetlights that cast a surreal yellow glow over the cement desert. I feel as though I've stepped into the set of a science fiction movie and it's the scene after a nuclear holocaust. I look at Belal and the others and we all seem to be feeling the same sense of unease.

Nablus is not under curfew but Belal explains that most people opt to stay inside anyway, at least in this part of the city. The residents are acutely aware that large numbers of Israeli soldiers now patrol their city searching for the senders of the recent bomber in Tel Aviv, and from past experience they know it's better to stay clear of trouble, that anything can suddenly happen.

Belal tells us that we'll have one meeting with his Fatah contacts, and then if things go as he plans, we'll go to the safe house. At this point, we are in his hands and follow his lead. We pile into another taxi, this time with a cracked windshield, and drive through the empty yellow and gray streets to a residential area. We get out and walk down a narrow stone lane, passing through a painted wooden door into a courtyard where there is a bench and some potted blooming flowers and then through another door into the home of Belal's contacts.

A man, his wife, and his sister are present, as well as the couple's two young daughters, ages two and four. The couple greets us and offers us seats on their sofa and pull up easy chairs and small tables to make a cozy seating area. A fire glows behind our hosts, and Hala, the aunt of the small girls, begins offering us food, saying surely we need to eat after our journey. One thing I've noticed is that it doesn't seem to matter how poor they are; all Palestinians are hospitable, offering food, coffee, tea, sweets, so much so that I doubt if we'll ever be hungry during our stay in the West Bank. This family doesn't seem too poor and as Hala passes us dishes of delicious vegetables and rice, we accept them and eat heartily. Everyone is hungry and we enjoy the honor and pleasure of breaking the Ramadan fast by sharing this evening meal together.

Hala is very talkative. She begins to tell us about her younger brothers, both of whom she calls "martyrs."

"Look," she says pointing to the young girls' necks. "They wear their martyr's necklaces all the time." Then she turns to the girls and speaks about the young men in Arabic, impressing upon them who their uncles were and how they died. Yousef and Jamilah take turns explaining to us what is being said. Both of the uncles it turns out were militants plotting against the Israelis and were killed in skirmishes. The little girls are wide eyed as they listen to their highly emotional aunt tell her stories. Clearly she is instilling an emotional message of wrathful hate that they are far too young to understand.

"Our brothers used to come here at Ramadan and bring sweets and gifts for them, but now the girls don't want Ramadan gifts anymore," Hala explains. "They think whoever brings them gifts will be killed next."

I begin to get angry listening to her. It's emotionally abusive what she is doing to her young nieces. Children don't understand causation and clearly these little girls have become confused about receiving Ramadan gifts and the cause of their uncles' deaths—they feel there is a connection between the two and know they are supposed to hate Israelis. But they are far too young to comprehend all their aunt is drilling into them.

I am angry to see martyrs' necklaces on their necks and I want to replace them with normal childhood baubles, but I can do nothing. One of the girls comes over by me and I lift her up onto my lap. She sits there happily and I whisper sweet messages to her in English even though she cannot understand—willing life-affirming messages into her little spirit, rather than the death messages her Aunt Hala is sending. Al sits beside me and is upset too. He undoes his necklace and places it around her neck. I tell Yousef to tell her that this is his Ramadan gift and that Al is going to stay alive, no need to worry this time.

We listen as the adults discuss the situation in Nablus. Evidently the Israelis have clamped down on the crossings, and it's been really hard getting people and supplies in and out. They ask about the checkpoint and we tell them how we crossed.

Hala tells us, "I work for the Red Crescent. Next time you want to come, we'll smuggle you in an ambulance, no problem." This makes me think about how the Palestinians frequently complain that the Israelis block Red Crescent ambulances and have even fired upon them, but the counter to that is that the Israeli soldiers have had many problems with the misuse of vehicles designated for humanitarian purposes.

At counter-terrorism conferences, I've learned that Israeli soldiers train in how to respond to the many ethical dilemmas they face, using filmed staged scenarios where they must decide in milliseconds what to do. For instance should they decide to be generous and humane to what looks like a laboring mother and cause no delays as she rushes across the checkpoint to give birth at a hospital or potentially err on the side of security precautions assuming she may not be pregnant at all but instead loaded with bombs? If she is indeed pregnant the delay may cause her to birth unsafely on the roadside and enrages even more Palestinians. If she is not pregnant and carrying bombs, the search and delay can save many Israeli lives. There are no easy answers and this is a prime example of why.

"Thanks," I tell her, "but I don't think I'd feel right using a Red Crescent vehicle that way."

"Why?" she exclaims. "We do it all the time!" I decide there is no point in explaining.

This is the first Palestinian we've met who I really don't like. It's not often that I don't like people. I almost always find some point of contact, something to join with and expand into a good rapport. But I'm so disgusted by what she has done to these young girls in front of us that I don't want to hear anymore from her. I assume it's a constant daily harangue of hate that will ultimately brainwash them. I just want to leave.

I ask Ken where the bathroom is and he shows me to the stairs. He's already been and informs me that he's searched all the upstairs rooms and cabinets in the bathrooms and that there are no guns.

"What?" I ask him. "You went in their cabinets? We are guests here, Ken!"

Ken shrugs and laughs, "Yeah, but they are terrorists!" It's so Ken to do something like that. He has no shame and no boundaries. I scowl at him and go upstairs to use the bathroom.

When I return Hala has locked on to Al and is seated beside him, flirting heavily. This makes us all laugh because she is at least eight years older and Al is clearly uncomfortable. Al shaves his head and always wears a smart Gatsby cap to cover it. She takes his hat and plays with it as she tries to draw him out, telling him he's handsome and looks like a famous movie star. Al can't resist smiling at the compliment, although he is squirming. To Al's chagrin, when it's time to leave for the safe house, Hala takes Al's arm leading us back out along the garden path. Ken and I follow behind joking about Al's new "older" girlfriend. Jamilah does not seem pleased.

Funny though, it sparks something new in me. I've never really noticed Al before. He's been my student for almost a year now and I know him very well. I know about his family background, that his parents were tough on him and although he's Belgian, he grew up in Africa. I also know that he sometimes smokes weed on class breaks and that he's very smart and very sensitive and that he loves his girlfriend, and so on. I've had to intervene for him with the college administration that wanted to expel him when he failed half his classes and received A's in the rest because I knew he was smart and thought he was having trauma-induced responses from his childhood with the professors he didn't get on with. I think he is probably the smartest kid we have at our small college. He's also reserved, sometimes hides himself inside the large jacket and hat he wears to class, and that he's funny when he smiles shyly. I always know he feels deeply what we discuss in class and cares about us all a great deal. But I've never noticed him physically as a man; I don't know his body or his face from that perspective. To me he's just a student I care about.

Suddenly as Hala walks ahead of us with her arm in his, chatting him up, having taken his hat now and wearing it, I notice that Al *is* handsome. He's tall, sweet and protective in the way he walks, and he's got a gorgeous smile. His jaw line is strong, and his face does have that broody movie star quality to it. It's a revelation to me. I laugh at myself, noticing it only at this moment in Nablus.

As we walk through the now crowded section of town that leads to the safe house, it turns out I'm not the only one noticing. Yousef told us before coming, that Nablus is believed by many to be the biblical city of sodomites, that many Palestinians here are homosexual and that they get excited over foreign male visitors. According to Yousef, it's a place that men from Palestine and foreigners also go to have homosexual "adventures". It seems he's right because Ken and Al are getting all kinds of attention and cat calls from both older and younger men.

Making our way through the narrow crowded stone paved lanes, all brightly lit with Ramadan lanterns, I have the feeling of being in Marrakech. There are food and jewelry vendors, spice dealers, snake charmers and conjurers all about us on the streets. It's festive, but there is another feeling as well. In Ramallah, the women were also out under the Ramadan lanterns, but not here. It is only men and has a feeling of "sin city". I feel anxious to leave the street. Ken and Al look uncomfortable too with all the male attention, although they cover it with many jokes.

As we approach the safe house, Ken fills me in on what we could possibly expect. "You know if the Israelis raid this place the first thing they'll do is break down the doors or the windows and throw in stun grenades. When they go off they are so bright and so loud that you are temporary deafened and disoriented. The best thing is to get under a heavy piece of furniture and freeze. You don't want them to think you are a militant fighting back."

I nod to Ken and imagine hiding powerlessly under a table, but as I do, I can also imagine an innocent party getting threatened enough that they pick up a weapon and begin to fight back, getting killed as result.

"Let's just hope they have no idea this place exists and we get in and out fast," I say. "Or if they know it exists, that they also know that we are here and wait until we leave."

Ken and I exchange smiles and we follow Hala through the small iron door and down the narrow cement staircase leading to the Nablus "safe house".

CHAPTER 17

Nablus Safe House

We navigate the narrow, cement steps and turn to enter a passageway that leads into a basement apartment. A middle-aged, heavyset woman dressed in an abaya and headscarf opens the metal door admitting us in. We enter a long hallway, pass an unpainted grey wooden ladder that hangs alongside rusty painted water pipes and turn into the main rooms. It's a cozy apartment, but poor. The linoleum floor is cheap and worn, the upholstered furniture is dated and tattered, and the curtains that cover the ground level windows are simple cotton. The walls are painted in shiny enamel paint, grey up to waist height, and white above. Some artificial red flowers are draped along one wall and traditional Palestinian embroidered items hanging on the others.

The hostess's daughter, a dark-haired five year-old girl in soft blue denim overalls, trails behind as we enter the small apartment. Our hostess offers us a seat, Hala offers us drinks, and we meet the woman's husband, who looks tired and mentally absent.

The two fugitives who sent the suicide bomber into Nablus haven't arrived yet. Remembering Ken's words about the Israelis using stun grenades in a possible raid, I quickly scan the room and see only the entrance we've just used and the windows above our heads. Not much of an escape route. There isn't much furniture to hide under either: a few end tables, a coffee table, and the easy chairs we are using. It feels a bit like being in a firetrap.

I decide to put it out of my mind and stay in the moment. Hala takes over serving glasses of juice acting in behalf of our hostess, who sits heavily in her chair facing us. I get down to business, retrieving my pen and tablet and explaining who I am and what I'm doing. Our hostess trusts us based on Hala's introduction and tells us that she has been taking care of fugitives and militants hiding from the Israelis at this "safe house" for years and the Israelis have never managed to discover it. More recently, she says, many suicide bombers have also been staying for a few nights before they left on what she calls their "martyrdom" missions. Most of those who stayed here were either captured, killed, or killed themselves (i.e. self-detonated) upon leaving.

"Can you tell me a little bit about the suicide bombers," I ask. "What they were like? How did they feel? What did they talk about and how did they act in their last days?"

She doesn't really connect to the question. Instead she stands and takes out a balled up pair of heavy knit socks from an embroidered sack hung on the wall, and as she begins to speak of the "martyrs" she cared for before their deaths, she cradles the socks to her face and begins to cry.

"These are Hamid's," she says holding them out like a sacred object. "I did his wash and cooked for him. He left these here. Now he'll never be back." She stifles a sob.

She takes a second pair of knit socks and tells another story of a "martyr" she cared for. I have the feeling the whole sack is filled with "martyr's" socks. Aside from her tears and obvious grief, I find there is something very bizarre about watching her hug the socks of young militants she helped to send to their deaths.

In fact, the whole situation is very strange. From time to time our hostess tries to engage her husband who sits in the corner silently. He weeps momentarily but is so detached from our conversation that he doesn't seem to be upset about what she is telling us, and it's obvious he doesn't want to speak about why he is weeping. When Ken can't stand it anymore and asks why, he waves his hand for the interpreter to leave him alone.

For some reason everyone's emotions feel far removed in this place. Usually, once I begin an interview I am so immersed in the material that I feel only what's going on in the room and I become empathetically locked on to the emotions of the person I'm talking to, so much so that I begin to feel what they are feeling. Now however, I just can't move my mind into how she feels and am surprisingly unmoved by her tears. Perhaps it is because I am baffled by how she can stand to help launch young men into enacting suicide missions. Or perhaps I am more afraid than I realize and have numbed my own emotional responses in order to be able to conduct this interview while simultaneously knowing that we might at any moment be subjected to a terrifying military raid. Whatever the reason, I feel nothing for this woman. I notice that it's not only me though—my students and our translator also seem unaffected by the old woman's tears as she speaks.

Suddenly the little girl appears again in the living room. She is carrying a small black toy pistol that looks very real. She takes it shyly to her mother and asks in Arabic about us.

Belal interprets aloud, "She thinks we are Israelis come to interrogate and arrest her mother.

The little girl aims her pistol at us. Seeing that she feels it is her duty to protect her family members by bringing a pistol to shoot "the Israelis," I take my camera to quickly capture on film the child with her gun. It's a picture so juxtaposed with innocence and aggression. It touches me deeply that she feels at so young an age a need to protect her family.

Hala, on the other hand, has a completely different response. She moves quickly to correct the way the girl holds her gun, showing her how to stabilize her firearm with the other arm, holding it steady. I am sickened by Hala's behavior toward children, how she encourages the girl in her belief that she has a duty to protect her family by wielding a gun against "the Israelis". Is this how young Palestinian children are socialized into violent responses?

The mother tells her daughter that we are not Israelis and not to worry, to put the gun away. After an hour of talking with the women, Belal goes outside where there is cell phone reception to call his contacts, who confirm that the militants won't be coming after all. They fear detection and have decided it's too dangerous for them to move and also for us to come to them. I am frankly relieved, as I've found these people hard to take. We thank the women and depart quickly.

We return to Hala's house and discuss with her what to do next. She offers to help us make more interviews tomorrow, but advises that we should leave Nablus for the night and return again the next day. Everyone is expecting military action to happen in Nablus soon—there could be gunfights, raids on homes, even whole areas of the town encircled by soldiers, and these things usually happen at night, she tells us.

I remind her how we came from Beit Fourik, crossing the meadow illegally and tell her, " We don't want to do that again." I turn to her sister-in-law who seems more grounded and say, "You're a mother. Please give me your best advice on what is the safest and best thing to do now. I want to be safe, but I honestly cannot judge if it's safer to stay here or leave."

"It's better to leave tonight," she confirms and Hala advises, "You can cross back the same way you came. You'll be fine, we do it all the time."

"What about the checkpoint?" I ask. "They wouldn't let us cross into Nablus but what about going the other way into Beit Fourik. Is there a problem going that direction?"

"You can go," Hala answers indicating with her eyes Ken, Al and me. "But they cannot," she says indicating Yousef, Belal and Jamilah. "The soldiers would realize they crossed into Nablus illegally and arrest them."

"You can take the checkpoint, and we'll recross the meadow," Yousef interjects in a downcast voice.

"You'll be safe that way," Jamilah adds trying to sound cheerful but her face belying her anxiety.

"I can't do that," I answer knowing I cannot abandon them after they risked so much to help in our research.

"No way," Al adds. "We stick together."

"It sucks about the checkpoint," Ken says inhaling deeply on his cigarette and flicking it down to the stone courtyard. "But we can't leave you guys," he adds with a grim smile.

Maybe Belal deserves to be abandoned to recross on his own, but Yousef and Jamilah certainly do not. We say thank you and goodbye, hugging each other as we depart from their courtyard under the star-filled sky to enter a taxi they've called for us.

The driver takes us back to a spot near where we crossed earlier, but it isn't until after he drives off that we realize that no one recognizes the dirt road. And it's pitch black. Belal calls Hala and she tells him to look for a cement barrier in the meadow, a fence that we can hide behind as we cross.

We walk in darkness along the dirt road trying to find the fence. The only things we can make out is a guard tower up ahead and a searchlight sweeping across the meadow on our left, likely mounted on a tower at the checkpoint and put there to find anyone trying to cross the meadow illegally. Suddenly the beacon turns and sweeps the road up ahead of us. I feel alarmed watching it sweep back and forth across the road, as though someone knows we are here and is trying to spot us. Thankfully we are not yet in range of its piercing beam.

Belal explains, "It's the Israelis at the checkpoint searching the area to make sure no one crosses outside of the checkpoint."

The searchlight beam, coming from about a quarter mile away, is strong and concentrated. It seems that if we walk much further forward along the road it will surely expose us. Al and Ken nervously put out their cigarettes.

"No sense making ourselves an easy target," Al jokes as he throws his cigarette down to crush it on the soft dirt road.

I can't decide if we are in real danger or not. We are on a dirt road, not crossing the meadow, and now I can see that there are large buildings on the right side of the road—factory buildings or warehouses, I think. Surely Palestinians must be able to walk along their roads at night, as long as they stay away from the settler's road. Or not? Is simply being out late at night justification for being shot dead? I can see that Belal is clearly nervous about walking toward the searchlight, but I don't trust his judgment anymore so I don't bother to ask him.

We walk a bit further joking nervously in soft voices, and Belal finally says, "No, the cement barrier is further back. We need to turn back."

I don't know how he can get any bearings in the darkness but we gladly turn and follow him away from the searchlight. Belal spots the barrier on the far side of a ditch, leaps down and, scrambles back up some grass on the other side, and disappears behind the shelter of a five-foot-high cement barrier, which meets a long, winding cement fence that trails across the meadow.

We scramble after him as he says, "Quick the searchlight is on us!" We leap and cower together behind the cement barrier as the searchlight sweeps over our position. The fence blocks its beam, but if we stand our heads will be caught in the searchlight. If we are spotted, can we be shot?

"Shit!" Ken cries out softly as it sweeps past us, and we all crouch even lower.

"What should we do?" Al asks crouching low.

"We can move along behind the cement barrier. Keep your heads low; they could shoot if they see us," Belal answers.

Without much choice, we continue on, following the barrier across, but as we move forward crouching below the cement fence, we realize that the cement wall is not a solid shield. Every twenty feet or so, there are decorative wrought iron openings in the cement barrier where we are exposed to the searchlight and the fence is also angled so we are moving toward the checkpoint, bringing us closer to the searchlight than if we remained on the road.

"Fuck!" Ken swears as he sees the first gap in the barrier.

"Come on! The light's moved away," Belal hisses as he leaps across. Ken follows then Al.

"I never expected this, Speckie!" Al says using their pet name for me while turning back to make sure I get across. The others leap forward, and we continue on for three more gaps until we stop to rest as the spotlight moves back and forth just over our heads.

"Shit, they know we're here!" Ken says, and we all feel it's true.

Then for some strange reason we all start to giggle uncontrollably. Maybe it's the complete terror of facing our deaths and the absurdity of it. Maybe it interjects some normalcy—like this can't possibly be real, can it? Whatever the reason, it seems there is nothing else to. Ken makes it worse by softly cracking profane jokes as the searchlight hovers back and forth over our position, making us laugh so hard that I suddenly feel I have to use the bathroom.

"Don't!" I cry. "I'll have to pee my pants."

"I already shit mine a long time ago!" Ken says which just makes us laugh harder.

"I need a cigarette," Belal says.

"Oh God don't light up here!" Yousef says.

"They'll fucking blow a mortar into this fence if they see your cigarette," Ken quips, and I wonder just how much fire power the Israelis have and how willing they are to use it.

"Great research project this is turning out to be, Speckie," Al adds.

"Oh fucking shut up!" I say joining them in their profanity.

We continue onward, moving in fits and stops, our hearts racing as we wait at the openings in the fence until the searchlight has swept over us, timing our runs across the exposed areas to after the searchlight has moved away. The problem is that it sometimes jerks back suddenly—it's not automatic; a soldier is manning it in pursuit.

We progress along the barrier and are now about a hundred yards across the meadow. My mind is racing, thinking we just have to make it across the meadow past the checkpoint, but there is still a long way to go. Ken and Al continue to release the tension by cracking more jokes about getting shot up. I double up laughing so hard at one point that I think I might actually wet my pants and tell them, "Please go on ahead, I'm going to use the outdoor facilities."

"Speckie, you better hope they don't shoot you with your pants down," Ken quips as they move along leaving me to crouch alone in the tall grass in the darkness to relieve myself.

As I catch up and we continue onward the searchlight appears to narrow in on our position, again sweeping back and forth exactly over where we are hiding. I begin to wonder if they have sensing equipment that allows them to hear us as well. We don't know whether to be terrified or to keep laughing at the absurdity of hiding behind the cement wall like hunted beasts, and so we just continue on hugging the inner wall of the fence. After about two hundred yards the wall suddenly terminates into hilly mounds that were probably bulldozed into place when the Israelis made their settlers' road and are now covered with long meadow grass.

We wait for the searchlight to sweep over us again and quickly in the cover of darkness move from behind the fence to throw ourselves down inside the hilly mounds, into their soft grassy shelter. As we spread out hiding from the searchlight, we discuss what to do now.

Belal says, "See those lights over there? That's Beit Fourik. When the searchlight moves we have to make a run for it."

"No way, Belal," I protest. "Do you want to be shot running across the meadow?"

"This is how everyone here crosses," he answers. "You have to wait for the searchlight to move to the other side and then we run like hell." I don't think he knows anything and is being reckless by willing to risk all our lives with nothing but his best guess.

"Belal, if you want to run, go ahead, but I'm responsible for Ken and Al, and I advise we stay put for a bit and think this one through."

Ken and Al are happy to comply, Yousef and Jamilah too. They move a bit away from me, still inside the cover of the hillocks to light up cigarettes and begin a heated discussion. Al, whose dream is to become a paratrooper runs crouching over to me and says, "Belal and I are going to make a short reconnaissance mission there between the hills," pointing to the small hillocks nearby.

"No." I tell him firmly. "You could be shot!"

"No they can't shoot us there," Al says pointing to the larger hill that blocks their view of the path he wants to take. "I'll be fine." He runs off with Belal before I can stop him and returns to report that there is no way to avoid the searchlight once we leave the cover of the small hillocks we are hiding in. I tell him, "We'll stay here. Don't move."

Al goes back to join the smokers, and I listen as they discuss all the possibilities of getting back to Beit Fourik. Meanwhile I lay back on my hillock watching the searchlight beam passing our position, swathing the hillocks above us in bright light and jerking back again, still searching. The soldiers are unable to detect us hidden among the grassy mounds, yet I feel like a deer, frozen in position, waiting for a hunter to pass by.

After awhile, I begin to gaze up at the stars as I feel the soft grass cradling my back, thinking over what to do. It's a clear sky and a balmy night, and it amazes me that even though we are here caught between Nablus and Beit Fourik and may be killed if we make a wrong decision, the constellations are the same here as they are back home in Brussels. I lie back looking up into their mystery trying to discern a good answer and draw a strange comfort in their constancy and familiarity.

While I'm enjoying the stars, the young men have worked themselves, with male bravado, into a kind of "last battle" mentality and have decided to make a run for it, with Belal and Al being the strongest proponents. I'm not much of a runner and I know it's a mistake. I've listened to them for about a half hour and finally when they reach their stupid consensus, my adrenaline is flowing freely.

"Belal, fucking Rambo, shut up," I hiss at him, keeping my voice low. "It's your fault we are here in this situation to begin with, and no one is going to take your advice now. Maybe you think you *are* fucking Rambo but I can guarantee you that if they catch us in the searchlight they won't think twice, and we'll be shot, no questions asked! No one on my watch is going to run across that field and get shot up tonight. If you want to run, be my guest, but Ken and Al are staying here, unless you guys think you are fucking Rambo too now?"

They laugh, but I continue. "Listen guys, it's much better to stay here tonight. We can wait for sunrise; even sleep here if we need to. Then in the dawn we can walk slowly and peacefully across the meadow. That way they can see who we are, that we are not doing anything criminal—walking, not running and not looking like militants in the night. So, Belal, I will repeat myself one more time. If you want to fucking run, be my guest, but no one else in this group is joining you."

My little speech shakes Ken and Al to their senses, and they immediately agree. We discuss our plan some more and decide maybe it's not safe to stay here until daylight since the Israelis seem to know we are somewhere in the meadow and could send out an armed search party. Better to retrace our steps and go farther along the dirt road where we were dropped off to find where we originally crossed, far from the checkpoint and the searchlights. We get up and begin the trek backwards, again anxiously cracking jokes and laughing as we run between the open spaces in the fence. When we get to the ditch and the edge of the road where the fence ends, we wait for the searchlight to move and we scramble back up to the road. Belal phones Hala and they agree the taxi has left us off at the wrong place. She says she will call the driver and send him back to pick us up again and take us to the right spot.

We wait for about fifteen minutes and the driver arrives. He is upset and tells us it was the right place. Belal argues with him explaining where we crossed earlier in the day. He finally understands and takes us ten minutes further down the road, thankfully far removed from the search-light, and drops us off again. This time we step off the road into the same muddy soil that we traipsed across earlier.

Belal points ahead, "See we have to climb up this big hill and then we'll be back in the meadow where we originally crossed." In Belal fash-ion, he omits several key facts: the settler's road runs along the top of the hill and all this area has been bulldozed to keep Palestinians from getting anywhere near it, and we won't be crossing back through the culvert but running illegally in full view across the road, this time as fugitives in the middle of the night.

We begin climbing up the mud, rock and dirt cliff, anxious to get out of this situation. The muddy cliff is about twenty feet high and consists of highly unstable soil and rocks. The boys are wearing sneakers and Jami-lah is tiny so they help her up as they also climb up easily.

In my slip-on shoes, I can't get a grip. I push the pointy toes into the soil and reach for the more solid parts of the cliff to climb up, determined to rise. My brother is a world-renowned rock climber, blazing trails on ten thousand-foot-high cliffs, and he's taken me climbing a few times, so I know how to search out and take advantage of a foothold, and I know that I have it in me to get to the top. But I'm dressed all wrong, not as fit as I should be, carrying a briefcase and on an unstable cliff that no serious rock climber would ever climb.

Ken is looking out for me again and Al, too, this time. Al is ahead and reaches his hand down to pull me up. Ken circles around behind and tries to tell me where to place my feet. I reach up and get a grip on a large stone with one hand and pull hard to reach Al's hand with the other, push-ing with my legs. But I have chosen my hand hold badly. The big stone pulls loose from the soft soil and as it dislodges it begins a sickening slide straight for my face and shoulder. I hang on to Al's hand and try to turn

Anne Speckhard

away while flattening myself into the cliff trying to dodge it, but the heavy stone scrapes over my upper arm, shredding my skin, then thuds on my shoulder and begins pulling me down with it, until it falls free leaving me dangling from Al's hand. I regain my footing and pull hard on Al's grip willing myself up. He pulls too, and Ken comes alongside and all together, we push and pull me to the top of the cliff.

Scrambling, over the ledge, we stand above the twenty-foot soil cliff and find ourselves upon a strip of small boulders. The settlers' road is ahead of us. I understand it's dangerous to cross, but no one is here, so that's good.

Belal is running already. "Run, quickly now!" he hisses.

Al runs and the others run with him, but I freeze, too terrified to run in my slippery flats on these large loose slippery stones. I'm a bit night blind and have frequently twisted my ankle in dark settings. My body says, 'No don't run here – too dangerous, you'll get hurt.'

Ken sees my fear and misunderstands my concern thinking I'm afraid to cross the road. He does the right thing speaking calmly "Speckie, we have to run now. This is their road."

"I'm afraid I'm going to twist my ankle and fall," I say as I balance on the slippery stones trying to walk quickly toward him.

Comprehending he holds out his hand for me to grab and answers, "I've got you. You won't fall, come on—run!"

"I can't," I say, taking his hand. He pulls me forward, walking fast but not running. I can feel Ken's urge to dash ahead, but he forces himself to stay with me. The rocks thin out and we run across the paved road, but as the cragginess resumes on the other side, I slow down again.

Ken has lost his patience and pulls me hard, running across the slippery stones while keeping me upright until we get to tall but sparse grass.

"Get down! Get down!" Belal and Al call to us from a distance away in the grass as we flatten ourselves on the dirt. Ken pulls me down and we both hit the ground.

A vehicle is coming. We all lie flat on our bellies, Ken and I closer to the road than the rest of them. As I stare ahead at the settler's road I realize how sparsely the grass grows here—it's less than a foot tall. There is a very good chance we can be spotted, but there is no time to move anywhere better. We hold our breath as the settler's jeep approaches, a searchlight mounted on top, scanning the area.

"Shit!" I hear Ken swear beneath his breath.

162

Frozen, we lie silent waiting. The jeep is moving fast, and the searchlight is thankfully sweeping the other side of the road. Someone obviously knows we are here; it's been sent out to look for us.

As it gets closer I paste my face into the dirt and stop watching, waiting an eternity to hear or feel what comes next. The car speeds past and we all begin to breathe again, though Ken and I don't move for the next five minutes.

"It's okay," Ken says, finally. We get up and see that Belal, Yousef, Jamilah and Al have already gone and are running ahead of us toward the village.

We take off running too now. The meadow is basically flat so I am able to keep up, and Ken and I sprint until we catch up to the others. Together we enter the village, exhausted, in shock and emotionally drained, but also amazed that it's over and we are okay.

We head back to the house where Belal has arranged for us to stay the night. Our host is a senior head of one of the factions in his village and another of his guests is also a militant. They've both agreed to speak with us and have been waiting, so despite feeling a nervous wreck, I get out my tablet and start again.

They repeat a lot of what Shakespeare and the men in the culture center have already told us, adding more details about how aggressive the settlers are and how young men up to a certain age are basically prisoners in the town.

Our host listens as Belal tells how we crossed the meadow tonight and what happened with the Israelis. He looks very seriously at me and asks sternly, "You know how dangerous that was? I wouldn't have done it myself. You could have been killed! They will shoot anyone they find by the road, especially at night."

I feel a chill as he says it and realize the reality of what we've just been through hasn't hit me yet.

The Palestinians pull foam mattresses down and make beds for us to sleep. They put me in a small room on my own. My clothes are filthy so I strip and sleep naked in the sheets, too exhausted to care. Stupidly I leave my shower until the next morning, learning then the risk with Palestinian water heaters. It's freezing in the mountains at night so even with the faucet turned full blast to hot, the shower water comes out icy cold. It takes me some time to figure out that it's never going to warm up. It's a fitting finale to the rest of the trip.

After a hot coffee, we leave at the driver's insistence to depart immediately. Doing so means we forgo any more interviews, but when the
dangers are laid out for us clearly, we have to choose safety. We head
down the mountain to Ramallah, taking the same route and many detours
again to avoid the Israeli patrols. After what we have just been through it
somehow no longer feels alarming.

CHAPTER 18

Emergency Sex, Sodomy and Palestinian Virginity

After our return home from Beit Fourik, Yousef and Jamilah attend their classes at Birzeit University; Ken, Al and I hang out in downtown Ramallah waiting for them to return. We're seated on a park bench near the square with the big brass lions in the shade, and Ken and Al smoke as they confide in me their feelings about the Nablus crossing the night before.

"I still can't believe what happened last night," Al says, shaking his head, "The whole thing that Palestinians can get shot on the settler's road—that's fucked up."

"I think we need to vet our guides better," I say, referring to our displeasure with Belal.

"You meaning fucking Rambo? I'm never going anywhere near him again," Ken says, throwing his cigarette to the ground and crushing it in the dirt.

Inhaling deeply on his cigarette Al looks at the ground and jokes shyly, "Last night was one of those moments we talked about before in class—it was a moment for emergency sex."

Al is referring to the book Emergency Sex and Other Desperate Measures: True Stories from Hell on Earth,[63] written by a group of three United Nations (UN) relief workers who had seen some pretty dicey moments in their service in conflict zones. Their responses to working in a conflict zone were psychologically interesting so I brought the book to class and read a section of it in which Heidi Postlewait, one of the authors, describes how she and her male co-worker from the UN got caught in the crossfire between two armed militia trucks who suddenly converged. Heidi and her co-worker dove for cover under a nearby, parked truck as bullets flew. Lying there terrified and sure they will be killed, the militias ceased their gunfight and roared back out of town as quickly as they arrived. Heidi was overcome by both amazement of their survival and a sudden and unexpected carnal instinct. She ripped off her and her co-workers clothes, thinking to herself, 'I have to have sex and I have to have it now.'

I found it psychologically interesting that being faced with her own imminent death, Heidi responded with such a strong urge to engage in sex. Was it an instinct to reproduce perhaps that was activated by the threat of dying?

My students had thought it funny and Al borrowed the book and read it cover to cover as he did often when I brought books to class. He said the rest of the book was boring, but he and Ken joked before embarking on this trip that if I wanted to write a bestseller about my research I should put a lot of sex in it. I generally let my students speak openly to me so they ribbed me about how they'd be happy to volunteer themselves to go out and "make" juicy stories and said if things got really bad, we could always engage in "emergency sex".

"Yep, I was ready to pile on top of you, taking turns of course," Ken says puffing on his next cigarette, his eyes sparkling with mischief.

"Oh right," I laugh through embarrassment. I find the thought graphically distasteful, but I understand they are just trying to joke through their anxiety, just as they had done on the trip.

As they carry on, I remember going to sleep after our misadventures feeling somewhat "buzzed" by all that had occurred. I guess there is nothing like facing your own death to make you feel really alive. Perhaps it's what keeps so-called "adrenaline" junkies hooked on risk-taking. I can't say I had any of the feelings the UN workers describe, but they were colleagues who had already slept together before the incident and related on an equal basis, whereas I am in a parental or protective role with my students, far older than them and more conservative by nature when it comes to promiscuity. Now my students are just pulling my leg, using the joke to drive away the terror we all felt the night before.

I laugh and tell them, "Well, it's good we all survived!"

That night, after Yousef and Jamilah return from university, I offer to take his family to a restaurant in Ramallah for dinner but Al asks first if we can see the Mukata'a, Yasser Arafat's compound. Arafat is the leader of the Palestinian Liberation Organization, and at this moment, he is in Paris dying—transported there for emergency medical treatment just days before we arrived and has since lapsed into a coma.

"You know if Abu Ammar dies while you are still here, all the checkpoints will be shut and you will be trapped in Palestine," Yousef tells us referring to Arafat by his familiar name.

"They say on the news his condition is worsening," Al adds.

"Geez, just what we need, to be locked in Palestine," I say, looking at Ken and Al to gauge their reaction.

"Hell, we'll just keep interviewing," Ken says, smoking as usual.

"Yeah, I bet it will be really interesting if he dies," Al adds. "But how long would they keep the checkpoints closed?"

"With the Israelis you never know," Yousef answers.

The sun is setting around us as we walk along a two-lane street toward Arafat's compound, the sky deepening from a deep pink to violet. As we pass still-open stores with Ramadan lanterns strung up over their sidewalks, I think to myself maybe it's better to go back to Jerusalem rather than risk being caught in Ramallah. The other side of me thinks it would be a shame to abandon what is turning out to be an amazing research trip. As we walk, Al, our news hound, continues to discuss Arafat with the two Palestinians.

Arafat has many titles: Chairman of the Palestine Liberation Organization (PLO), President of the Palestinian National Authority (PNA) and the leader of the Fatah political party, which he founded in 1959. A complex and controversial figure, Arafat was originally opposed to Israeli's existence and spent most of his life fighting against Israel for Palestinian independence and self-determination. In the late 1960's and early 1970's while based in Jordan, Fatah engaged in a brief civil war with Jordan, and Arafat and his cadres were forced out of Jordan into Lebanon as a result. From Lebanon, the Palestinian militia groups were again responsible for armed incursions into Israel, triggering Israel's 1978 and 1982 invasions of Lebanon, with Arafat and Fatah as the major targets and causing Lebanon to disintegrate into civil war. Yet, after all was said and done, Arafat received the Nobel Peace Prize for his work on a brokered peace agreement between Palestine and Israel. Israelis generally consider him a terrorist while Palestinians revere him, seeing him as a freedom fighter and icon of their fight for statehood, despite the ways in which he set back their cause. They refer to Arafat as "Abu Ammar" as Yousef did, which literally means Father of Ammar, Arafat's oldest son's name, and is in Arabic the familiar way of referring to a person.

In his later years Arafat claimed that he swore off terrorism and military actions against Israel, but as the second Intifada continues to grind on, the Israelis have activated Operation Defensive Shield, an all-out offensive in which they have made repeated incursions into the West Bank. During one of these, they discovered RPG launchers, documents, and other items inside an office in the Mukata'a. The Israeli government claimed these as evidence that Arafat and the PLO actively support the al Aqsa Martyrs Brigade, or the armed wing of Fatah, and aid in sending suicide operations against Israel.[64] As a result, Israel's Prime Minister, Ariel Sharon, ordered Arafat to be confined in the Mukata'a from January 2002 onward until recent days (in 2004) when he was evacuated to Paris for medical treatment.

When Israeli Minister of Tourism Rehavam Zeevi was killed, the Israelis were angered that Ahmed Sa'adat and Hamdi Quran (Palestinian militants from the PFLP who we are scheduled to meet the next day in prison in Jericho) and four other men involved in Zeevi's assassination were hidden inside the Mukata'a. This incited the IDF to place it under siege from March to May 2002 until an agreement was made for the six fugitives to be handed over to authorities to stand trial.[65] In September 2002, the fugitives had still not been handed over, and the compound was again placed under siege and later partially demolished by IDF armored bulldozers.[66]

As we continue toward the Mukata'a we walk along a poorly lit sidewalk. Ken, who is looking up at the buildings, fails to see a large hole in the middle of the sidewalk and walks right into it.

"Fuck!" he swears as he leaps back out, hopping and holding his shin. "Geez I could have broken my leg!"

Al starts laughing and I bend down to check Ken's leg. It's bloody but okay.

"I guess they don't see any need to put up a barrier or warn people when the sidewalk has two foot deep holes!" Ken says rubbing his shin.

Meanwhile, Al asks to borrow my camera and begins snapping pictures of the billboards that simultaneously advertise female products and remind us that Palestinian girls are irresistibly beautiful. I laugh, remembering I am in the company of testosterone-driven young men and remind him that he better not photograph any actual girls, as I don't want trouble.

When we arrive at the Mukata'a, it's late, but Yousef talks the Palestinian guards into allowing us into the compound. We walk around it under the light of a full moon and feel eerie being there, knowing that if Arafat dies, we may become trapped inside Ramallah. Like the other destroyed homes we witnessed in Beit Fourik, we see that blasts and bulldozers have destroyed half of the main compound here, leaving gaping eyesores of holes and collapsed concrete. What remains however is still regal and I can imagine it functioning as the seat of government.

After the Mukata'a, we pick up Fatima and Bashar for dinner. Yousef's mother has to work so she cannot join us. As we walk from the parking lot by Yousef's house we pass some boys between four and twelve-years-old who are running and throwing firecrackers. As we pass, they dare to throw one near us—playfully trying to scare us. It makes a loud noise and I startle. The Palestinians with me don't even react—they are used to much more aggressive bangs than these little firecrackers.

It's Ramadan, and all the stores are still open and brightly lit. As we round the corner by one of the stores, we come across piles of wooden crates blocking the sidewalk. In between them, five or six little boys from five to ten-years-old are playing with small guns that have been cut out of wood. One of them comes out suddenly from the crates and points his toy gun at us. I laugh, but he continues and says in a loud and menacing voice in English, "Who are you? Where are you going?" His friends join him and they all level their "automatics" at us. The smallest one points his gun expertly and also demands, "Who are you? Where are you going? Where are you from?"

I cannot resist. I pass my hand behind his head and touch his neck and hair and answer "America" and smile at him. He is intent on his play and does not come out of his role although he also does not pull away from my caress. He asks us again sternly, and they all join in, repeating their demands. I touch him again and ask, "Is this your checkpoint?" They are confused with English, but they understand "checkpoint" and laugh gleefully and demand even louder, "Who are you? Where are you from?" They follow us with their wooden guns trained on us as we move.

I reach out to another one of the small boys and gently hug him, repeating softly back to him as I rock him gently side to side, "Who are you? Give me your documents, please." I can see he is like all children who need play to work through their anxieties. In traumatized children we call this "posttraumatic play," which usually consists of the child repeating over and over again in play the traumatic episodes they have endured until they are mastered in fantasy.

I get my camera and ask if I can take their picture. They all point their guns at me as menacing as possible, and I snap the photo. They want to be strong men, but they are just little boys. I've been able to put my emotions aside for everything we have heard on this trip so far, but it must be adding up inside because as I walk away tears start to fall from my eyes.

• • •

During this trip I've been surprised to learn that Palestinian society is not as conservative as I would have thought. Every night the guys stay up late drinking with their new Palestinian friends, including Jamilah, whose crush on Al has deepened.

Tonight, I'm going to spend the night again with Yousef's family, and I learn from Ken and Al that they are again staying at Jamilah's place. I've learned that many Muslim girls in Belgium, who must "prove" their virginity at marriage, engage in anal sex in order to keep their hymens intact or they have a doctor put a surgical stitch inside their vaginas in order to recreate a broken hymen. I ask Al if he is sleeping with Jamilah, as I don't want any trouble. Al smiles, laughs, then protests that he has a girlfriend back home. Later when it's obvious they are getting closer, I press him and he laughingly tells me that he knows not to compromise her virginity—that there are other ways to be together. I don't know if he's pulling my leg or if they are "together", but I don't ask for more details.

Sex, however, is something I probably should be asking more about, as it does play a prominent role in many theories of suicide terrorism. This is because senders of suicide bombers in Islamic populations often invoke the Koran and the Hadith[67] in their "martyrdom" ideology, making promises to would-be "martyrs" about the afterlife. Aside from instant admission to paradise, male suicide bombers can expect to meet seventy-two virgins waiting to serve them upon arrival. Many terrorism experts take this promise as a serious motivator for suicide terrorism, concluding that Muslim young men are eager to bomb themselves while killing others in order to reach the "virgins".

I personally find this laughable. After all I am learning, seeing and experiencing here I simply don't believe it. In my research thus far, especially in conflict zones, I have not found "getting to the virgins" prominent in the thinking of anyone I have studied; the traumas, the daily humiliations and losses suffered by Palestinians and Chechens alike, and later Iraqis and others who are inside conflict zones, are always front and center in the extremists I am interviewing. The episode of the little boys playing checkpoint also exemplified the deeply traumatized youth and convinces me that the greatest vulnerability for induction into suicide terrorism among this population is trauma and not promises of sex.

As we saw with Che, trauma survivors often use sex as an escape from the pain of flashbacks, intrusive thoughts or nightmares, which are often described as unavoidable, inescapable and as horrific as the original event. Flashbacks usually feel like a full sensory film with the color, smells, sounds and sensations of the original trauma, ignited whenever posttraumatic reminders are encountered. And just like the UN workers who responded with an urge for sexual activity, sex can be an instinctual response to threat and can also be used as a way to drive away painful feelings and calm the body. The promise of virgins is surely alluring because the sexual outlet for soothing emotional pain is one that is forbidden in this society for unmarried men and women, but it seems to me to be more of a bonus than the reason to volunteer oneself for suicide terrorism.

It isn't easy to ask about sex as a motivator to suicide terrorism, and that isn't our primary goal in the interviews, but as I go along, I find that maybe I should try to explore the subject. When I submit one of my academic papers on the general subject of suicide terrorism for scientific review, the journal editor, Lloyd deMause, jumps all over me saying, "You know terrorists only become violent because violence has been enacted upon them." He claims that among Arabs, those who become terrorists do so at least in part because they have been abused in their families and have been sodomized. I can basically agree with the idea that violence often begets violence; however, the claim that all terrorists have been abused within their family settings and that acts as a primary motivator to terrorism seems to neglect the very real and painful political realities of their lives and seems ridiculous to me. Yet I do know that in Arab countries sodomy is rumored to be rife between men and boys.

To prove his point, Lloyd sends me twenty or more scholarly articles about practices of sodomy among Arabs. Much of it's dated, but as I sickeningly make my way through it, I have to acknowledge the societal acceptance in some Arab populations of men and older boys sodomizing young boys up to a certain age, practices that may continue up to now. The researchers point out that in most Arab cultures, preying upon younger boys in this manner is not considered homosexuality, but rather a means of meeting sexual needs given that women are off limits. And it is only of concern in their culture if the receiving boy grows up to "like" being sodomized and starts to invite such acts. Then he is considered deviant and a homosexual.

Lloyd writes to me, "You don't understand what motivates your subjects because you haven't asked them about their sexual and childhood abuse histories." When I tell his views to Khapta as we also continue our interviews there, she becomes incensed and answers, "Tell him there are many healthy families in Chechnya where a son or daughter becomes a violent extremist, and it's not because of the family practices. It's because of torture, having your family members and neighbors killed and all the other political violence they have been exposed to on a society wide level during the wars here. Tell him human rights abuses are enough to motivate young men and women to join militant groups and to enact terrorism—no family abuse is needed as the main motivator!"

I also tell Lloyd that I've stayed in the homes of many of the suicide bombers' families and have observed the interactions between parents and children in normal family settings. I tell him that they, for the most part, appear to me as loving, despite the use of corporal punishment with their children, used similarly to how many American parents disciplined in the fifties and sixties. And while I tend to agree with Khapta, I realize I am not a serious researcher if I don't at least try to ask these questions and explore competing theories of the motivations for terrorism.[68]

On our next trip to Palestine during the spring of 2005, when we return for additional research interviews I begin to ask those with whom we have gained the most rapport about whether sexual relations between unmarried men and women in Palestine are completely taboo, and if child sexual abuse and nonconsensual sodomy is widespread. I also keep my eyes wide open to see how Palestinian parents interact with their children, especially when they think I'm not paying attention.

In Ramallah in Spring of 2005, I say to our new translator, "Listen, Alla, maybe you think this is a strange question, but I've read that sodomy is commonplace in the Gulf countries and other Arab countries. Is it the same here?"

Alla looks at me with wide eyes and a quizzical face. "What? No I've never heard of that here!"

"But you have heard of it in the Gulf states?"

Yes," he concedes, chuckling. Alla is clearly uncomfortable with where the discussion is going and is fidgeting with his keychain as we talk, but I press on.

"What about when a man here cannot find a woman to be with. Does sodomy happen then?"

Alla screws up his face and answers, "But in the West Bank it's easy to get laid; you just don't talk about it." He's clearly not happy discussing it, so I back off and leave it at that.

Later, as Jamilah and I prepare a meal together in Alla's kitchen, I broach the subject just as she is closing the refrigerator door. "Jamilah," I say, "today I was talking to Alla about sex in the West Bank, and he said that it's easy to get laid. Is that true?"

Jamilah suddenly freezes, and she holds the door ajar, gripping it tightly and staring at me in horror. "What did he tell you?" she asks.

From the look on her face, it's obvious something has passed between them and she is terrified that he has told me.

I quickly relieve her by answering her with the truth, "He told me it's easy to get laid, but he also said if you sleep with a Palestinian girl, it's very important that you never reveal it to anyone."

Instantly, Jamilah relaxes, her arm unfreezes, and the refrigerator door swings shut. We go back to chatting normally as though I don't realize what her face just gave away.

I do quiz her on different points, first asking her how hard it is to get contraception.

"You can get birth control pills at any pharmacy," she says, "But it's better not to go to your local one, so no one there knows you."

"And abortions?"

"Abortions are performed in Jerusalem," she answers.

That (third) trip we all stay in Alla's apartment; I sleep on a twin bed in Alla's room, while Ken and Alla take the living room sofas. One night, Jamilah joins us with an Israeli young man who is working on human rights causes in Palestine. They sleep over and stay up much later than everyone else. At one point I get up to use the bathroom and as I enter the hallway they jump from what looks like an embrace to at least two feet apart. I pretend not to notice, although its highly amusing, and go on to use the bath room.

When I come out, Jamilah is obviously frightened as she asks me, "Were we too loud? Did we wake you?"

I smile knowing she really wants to be reassured that I didn't see anything so I answer, "Oh no! I was so deeply asleep I didn't even see you guys in the hallway! You surprised *me!*"

I see her face relax in gratitude and with the hope that I'm telling the truth. I have no idea if they were "making out" but judging from Jamilah's face it seems that she's terrified of anyone finding out. I don't know if the terror is over the sexual contact or that he is an Israeli.

I also don't know if Jamilah is an anomaly; she seems a bit more "wild" than the other girls we are meeting, but she is also the one we are getting the closest to. She tells us that at one point her parents forced her to leave Birzeit University because one of her male cousins was telling her parents that she was acting out. She hated being called home to live with her family and spent her semester convincing her parents that she was being as proper as necessary. They decided to let her return to university.

On our first trip into Palestine, Ken and Al spent their first night with male students but stayed at Jamilah's house for the remainder of the trip, where I was not present. On our second trip, we all stay in her apartment for two nights and I notice that she goes to great lengths to hide the fact that she has male overnight guests, even though I am there as a chaperone of sorts. She sleeps on the floor in blankets near Ken and Al, obviously thrilled to be with them. When we travel and are invited to stay in other homes she is always given a place to stay separate from the boys, but she manages each night to sneak down to where they are staying and sleep near them. I can see she is enamored with Al, but as far as I can tell he is committed to his girlfriend. Perhaps she hopes to turn his heart.

Though Alla had assured me that Palestinian young men are not sex deprived in the West Bank, I begin to doubt him when we are invited to a party in Ramallah one night. There are perhaps twenty men, ages eighteen to thirty, and some young women who are with their boyfriends. There is alcohol being served, and I make a point of not accepting it, as I generally try not to drink with my students and also don't want to be misinterpreted as "wild".

Despite my refusal of alcohol, the men assume I am an "easy" target for sexual relations, perhaps because I am the only Western woman present. There are two occasions in which I strike up a conversation with a male that evening: one tries to steer me out the patio door into the darkness; the other physically pushes me into a bedroom. As a result, I make a conscious effort to avoid standing anywhere near doorways, but as the evening wears on, they become even more aggressive and repeatedly push me toward the open sliding glass doors. Frightened of being shoved out into the darkness and raped, I find Ken.

"I don't care if you party all night," I say, "but I need to leave now and I don't want to walk home alone. Can you walk me home, please?" At this moment I'm very glad Ken is training for the Special Forces and has studied martial arts.

Ken complies, and as we walk home I explain, "I don't think these guys are getting laid as easily as Alla is telling us. They seem desperately horny to me."

"Yeah, well Alla is young, good looking and lived outside [in Tunisia when the PLO leaders were all exiled there] all those years and his father's a big guy in the PLO. Maybe that makes a difference for him," Ken says laughing. "So, were they coming on to you?"

"Geez, I thought I could be raped," I say and tell him about the men's aggression. "I'm glad you're here."

"They probably think all Western women are loose," Ken says.

In my end analysis I can't say for sure that all the Palestinian men who go to "martyr" themselves haven't done it for sex, given that it doesn't seem so easy for them to find willing partners, but it also doesn't seem like a main motivator to me.

Neither can I say that suicide bombers were not victims of child abuse. Even in therapy, it takes a long time for people to open up about their child abuse histories. Often third world cultures still adhere to domestic practices that first world countries would label as family violence, and violence in the home certainly opens the gateways to accepting violence in other venues as well. And a personal history of being sodomized might leave a person with enough despair to want to die. But, as I told Lloyd later, I didn't witness any child abuse but rather warm loving families, bestowing a lot of physical affection and nurture on their children, despite the occasional mild slap to keep young children in line. That there are much more serious incidences of domestic abuse in Palestinian families I have no doubt, but I am not sure their incidence of domestic abuse differs dramatically in comparison to other societies thereby explaining the huge number of terrorists emerging in their society. Sadly when one looks at child abuse statistics across the world almost all societies have problems in this area. What I saw more than anything else is that the political struggle for freedom, the daily humiliations and hardships and the violence: inter-faction violence, violence enacted on suspected and known collaborators, violence enacted by Israeli soldiers, interrogators and prison guards, and yes, in some cases also family violence—all of which likely had an effect on opening the doors of terrorism to young Palestinians. And I saw that here in Palestine and earlier when we inquired in Chechnya, there are terrorist groups ready to provide an outlet for young men and women, to pass on the violence they have encountered in their lives and to glorify them for doing so. For me, sex and the promise of the "virgins" just doesn't seem at all like the main reason inside conflict zones behind agreeing to become a "martyr" and enacting suicide terrorism.

CHAPTER 19

Jericho Prison-Ahmed Sa'adat

The next morning, Jamilah has arranged for us to interview Ahmed Sa'adat, the secretary general of the PFLP. The PFLP is the second largest of the groups forming the Palestinian Liberation Organization (Fatah being the largest) and is listed as a terrorist organization by both the U.S. and the EU. It has been responsible for numerous plane hijackings, bombings, the assassination of an Israeli cabinet minister and many other militant and terrorist acts.

Sa'adat has agreed to meet with us; the only problem is that he is an inmate of a Palestinian Authority prison in Jericho.

"Can we get inside?" I ask Jamilah. I have previously made repeated official requests for access to Israeli prisons to interview terrorists, including failed suicide bombers and their senders, but none of my requests have been granted.

"This prison is not controlled by Israelis," Jamilah answers. "It's a PA prison and it's guarded by American and British soldiers. I know people there. We'll get in," she says, tapping her cell. She's phoned her contacts earlier and is confident that we'll be admitted, but I, on the other hand, am not so confident.

Regardless, we board a minibus in the center of Ramallah. As we hand our shekels to the driver, Yousef explains, "This bus can take us only to the checkpoint in Jericho. We'll have to cross on foot and get another one on the other side." It seems so inconvenient to me and hard to plan our travel—how do we know we'll find another bus there? But there's no choice when it comes to crossing the Israeli checkpoints, so we carry on.

This time we are headed east. We pass over dry, rocky terrain and climb between reddish cliffs, finally descending toward the lowest point on earth: the Dead Sea. When we encounter a temporary checkpoint, Israeli soldiers wave us to the side of the road, instructing the driver to turn off the engine. He pulls our bus in line with other vehicles already stopped by the side of the road. We swing the doors open but even then it quickly gets too hot inside the minibus.

One of the soldiers comes and pokes his head in the window demanding, "Documents?" The driver takes everyone's documents and hands them to the soldier before I even have time to find mine. I don't protest and wonder if the soldier will notice that mine is missing. He doesn't.

It's too hot to stay in the bus so we get out and sit on large rocks near the road. Ken takes off his shirt to suntan and says, "Now this is really an Israeli thing to do. An Arab would never do this." It's true, Arabs are more modest about nudity.

Nearby, an ambulance has been stopped by the authorities and sits on the side of the road with its doors wide open. A man with dusty boots lies inside on a stretcher. "He must be suffocating from the heat," I say.

"Maybe he's a corpse," Ken jokes, dragging on a cigarette.

"No, it's an ambulance," I point out, wondering if he will be okay.

"How long can they keep us?" I ask Yousef.

He shrugs. "No one knows how long we will wait here, it could be hours; it could be the entire day. It's up to the soldiers."

A young Palestinian man and girl from our minibus walk toward the checkpoint to speak with the armed Israeli soldiers. Both wear tight, form-fitting clothes and have no hand or shoulder bags, so it's clear that nothing is hidden on them. They say something to the soldiers, who wave them away before they get close.

"What did you go to speak to them about?" I ask as they return.

"The boy on our bus, the one with his mother…He has a fever. He is three years old, and his mother says he needs an operation. We asked them to let our bus through to help them get to the hospital."

The soldiers must feel sympathy, because they allow us to continue onward quickly thereafter.

In about twenty minutes, we approach another informal checkpoint where an Israeli jeep is parked on the roadside. The soldiers wave to us, signaling for the driver to turn our minibus around; the checkpoint is closed.

We turn and try another road and encounter yet another checkpoint. It's also closed, and we pull over on the shoulder of the road behind a line of other cars that are waiting for it to reopen. Again, it's too hot to remain inside so everyone gets out and begins to socialize.

Our minibus driver is a stout Arab Israeli dressed in worn western clothes. Hearing about the sick child, he advises, "Send the foreigners to go and ask if the woman and her child can be allowed to pass."

Ken and Al agree and walk toward the checkpoint, the distance of about two city blocks. Ken has his shirt off again, and both have their hands raised as they walk slowly toward the armed Israeli soldiers. They look very vulnerable as they approach the soldiers in full gear, armed with automatic rifles. I trust that Ken's Hebrew and charm will protect them.

Ken and Al return and report that soldiers said no, naming two other towns where she could take her son instead. Our driver shakes his head. "She can't go to either of those towns; the checkpoints are closed for both."

A press photographer riding in one of the minibuses is frustrated that he failed to capture the picture of Ken and Al walking "hands up" toward the Israelis.

"Could you walk toward the checkpoint again so I could photograph it?" he asks.

They agree, walking only halfway the second time – just far enough for the photo and then they return.

We continue to wait on the rocks when an Israeli soldier in a jeep sees there are westerners present and stops alongside us.

"Everything okay here?" he asks. The Arab Israeli driver talks to him and asks him to please help the woman pass with her child. He arranges for them to cross the checkpoint alone in our minibus, which will return for us later.

Boiling under the hot sun without our minibus, we realize life as it must be for the average Palestinian: boring, hot and frustrating. Another Israeli jeep pulls up with two senior military men who are obviously curious about the foreigners held at an informal checkpoint. Ken goes to greet them and asks in Hebrew if we can please drive on into Jericho, explaining our situation with the minibus.

"Sure, you can pass," they say. "We'll go ahead and tell the soldiers to let you through." Worried about our return, I ask the senior Israeli, "Listen, I don't want to get stuck on the other side. Can you assure us that we will be able to return to Ramallah if we cross now?

"I can give you permission to return across the checkpoint," he answers, writing his name, Hamit, and phone number on a piece of scrap paper. "If you have trouble let me know." He pauses. "But I cannot guarantee that you can return, even with my note."

Not very reassuring.

Our minibus returns, and with Hamit's permission, we proceed to the checkpoint. When we get there, the Israeli soldiers are upset.

"Why do you come and speak Hebrew to us and then you turn around and make it into a photo shoot for those people?" they ask Ken angrily in Hebrew.

"Sorry, man, we didn't mean anything by it," Ken answers, but the soldiers are not placated. We pass through the checkpoint and Ken translating what they said, wipes his shirt over his eyes groaning, "Ah that was a shitty way to repay them for letting the sick baby through their checkpoint!"

"But the photo was accurate—it was exactly what it looked like the first time," I answer.

"Yeah but we didn't need to mess with them." Ken says, squirming in his seat.

He feels bad; we all do. Yet I keep thinking that it's also not right for them to be angry that we captured reality on film.

When we approach the next checkpoint our minibus stops and we are told to disembark and cross on foot. As we emerge on the other side, there is a crowd of angry Palestinians demanding to cross. Some of the men are shouting in Arabic at the Israeli soldiers, and it looks like it could become violent. Yousef translates, explaining that everyone is upset that the checkpoint is arbitrarily closed from that side and that they are blocked from getting home or going on to work or school. It seems the Israelis open and close checkpoints in either direction according to their security concerns, and no one can do a thing about it.

We cross and pick up another taxi, instructing him to take us to the Jericho prison. The road here passes high above the Dead Sea, and the sparkling expanse of water with mountains rising dramatically on the other side is breathtaking.

"That's Jordan on the other side," Yousef points out. When we get to the end of the water, there is a wide swath of fenced land with occasional outpost stands dotted along the way. "What are those guard stations?" Al asks.

"That's "no man's land," Yousef answers, the area between Jordan and Israel heavily manned and guarded by soldiers on both sides.

As we arrive at the prison gates, the Palestinian soldiers ask why we have come, and Yousef and Jamilah discuss our mission with them in

Arabic. Apparently satisfied with our answers, they let us enter. In the courtyard, a sentry box towers over us, manned by British soldiers who watch us pass.

Another searches our belongings, telling us to leave our phones and cameras behind. He takes my phone upon inspecting my purse, but doesn't notice my disposable camera. It's not caught as I am sent through a metal detector, so I keep it with me.

• • •

Ahmed Sa'adat is seated somewhat regally in a well-worn yellow armchair facing us as we enter his prison cell. The room is spacious with a faded sofa, table, and another armchair. Ahmed is fifty years old but still slim and looks in good physical shape. He is wearing a collared grey Lacoste short-sleeve shirt over sports pants. His hair is white although his bushy eyebrows are still dark black. He has a kindly face and intense eyes that seem to notice everything.

"Welcome," he greets us as though we have entered his diwan, the reception room of an Arabic sheik, and with a sweep of his hand invites us to sit down. His fellow prisoners bring drinks, and I thank him for his hospitality and agreeing to meet us, using Yousef as my translator. I explain to Ahmed why I am here and ask him to tell us his story beginning with his birth.

"I was born in Ramallah in 1953. The misery was already there when I was born. The minute I opened my eyes in this world I heard about Israelis killing people, kicking them out in the occupation. The situation was already bad. It was a duty to fight and go to prison." Ahmed tells me he first went to prison at the age of sixteen and has spent eleven of his fifty years in prison.

"But no one is born a militant," I say, careful not to call him a terrorist. "What were the experiences and events that propelled you into this role, leader of the PFLP? Can you go way back in history and start with your childhood so we can understand how you grew up and what influenced you?"

Ahmed nods and smiles. "When I was five years old I saw a crowd of people," he begins. "Everybody was there—women, men, children—cursing and shouting; cursing King Hussein, the American government, the Israeli government. They were just words then, but they took in my mind, even if I didn't understand them. I went to the crowd, but my mother pulled me back. They were yelling about Nasser and that guns will protect us. I heard it and took it. What I understood several years later was that they were yelling about the union of the government in Jordan and that King Hussein had jailed all the opposition."

Ten years later, Ahmed's school closed in a strike. When young Ahmed asked what is a strike, a classmate told him, "We go to curse Hussein."

"I hate King Hussein," Ahmed says. "He gave up Palestine. I grew up learning this from childhood."

Listening to Ahmed, I can see the power of emotionally-charged events upon small children and how adults can color a child responses, both then and later in life.

"These experiences and how the people around you framed them, defined reality for you," I say.

He nods and continues, "In that event, I saw killing, blood and smelled the [tear] gas that the soldiers used to throw on Palestinians. That's what created me."

Indeed, the events that children witness, particularly violent ones, are often galvanizing events that define and form important parts of a child's personality. Children often feel disabling fear every time a trigger reminds them of the terrifying events they witnessed. Conversely, they may cope with their terror and complete feelings of powerlessness and helplessness by casting those feelings aside and identifying with the aggressor, which is how Ahmed coped. He decided violence was power, and when faced with the aggression of others, he became a fighter, which helped keep his fears and feelings of vulnerability at bay.

Ahmed explains this psychological mechanism in his own words. "I lived through two occupations, British and then Jews. When we went to Jordan there was an aggressive government. Now when there is aggression, I fight back. Aggression gives me both the motive and the fear of going on."

Interestingly, when we interviewed Ahmed's daughter, Sharina, she expressed the same sentiment—that anger helps control her fear, and without it, she becomes engulfed in terror.

As Ahmed speaks, one of his fellow inmates, Hamdi Quran enters the room, takes a chair and sits down behind Ahmed. In clear opposition to Ahmed's kind, humble and intensely intellectual manner, Hamdi looks like a slick Mafioso. He is tall, well built and dressed in an immaculate white suit, his black hair slicked back. He is super relaxed—possibly stoned. Hamdi is the assassin of Rehavem Zeevi, the Israeli Minister of

Tourism. Knowing that he is a cold-blooded killer and watching his arrogant demeanor creates a feeling of disgust for me, but I don't want him to destroy the good rapport with Ahmed, so I ignore him. Soon, Hamdi grows bored and leaves again.

Ahmed continues, "The whole situation for all Palestine was aggression against us. It's a feeling of injustice that is felt by the whole people. Any people whose rights have been taken away will fight back."

"But does it work?" I ask. "I heard that you spent many years in prison."

"Israeli prison is our training ground. As long as we have prisons, we have training camps for our youth," Ahmed answers. He then surprises me by quoting Moshe Dayan, a former Israeli Minister of Defense: "We must lower the aggression inside jails because if we continue in this way the tough will become tougher, and the weak will vanish. We will have only the tough fighting back." He continues to discuss his views of Marxist revolutionary theories and I quickly see that Ahmed is a well-read and ardent student and believer of Marxism. I lived in the former Soviet Union for two years and saw how the high-ranking party members had all the privileges while human urine stunk up the hallways of most apartment blocs that housed the post-Soviet poor. I find it laughable that anyone could still believe that communism works.

Ahmed explains that the Israelis can prevent militancy of young men for a year or two by imprisoning them, but if the situation does not change during that time, the youth will return to their activities. Even in prison, Ahmed continued to work for his party.

"I never quit. The party was so strong, and it worked in a rational way—it was not emotional. It's not just me, but hundreds like me. We will never quit."

Indeed prison for Ahmed was his launching pad into militant activities. "It was the point when I begin my struggle," he explains. "It was my first organization."

According to Ahmed, he was first arrested for taking part in a strike, specifically for throwing rocks that he says no one saw him throw. Prison was Ahmed's first direct contact with politically-oriented violence directed at him.

"During the interrogation they beat me to try to force me to say I was there throwing rocks. I saw soldiers swearing on the Torah that they saw me. I didn't tell anything."

Ahmed's first time in prison, at sixteen, lasted three months.

"What was Israeli prison like at that time?"

"I had never seen a jail before," Ahmed explains softly. "I entered with a group of eleven boys from different schools. They put us in a column against a wall and yelled at us and punched us, shoving us forward. They told our group to get naked. I thought it was to beat us, but the first thing they did was put DDT powder on us and told us each to grab four types of bedclothes. They yelled at us so loud, and we were so confused, we just grabbed any four things, and often they were not even useful ones." He chuckles remembering.

"They put us in a one-meter by two-meter cell with four guys inside. We wanted to use the toilet, but when we asked the guard, he replied in Hebrew so we could not understand. The only thing in that room was a small barrel. We knew after awhile that this is our bathroom. In the morning they brought food for the four of us. Everyone was given a small dirty plate with Jell-O, cheese, yogurt, and one olive."

"Were you afraid?"

"Everything was frightening for us," Ahmed says. "The day of our trial the [Israeli] captain and soldiers came and said, 'You will be transferred to court and all of you must say you threw stones. Anyone who denies this we will beat and put in prison for ten years. If the judge asks you, you have to say 'I'm very sorry that I did it.' We understood that this is the first move to break us. So when the guards left we talked between the prison cells. We all had fears. Some said we have to do it, others no.

"Then we went to court. We were surprised. It was orchestrated like a play. The headmasters of our schools, the magistrate of our village, and other leaders were there, brought by the Israelis to sit and hear our guilt. We were too proud to say these false things in front of all of these people. We went back to our cells and felt our victory. We had done something magnificent!" Ahmed's eyes shine with the pride and exhilaration of his resistance. "I served about eleven years total in prison, in and out about fifteen times. From the group of eleven, ten of us continued our struggle."

For Ahmed, the galvanizing event for becoming a militant in his society was a civil demonstration against what the people viewed as an injustice, but it was his arrest and time in prison that set him on his path.

"Everyone who lives in the occupied territories knows that the main station of organization is jail. We all didn't have any idea of political parties when we were in the strike, but in jail we all learned and were organized into existing parties," Ahmed explains.

"You are very charismatic," I tell him noticing that he has a calm kindness, which coupled with his intellectual ways could strongly sway a young person. "I can imagine you having a very strong influence on young minds."

"Yes," he nods. "I was able to recruit and organize many young people during my years in prison."

The PA prison he is in now holds only two other prisoners, Hamdi and another, so Ahmed can no longer continue such activities. However, he admits, he is able to receive visitors and has a contraband telephone. So he still coordinates activities of his group from inside the prison.

"How do you feel about the people who bomb themselves, the 'martyrs'?" I ask again choosing my words carefully.

"It is the 'tax' for the struggle, but it is only a small part in the big picture. There is no party who makes a martyr. Many are volunteers." I realize he is sensitive because he just admitted to me that he is a charismatic figure among the youth and it's the youth, for the most part, who bomb themselves.

Taking a sharp breath, he carefully explains. "A martyr goes to die. A soldier is *ready* to die. It is all the same. In any army in the world there are those who volunteer to make a road for the others. The reason the Palestinians have more and more of these guys is that the Israelis are well trained, they have high-tech equipment—Apache missiles. These volunteers go to be Palestinian Apache missiles. They go and search for their targets. It hurts that a person dies this way, but we have no alternative. No one likes his army to die. Any army likes to keep its soldiers, but we have no alternative."

"Does it work?" I ask.

Ahmed answers thoughtfully, as if he is a general surveying a battlefield, comparing his fallen men to the enemy's. "It makes some kind of balance. If you calculate losses of the Israeli occupation to martyrdom you will see it is the most effective thing to make losses. In the Vietnam War, they had one American loss to every forty-seven Viet Cong. In our conflict it is one Israeli to every three Palestinians.

"We have a political goal to achieve. When a [Palestinian] person gets killed in his own city, in his own house, in his own bedroom; when women and children are victims, when they burn his land, uproot his trees, destroy his homes, it is normal for Palestinians to hate Israelis in our core as they hate us in their core. When we realize that the answer for all of this is so simple—for Israelis to leave the land—rage builds up. Rage also builds when the world looks at us as criminals and blames us.

"The occupation is against all international law and human rights! The American and British governments can press on any country of the world for what they want, but they cannot push such a wrong thing as for this occupation to end? We need help to gain security, for our children to live in peace"

Ahmed has a point—people who feel unsafe will resort to extreme measures if they believe it will restore their security. As he says, Palestinians feel pushed up against a wall and when they wish to fight back it's upsetting to be labeled as savages and denied the support of the major powers of the world. Yet he does not own full responsibility for the many terror acts Palestinians, including his own group, have committed against Israeli civilians resulting in a general backlash against Palestinians.

"Is a political solution possible?" I ask.

"If there is a problem, when do we say that it is over, solved?" he asks, then answers. "If we don't get to the bottom, it won't be solved. The South Africans used everything to fight and in the end they were given one country and elections also. My solution is to see Palestine as a democracy. No racism in it at all; not color, religion, nothing. I want the same thing that happened in South Africa to happen here."

Ahmed is advocating for a united state—not a two-state solution but Israel and Palestine united as a true democracy. It's a radical idea from the Israeli point of view, as it would do away with the "Jewish" state and everyone knows this "solution" would eventually end with Arab dominance due to the higher birth rate of Arab Israelis.

He explains that most Palestinians want what the United Nations General Assembly decreed for them: the occupation to be withdrawn, a country for Palestine, restoration of the 1967 borders, and the right of return for all refugees since 1948. However he does not think the UN decree can bring a lasting solution, only an end to the current violence.

In that scenario, he says, "There is still Jerusalem. In the West Bank there will be only Palestinians, but one million-and-a-half Palestinians live in the occupied territories [he is referring to Israel]. Of these, one million will probably return to us, the half-million that stay will still be Palestinians. How to resolve it when these Palestinians become one million, and then in another ten years they become two million, and in another ten years three million? The one and basic reason for the struggle will remain. To come to a real solution, we need a democratic country over all the land. Two people who live together. In democracy, it is not the occupier and the occupied."

"So you favor the one state solution?" I ask.

Ahmed nods. "I don't see this solution as near. It will come, but not now. Maybe in non-violent ways because we are not a violent people. In peaceful ways will be better," he says, but then contradicts his own words, "But we won't be satisfied with just talking. Maybe there are peaceful ways to struggle, but the occupation can only be fought in its way. The occupiers will not go out of the land by giving them flowers as in Prague. The Palestinians went to give flowers to the tanks and the Israelis answered them with rubber bullets and gas."

Al, whose hero is Mahatma Gandhi, is anxious to ask a question and whispers to ask me if he can. I tell him to go ahead.

"What about gaining world opinion by using Gandhi's methods? If you do, the world will see the Israeli violence and a non-violent response?"

Ahmed answers after a moment of thoughtful consideration. "Yes, before this Intifada there was peaceful talking. Even when Sharon went to the al Asqa Mosque, we just went to stop him. They started the violence. If I throw a stone at a tank what harm does it do? They still shoot the little boy who throws the stone. We go on strike, but after we go to the hospital wounded; we go on strike, but after we take the martyrs [those innocents who were killed] to bury them; we go on strike and it just goes in circles. The violence comes from them."

"But how do you justify sending bombers to civilians?" I interject.

"Our losses are civilian too," Ahmed says calmly. "We are allowed to die, to have no birds, no trees, bullets in our kitchens, all of this; but we are not allowed to hurt a civilian? We are civilians too!

"If you give us tanks, military trainings, jets, etcetera, then you will see that we fight with their army, not with their civilians."

"What's a rifle against a tank? And it's a rusty rifle! If you put a cat in a corner it will attack. So, what will happen to a human being?"

"It's their violence, Sharon's fault. It's so savage. If they elect a peaceful government then we will be able to talk. It's the Israelis themselves who elect and reelect Sharon."

I think how many times I have heard the Israelis say they have no partner for dialogue among the Palestinian leadership and now I am hearing the same from him.

As he speaks I recall the famous statement, "One man's terrorist is another man's freedom fighter." While terrorists are basically defined as non-state actors who target civilians with violence for political reasons, it is never simple and defining both them and their acts very often depends at least in part upon perspective. And Ahmed Sa'adat seems completely convinced of the righteousness of his cause and the legitimacy of his methods even though his group targets civilians.

"When people say, 'We fight only with the settlers'," Ahmed explains, "It's no different in any part of the whole country. They are all settlers! What we ask for is so simple. We want the occupiers to get out."

"How do you feel about the targeted assassinations?" I ask, knowing I am on sensitive territory because his friend and colleague Abu Ali Mustafa, the PFLP's former Secretary General, was killed by an Israeli targeted missile attack in 2001.

Ahmed answers, "It's one way of violence against the Palestinians—a very crude violence. Just to see the body afterward, it fills you with so much anger. They think it will solve problems, stop organizations, or terrify the people but the facts are against that. Occupation always goes for unreasonable things to justify its reasons."

Research supports his view. Scholarly analysis of Palestinian terrorist acts charted against targeted assassinations in the second Intifada shows that the Israeli policy of assassinations caused terrorist groups to suffer temporary setbacks in leadership, including the loss of bomb-making and other tactical skills and a delayed rebuilding of their capacities. The studies also showed, however, that the overall level of attacks did not diminish in response to targeted killings, and many groups also quickly replenished their ranks with even angrier young men[69]

I know that Ahmed ordered the assassination of Zeevi in retaliation for the killing of Abu Ali Mustafa,but I don't want to ask him to incriminate himself in case we are being recorded by the PA prison authorities. Instead I ask, "*If* you ordered Zeevi's assassination, how do you feel about it?"

"I don't believe in political assassinations," Ahmed answers with perfect calm, holding his hand to his heart in what looks like a genuine gesture to show the subject is a very painful one for him. "I'm just one of the people fighting for my freedom. The one who is forced to do something is not a hero. Any decision to kill is very hard, even if it was our enemy and he was so bad. But we have no other choice, because the pain is in every one of us and every one is forced to take this decision. If we don't kill him first, he will kill us."

"Abu Ali Mustafa was killed in a targeted assassination?" I ask referring to the former PFLP Secretary General.

Ahmed nods, his face filled with sorrow. "I saw it on the news. They fired two Apache missiles at him through his window in his office in Ramallah. He was alone in the room, so it was only he that was killed, but there were people all around, working nearby. I came after it happened. They wouldn't let me see him. It was so devastating for me, as for all of us."

"Do you know why the Israelis did it?" I ask.

"They said he had to do with violence. What does that mean?" Ahmed's voice becomes angry. "He was a leader of a political movement. It was so ridiculous what they said."

But it is not ridiculous because Mustafa and the PFLP have long been involved with violence so I ask, "Did he send "martyrs"?

"Yes of course," Ahmed answers, "but they are volunteers."

I am suddenly curious about this volunteerism and Ahmed Sa'adat's and other terrorist group leaders part in it. I impulsively ask, "If I ask to become a 'martyr' for you, will you give me a mission?"

Ahmed stares at me blankly and then turns to the others in the room. He is momentarily shocked by my question but recovers his composure and answers softly, "For me I prefer this person to do more than one thing. I want him not to die in only one strike, but to strike many times. But if one comes serious and wanting to, I will send him."

"And me?" I push.

Ahmed looks me carefully in the eyes, trying to gauge if I'm serious or just playing with him. He answers softly, "Yes, I will give it to you and love you. A person who dies for a noble cause deserves to be loved."

But then he quickly laughs, saying, "But what a shame for such a beautiful girl to die." Indeed, his party does not send women.

I can see his "love" for the person that would volunteer to carry a bomb. It's powerful and I can understand how volunteers come forward to receive his "blessing". For a young person who doesn't have much to lose, gaining Ahmed's approval could mean a lot.

I change the subject, as I don't like to think of offering myself—even in fantasy—to his cause. "You said you respected Abu Ali Mustafa so much and said he was not corrupted. Can you explain?"

"He was a volunteer for our political struggle, and he did not take financial benefit. He fought corruption inside and out. He was a real democrat in his leadership. He respected others and did not get angry easily. He treated his comrades with so much respect and lived like all others. He made less than one thousand dollars per month even though he was a leader."

"And Zeevi?" I ask. "There was no Apache missile for him, only bullets?"

"Mustafa agreed with me," Ahmed says. "He hated assassinations. But if we don't do to them, as they do to us, they won't stop."

"This is what Al was trying to suggest—that Gandhi taught the opposite and that by responding with nonviolent protest it shames the opponent and make his violence glaringly obvious in contrast to a nonviolent stance. You don't see it that way?"

Ahmed shakes his head. "When they killed Mustafa, we had to go back with the same or greater response, if possible. Our leaders are not as well guarded as theirs, but we can still reach them. Killing General Zeevi was the first action of its kind initiated by our group. He was a criminal. He killed Egyptians in jail. He was a racist also—the leader of Israel is our Home; their solution is to kick Palestinians out and have a pure Jewish country. He was one of the people who ordered the assassination of Mustafa and others. That's the point."

As we are speaking, the other prisoners begin to bring out food. There is a tray of tasty fried chicken pieces being offered around and another of drink soft drinks and juice. It's clearly time to wrap up our time together.

"How long have you been in this prison?" I ask as we wind our interview down.

"Since the first of May 2002."

"And how long are you in for?"

Ahmed shakes his head and raises his hand. He doesn't know how long he will be held this time. He explains that he, like the others we interviewed earlier, is an "open check" prisoner and that he could be released in a prisoner exchange.

"Bargains turn into political issues," he says. "I don't think it's for life, but Israel doesn't want Arafat to release me. There are two cases with Israel. If they take me [into their prison], they can keep me, or they will kill me; the easiest thing is to kill me. At any time they can do anything to me. Even if there is an international intervention, we are prisoners held outside of the law—without clear limit—we don't know if we are here for a definite time period that keeps renewing or an unlimited time."

I ask Ahmed about fear. He answers, "I try to defeat my fear in order to be able to defeat the enemy. But fear is a normal thing found in every human being. I always hope I can control my fear, although I believe in the duality of weakness and strength together. I cannot judge myself. Others will give the right judgment."

As far as terrorists go, I find Ahmed to be a very thoughtful leader. He is emotionally connected yet appears firmly in control of his emotions and able to reflect on his own actions. For the most part, he has not spewed rhetoric at us but tried to show his position, while still being able to step out of it to see other points of view. I tell him he is different from others we interviewed and he becomes shy responding, "The thing that confuses me most is to talk about myself."

I ask Ahmed if I can take his picture. As I snap his photo he no longer looks regal and expectant in his armchair, but rather vulnerable and alone. We shake hands, say our goodbyes and leave the prison, again walking underneath the sentries, this time waving to the British soldiers who stare down at us. We find a taxi on the street to take us back to the checkpoint.

The checkpoint is still closed, and there are twenty tense soldiers spread across the entry, blocking it and keeping the Palestinians at bay. From their stance, it's clear that no one should approach them, but I want to return to Ramallah so I walk slowly toward one of the soldiers with my American passport held out in front of me. The soldier waves aggressively with his gun, signaling for me to turn back. I don't obey and keep approaching slowly, warily watching his every move. When I get close enough for him to hear me, I call out, "Please, I am American and I have the phone number of one of your superiors. Can you call him, please, to get his permission to let us pass the checkpoint?"

The soldier comes to me and looks at the paper confirming I have an Israeli number. I tell him that Hamit told us to call if we have any trouble passing the checkpoint on our return trip.

"Are you all Americans?" he asks.

I indicate our group and pointing to each I tell him, "Al is Belgian, Ken is Irish and Jamilah and Yousef are Palestinians."

Vexed he cuts me off. "Just cross and get out of here."

Jamilah and Yousef point out that because the checkpoint is closed, there are no taxis waiting on the other side and that I must also ask for our taxi to come. He calls for it, and we cross.

As we make the drive back, the mountains on the Jordan side are lit in bright shades of red by the setting sun shining across the Dead Sea. I'm tired and watch peacefully as the glowing orb slides between the mountains, the Israeli sky burning with the last rays of daylight. The relaxation flows through me—until Al's highly agitated voice breaks it.

"He's a killer! He sent Hamdi to kill the Israeli tourism minister in cold blood," he says. "We shouldn't be listening passively to them spew hatred and their plans of violence. We should be talking to them about Gandhi."

"Yeah, like they are going to listen to us about Gandhi," Ken snorts. Al argues that we are complicit if we do nothing, his voice rising in anger. He suddenly turns to me.

"We have a responsibility to confront these terrorists!" he shouts. "You're just listening and taking notes like they are talking about the weather! What are we doing listening to these killers and doing nothing to stop them?"

"Al, we came here for research, not political activism," I answer as calmly as I can. "Maybe by learning and understanding we can make a difference, but that requires setting aside any agenda and just listening. If you disagree you are free to come back as a peace activist." This just makes Al angrier.

"Do you even know anything about Gandhi? Have you read his books?"

"I've read one of his books, Al."

"But did you understand it? Do you know what nonviolent movements are about?" I'm starting to get irritated back.

"I didn't memorize it word for word and I can tell you for sure he's not the only advocate of nonviolence that ever existed. There was Jesus Christ, there was Martin Luther King, there were many, and yes I do understand his ideas and I get what you're saying, but I don't share your agenda for our trip."

Al continues to lecture us, imploring us to read Gandhi, to understand his words, to teach the Palestinians to carry out his ways. If we don't, he says, getting even angrier, we are guilty as well. Yousef and Jamilah try to jump in but are quickly shut down.

"I actually found Ahmed Sa'adat a thoughtful person," I say.

"Did you see Hamdi, the killer of Zeevi? He's a cold-blooded assassin!" Al yells.

"You're right. I didn't like him either," I answer, starting to wonder what am I going to do if Al melts down on this trip. "Hamdi gave me the creeps. Listen, Al, I will read Gandhi's books again. It's a good idea. You have many good ideas. Let's try to think of the best ways to implement them. But for now let's give it a break, okay?"

Al goes sullen and silent, still highly upset.

After some time on the road, we are stopped again at an informal checkpoint. We all get out of the taxi to stretch our legs. Al is not speaking to any of us and when he wanders off to have a cigarette, Ken goes and smokes beside him. Al apparently gives Ken another earful, and after, the ever-provocative Ken comes swaggering back to me.

"Don't get too upset about Al," Ken says with mischief gleaming in his eyes. "I'll take him out tonight and get him drunk on his ass, and when he's good and drunk I'll take a swing at him. When he hits me back I'll ask him what happened to your fucking Gandhi?"

We both double over laughing, and Al catches us, his face getting even darker. I smile and realize Al is our sensitive one and that we have to love him as he is. As it turns out, all of us will have our own version of cracking under the pressure of these interviews.

CHAPTER 20

"I was Dead Three Times"

Following our interview of Ahmed Sa'adat, the guys head out to the student housing and I go back home with Yousef. The next morning Yousef and I make our way back to Birzeit University to hold a few more interviews in the cafeteria. The guys are nowhere to be seen, but I'm used to them dragging in late in the mornings.

I begin with a young man who wants to be called "Bashar". He is a slim dark student with a small beard on the edge of his jaw.

"I was [nearly] dead three times already," Bashar starts, leaning forward on his chair. "The Jews came to the university. We threw rocks and they shot bullets."

"What kind of bullets?" I ask.

"The first time they were real, the second and third times were rubber; but it's all the same [to me]. The first time I was behind a tree and the bullet hit my pants leg, the second time I was behind a railing and the bullets hit the metal, the third time I was by the phone booth and the bullets shattered the glass."

Bashar is studying political science but is an artist by inclination. He pulls out a collection of his drawings and explains them to me shyly. The first is a gallows.

"What does it mean to you?" I ask.

"It's what I expect of life,' he answers.

The second is a drawing of a man with disconnected parts lying on the ground and footprints all around him.

"He's been stepped on by everyone," Bashar explains. "The occupation, his own government, his people."

It seems to me that Bashar has drawn an image that represents a state of "dissociation", when the body no longer feels connected normally or parts of the mind, like the ability to think, feel or remember, drop out. His drawing reflects how many Palestinians experience themselves.

Next there is a hanging man in a shroud. With this one Bashar tells me, "I love death. I love drawing death, because it's strong."

"After death there is no more they can do to you?" I ask. Bashar nods and smiles, pleased to be understood.

"Death is stronger than life," he explains. "Hate is stronger than life. It's not that I love death and hate. I love these emotions because they are strong. They are wrong, but strong."

Bashar has explained the psychological concept of identifying with an aggressor. Victims often cannot stand to face their powerlessness and instead identify with the power of the aggressor, preferring to remember what hate and power feel like versus powerlessness and pain. As seen with Ahmed Sa'adat, this identification can result in re-enacting the aggressor's actions when memories of pain and powerlessness are triggered. Instead of feeling pain, the people choose to put themselves in the opposite position and aggress on other, new victims. It is why some child abuse survivors grow up to be abusers, why violence gets repeated over and over again, often being carried out by victims who should have empathy, but who cannot stand to recall their own powerlessness.

"Love—you can never express it enough," Bashar continues. "Hate you can. You can keep going perfectly.. . . Before the operation in Gaza, they shot a little girl with twenty bullets."

"Geez," I say reflexively.

Then he becomes reflective and says, "What they suffered under the Nazis makes them do this to us...all this hate they have."

"You really think so?" I ask.

"In the first Intifada they used to break bones," he continues. "If they caught someone throwing stones, they took a heavy stone and crushed your bone with that stone. They found it was of no use and now they stopped. I can show it to you, a guy from the French press made a movie of it."

"No I don't think I could bear to see it," I tell him. Later I will meet a Belgian extremist who did watch such films and was radicalized into terrorism as a result (see Chapter Fifty-five).

"I study Hebrew because I want to know the language of my enemy," Bashar tells me. I want to understand on the common level what they think."

I nod listening.

Bashar then tells me "The Jews see themselves as people. They teach their children a good Arab is a dead Arab." I am surprised to hear a Palestinian say this, as the usual outcry is the opposite – about Hamas materials indoctrinating Palestinian children to dehumanize and hate Jews.

"Will you teach your children to hate Israelis?" I ask.

"No," he says. "I will teach them their rights."

"So, are there are other ways to be strong besides hate and death?" I ask.

"I hope, maybe," Bashar answers. "What gives me hope is the difference between them and us. The most important thing to say to the world is that, in Palestine, we are living people: we laugh, we live, we cry. We don't *just* throw stones, fight, and explode ourselves. We are willing to die for our people. They are not.

"Bashar, if you carried a bomb, would you feel pity for your civilian victims?"

"No, because every one of them, if they have the chance to kill me, they will."

Bashar says he doesn't think he would ever have the courage to do a mission, but explains, "The minute [a bomber] thinks to do it, he's dead—a walking dead man. That's the strength of it. You can't stop martyrs from doing it because he's already dead."

"Do you personally ever feel this sense of living death?" I ask of what I would clinically label a dissociated sense of being—derealization or depersonalization—when normal sensations, emotions, even thoughts, drop out of everyday consciousness, or in the most extreme, when one feels that they are no longer even a person, alive or real.

"I feel it sometimes," Bashar tells me. "It lasts about an hour. It is all very black at those moments. But when I feel this way, I take all my feelings to motivate me to do good. I draw, I speak, I always change it to a good action."

I nod seeing that even though he admires death and hate for the strength he thinks they possess, he hasn't given up yet.

"Have you been in prison?" I ask.

"No," he shakes his head, "But I expect it everyday. Anytime they can grab you and take you. In prison I'm afraid of myself; that I will talk and betray others. I'm not afraid of torture. I think most of it is psychological, to find a weakness. They try yelling, sweet talk, even beating to find something weak. They try to give you the idea that they know everything. Some guys fall for that and start talking."

"Have you been stopped often by the Israeli soldiers?" I ask.

Bashar nods. "Once I was wearing the Palestinian necklace," he says, referring to a leather strap with a medallion hanging from it in the shape of the territories of Israel and Palestine combined that was covered completely in the colors of the Palestinian flag. The soldier who stopped me asked, 'What is this?' I said, 'Palestine.' He got angry and said, 'No it is Israel.' I thought if I agree I am nothing. If I argue maybe I will die. I said, 'No it's Palestine,' and we argued back and forth to the point where he pointed his automatic gun at me. I refused to agree. He saw this strength in me and he stopped. He let me go because he had no other choice but to shoot me."

Nadia, our translator from the first days, joins us and asks, "How can people in the West don't understand our situation? If they kill your brother, will you just sit there? Sharon keeps killing our people because he doesn't want us [Israelis and Palestinians] to live together."

Ken and Al finally arrive and greet us, breaking up the conversation. We catch up and it turns Al out has been doing interviews of his own with the Palestinian students he and Ken hung out with last night. One of the young men, Aziz, told Al that he would love to go as a "martyr" to avenge his father's death. Aziz said, "My father was a leader. When the Israelis killed my father they didn't consider that he had babies who would grow up without a father. It would be an honor to go to jail. If I carry a bomb, I want it to be a very big operation, like in Sharon's bedroom. I don't want to kill civilians, only people in power because they are the ones that make the difference." Al says Aziz quickly justified those who target civilians by pointing out, "Israeli kids grow up to kill our children."

"How would your mother feel if you went to be a martyr?" Al asked.

"If my mother knew that I want to be a martyr, she would encourage me and be the first one at the [obituary] demonstration."

"And if they destroy your home?"

"Even if Israelis come to destroy our house, it doesn't matter. Every Palestinian house is my house. Palestinians are one family so my mother will still have a family."

Al asked who will send him and Aziz answered, "I will go by Fatah or al Aqsa, and I will go to them, they won't come to me, but they will give me instructions on how to detonate."

"Will you tell your mother?"

"My mother doesn't know now, but she will be happy," Aziz said but then contradicted himself. "The time is not right to tell her. I would not tell my mother before it happens, because her first reaction would be to tell me 'Don't go'."

• • •

Our plane is leaving the next day and we need to get back to Tel Aviv. As we depart the university we make the rounds and say fond goodbyes to those we interviewed. I tell Mustafa to stay alive and am emotional as I wonder what will happen to him. We part from Yousef and Jamilah with even more emotion, promising that we will return soon.

As we leave, I am concerned that after all our success in the interviews, our materials could be confiscated at the airport. I don't want to be the cause of the Israelis making any arrests, and I also don't want to lose our work. We agree to go to an Internet café and type up the most worrisome of our interviews and e-mail them home from one of the Palestinian's e-mail accounts to Al's girlfriend. We figure that makes them untraceable to us if the Israelis go snooping into our e-mail accounts. I also Xerox all our handwritten notes and then we divide them into packets of originals and copies and send them home in two separate packages along with my disposable camera. We go to the airport without any evidence of our research trip in Palestine.

We take a taxi from our hostel in East Jerusalem to the airport, not realizing that a taxi with Palestinian license plates will arouse suspicions at the airport. Al has been given a PFLP flag from his new friends and has it folded in his pocket. We discuss briefly our anxieties about going back through the airport; if we will be searched, if the flag will be discovered, and if that can be cause for detainment. Al seems especially worried.

Ken is in the front seat with the taxi driver, and I'm in the back with Al, who has nodded off. Suddenly Al starts punching himself in his sleep, giving himself some pretty good hits to the face. I know that Al was hit as a child, but I've never seen anyone do this before.

"Ken, look at Al," I say, alarmed. Al continues to hit himself, and Ken and I gape at him in disbelief. The Ken characteristically begins to laugh raucously. "Look, he's beating himself up!"

"Al, Al! Wake up!" I say, shaking him gently. Al continues to hit himself, and then suddenly wakes up.

"Al, you're punching yourself in the face!"

"What?" he says groggily and laughs shyly when we explain what he was doing.

"Are you worried about the soldiers at the airport?" I ask him, rubbing his back soothingly.

"I don't know, maybe?" Al answers.

"Here go back to sleep," I say letting him rest his head on my lap as I continue patting his back. Al falls back to sleep again, this time peacefully. I think to myself, now *here* is childhood reenactment—when he anticipates being confronted by authorities he begins punching *himself*!

We arrive at the airport, and the soldiers at the checkpoint outside the airport become alarmed by the East Jerusalem taxi's license plates. They ask us to get out and take our passports. We look at each other each silently thinking,*This is it—we are about to be found out.* Ken nonchalantly tells the soldiers in Hebrew that we are in a Palestinian taxi because we had just been having a look at the Damascus Gate and caught a taxi from there. The soldier is reassured by Ken's Hebrew and charm and lets us pass without further questioning.

Inside the airport, we begin searching for our flight on the departure screens only to realize that I have misread our itinerary and we've missed our flights.

"Good one, Speckie," Ken says as we begin to realize that our flight does not leave at six p.m. today; it already left at six a.m.! I go to talk to the airline agent and she is kind enough to re-book them for us, but we head back to Tel Aviv with an unexpected extra night on the town. The guys are delighted.

"Let's go clubbing," Ken says. "The nightclubs here are great."

Al agrees but I have a better idea.

"Let's try to see Reuven," I say. My colleague, Reuven Paz, is an Arabist, world-renowned expert on al Qaeda and former Shabak intelligence officer who has spent years studying religious and political fanatics. His early career focused on the Palestinians and he is interested to hear about our trip. I trust him, so we meet that night and tell him where we have been and some of what we learned, careful not to reveal anything that could cause problems if he reports it to the authorities.

Reuven is fair, and it's good in a way to have an Israeli sounding board after being so deeply immersed in the Palestinian mentality. He acknowledges that many of the Israeli security practices, such as destroying homes or being too harsh at checkpoints, incite rather than curb violence. Reuven is amazed that we were allowed entry into the Jericho prison to meet Ahmed Sa'adat and also interested to hear how openly many Palestinians spoke to us.

"What should we expect at the airport in terms of search?" I ask. "We have a few things they might think is contraband."

"What kind of things?" Reuven asks. Al explains about the PFLP flag.

"I don't think it would go well for you at the airport if they find you carrying that flag," Reuven says. "I think you could be arrested."

"I have a few things as well," I add, remembering the wristband bearing the Palestinian flag I've been given by a child in Beit Fourik.

"I really don't want to give up the flag," Al says.

Reuven nods. "I could take these things and mail them to you if you want."

We agree and I take mine out of the bag I'm carrying, removing them from inside female toiletry items that have been wrapped up in underwear—all things that a security agent might be loathe to search. Reuven watches and says appreciatively with a big smile as I hand them over, "You'd make a good smuggler."

After dinner with Reuven, Ken, Al and I walk around Tel Aviv and because I don't want to be left alone at the youth hostel, I agree to go with them to a dancing club. There they drink and watch the Israeli girls dance, while I sit quietly sipping glass after glass of water, occasionally getting up to dance a bit to the music, soothing away the tension, until I also finally succumb to a couple of glasses of wine while waiting for them to be ready to return to our hostel.

Finally at three a.m., they are ready, and we walk a couple of miles through the city of Tel Aviv toward our hostel by way of the beach. When we look at the water beckoning in the moonlight Ken says, "What do you say to a midnight swim?"

"I'm game," I say and Ken and I toss our things down, throw off our shoes, and run into the lapping waves, laughing and diving beneath the water. Al stands back completely amazed and laughing.

"Come on in Al, the water's great!" I call.

"You guys are crazy," he argues.

"Suit yourself," Ken calls and slowly Al throws his belongings to the ground as well and dives in laughing alongside us.

It feels wonderful to be immersed in the warm seawater, rinsing off all the horror and sadness of what we have just taken into our souls. We swim and laugh together for about an hour, telling each other we are definitely *crazy* and then as the sun just begins to rise we head back along the beach to the hostel, arriving with our clothes dripping wet, exhausted and ready to flop down to sleep soundly anywhere.

After a short hour of sleep, we rise again and head out to Ben Gurion airport. Al is calmer now that he is no longer carrying the PFLP flag hidden in his back jeans pocket, but we all get nervous re-entering the airport, anticipating an encounter with security. Now we are aware that there are hidden cameras and plain-clothes security everywhere. As we stand in line to check in and put our suitcases through security detectors, female border police walk down our line, examining passports and asking questions.

"Where did you travel during your trip to Israel?" the soldier asks us. "Did you meet any Palestinians while you were here?"

"No," we answer, trying to remain calm and stick to our story about research. The woman asks pointed questions about where we stayed and is clearly not pleased to hear we used a hostel in East Jerusalem. Ken covers this, saying the others were fully booked. She obviously isn't sure about us but between my Holocaust research story and Ken's charm, she lets us pass.

On the airplane, Al orders hard drinks as fast as the stewardess will bring them. He's clearly agitated—it looks as though he's battling post-traumatic stress in full swing. The stewardess finally gets fed up and cuts him off. He turns to listening to music and the three of us try to coordinate our music players to all play the same songs at the same time, laughing as we pretend to dance in our seats. When we land in Zurich, Al says, "I'm so glad to be back in a democratic country and out of that fascist place." Ken and I look at each other a bit dumbfounded and begin to laugh.

In Brussels, we part with a big group hug and don't see each other until we meet after class in the student union a few days later to discuss how everyone's doing over a few beers.

"I've been having nightmares," Ken confides. "One night I saw Israeli tanks and babies being shot up. And the first day when we got home I flopped down on my bed fully clothed and I woke up with my thumb in my mouth!" He lets out a snort. "Now my roommates are razzing me about 'sleeping like a baby'."

"So much was really fucked up there," Al says with a shudder. "I keep thinking about it all, especially what happened in Nablus."

I also feel a nervousness I can't shake, my mind replaying the scenes of climbing up the embankment to the settler's road and lying on the other side in the short grass as the Israeli vehicle passed by searching for us.

"I can feel the fear and arousal still in my body. Can you?" I ask Ken and Al. They both nod. "I think we all have posttraumatic stress symptoms, but none of us will get a full blown case of PTSD as long as we let the experiences flow through us, and don't try to avoid dealing with all that we experienced: the fear, horror, inescapability and helplessness."

I point to the beer they are drinking and say, "That will help to relax for now, but the true healing is from being in safety and not avoiding the posttraumatic recall, letting it become part of our narrative."

It's true. We recover quickly from our small traumas but remain haunted that those we interviewed don't have our safety or luxury to recover from the many more traumas they have endured.

Chapter 21

Reentering Palestine - Hasharon Prison

It's March 2005, five months since our last trip, and we land again at Ben Gurion Airport on our way into Palestine for our second round of interviews. This time Ken, Al and I have a much better idea what to expect, and we pass through security uneventfully, exiting into the bright March sunlight. We hail a taxi and take it to a hostel in Tel Aviv not far from the beach. The hostel owners welcome us, handing us clean sheets and directing us to our respective communal rooms.

"Let's go for a swim!" I say, after wandering down the narrow bright blue painted hallways where I find Ken and Al emerging from the men's wing.

"I need a coffee first," Al says and Ken argues for a falafel so we agree to meet all needs and then hit the beach. After swimming, Ken remembers a certain bar from his days when he was studying at Hebrew U and thinks that it is on Allenby Street, so after showering and changing clothes, we head off down Allenby traipsing for miles in search of it.

"Listen Ken, I don't think we are ever going to find this place," I say after a few hours, my legs feeling as though they will give out.

"Yeah, man, we need to change the plan," Al says exchanging glances with me. We both know Ken is locked on to finding this bar and won't be easily talked out of it.

"Let's ask someone," I suggest and Ken rolls his eyes. When I turn to look around for who might help I settle on two nice looking girls their age to ask. As it turns out they are going to the *same* place and offer for us to follow them there.

"How did you do that, Speckie?" Ken asks a smile of amazement lighting up his face as we fall in behind them. "I think you are a witch! How of all the people on the street that you could have asked did you manage to pick these two girls who are going to the very same spot I've spent hours trying to find! And not only that, they are damn good looking!

"I guess I'm just a chick magnet—lucky you brought me along," I answer, shrugging it off as coincidence. Ken and Al laugh and agree that if I can keep finding them such nice looking girls to hang with, they'll never leave me back at the hostel.

This incidence of intuition doesn't particularly catch my attention - I simply want to sit down and enjoy a nice drink with my students and their new Israeli "girlfriends". Later though, when I do have time to reflect, I notice my intuitive gift becomes increasingly apparent as we travel in this free-fall sort of manner. It seems that when things are left open or when there is a need to find something I seem to have some sort of knack for asking the right people the right questions, finding the right interviews, or at least, empathetically or intuitively getting to the heart of the matter with my subjects.

At the bar, the guys have a few drinks and flirt shamelessly with the Israeli girls. At first, they talk about their work and school lives, but as they all drink more, the conversation veers into sexual topics. I sip my water, grateful to be seated on my bar stool and listen and laughs they banter back and forth.

"I was in love with an Israeli girl the year I was studying at Hebrew U, and we talked about marriage," Ken tells the girls. "I was willing to convert but I didn't know about getting circumcised!" That brings a heated discussion about adult male circumcision and if religious intermarriages are a good idea. Then the girls go on to say they admire northern European girls and wish to be more like them—flat-chested and less curvaceous. I crack up laughing and can't stop my maternal response, "But you Israeli girls are so beautiful with your long curly hair and hourglass figures!"

Of course Ken and Al second that opinion. After an hour or so, the girls invite us all back to their apartment. Unsure if I should continue tagging along, I ask Ken and Al their view. Without hesitation they answer, "Come on, Speckie, you have to come!" So I do.

The girls' apartment is in the city not too far from the beach near our hotel. It's on the second floor of a stone building, sparsely decorated inside with a trendy area rug, college style furniture, a few plants and hanging lamps finishing the look. After opening a bottle of wine, one of the girls brings out a bong asking, "You want to smoke up?"

Ken and Al enthusiastically agree while I groan inside. Marijuana smoking is decriminalized in Belgium so most students smoke freely whenever they wish with no worries about criminal penalties. I've already spoken to both of them about this: we need to obey the laws in Israel regarding pot smoking and all else, especially because we are going into Palestine to interview the sworn enemies of Israel on our trips—something that could make us targets for particularly harsh punishments. Steamed at how quickly they forget our agreement to only drink moderately and forgo all illegal drugs while in Israel, I watch as Ken starts preparing the marijuana leaves for the bong.

"Your weed is so bad here!" Ken says, laughing at how the packet of marijuana one of the girls has handed him is filled with seeds and other plant debris. "You should see what we get in Belgium. It's nothing like the crap you get here!"

I see that they are committed and I don't think I can stop them without making a scene so I lean back on the couch and think of all the other times they've smoked up and didn't get in trouble, and I hope this will be the same. As they smoke, the conversation mellows and eventually everyone is tired. We leave, Ken and Al promising to call the girls again tomorrow.

The next morning while Ken and Al sleep off their revelries, I get up early to stand on the main road near our hostel waiting for a good friend and colleague, Yoram Schweitzer, to pick me up. Yoram, who has been going in and out of the prisons for the last year obsessively interviewing the hard line militants of Palestinian Islamic Jihad and Hamas, has promised to take me with him today inside the Israeli prisons for interviews.

We frequently meet at international conferences and compare notes, and up to this point, I've heard a lot about Yoram's work from him directly, by reading his papers and from his international reputation as a terrorism expert. Yoram often sits unguarded in prison cells with ten or more tough male terrorists and uses an aggressive male-style of goading the prisoners with his strident Israeli views to provoke them into talking about their rationale, operational mentality, motivations for terrorism and world views. His approach is politically oriented and systematic, interviewing and re-interviewing prisoners to ask them details about information he learned in other interviews. I am a bit envious of Yoram's captive sample and his ability to circle in on each terrorist act, especially since I don't have the luxury of repeatedly interviewing my subjects. And my interviewees aren't gathered in prisons, bored and eager to talk to anyone who will listen. Instead they are free, wary and too suspicious to be approached more than once, often developing fantasies of me possibly being a spy or working for the security apparatus who may come to arrest them.[70]

Likewise, after our first trip into the West Bank, I've decided I'm no longer comfortable seeking out would-be suicide bombers. The ethical dilemmas posed by interviewing more like Mustafa and then walking away without knowing if they will go and blow themselves up are insurmountable. But Yoram's subjects are failed bombers, some who have even been suited in their suicide vests prior to being arrested, and the worry about them going active is removed.

In our discussions Yoram once said, "The failed suicide bombers are stupid, but the leaders are bright."

"To volunteer to carry a bomb you have to be traumatized enough to easily become dissociative," I had answered. "You think they are stupid when probably they are just going dissociative in response to your aggressive interviewing approach. Why don't you let me come along with you into the prisons sometime and I'll show you that this is the case?" All my requests to gain access to the Israeli prisons previous to this had gone unanswered and this was my way in.

I hop in Yoram's car, greeting him warmly. Yoram smiles brightly at my excitement, giving me background as he drives north of Tel Aviv to the Hasharon Prison. "There's no guarantee—we might not get in," he says as he weaves his car through traffic. "You never know, it's always touch and go with this work."

As the Hasharon Prison comes into view, I notice the sun is sparkling along the razor wire curled high atop the cyclone security fences. Yoram drives into the complex and I see multiple buildings nestled within the security perimeter. Outside a young female Israeli soldier has been waiting. She greets Yoram and escorts us into the first entry point. As we follow her I cannot help but notice her figure. She is tall, with long lean legs, her hour glass form fitting into a khaki top tucked into tight fitting khakis pants, all of it topped off with her long black curls flowing down to her waist. Walking behind her brings to mind Ken and Al's fascination with female Israeli soldiers.

"Chicks with guns" they drawled last time we were in Tel Aviv, nodding with appreciative smiles whenever we saw female Israeli soldiers toting their rifles in the city. When I asked them what exactly it is about pretty Israeli girls with guns, they became embarrassed muttering explanations about a girl with a gun being powerful, sexy and able to take control.

They'd like this one, I think to myself as we follow her, *especially with the pistol hanging on her hip and handcuffs dangling from her cinched waist.* It is definitely a juxtaposition, the gun and her beauty, and there's no question—she's strikingly beautiful. I smile to myself following her, unable to shake the label they have already planted in my mind: *chicks with guns.*

Yoram, I notice, is completely unaffected. Perhaps it's because most of the young women in Israel are exceptionally pretty and he is inured to it. He leads our way ahead to speak to another type of girl: the Palestinian failed suicide bombers housed in this high security prison. I wonder as we walk toward the security desk, *What they will look like? What will they tell us?*

Approaching the armored glass security console, Yoram speaks through the thick window to the guard and slides our passports through the small slot. I watch to see if there is any reaction to my American passport. Yoram shoots me a glance with raised eyebrows, shrugging his shoulders as if to say, *"Here's the critical moment."* We wait and then are passed through without question. We move through a metal detector and place our things into an x-ray machine. I put my purse through, deviously pleased that the guards don't notice my mobile phone or the plastic disposable camera in my purse.

"Switch off your phone," Yoram instructs after we pick up our things. Evidently phones are allowed. I decide not to mention the disposable plastic camera. It's the second time I've passed an x-ray machine with one of them—the cheap plastic must not show up in the machine. *Who knows,* I think to myself, *it may come in handy,* although I know I won't use it without Yoram's permission.

We move through a huge metal door of the type on ships or security vaults in banks, thick with heavy reinforced metal and huge rubber seals. The dull sound of its seals closing behind us gives me an uneasy feeling, like I'm being locked up. It's sobering and despite the discomfort, I force my mind into feeling what it must be like to be a prisoner brought through such doors.

We continue down a corridor and out into a garden area lush with green grass and potted flowers. It's a bit surreal for a prison yard, but we are not yet in the area where the prisoners are kept, and we continue along a sidewalk and into the offices of the prison director. The walls here are hung with colorful paintings, tastefully chosen, humanizing the place. Of course this is not where the prisoners live but private offices. Yoram introduces us and we shake hands. They speak in Hebrew and I wait silently smiling. So far, so good. We are in.

From there, I lose track of all the gates that we pass through, each briefly unlocked and swinging shut again, locking us in from behind. Repeatedly I feel a chill. *This is how it feels to be a high security prisoner locked within embedded cages.*

At the sixth or seventh door we are outside again, but there are no flowerpots or lush greenery here. We are in what seems to be the center of the complex approaching one of the wings—the women's, I assume. As we approach I notice someone has painted in blue a rather crude depiction of the Israeli flag with its prominent star of David on the white wall. It seems like an unnecessary reminder to prisoners that this is Israel where you are caged.

We pass through two more locked doorways and finally into a chain-link fenced-in reception area. "There are three women's wings here, but the one we go to now is the most difficult for me because of that witch Muna," Yoram explains. According to the agreement with Israel, Palestinian political prisoners have arranged for self-governance, meaning that the prisoners wear street clothes, cook their own food and appoint one of their own to be in charge of each cellblock. Muna is imprisoned for presenting herself over the Internet as "Sali," a newly immigrated Moroccan Jew, to sixteen-year-old Israeli Ofir Rahum and offering him "a good time." She invited him to bring condoms saying, "I don't want to get pregnant." When they met she persuaded Ofir to accompany her into the West Bank, to Ramallah for their sexual tryst, where he was ambushed and shot on his knees at close range begging for mercy.[71] In prison Muna has manipulated herself into a position of control and continues in her cold-hearted ways; she allegedly retaliated on one girl who challenged her authority by throwing boiling oil in her face and she dares anyone else to stand up to her.[72]

"You must be very polite to her," Yoram cautions as we wait in the hallway for the guards to bring Muna to us so that we may ask permission for today's interviews. "But don't show her too much attention either, as she is very egotistical and might insist on spending all our time being interviewed herself." He has already interviewed her extensively and I can see that he is disgusted and already bored by her. I nod while quietly looking around, getting my bearings and begin to walk around, testing the limits. Further down the hallway I see the prison cells, circling around an inner courtyard below us, caged completely by cyclone fencing and a grid of bars above, through which you can at least see the blue sky. In the courtyard are thirty or forty Palestinian women going about their activities, doing their wash, hanging brightly colored robes up on lines that have been strung along the perimeter of the courtyard. *How normal it seems and yet how odd,* I think. *It's like looking at a small village of Palestinian women.* It's also a bit like a zoo, and I feel deeply ashamed and at the same time excited by them. Some of them catch my eyes and smile greeting me in Arabic.

"Wa-Aleikum Salaam," I say in response and smile when they greet me. My fingers curl tightly into the fence as I squat down and bring my face close as I look at them and smile brightly in recognition.

Yoram finishes checking us in and calls me back. "Here's the room we'll use. Muna is here and she is giving me trouble already. Just be quiet and don't speak to her." I glance about the room taking in its furnishings: four plastic chairs, a wooden desk and huge fabric Israeli flag hanging on the wall behind the desk that faces the doorway. *That's lovely,* I think to myself as I imagine being a Palestinian prisoner facing the Israeli flag hung behind the interrogator. Yoram puts his things down on the desk and pulls another chair behind it saying, "Put your things down. We can sit here together."

"No Yoram," I answering laughing softly. "I won't be sitting *there* with you," indicating the chair he has pulled under the Israeli flag. I pull my chair to the other side of the desk and place another two chairs close by my chair—one for our subject and one for the translator—and explain, "This is how I do interviews. I sit beside and with my subjects, not separated from them, and certainly not under that flag!"

Yoram laughs. "Okay, do as you like. Today you are in charge." I wonder how long that will last, as Yoram is strong-willed, but I hold my ground for the moment. Yoram leaves again to speak with Muna, and I return like steel drawn to a magnet, a moth to light, back to the fenced in courtyard. This time the women speak to me in English.

"Pretty English woman, where are *you* from?" one of them says as she clips a colorful just-washed shirt up on the clothesline.

"Where are you from?" I ask in reply, deciding not to challenge their misperception that I am from England. They don't seem to speak much English but they understand enough to answer, "Ramallah ... Hebron ... Nablus," and I smile brightly as they rattle off the names of towns and villages in Palestine where I've been.

"I've been there," I nod excitedly. My heart moves with shame and pity. "I'm going over to the West Bank tomorrow," I say knowing I shouldn't say that here in the prison, but I can't stop myself. "Tell me your names and your towns and if I go there I will kiss your mothers for you. I'll tell them I've seen you here and you're okay." I know how few of the Palestinian families can visit their imprisoned relatives and how many of them long for any news of their jailed loved ones. I hand my tablet and pen through the open slot at the bottom of the cyclone fencing saying, "Write down your names and towns for me."

One woman climbs up on a bench and takes it from me. Eagerly they begin saying their names and where they are from as she records what they say on the tablet. Then suddenly the eager chatter goes silent. All the women turn and I see that a formidable young woman had suddenly entered the scene. She is tall, regal and wearing an abaya made of a rich purple fabric.

"Stop talking to her!" she orders firmly, gesturing for them to go away. Shocked and worried that perhaps this is the difficult Muna that Yoram has warned about, I struggle to come up with something to say to her.

"We were just chatting," I explain. "I asked their names and if I could kiss their mothers for them when I travel through the West Bank tomorrow and in the next days."

"We don't need *you* to kiss their mothers," she replies, anger clouding her brow. Our eyes lock as I read her fury and search inside for how to answer in a way that can dispel her rage.

"Your dress is very beautiful," I say, stupidly grasping for anything that comes to mind. "Purple is my favorite color."

Disarmed by a compliment, she spins on her heel and walks away. The Palestinian "village" of busy and animated women has disbanded and there are now only a few women left, all gathered far away on the other side of the courtyard. No one dares talk to me now and my tablet on which they were writing their names has disappeared.

I understand immediately that I have made a huge mistake. I walk back to the small room designated for our interview and wait for Yoram to return, fully expecting him to read me the riot act about how I have screwed up our interviews.

While I sit stewing anxiously, Muna and Yoram come up to the door still negotiating about who she will allow us to speak with. Muna is another woman altogether, dressed in western clothes, tough-looking and hardened. I meet her briefly and then sit down, still shocked by what has happened. I can see already I am going to have some difficulty processing all my own emotional responses to being inside a prison.

"Okay, Muna has agreed," Yoram says, returning to the room to take his seat under the flag and behind the desk. "Our first woman speaks Hebrew quite well so we won't need a translator."

I'm not sure that's a good idea, I think to myself. Isn't it a bit difficult to be interviewed in the language of her enemy? Can she really express in Hebrew what she feels about wanting to bomb herself? But I am in no position to protest and I am just glad to learn that I have not blown the whole thing by my curiosity overlooking the courtyard.

We begin with our first interview, a young girl named Suad who was slated for a suicide mission but arrested before she could carry it out. She tells us about being deeply affected by the images she viewed daily on television. When we finish she asks who to send up next.

"The woman in the long purple robe who turned everyone away," I say wondering if she would ever agree to speak to us. Obviously she is a powerful presence, fiery and full of things to share, and she speaks English.

"I'll ask her," Suad says as she leaves the room.

As we wait I begin sketching the prison interior and courtyard on my paper, trying to memorize it so I can later accurately describe it. As I am drawing I am surprised when the woman I asked for does indeed walk through the door with the same proud air. I shuffle my papers aside and sit up expectantly waiting to see what this one will have to say.

CHAPTER 22

Arin Ahmad

When Arin Ahmed, the woman in the purple abaya that reprimanded me in the courtyard, tells us her name, Yoram immediately recognizes her as the young woman who on May 22, 2002 wore a bomb-filled backpack strapped to her body for six hours while walking around Israel before deciding *not* to detonate. After the young man she had gone with had already exploded himself, Arin called her senders, Ibrahim Sarahne and his wife, to tell them she wanted to be taken back home. Yoram briefly explains this to me in a low tone as Arin sits down. Then I explain my study to her smiling appreciatively that she has agreed to an interview while I also wonder why she has now decided to talk with me. Perhaps she is curious about us as well?

"Where are you from?" I ask. "How long have you been here in prison?"

"Nazareth," she answers then clarifies that she had been living most recently in Bethlehem. "I have a seven year sentence. I've been here for three and a half years." She then turns the questions on me, making sure I come without condescension.

"How do you see us? We are human beings, we have minds, thoughts, beliefs."

I smile, appreciating her intellect, and nod in agreement. "Can you tell us about your history, your childhood and growing up?" I ask.

She seems mollified that I want to know her as a complete person, not just as a terrorist and begins. "My father died when I was six months old in a car accident. We moved to Jordan with my Mom. But then she remarried and I came here to live with my father's family."

What Arin is describing is normal in Arab culture. A divorced or widowed woman who remarries often leaves the children she had in her previous marriage with her husband's side of the family. As I listen to the break up of her family, losing first her father, then her mother, and the relocations that came with each, I note that these are a series of heavy psychological losses for Arin.

"They loved me," she continues, probably defending herself from the emotional pain that recalling her early years brings up. "My aunts love me so much. They gave me everything. I lived with them to twenty years old."

"How old are you now?" I ask.

"I will be twenty-four in two days," she says.

"Happy birthday in advance!" I say smiling.

"I don't like my age," Arin says. "I want to be older." Indeed her stature and intellectual presence is of an older more settled woman, someone who is cool and sure of herself.

Yoram jumps in, asking about her life in Jordan. "Where did you live? Wasn't life better there?" he asks.

"Amman, [in Jordan]," she answers. "It *is* a more difficult life in Palestine, but I was still young [when I moved back]. In Jordan we lived in a home. Here, there was more freedom. Males and females can be friends so it was better in Bethlehem."

It seems she tries to find things to compensate for all her losses, which is normal.

"And how are you withstanding prison?" I ask.

"If I don't stand [it], then I go to isolation," she answers. "I was just two months in isolation. You live your life with nothing, no hot water, no TV, no nothing."

"Can you tell us about what happened leading up to your imprisonment?" I ask.

"I was in university in business administration and accounting in Bethlehem," Arin begins. "I saw my friends living a very bad life," she says, contradicting her earlier statement that life is better in Bethlehem. "They would go at three a.m. to the checkpoints to reach the university at ten a.m. They suffered a lot of humiliations at the checkpoints—the soldiers told them bad words. We have to suffer and sacrifice our dignity."

"Were there other things you saw as well?" I ask.

"I had a boyfriend who was killed by the IDF." Arin's eyes pool with tears as she begins wringing her hands. "I don't want to talk about this," she says, glancing at Yoram and the Israeli flag displayed behind him. I smile, understanding it's probably too hard for her to open up about her posttraumatic grief in front of him given that Israelis killed her boyfriend, and wait in silence to honor her sorrow.

"Is this the thing that pushed you over the edge?" I ask gently.

She nods and begins again, this time a bit jumbled by her emotions. "I thought that my home will come in danger. That [the Israelis] can come and fight us. There is nothing to do as a girl. I haven't any weapon and I have to save my world. This was the only way to play my role, my responsibility to my nation, my family..." She pauses. "At the last moment I changed my mind.

"We deserve a lot more than anyone else . . . I have to fight for my life. I have to live my life as any girl. I wanted to work in a bank. It's my right in my country to go to the disco, the park, a garden, in a car, to go to the sea whenever I want. All of these desires are forbidden because we are under occupation. All things are forbidden. You cannot go anywhere. I like to smoke and dance with the girls."

"You took the bomb after your boyfriend was killed?" I ask.

"Yes," Arin answers. "It was two months [after he was assassinated]."

"What was his name?" Yoram presses in his interrogator style, but Arin answers, "I can't say his name!" She has tears again in her eyes and looks at me as if pleading with her eyes to change the subject. "Not yet. He's still a part of myself."

"His death was really traumatic for you?" I say trying to deflect the pressure from Yoram's question.

"My mind was stopped. My thoughts, my life was stopped. Everything was black. I cannot sleep," she says, slipping into the present tense as she recalls the memory of that time.

"Did you see pictures of the assassination?" I ask.

"Yes, many times." I later learn Arin's boyfriend, Jad, was found incinerated in a car that Palestinians claim was hit by an Israeli missile, a targeted assassination aimed either at him or the other militant occupants of the car. Israelis say it was not their missile that killed him and claim he was rigging the car with a bomb and it exploded on him. All that was left of the passengers were their charred remains.[73]

"Once he came to me [in a dream or daytime hallucination]," she reveals.

"'Arin, I'm here,' he said. 'Look at me. I am here,' he said.

"I feel him all the time." Arin inhales deeply.

"Who asked you to take this mission?" Yoram jumps in interrupting the moment.

"I wasn't asked," Arin corrects him. "I went to the group and said 'I want to make a suicide bomb'. I didn't have to explain anything, only this one sentence. They gave it to me in three to four days." *How quickly they become activated!* I think to myself.

"Do you think becoming a hero in your society gave you any motivation?" I ask.

"I didn't care about [martyr's] posters," Arin says, smiling and shakes her head. "They will fall off [the walls]. I wanted my family to remember."

"How did you feel and what did you do between the time you asked for the mission and the time you went?" I ask.

"I was not talking with anyone, just in my imagination. I looked at my aunts and said goodbye to everything," Arin explains.

"You felt a bit dissociated, disconnected from your normal feelings and normal sense of self?" I ask.

"Yes, I was not normal," Arin answers. "I felt disconnected from them and they felt it. They asked, 'What's going on with you?' I said I was sick. I wrote a letter for them saying, 'Forgive me and I'm really sorry. This is my life, and I want to end it in my own way.' When I came back, I destroyed it."

"Can you describe what you felt when you put this bomb on?" I ask.

"I wore it for six hours. I went out of the house to Yehuda," Arin explains referring to a city in the Tel Aviv district of Israel. "I was not in consciousness. When I meet bad things, I move away. I collect the bad things and I work them out inside myself." I nod—I have already seen her avoiding thinking and talking about negative thoughts in this interview.

"What brought you back to feeling again?" I ask.

"I was very nervous," Arin answers. "I felt my mind stopped. For these six hours I can't think. Just at the last moment I looked at the people, looked at babies—I saw babies! I thought, *If he dies what should I tell Allah? What should I tell him?* If he wants to cut my life and take my soul, [he can], but I don't have the right."

Arin says she took the bomb-filled backpack off herself but explains that turning back was complicated.

"I made a video. [After that,] it's forbidden to come back," Arin states, confirming what Israeli counter-terrorism expert Ariel Merari argues—

that making a video before a mission locks the would be bomber into the mission, although in Beit Fourik our earlier interviews disconfirmed this view.

"What happened when you said you wanted to return and not carry through your mission?" Yoram asks.

"I argued with them. [Sarahne's] wife screamed at me but eventually her husband gave in. They took me back [to the West Bank] after three hours. I can change my mind anytime! It's my mind! It's my life! No one can tell me! It's my life, my decision," Arin states, her eyes a bit unfocused as she seems to relive the argument.

"What do you want to be now that you have the rest of your life back?" I ask.

"I don't know," Arin muses. "I have to be unique." She ponders a bit and then asks herself, "How to get there? I don't like my life. I don't have any rights. I can make from myself a bomb just to tell you and all the world [that] there is a nation that wants to live his life the same as any other nation."

"So for you, blowing yourself up would be an act of expression?" I ask.

"Yes," Arin nods eagerly, happy to be understood. "It's the most important.

"But now you are against it?" I ask.

Arin nods. "If I hurt from something, it's not the answer—of course not! I don't want anyone to repeat this experience! We are here [in prison] now to change, to dream what we want when we get out. There is a message here for me."

"Your boyfriend understood you, that you wanted a career and wanted to be free as a woman?" I ask.

Arin nods smiling quietly as she remembers him. "Yes he understood me and supported me."

"That's not so easy to find among Palestinian men?" I probe to see if she will open up further about her boyfriend.

"If you have a special idea," Arin says, "and don't look like all the others, it's very difficult to find others who will understand you. Our society doesn't understand us. [But] if not today or tomorrow, they have to say Arin is one of us."

Arin is talking about feminism;[74] a journalist, Barbara Victor, has just come out with a new book called <u>Army of Roses</u> that is based on interviews about the recent Palestinian female suicide bombers that makes an argument that feminist strivings are integral to understanding the motivations of female suicide bombers. Victor states that Palestinian women volunteer for suicide missions because they have no fulfilling roles in society and furthermore are "damaged" or "compromised" in some way, so they volunteer to escape their constricted roles—taking on this one open role for them as a form of feminist protest. I don't agree with Victor's thesis given all the other more compelling reasons active in the conflict zones like trauma, dispossession, outrage, etc. that seem to motivate both men and women to go as bombers, but I feel I must ask Arin about it, especially since she obviously is concerned about feminism.

"Did the struggle for women's rights affect you at all in your choice to go as a bomber?"

Arin laughs outright at the idea, shaking her head as she laughs and answers, "No!"

"Your act was not a feminist statement?" I clarify.

"No! That's stupidity!" Arin says. "I give my life just to say 'No!!' [to the occupation]." Arin contemplates a bit then adds, "I can fight in my own society to express my rights as a woman. Anyway I can get my masters degree, a good job and go where I can affect our society's mindset."

"Barbara Victor wrote that women who take bombs have been sexually compromised, are infertile or somehow cannot fit into Palestinian society because it's oppressive to women, so they fight for feminism by becoming equal as suicide bombers. Do you agree with her?" I ask again, pressing the point.

"You want to explode yourself for infertility?" Arin asks, her eyebrows raised and her face aghast. "That's stupidity! You have to deal with Allah!"

"What about for sexual relations?" I ask, hinting at the rumors of some women having been sexually compromised.

"You will die for this?" Arin asks, throwing her hands up.

"What about adultery?" I ask.

"No!" she answers. " I can speak to Allah, and he will forgive me."

While it seems that Arin is making light of getting caught in illicit sexual relations in a religiously conservative society, she is also making it clear that she would not chose suicide as the way to resolve these issues.

"Take Ayat [al Akhras]," she continues. "She was engaged and very clever in school. She was a very unique girl, very polite, very respectful and loves life. Then she became a bomber. Why? Some people said that she slept with her fiancé and wants to break up. It's not true. I know she was in love with him for four years before the engagement. I know it is so."

Arin rolls her eyes. "If people believe these rumors . . . There doesn't have to be that type of reason. Every girl can decide for herself."

"All the journalists say we have a bad [oppressive] culture. We are normal people. We live our lives as you do. Before I did this, I dressed the same as you [in Western style]. But one day after my boyfriend died, I changed [and took the hijab]. Maybe things were needed to change in my life. When I dressed, I thought I can live my woman's life with a cover or without a cover. When I want to be in touch with Allah, I have to give him all his rights."

"Looking back now do you feel the senders used you in your moment of grief?" Yoram asks.

Arin looks down at her hands for a minute and then looks at Yoram with sad eyes answering, "Yes, they definitely used me! They exploited me at a very vulnerable time. I would never have done that at any other point in my life."

Yoram signals that he wants to end the interview and go on to the next one, so we end thanking Arin and I thank her for speaking English with us as well.

"I speak German, too," she says modestly.

"I hope the best for you and that you will be released soon," I say as we stand up to part.

"Please pray for me to get out, and if you go to the West Bank please light a candle for me," Arin says. Then she adds, "I was taught in Christian school. Many nights I say Christian prayers. We all talk to one God. He can speak all languages."

Later, when Israeli criminologist Anat Berko publishes her research findings from her extensive and creative work interviewing Palestinians inside Israeli prison, I find Arin's case among them. Berko also found Arin, who she referred to using the pseudonym Shafiqa, as "charismatic, fluent and full of self-confidence and determination".[75]

Arin confided in Berko as well about her feelings of abandonment at age ten when her mother remarried. "I was very angry with my mother," Arin related. "She deserted me and remarried, even though she knew that my father's family would take me from her". Arin also shared with Berko that shortly thereafter her mother had another child – a boy - with her second husband making her feel even more abandoned and replaced.[76] Likely these early abandonments made the loss of her boyfriend – yet another abandonment of sorts – even more painful to Arin.

Arin also elaborated to Berko that she had been afraid to marry because she feared that Jad would be killed by the Israelis for his militant activities. Contemplating that crisis time in her life after Jad's death and wishing then to die as a "martyr", Arin told Berko, "I thought I would meet him in paradise". Reflecting on her thoughts once she had accepted the mission, Arin recalled, "It was wonderful to say goodbye to life. I felt I was up in the clouds from the moment I knew I was going to become a shaheeda [martyr]."[77]

Arin also recalled the actual operation to Berko. "I was in a car with a sixteen year old boy," she said. Dressed by her handlers in tight pants and a midriff top with the bomb strapped to her in a backpack the pair were driven into Israel to carry out their joint suicide missions.[78] "The two of us were supposed to blow ourselves up in the same [general] area," Arin told Berko.[79] The plan was for Arin to detonate minutes after the boy in order to cause maximum carnage as civilians ran from the first explosion toward her.[80]

Arin recalled that they were each prepared separately and she met the boy only two hours before their attack. "He was only a boy; what had he seen of life? I could also see he didn't know why he was going to do it.[81] He didn't say anything, he was closed off within himself and sad," she recalled to Berko. "I couldn't stop thinking how young he was and about how he hadn't lived at all and about how he really didn't know what he was doing to himself and his family. . .When we got there, I asked him if he was certain he wanted to [do it]." Arin recalls that she couldn't get through to him because "he was focused on what he was going to do."

To me this sounds like the typical dissociative trance that suicide bombers seem to enter before exploding themselves.[83] Her normal emotions and cognitions dropped out until Arin encountered a woman with a little baby in a carriage and was brought to her senses realizing what she was about to do was not right.

At that point, Arin told Berko that she called her senders telling them to come take her back.[83] "They hung up on me, they told me that lots of people were waiting for me to blow myself up, so I had better do it." Arin called them three times until they finally came to take her back.

As Arin recalls that tragic phase in her life when she almost exploded herself among families and takes total responsibility for her actions. But she also places clear responsibility upon those who took advantage of her in her moments of unbearable grief. Arin told Berko, "The people who recruited me and dispatched me, used and abused me."[84] Indeed after her grief subsided Arin no longer believes in suicide missions and confirmed to both Yoram and I that she longs for peace.

CHAPTER 23

Omaia Damaj

As Arin exits her interview, Yoram follows her out of the room asking, "Say, given your English is so good, would you be willing to help translate for our next interview with Omaia Damaj?"

Arin agrees and goes off to fetch Omaia, a twenty-seven year old Palestinian who has been imprisoned for two and a half years for attempting to carry out a suicide bombing inside Israel. When the two appear together I can see that we have already received a favorable report—Omaia, a petite young woman dressed in a striped blue abaya enters the room in an unguarded manner and seats herself in a relaxed way, smiling to signal that she is ready to speak openly with us.

Yoram sits back as I explain my study to her with Arin translating into Arabic. After receiving her consent, I ask, "Can you tell us why you are here and how long you've been in prison?"

"I was a suicide bomber," Omaia answers belying her petite frame and soft voice. "I planned to make it, but I did not succeed," she explains. Her sweet smile seems as though we are discussing some kind of athletic event, not the explosion of her own body intended to murder as many innocents as possible. "I was a volunteer to Fatah in April 2002 during the IDF operation [in the Jenin camp]."

"Did the sending organization matter for you?" Yoram asks.

"I wanted to be Fatah," Omaia answers. "I believe in Fatah. I believe like them."

"How did you know how to volunteer?" Yoram fires off his question. I squirm uncomfortably at his interrogation and constant confrontation, though I know he has had successful interviews in these prisons.

"I knew he was a sender. He was someone that everyone knows does this," Omaia answers her brown eyes widening as she recalls. "He's dead now. He asked why I wanted to do it and I said because of the poor babies who died in this operation," she says referring to the blockade of Jenin during *Operation Defensive Shield.* "He took care of me until I was ready to go explode myself."

"How long did it take for him to accept and train you?" Yoram asks.

"After requesting it, I was mobilized for the operation in two weeks time," Omaia answers. "There was no preparation. He took care of what I needed. He wanted me to live a normal life up until going on the operation. He took the time to ask about me from others during those two weeks—he checked on me."

"Why did your sender check on you?" Yoram asks.

"Because I worked inside Israel," Omaia answers. "He asked me why I wanted to explode myself because I was the first girl in my area to volunteer." Omaia suddenly draws herself up proudly, relishing the distinction and honor that would have come to her posthumously had she completed her task.

"And your reasons were?" Yoram asks again.

"There were two invasions in Jenin: the first around the borders, the second one was the heavy one," Omaia answers.

Omaia explains she made her decision after the first invasion into Jenin, and the second one, which occurred while her sender was checking her background, confirmed her desire to suicide bomb.

"The tanks, guns, helicopters, the heavy operation in the camp—these all made my decision," Omaia answers. I have the feeling knowing Yoram is Israeli, and maybe even the large flag on the wall behind him, figures into the grit that has entered her voice as she continues. "It was a Holocaust in my eyes. I can't imagine how I can live in this humiliation. The Jenin operation and destruction made it absolute in my mind. It was normal for us to see soldiers killing [Palestinian] people at the checkpoints. I saw so much on television—bodies killed in Gaza and the little baby girl [killed]. This was a big thing for me."

"Did you see the baby die?" I ask knowing much of what she has listed are things she only heard about or viewed over television.

"The baby was killed in front of my eyes!" Omaia answers, fear crossing her face—although I think she is still referring to what she saw on television.

"You had been involved in Fatah previously?" Yoram asks, as I laugh to myself at how we are conducting this interview. I am so much more interested in who she is and what she has experienced to make her into a terrorist but he wants to know operational details: how the groups work, who they recruit, how they train and make their decisions on who, when and where to activate a suicide bomber. These are all important questions, but his manner of shooting them off somewhat aggressively interrupts the flow I would like to establish, which would help her reveal her inner life. Yet, I cannot be upset with Yoram for his continually peppering her with the questions he wants asked because it is only by his grace that I am even here.

"No I was never before involved," Omaia answers meekly as she turns herself back to Yoram. "I was working the vegetable fields [inside Israel]. I don't have any weapon," Omaia continues, her small voice and hands flailing powerlessly as she becomes agitated. "I don't know how to obtain a weapon and fight against this injustice. This is what I could do."

"Why did Fatah agree to send you?" Yoram asks after musing over the operational components again.

"In our religion we have the right to fight," Omaia answers.

"How did you communicate with your sender?" Yoram asks, cutting off her religious justifications.

"There was a connection between us," Omaia answers. "By phones."

"How did he check you?" Yoram asks.

"In the camp, in our culture, if the girl is polite and has nice manners and comes from a good family this makes people believe in her and fight for her," Omaia explains.

"Did he become your boyfriend?" Yoram challenges. "Did you make love with him?"

"No! Absolutely no!" Omaia exclaims and both Arin who is translating and Omaia look completely shocked at the question.

"So how long was it between learning you would go on a mission and actually going to get the bomb to carry it out?" I ask, shifting her focus.

"Fifty-five days," Omaia answers. "Three months."

"How did you feel during that time when you knew you would be given a bomb and were waiting to go?" I ask.

"I felt myself above the ground." Omaia's face takes on a look of elation. "I felt myself as a soul, as if I was playing. I felt happiness. I felt like there was something running in front of me—my destiny." Omaia begins to act giddy and giggles with delight.

"Did you waver during that time?" Yoram asks.

"No, I never wavered," she answers. "I never wanted to change my mind."

"What if you wanted to back out?" Yoram asks.

"If I wanted to change my mind?" she asks. Yoram nods and she continues, "Yes, I can. It's not forbidden. But I did not want to at all. It's forbidden *inside of me* to change my mind after making it."

"So you could back out if you wanted to?" Yoram asks.

"Yes. They even told me that if I feel tired and do not want to make it, don't. No one forces us," Omaia explains. "I forced myself."

"So how did you psychologically deal with this long time of waiting to carry your bomb—fifty-five days of knowing that any day they could call and say today is the day that you will go to explode yourself?" I ask.

"It was the nicest time that I lived in my life," Omaia recalls her face beaming. "I was so happy. I was thinking only of this, not at all of material things. The happiness comes from [knowing] that a high-up man will trust me with this mission. It is a very big honor."

"Did you behave as usual?" I ask.

"Yes," Omaia answers. "There was no work [due to the invasions and closures]. I stayed at home. I wanted to stay sitting with the family, talking and laughing and looking at them in a deep way. I was looking at them as if saying goodbye, that I would never see them again," Omaia becomes more serious. "My mother felt the change in my heart and commented on it.

"Then the invasions solidified it. Our home was destroyed so my mother was busy. She couldn't notice and all the changes [in me] could [also] be from the invasion."

"What were your thoughts during this time?" I ask.

"My thoughts were [about how] I would take off the suffering from my camp and my people. This is the only way to make a message. I didn't want to kill any women, old people or babies. My explosion was supposed to be inside a camp of soldiers."

Her desire to make a message tells me that the expressive act is important in her motivations—she wanted the Israelis to understand the suffering and outrage they had caused in Jenin and in the West Bank during *Operation Defensive Shield*. Of course the militants and terrorists were in large part the reason the Israelis had come to invade these cities, but from her point of view, she believed her act might make a difference and cause the Israelis to think twice.

"You wanted to send a message?" I ask.

"Yes," Omaia answers her face scrunched in anger. "To send the message to those people who destroyed our camp, 'We killed you in our place.' I wanted to let their parents know what they did and feel the same that we suffered."

"You wanted revenge also?" I ask.

"Revenge?" Omaia reflects. "Yes, of course! When you see all your life destroyed, of course there is nothing to think of except revenge."

As a psychologist, I find this revenge mentality interesting as it misses the point of understanding why the other side acted and instead, just blindly strikes out again perpetuating the cycle of violence.

"Was any of your motivation out of a desire to be equal to the men, any desire for feminism?" I ask, picking up on her earlier comment she made about being honored by a high-up Fatah operative allowing her to carry out this mission. I catch Arin's eye as she translates. She smiles sarcastically but translates the question without commenting.

"No," Omaia answers and then adds, "If this helps women's rights, that's okay."

"How did you feel about Wafa Idris [the first Palestinian female bomber]?" I ask.

"I wanted to be like her," Omaia answers. Indeed it seems that had Omaia's operation not been delayed she may have had Wafa's place of distinction in Palestinian memory. "I was the first woman in the West Bank to try [for a suicide mission]," Omaia states implying that she volunteered before Wafa has gone on her mission.[85]

"What do you think about the other female bombers, about why they go?" I ask.

"All of us are the same," Omaia answers. "We are sisters refusing occupation."

"Do you see a difference between the men and the women who volunteer themselves for these missions?" I ask.

"It's the same," Omaia answers. "What he gives, I give. But he has many more choices. We have not. He can fight in other ways." This for me answers again the question that Barbara Victor posed and answered, claiming that Palestinian women go on suicide missions as an act of feminism trying to become equal in death to their men. I don't see it that way. It seems Omaia is honored that she can fight like the men and give her life, but her motivations for volunteering are not to express a feminist yearning, nor to overcome, as Victor argued, any deficit she has as a Palestinian woman, but pure and simply to express her outrage over the injustices of the occupation and to fight and revenge for it.

"Did you make a video during this time?" Yoram asks.

"Yes, it took a long time to make it. There was also a letter to my family in which I was saying goodbye. My family found it that night [that I made the video]. [After she found the note] my mother was praying for me to return. I came back at ten p.m. All my family was crying. When they saw me they were happy. My mother asked, 'Why did you write this?!' I said, 'Oh it's just imagination that I am shaheed [a martyr].' They didn't believe me and I was kept home [for some time] after that.

"But as time went on, I convinced them about the letter—that it was just my imagination. I'm so soft and cute at home that they believed me."

"Tell us about the video tape," Yoram says.

"I posed with the Holy Quran and a gun," Omaia answers. "When I made the tape it all came closer and became more real. I became more happy. I liked that feeling!" she says clapping her hands together in delight and laughing somewhat drunkenly.

"You felt a sense of being high—like drugs, bliss perhaps?" I ask, watching her carefully as she becomes increasingly giddy.

"Yes, yes," Omaia says. "It's very strong! A high, yes; bliss yes!" She laughs describing her "high" now in the present tense.

Curious at what is happening in front of my eyes I turn to Arin. "Arin do you see what has happened just now—her giddiness as she recalls this waiting period?" I ask. Arin nods, her expression serious, confused to see Omaia become almost drunk before our eyes. "I think she is reliving this emotional state she was in and I want you to ask her please if she was using drugs, drinking or having sex at all during this time to create this intoxicated kind of high, okay?"

"No," Arin says glancing at Omaia and shaking her head. "That is an extremely insulting question, and I'm sure the answer is no."

"I'm also almost sure it's no," I explain, locking eyes with Arin so she will listen and do as I ask. "But you see this change in her, this almost drunkenness as she recalls?" Arin nods glancing again curiously at Omaia. "I think it is endorphins," I explain, "that her brain produced this state to cope with the horror of waiting so long under the stress of knowing she could be called at any moment to go explode herself, and I think she is reliving this endorphin high right now in front of us, producing it again right here as she recalls it. That's why she looks drunk now in front of us! Look Arin, if she can reproduce this state of being at will, it might be useful to her in surviving years in prison," I explain, trying to get Arin's buy in.

Arin nods agreeing that what we are witnessing is very strange, as though Omaia has imbibed a few shots of hard alcohol or drugs as the interview went on. Arin turns to Omaia and delicately frames the question explaining why I'm asking it.

"No!" Omaia answers shaking her head, her eyes wide in amazement and smiling sweetly, "I never took drugs or drank or had sex! It was just *a very precious time.*"

"But you did feel a sense of giddiness, as though you were almost high or drunk as you waited?" I ask.

"Yes!" Omaia giggles. "I don't know what drugs and alcohol feel like but I felt very, very high. Yes!" she explains giggling again.

"And you feel it strongly again here when you recall that time?" I ask.

"Yes," Omaia answers. "Many times I make this, but it's not as strong as the first time."

"Tell me how to do this!" Arin exclaims, turning to me. "Tell me how to make this in my mind too!"

I look at them and then at Yoram, realizing I won't have the time or luxury to teach them this, although I would like very much to give these young women something back to help them cope with prison life.

"You can create this state of mind through self hypnosis or by facing your own death by explosion," I say. "If you felt it before, the best way to get it back is to reenter the memory and reactivate it that way. For you," I look at Omaia, "you can reactivate it very easily by going into the memory as you did today, although likely that will fade over time," I add knowing that the more times she reactivates this memory-brain-body state, the less powerful it is likely to become.

"Did you feel that sense of high with the suicide belt on?" I ask turning to Arin.

"No, I knew my boyfriend had died so I can die anyway," Arin explains, her voice dulled with depressive pain of remembering her reasons for volunteering. In contrast to Omaia, Arin had been deeply bereaved and felt no euphoria over the perceived glory of ending her life. She simply wanted revenge and to reunite in death with her dead boyfriend. "I can live through it for revenge and to fight back for our humiliation, and to make a message [to the Israelis]," Arin answers. "I was willing to die, but it was not suicide. It was that I have a message. If I wanted to commit suicide I can cut my wrists, but I have a message."

"When you were arrested you were disappointed?" I ask Omaia.

"Yes," Omaia's giddiness fades suddenly as she adds, "All my dreams were gone."

"How were you arrested?" Yoram asks.

"It was one month after the invasion," Omaia answers. "I went to the Israeli checkpoint on the day of my explosion. I was going inside Israel to meet with the person who had the bomb, to put it on, but I was arrested on my way to the mission."

"What is attractive in dying?" Yoram asks.

"It's not attractive to die," Omaia explains, "but the happiness when others explode—this happiness, I wanted to give to other people." Omaia is referring to the jubilation among Palestinians when a suicide bomber strikes leaving terror in the hearts of their enemy.

"Were you worried about your family?" Yoram asks, referring to the Israeli policy of home destruction after a family member strikes.

"All the time they say they will destroy our home, but it was already destroyed!" Omaia says, challenging him with her eyes. "I knew they will cry, punish themselves and so on. They will ask why? Maybe my brother and sisters will forget, but my mother never will!"

"Looking back now do you have another opinion of your actions?" I ask.

"I don't second guess. What happened, happened," Omaia answers. " I don't feel it's wrong to explode."

"Is carrying out suicide operations the only way to fight occupation?" I ask.

"After I think in my mind," Omaia answers, reflecting on her time spent in prison contemplating her choices, "now I see that I can fight in another way. I can teach my sons to be doctors and lawyers. I can help babies and children to be happy."

• • •

With that we end our interview, thanking Arin and Omaia. They leave back to their prison cells and Yoram turns to some business with the guards so I exit and walk along the fence over to the prison cells that line the walls on the left of the courtyard. The cell doors are heavy metal with a small barred opening at eye level. I walk up to one of the cells and look into the opening. Inside there is a Palestinian woman dressed in a green abaya who smiles when she sees me.

"Salaam Aleikum," I say, smiling back to her. "Is it okay if I look in?" I hope that she will understand some English.

She doesn't. But she beckons for me to have a look and begins to pantomime so I can understand: showcasing her small cell while describing each feature in Arabic and smiling cynically. She points out the old tube-style television placed on a small table against one wall, her bed against the other and a small chute that is in place of a window and I assume she is saying, "Here is my television, here is my bed, and here is my window, if you can call it that."

"Come in," she seems to say as she beckons, speaking in Arabic, and I understand that she is inviting me in. The heavy door to her prison cell is bolted with a large lock, so I go back to Yoram, telling him to come.

"Noooo!" he says. "I cannot even walk down that corridor. I could be accused of impropriety!"

"Let's ask the guard," I say. "One of the prisoners invites us into her cell!"

The female guard approaches and offers to help. She goes up to the cell I point out and speaking through the small opening asks in Arabic if we can enter.

"Yes it's fine," the guard says after consulting the prisoner and gestures for us to come. Meanwhile the female guard struggles trying to open the lock and when it sticks she calls out in Hebrew for assistance. It takes two male guards to pry the lock open. Once inside I see the details of her room: the bed has a quilt from home and there are a few toiletries laid out in the very tiny toilet room that has a nozzle to shower from as well. On the outside wall across from the cell door there is a small air chute. I walk over to it and see that by bending and glancing inside one can breath fresh air and see the blue sky overhead, but only by significantly contorting one's body. As I straighten up, the room suddenly feels claustrophobic and as I look at the heavy door I think to myself, *What if there had been a fire here? How long would they have struggled to open the door before abandoning her to burn inside? I would go crazy locked in this small cell day after day!* Shaking the revolting feelings off, I thank the Palestinian prisoner for this unique experience. We exit and the two male guards bolt her door shut again, throwing the heavy lock back into place. Yoram and

I leave the prison together, me silenced by the reality of human beings locked in steel cages.

CHAPTER 24

Prison Blowback

On the drive back from Hasharon Prison to Tel Aviv, Yoram and I compare what we learned today to our general understanding of terrorists and to what the other experts in the field are saying. I continue to reel inside from the emotional impact of the day..

"I can't get over how horrible prison is," I say, trying to be diplomatic. "I mean your prisons are fine—just the whole idea of prison, what it really means to be locked up in a steel cage. It's pretty horrible!"

"I had a bad reaction the first couple times I went as well," Yoram confesses. "It was hard to sleep knowing I went home and they were locked in cells. But I got over it!" He laughs cynically. Yoram is a rare combination, capable of being exquisitely sensitive while outwardly always coming across as extremely brusque. His experiences growing up in Israel under numerous wars, serving in the military, and now witnessing heavy terrorists attacks have certainly hardened him. I doubt I will ever be so hardened and capable of laughing about human beings in prisons.

I don't want Yoram to feel bad or think I am judging his country unfavorably so I keep my emotions bottled inside while we continue to chat about our research. As we enter Tel Aviv, Yoram takes a busy street leading along the beachfront. We have arranged to meet Ken and Al for drinks and dinner at Mike's Place, a popular bar right on the beach next to the US Embassy. It's an appropriate venue given our research—Mike's Place was the target of a Palestinian suicide attack in April of 2003, carried out by two British bombers (Muslims of Pakistani descent) in which three were killed and another fifty wounded. After the first bomber detonated, the second ran off when his suicide bomb malfunctioned. His body eventually washed up in the sea nearby, cause of death unknown. When Ken hears the story he snorts saying, "I know for sure who killed him! Or the fucker couldn't swim, but come on - it was the Israelis! They beat the fuck out of him and tossed his body in the sea." Despite the huge bouncer outside checking everyone who enters, whenever we show up here, I always wonder if it will be targeted again.[86]

But our gathering is filled with light banter. Ken and Al dream of becoming Special Forces and Yoram loves to engage with them on all things male. I try to join their conversation, but I keep feeling strong waves of emotion welling up inside. Somehow the overwhelming sadness and trauma we listened to today has hit me hard. I know what those women were about to do was terribly wrong, and no country on earth would fail to lock them up, but right now I am without logic and just awash in emotions from our interviews. Having empathetically gone so deeply into their minds today trying to understand the pain that can drive a suicide mission, I have temporarily taken on their thoughts and emotions to a certain extent and now I just want to scream and perhaps explode emotionally at all the injustices Palestinians suffer. Later I will regain my objectivity, but right now I'm heavily under the influence of their pain and as I keep feeling these waves of emotion, I know that somehow I need to let it wash through me as I sort it all out. But I can't let it out here as I certainly don't want Yoram to hear this overwhelming and wrongly placed one-sided sympathy for the Palestinians and my anger over all that they suffer, as it is purely an emotional reaction to all we heard today rather than well thought out sympathy and it would also be ungrateful to him to voice what I'm feeling after he's been so generous to share his access to the prison with me.

It's very important to me to be objective in my research, but sometimes in the short-term it just isn't possible. Israelis who hear about my study ask me why I don't interview the victims of suicide bombings, suggesting that to do so would make me more objective on the subject. I am sure they are right but I've spent my whole career working clinically with victims of homicide, rape, childhood abuse and other trauma, and I know well how people suffer when their loved ones are torn from them, wounded, killed or left emotionally devastated. I don't need to interview victims of suicide bombings to empathize deeply with them.

But with the Palestinians, Chechens, Iraqis, Sri Lankans and all the others who have joined in the recent concert of enacting suicide bombings—these people and their choices are so alien to anything I can imagine that I only began to understand them once I went out into the field to meet and talk with them, their loved ones and those who knew them well. By trying to empathetically enter their warped realities that drive such horrible decisions as strapping on a suicide bomb, I am beginning to understand their side of the equation, and from time to time, I get temporarily lost in their pain and lose my objectivity. This is one of those times.

I become so overwrought, my eyes welling with tears, that I have to leave the table. In the bathroom, I look at my tear-streaked face in the mirror. *I can't stand this unjust world*! I think to myself as I hang my head over the sink rinsing my face with cold water. My hot tears splash down into the hard ceramic bowl and wash down the drain. I look again at my face in the hard grey glass and struggle to compose myself. *This is stupid, get a grip*! I tell myself as I wipe my face off and head back to our table.

"You okay?" Al, always sensitive, asks when I return. That just makes me feel another round of tears welling up in response to the sympathetic tone of his voice, but I beat them back.

"I'm fine," I say lifting my glass. "A toast to Yoram! Thanks again, *so very much* for taking me along with you inside the prison. That was an amazing experience!"

When the dinner ends, Yoram walks me back along the beach while the guys go off to have a smoke and then we say our goodbyes at his car. "You going into the West Bank tomorrow?" he asks.

"Yes," I answer softly.

"Where this time?" he asks.

"I never know ahead of time," I say, "And I wouldn't tell you anyway." I trust Yoram, but he is still an Israeli and I am a researcher who the Israeli security services consider a thorn in their side. It's not wise to disclose our interview plans, even though all we have are just promises from Jamilah to introduce us around again. I give Yoram a kiss on the check and he gets in his car and drives off. Then I turn back to the beach to find Ken and Al.

"So Speckie, you want to go out with us and hit the town?" Ken asks.

I nod. "Where are we heading this time?"

Al explains that they've made plans to meet up with the same girls we met last night and we head off walking to their downtown apartment where we have some more drinks. Still overwhelmed with emotion, I can't drink mine and tell the guys I am going to beg off. I know I can't discuss my feelings of sympathy for the Palestinians here either, as both of these girls have done their military service and are highly unlikely to relate.

"I'll be fine getting back to our place," I say, trying to get out the door quickly before the tears start up again. As I walk down the steep stairs from their apartment to the street below, Al comes bounding along behind me.

"Are you okay?" he says as we both spit out the door onto the sidewalk beside their stone building.

"No!" I say, covering my eyes and leaning back against the stone wall. "No, I'm not okay!" Tears are streaming again now and there is no way to stop them. I feel so stupid but I know that until I have a good cry I'm not going to be good for anyone. "Go back inside. I think I'll just go for a walk along the beach." I turn and head off down the sidewalk.

"No," Al says. "I'm not going to leave you alone."

"I'm fine, Al," I say, choking on the words. "No actually, I'm really messed up, totally messed up. If you want to come along that would be great."

Al and I walk down to the beach where it all gushes out of me in one long almost incoherent stream of tears, anger and confusion: what the women said, what the prison looked like, how there were so many doors locking us in and razor wire everywhere and how I felt when I saw the painted star of David on the prison wall—that it seemed it was put there just to taunt the prisoners—how I felt seeing the women in the courtyard, the way the prison was designed so that when I stood above the courtyard the prisoners would be eye level with my shoes and how abusive that seemed, and how I felt when the cell door of the woman could not be opened.

"I would never make it in one of those cells, Al," I say, tearing up as I pick up handfuls of sand and throw them back down again on the beach where we have seated ourselves. "I know Israeli prisons are actually humane, and that they are guilty, but they sit in there for half the day and all the night. I would go crazy with no fresh air, no window, just a small air duct to stick your face in to try to breath fresh air and see the sun!

"You think I'm too sensitive for this kind of work?" I ask, laughing cynically. "I don't know what's wrong with me, but something is terribly wrong with this world, with prisons, with everything in this world." I see a giant stick and go to pick it up and angrily hurl it into the sea.

Al listens quietly, asking questions and reflecting in a soft voice and as the time passes I become calmer. Al's kind, sensitive, a good listener and I know he is disturbed—maybe even more deeply than I am—by all of the same things. I don't have to defend my thoughts as I just let them wash over me and spill out of my mouth uncensored.

Eventually I calm down and our conversation turns to other things: my marriage that hasn't been going too well ever since my husband hit his mid-life crisis, Al's up and down relationship with his girlfriend, the fact that we like each other a lot but it would be stupid to think about crossing lines that aren't meant to be crossed. Al is the only guy who has ever managed to cross into my extremely well guarded self-protective system of repelling "all men who try to seduce me when they realize I am in a vulnerable state". I've never been the fooling around type and I've erected strong psychological barriers that let me laugh and flirt up to a point, but beyond that no one gets past—except Al—who managed to do so just recently. It's probably because he's a young man, my student and barely older than my oldest daughter that I hadn't ever put him in the category of someone I could fool around with until we started these trips and shared so many emotions together and until he hinted after the last trip that he had a crush on me. I had laughed in shock at the time since I am so much older than him and I passed it off as just kid stuff, or maybe a result of that we were all traumatized together with our last trip into Nablus and back, but somehow he seeped under my "man repelling radar" and made me notice him.

"You sure you aren't upset by more than just the prison?" Al asks bringing that subject back up. "Maybe some of these tears are because you want something more from our relationship?" he asks. I laugh thinking again of that cell door and the two Israeli soldiers struggling to open it. The image won't leave my mind. The kind of posttraumatic flashbacks I've been having all night and this outpouring of emotion isn't from frustrated sexual tension—I know that.

"You are a good guy, Al," I say looking up at him with a tear-streaked face and smiling sweetly as I laugh and wipe the tears away. "You know I really care about you," I say, referring to the love of a professor to a student, the love between friends but nothing more. "While I'm sure we could have a very good time together, it would be a shame to ruin a great relationship by being stupid. Let's not be stupid, okay?" Al laughs and mumbles something about his wish to be true to his girlfriend as well, which I also appreciate. The moment is passed as we stand up to walk back along the beach. We head back to the hostel where Al drops me off, and I fall into a deep restorative sleep while he heads back downtown to find Ken and party the night away.

CHAPTER 25

Back to Ramallah

The next morning I wake up in the bunk and notice another woman in the room. She is slim, blonde, mid-thirties, unmade up and wearing old jeans and a worn t-shirt. She's pretty in a rough sort of way, but when she smiles shyly at me, I see that her front teeth are broken off stubs.

"Hi, my name is Anne," I say. "Where are you from?"

"Romania," she answers, and although her English is not so good she manages to convey to me that she immigrated to marry an Israeli who beat her and broke her teeth, so now she lives and works here as a maid.

"Oh, that's tough," I say as I gather my toiletries and towel to go down to the communal shower. As I walk down the long brightly painted blue hallway I wonder if Ken and Al are awake yet. They tend to sleep in after partying but I want to get going. Today we are going back to Ramallah to meet Jamilah and the new translator she's found for us.

We have planned ahead to stay in the West Bank this time and to use Jamilah as our main guide as she seems to be the best connected. Since our first trip, Jamilah, Al and Ken have stayed in touch by texts and Internet and Jamilah has told Al that she no longer hangs out with Yousef, the college kid who translated for us last time.

"I have someone else we can use as a translator—someone I trust," she writes. I'm sorry to lose Yousef, but we must honor Jamilah's choice.

"You can stay with me," Jamilah has told Al when he inquired about where to stay this time. Al assures me that Jamilah has a nice apartment and that there's room for all of us.

"You can even have the bed," Al jokes. "Ken and I and Jamilah will camp on the floor. We just have to keep it quiet because last time a few people were asking where we were staying, and she didn't want problems so she snuck us into her place after dark." I don't like the sound of that, although I would think having an older adult woman present this time would qualify the whole thing as being "chaperoned", although possibly not given they are boys from outside her family and I'm a Western woman.

In any case we don't have too many choices, and I'm happy to have Jamilah guide us.

After showering I walk down to the men's wing and call into their dormitory for Ken and Al to wake up. Al emerges to take his shower saying with a laugh, "Ken is still out of it, but I'll wake him up after my shower." Then I go down to the hostel lobby and drink a coffee while I wait for them.

When the guys appear, we walk to the bus station, and once aboard, the bus pulls away from the station. Al and I exchange glances and I know what he's thinking. I turn to Ken and ask, "So Ken, if a bomber appears on this bus, who are you going to throw into him—me or Al?"

"Oh hell, not that again!" Ken says. "Neither of you!"

"No, really," Al persists, "Whose it going to be?"

"It would never be someone I *know*!" Ken protests. "Anyway I'm over that now."

As we travel into Jerusalem I wonder if we are stupid to be riding busses in Israel. *So many of them have been blown up by suicide bombers. Could we be next?* I ask myself.

We make our way on foot from the bus station in Jerusalem to the East side where we pass by the Eastern Gate. We pass near the Palms Hostel where we stayed last time, and I smile nostalgically as we stop briefly to buy some hot Arabic style bread baked in the shape of a flat donut from the vendor at the corner.

The bus from Jerusalem to Ramallah, the Kalandia checkpoint, and all the rest is much the same as last time—lots of hassles and time consuming. As we finally arrive in downtown Ramallah, Al texts Jamilah and we meet up in a local restaurant, trendy and modern with Mexican food on the menu, which seems strangely out of place here.

Jamilah introduces us to our new translator, Alla. Alla is tall, dark, has a charming smile and is obviously "cool"—he easily uses all the poses and catch phrases for his age set. Alla is studying in Birzeit University, and although Palestinian, he's only lived in the West Bank since 1993 when the PLO leaders returned to Palestine. Alla's father works for the PLO and Alla has lived a more privileged life than most, living in Jordan, Lebanon and Tunisia with Arafat until the group returned to Palestine,and its clear that he enjoys a degree of respect garnered by his father's position working for Arafat.

"The al Aqsa Brigade shot this place up just last week," Alla points out as we are seated. We glance around the room as he continues, "There's still bullet holes in the walls."

"Why?" I ask wondering if this is a safe place to be dining.

"They said they were not getting their share of the money Fatah owed them and they came here to threaten some of the political leaders. They shot it all up and they had to close the place for a week," Alla says, munching on the snacks the waiter has brought us. You'd never know, as the place is hopping right now. Everyone orders and Alla joins Ken and Al in ordering beers. Jamilah says she won't order a drink but tells Al that she plans to drink from his when no one is looking. It's her way of getting away with drinking in public.

As we eat, Alla tells us about how hard it's been for him to move back to Palestine. He feels a bit like a foreigner in his own country. Alla mentions that he did a study year abroad in Russia. As I lived in Belarus and speak Russian, I think to myself - *that may be handy as he can always tell me in Russian if he can't find the right English words to translate.*

What we don't have in common is Alla's negative views of Chechens, clearly picked up in his days rubbing shoulders with Russian students. "Come on," he says as we discuss my research studying the Chechen suicide bombers. "They do these things because they are wild, uncivilized people."

"I can't believe you just said that!" I say. "How can you say such things? Do you know the Chechen militants consider themselves under occupation—just like here?"

"They are uncivilized and wild people!" Alla repeats brusquely as though the conversation is closed.

I can't decide if I should laugh or get angry, so I try something in between and toss one of the dried beans we've been snacking on at Alla. "Here take that! I cannot believe that I am hearing a *Palestinian* tell me that Chechens are wild uncivilized people! Do you realize you just accepted the Russian stereotype hook, line and sinker?"

Alla laughs and says, "But it's *true!*"

"No it's not!" I say. "Have you ever met a Chechen? Do you know anything about their lives? I toss another bean at him and try to keep my anger at bay by doing so.

"No," Alla says with a twinkle in his eyes, "but I know it's true. I lived there!"

"You lived in *Russia*!" I answer anger beginning to tinge my voice. "And you accepted their mentality completely on this subject! Do you know what Israelis say about Palestinians—that you are violent people with a sick religion that tells you to kill others?"

Alla looks taken aback and doesn't reply.

"You think everyone who lives in Israel or is friends with Israelis should swallow those lines about Palestinians uncritically?" I ask.

"It's different here," Alla protests and Al intervenes, embarrassed by my outburst.

"Okay," I say, deciding I've gone too far. "I guess we'll just have to disagree, but please keep in mind when you are talking to me about Chechens that Khapta,my Chechen research colleague, has risked her life in Chechnya documenting our research interviews. Right now her sister, Seda is living with me at my home in Belgium, and both of them are highly educated, gentle, kind and intelligent people so I don't want to hear anymore talk from you about Chechens being wild uncivilized people. I'm a very loyal person, and I take it as a personal insult, okay?"

"Sure, we can leave the Chechens out of it," Alla nods, smiling and obviously glad to make peace.

We finish our lunch but I am rattled. With all the emotions of the prison interviews yesterday and now having crossed into Palestine, a passage that is always emotionally arousing, my nerves are on edge. And sitting here in a place that was shot up last week while listening to a Palestinian tell me Russian canards about the Chechens has wound me up even more.

But I can see that Alla's English is great, he has a good sense of humor and he's willing to help us. I need to be grateful so I pay for the lunch and try to forget it. Leaving the restaurant we part with Alla, agreeing to meet again tomorrow for our first interviews as we head off to Jamilah's place outside of Ramallah. Jamilah tells the taxi driver to let us off well before her house explaining to us that we should not attract attention.

"Please be quiet and don't smoke right now," she warns as we walk toward her house. "I don't want my neighbors to see us and to know Ken and Al are staying the night." Then she asks us to wait and follow her one by one around the stone courtyard to the lower level of the two-story house where her apartment is situated. I feel silly doing this, like we are playing a spy game, but wait with Ken and Al while she goes to unlock the door. Then Al slips quietly across the darkness into her apartment, then me, then Ken.

Jamilah's apartment occupies the lower floor of a large house and has big windows that overlook the terrace. Red cotton curtains are now drawn tightly over the windows hiding the party that is just beginning inside. There is a large rough cut, wooden table near the door that seats six, and beyond that a kitchen and living room. Up a few stairs is a low loft area that makes up Jamilah's bedroom where she has a twin bed, a few dressers and a closet overflowing with her Western style clothes. The outer walls are exposed stone and the big wooden beams inside give it the look of a Swiss ski chalet.

We've brought a couple bottles of wine and snacks that we put on the table, and Jamilah gets bowls and glasses out. We all gather around the table and begin to chill out. Most of the evening is spent catching up, with a lot of flirting and laughter between Ken, Al and Jamilah. They pepper Jamilah with questions about all the students they met last time and reminisce about partying together. Jamilah asks about life in Europe, and they compare notes on their college experiences. Most of it I can't relate to, but I quietly enjoy their reunion, glad to have a place to stay and curious about what will unfold in the next days. When I go off to wander about her apartment looking around at the walls and bookcases, curious about what a Palestinian college girl keeps in her living space, I notice that she has "martyr's" posters on many of the walls. When I ask her about it she answers, "Those are my five best friends. They are all martyrs." When I ask how they died she answers, "The Israelis shot them all." I wonder what it's like for her to look everyday at these posters of her friends who were all shot to death.

At some point we get around to discussing Alla and the subject of Chechens comes up again. I point out that Khapta won the award "Chechen Woman of the Year" for her humanitarian work in the last year. Now Al becomes critical stating that if the Russian propped up government gave the award, it was not likely the honor I am making it out to be. I find myself getting irritated and tearful again as I tell Al he doesn't know what he's talking about. I go out on the terrace to sit alone and think, *Geez I'm really not myself this trip. I hope I get a grip soon!*

"Looks like you're the one that's going all spastic this trip," Al kids as he follows me outside, reminding me about how he lost it last trip after we drove away from our interview with Ahmed Sa'adat.

"I guess we are all probably going to have our meltdowns!" I say laughing.

When we turn into sleep, Jamilah offers me her bed, and they take pillows and blankets putting them on the floor in the living room where they camp out together. There is a lot of laughing and Ken, always a potty mouth begins passing stinky gas and telling loud jokes about what a prolific "farter" he is. They shriek over the odor, laugh and joke until finally after many false bouts of silence, it really does become silent and I think, *Okay now we will all get some sleep*! It will be a short night because Jamilah's arranged for us to get up early to visit Ahmed Sa'adat again in the Jericho prison, so I'm relieved that they've finally settled down. But the silence is suddenly broken by Jamilah's crying.

"What's wrong?" Al asks her.

"I want a gun!" she wails.

"What?" Al asks.

"I want a gun, I want them to give me a gun so I can shoot as many as Israelis as I can!"

"No, you can't do that!" Al says.

"They killed all my friends!" Jamilah answers.

"But Jamilah, you want to go on a suicide mission?" Al asks.

"Not with a bomb." Jamilah answers. "I just want a gun, and I want to shoot as many as I can."

"That's a suicide mission!" Ken answers.

"I want them to give me a gun," Jamilah wails, "but my group won't give girls a gun!"

I sit up, foggy-headed but alarmed. We are going to meet the PFLP leaders tomorrow and Jamilah very well might successfully beg them for a gun. I listen as they continue and finally jump in. "Jamilah, I know you are so sad about your friends, but you have to stay alive! Things will change eventually and getting a gun is no answer."

Ken and Al are both now also wide-awake. They take over and reason with her as well. Jamilah cries some more but is eventually mollified. I hear Al comforting her, talking to her like a tired child. I lay back down in the bed exhausted and begin to cry as well. *How people suffer in this world!* I think as all of our tears finally dissipate and once again there is silence in the room lined with posters of all Jamilah's dead friends.

CHAPTER 26

Ahmed Sa'adat and our Return to Jericho

The next day everyone wakes up in a good mood;Jamilah's suicidal and terrorist yearnings have apparently passed, I feel recovered from my prison visit and refreshed and ready to begin our work. Leaving Jamilah's place we repeat our single file exit after she goes ahead and checks to be sure no one is watching. At Birzeit we exit our taxi on a busy corner in Ramallah, and I buy two large cups of fresh pressed orange and carrot juices from the sidewalk stand.

"I think we both need to keep our blood sugar steady today," I say handing one to Al, catching his eyes and smiling.

"Thanks!" Al sips appreciatively. "You think I lost it last time because we weren't getting any sleep and not eating regularly?" he asks in a cynical drawl.

"Could be," I shrug. I know now after more experiences with Al that he needs to eat regularly to stay steady and the same is true for me.

After making it across the official checkpoint in Jericho and changing taxis, we arrive at the prison and pass through the Palestinian security check, entering into the prison area.

"Welcome!" Ahmed Sa'adat says, smiling and shaking our hands as though we are long lost friends. He gestures for us to come and sit down while one of his fellow prisoners begins offering us drinks of soda and water. We ask how he's been and he assures us things are well with him. Al, always an avid reader and an ardent student of terrorism, has a keen interest to ask Ahmed about "Carlos the Jackal", the PFLP undercover operative whose real name is Ilich Ramírez Sánchez, and whose story has been the basis of numerous spy novels and movies. While Carlos's story is the stuff of spy novels, I am more interested in how Ahmed's group, the PFLP—now sidelined by Hamas and Palestinian Jihad—was once front and center among the Palestinian groups, having pioneered Palestinian terrorism beginning with plane hijackings in the seventies. It turns out the stories are intertwined.

The story of Carlos, who Al asks about first, starts with Wadid Haddad,[87] deputy founder of the PFLP. Haddad planned the first PFLP (and first Palestinian) aircraft hijacking in July 1968, in which an El Al (Israeli Airlines) plane carrying thirty-two passengers and ten crew members departing from Rome and headed for Tel Aviv was overtaken and successfully diverted to Algiers. While most of the passengers were released relatively quickly, the seven-crew members along with five Israeli male passengers were held hostage for forty days until negotiations for the release of imprisoned Palestinian militants were settled. Haddad carried on, implementing the Dawson's Field hijackings of September 1970, in which PFLP members hijacked five passenger planes headed to New York City, landing three in Dawson's Field, a small airstrip formerly used as a British airbase in Jordan.[88] Though the dramatic nature of these events brought the PFLP and Palestinian claims of dispossession onto the world-wide stage, Haddad's activities further provoked the already deteriorating relations between the Palestinian factions and King Hussein of Jordan, culminating in the bloody fighting of Black September between Palestinian militants and the Jordanian army. This ultimately resulted in the PLO's expulsion from Jordan. During this time, the PFLP leadership was under pressure from the rest of the PLO to bring Haddad under control. Haddad refused to stop his kidnapping and terrorist attacks abroad and continued his external activities under a new name PFLP-EO, the last letters standing for External Operations. It was during this time frame that Wadie Haddad employed the services of "Carlos the Jackal", whom he trained in guerrilla warfare techniques and engaged as his executioner.

"Did you know him?" Al asks, explaining his fascination with Carlos's ability to disguise himself and thereby evade detection and capture for decades.

"No," Ahmed smiles charismatically, his bright eyes sparkling with appreciation for the glamour surrounding certain spies and terrorists. In that gentle smile I see hints of Ahmed's power as a terrorist leader interacting with young men.

"I couldn't travel to Lebanon to meet him," Ahmed answers. "But if you did meet him he changed so incredibly each time that you wouldn't recognize him! It was the needs of his work." He reminisces over those times when the PFLP was a much more well-known and politically influential organization than it is now. Ahmed's group lost much of its former significance with the demise of their Soviet backers, their rejection of the

1990s Israeli-Palestinian peace process, and the rise of Hamas and other Islamist groups in opposition to Fatah.[89] Only recently, in the Second Intifada, did the PFLP reassert themselves as a formidable terrorist force by carrying out the 2001 assassination of Israeli Tourism Minister Rechavam Zeevi and by just recently joining the fray of sending suicide bombers into Israel.

"Carlos was very successful," Ahmed continues, "but he believed armed revolution can make changes. This situation did not fit the PFLP, not because we don't believe in revolutionary work, but [because] it was not tactically correct [for us]. To accept comrades from the world is good," Ahmed says referring to Carlo's Venezuelan nationality, 'but the struggle is here. He took the PFLP and started operations outside [internationally] and kept up operations against the Israelis everywhere. While we [the PFLP] stopped hijacking airplanes because we thought that period of time had passed and we had achieved our aims. [What became the splinter groups of the PFLP, including Haddad and Carlos] were in a struggle along with outside organizations. In 1977 Carlos went out [of the PFLP]. But Carlos kept working and always considered himself part of the PFLP."

Ahmed is referring to disagreements within PFLP history over how far to go in carrying out terrorist acts and whether the gains in garnering media attention to the Palestinian cause and of extorting money for the release of hostages was worthwhile given the blowback from many of their host countries and supporters of the Palestinian cause. A year after its formation, the PFLP joined the PLO (the Palestinian Liberation Organization - formed in 1964), which at the time was committed to liberating Palestine by armed struggle.[90]

Harkening back to this time and the split in the PFLP that occurred with Haddad's insistence on continuing terrorist attacks, Ahmed continues, "The Israelis killed Wadid and the [terror] cells got separated. One group got aligned to Fatah—Black September. They used to criticize the PFLP, but later they allied themselves with us." Black September was infamous for its 1972 terrorist attack during the Summer Olympics in Munich where they infiltrated the Israeli Olympic team headquarters, took hostages and murdered eleven Israeli athletes.

After Haddad was expelled from the PFLP he persisted in his terrorist activities and in June 1976 helped to organize the Entebbe hijacking of the Air France plane carrying two hundred forty-eight passengers who were diverted to Entebbe, near Kampala, the capital of Uganda. Despite the blowback from Jordan for landing the Dawson's Field hijacked planes on its territory and the resulting expulsion of the PLO from Jordan, Wadie Haddad, "Carlos the Jackal" and the PFLP was, in it's heyday of terrorist hijackings, highly successful in capturing international headlines and the fantasies of anyone mesmerized with the terrorist's mentality. Consequently, the demands for Palestinian liberation became an internationally recognized cause.

Another actor in the Dawson's Field drama included Leila Khalid the notorious svelte female PFLP terrorist who was an early precursor to the female suicide bombers of today. Leila and Patrick Argüello pretended to be a married couple traveling to Honduras when she was in fact smuggling two hand grenades (believed to be hidden in her brassiere) onto the plane. Their hijack attempt was foiled but nonetheless dominated headlines as three other planes were hijacked by the PFLP in the same time frame, one purposefully in order to affect Leila Khalid's release.[91] Khalid became a poster girl for Palestinian terrorism when she posed for a photo wearing a keffiyeh (Palestinian head dressing) and holding a Kalishnikov. Both she and Carlos the Jackal grew into iconic figures in the terrorist fight for a free Palestine and were the subject of much media fascination—something that terrorists are often looking to capture.[92]

"Until now we are looking at Carlos not as a criminal but as a revolutionary," Ahmed continues. "He was independent minded and world revolutions need such persons, despite that he is not one of us now. Carlos had his own ideas, new ones, about Marxism and religion."

"He also likes the operations of bin Ladin," Ahmed explains. "He cannot give up Marxism, but he sees Islam confronting capitalism. That's why he supports them."

Marxism, once believed by many Arabs to be the way to bring world revolution and restore rights to the people, including Palestinian freedom, is no longer in vogue among young Palestinians and Arabs who watched Marxist leaders collapse in the USSR during the end of the Cold War and fail to bring Arab countries freedom from despotic dictators. Political Islam has since risen and captured the minds of the former Marxist cadres and the PFLP, which still remain strong in Ramallah. Throughout Palestine and Gaza, however, Hamas has greatly overtaken Marxist groups, appealing to the masses by promoting Islamic "martyrdom" and suicide missions (much like al Qaeda does) as a legitimate way to win the Palestinian nationalist struggle.

Of the rise of Islamic political movements that have overtaken Marxist groups, Ahmed says, "There are only two religious movements: the
Taliban and the Shia Jamaat [brotherhood] from Iran. From my point of
view [our] struggle is tied to ideology, and theirs doesn't lead anywhere."
In other words, the goal of both Sunni and Shia militant jihadi groups to
restore the Islamic caliphate isn't a political objective that resonates with
Ahmed.

"Carlos knew Osama bin Ladin?" I ask.

"It's a strange thing," Ahmed raises his eyebrows. "He was in Sudan.
Maybe he met Osama in Sudan. Sudan was a shelter for the revolution."
Osama bin Ladin also found shelter in Sudan during those years. Ahmed
shakes his head to indicate he doesn't know if the two met or not and
continues, "There was pressure on Sudan from the US, and [the Sudanese
government] gave [Carlos] up in a special deal.[93]

"Carlos had a network with groups in Iraq. He used to work with
all revolutionaries. He was top secret, he works on his own." Ahmed
reflects in silence for a moment, a sad smile on his face as he reflects on
his comrade in arms. "I think Carlos is great. He's an intelligent man and
we should struggle to set him free. Maybe not at this stage—it's too hard,
but we always have to think of ways to set our fighters free. He helped
many people."

"How did your group fund its operations?" Al asks.

"In 1972 for the hijacked German airplane, [the PFLP] took five million
French francs to return the hostages," Ahmed explains. "There are many
revolutionary ways to fund operations, to use donors as well."

Referring to al Qaeda, Ahmed states, "At the beginning Osama was
a man of America," Ahmed continues. "In Afghanistan there were many
conflicts [among the terrorist cadres] and they crossed their processes
together . . . there is a vacuum and now the ideology of Osama bin Ladin
can fill it and unite the people."[94]

Indeed the ideological appeal of militant jihadi terrorists groups is one
of the issues that the PFLP currently faces. According to renowned terrorism expert David Rapoport, historically there have been four waves of
terrorism that have emerged over the decades, each wave having unique
goals and actions that reflected the political climate and the way the states
they were attacking responded to them.[95] According to Rapoport, the first
wave began in the 1880's with the Russian anarchists. The second wave,
occurring from 1920's through the 1960's, was anti-colonial and involved

many small states using terrorism to win independence from their colonial masters. The New Left emerged in the 1960's uniting terrorism with communism. Ahmed's PFLP party formed in 1967 and belongs in this wave. The fourth wave of terrorism emerged in 1979 with the Iranian revolution, binding religion and terrorism, and includes groups like Hamas and the many permutations of al Qaeda (or militant jihadi terrorism) that we see throughout the world today.

So, as Ahmed's PFLP party struggles for political influence through traditional means, ideological influence and terrorist tactics, he is facing the ascendancy of Hamas and Palestinian Islamic Jihad, groups already on the more modern wave of terrorism that use an Islamic "martyrdom" ideology to attract recruits. It's noteworthy that it was only when Hamas, Palestinian Jihad and other Palestinian groups began using suicide terrorism that the PFLP joined their ranks, enacting what seems to be what terrorism expert Mia Bloom refers to as outbidding to keep up with the other groups and maintain their influence.[96]

"We don't worship the struggle," Ahmed says, "but the belief that forms the struggle is based on tactics and they are changeable. What we can achieve from the tactic is based on our objectives. It's a moveable tactic and it's always better to accomplish our objectives without blood."

This is indeed always the problem with terrorist groups—they push forward their political agenda with violence and then when terrorism is no longer useful transition back out of violence. But it takes great self-discipline for a political group to restrain it's armed wing because terrorist acts always grab headlines, creating a strong popular response among constituents and sympathizers and can seem to be accomplishing objectives when compared to the often slower and more arduous processes of traditional politics. But leaders who have endorsed terrorism as a means to fight for freedom eventually will, if they begin to win their objectives, try to take the reins of the independent nation they fought for, though it is often made impossible by disagreements among the factions and the inability to negotiate peace among all the terrorist groups. Indeed this very issue plagued Arafat and the PLO following the Oslo accords. The negotiated agreement was hoped to lead to Palestinian self-governance and renunciation of terrorism by all Palestinians but, in actuality, it led to an escalation of terrorist attacks by Hamas, Palestinian Jihad and to a lesser extent by the PFLP (alongside of the Israelis continuing to build settlements) spoiling the peace process.

"I can't claim we were planners of the Intifada of '87, but we were ready for it. The first martyr was from the PFLP." Ahmed's eyes blaze. "So a national movement was formed and we put a plan for the Intifada."

"Did you ever consider nonviolent movements of struggle, perhaps like Gandhi or Martin Luther King?" I ask, hopeful that maybe such an intellectual mind can see better alternatives than terrorism.

"The first Intifada *was* based on a method from Gandhi – to sit down," Ahmed answers excitedly. "Women had a very important role and even leadership. There were two direct [political] aims. The first was to break down the employee sharing between Jordanian and Palestinian [peoples] that was based on their policies. The second direct request was to have local elections for municipalities."

While the aim may have been to follow Gandhi's nonviolent methods, Ahmed acknowledges it didn't last long, giving his perspective on what happened. "We used to talk about a peaceful struggle. When the demonstrators clashed with the Israelis, the Israelis put their hands on weapons. [They] killed and arrested people in the hundreds, but we preserved ourselves in one direction. There was no violence [from the Palestinians] at first."

Ahmed explains how his group went on to organize Palestinian employees to strike against their Israeli employers and encouraged the people to prepare kitchen gardens so they could avoid purchasing Israeli products.

"Our idea was to try to raise a budget for a Gandhi-type project based on his concepts of strangling the economy of oppression and not being slaves [laborers at poor wages] or to buy [Israeli] products. The Palestinian streets were in flames but we failed to pass this project [in the legislature].

"Our beliefs are [also] always to look at the case of Nelson Mandela's struggle against apartheid," Ahmed tells us. "It's always been in our heads, the question of how can we gather a peaceful struggle of local people and follow Gandhi."

"Don't you think you *could* find a way to lead a powerful nonviolent movement?" I ask. "I've been thinking of how excitable Arab men are, perhaps it would be better to organize the women into a nonviolent movement against the occupation that would capture the world's attention?"

"The first demonstration against the Israelis in 1968 was one year after the Israelis occupied the West Bank," Ahmed recalls. "We had the women organized into a demonstration. They were wearing black and they went to the cemetery to [the graves of] those killed in the [Six-Day] war and put flowers on their tombs and walked in a silent demonstration. The [soldiers of the] occupation got really pissed off. They attacked the women and it exploded into revolution."

"What about if you had cameras and the media present?" I ask "Wouldn't that help?"

"I'm completely convinced of the importance of the media," Ahmed answers. "In the first Intifada I was in jail and I read of it in the Hebrew newspapers. I saw the echo of the Intifada on Palestinian streets within the Hebrew [Israeli] government."

"We put Gandhi's method on the table in front of us. The revolution in Iran [was also happening] at that time and we had a problem. I followed the Iranian revolution day by day," Ahmed states, reflecting how influential it was to watch the first Middle Eastern regime change occur in response to Islamic revolution. "The last lieutenant in the army worked in the military wing of the Immortal Lieutenants [the Shah's imperial guards] and he refused to shoot [his own] people. So the institution [of the military] got separated [from the ruling government] and the people won. In South Africa the military institution was quarantined from [attacking] the people as well. But the Israeli military—it's hard to separate [the Israeli political leaders from the occupation]," Ahmed explains. "We had a plan to put [the IDF] aside by making them make mistakes in front of the international community and then by raising the struggle against them. The chances were there but we didn't make good use of them. Unfortunately in the first Intifada, pictures of Israeli violence were filling up all the world and the violent logos were on the tongues of the high Israeli leaders, for instance the policy of Rabin of breaking bones [of young people throwing rocks]." As Ahmed points out, terrorist groups often try to provoke police and military brutality, hoping to turn citizen outrage back onto their own military and police sometimes leading also to insurgency and revolution.

"It's why I say we are a great people with bad leadership," |Ahmed says ruing that the Palestinian Liberation Organization (PLO) leaders didn't do better using the international media to their advantage in the Intifadas. "Our other chance [to skillfully use the media] was in the second Intifada," Ahmed continues. "There were two political speeches by Yasser Arafat. He talked about continuing negotiations based on Oslo and brave peace based on Rabin. But [after those words] we failed to have only one strategy that concentrates on organizing the people. So now after four years we have returned to the same point, the same struggle at Sharm el Sheikh where we agreed on the road map and agreed to cooperate with Sharon." As Ahmed speaks it all sounds so hopeless – that the Palestinian leadership is too divided and that they will never find a way to have true peace with Israel.

"[Also the settlements] are too expensive for Sharon," Ahmed says. "If Sharon evacuates the settlements in Gaza, he will try to evacuate the Arabs from some of the areas of the 1948 zone in return. He will try to make an exchange of lands and people and redraw the borders. He wants to be as far ahead as he can be of any international solution that can be forced upon the Israelis from the outside. They are scared of the future of a choice of two states, two nationalities. Leiberman [a conservative Israeli politician] said, 'two states means separating two peoples' and that means the transfer of Palestinians." Ahmed goes on to explain how his party believes in building democratic institutions, supporting the PLO because "it reunites Palestinian people inside and outside of Palestine", using the UN to support a Palestinian state according to the 1967 lines and activating worldwide concern in the international community, as well as among the four and a half million diaspora of Palestinians worldwide.

Ahmed also argues that the Palestinian people need "one leader and one decision" to win their case. He states that if the political leadership in the case of a united Palestine allows armed struggle, his group would not separate over this point.

Ahmed goes on to explain that alongside the PFLP, Hamas has risen as a serious opposition group to those in the Palestinian Authority (PA) who he sees as corrupt, explaining that they "rush and translate the Palestinian Authority into cars, money, houses and economic projects." Hamas, in his opinion, and the PFLP are among the far less corrupted political parties and oppose the dishonesty and greed Ahmed sees in the Fatah leadership of the PA. He states, "The surfacing of the Islamic movement is dogmatic but pragmatic," underlining the fact that Hamas, although a fundamentalist movement, does serve the people, winning their trust.

Speaking of his own group he adds, "Our main focus is on real public movement and modern and capitalized democracy that has a relationship with advancement. Like revolutionary and public parties it is anti-capitalism. Abu Mazen [Mahmoud Abbas, referred to in the Arabic style as "father of Mazen"] goes to the [World] Economic Forum of Davos with the big capitalism countries," Ahmed complains about the Fatah leader. "I cannot make a relationship between Davos [the World Economic Forum] and the people's movement. That's why we tried to reunite the [opposition] parties but we failed unfortunately. So the choice before us was to support Barghouti [a candidate for President of the Palestinian Authority] not because he is [on the] left but because he has lots of independent, democratic characters surrounding him. After we agreed on a program with him our results were good. He got twenty percent [of the vote]. Right now we are trying to construct ourselves to be strong in the elections of parliament and in the local councils. Our plan is to have a strong presence that would create a real democratic face to show to the world so we can change the picture of democracy. Any political party that is honest to the people's needs gives power to the people and respect," Ahmed concludes.

"Will your group break the "hudna"?" I ask about the recently declared ceasefire between Palestinian groups and Israel.

"We haven't quit our struggle," Ahmed answers. "We are Marxists. We belong to Lenin's school and Gramsci[97] and we strengthen our relationship with the people. We are controlling a media fight in order to construct an ideology and raise up the psychological consciousness so that we can continue our struggle. We had good experience in the first Intifada. It does not necessarily mean bombs in Tel Aviv," Ahmed explains, "but rocks and Molotovs in the demonstrations."

As Ahmed speaks, I think about how enamored he is with the Marxist ideology—his face lights up when he speaks, and he reminds me of a college professor discussing his favorite subject. But now with the emergence of a "cult of martyrdom" and the people's belief that suicide bombs can turn the tide, I wonder how much his outdated Marxist views reach the average Palestinian.

As I reflect on Ahmed's words, I realize that terrorists who see themselves as freedom fighters often one day do hope to take the reins of government. But terrorist groups that are strongly dedicated to their political aims will often, only ever lay down arms to come to the negotiating table, to run party members for political office or to use another nonviolent way to influence the political process if they believe strongly enough in it to give up whatever benefits terrorism is winning for them. As Mia Bloom points out in her latest book, the transition terrorists make from purveyors of violence to political leaders in their countries makes it difficult to say who is a terrorist and who is a freedom fighter. And as she states, "This is particularly evident when one considers that more former terrorist leaders than American presidents have won the Nobel Peace Prize."[98]   Indeed, former PLO chairman Yasser Arafat is among them. And Ahmed Sa'adat remains committed to his cause willing to stick it out for the long haul while being pragmatic, thoughtful and willing to use whatever it takes, violence or traditional political methods to achieve his goals.

Ahmed does manage in January 2006 (nine months after the time of our interview) to get himself elected—from prison—to the Palestinian parliament. At the same time, he also witnesses the landslide victory of Hamas, overtaking the corrupt Fatah in national Palestinian elections. And a year after our interview, his situation and future prospects change dramatically, but before we move to that story, there is one more interview in the Jericho prison.

CHAPTER 27

Hamdi Quran - Zeevi's Assassin

As we finish up our interview with Ahmed, I ask if we can also inter-view Hamdi Quran, the slick assassin I recall being revolted by last time we were here.

Hamdi Quran is here in prison for shooting Israeli Minister of Tourism Rehavam Zeevi in a Jerusalem hotel where he had been staying and then fled with his accomplices to the West Bank. Israeli leaders made clear they would not tolerate the assassins and their political leader going free inside Palestine so the Palestinian authorities apprehended and at first held them in Arafat's Mukata'a in Ramallah. There they tried and convicted Hamdi and the other three of his henchmen in a hastily contrived military tribunal inside the Mukata'a and sentenced Hamdi to eighteen years.

Sa'adat, however, was not tried with the assassins as Arafat viewed him as a political, rather than a military, leader. The Mukata'a, as we heard on our first visit to Arafat's partially destroyed compound, was then placed under siege by the IDF to try to force Arafat to hand over the suspects. Arafat himself finally gave in, gaining his own freedom by agreeing to a US brokered deal where the four accomplices and Ahmed Sa'adat were jailed in the PA prison in Jericho under UK and U.S. prison monitors. Later in 2002, the Palestinian Supreme Court addressed the case and ordered the PA to release Sa'adat since he had never been charged or brought before a judge. The Israeli government's response was harsh; Ra'anan Gissin, an Israeli spokesman, said that if "[Sa'adat] is not brought to justice, we will bring justice to him," implying that if released Sa'adat would be subject to a snatch operation or targeted killing by the Israelis.[99] We are in the Jericho PA prison now.

Ahmed nods in response to my question about interviewing Hamdi."You can ask him. I think he'll agree," he says as he signals for the others to check with Hamdi. In the meantime, we say our goodbyes to Ahmed, telling him we will try to visit him again on a future visit—something that will turn out to be impossible.

The assassination of the Israeli Minister of Tourism Rehavam Zeevi was organized in October 2001 by the PFLP in retaliation for the targeted assassination of their leader, Abu Ali Mustafa. Zeevi was the most likely of the Israeli ministers to be assassinated due to the inflammatory nature of his remarks. In July of 2001, he referenced the one hundred and eighty thousand illegal Palestinian workers and residents inside Israel as a cancer and said Israel should "rid itself of them the same way one gets rid of lice."[100] Zeevi's extreme right wing political views also included advocating for the mass expulsion of the Palestinians from the West Bank and Gaza to neighboring Arab nations by military force or otherwise.[101]

We go to Hamdi's cell where he motions for us to sit down. Hamdi is a nice looking man who seems to know he's attractive. His hair is oiled back and his t-shirt is worn tight over his muscled chest. I estimate he is in his mid-thirties.

He has not yet been tried in Israel for his crime, and if there is any possibility of Israeli surveillance inside this prison, I do not want him to admit to anything in our interview that could later be played back and used against him in a court of law. I explain this to him and he nods, starting out cautiously, "I was accused of killing one of the Israeli ministers."

Instead of probing on that, I ask him, "Can you tell me about your beginnings—your childhood and how you got to this point of ending in prison?"

Seemingly relieved to start with better memories, Hamdi smiles. "I was born in 1974 in Ramallah. My childhood was normal. When we were little kids we never knew occupation. Then when I was thirteen years old the first Intifada occurred, in 1987. The first martyred woman was my neighbor, Imid. The Israelis killed her, those sons of bitches at a demonstration at al Manara Center. She was a mother and had four children. Her sons were my friends. I was in school. When I got home from school she was already dead.

"You were shocked?" I ask.

"Yes of course," he replies. "I was a little child. Since then, I started to ask myself what and why?"

"Was that the event that radicalized you?" I ask.

"That was the first incident that opened my eyes," Hamdi answers, "but after that there were many more."

"Can you tell me about them?" I ask.

"When we were little children," Hamdi says, "Our father spent two months in jail. Then they arrested our mother. She also spent two months in prison during the same period. We were, like, in the street."

"Why were they arrested?" I ask.

"They were both involved in the party Fatah," he answers.

"[Then] they shot my brother in his mouth," Hamdi continues, his voice constricting in pain and his eyes averted. "They tied him and put the gun in his mouth and shot him. I saw him in the hospital. Another neighbor got martyred. People got arrested."

"What happened with your brother?" I ask, horrified.

"It was in Ramadan after the evening meal. He was hanging out with our cousins. [The Israeli soldiers] just took him and shot him [in the mouth]."

Hamdi says that his brother was sixteen or seventeen at the time, which made him thirteen or fourteen.

"How did your mother react when her son was shot?" I ask.

"She went crazy," he answers. "She started slapping her cheeks."

"We got his entire jaw rebuilt. It's platinum now. My father sold a piece of land in order to make the operation. It cost a lot of money."

Hamdi's brother was later arrested.

"He stayed in jail for five years. He had many charges against him for being involved in Fatah and should stay longer but we sued the Israeli soldiers who shot him. The Israelis told us they would give reduce his sentence to twelve years if we gave up the case, so we agreed to drop it."

"I was also in jail in 1991," Hamdi adds. "I was nineteen. It was for having a gun I found. I used to it shoot at a police station in Ramallah."

"So after all these things, making an assassination attempt on the Israeli minister is something you would do with pleasure?" I ask.

"Yes," Hamdi nods. "It's not wrong."

"Did you volunteer for the mission?" I ask, forgetting caution as he opens up.

"I'm originally from the PFLP," Hamdi explains. "They came up with the operation, and I did it because I was the most suitable person. I had been living in Israeli and I speak their language. I had friendships with Russian Jews. When you have to do something specific, the person must know the language and the area. Also, I was being chased by the Israelis and I was experienced with them. I was chased since the beginning of the second Intifada. I was a fugitive."

It's interesting that once again we hear of a fugitive volunteering for a mission that will likely end in his own death.

"Was this your first assassination?" I ask.

"What is assassination?" Hamdi asks blinking his eyes sharply and bristling at the term. "I killed many people."

"Like this?" I ask.

"I didn't kill this way before," he clarifies, calming down. "I killed with bombs and by mining cars before this."

"How far in advance did you know you were going to do the operation?" I ask, wondering how he prepared himself psychologically.

"I knew for two months that I will do it," Hamdi says, his eyes becoming unfocused as he returns in memory to that time period. "I rehearsed it. Everything was ready. I went twice to the hotel. I slept there and got familiar with it."

"How did you feel leading up to the operation?" I ask.

"The feeling of getting revenge," Hamdi says his voice resolute. "It made me not feel anything. I was really focused on success, no way to fail."

As he speaks my mind returns to the student interviews we did in our Belgian thought experiment. Hamdi sounds like they described imagining themselves on a suicide mission—their focus narrowed in on the mission and on revenge and all other emotions dissociated from consciousness. Only this is the real thing.

"It went according to the plan," Hamdi continues. "I went to the hotel. I called before and ordered a room and I went to the hotel with Basel [my co-conspirator]. We slept in the hotel. I saw Zeevi in the morning having breakfast with his wife. When I saw him in the lobby I went outside to check if his bodyguards were in his car. Then I went back inside. We were waiting for him just in front of his room."

"Did you say anything to him when you shot him?" I ask.

"Yes, I wanted him to see me," Hamdi says, his eyes burning as he switches into the present tense as he momentarily relives that moment. "This is most important. I want him to see that I am Palestinian and that I kill him. I call out to him, 'Hey!' I want him to look at me. And I look at him in his eyes."

"What did you feel at that moment?" I ask.

"Nothing," he answers still entranced in memory, then coming out of it he looks at me and says, "I don't know," while shaking his head.

"Fear?" I ask.

"No," he answers with a faraway look.

"Anger?" I probe.

"Yes," Hamdi nods, still caught in the memory and moving backwards in time to speak as though it's happening right now, "Because I know the person I am going to kill. I know he's a butcher. I don't want to hurt just anybody, but him I want to kill."

"Where did you shoot him?" I ask, already sensing the answer. I feel certain even before Hamdi answers that he will have revenged for his brother by shooting Zeevi in the neck or jaw just like his brother was shot by the soldiers.

"I shot him in the throat," Hamdi answers "and his forehead, twice."

"Did you shoot him in the throat for your brother?" I ask.

"No," Hamdi says snapping into the present as he vehemently denies the connection. "It wasn't about the past. It has nothing to do with this. I wanted him to die. I shot him also in the head."

His strong emotional response to my question tells me I probably have it right, but I decide not to push on his lack of self-insight and accept his answer.

"Your gun had a silencer?" I ask.

He nods.

"What happened then?"

"I went downstairs and turned the engine on and left," Hamdi answers.

"And his wife?" I ask, wondering about the poor woman who is about to learn her husband has just been murdered.

"I didn't see her on the way out," Hamdi answers.

"Where did you go?" I ask, knowing his escape was short-lived.

"I drove the car," Hamdi replies, his face showing the intensity of those moments. "I was sure of going back home [to the West Bank] because before there was a car chasing me many [other] times and I knew that I can evade."

"And the others?" I ask, wondering about his co-conspirators.

"Mohammed was caught," Hamdi explains. "He was waiting outside of the region to change the car and pick us up. They caught him and he confessed. Otherwise they wouldn't know it was me. After that, I knew

I will be caught. It's a sacrifice. If I can sacrifice [for my country] I will do it."

"Where did they finally catch you?" I ask.

"In Nablus," Hamdi answers. "The PLO caught me, not the Israelis," he explains, a look of disgust crossing his face. "If the Israelis caught me I wouldn't be speaking to you now. I wouldn't be alive." After being caught, Hamdi and his coconspirators holed up in Arafat's Mukata'a inciting Israeli retaliation against Arafat.

"Did you expect to survive this operation?" I ask, truly amazed that a Palestinian team of assassins was able to infiltrate the Jerusalem Hyatt whilst an Israeli minister was staying there and assassinate him right under the noses of his bodyguards.

"I had a fifty-fifty chance of living," Hamdi states.

"Why do you call Zeevi a butcher?" I ask. "Do you mean from the physical or mental point of view?"

"Both," Hamdi answers. "He believed we Palestinians are not humans and have no rights. He had only one idea: transfer." Hamdi is speaking about Zeevi's radical proposition of forcing Palestinians to exit the West Bank and Gaza and emigrate to Arab countries, either by military means or just by making life miserable for them. "On the physical level he was a General in the Israeli army and killed Palestinians in Lebanon, Egyptians in the Sinai and Palestinians in the West Bank and Gaza."

"And you wanted revenge and to stop him?" I ask.

"This is the only way that I can protect myself. We don't have anything—no tanks, no Apaches, only small guns. And with only a gun we are facing the most powerful country in the world," Hamdi states. Then with his hands moving in agitation he adds, "The Israelis cannot control the U.S. Before the first election, they brought Bush from the bars, cleaned him up and asked him for only two things: take Iraq, give us revenge and delete the right of [Palestinian] refugees to come back. For this you will be President."

I laugh outright at this characterization of President Bush. I am living in Europe and traveling a lot in Arab and Muslim areas and used to the U.S. President, in particular, being maligned for his "war on terror" and invasion of Iraq, but this really hits my funny bone. It's true that as a young man Bush drank alot and perhaps used drugs but implying that the Israeli lobby picked him up and made him president on these premises makes me laugh heartily.

"Bush is not my favorite president either," I tell him, and he laughs too.

"We don't have our borders," Hamdi continues, becoming serious again. "We cannot fly [through Ben Gurion airport]. We have no real independence.

"It's because of the media," he continues. "All the films show some humiliation to Arabs. Show me if you find any films with humiliation to Israelis and Jews! And we have the occupation. Everyone knows about it, and they don't do anything. They don't want us to fight. They are on our back. What to do? The Jews always scream about the Holocaust. But they give *us* numbers when they catch *us*. We are getting killed in front of the world."

Many times as I've traveled through Palestine I've felt echoes of the Holocaust history in the ongoing confiscation of Palestinian homes and lands by settlers and the like, and through the separation barriers, dispossession and widespread discrimination. Of course there are no mass round-ups, no mass killings as in the Holocaust, and the Palestinian militant uprisings and terrorist responses hardly resemble the passive response of Jews in Europe. Yet the way Palestinians are treated and the ghettos of Gaza and the West Bank still strike a chord. Amira Hass, an Israeli journalist who comes from a family of Holocaust survivors, writes often about her own concerns on this score saying that whereas the Holocaust ended, the Palestinian dispossession of lands and homes continues to this day. Having abandoned Israel to live in the West Bank city of Ramallah, Hass contends that Israel uses the Holocaust as an excuse to make some of the same types of violations against Palestinians, arguing that security for Jews is a paramount concern because of the Holocaust. She writes, "Israel provides itself with the license to come up with more kinds of fences, walls and military guard towers around Palestinian enclaves..." and that "in Hebron, the state carries out ethnic cleansing via its emissaries, the settlers, and ignore [sic] the enclaves and regime of separation it is setting up."[102]

It's always disturbing to me when Palestinians argue that the Israelis are repeating some of the same things that were done to them. I don't think it's the same at all, yet as a psychologist, I know that victims often do reenact their traumas and at times become the aggressor repeating what was done to them. Inwardly I wince listening to Hamdi but I say nothing.

"A Palestinian killed an Israeli girl in Hebron, a baby girl," Hamdi says, his face clouded in anger. "He didn't mean to kill her. He wanted to kill her father. Since four years they [the Israelis] have been making a big deal of the little girl. But everyday our children are killed."

Again I hear echoes of other militants who say they are facing a much greater army and are "forced" to resort to terrorist acts. For instance Shamil Basayev, the Chechen terrorist who planned the takeover and hostage taking of an elementary school in Beslan- North Ossetia, was angered over the worldwide outrage over the three hundred mothers and children killed saying after the fact, " Officially, over 40,000 of our [Chechen] children have been killed and tens of thousands mutilated. Is anyone saying anything about that?"[103]

Palestinians, Chechens and other minority or disenfranchised groups who want their independence often feel the only way they can gain worldwide attention to their cause and force the hand of their much better equipped adversary is to resort to terrorism. Hamdi continues his lament, pointing out the world's inattention to the Palestinian cause and to the United Nations' efforts to make some resolution in their case, "We have one hundred and fifty decisions from the UN and no one talks about it. What is this? It's lunacy, I think!"

Hamdi continues his diatribe, returning again to the U.S., "Bush says our bombs didn't kill them—we bring democracy for Iraq. This is the way the West understands democracy. If you have the power you can do as you like." Hamdi's eyes burn as he asks, "But what do I do for the pain in my heart? For the silence of the world? Don't they see *me*?"

I know indeed most Americans have no idea where Palestine is and what Palestinians suffer on a daily basis. And I realize that he feels he can disappear, that his life seems as nothing more than meaningless suffering unless he fights back.

"The most important thing is we don't shut down," he continues. "We do something to feel life."

"If not?" I ask trying to get at these feelings of disappearance and nihilism that he fights by using his anger.

"I have a lot of anger inside me," Hamdi's asserts even as his voice fades in pain as his hand wipes his brow. "Forty percent of the children here have psychological problems. Many have asthma. They cannot breathe. It's not from nothing!"

I nod, knowing it's true.

I don't want to prolong Hamdi's political diatribe so I change the subject asking, "How long is your sentence?"

"Eighteen years I should be here," he answers referring to his PA sentence.

"And if there are two states?" I ask, musing about what would happen to political prisoners held inside an independent Palestine. "Would you be freed?"

"I don't think so," Hamdi says, shaking his head. "The problem is with the Israeli government—they will always follow me and try to kill me."

"So you are safer in prison?" I ask.

He nods. "My wife comes here to visit. I live here better than in my life. I miss my freedom of course. This question cannot be asked. For my mother it's most important to see me alive. Every week they come to visit us."

I nod, understanding the bitter sweetness in his acceptance that his life will likely be lived out within these prison walls, his trade for fighting for his country and now for staying alive.

"Do you think they will transfer you out of this prison?" I ask, wondering if the Israelis will come here for him.

"It's a matter of time," Hamdi says in acceptance of his fate. "If you put a hundred shekels in a safe you won't lose it. You can always pick it up."

Indeed that is exactly what happens in March of 2006 after the Hamas electoral victories. The UK and U.S. monitors, fed up that "the Palestinians Authority has consistently failed to comply with core prevision [sic] of the Jericho monitoring arrangement regarding visitors, cell searches, telephone access and correspondence" and "failed to provided secure conditions" for the U.S. and UK personnel working at the Jericho Prison, decide to no longer guard it.[104] The monitors and the Israeli government, are also concerned about the hand over of the prison to the newly elected Hamas government who have expressed their possible intent to release the prisoners. In response to their withdrawal, the IDF quickly raid the prison to "pick up" the killers and plotters in the Zeevi assassination.

Indeed as I had understood in our first interview with Ahmed Sa'adat, the prison was extremely permeable to visitors and Sa'adat could easily continue his terrorist and political operations from inside it. In an official statement as they embark on their IDF raid called *Bringing Home the Goods*, the Israeli government states, "Both Ahmad Sa'adat and Ahed Ulmeh continued to guide and direct the organization's terror activity from within the jail."

In response to the monitors leaving, the Israeli military charge into the Jericho compound surrounding it with soldiers and armored vehicles. When Sa'adat, Hamdi and the others refuse to surrender and even fire back at the Israeli gunfire, Israeli bulldozers begin knocking down the walls. I hear of the siege as it is happening and watch it on the Internet and television, sickened as I see the military helicopters flying overhead, bulldozers crumpling the prison walls and black smoke filling the desert sky. It doesn't seem possible that any human being inside can survive. I write frantically to Jamilah, telling her that if she has any way to communicate to Sa'adat to urge him to surrender, to tell him it's better to stay alive than to die this way, and that I will do my best to visit him in Israeli jail. Likely it means nothing to him but it feels good to do something at least. Jamilah writes back saying that she has conveyed the message and after ten hours I see on the television that Hamdi, Sa'adat and the others emerge from the nearly destroyed building to surrender to Israeli custody.

The Israeli raid triggers massive riots throughout the West Bank and Gaza, including Palestinian attacks on sites linked to the U.S. and UK who were blamed for the departure of the prison monitors. Likewise westerners in Gaza and the West Bank are temporarily kidnapped in retaliation for the raid but then quickly released.[105]

Once in Israel, Hamdi is tried in Israeli courts where he pleads guilty, readily admitting to how he had carried out the assassination plot and killed Zeevi. Hamdi is sentenced to two life terms and an additional one hundred years for bombing and shooting attacks against Israelis. In court Hamdi does not express sorrow for his actions stating, "I am being tried because I carried out my basic right to defend my nation against the Israeli occupation—the same right that you grant yourselves daily, to kill us, the Palestinians." He goes on to say to the Israeli court, "I blame you for activities against all of humanity."[106]

Ahmed Sa'adat is also tried in Israeli court and sentenced to thirty years for heading an illegal terrorist organization. When he had been taken from the Jericho prison the Israeli government accused Sa'adat of planning the assassination of Zeevi, but once in court he is tried only for heading a terrorist organization. The court rules, "The offenses the accused has been convicted of indicate that he initiated and participated in military activity with the aim of killing innocent people." An Israeli military source adds anonymously that "as chief of an illegal terrorist organization,

Ahmed Sa'adat is responsible and guilty of all actions carried out by this organization."[107]

True to his word about Israeli prisons being a training ground and that he would remain active inside or outside of prison, and still charismatic behind bars, Sa'adat continued to carry on his political and militant activities and was elected to the Palestinian parliament from Israeli prison later in 2006.[108]

In our taxi leaving the Jericho prison that day in 2005, I turn to Al saying, "You were so right to insist we interview Hamdi. I thought he was just a cold-blooded killer—he looked so cold and superficial last time we saw him that he really turned my stomach, but now that we talked with him, I see a much more nuanced man."

Al nods as we drive toward the checkpoint both of us hoping this time we can cross smoothly. Here only a few days in Palestine we are already sick of the hassles.

CHAPTER 28

Missing Passport

After our interview with Ahmed Sa'adat, we pass back through the Jericho checkpoint, get another taxi and return to Ramallah. It's late so we have something to eat in one of the local restaurants and then head over to Alla's house for a while, making a stop for beer and snacks. We have the house to ourselves as Alla's divorced father, with whom he lives, is out late. As Jamilah and the guys settle in to drinking and playing video games, I read.

Jamilah gets a call from her contact in Jenin. After a short conversation in Arabic, she snaps her phone shut. "We can go to Jenin tomorrow and we *may* be able to interview Zakaria Zubeidi," she informs us. "But we won't know until we get there. We can *for sure* interview some martyrs' families."

"That's great!" I remark. It would be very interesting to interview Zubeidi, who is the head of the al Aqsa Martyrs Brigade in Jenin and responsible for sending many suicide bombers into Israel. "Is Jenin safe?"

Alla and Jamilah glance at each other and shrug.

"I think so," Jamilah answers, "As long as we stay with my contact."

Ken pats his back pocket as his face suddenly screws up. "Oh shit! I don't have my passport!" He jumps up and runs to check his jacket pocket, then rifles through his backpack, dumping the contents and frantically searching all his belongings. "Fuck!" he says. "It must have fallen out of my pocket when I leaned over to pay the taxi driver! It was so dark I didn't see it. It must be sitting on the seat of the taxi right now. Oh fuck!" Ken slams the back of his hand into his forehead. "Jesus, what if somebody tries to use it crossing into Israel pretending to be me. I can be a fucking terrorist! Alla, can we call the taxi company to see if anyone has turned it in?"

Alla and Jamilah call the taxi companies servicing Ramallah, but none have found Ken's passport.

"I've got to call my consul," Ken says, repeating his worries of a terrorist or militant using his passport. Hours later, Ken reaches the Irish consulate's emergency contact person, who cancels Ken's passport and tells him if he comes in the next day he should be able to get a new one made for his flight home.

"I'm going to miss going to Jenin," Ken says, putting his hands in his jeans and standing dumbstruck. "I've got to go back to Tel Aviv to get a new fucking passport."

"Do you want us to come with you?" I ask, but Ken refuses.

They return to video games and I type up some of my notes from the day on my laptop. Jamilah and Alla begin to tell about us what it was like to live through the invasion of Ramallah during *Operation Defensive Shield* in the Spring of 2002, and I document their memories of the IDF troops and armored vehicles entering Ramallah and occupying the Mukata'a, sealing Arafat and much of his staff inside. Ramallah itself was occupied too after street fights in which thirty Palestinians were killed. A strict curfew was placed on the city while searches and more than seven hundred arrests were made.

"I was under the curfew in Ramalla," Jamilah states. "I stayed with friends. At one point we ran out of cigarettes and [my friend] Bashar and his brother [Mohammed] went out to get some. A tank surprised them and they spent three hours hiding on the ground, but finally they came with our cigarettes."

"I decided to go home," Jamilah recalls. When I opened the door to go out, his sister asked me where I'm going and I said, 'I'm going to the phone booth.'

'Be careful,' she said.

"The street telephone was near their house," Jamilah continues. "While I was outside, they announced on the television that the Israelis had entered the Mukata'a and the house we were staying in was *right next door*!

'Where is Jamilah?' everyone asked.

'She went to phone her mother,' the sister told them and then everyone went out to find me and they all left their mobiles inside. [Bashar's] mother became hysterical. When I came back to the house she [was so happy that I was alive that she] made a party for me.

"Then the Israelis came and took all the men. Their mother got hysterical [again]. It was ten days with her asking all the time, 'You think Bashar and Mohammed eat now? Smoke now? Sleep now?'"

"How was it for you to live through this?" I ask, wondering if it was as scary as it sounds given that she and her friends sound a bit blasé about being outside during the curfew to get cigarettes.

"At first we were really happy," Jamilah recalls. "All of us friends were in one house. We said to the helicopters, 'We win! We win! You try to make us unhappy but we are happy together! But after forty days it was harder. They took the boys; we had no cigarettes, no phone, and we fought. Most of [the boys I was with] are dead now, but we became very close friends during this time," Jamilah recalls, crossing and uncrossing her arms as she speaks. "All of us in the same situation and we don't know what to do. They opened [the curfew] for one hour [each day] but we don't have money. We don't have food. My family tries to share everything. We bought chocolates and cigarettes. Our families were too worried."

"How about you?" I ask. "Were you scared?"

"When we were in curfew we don't feel anything," Jamilah answers. "But after we feel how much it hurt us. Oh my God, after this we couldn't go to school! There were soldiers standing at [newly-made] checkpoints. We don't know if we have to study or not. All the night we called each other, 'Can we go or not? Curfew or not? Maybe yes, maybe no?' Oh my God, this is the worst! We don't know what we have to do and PA [the Palestinian Authority] doesn't have money so we don't get salaries. Everyone tried to help everyone else at that time. And the fighters close their phones [during that time] so we don't know if they are alive or dead, taken or not. We tried not to let them make us sad. We tried to make a party, play cards, but in the end we became tired."

"What was the worst part?" I ask.

"When our house got bombed," Jamilah answers. "We were near the Mukata'a. There no one can go out. Soldiers enter the building every two days to search. We suffer too much then!"

"The house you were in *was bombed*?" I ask.

Jamilah nods, her eyes wide with fear and her limbs shaking in an agitated manner as she recalls, "We were sleeping at four a.m. We heard a very loud sound. After this I am deaf but I saw the roof coming down! I thought all the girls had died. I was running to get out but then I heard the others. [After being outside in the cold] we finally went back in to sleep. We didn't think that the rest of the building could collapse on us. All the doors were opened and all the windows broken. Later we called an ambulance to take us to Birzeit."

Jamilah gets up and walks out of the room briefly, obviously upset about what she's been recalling.

When she returns Ken asks, "You didn't want to go to your family in Hebron?"

"We were in Hebron first but all my friends are far away and I thought if they die, I want to die with them."

Jamilah's parents told her she was not allowed to go back to Ramallah to be with her friends, but she was too worried about them and went anyway.

"Two tanks stopped me. If you are scared [they don't let you pass]; if you are strong the soldiers become scared," she tells us underlining once again how anger serves individuals in conflict zones, helping them keep their wits about them rather than falling into dissociated and passive states of powerlessness. Indeed each of the persons describing using anger this way is forcing themselves to stay in the "fight" versus "flight" or dissociated "caught in the headlights" frozen responses that are all potential instinctual brain responses to posttraumatic threat and overwhelming terror.

Our conversation is disrupted as Alla's father Ahmed returns home and greets us, welcoming us to Palestine. He is in a jovial mood and goes to his study to bring back a bottle of Russian vodka. After everyone has a "bottoms up" toast, Ahmed retires in his study but comes out intermittently, offering more drinks and getting progressively drunker, obviously drinking in his study as well. He finally dozes off and around two-thirty a.m. the guys finally become tired as well.

We begin to gather our things to leave for Jamilah's house where we will spend the night, and Alla stands to go wake up his father who offered to drive us. I pull Alla aside and say quietly, "Listen, Alla there is no way we can get in a car with your Dad. He's been drinking all night."

"No, he's fine!" Alla says wide-eyed.

"He's been drinking too much to drive," I argue back.

"He drives like this all the time!" Alla protests, honestly not seeing my point at all.

"Well he may be a very good driver, Alla," I explain gently, "but I have a rule that I don't get in cars with people who have been drinking. Let's call a taxi."

"All the taxi drivers are doped up this time of night," Alla says laughing, and Jamilah seconds his opinion.

"Really," Alla protests, "He'll be fine!"

"But the road to Jamilah's house is a winding one with lots of steep cliffs alongside it," I say.

"He can do it," Alla insists adding with a totally straight face, "He drives drunk all the time!"

After more discussion in which I get the point across without being insulting that in our culture getting into a car with someone totally inebriated is just not cool, Alla finally agrees that since I'm the only one who hasn't had too much to drink, I should drive us home and Alla will pick up his father's car at Jamilah's tomorrow.

"Is my driver's license even valid here?" I ask.

"Hell, you're the only one who isn't drunk!" Ken answers.

"I just don't want to be the foreigner who ends up in Palestinian jail!" I answer, wondering how I would defend myself for driving without a license.

Finally at three a.m., I get behind the wheel realizing that I'm a bit rusty with a stick shift, but with Jamilah's help on directions, I manage to get us onto the winding hillside road leading from Ramallah to Birzeit. As I drive along its snaking curves and see the sharp drop-offs close to the edge of the road, I lose my breath imagining Ahmed trying to maneuver this road drunk, and I'm really glad I stood up to Alla.

In the morning, we get ready to go to Jenin, and Ken heads off to Tel Aviv. He stands in line at the Kalandia checkpoint and when he finally gets to the front of it, the Israeli soldier smirks and says. "Did you know you're in the women's line?"

"Oh shit!" Ken says, embarrassed. He allows Ken to stay and asks for his passport. "Uh, my passport—I lost it last night in a taxi cab in Ramallah. I've called it in to my consulate and they cancelled it already,but I have to get to Tel Aviv to get a new one."

"So you're in the West Bank without a passport?" the soldier asks, rolling his eyes.

"Yes," Ken answers, and seeing his usual charm failing him, he jokes, "I'm Irish God damn it, you can see I've got blue eyes and freckles!"

"Okay, prove it," the soldier challenges. "Say five Hail Mary's at the top of your voice."

Ken luckily knows the words of this Catholic prayer from Jesuit reform school and starts shouting it out at the top of his voice. When he finishes his first Hail Mary he stops.

"Four more," the Israeli demands and Ken, to the consternation of all the Muslim Palestinians also trying to make their way across the checkpoint, keeps yelling the Hail Mary at the top of his voice four more times. When he finishes the Israeli jerks his head saying, "Okay get out of here!"

Ken takes the bus from the checkpoint to East Jerusalem and when it's stopped and searched by soldiers he repeats the same story. He's hauled off the bus but finally allowed back on. Ken continues onward to Tel Aviv where he fills out the paperwork for his passport and then begins a drinking binge that continues until the next night when we meet up with him at Mike's Place.

Meanwhile, our taxibus is speeding us along into the Jenin refugee camp.

CHAPTER 29

The Battle of Jenin

"Jenin and Nablus are the two hotbeds of extremism from where many of the suicide terrorist have been launched," my colleague Nichole Argo wrote to me when I asked her about where to travel in Palestine and where to avoid. "The situation there changes from day to day and you have to be very careful about going to either." Her words were a good warning for Nablus— no question on that—and now I am on my way in to Jenin, the site of the biggest Israeli incursion: the Battle of Jenin, which occurred during *Operation Defensive Shield*, and the camp that still undergoes frequent incursions.

During the Second Intifada, Jenin had become what Palestinians referred to as the "martyrs' capital," leading all other West Bank cities in attacks upon Israel. Fed up after Fatah, the al Aqsa Martyrs Brigades, Hamas, and the Palestinian Islamic Jihad (PIJ) groups based in Jenin dispatched twenty-three suicide bombings and six attempted bombings on Israelis, the IDF was determined to capture or kill the two hundred militants in Jenin who were responsible for so much Israeli suffering.[109]

At the end of March 2002, the IDF encircled the Jenin refugee camp, declaring it a closed military area and sent troops in to route out the militants. But the militants had prepared in advance by booby trapping buildings and planting explosives in cars and trash cans, and the ensuing street battles were fierce. The IDF responded by calling in assault helicopters and armored tanks to bulldoze the rigged buildings, ultimately flattening a two hundred square meter area inside the camp and damaging additional structures to allow the commando troops to enter safely. The fighting lasted for ten days until the militants began surrendering. Zakaria Zubeidi, head of the al Aqsa Martyrs Brigade, was among the few militants who eluded capture, slipping away among the rubble to pass through the tightening Israeli noose. Fifty-two Palestinians—half of them civilians—were killed in the battle, and thirty-two Israeli soldiers also lost their lives, an unusually heavy toll for the IDF.

Israel ordered a news blackout during the battle and wild rumors circulated. Palestinians referred to the battle as an "Israeli massacre", claiming hundreds if not thousands of Palestinians had been killed. When investigators were later sent in, the numbers were far less, although many of those killed were civilians. Unquestionably it was a heated battle in which the Israelis, as usual, had overpowering force. Civilians had been encouraged to leave ahead of time but many did not and militants were allowed to surrender—though they were forced to strip naked when turning themselves in due to the Israelis' fear that they might be wearing bombs to explode themselves. Now I'm here to hear their stories.

As we arrive and our taxi takes us into the heart of the Jenin refugee camp, Jamilah reminds us, "This place is filled with fighters." I look around and notice that the "camp" no longer consists of tents as the name conjures, but is comprised of two-to-four-story stone buildings, housing sixteen thousand Palestinian refugees, most of whom came in 1948 from the Carmel mountains and region of Haifa (areas that are now in Israel proper) at the time of the "Nakba", or the disaster as Palestinians refer to it.[110] According to the United Nations Refugee Relief and Works Agency (UNRWA) the Jenin camp residents are poor and most work in the agricultural sector, but as I look around I think their poverty isn't evident from the outside. The limestone buildings look nice and while the children playing in the paved streets are wearing worn and faded clothes and some are barefoot, they look otherwise normal. Some of them gather curiously around our taxi, staring at the foreigners and probably hoping for candy. I reach into my purse as we step out of the taxi, stretching from our two-hour journey from Ramallah, wondering if I have any gum for them, but decide being mobbed by even more children isn't smart. Jamilah calls her contact, and our Jenin handler soon appears.

"Marhaba! Welcome!" he says and after we are introduced, he confers briefly with Jamilah in Arabic. Jamilah then introduces Mahmoud[1] who has arranged for us to meet some of the men who were here during the Israeli invasion. Mahmoud leads us into a first-floor room in one of the nearby stone buildings into the community room. We take seats on the empty metal chairs while he brings in five men from a nearby room. They are all darkly tanned, muscled and their grizzled hands, worn pants and button up short sleeve shirts look like those of men who are laborers. Mahmoud introduces us but withholds their names.

---

1 Mahmoud is a pseudonym

"What would you like to know?" Mahmoud asks, gesturing to the men who sit ready to answer.

I explain my study, with Alla translating, and after getting their consent to participate I ask them somewhat tentatively, "You all are fighters? You participated in the battle of Jenin?" As I wait for them to answer I notice they seem proud and tough. They smile and squirm a bit, then one answers, "Am I a fighter?" he smiles as though to say yes, answering, "We did not leave the camp. I was in the camp and very proud of it. I was not objecting [to the fighting]."

I realize that given that they were militants targeted by the Israeli army, they may not want to admit to their activities, so I back off.

"I am trying to understand what motivates Palestinians into political violence and terrorism," I ask, changing tact.

"Mahmoud was named after his uncle who was assassinated by an Israeli soldier," one of the men begins. "If you ask him why he is named Mahmoud he will tell how he grew up with a struggle [for freedom] and that he believes in sacrifice and revenge. Ninety-five percent of our children have martyrs' names."

I nod. "Do you teach your children to be fighters then? Do you agree with some of them going to 'martyr' themselves? So many bombers have launched from this camp, no?"

"Of course I raise up my children to understand that our case is fair and to protect this case [i.e. to end the occupation, to free Palestine]," one of the others answers. "But I am not going to choose the way for him and his generation. The past generation did not choose our way. We chose it. We joined a revolutionary movement, a struggle. Our generation started twenty years ago with Molotovs and rocks thrown on the [Israeli] jeeps, but today you have martyrs and bombers operations. In the future I cannot tell what can happen."

"What about nonviolent protest?" I ask. "Do you ever consider the chance of following nonviolent methods like Gandhi or others used to achieve their political struggle?"

"Every struggle has its stages," a third man answers. "Only thing that stays the same is our case is fair and we are trying to defend it. The methods of defense are open—all methods from violent to nonviolent. Gandhi stood up to the British occupying India for them to go out. I will never forget that the Israelis took my ancestors' land. The solution for me is to go back to my house. But he doesn't have the will to leave it. I don't expect any Jews to give my home back."

"Can you tell me what happened here in the Battle of Jenin" I ask, adding with a smile, "even if you were not fighters in it?"

"The battle was for fifteen days," the second one answers. "It was nine days of fighting."

"It's very important to say," the first one adds, "that before the fighting began we decided together as a group—and the women decided as well—to stay [rather than take the Israeli offer and evacuate before the battle ensued] and to die with us if necessary. It was an extremely courageous decision on the part of the women."

"What did the women do during the fighting? Did you keep them to be human shields for you?" I ask horrified.

"They were both shields for us and assisted us in the actual fighting," he answers. "They were very instrumental in the fighting actually. They brought guns, made meals and ran with things we needed."

"We fought five at a time for one to two hours at a time," the second man adds, admitting that they were fighters. "There were fifteen thousand Israeli soldiers in their detachment, and we were one hundred and fifty to two hundred men resisting with our weapons. They could fight for a short time and then rest while others went in for them, but we kept fighting the whole time. We didn't have any relief."

The men then offer to take me through the camp to show me how the street battle was fought and to the cemetery where the fifty-two camp residents who were killed—women and children among them—are buried. As we walk through the camp, the men stop proudly to point out bullet and mortar holes in the walls and explain how they had placed bombs in some of the buildings at one particular juncture in their street and ambushed the Israelis, killing thirty-two soldiers—a far greater ratio of Israelis to Palestinians killed than is normal for the IDF.

As we walk up the hill, one of the men points out all the newer buildings saying, "They brought their bulldozers and destroyed all these homes. It was a great swathe of destruction from the mosque to the trees."

At the crest he tells us, "Sharon stood here on the top of this hill [overlooking the camp] and ordered the army to destroy the houses. An Israeli media unit was allowed on the hill so they saw all of it." I understand that the Israelis allowed only their own media in during the news blackout, as their media is heavily censored and answers to the IDF.

"During this time the army didn't allow ambulances and relief workers in to help the people, and many ambulances were destroyed," he continues. "After it was all over, a European artist came and made two statutes using pieces of metal he cut from the destroyed ambulances. One was a huge sculpture of Sharon depicted as a monkey shaking his fists, as if he were watching it all. We placed it here as a monument to that moment [when Sharon was ordering destruction from this place]." He indicates an empty spot on the top of the hill. The men laugh as I imagine this giant metal monkey overlooking the camp. "When the Israelis learned about it," the man continues, "they came and bulldozed it too."

As we walk back down the hill, we stop in at the community graveyard. It's a small plot of land, but there are a considerable amount of graves. The men become emotional pointing out where children are buried. As we stand in silence, Mahmoud reminds us that we need to move on, as he has lined up an interview for us with the parents of a suicide bomber.

At the bottom of the hill, we thank the men for sharing and part ways. It was a tough battle from the sound of it, and I wonder how Zakaria Zubeidi managed to sneak away from it.

CHAPTER 30

A "Martyr's" Birthday

Next we move to the family home of Nidal Abu Shaduf, who at age twenty-one carried a bomb into Israel on July 16, 2001 and exploded himself at a bus stop in Binyamina (a town in the Haifa district of Israel), killing himself, two others and wounding eleven more.

Nidal's father, dressed in khaki pants and a button-down short-sleeve shirt, greets us at the door and ushers us into their living room, which is furnished with typical upholstered sofas. Nidal's mother, dressed in a traditional Palestinian abaya and headscarf, rises to greet us and points out chairs for us. Mahmoud, our handler in Jenin and friend of the family, is also welcomed to take a seat.

"We are refugees from the village called Sulim in the area of Ala Footi," Nidal's father explains to us as we take our seats. "We are 1948 refugees," he adds referring to the voluntary and involuntary exodus of hundreds of thousands of Palestinians from Israel and the emptying of over five hundred Palestinian communities at the time of Arab-Israeli war and the civil war that proceeded it. "Nidal was born here. He is our eldest and has two brothers [Ishmael and Mohammed]."

I nod, glancing around as I get settled.

"This house is new," Nidal's father comments. "[The Israelis] destroyed the previous one."

"We celebrate Nidal's birthday *today*," his mother tells us as we take our seats. I nod and confused by her statement, confer with Alla as I pull out my notepad.

"They are celebrating his birthday today even though he is dead?" I ask.

"Yes," Alla nods. "She says that she won't accept his death as real until she receives his body back from the Israelis, and yesterday was his birthday so she has made a big meal and cake for the family."

I take a deep breath and turn to Nidal's mother saying, "Thank you for allowing us to come today. I understand it's a very special day for you and your family."

She smiles sadly.

I smile back, trying to comprehend her pain.

"It comforts you to remember his birthday?" I ask gently.

"I cried and had a nervous breakdown all day yesterday," she answers. A sob catches in her throat as she wipes more tears and then continues with her eyes glistening, "The culture of the birthday party does not exist in our society. I don't make a party for the others, but for him I do. I always make some kind of gathering. His birthday was the same day as the visiting day at prison [where her son Ismael is currently held], but we were not allowed to go, so our younger son, Mohammed, went to visit him. In general we are forbidden [by the Israelis] to see our son. It's because of Nidal." It is unclear if the parents cannot visit their son because they are considered a security risk or if this is another Israeli way of collectively punishing the families of suicide bombers.

"What is a prison visit like?" I ask, curious after having observed visiting day in Hasharon prison.

"I grab a microphone and talk through the glass to him," she answers and then throwing her hands in the air adds, "But his brother [Mohammed] is the one who goes. Such a visit for a little kid to his elder brother! Ishmael won't tell him what he needs, like 'I'm hungry,' or 'I'm suffering.' I always want to know what I can do to help. Since the beginning when he got locked in jail, I bought him a gym suit and I keep sending it to him and they [the Israeli prison officials] keep sending it back. Five months he's been under torture in the black hole."

"What is the black hole?" I ask.

"During investigation he is locked in a small room," Nidal's father explains. "They take him back and forth on a gurney. They are really interested in him. They thought that he's a sender [of bombers]. We don't see him, but others who visit hear that the Israelis mistreat him. He wanted to be taken to the hospital to stop the bleeding, and he wrote a letter [apparently smuggled out from there] saying, 'My hands—I just newly feel them.'"

"How do you know what is happening to him—that he is being tortured?" I ask a bit aghast at their allegations.

"Through what he tells our friends and family," Nidal's mother answers as she nervously wrings the loose folds of her abaya in her hands.

"The Israeli torture process," Mahmoud jumps in to explain, "consists of putting the prisoners in stress positions in plastic chairs and very tightly tying their hands together with plastic cuffs. The prisoner can stay in this position for fifteen days! The plastic is really tight so if he tries to move, it digs even further into his skin." Mahmoud pulls his chair next to mine and uses his hands and body to demonstrate how a seated stress position looks. "They also cover his head with a sack made of tenting material so it's very difficult to breathe. The sack is always wet so it has the smell of decay. There are also direct beatings. And they make the prisoners sit on a chair inside a small cupboard in a stress position with their hands tied behind them. They are locked in a cupboard so tight that it barely fits the body. The prisoners stay like this one to two days and the chair is really short so their legs tire. There is no bathroom, no food and sleep is forbidden. There is a microphone in the cell and huge speakers playing very loud music right by their ears so it is impossible to sleep. Then there are showers with very cold and very hot water."

"What are the other stress positions?" I say, trying to keep my cool as I listen.

"They tie his hands on a pipe overhead and put the prisoner on his tip toes so he can't relax," Mahmoud says. "They tie your hands and legs together and your chest toward the floor so you cannot stretch out. They use this hanging and humiliation and spitting on your face and cursing. They also make very small cuts on your face or neck so it gets inflamed and then they beat on the sore place. This can go on for fourteen days or five or six months."

"You've seen this with your own eyes?" I ask horror struck.

"I've tried it three times!" Mahmoud says, laughing kindly at my naiveté regarding the Israelis' use of such procedures. "I've spent five years in jail. I saw this and much more with my own eyes. They yell, 'Fuck your mother!' and 'Fuck your wife!' and all these humiliations on your relatives. And they use the family as material for pressure on the prisoners. They might arrest the father and mother and bring them during an investigation and let you see them with the implications that 'we won't let them go unless you confess.'"

"With Ishmael [Nidal's brother], the Israelis brought pieces of *Nidal's corpse* in order to put him under pressure to confess as well as threats of destroying his house!" Mahmoud continues. "In fact, they destroyed the house of his father. Their torture can be on high levels. They press on the prisoner with psychological methods. For instance, they take pictures of you entering prison and another one when in miserable shape one month after the torture and show it to you. It's some kind of psychological torture. They want the prisoners [under interrogation] to see only the detective and to listen to loud music so you feel you are all alone in this world. And of course they bring you fake news of your parents. 'Your father has died.' 'Your brother died.'"

"They came three times and destroyed our home, our furniture, our photos, Nidal's father says anger burning in his voice. "They burned our mattresses and blankets, and oil was mixed in with our flour."

"They wanted to kill Ishmael at first," Nidal's mother adds, her voice becoming hysterical as she recalls the time when the soldiers came to arrest her sons. "They didn't want to take him, they wanted to shoot him by a sniper. And Mohammed was shot by a sniper right behind the ear. He was very quick and laid on the floor. Then we started crying because we thought he got martyred. The soldiers did not come inside. So my husband went out to see what's happening. Then the army [IDF] came. They came into the house and were about to shoot Mohammed. We ran to him. The army was already there, and one of them was about to shoot him but when they heard us calling out his name, 'Mohammed!' they stopped. 'This is not the one we want,' they said. [But still] they took him in the car and beat him. They took Mohammed for eighteen days, and they took all of us outside under the rain, sleeping girls and babies. Then they entered the house and fired all around the house, shooting randomly."

I nod, scribbling down what they are saying and ask, "Can you tell me about your son? About what happened with him? Do you know why he went on this mission?"

"Nidal didn't finish high school," his mother answers. "He transferred to work instead. Then a rocket from a tank martyred the friend of his cousin. Two of his best friends were martyred as well. His cousin used to work for the Palestinian national security [forces]. He was on the check-point for Palestinians and a tank bombed them with a rocket. That was just at the beginning of the [second] Intifada."

"Do you know why Nidal's friends were killed?" I ask.

"The two friends were throwing rocks at the army," Nidal's mother answers.

"These things upset Nidal very much?" I ask.

"Yes. He used to go to work and if he heard of a martyr, he got really affected," his mother recalls. "He would laugh and joke but you could never tell what was deep inside."

"Because of this behavior," Nidal's father adds, "we did not know anything. He was too polite. Everyone was proud of his character. He was really, really quiet. The day he did it, he was with me in the house. He was completely normal. With his good clothes on he looked like a groom!"

"[On the day of his mission] I made his breakfast," Nidal's mother recalls. "He woke up and didn't eat breakfast [and smoked instead]. I told him, 'I swear to Allah, for how much you smoke, you will die in a year!' Later I asked myself, *Why had I said this to him?*"

"You sensed it somehow, perhaps as a mother?" I ask, understanding how mothers often have strong feelings about their children that they cannot really put into words.

"Yes," she nods. "Before he got martyred, in three days we lost two martyrs. They had an operation planting mines. They were his friends. When he got home [from work], he found their martyrs' pictures on the table. He put them in a frame. He was really terrified by the pictures. When I saw him in this state because of the death of his friends, I prayed to Allah, *If you take my son, please take him as a martyr!* Now I feel like I cursed him or put a spell on him! I feel guilty! If they give all of Palestine to me it won't count for one look from him."

"Are you saying you had a sense that he was going on a mission, or that you somehow encouraged him?" I ask.

"No," she says, shaking her head. "We had no idea that he was considering going. When I look back I realize I understood on some level. It was mother's intuition that I felt it beforehand, but we had no real idea."

"He really used to like martyrs," his mother adds. "Whenever there were demonstrations for martyrs, he was the first in their processions. But when the mosque made the call [saying he had suicided], I never thought he would, or could, bomb himself. Not in this way!" Her face screws up in pain and she clasps her hands to her heart.

"Can you tell me what happened with Nidal that day?" I ask.

"He went out at four p.m., and the operation happened at seven p.m. It happened pretty fast," she recalls. "It was well organized. I never thought it could be that easy!"

"Did he make a 'martyr's' video?" I ask.

"No, there was no video." Nidal's mother shakes her head. "I always ask myself why they all made videos and he did not."

I think to myself that often when a group decides to act quickly, they send a recruit without taking time to record a video. However, Nidal's father explains that he learned from Nidal's sending group, Palestinian Islamic Jihad, that Nidal didn't want to make a video in fear the Israelis might learn of his mission and arrest him before he could carry it out.

"Did he leave a letter that explained any of his reasons for going?" I ask.

"Yes," his mother nods. "He wrote a letter that same day. He came home, took a shower and prayed. Then he called his sister [at university] and asked her to proofread it but she said, 'No, I'm busy with my studies and I don't have time. If you wanted me to read it right now you should have stayed at school.'"

"When my daughter learned afterward about the letter," Nidal's father explains, "she went to her mother to tell her that Nidal had called asking her to proofread it. Her mother said, 'Get away from me! If you had just read his letter ahead of time we could have stopped him!'"

"What did it say?" I ask.

"He wrote, 'My mother, don't wait for me in the afternoon. My father will drink my coffee in the afternoon, my little brother will eat my food,'" Nidal's father answers adding, "He wrote, 'My mother don't wait for me in the night'—it means I will never come back.

"'Hopefully we will meet at the gates of heaven,'" his mother adds as she takes the long ends of her scarf and dabs at her eyes catching her tears before they roll down her cheeks.

"How did you receive his letter?" I ask.

"They gave us his wallet and the note was inside," Nidal's father answers. I fail to ask, but assume "they" are either the Israelis since he exploded himself inside Israel, or his senders with whom he left his wallet.

"How did you learn about his operation?" I ask.

"We learned about the operation from the radio," Nidal's mother answers. "When I heard about the operation I was happy, but I didn't [yet] know it was my son. The neighbor brought an ambulance to check me. I told him, 'I'm not in need of a doctor!' When I first understood that it was my son, people [had begun] making demonstrations down the streets. I was in a terrible situation. I wanted to cry for my son. The doctor was going to inject me [with a tranquilizer] but I didn't want that." She breaks down into sobs.

"Maybe you don't believe me," she says after composing herself. "For four years I didn't see his body! I still think I can see him. I don't believe he got martyred!"

I nod, understanding a mother's wish for her son to be alive when clearly he is dead.

As Nidal's mother wipes more tears from her face, their neighbor explains, "The Israelis keep his body as punishment to his parents."

"In the cemetery, [there is] a crypt with his name on it," his mother says. "He's not under there. We stopped going to visit it.

"His friend had a house he built on his own from his own money," she continues. "He paid for it himself. Now they are together in the fridge!" his mother wails, referring to their corpses lying in Israeli morgues. "A few days ago they handed some fifteen bodies back," she adds. "I always have the hope that they will release his body. I keep expecting it."

"How do you feel about the organization that sent him?" I ask.

"Everyone will die," Nidal's father states, "and he was always into it. I don't feel anger toward them. I sat with the person who gave him the belt. I knew Nidal asked for it. My son was really happy for this, and it was from deep beliefs."

"I talked with the sender also," Nidal's mother states. "I asked him, 'Tell me exactly how did he go there? Was he in happiness or not?' Nidal said to them, '[If you don't give me a bomb] I will go with my knife.'"

"What was his urgency from?" I ask.

"We don't know," his mother answers. "But there were two martyrs the day before, both his friends."

"What you should understand about his motives are that they are tyranny and inhumanity. We are suffering under it," Nidal's father explains. "[The Israelis] raped the land of a whole people."

Nidal's parents share with me a bit more about the person Nidal had been.

"At his funeral procession I cried and cried and cried," his mother says. "Nidal was so sympathetic with me."

"He was the perfect son with his treatment of us," Nidal's father states. "In Arab society the first child is honored and given a special position."

"He used to give up his food for me," his mother adds. "He used to give a lot of money to his brothers to buy sweets and snacks."

"The first day of his salary, the first thing, he gives money to his mother," his father adds.

"Nidal worked because of our family circumstances," his mother explains. "His father was sick and he had to feed thirteen members of his family. At thirteen years old, he worked for us. We felt actually we were unfair with him not to push him to do only school. He stayed in school but on Thursdays, Fridays and holidays he worked. When we collected vegetables from the farm he came out of school and ran straight to help out."

I nod. "It's his birthday today? You make a party to comfort yourself?" I ask, choking down the emotions engendered by their grief.

"I gather the family," his mother answers. "I feel he is with us right now. When something [bad] happens, some people hide the things that remind them. I want to see his things. I open his closet and run my hands over his clothes. I have Nidal's shirt and I don't wash it," she says, beginning to wring the ends of her headscarf in her hands using it to wipe the tears streaming down her face. " I always ask Allah to bless my son as he blessed me."

Alla, our translator, breaks into tears.

"Are you okay?" I ask leaning over him. Up to now I've been looking in the faces of the speakers watching them intently and only hearing Alla beside me translating their words, not paying attention to how this is affecting him. Alla is weeping and waves his hand gesturing me to leave him alone to compose himself. He turns to Jamilah speaking in Arabic, and she looks at me signaling that she will take over as translator. Her English is not nearly as strong as Alla's, but I nod and wait for her to take over.

"Did the Israelis destroy your home?" I ask.

"His operation was on the sixteenth of July, 2001," Nidal's father answers. "They destroyed the house on the third of November, 2002.

"The most expensive thing to lose is sons and daughters," his father says comparing the loss of Nidal to that of his home. "I had to sell a piece of land to construct our house and I gave up my work to build it myself. Then they came at one thirty a.m. The soldier said you have fifteen minutes to evacuate the house. In fifteen minutes we can barely take our own children out."

"They didn't come the day of the operation?" I muse.

"The operation was at the beginning of the [second] Intifada, [so] we didn't expect the Israelis to destroy our house."

Nidal's mother is still recovering herself and Alla sits with his tear-streaked face. I think we have asked enough of this family today. I'm actually amazed they agreed to an interview with us at all on Nidal's birthday. I thank them profusely and we begin to gather our things, feeling the heaviness of the emotions in the room. Then suddenly Al asks, "Could I use the restroom, please, before we leave?"

The neighbor shows Al where it is, and as we wait for Al, I transition from my clinical interviewer self who keeps her emotions at bay to be able to observe, sense and work more objectively with the emotions of those who are being interviewed, back to "just me". Nidal's mother gazes at me and I gaze back at her when suddenly I feel a sudden rush of emotion and a strong intuitive insight.

"I know what you do when you go in Nidal's closet touching his clothes," I say kindly to her.

She nods, and I feel we are communicating beyond languages and cultures somehow—our gaze relaying information across the wide abyss of our linguistic limitations.

"You hold them in your arms and smell them," I say.

She nods and begins to cry and at that moment I crack also. Tears burst out over the strong dams I was holding them behind in my "clinical persona" and I choke back a sob.

"We are both mothers," I say, looking into Nidal's mother's eyes as I take a tissue and dab at the tears that are now falling.

I can see the family is very moved and surprised by my emotions. I don't explain anything to Al when he returns, though he is surprised to see me in tears. I stand up, hug the women and hold my hand over my heart to say goodbye to the men. Later I realize that this moment of humanity is likely what convinced Mahmoud, Jamilah's contact and our handler in Jenin, to trust us enough to arrange for us to meet Zakaria Zubeidi, the leader of the Jenin al Aqsa Martyrs Brigade.

CHAPTER 31

Zakaria Zubeidi

"He's agreed to see you," Mahmoud tells us as he puts his mobile phone back into his jeans pocket. "But you have to agree to meet him with his cadres. They are carrying machine guns." He looks to see my reaction.

"It's okay. Let's go," I answer, already prepared for that by Jamilah. We pile back into our car and Mahmoud drives to the location where Zubeidi has agreed to meet. It turns out to be the same place where we interviewed the fighters earlier this morning.

"He'll be here soon," the handler says as we enter the room. The metal folding chairs are still there and I sit with Alla on my right, Al to the left and Jamilah beside him. The rest of the room is empty. The handler pulls the blinds on the windows and checks the outer door to be sure it's locked.

Soon we hear voices and boot steps in the hall; Zubeidi, flanked by fifteen of his cadres, saunters into the room. He's wearing jeans and a blue zip-up military style jacket with a grey furry collar. He and his cadres do, indeed, carry automatic rifles.

Two of them take post by the windows, peering through the plastic slatted shades, their automatic rifles ready to fight in the event of a sudden Israeli raid. Zubeidi is the local head of the al Aqsa Martyrs Brigade, the umbrella organization that has equipped and sent twenty suicide bombers who have killed eighty-three Israelis and wounded an additional six hundred and eighty six.[111] Zubeidi, age twenty-eight, is on the Israeli hit list and I know that if the Israelis learn that he's here now they may not hesitate to take him out, never mind that my students and I would be their collateral damage.

Zubeidi takes the seat directly across from me, his legs spread wide and his M-16 slung across his legs vaguely pointed in my direction. He drums on the body of his gun venting his nervous energy.

Mahmoud introduces us as Alla translates. Zubeidi leans back in his chair, looking arrogant as he waits for me to begin. I hesitate, remembering that my mobile telephone is still in active mode in my handbag. I know that it could serve as a listening device for the Israelis and that if any collaborator has informed them of our meeting, the Israeli army could also triangulate onto my phone to zero in on to Zubeidi's location. And that would mean a missile for both of us. I reach into my bag to retrieve my phone, keeping my gaze on Zubeidi and switch it off.

Zubeidi immediately challenges me, his tone rough. "What are you doing?"

"If the Mossad wants your interview, they can come get it themselves," I say.

He laughs derisively and tosses his phone on a small coffee table between us, leaving it switched on. I wonder again if the IDF will strike knowing that we are with him.

I'm here to learn Zubeidi's thoughts about the young men and women that he has been actively sending into Israel to bomb themselves under the banner of the al Aqsa Martyrs Brigade—at least until the Palestinian's just-declared "hudna" while they assess the situation with Israel and look for avenues to peace.

Looking at his rifle and his armed cadres, I begin. "It must be hard to suddenly lay down arms, to stop the struggle."

Zubeidi jerks up in his chair and looks at me angrily. "It's not hard at all," he answers, a cold edge to his voice. "We do what the people want us to do. If they want us to struggle, we struggle; if they want us to lay down arms, we lay down arms."

I feel badly that I've started with a wrong assumption about him, so I ask, "How do you know what the people want?"

He spits out his answer definitively, "They tell me."

I can tell that the interview is about to falter and that my opportunity to build rapport is waning.

I soften my voice to indicate that I don't mean to offend. "How do they tell you?" I ask gazing directly into his eyes. "How can you know what they really want? Do you have some way of talking them, to get a good indication of what they want from you?"

He responds more thoughtfully. "I sleep in a different house each night. I stay with many families and every night we talk about the situation, so I have a pretty good idea of how they feel."

"Can you tell me what the feelings are right now?" I ask, hoping that we are starting to make that essential connection.

He leans forward slapping his rifle with his hand so that it bounces lightly on his leg as he talks. "Right now the people are tired. There has been too much fighting, too many deaths. They are tired. They need peace right now."

I can see his growing frustration with my questions, and I struggle to recover, thinking about how to proceed to regain my footing. And then his phone rings.

Zubeidi answers, "Hello?" He's silent, waiting, but there is no reply.

"Hello?" he says once more.

I eye the table between us, mentally measuring the distance. Fourteen centimeters. It can't be much more than that. I feel a strong urge to back my chair away from him, panicked that a missile may be coming any second now. I know the Israelis can hone in on their target after identifying him on the phone with the precision of less than fourteen centimeters. *Are they launching a missile now?*

"Hello?" he says once more.

The room is completely silent, bodies tense. There is no answer. It seems it can mean only one thing. I resolve to stay in place. I don't move my chair. *If a missile is coming we will be killed together.* Curiously, I feel ready, unafraid.

Zubeidi repeats "Hello?" again, this time angrily.

Silence. He switches off his phone and slams it down on the table, cursing. At once he looks up, his flashing black eyes lock with mine. I don't move, just hold his gaze. The moments tick by. No missile. Zubeidi has noticed that I haven't flinched, haven't backed away, that I am still here with him. I see the sudden respect in his eyes. He curses at the phone and at the Israelis. I proceed.

"What is it like to be a hunted animal?"

"I'm chased," he answers. "Every night I stay somewhere else—since I almost got caught three years ago." He reflects for a moment. "Right now the people need this hudna. As long as the people want this we go along with it."

"I know you are a sender of 'martyrs,'" I say using the Palestinian terminology in order not to offend him. "Can you tell me when these men and women come to you asking to go on a mission how do they appear to you psychologically? Can you describe their mental states, what they are like?"

"They are martyrs!" Zubeidi answers, looking a bit astounded at the question. "How can I describe their mental state? This is like me asking you what does the person appear like psychologically who is standing on the twentieth floor about to suicide?"

This is a question I can answer, and I am delighted with the opportunity. "Actually I can tell you how a person is psychologically who is standing on the twentieth floor ready to jump. Most people who commit suicide are in deep psychic pain and they've detached themselves emotionally and mentally so that they feel numb and at a distance from their emotional pain. As psychologists we speak about that mental state that comes from being traumatized or in overwhelming psychic pain as dissociation. Do you understand what I mean by this concept—dissociation?"

I see a sudden click of recognition on his face and Zubeidi becomes highly animated leaning forward and speaking quickly. "Yes, I do understand! I had this 'dissociation' when the Israelis tried to arrest me last time. They surrounded the whole house. I had a decision in my mind that I won't go back to prison. So I opened the door and jumped out firing at them [expecting to be killed]. I had not even one percent chance of getting out alive. They ran away and I did, too. As I ran they shot at me from the back. I had normal injuries."

"You can say this [dissociative episode] happened in two stages," Zubeidi explains, his black eyes flashing. "It's a point you reach. The first stage was when I was inside the room. I took a look from the window. I decided I want to die. But when I got my weapon ready and jumped up, I decided not to die. I felt like the feeling of being a martyr when I jumped up, but it changed just when I opened the door. In one flash my feelings changed from asking to be martyred to cursing."

It's interesting to me that he also like so many others we've heard from countered his dissociative state with anger.

"It was in the first moments when you decided you'd rather be killed— be 'martyred'— then go back to prison?" I ask.

"Yes. All my options were available but going back to prison is like going to a piece of hell. Prison, even if only a cage with no torture, takes all your achievements. In one moment it all disappears. You always keep remembering the outside, the outside…You start to hallucinate. [At that moment] I got the whole tape rewound, the whole prison, flashbacks of the prison."

Zubeidi's face is aglow as he recalls this incident and I see recognition on his face—he is now beginning to understand mentally and emotionally what happened at that time.

"You get flashbacks and feel dissociative often?" I ask.

He nods, absorbed in the sudden self-understanding. "All the fighters get flashbacks all the time," he says, his attention still turned inward.

"When does it happen for you?" I ask.

"I speak normally with you now, but at twelve a.m. I cannot speak with you. You might talk to me and my brain is somewhere else. If you speak too fast..." he slaps his gun nervously on his leg. "All my senses are aware. The Stealth goes overhead then. They load it with two rockets. Sometimes it kills," he states, referring to his belief that the Stealth bomber is used for Israeli targeted assassinations. "For one hour it flies overhead, but the sound keeps echoing in my mind. The people I'm with tell me it's gone, but I say no. I try to get rid of the sound. I spend thirty minutes [calming] and then before I agree to move I make the person go and come back many times to be sure."

"So when you think the Stealth is overhead, you get agitated and then dissociative?" I ask.

He nods. "The Stealth has a laser that gets the aim. I don't know where it comes from, the right or the left. So my thoughts are all right there, right then. I am caught in a box in my mind."

Unable to get back to sleep, Zubeidi then roams the city alone.

"I sit up by the edge of the city [where the statue of Sharon as a giant monkey was erected] and look at the stars. It's the only diversion I have. The stars are my comrades at night. Then I walk all around the city. It makes me release what's inside."

"At three a.m. I am still awake under chase [as a fugitive]. I sit in one place and say the Israelis can come and take me. I keep shooting my gun until I get exhausted. I stay waiting. At five a.m., I forget this mood and I get reborn."

"What do you shoot at?" I ask.

"At night it's only me and the dogs," he says emerging from his self-hypnotic trance and looking at me with a shy smile. "Sometimes I shoot dogs!"

"You are the one who shot the dog last night?" one of his cadres interrupts as he gasps with amazement.

Zubeidi nods flashing a charismatic but shy smile. "He made me annoyed. He keeps barking!"

"Do you get dissociative when you are in a gunfight?" I ask curious to know when else he feels detached from his normal modes of consciousness.

"In the issue of shooting I don't think twice," he answers. "I lost many comrades in operations. When I am under danger I shoot anything. When you shoot and fire directly, you get out the tension. You mustn't shoot from the eyes but from inside," he states alluding to an automatic focus that most militaries train for.

"Sometimes in Ramadan when it's time to eat in the morning I look at houses not lit up, and I start shooting to wake them up. When the people wake up then I'm not alone anymore," he explains, flashing another bright smile.

"Sometimes, a person feels crazy," Zubeidi adds, his voice soft again as he reflects on his internal state once more. "Sometimes I go up the mountain. Everyone is sleeping below. It's like I talk to them saying, 'I'm the king! You are all sleeping.' A person at night goes insane; he is annoyed and feels aware."

"This is a state of hyperarousal," I say explaining. "It's normal after traumas to feel intensely attentive, to be in a heightened state of awareness."

He nods. "It happens to me daily. Sometimes you are the king, sometimes something else. At those moments I put my weapon down and have nothing to do with it."

"Do you know what posttraumatic stress disorder is, the psychological states that happen to fighters sometimes after many battles?" I ask.

He nods.

"You think you have it?" I ask softly.

"Yes, I think so," he answers.

"Is the 'martyr's' mental state the same as you describe?" I ask.

"No," he answers. "They are completely different than us [fighters]. They have only one decision. We have many options. [For the fighter] the thought of running away is always available. [The fighter's] thoughts are always offensive. We go and shoot."

"When a young man or woman comes to you asking to be sent by the al Aqsa Martyr's Brigade, do you find them to be people who are in a lot of psychic pain or traumatized? Are the people who come to be 'martyrs' also dissociative?" I ask.

"Yes, but he has already reached some higher level. I don't know what it is," Zubeidi says, his tone reverential again. "This feeling no one can tell about it."

"This dissociative mode, it comes from suffering?" I ask.

"Yes I had suffering from my mother [when she was killed by Israelis][112] but I couldn't reach this level of the martyrs yet."

"It's a stable state or it fluctuates?" I ask.

"For the martyr all the cells in his mind are dead except for one," Zubeidi states, meaning they are locked into their decision for "martyrdom". In contrast he explain that his and the fighters' dissocation is an "on/off thing".

"Do they seem to be people who have seen a lot of death, been traumatized or have PTSD?" I ask.

He nods. "They have flashbacks all the time and for them death is a mercy," he answers. "Most martyrs don't have a group and don't care who sends them." Slapping his gun lightly he explains, "They are in a special state," his tone turning reverent again as he adds, "They are martyrs!"

It seems Zubeidi sees things along the same lines I've picked up from studying suicide bombers in both Chechnya and Palestine. In conflict zones the individuals volunteering for suicide missions have too much trauma and pain to cope. In their hyperaroused states, they become totally fixated on carrying out what they view as acts of community defense, which also allow them to revenge, express their pain and ultimately escape from it. Zubeidi explains the difference between the inflexible dissociative states that "martyrs" are in compared to the flexible dissociation that the fighters experience:

"When I feel this way I stay there one or two hours, but [a martyr], after all that he has observed, there is only that one thing."

"Will you start sending bombers again?" I ask curious about his next moves.

"Under the [current] policies of Israel there won't be peace," he answers.

"How will you know when to start fighting again?" I ask wondering what specifically would trigger him to send bombers again.

"If there is an assassination we will counter it," Zubeidi says.

"We don't advertise ourselves," he adds changing the subject a bit. "And these operations cannot be stopped by the [Palestinian] leaders. The thing that stops them is that there is freedom and peace."

"What kind of person comes asking for missions?" I ask.

"They come begging – we reject more than we accept. There are hundreds of them," Zubeidi says almost wearily, without a hint of bragging about the scores of young men and women who want to fight the Israelis by suiciding.

"Are there as many girls as boys who come?" I ask.

"There are many *more* girls than boys who come begging for such operations!" Zubeidi answers.

"Why do you think that is?" I ask, genuinely perplexed.

"The emotions of girls are higher than boys," he suggests, shrugging his shoulders.

"Girls are defensive of their families —like 'she bears'?" I ask.

"Yes," he answers smiling. "The feelings of girls are much deeper than of the guys."

"How do you know this?" I ask curious how he has arrived at his stereotypical gender conclusions.

"Allah created girls more sensitive," he answers.

"How many more girls ask to become 'martyrs' than boys?" I ask.

"The girls who ask are double the guys who ask," Zubeidi answers. "No one took them into the Intifada [as fighters], so this pool increases. A young man can let out a little bit of what's inside by going to shoot. He can go on an operation, shoot and come back. But a girl has fewer options. She cannot go and shoot. Every girl [who wants to fight] has just one way: a martyrdom operation."

Zudeibi tells me his sending group has decided not to take girls despite the many who beg to be sent as suicide bombers. I ask him about Omaia Damaj who we interviewed in Israeli prison who was intercepted from Jenin.

"She used to live here before the invasion, but she moved," he answers implying that another group sent her, not his.

"These girls who are in jail now," he continues. "As much as they ask for an operation, they get caught. Girls talk more. Maybe she goes to many leaders and everyone rejects her and the information spreads. We don't look for them."

He has a good point—stereotypically women tend to talk more then men in order to process their emotions and therefore may be more of a security risk, especially on a mission that often requires waiting periods.

I ask how Zubeidi knows the men he sends are certain about their choice.

"Before I agree [to equip someone]," he explains, "I make this person go and come back many times to be sure." Evidently he is testing them to find the ones who are truly locked on, committed to dying and ready to take on a mission—it's likely these are the ones most traumatized and dissociative.

He taps his gun again.

Suddenly, Al leans in asking if he can say something. I nod.

"Please, can you point your gun away from my professor?" he asks protectively. "I'm afraid when you hit it like that it could accidently discharge."

Horrified I look down to see it is aimed right at me. Zubeidi smiles at Al and nods, moving it across his lap so that it is now aimed at the wall to the side of us. He continues to tap it nervously.

Zubeidi's cadres have all been listening intently to our conversation amazed to hear their leader reveal so much of his vulnerability and inner life.

"Your body guards seem to really care about you," I note.

"I run from prestige, from body guards, etc." Zubeidi states. "I have a bunch of comrades—not bodyguards. If I put them as bodyguards I am a coward, and then they will be cowards too." He turns to them and says, "I make them laugh at me to make them feel they are smarter. Then they are reassured in themselves." He flashes another charismatic smile.

Jamilah leans over and whispers to me that the cadres are nervous that they have stayed in one place too long and want to get moving. I nod and turn to ask my last questions.

"How do you deal with all the people who come to you asking for missions?" I ask preparing to wrap up the interview.

"It's his choice. I cannot convince him otherwise. I cannot give him freedom, nothing," Zubeidi says shaking his head sadly.

"Do you argue with those who come asking for bombs?" I ask.

"Yes sometimes," he answers. "But the bomber doesn't ask for an organization. I told you before that ninety-five percent of them are not organized. They come to any organization that they think will send them."

Evidently arguing may be futile, as the committed volunteer will simply find another organization to send him.

"Once you've equipped him, if he decides he doesn't want to carry the mission through can a bomber change his mind and return?" I am curious for more confirming information.

"Yes, of course you can change your mind," Zubeidi answers. "There is no penalty. There are some people who were in the heart of the beast [inside Israel] and return. We treat them normally. It's his decision [to self-martyr], not mine."

"I see you need to leave," I say wrapping up the interview. "I really appreciate your honesty and willingness to talk to me," I add as we rise. We shake hands and Zubeidi agrees to let me photograph him. After I snap a photo of him alone and have Al take one of us together, his cadres surround me thanking me and telling me that I am an amazing psychologist, that they have never seen this side of their leader.

I feel honored and relieved as they file out of the room with their automatic rifles. No missile. We are all still alive.

When I return home I read more about Zubeidi. According to an interview he gave a year after I visited him, he spoke about his family and how he entered the militant movement.[113] According to what he told journalist Christine Toomey, he had educated roots. His father was an English teacher but was arrested by the Israelis for his Fatah membership and thereafter blocked from teaching. He resorted to work as a laborer in an Israeli iron foundry instead. Zubeidi's mother, later a widow and mother of eight children, believed peace was possible. When Israeli human rights activist Arna Mer-Khamis created an initiative to foster Palestinian-Israeli understanding and set up a children's theater in Jenin, using psychodrama to help Palestinian children work through their traumas, Zubeidi's mother opened the top floor of her house for the children's theater rehearsals. Zubeidi and his brother were key players in it and he recalled his time with it fondly to Toomey.

But Zubeidi's young life was marked with its fair share of politically connected traumas starting at age thirteen when he was shot in the leg as he threw stones at Israelis at the onset of the first Intifada. The injury required six months of hospitalization and left him with a permanent limp. At age fourteen, he was arrested for throwing stones and was imprisoned by the Israelis for six months. Upon his release he was arrested again for throwing Molotov cocktails[114] and that time served four and a half years in Israeli prison. It was in prison that Zubeidi was recruited into Fatah. Toomey quotes Zubeidi as mourning the loss of his childhood saying,"I was injured at thirteen, put in jail at fourteen. Where is my childhood? Where has my childhood gone?"

A smart boy, Zubeidi served as the spokesman for the other children in prison. He also learned Hebrew and upon his release worked briefly for the PA. But he soon became disillusioned with their politics and went to work illegally inside Israel until he was caught and deported back to Jenin. There he engaged in car theft, was arrested again and served more time. He found a job as a truck driver in Jenin but had no work when the West Bank was sealed off due to the second Intifada.

Zubeidi entered the militant movement in late 2001 in response to the killing of a close friend. He learned to become a bomb maker. Shortly after, in 2002, Zubeidi's mother bled to death after being hit by an Israelis sniper during a "lightening raid" into Jenin as she stood near a window. Soldiers in the same time frame also killed his brother, Taha. Zubeidi bitterly recalled their deaths and the failure of the Israeli peace activists who had been fed by his mother to pick up the phone and express their condolences.

"That is when we saw the real face of the Left in Israel; the Left who later joined the Sharon government," Zubeidi told Toomey. Having lost his confidence in the peace movement he stated, "When you lose hope, your options are limited," adding, "So this is how suicide attacks happen. When people lose hope. When a suicide bomber decides to carry out an attack, he's fully convinced there is no more hope." He went on to tell Toomey that suicide attacks as a fighting tactic were necessary given the imbalance of power.

Israeli actor Juliano Mer-Khamis, the son of Arna Mer-Khamis, returned to Jenin in 2002 to look for the six boys who had been the core of his mother's theater group. In his award-winning documentary *Arna's Children*, he found that Zubeidi had turned to armed resistance, his brother Daoud was serving sixteen years in prison for militant activities, and the other four were already all dead.

In 2007 Zubeidi was included in an amnesty offered to militants of Fatah's al Aqsa Brigades,[115] and in 2008, he and Arna reestablished the Freedom Theatre in the Jenin refugee camp. But even as they worked to raise emotionally healthy children and foster peace, Arna's son (Juliano Mer- Khamis) was assassinated in Jenin in 2011 by a masked gunman.

It seems that Jenin alternates between hope and despair and the cycle of violence between Palestinians and Israelis carries on.

CHAPTER 32

Evening in Jenin

It's late when we finish our appointment with Zubeidi, too late to travel back across the checkpoints to Ramallah and Jamilah has arranged for us to stay with a local PFLP leader's family. That night we are invited for supper in their diwan with many of the men from their group. When we arrive, we are ushered into the room and seated on one of the large sofas, while the women prepare food in the kitchen. Jamilah and I are the only women sitting amidst the men. The women sumptuously place a large meal on the large dining room table and retreat while we are called to fill our plates. We help ourselves, return to the living room and continue chatting. The men discuss the politics of the Palestinian situation and are keenly interested in how an American views them and ask me many questions.

After some time I get up to use the restroom and when I return Al's face is serious.

"They've just been discussing taking you hostage in exchange for Ahmed Sa'adat," he says.

I look from Al's face to the others. Twenty men fill the room and everyone is looking intently at me, totally silent. I laugh and say, "You're joking right?"

"No," Al says, shaking his head, "I don't think it's a joke."

Smiling I look around at the men and take my seat on the sofa again.

"I don't think it's a very good idea," I say, seriously considering the idea of it. "Of course if you wanted to keep me I guess I could just continue my research interviewing all of you, but I don't think the Israelis would consider me a very good trade for Ahmed and while I'd be happy to stay with you, I think it would end in blood. We'd all be killed!"

I look around at them grimly and realize they are weighing my words carefully as Alla translates what I've just said. When he finishes they start an animated discussion in Arabic that Al and I cannot follow and that Alla cannot keep up with.

After some time Alla and Jamilah tell me that they agree with me—the Israelis probably wouldn't give them Ahmed Sa'adat for me and it would end badly. The men, however, seem pleased with my conciliatory answer and one of them goes to get a Palestinian red and white checkered keffiyeh and presents it to me. I think he is genuinely grateful that I haven't objected to be taken in trade for Sa'adat, and he places it around my neck in a gesture of honor. I accept it graciously, but when they ask to take my picture in it, I decline, not sure what wearing it might possibly mean to others and I don't want to unknowingly make a political statement in photos I have no control over.

As the evening wears on, the men tire and leave and we are each taken to our rooms, me to sleep in the room of one of our host's daughters. It's freezing cold at night in the mountains of Jenin, and I'm grateful for the warm pajamas I've been lent and the heavy quilts covering the bed. As I fall into sleep, I smile thinking about how sometimes it can be a good thing to be an undervalued woman in a male dominated sexist society—my value in their eyes as a hostage wasn't high enough to justify keeping me!

CHAPTER 33

Fadi Ziad al Fahudi and the Jihad Mosque Soccer Team

It's March 2005, and we are back in Palestine for the third time. Al could not make it, so it's just Ken and I. We pass through the airport without problems and go immediately onward to Jerusalem and then to Ramallah, where we are staying with Alla at his father's home. Upon our arrival, Alla takes us in a taxi bus from Ramallah heading to Hebron to interview two "martyrs'" families.

Hebron is a city of approximately one hundred twenty thousand Palestinians and five hundred Israelis, comprised of forty-five Jewish families and around one hundred fifty yeshiva students. An additional six thousand Jewish settlers live in the adjacent community of Kiryat Arba[116] and other small settlements are springing up in the area, a constant irritant to Palestinians who see it as Israelis grabbing land from them.

Hebron (al Khalil in Arabic) means the "friend of God," referring to Abraham, the patriarch of all three faiths—Islam, Judiasm and Christianity—that claim their heritage from him. The cave of Machpelah (also known as the Cave of the Patriarchs, now enclosed by the one-thousand-year-old Mosque of Ibrahim) is considered the traditional burial place of Abraham and Sarah, Isaac and Rebecca, and Jacob and Leah. For Jews, Hebron was both the capital from which David ruled the Hebrews for seven years before moving his capital to Jerusalem, and the place where Absalom, his errant son, also began his revolt against David. For Muslims, the Koran mentions that the Prophet Muhammad made a miraculous night journey to Jerusalem where he received a revelation from Allah. In this journey he stopped in Hebron at the burial site of Abraham. For these reasons, the Sanctuary of Abraham is considered to be the fourth holiest site in Islam, and for Jews, Hebron is often claimed as their second holiest site after Jerusalem. Israeli settlers lay claim to the area,[117] hoping one day to include these sites in Israel proper, creating tensions that we are on our way to learn about.

Twenty-six miles[118] from Ramallah, Hebron is not a long trip by car, although it's made much longer by the five Israeli checkpoints that we hit along the way. At least this time, as we wait alongside the road, we are surrounded by the beautiful blue Judean hills.

After two hours of travel time, Ken, Alla, and I arrive to the outskirts of Hebron. Rather than heading into the old, stone historic city center, we veer off the highway onto a thoroughfare that leads into the rural village of al Khalil where we have scheduled our interviews. The village appears dusty, depressed and empty; the few shops sport faded signs and dilapidated storefronts. We leave the taxi bus and take another taxi from al Khalil further into the countryside, finally arriving at a two-story stone home on a dirt road surrounded by other equally nice homes that all seem fairly new. There is no landscaping between the homes, just weeds growing between rocks.

Alla has arranged for us to talk today with two families of martyrs from Hamas. Hamas is a Palestinian political organization and resistance movement formed in 1987 as an offshoot of the Muslim Brotherhood that sprang up during a time when Islamist movements became popular and overtook parties that followed Marxist ideologies. Popular in Gaza and parts of the West Bank including Hebron, Hamas runs extensive social service programs such as schools, health care clinics, orphanages, relief work, soup kitchens and sports leagues—services the Palestinian Authority has often failed to provide. Although it is an organization with benevolent goals, it is also a militant one. Shortly after its inception in 1988, the Hamas charter announced its purpose of liberating Palestine from Israeli occupation and establishing an Islamic state in Israel, the West Bank and Gaza.[119] For that purpose, Hamas runs a military wing, the Ezzedeen al Qassam Brigades, responsible for many attacks, including large-scale suicide bombings, against Israeli civilian and military targets, suspected Palestinian collaborators and even Fatah rivals.[120]

Our first interview is with Ziad al Fahudi, the father of Fadi Ziad al Fahudi, a young man who joined nine other members of his fifteen-man Jihad Mosque soccer team in executing suicide attacks inside Israel proper and upon Israeli settlements in the Hebron area.

Fadi's father is expecting us and waits at his door as we arrive. He's a slim man nicely dressed in Western clothes with grey hair. His eyes are bright as he greets us warmly saying, "Welcome," and ushers us into his "diwan" or formal sitting room. His five or six younger, school-age children gather around him as we are seated on brown velvet couches. We are offered tea and coffee but there is no wife present. The house and the children are clean and tidy and everything is tastefully decorated leaving little doubt of a woman's touch. She is following Islamic traditions and not showing herself to male strangers, or she is out of the house.

One of the boys is proudly holding up the family's baby girl, no more than eighteen months old, on his lap for me to see. Ken points out that she is sporting a green Hamas headband that proclaims in Arabic lettering: "There is no God but Allah, and Muhammad is the messenger of Allah". I am not sure if her being dressed in the Hamas headband is an allusion to her as a small "martyr" or if she is just wearing the "team" colors, but I am reminded of the Arab children whose parents dress them in fake suicide vests for demonstrations.

I introduce Ken, Alla and myself, and Alla translates and explains my project.

"We've had problems with journalists," Ziad says. "They told us, 'We are press. We will listen and give the right picture.' But then they pictured us as terrorists and that we love killing Israelis, and they ignored the occupation."

I tell him I will do my best to be fair. Ziad nods his agreement and tells us parts of the story that he knows—the missing pieces I fill in with research to piece together a more complete story of Fadi's trajectory into suicide terrorism. Fadi, who was twelve at the end of the first Intifada (1987-1994) as Ziad tells us, had witnessed his fair share of Israeli violence while young and impressionable.

"When the first Intifada started," Ziad explains, "Fadi cooperated in some activities without my knowing. Later on news got to me. In the first Intifada he was involved in throwing rocks."

"Do you know what made him want to throw rocks?" I ask, although after having lived and traveled throughout the West Bank it's becoming obvious to me.

Fadi's father points out, "Until 1997 we lived next to the Kiryat Arba settlement. After that I came to buy this house in this area and started fixing it up. I didn't have the means to pay for repairs so I made favors (bartered) and others built for me. Fadi helped me."

The Kiryat Arba settlement is one of the first settlements formed in the West Bank and was co-founded by former U.S. military officer Dov Dribin who established illegal settlements that claimed even more Palestinian-owned land, evicting the Palestinians and demolishing their homes. These settlements eventually became legalized by Israel, angering the local population.[121] According to international law, the hundred or more settlements in the West Bank, housing approximately two hundred thousand Israeli settlers, are illegal, yet Israel persists in building, supporting and protecting such settlements. At this time in 2005, the Kiryat Arba settlement houses approximately five thousand illegal residents, further inflaming local tensions.

Indeed the settlers in the Hebron area are known to be some of the most hardened and aggressive Israeli settlers in the West Bank, notorious for stunts like taunting elementary school children, upending their book bags and strewing their articles about on their way home from school, and stoning them in an effort to get them to give up going to schools near the territory the settlers have claimed as their own.[122] Ziad's mention of Kiryat Arba explains so much. Fadi was twelve years old when the first Intifada ended and likely heard and witnessed these types of violent interchanges with settlers and was aware of their land-grabbing schemes before his father moved the family.

When Fadi was in tenth grade, he stopped going to school to help his father in his electricity business, but as the Second Intifada began, Ziad, like most Palestinians, suffered economically when Israel shut down its borders in response to the many suicide bombers who detonated themselves inside Israel proper. This caused the flow of Palestinian laborers into Israel and the wages that came with them to decrease, slowing the entire Palestinian economy and causing unemployment to soar.[123] Ziad was forced to return his house back to the person he bought it from and become a renter instead.

"My work was down. It created an empty space and spare time for Fadi, so he went to the coop [a community center] for physical activities, and he participated in sports. He went in the Islamic direction with the youth of the Mosque," Ziad explains, his face troubled. "I didn't watch him too much." He meets my eyes to see if I understand how hard it is, as a parent, to steer a child in the right direction, particularly when there are other societal influences that can take him where you do not wish him to go. I do understand and gaze back at him without any judgment, knowing all of the times I too could have lost my children—when I was distracted, busy, unable to keep tabs on everything about them, their friends, their activities. Parenting is always a challenge, but even more so when there are financial challenges at home and the surrounding society is troubled.

Fadi's first step toward becoming a suicide bomber appears to have been when he joined the Jihad Mosque soccer team.[124] In 1998, the team leader, Muhsin Kawasmeh, a young, devout member of the Jihad mosque who dropped out of school at age sixteen to run a small bookstore that specialized in computer and Islamic texts, founded the team and recruited fifteen other boys and young men from the neighborhood. There was only one requirement for membership: that all members pray five times a day and fast on Mondays and Thursdays.[125] The boys would gather once or twice a week after morning prayers under Muhsin's leadership and practice soccer.

During the second Intifada in November 2000, Israeli troops shot and killed team member Hamzeh Abu Shkhedeh in the head while he was throwing stones. Then in January 2001, Israelis killed a second teammate during another clash.[126]

"There were many obituaries in the second Intifada," Ziad says.

By obituaries, Ziad is referring to the communal mourning ceremonies for "shaheeds" and "martyrs" (terms used interchangeably by many) for those who killed themselves in suicide missions—and for those who were killed by the Israelis in actions against the Palestinians. Usually the entire town turns out to lament for the deceased, and a casket is carried throughout the town with mourners following in a procession behind it, the women making ululations (long, wavering, high pitched cries of joy) celebrating their belief that the deceased "martyr" has gone to paradise.

"What do you think pushed Fadi to do it?" I ask.

"What pushed him to do it?" his father repeats mulling the question over. "Humiliations . . . any Muslim is our brother, what happens to one, happens to all of us. It was based on these things: patriotism and he was religious." Then his eyes suddenly become fiery. "When they killed Hamid Durrah wasn't the whole world affected by it? He was no threat to them. The Israelis just love to kill!"

The killing of Mohammad al Durrah, a twelve-year-old Palestinian boy in the Gaza Strip, the event Ziad is referring to, took place on September 30, 2000 on the second day of the Second Intifida during heavy rioting throughout the Palestinian territories. Mohammad and his father were captured on film (by France News Channel 2) as they huddled behind a concrete pillar, caught in crossfire between Israeli soldiers and Palestinian security forces. The minute long footage shows father and son clinging together--the boy crying and his father waving for help--as the shooting continues unabated. A burst of gunfire and dust erupt and Mohammad is seen in the last moments of the film slumped across his father's legs, apparently killed by a stray bullet.[127] The footage with a voice over telling viewers that the child had been a target of Israeli fire went viral and pictures of the small boy huddled in his father's arms just before being shot to death are even now widely accessible on the Internet. A huge emotional obituary was held in Gaza for the boy and Muslims worldwide still hail Mohammad Durrah as a "martyr" and use his picture to deride Israelis as cruel killers of innocent children.

The Israeli Defense Forces at first accepted responsibility for the killings but later after investigating the incident concluded that they had probably not shot the al Durrahs. Further controversy arose when it was discovered that the France 2 footage had been cut and that in the final few seconds of the filming, Mohammad appeared to lift his hand from his face and was still alive.[128] The France 2 editors said they cut this part because the child was obviously in his death throes. There was also controversy over the killed boy's identity. In 2007 the Israeli Defense Forces renounced responsibility for having killed the pair, and the Israeli government claimed the entire episode was a staged propaganda stunt.

This death of Mohammad has been used as a rallying call to incite many to violence. It was invoked as the reason for the October 2000 lynching of two Israeli army reservists in Ramallah. When al Qaeda operative Sheik Mohammad Khalid filmed himself beheading Jewish-American journalist Daniel Pearl in Pakistan, the picture of Mohammad Durrah crouching in fear was shown in the background. Even Osama bin Ladin invoked al Durrah's name in a "warning" communiqué to President Bush after 9-11. And now Fadi's father is invoking the child's death as a possible reason that his son volunteered to retaliate against the Israeli settlers in their area. I don't doubt that it was one, among many, motivating forces in Fadi's mind, given the strong motivational force of identification with "fictive kin".[129]

Fadi, Mushin, and over time, eleven of the Jihad Mosque soccer team members joined the Qassam Brigades, the militant wing of Hamas, under the recruitment of Abdullah Kawasmeh, a quiet but intense Hamas militant who grew up in the neighborhood.[130] Years earlier, Abdullah was in the group of four hundred and seventeen Hamas militants who the Israeli army rounded up and expelled to southern Lebanon in late 1992. According to his older brother, Abdullah's time spent living in Lebanon "was the turning point in his life."[131] He lived a year in a tent on the border studying the Qur'an, building a mosque in the camp and steadily became increasingly committed to the destruction of Israel.

In hindsight, exiling the Hamas militants to Lebanon was a terrible mistake on the part of the Israeli government because there Hamas militants mixed with and learned from the Hezbollah operatives who were already well versed in suicide bombings. When the Hamas exiles were permitted to return to Palestine after the 1993 Oslo accords they quickly put their newfound knowledge to work. Upon Abdullah's return from exile, the Palestinian Authority locked him up for another two years. Upon his release he became a leading member of Ezzedeen al Qassam in Hebron. At that point in 2002, according to the cousin of one member of the Jihad soccer team, "The Jihad mosque became a factory for martyrs."[132]

During this same time period, the Israeli Defense Forces reoccupied Hebron as part of its massive sweep through the West Bank and took hundreds of men and boys into custody further inflaming Palestinians. The team coach Muhsin Kawasmeh and player Fuad Kawasmeh were both arrested and spent six months in Ofra Prison where they were further radicalized by Hamas activists inside the prison.[133]

Fadi still on the outside, learned to handle light arms and explosives under the tutaluge of Abdullah Kawasmeh who, preying upon the psychological vulnerability of these young boys, welcomed their anger and enthusiastically equipped them to take on suicide missions to kill settlers in the West Bank and Israelis inside the green line.

"Can you tell us what happened with Fadi?" I ask, trying to convey my sympathy for reopening his wounded father's heart.

Ziad nods, swallows deeply and continues, "It happened after our Ramadan in 2002. We are used to fasting with the six days after as well in Shawwal." Shawwal is the month following Ramadan, and Ziad and his family followed the Hadith in which the Prophet said, "Whoever fasts Ramadan and follows it with six days from Shawwal, it is as if they fasted the entire year."

"Fadi was fasting," Ziad explains. "We broke our fast in the evening, but he did not come back. I kept calling his mobile—no response. Then the Palestinian intelligence called our house and told us, 'Fadi is locked up at our department.' I went there to meet my son. They told me that Fadi was gathering weapons with some of his friends. I asked for his release but of course they refused. They said it was forbidden by an agreement with the Israelis. Fadi stayed in the Palestinian Authority intelligence unit for five months. We visited but the PA could not help him. They gave me information from time to time."

The Palestinian Authority had at that time, in an effort to move toward self-determination in the occupied West Bank and Gaza, entered into an agreement with Israel to hold and detain anyone who was plotting against Israel. Fadi thus was not arrested by Israelis but by his own government and was likely interrogated daily for hours at a time and beaten as well. For many Palestinians, this PA cooperation with Israel continues to be a thorny issue as many regard violent resistance against Israel as patriotic. It must have been a very bitter pill for Fadi to be locked up by his own people for amassing weapons to fight for his country's freedom.

As is often the case with parents, Ziad perhaps only knows part of the whole story about his son and other sources provide more details about this time in Fadi's life. In 2011, his biography displayed on the al Qassam website proudly states "Fadi was recruited by Ezzedeen al-Qassam Brigades, where he worked in preparing explosive devices. In addition, he became good in using light weapons. As a result, the Palestinian security forces detained him for 3 months."[134]

Thus according to the military wing of Hamas, Fadi was already working for them at the time of his arrest by the PA—and not only gathering weapons as his father had learned, but also gaining skill in making explosives. According to the al Qassam website Fadi was released during the second Intifada only a few days before the Israeli forces attacked his village near Hebron.[135] This is what his father also recollects.

"After this," Fadi's father states, "There was the invasion of the Israeli army in April of 2002. There were too many arrests. All of his friends were arrested and those who had been released from the P.A. jail also got arrested [by the Israeli army]. The Israelis did not arrest Fadi. I told him to keep working as an electrician, that we don't want any problems."

Fadi's father pauses and gazes off in the distance remembering this time before his son's death. I wait quietly.

"He convinced me that everything is okay. He was a very good Muslim and always worshipped in our house and in the mosque, and he often stayed awake all night reading the Koran and making prayers. This was very important to him until the day of his martyrdom." [136]

Throughout the second Intifada, Fadi's team kept playing and winning just like other boys the world over who enjoy a good game of soccer. But they couldn't take full pleasure in the normal joys of teenage boys enjoying a sport together. As they played on, they witnessed their team's members shot dead while throwing rocks in skirmishes with the Israelis, rounded up, arrested, imprisoned; and finally one by one they became angry and demoralized enough to volunteer for and carry out suicide missions that Abdullah Kawasmeh, their local Hamas operative was only to happy to equip them to carry out.

In September 2002, teammate Mohammed Yagmur became the first volunteer for a suicide mission directed by Kawasmeh against a Jewish settlement near Hebron. He became the third member of the team to die.[137]

Three months later, Hamzi Kawasmeh, who had already quit the team, crept into the isolated Kharsina settlement northeast of Hebron to carry out the team's second suicide mission. Hamzi shot dead one settler and wounded three others before he was killed. Both Mohammed and Hamzi were effective in breaching Israeli security because they, like the other teammates that followed them, donned Abdullah Kawasmeh's trademark disguise of dressing as a Jewish Yeshiva student—a look that was unlikely to arouse Israeli suspicion.[138]

Ziad knew the deep emotional impact to his son of losing his team-mates to Israeli violence and then to suicide missions. But he didn't real-ize his son had been caught up in the group contagion of suicide.

Even with normal suicide this contagion effect is surprisingly strong especially among teenagers. School psychologists know that when one high school student commits suicide it's important to intervene quickly in the student body to prevent others from following in the first one's foot-steps. Without an intervention it's not uncommon for one suicide to turn into two or more. This group contagion effect can operate in families as well. In the case of the Jihad Mosque soccer team, once one member decided to strike back for the deaths of their teammates and all the other injustices involved in the occupation; one by one, the others followed. Probably Abdullah Kawasmeh also played upon their already strong reli-gious sentiments and told them that to "martyr" themselves was to attain the highest honors as a Muslim. It's clear that Fadi had been caught up in radical ideas that his coach and teammates (and he also may have) picked up in prison, that his Hamas sender had learned in Lebanon and that his imam extolled. In a vulnerable state Fadi was receiving multiple messages from many esteemed sources, eroding his barriers to suicide.

"Did you know something was wrong?" I ask.

"Yes it was an inner feeling," Fadi's father answers. "I could not tell the specifics, or exactly what it was. And this feeling is sometimes true, sometimes wrong."

Ziad's feeling was true. On March 8, 2011 teammates Fadi, Mushin, Hazem and their close neighborhood friend, Sufian Hares, went together to carry out an attack organized by Abdullah Kawasmeh. Splitting into pairs to carry out nearly simultaneous suicide attacks upon two different settlements near Hebron, the boys carried weapons and wore suicide vests to explode after breaching the settlement's perimeters. They comprised the third to sixth suicide attackers from the Jihad Mosque team. The Israeli security service had a hard time detecting the tight knit group because they communicated in person, an advantage that kept their terror cell functional until nearly the entire team had taken on suicide missions.

"If a group is closely knit, doesn't use cell phones and keeps itself tightly compartmentalized as this soccer team did, it can be extremely difficult to penetrate," former top Israeli military intelligence officer Eran Lerman comments.[139] It wouldn't be until after the eighth player blew himself up in Jerusalem that Israeli intelligence officers began to understand that the players of the Jihad Mosque soccer team were more than just fierce opponents on the football field.[140]

"On the day before [it happened] I had the night shift," Fadi's father says. "It was Friday. I came home early and saw Fadi.

'Good morning,' he said and hugged me. I felt deep inside me, 'My son, something is wrong!' He is sick or something. He is not normal!

'Are you sick? I asked him, 'You have a problem?'

He answered, 'No.'

Then I went to the market. Friday is our holiday."

The weekend for Muslims, like Jews, begins on Friday, and devout Muslim men typically go to mosque on Fridays to pray and hear the sermon. The Friday sermons at some mosques in troubled areas inside Palestine are filled with hatred for the Israeli occupiers and the imams incite the young people into "martyrdom" missions glorifying those who volunteer for suicide.

"We prepared lunch," Fadi's father continues. "I ate my breakfast, but Fadi did not eat—only a little. 'Let's work and pray,' he said."

By that time, Fadi had gravitated from his father's mosque to the extremist Jihad Mosque,[141] and each went to their separate mosques for prayers. Later that day, Fadi asked to return to his mosque for afternoon prayer.

"'Go, but don't be late so we can eat together.' I told him.

'Inshallah, when I come back.' He answered."

Inshallah, which literally translates to "Allah willing," is a typical Muslim answer regarding the uncertain outcome of future events, conveying the belief that it is arrogant to announce one's future when it is Allah who ordains the future. Ziad is highlighting perhaps that his son used this answer when referring to his return for the evening meal, because Fadi knew but did not want to say that he wasn't planning to return at all.

"But he didn't come back before the evening prayer," Fadi's father states, a crease settling between his eyebrows. "His mother got worried and called him.

"'He is probably waiting for the final prayer,' I told my wife.

"She called him, but his phone was closed. While we were speaking, the exclusive news of an action in the Kiryat settlement came on. After that, in ten or fifteen minutes, they gave news of an operation in another settlement [Negohote]."

Ziad rubs his forehead. "His mother felt it."

"'Fadi is in this operation.' She told me.

'It's not true,' I answered.

'My heart feels this operation,' she said, crying."

Ziad and his wife watched the news for forty minutes. Then Ziad called his father.

"My father lived near this settlement. As we spoke I heard the sound of an explosion on the phone. This was Fadi exploding himself, but I didn't know it."

I am shocked and sit silently listening. "Then people who we didn't know telephoned and said, 'Fadi went as a martyr in this operation. Allah finished his life.'

"Do you know how he carried out his mission, what happened?" I ask.

"He started shooting until he ran out of ammunition and then bombed himself," Ziad says, which explains why he first heard the news on the television but believes he heard the actual blast of when Fadi exploded himself over the telephone when he was speaking to his father.

"The Israelis say he killed five," Ziad says. He justifies his son's action adding, "These settlers in Hebron, they are the cruelest and deadliest people man has created."

According to the Ezzedeen al Qassam Brigades' Information Office website, Fadi's "martyrdom" operation carried out with his friend Hazem al Kawasmeh is described thus: "Having grown up near the settlement of Kiryat Arba, Fadi was selected to carry out an infiltration operation against that target. In the evening of March 8, 2003, Fadi and Hazem geared up and moved to their target. They succeeded in passing through the security perimeter of the settlement and fought an hour-long battle with the guards inside the settlement. Hazem was killed during the battle; and Fadi moved on to where settlers were gathered inside the settlement. He broke into their gathering and detonated his explosives belt."[142]

At the time of their "martyrdom," the Jihad Mosque team was sporting blue-and-white soccer shirts emblazoned with a hand wielding an axe, ringed by an inscription which read: "Prepare for the enemy and to fight the occupation."[143]

Upon receiving the news of Fadi's death, Ziad says he and his family prayed.

"We thanked Allah that he is a martyr."

Fadi's obituary commenced and Fadi's friends and their parents arrived at the house to offer condolences and congratulate the parents of the new "shaheed",–who I am learning do mourn, and deeply so, but they also feel obligated to play a societally-prescribed role in which they must claim pride for the sacrifice of their child in behalf of country and religion. It's not so different from American parents of fallen soldiers who put on a brave face when receiving the flag-draped coffins of their military sons or daughters. At that symbolic moment, deeply bereaved parents often hide their grief and make proud patriotic proclamations about their child's service on behalf of their country. But if privately interviewed afterwards, they admit to their anguish, and even their anger over the operation their son or daughter took part in.

Ziad, like many bereaved parents, clings to the hope that his son is in paradise and that he can join his son there when he also dies, as seventy family members may be elected by the "martyr" to sidestep the final judgment and enter paradise directly.

"In our religion we believe in the benefits and recommendation for the martyr," Ziad states.[144]

The father of Hazem al Kawasmeh came to Fadi's obituary looking for answers, and the next morning, he and Ziad went searching for their sons' bodies together.

"I found the corpses of three people," Ziad recalls. "Fadi was not one of them. They told me the fourth corpse was completely torn up because he was wearing an explosive belt.

"Then the municipality and the Red Crescent got involved. Around two p.m. they reported that they received his body in the hospital of Hebron. His cousins and uncles did not recognize the corpse and said, 'This is someone else.' I went myself and of course I recognized him. No one can mistake his son."

Fadi's father looks down to his hands and we remain silent.

"We took him and prayed over his body in the mosque. He wrote that he wanted his prayers said in the Halsa mosque and to be buried in Ribat mosque. He and all his friends were buried together in the same tomb."[145]

Fadi's obituary services resumed but were cut short.

"At that time many soldiers from the Israeli army came and invaded our house," Ziad states. Now, in the second Intifada, "martyrs's" families expect the arrival of the Israeli soldiers, who promptly arrive to destroy the family's home and sometimes arrest the men of the family. Therefore, those who gather at the "martyr's" home after learning of the operation immediately begin emptying it of all its furniture, appliances and other valuables preparing for the short time before Israeli soldiers arrive.

Ziad left the obituary processional in the streets when he heard that the Israeli soldiers had already overtaken his home.

"I came back here to the house," Ziad explains, "and they investigated and arrested me." The fathers of the other "martyrs" were also arrested along with him.

Ziad adds, "[The Israelis] choked me and put a gun right next to my head and asked, 'Would you like to go to jail or I kill you now? Your house will be destroyed now.'

"They covered our eyes and took our hands behind our backs and took us to an unknown address. It was completely dark and cold." His face twists in anguish. "The plastic cuffs were very tight on our wrists and they tightened more each time we moved our hands." Indeed many Palestinians have shown me scars on their wrists and forearms from these self-tightening plastic cuffs. "They treated us as terrorists who did not know how to raise kids." Disgust resounds in Ziad's voice.

The Israelis drove Ziad and the other shocked and bereaved fathers around in the cold for hours and then arrived at the prison of Asuon, which is only about ten minutes from their homes in Hebron.

"I stayed in jail thirteen days. They investigated us, but we actually knew nothing.

'How can you let your son do it?' the Israeli detective asked me.

'Your son is in danger. Would you protect him or not?' I answered him. He believed me.

"You speak one way, but your heart is different," Ziad adds. I am not sure if Fadi's father means that he felt hatred for the Israelis and was glad his son had struck them a blow but could not say so in the circumstances, or that he means that he spoke calmly to his incarcerators when inside he was torn up with grief wishing he had known and had protected his son. I don't want to interrupt him at this point, as he is reliving the story, telling it unprompted from me.[146]

"After thirteen days in prison, the soldiers dropped us on a country road and we don't know where we are. They cursed us and drove away. There were Arabs there and they helped, giving us a telephone to call our families. When I reached Hebron, the Israeli army had invaded Hebron. All our furniture was taken out of our house because the Israelis threatened to destroy our house. They destroyed all the others [of the three other suicide bombers].

"'It's not mine.' I said to the Israeli detective.

'You are a liar! You've bought [this house].' the Israeli said.

'Okay, your collaborator told you correctly,'[147] I said. 'But I lost it to the landlord. It's reverted back to a rental property,' The Israelis then arrested my landlord."

Ziad looks around the diwan and our eyes follow his. It's a very homey room with overstuffed furniture, thick oriental carpet and embroidered cloths on the end tables. It gives me a pit in my stomach when I look at his children.

"If you had known he was going to do this, would you have stopped him?" I ask.

"As a fact, if I knew my son was going to do this, I would stop him," Ziad answers without hesitation. "Every father would."

But then he qualifies his statement. "We have the strong belief that if I stopped him, he would have finished his life no matter what." I have heard this numerous times—that once an individual has locked on to the decision of "martyrdom" and gotten so strongly into the euphoria, power, glory and dissociative mindset, it's hard to turn them back, especially if his closest friends are in the same mindset and other important adults are encouraging him forward.[148]

"Did Fadi leave a last will and testament?" I ask.

"Yes there was a letter for the family, a long one. He wrote something for every member of his family."

"What kind of things?" I ask sensitively.

"For his mother to hang on and read the Koran and to pray for his soul, to pray he waits in heaven for her," Ziad answers. "He wrote the same to me. To his sisters he wrote to follow our religion, take hadjib [wear the Islamic headscarf] and listen to their parents. For the youth of the mosque he wrote for them to become members of al Qassam [the military wing of Hamas]."

As we speak about al Qassam, Ziad's adolescent son Thaer brings the Hamas flag into the room, mounted on a brass pole. Ziad smiles appreciatively to his son and the boy beams.

"What do you tell your children about Fadi's actions?" I ask, seeing Thaer boasting the Hamas flag and evidently proud of his older brother's actions.

"What my son did is right," Fadi's father answers and then looks lovingly at his still surviving son, "but I don't tell my kids this. I tell them that it was his way and his decision. We have presented one martyr [to Allah]. At the end everyone will die, but a normal death is different. We completely believe [Fadi] will be in heaven and save seventy of our family members. I tell my son this is enough."

"It's enough," Thaer repeats, as he smiles and nods.

"I'm forty-five years old," Fadi's father continues, "and I know my son has to take care of the family after me." He smiles again at his son.

"Is it dangerous for you to have the Hamas flag at home?" I ask, curious if having the flag of a U.S. designated terrorist organization in his hands is unsafe for Ziad's young son.

"Yes, of course it's dangerous!" Ziad answers. "But this flag to me means to me there is no God but Allah." Ziad refers to the inscription on the Hamas flag and headbands, the shahada that proclaims the Islamic belief in the oneness of God and the acceptance of Muhammad as God's Prophet: "There is no God but Allah, and Muhammad is the messenger of

Allah."This is the prayer that a person must make to become a Muslim and it is repeated daily.

I nod and turn the interview back to Fadi. "Do you know who gave your son the suicide belt?" I ask.

"Yes and I have total respect for him. He came and confessed to me, 'I am the one who recruited your son.'

"When he says he recruited Fadi what can I say?" Ziad explains with misty eyes. "It's true that they recruit themselves. Not anyone will go for it—just one with strong, deep beliefs. We have an ayah [verse] in the Koran that says, 'Allah chooses his martyrs.' We don't call people who died that way dead; they are living in Paradise. We also have an ayah that says, 'Some of them have got martyred in Allah's way while others are waiting (to fulfill their obligation).' These are our scriptures. Every people has their beliefs. We Muslims respect all people of the book [meaning all of the Abrahamic traditions]—Christians too, but the Jews corrupted the book."

"How did it happen that you met Fadi's sender?" I ask.

"He came in order to see how I feel. Am I upset or pleased? The situation is already finished for me. If I got angry it will change nothing. I knew I should welcome him with respect and I knew he would get martyred, because he was a fugitive."

Indeed, Israeli soldiers shot Abdullah Kawasmeh dead in June of 2003 as he left evening prayers at his mosque near Hebron, four months after Fadi's suicide operation[149] making him, in Ziad's beliefs, a "martyr" as well.

"Are you angry at all with the sender?" I ask.

"No, I have no anger inside now," Ziad answers resigned to the fate that befell his son. "I could never encourage him to do it. But I would not be angry. If he told me the truth I would have convinced him, no don't do it. He was twenty-one years old. Do you know what it means? Your son you used to hold. It's twenty-six months now since it happened. We are not normal. At Eid, Ramadan, all the big occasions we miss him. We can do nothing. We always thank God." Ziad is falling back on the common Middle Eastern acceptance of fate—that what is done is ordained by God and that in all circumstances he must thank God.

I nod listening, impressed by his charity to the sender of his son, also realizing that Ziad is probably loath to speak ill of the dead and feels pity for how he died.

"[Fadi] knew one thing. If Israelis caught him they would lock him in jail for the rest of his life. He prefers to live in heaven and eternity."

"When you think about what motivated Fadi the most do you think it was the traumas he witnessed under the occupation or his deep religious conversion?" I ask.

"His friends were killed and their houses destroyed," Ziad answers. "I want to go pray in al Aqsa Mosque [in Jerusalem] but I cannot. The checkpoints are like a big prison. You noticed how many checkpoints there were to Hebron."

"Yes, five!" Alla our translator shouts out without waiting for me to answer, reminding me how difficult it is for our guides to hold themselves emotionally together as they take part in these interviews that pertain to their live circumstances as well.

"We are in a prison! We don't agree with killing kids. We encourage getting revenge from those who kill us, who beat our kids. But we are peaceful people. I work in electricity and I have a relationship with an Israeli businessman. I don't even think of harming him," Ziad continues. "Why? He treats me as good as I treat him. As a Muslim, I give all good things for people. Life and humanity requires doing good things for others. The Israelis consider they are better than all others. Of course this is unacceptable. I want you to know, I always depend on God. I don't fear any Israeli, nor any human."

"Did Fadi make a 'martyr's' poster? I ask.

Ziad turns to a collection of photos of Fadi on the side table, picks one and shows it to me. Wearing blue jeans and a turtleneck under a fleece sweater with a Hamas headband, Fadi, looking calm and soft, holds an M-4 assault rifle in front of the Ezzedeen al Qassam Brigades banner that pictures the al Aqsa mosque in the background. Another photo taken at the same time shows Fadi and his friend and fellow operative, Hazem al Kawasmeh, both on bent knees holding M-16 assault rifles, Hazem is smiling sweetly while Fadi's arm is draped lovingly over his shoulder.

Later I learn that the two boys went with their Hamas operative to a photo shop in the area and made this picture as a gift for their parents before they "martyred" themselves in the Kiryat Arba settlement. The photo in a gold frame was delivered by Hamas and left on the doorstep for Fadi's family along with his last will and testament attached,[150] an unusual gesture as Hamas usually makes martyrs posters and releases a video with the "martyr" reading parts of his last will and testament. Perhaps in their case there was no time to carry out the usual practice or something else interfered.

"Once [the Israelis] stopped me in my car," Ziad adds. "I had pictures of my son with me showing him on his mission. They could have killed me. I didn't lie. I said this is my son. [The Israeli soldier] could kill me and there is no one to judge him. He would probably get a promotion!

"The Israelis and Americans say we are sending our children to be martyred to get money," Ziad continues. "I swear I got nothing. The [Hamas] movement made the obituary and that's it."

I nod, although on this subject, I have no way to know if he is telling the truth.

Sensitive to he and his family being portrayed as horrific terrorists without the other side's actions also being shown, Ziad tells us, "These settlers in Hebron, they are the cruelest and deadliest people man has created. In 1994 Baruch Goldstein went to the mosque and killed thirty martyrs while kneeling [for Muslim prayers]." Ziad is referring to a horrific act in which Baruch Goldstein, an Israeli settler who lived in the Kiryat Arba settlement, went to the holy site at the mosque in the Machpela Cave where eight hundred Palestinian worshippers were kneeling in the mosque for Ramadan morning prayers.[151] Goldstein sprayed up to one hundred bullets for over ten minutes from his automatic rifle.[152] Mosque inhabitants eventually stopped him by beating him to death with iron bars.

The guard at the mosque (Mohammad Suleiman Abu Saleh) told journalists that he thought that Goldstein was trying to kill as many people as possible and described how there were bodies and blood everywhere. The injured Palestinians were taken to the hospital but when outrage and rioting broke out there, the Israeli army killed an additional twelve Palestinians[153] and the week of ensuing riots culminated in the death of an additional twenty-five Palestinians and five Israelis.[154]

To his credit, Israeli Prime Minister Yitzhak Rabin immediately telephoned Yasser Arafat (the then head of the PLO) and called the attack a "loathsome, criminal act of murder" and pledged to take "every possible measure to bring about calm". The Palestinian Liberation Organization publicly decried the desecration of the holy site and mass murder of innocent and peaceful worshippers, demanding that Israel disarm all the one hundred and twenty thousand Jewish settlers then in the occupied territories and that the United Nations act to protect Palestinians.[155] But not all Israelis, and particularly the settlers, agreed with Yitzhak Rabin's sentiments. Settlers in Kiryat Arba established a shrine inside Goldstein's tomb there with a plaque inscribed, "To the holy Baruch Goldstein, who gave his life for the Jewish people, the Torah and the nation of Israel." The Israeli government forcibly removed the plaque and the shrine area in 1999[156] but that hasn't deterred the thousands who continue to come and pay tribute to his violent deed.[157]

In bringing up Goldstein's crime, Ziad wants us to understand that if Goldstein was at all representative of the settlers of Kirayat Arba, these were the neighbors that Fadi had attacked in his suicide mission. In these two acts we see what looks to be an unremitting cycle of hatred, violence and revenge.

"They killed my cousin, my neighbor, and my friend,|" Ziad cries out. "What are we to do? Just surrender until they kill us all!" Ziad throws his hands up in disgust. "The whole world security, the international Security Council are all with Israel. We have the decision of the United Nations Security Council but [the Israelis] never carry out agreements. For Iraq they carry out their agreements. But the whole world stands with Israel. The European people stand for Palestinians but their governments support the world Zionism movement. Governments are angry that Iran tries to have nuclear weapons. Israel has them but no one talks!"

As we ready ourselves to leave, we mention that we are going to speak to the father of Fuad al Kawasmeh next. Ziad shares his views about Fuad and then mentions that Fuad's younger brother, Whalid, is no longer psychologically normal after being heavily traumatized by the repeated Israeli incursions into their home and all that he has witnessed.

"The boy's case got worse after my son was martyred. [The Israeli soldiers] treated their family wildly. His brother got martyred. He is psychologically abnormal now and there is no help for him. It's all because of the occupation.

"Here we have fifteen suicide martyrs," he continues referring to his community. "We never have the chance to sleep peacefully while Israelis make terror outside. The kids view it of course and feel hatred..." his voice drifts off in sadness.

We finish our interview with Ziad, thank him for sharing with us and say goodbye to him and his children. I smile at Thaer as we leave thinking, *I don't believe his father encouraged Fadi to be a "martyr" nor will he encourage Thaer to follow in Fadi's footsteps.* But sometimes a father's influence is not enough to protect his son. In Thaer's case I leave hoping it will suffice.

We leave Fadi's house and walk a short distance under the blazing sun along a dirt road edged by weeds to the home of Jawwad al Kawasmeh, father of Fuad, the seventh Jihad Mosque soccer team member to go on a suicide mission. After Fadi's death, Fuad kept playing soccer and would regularly visit Fadi's father, Ziad, mourning together. Ziad recalled to a journalist that Fuad said to him "Think of me as your new son." Sadly, Ziad lost his substitute son only months later.[158]

I am eager to hear more about Fuad, but Alla tells me about a glitch that might prevent the interview.

"Listen," he says. "Ziad told me that there are too many checkpoints and we won't be able to travel back to Ramallah before the last one closes if we make this next interview."

"Oh. What should we do then?" I ask. With all the Israeli obstructions it looks like we can only collect one interview a day—not an efficient way to do research.

"Don't worry," Alla answers. "These people have a large house. Ziad called over here and said we're good people, so they invited us to stay the night."

"You think it's a good idea?" I ask. I've become accustomed to staying among Palestinians, but this would be the first time boarding in an actual suicide terrorist's family home.

"Sure, it's fine!" Ken says, throwing his cigarette stub into the weeds. Alla looks to me for confirmation.

"Okay, why not?" We continue on toward their recently constructed house of concrete and Jerusalem stone. The steps leading up to the front door haven't yet had a railing installed and a rooster pecks at the dry earth in a weeded area below. We make our interview there as well and are touched deeply by Whalid – the boy Ziad told us is no longer normal after being dragged from his bed by Israeli soldiers, learning of children his own age shot and killed and observing all the violence surrounding him. In the morning we return to Ramallah.

CHAPTER 34

Darine Abu Aisha

I have now returned from so many trips into the bustling taxi center of Ramallah, I begin to feel like we are "home" as we arrive from our latest visit in Hebron. From the center, we grab another taxi that drops us off in front of the white iron gate to Alla's apartment building. Alla swings it open and we pass red hibiscus bushes in bloom and yellow flowers in planters, then take the terrazzo steps up to the second floor. Alla's father, Ahmed, is already home when we arrive and cooking dinner. Alla kisses him and they catch up briefly in Arabic.

"Marhaba, welcome!" Ahmed says turning to us. "Do you like Palestinian food?"

"Yes, of course! We love it!" I answer, smiling widely.

Ken also nods in appreciation and wanders into the small kitchen to gaze at the chopped lamb and onions frying in hot oil. He inhales deeply, a scent of nutmeg, cinnamon and allspice coming from the pot. "I'm starving!" Ken says, smiles and rubs his stomach.

"Do you know maqluba?" Ahmed asks as he arranges freshly peeled eggplant on his cutting board and begins to cut them into round thin slices.

"No what is it?" Ken asks.

"In English it's called upside down," Alla says.

"You're going to love this dish," Ahmed brags with a wide smile as he rinses small ripe tomatoes under the faucet.

"Can we help?" I ask.

Ahmed refuses. Ken and Alla go to the living room and begin playing a video game and I retire to the bedroom, organizing my notes and getting ready for our interview tomorrow that Alla has arranged for us. We will be meeting the mother of Darine Abu Aisha, the second Palestinian woman to join the sudden emergence of Palestinian female suicide bombers—eight who had completed missions thus far. Journalist Barbara Victor author of the book <u>Army of Roses</u> has written about her interviews of the families and friends of the first five Palestinian female suicide bombers including Darine's mother, Nabila, as well as friends of Darine's. I pick up her book,even though her thesis that Palestinian women are motivated to suicide terrorism to achieve equal rights has been denied by three of my female subjects, studying it intently to prepare for tomorrow because she may have other insights I can benefit from.

Victor claims that an Israeli soldier forced Darine to remove her head scarf at a checkpoint and allow her male companion to kiss her in public— a scandal that made Darine's mother insist she marry immediately and give up her university education. I'm interested to hear Darine's mother's perspective and wonder if forcing marriage over education would in itself be enough motivation to become a suicide bomber.

The doorbell rings, interrupting my reading. It's Jamilah. Together we set the table, anticipating the maqluba that is filling the room with a wonderful aroma. We sit as Ahmed serves fills our tall stem glasses with white wine as I see once again that in less conservative Arabic communities, religious rules are often respected publicly but forgotten in private.

We toast the cook enthusiastically as Ahmed carefully places the 'upside down', a dish made of rice, eggplant, succulent braised lamb and tomatoes. When the casserole is inverted, the top is bright red tomatoes that cover golden eggplant. Ahmed serves us. Everyone is starving so it becomes quiet as we begin to eat, but as we fill up, we animatedly discuss our plan for the next day as I fill them in on what I've read already from Victor's book.

We rise early the following morning and take a taxi to the center of Ramallah near the bus station. Alla negotiates with the taxi drivers there to find one who agrees to take us to the outskirts of Nablus. I watch nervously, recalling our trip to Beit Fourik, and Alla laughs when he sees my anxiety.

"Don't worry! No illegal mountain roads this time!" Alla assures us. "But there will be many checkpoints so we may only get this one interview today. "

We climb into the taxi and as we speed along the highway, we ask Alla about growing up in Tunisia and coming to Palestine as an adolescent.

"I was eleven when we returned," Alla recalls. Alla's father works in the Palestinian Liberation Organization and they lived in Tunisia from 1982 – 1991, when Arafat was exiled there. Ken and I have noticed that Alla has a certain confidence and carries himself with the pride that comes with sons of highly placed officials. I've seen the same in my own children—the children of a U. S. Ambassador.

"You were in Ramallah during the Israeli *Operation Defensive Shield*?" I ask.

Alla nods, his smile fading from his face as he remembers.

"I think it began in 2002 in March and April. They were forty days in Ramallah. It was hell. During that time the soldiers opened the curfew for a few days, maybe two days, and at the end they opened for more days. At that time it would take eight hours to go to Jericho. "

Without checkpoints, Jericho is only twenty minutes away. Eight hours to cross such a short distance must have been maddening.

"There were four tanks at the gate of our building. " Alla continues. "Oh my God at night! There was mass destruction on the streets. They were shooting up buildings everyday, destroying whole roads, street lamps, and trees!"

"Did the tanks move around Ramallah?" Ken asks.

"They went over all the place, they destroyed cars and streets, hit ambulances... They were shooting all night. It was scary. You couldn't see them but there were snipers on all the higher buildings. The first week was the worst. " Alla's voice is filled with disgust. "We had soldiers around our building. For one week we couldn't open the door! We wore our clothes to bed in case they forced us outside. They called everyone above fourteen out to the street [in the night]. I didn't respond—I stayed in my room.

"I had a Palestine flag and a Che Guevara poster and a picture of Absolut Gaza - a kid with a Molotov. My friend had the same picture.

'Do you know this guy?' a soldier asked him.

'Personally, no,' he answered. "

We laugh, imagining the delight Alla's friend had smarting off to the enemy soldier.

"They punched him in the face, but he's really muscular," Alla continues, beaming with pride of his friend's courage.

"You were scared?" I ask.

"It was really scary but fun too!" Alla explains his voice lighthearted. "It was adventure—they were everywhere. "

Listening to Alla vacillate between memories of abject terror and laughing like it was a game, I understand how hard it must have been for parents of teenage boys to keep them inside and to impress upon them the dangerousness of the situation. Alla becomes serious again.

"They had tanks like hell—around two hundred! Every night they would strike or destroy houses. Sometimes I saw them through my window, the lights and the hissing. After they left we saw many rockets. They use tiny well guided missiles that use a wire. It never misses. I was so glad to get to Russia!" Alla says, referring to his year studying abroad.

"Did anyone fight back when you were here?" I ask.

"The resistance [fighters] were in the streets. But they couldn't defend. What can a Kalishnikov do against tanks and all these soldiers?" Alla throws his hands in the air. "No actually it really was fucking scary! It was the first experience for me like this. "

The time has sped by as we listened to Alla. We have been stopped for three checkpoints but they hardly registered. Now the taxi is nearing the village that Darine Abu Aisha's family lives in.

Darine, a twenty-one year old promising university student, was just months away from graduating when she self detonated on February 27, 2002. Together, she and two Arab Israelis,Hafez Mouqbal and Mousa Hasounaafez, arrived by car at the Maccabim checkpoint inside the West Bank, on route 443 between Modi'in and Jerusalem. There, they were asked for their identity documents. As Darine and the young men stepped out of the car, the Israeli border police manning the checkpoint sensed that something was off and distanced themselves just in time. Darine detonated herself as the two young men fled, her body exploding into gory pieces of flesh strewn over the entire checkpoint. The police were only lightly wounded and Darine's accomplices were shot and killed as they ran. [159]

Darine lives on in her martyrdom video. She appears in a green Hamas headband with Arabic writing on it that is tied around her white headscarf. She points a dagger at the viewer, looking angry and ready to strike, while her right hand points upward with one finger raised, the Islamic way of signaling that there is only one God and his name is Allah. In her video, Darine claims that she is on her way to paradise.

If I had only this photo to judge Darine, I would expect her to be a monster. But what I learned from Barbara Victor's account of interviewing both the family and a close friend helps me understand that Darine's decision was much more nuanced.

"Listen guys," I say as we approach her house. "Barbara Victor says that Darine's friends claimed that there was scandal at the checkpoint when Darine pleaded to get a sick young boy across the checkpoint. The Israeli said he would only let the boy pass if Darine removed her headscarf and let her boyfriend kiss her. She allowed the kiss but that led to a scandal, and Darine's mother then forced her to quit school to get married. Apparently Darine decided to bomb herself instead. "

"The soldiers at the checkpoints are so sick," Ken says.

"It's the Nablus checkpoint," Alla explains, "The soldiers there are the worst!"

"You think her mother would really force her to get married over something like that?" I ask.

"It doesn't sound right," Alla says.

"I guess we'll find out," I say as the taxi pulls up on alongside a dilapidated house, the first in Palestine I've seen with a porch.

Darine's brother Fadir is waiting outside for us.

"Salaam Alaikum," we call out in Arabic, meaning "Peace be to you. "

"Wa Alaikum Esalaam!" Fadir answers, sending peace back to us. The men shake hands, and I put my hand to my heart in greeting, as Fadir welcomes us into their home.

The inside is decorated ornately. Darine's mother, Nabila, sits on a green velveteen sofa with curved arms and carved lacquered wood ends and legs. She is wearing a long navy abaya and conservative white headscarf that drapes over her neck and shoulders. As she stands up to greet us I see that she is worn by age and sadness. I feel a sense of shame coming to trouble her about her dead daughter.

I sit on an identical sofa across from Nabila and notice that in the corner there is a shrine to Darine: a larger-than-life poster of her with the al Aqsa mosque at her shoulder, the flag of Palestine behind that and the al Aqsa logo photo-shopped artistically around her. Below this there is a small lace covered wooden table upon which sits pictures of Darine dressed for her mission, surrounded by what looks like awards or medals. If it weren't for the knife she is wielding and automatic rifles in the al Aqsa logo, the shrine could resemble a proud parent's collection of awards and photos of an academically gifted or sportive youngster.

"Can you tell me about Darine as a child?" I begin, noticing Nabila looks still so bereaved now, three years after her daughter's attack.

Nabila's face lights up.

"Since childhood," she begins, "Since she was one and a half years old, she became the most beautiful and clever among her sisters. "

"How many children do you have? Which one was Darine?"

"She was among the youngest," her mother answers smiling. "I have two sons and six daughters older than Darine and one younger girl.

"[Darine] finished high school with high grades and excelled ahead of her classmates. Every year they used to give her a lot of certificates!" Nabila says as she turns to Fadir telling him in Arabic to go and get them. "She specialized in English and had just two months to get her Bachelor of Arts degree. I never knew one day I could lose her!"

"Do you have any idea what motivated Darine to "martyr" herself?"

"Events that used to happen affected her a lot," her mother replies. "There were pregnant women on the way to the hospital that used to pass out at the checkpoints. The Israelis started to assassinate [Palestinian] leaders so she got offended and activated by what she saw. God bless her, she couldn't handle what she saw!"

"I've seen how hard it is here in Palestine," I explain, noticing that Nabila wears a "martyr's necklace" with Darine's picture hanging on a pendant around her neck. "Do you have any idea what were the events that pushed Darine over the edge? Was there any one event or events that were just too difficult to take?"

"It was the assassination of Jamal Hassein that happened in Jenin," her mother explains speaking of a Palestinian militant killed in a targeted assassination. "He was hit by an Israeli missile while in his car and incinerated. When they got his body back he was completely burned, it looked like coal. There were six of them and they had many kids with them. " Darine's mother explains that Darine knew Jamal personally.

I nod listening trying to imagine the feelings of learning that an enemy missile has incinerated a friend and his children.

"And the pregnant women who gave birth at the checkpoints because the Israelis didn't let them pass disturbed her," her mother recalls. "She would ask us,'Are we going to sit in the house as our men are outnumbered and we are watching them [die]? What can we do? We have empty hands and uncovered chests! We have to do something because our men are outnumbered!' She would tell us. I was scared for her when she spoke this way but I didn't expect that she would do this. "

"So you didn't know she was going to take a bomb?" I say.

"If I knew she was going to do it I would have hid her and locked her behind seven doors!" her mother answers, sighing heavily.

"Do you know her senders?"

"They are in jail: Nasser Shawish and Adul Kasin Awis," Nabila answers.

"Did you speak with them?" I ask.

"I spoke only with Nasser," Nabila says explaining that he told her, 'We tried to talk her out of it, but she rejected. ' And Nasser said that Darine told him, 'If you don't let me do it, I'll take a knife and go myself, do it and get martyred that way!'

These words are his, but I don't know what happened," Nabila says uncertain if it's the truth.

But Yoram Schweitzer, my Israeli research colleague also interviewed Nasser multiple times in Israeli prison and confirms his words. In his book about female suicide terrorists Schweitzer writes, "Nasser Shawish of Fatah was personally involved in sending three suicide terrorists, including a woman named Darine Abu Aisha. Shawish reiterated during all my conversations with him that in principle he opposed sending women, and had even continuously tried to persuade Abu Aisha to abandon her determination to carry out a suicide mission, saying 'I felt that she was a pretty and successful girl studying at the university, a future mother, who should marry and bear children, and help her people in other ways. But she wouldn't stop pressuring me. "[160]

According to Schweitzer, Nasser's fiancée, Obeyda, and Darine's best friend also tried to dissuade Darine from carrying out the suicide attack, but Darine also told them that if Nasser wouldn't help her become a *shahida*, she would "buy a knife, go kill soldiers at a roadblock, and die that way". Nasser told Yoram that he changed his opposition to sending female suicide bombers when he became bereaved and outraged over the killing of his closest friend, Muhanad Abu Haliwa, and after witnessing the killing of the family of wanted terrorist Nabil Quake.

Nasser told Yoram, "I looked for vengeance, and I wanted it to be special. Enough! I felt that a woman would be able to carry out this special attack that we planned more easily and pass through the roadblocks because of her innocent appearance. "[161]

Since women had not yet been activated as bombers in Palestine, soldiers were less likely to suspect them or search their bodies stringently.

"Are you angry with them that they sent her?" I ask Nabila.

"Of course," she answers her face clouded with anger. "When I lost my daughter I lost a part of my body!"

It's refreshing to hear a Palestinian parent of a "martyr" admit anger with the sender. I know that some feel they cannot, because in general they support the militant resistance in Palestine and because they know the senders also often get killed by the Israelis. But Nabila has no such compunction.

"Did you have plans for Darine to be married?" I ask,

"Many men came asking for her hand but she rejected them all," Nabila answers matter-of-factly. I sense no blame to Darine and perhaps a hint of pride in her daughter rejecting many suitors.

"Was she waiting for someone special?" I ask.

"She would say, 'Not until I graduate, until you eat from my sweat, I won't marry. Then maybe,'" her mother repeats, pride filling her face. It doesn't sound at all like Victor's story of a mother forcing her daughter to marry.

"You have other children in university?" I ask wondering how Nabila felt about Darine wanting to pursue her education before marriage.

"All!" Nabila answers sitting up proudly. "Her older brother got his Master's in the English language. My daughter finished in economics, the next daughter in Arab literature, the next in Islamic education, and I have two still in. One will graduate soon. "

"Fadi," she turns to her son who is sitting with us, "studied one course but did not continue. " Then to explain why she says, "His father is sick. They destroyed our house. His father works at our destroyed house today. This house we are in now is rented. We cannot rebuild our home. We have no money; [we rebuild] only by the help of foundations and people who come to help. "

Again I see that the money that is given to families by terrorist sponsoring organization after their son or daughter goes on a mission may not be that big of a reward as many think, given that after their home being destroyed the family must struggle to rebuild their communal home. The so-called "blood money" may, in actuality, be a bit more like getting an insurance settlement versus winning a big pay off for the "martyrdom" of a family member.

"The soldiers came at one a. m. " Nabila says of that time. "They pulled us out of the house and said, 'We will destroy the house. ' They didn't let us get any of our furniture out. They put us at a distance from the house. The explosion was very strong! Some parts hit the neighboring house!"

I wonder if there were young children present. "How old is your youngest?" I ask.

"Eighteen years old is the youngest," her mother responds. "I have two boys and eight girls—now seven. " With this remark she gazes down sadly at her folded hands.

"You said that Darine was upset about women giving birth at the checkpoint. Can you tell us more about that?"

Nabila explains that there was a laboring woman with her husband and father-in-law in a car speeding to the hospital and in their panic they failed to slow down. The Israeli soldiers shot the men as they raced toward the checkpoint.

Nabila takes a sharp breath. "We are not talking of only one woman [in childbirth] stopped at the checkpoints," she says. "There are many women. The Israelis make excuses,saying we found a woman wearing an [explosive] belt and so on. "

"If the woman was in an ambulance, there would be a medical crew to help her," Nabila explains. "But if in a private car as she was, no. " As she explains she makes it clearer why the husband and father-in-law were particularly in a panic with no help for her to birth safely if they were stopped at the checkpoint.

"What other kind of things happened that disturbed Darine?" I ask.

"She used to say she's affected by the situation that is happening and I could see that the emotions were growing in her and she would start to cry. For any assassination that happened she would cry. The day of the assassination in Jenin, she had a nervous breakdown. "

"She observed this on television?"

"Yes, TV. "

"Did she know the leaders who were assassinated from university?"

"Yes. Once she asked Jamal Hassein, 'Put me on an operation. ' He refused. 'No way my daughter!' he told her. 'We have men. If we run out of men, we'll think about it. '"

"How do you know this?" I ask.

"She used to talk with me because she was scared. She told me, 'If I would go [on a mission] I would go with PIJ (Palestinian Islamic Jihad) or Hamas. I never thought she would go with al Aqsa. " Nabila wrings her hands helplessly.

"So you knew she was deeply affected by the traumatic events happening around her—enough to want to go and 'martyr' herself, but did you know she was actually preparing for a mission?"

"No. " Nabila shakes her head sadly.

"What happened?"

"It was a Thursday morning. She was at home. 'I am going to get a book because I have an exam tomorrow,' she suddenly said. 'I won't be late. '

"She was going to Nablus to the university library. I won't be late,' she said. 'I won't be late. '" Nabila repeats her daughter's words as though by invoking her promised return she can somehow undo her daughter's tragic suicidal act.

"It was fourth day of Eid, our biggest holiday [the Eid al Adha or Feast of the Sacrifice following Ramadan]. It was the anniversary of her martyred cousin that day," her mother explains.

"'Don't be late. I'm making food,' I told her.

'One half hour,' she told me. "

After some time, Nabila tried to call her several times, but her mobile was turned off.

"When she saw the missed calls she called back and said, 'I'm on the checkpoint and maybe if it gets late I will sleep at my friend's place. ' She never went anywhere overnight. She was very religious. She taught religion classes. I felt strange because when she said 'I am on a checkpoint,' I knew she didn't go far away.

'Tell me exactly which one so I can send a car to come get you,' I said.

'I cannot tell you where I am exactly,' she said. 'Keep faith in Allah. '

"I began crying. I waited and she called back again.

'Come on back home,' I told her.

'No, I won't come back home,' she said. 'I'll come in the morning. ' I begged her to come home, but she didn't even listen," Nabila says breaking into sobs.

"She said, 'Keep faith in Allah. Don't be scared. '"

"She called to say goodbye, then?" I ask.

"Just to hear my voice," her mother explains between sobs.

"For courage?" I ask.

Nabila nods.

"After that, I sat and I couldn't sleep. I switched the TV on. All her brothers and sisters and father slept. He was sick and tired. I stayed awake. Around ten-thirty [p. m.] they said an operation occurred around Jerusalem. They did not announce the names at first, but I felt something, so I sat up. I had been circling in the room. I started thinking and pacing in the room. Her older brother awoke.

'Your sister has gone,' I told him without even knowing.

'Mom this is our share from Allah,' he said.

"They brought her name on NBC. He saw her name, but I didn't see it." Nabila stares blankly into space.

"They announced the name," Fadir explains. "It was through the video-tape she made before she left. The side that sends the 'shaheed' gives her video to the news."

"Have you seen her 'martyrdom' video?" I ask.

"Yes," her mother answers her voice filled with exhaustion and disgust. "I've seen it. When I saw it, I lost my heart from inside."

"She left a letter as well?" I ask.

"Yes," her mother sighs. "She asked her brothers and mother not to wear black and cry over her," Nabila recalls. "She asked the wives of our uncles to keep going to mosque and to dress in hidjab. 'I'm making this as revenge for the martyrs and for the Intifada of al Aqsa,' Darine wrote. 'All that I own is my body and soul to defend my country.'"

"Can you tell me about her cousin whose anniversary it was? The martyred one?" I ask.

"He got martyred one month before her on the twenty-fifth of January and she the twenty-seventh of February [a year later]. He was young, eighteen. He made an operation in Tel Aviv at the bus station. His name was Sufatat Fadl Rahkmen. He went with PIJ."

A cousin going to explode himself would certainly further erode the barriers for Darine to consider going as a suicide bomber, especially if she was close with him and if her family was proud of his act.

I am curious about Barbara Victor's account, so I say, "I have this book with me, <u>Army of Roses</u> by a journalist Barbara Victor. She writes that you gave her an interview?"

Nabila nods, smiling calmly.

"She told about a scandal at the checkpoint that compromised Darine," I explain and share the story of the Israeli soldier who ordered the boy, Rashid, that Darine was with, to kiss her. I repeat everything in the story except the claim that her mother was making her get married and drop out of university as I don't want to make Nabila defensive before hearing her explanation.

"It happened to her friend, not Darine herself," Nabila answers calmly. "Her friend told Darine about this story. I told this story to the press. I don't recall to whom. [When it happened] my daughter came and told me this story. It really affected her deeply. "

Darine's friend, Hemar, and her male companion, Rashid, had been trying to convince the Israeli soldiers to let a seriously ill child cross the checkpoint, Nabila explains.

"The baby they were trying to help was suffocating," Nabila recalls. "He was inside an ambulance and the soldiers did not allow them to pass. "

"Hemar was wearing a face covering and scarf.

'Take it off,' the soldier told her.

"Then he told the guy with her, 'Kiss the girl. ' But he refused. Then the soldier beat this guy. The soldier took the face covering from Hemar and her scarf as well. But her friend did not kiss her.

'You can kiss me,' Hemar said when she saw the soldier beating him up. 'You are just like my brother. You can kiss me. ' He did not and the soldier beat him badly.

"Darine was not there, but her friend came late to university and told Darine everything that happened. That's how she and I knew about it. "

"In her book, Victor claims this happened to Darine," I say puzzled. Nabila doesn't seem to be lying. She is calm, unbothered, and clear it was not Darine to whom this happened.

"Yes I told her this story," Nabila explains. "Maybe she misunderstood. She had two translators with her. One of them was an old man from Jerusalem, an Arab. "

"So Darine was never at the checkpoint with her cousin Rashid or forced to marry him later?" If Victor got it wrong, I want to be sure I'm getting it right now.

"No! No! She was not at the checkpoint when this happened with Rashid," Nabila confirms.

"And we have no relative named Rashid. " Farid chimes in.

"This is Darine's friend, Hemar, who had this experience," her mother repeats. "We gave this story as an example of an experience that affected Darine, but not her own experience. "

"So she was not forced to marry?" I ask.

"No! She needed to finish university!" her mother insists.

"So you wanted her to finish her studies rather than marry?" I ask now, adding Victor's version of the story that Darine was a frustrated feminist who wanted to pursue her education and bombed herself because she was being forced to drop out of university and marry because of the kissing incident at the checkpoint. The family all shake their heads laughing incredulously.

"I have three daughters who finished university!" Nabila states. "One of them finished and has children, and now her husband doesn't let her go and work. Another studied nursing and is in Saudi Arabia. She used to work here and now she applied there to get a job. My third daughter has only two months before graduation. She studies to be a primary school teacher. She will work. If she gets married, whether or not she works will depend on her husband," Nabila explains.

"You support them working professionally while being wives and mothers?" I ask.

"You give birth and then you can work," Nabila says matter-of-factly.

"And Darine, what did she study for?" I ask.

"She wanted to be a teacher of English in secondary education at a university. She wanted to get her Ph. D. ," Nabila answers proudly. "'I want to work and continue my studies,' Darine told me. She has a strong will and character and can do it. She used to work hard for her age and she was advanced. Going to graduate school was only a question of money. Their father paid for university for all of them. "

"Are you proud of your daughters?" I ask.

"Thanks to Allah!" she answers without hesitation. "Allah bless them! I really wanted them to learn! It was the thing I never had. I was very proud!"

Darine's sister has returned home from university and sits down to join us. She is a petite girl dressed like her mother in a black abaya with a white head covering that drapes over her neck, shoulders and chest. She wears silver wire framed glasses. We are introduced and she asks if we would like to see Darine's scrapbook. Together we look through a scrapbook of photos, special items pasted to the pages, poems and letters. It's in Arabic so I cannot understand it on my own.

"What is this?" I ask pointing to a handwritten piece.

"This is her poem," her sister answers. "She wrote it for the anniversary of the assassination by Israeli special forces of Abu Hanoud (a Hamas operative). [162] They published it. "

"This is the blood of her friend," her sister points to a plastic wrapped tissue. "She kept it in plastic. The Israeli Special Forces killed them at the checkpoint. She had his blood on this napkin. She was at the funeral and got some blood from his body. "

"Who was he?" I ask.

"His name was Zayi Zawata. He was a soldier in the Palestinian Authority. "

"Do you know why he was killed?' I ask.

"When the Israelis gave the territories under the Palestinian Authority, they had checkpoints also," Darine's sister explains. "The Israelis used to strike them with rockets too. "

"If you want to say something," Fadir adds, "say the Israeli army made us reach this point. We have no way to defend ourselves. They always come and rape us and the world does nothing about it!"

Darine's sister turns the pages on another scrapbook.

"This is her book of martyrs," she says and points to a photo of a child. "This is Ikram, a baby sister of someone at high school. Here is a martyred guy shot in his home lying in his blood. " The photos are awful to look at, not a normal college girl's scrapbook.

"This is Darine's ["martyr"] letter," her sister continues. "It says, 'I hope you will forgive me. ' Here is a photo of her. " The photo shows Darine in a headscarf, looking pleasant.

Darine's sister notices I have Victor's book with me.

"How could she think when Darine had only two months to finish university that I would want her to drop out and force her to marry?" Nabila shakes her head and laughs as her sister outlines Darine's clear plan for her life.

"She wanted to get educated and then marry after her twenty-seventh birthday," Darine's sister explains. "She had a good sense of humor. She said she wanted six babies and would raise them as she likes and raise them religious.

"It's her life," Nabila says, genuinely - still bothered by this account of Darine. "I cannot force her! She is on her own. "

"Girls here have wishes like a joke," Darine's sister laments. "We all know there is no future in Palestine. I was young in the first Intifada. I had ambitions. After that I felt all got lost and it's hard. At any moment I might be under threat of Israeli tyranny. I want to be an architect. I saw many bridges destroyed. Who is going to rebuild them?"

"Do you want to marry?" I ask.

From the look on her face I can tell she is clearly shocked by the question.

"No! I am only eighteen years old!" she answers.

Her reaction makes me feel as though I've asked a child if she is interested in sexual relations and that it confirms the improbability that Darine was being forced to marry young.

"Would it have been possible for Darine to find a husband who supports her to be a university professor?" I ask.

"Yes, of course!" her sister answers, and I realize I have met married female university professors at Birzeit University. Clearly it's acceptable to at least some Palestinian men to have professional wives.

"She was very popular," her mother adds. "You can ask about her at the university. We had many offers of marriage for her. We didn't want her to move too far away. "

Nabila goes and gets a framed diploma from one of the tables and holds it proudly up on her lap for us to see.

"This is Darine's graduation certificate. The university awarded it to her after her death and gave it to us," she says smiling. There is a calm courage in the way she sits erect holding it framed on her lap.

"May I photograph you with it?" I ask, wanting to capture this poignant moment.

She nods, a calm, proud smile on her face as I snap the photo. While I arrived deeply influenced by Victor's book, I am now convinced that Barbara Victor got this narration lost in translation and mistakenly mixed up the story of Hemar with Darine. Nabila seems too proud of her daughters' educations to have ever tried to compromise them. The sister also seems genuinely free when it comes to her education coming before marriage. Nabila appears to have a respect for her daughters and enjoys that they have the chance to get educated. Maybe they are all lying, but it does not seem so.

I thank Nabila, and Darine's sister and brother for their time and promise to do what I can to correct the record in my book. They express their gratitude and we part with goodbyes.

In the car on the way back to Ramallah I think over the case of Darine Abu Aisha and how she was affected by both personal and less direct experiences. It seems to me that Darine's fury built as she watched all of these traumatic events unfold and finally after watching her cousin carry a bomb, she decided that she wouldn't be powerless any longer, that she would use the only things she had—her life and her body—and sacrifice them to the cause.

On the same day that Darine carried out her suicide mission, Sheik Yassin, the spiritual leader of Hamas, issued a religious ruling or fatwa, that gave permission to women to participate in suicide attacks. Sheik Yassin also listed the rewards that these female "martyrs" would receive in paradise upon their deaths and promised many more female suicide bombers to come. This of course added legitimacy to senders of female bombers and social support for women to volunteer themselves.

Darine was only the second Palestinian woman to enact a suicide bombing, and Muslims worldwide reacted in different ways. Some celebrated Darine's courage and encouraged full participation of Palestinian women while others felt that sending women to explode themselves was not a good practice. As Palestinian women joined the cadres of suicide bombers (totaling ten who carried out their missions and another seven more who were intercepted) during the second Intifada, they opened the door for other Arab and conservative Muslim cultures in Iraq, Pakistan and Afghanistan to use them in missions as well. Al Qaeda "central" has also now resorted to using female bombers with Muriel Degauque, a blond Caucasian Belgian convert, being one of the first to be sent (see Chapter Fifty-four).

Authors like Victor argued that the use of female bombers is a sign of the rising status of women in Arab culture and that women participate in an effort to achieve equality. An opposing argument could be made that the bombers are simply low-level pawns and their involvement does nothing to raise their status. The comments of Zakaria Zubeidi, the sender from the al Aqsa Martyr's Brigade in Jenin (who refused to send women) bears this thesis much more strongly. He claimed that many more young women than men begged him to equip and send them as bombers because they could not easily become militants fighting with guns and had few other ways to fight back. His explanation underlines that women's interest in suicide bombing does not seem to be about equality because their involvement has not led to more leadership roles for females in these sending groups.

The feminist argument seems almost meaningless compared to the high level of traumatization among this population that deeply affects both men and women. Darine Abu Aisha appears to have clear and deep posttraumatic triggers that built steadily over time into a furious and desperate need to strike out at the Israelis. Gender equality was an issue for Darine in that she broke a glass ceiling allowing women to ascend to "martyrdom" missions, but feminism itself does not seem to be her main or even secondary motivator.

Yoram Schweitzer also disagrees with the claim that signing up for "martyrdom" missions advances the feminist cause among Palestinian women. He writes that when Palestinian women express their political and religious motivations to be a "martyr", their statements "may reflect their authentic need to take part in fighting against their people's enemy, but it does not in any way change their unequal and inferior social status as well as the reluctance of their traditional societies to include women in these operations. "[163] During the years I was interviewing terrorists, Yoram also became a close friend as well as a colleague, and we often compared notes, particularly Yoram's interview with Darine's sender, Nasser Shawish. [164]

In addition to the multiple traumas listed by Darine's mother, Nasser added others telling Schweitzer that Darine was deeply upset witnessing a Palestinian child's death over the television. Hearing that echoed the thought experiment we did with the students in Belgium who had also incorporated during their role-play what they were told they saw only on television as actual facts in their own lives. As I found again and again when I began interviewing outside of conflict zones, terrorists groups are adept at using video and still images from *inside* the conflict zones to create secondary traumatization, anger and a desire to enact revenge. While Darine lived inside a conflict zone, her sender recalls that a televised picture of a killed child affected her as deeply as the other deaths of people she knew personally.

Nasser also told Schweitzer that Darine was very calm and happy even as she was being equipped for her mission,[165] suggesting she had psychologically entered a dissociative state, seemingly emotionally detached from the horror she was about to enact and possibly even euphoric. This too reminds me again of the students in the Brussels thought experiment who exhibited signs of euphoria and lightness of being as they *imagined* in a role-play putting on a suicide vest.

It's unclear if Darine's act made any difference for the Palestinian cause. She certainly expressed the collective outrage of her people as she tried to inflict the pain Palestinians feel on the enemy Israeli soldiers, but she failed in her attempt to even seriously wound them.

Darine's act can be seen as one among many in a mounting inferno of acts of Palestinian resistance or terrorism. [166] She bombed herself just after fights between Palestinian youth and Israeli police broke out at the al Aqsa mosque in Eastern Jerusalem, a contested site that is claimed by both Muslims and Jews. [167] Also within forty-eight hours of her attack, one of the worst suicide bombings inside Israel occurred in the Dolphinarium nightclub at the beachside town of Netayna, killing twenty-two and leaving more than one hundred wounded. [168] In response to the events, speaker of the Palestinian parliament, Ahmed Korai announced: "Israel is pushing us more and more. If it continues, there will be a million suicide bombers. " Darine's act unquestionably added to the collective Israeli unease and showed that a suicide mission could happen at anytime, coming from anyone—even an innocent looking young woman.

CHAPTER 35

Ayat al Akhras - The Second and Youngest Palestinian Female Suicide Bomber

After speaking to Darine's family outside of Nablus, I ask Alla who else we can interview related to female bombers.

"We can try to speak to the family of Ayat al Akhras," Alla offers. "I don't know them personally, but I know they live in the Dehaishe refugee camp. It's on our way home. Do you want to try talking with them?"

"Yes!" Ken and I answer simultaneously.

Alla instructs our taxi driver to redirect his route.

"You know people are fascinated by the violence of women," I say as our taxi speeds along the highway. "After studying the Chechens who used female bombers from the start and have almost as many female bombers as male, I get asked all the time to speak on the topic of female suicide terrorism versus suicide terrorism in general. I think the conference organizers see it as sexy but I don't see a big difference between the male and the female bombers."

"It is sexy," Ken jokes. "Women with weapons."

"Maybe," I muse. "Or maybe because we don't want to accept that women can be violent. They are though. Men are generally violent and we accept that, but women are violent too, just to people smaller than themselves—to their children most often. Far more women than we like to admit abuse their children."

"Yep, getting slapped around by Mom is no fun," Ken quips.

"Maybe there's an underlying anxiety in all of us that women are not always the kind nurturers we wish them to be," I continue. "It's terrifying when you're a child and you get in touch with the possibility that your mother can lose it and she can take you out if she wishes."

"It is horrible," Alla says.

"And so many journalists write about exploding wombs and weird things like that. They never write about men exploding their genitals." I complain.

Ken bursts out laughing.

"You know, Wafa was the first Palestinian female bomber," I say, "but Yoram [Schweitzer] told me there was one planned for a long time before her. It was Atef Elian, a senior Islamic Jihad operative who planned to explode a car bomb at a target in Jerusalem in the late eighties. She was caught before she could carry out her mission."

"How about the female highjacker, the woman with the grenades?" Ken asks. "She hid them in her bra!" He laughs raucously.

"That was Leila Khaled," Alla says. "She was PFLP."[169]

"That was the late sixties," I say. "So some Palestinian women have been involved as militants before this current wave. And the Syrians and Lebanese were using women as suicide bombers in the eighties. But among Palestinians, sending women as human bombers is new."

Ayat al Akhras, whose family we are headed for to interview, was the third and youngest Palestinian woman to carry out a suicide attack. A pretty eighteen-year-old dressed in western clothes, Ayat walked into a supermarket in the Kiryat Hayovel neighborhood of West Jerusalem, the market crowded with Sabbath shoppers and those readying for the Passover holiday. She passed the first guard easily but aroused the second guard's suspicions with her behavior and the heavy bag on her shoulder. He confronted her and she responded by detonating her bomb.[170] The bomb only partially exploded, and as she had not fully entered the crowded store she killed only herself, another girl her age and the security guard, and wounded twenty-two others.[171] Ayat's and Wafa Idris's terror acts prompted one writer to comment that the terrorist movement had dramatically shifted, "Women and children are now killing women and children."

From what I know about Ayat, she was young, pretty, educated, engaged-to-be-married and seemed to have a good future. According to Ibrahim Sarahne, who equipped and drove her on her mission, he offered her the last minute opportunity to renege on suicide, but she declined. Instead she calmly told him, "I'm not afraid. I want to kill people."[172]

Alla doesn't know how to contact Ayat's family but he knows where she lived. He suggests we just go to her house and request an interview. That seems rude to me, but he assures us that if we are polite when we arrive, it will be okay.

We arrive to the Dehaise Refugee Camp in the afternoon. It's located south of Bethlehem and was originally established as a temporary refuge for only three thousand four hundred Palestinian refugees coming from forty-five villages west of Jerusalem and Hebron who fled during the 1948 Arab-Israeli War. At that time, the refugees lived in tents. They've since built cement block homes for themselves and the camp has expanded to eleven thousand inhabitants. UNWRA describes the inhabitants of Palestinian refugee camps as generally unemployed and impoverished, but as we pull in, the camp charms me. The narrow streets are paved with stones and the homes, three and four stories high, are arranged in rows much like an old European city center. Here and there lemon trees are growing in tiny courtyards. It's started to rain lightly as Ken and I walk with Alla through the narrow streets to Ayat's family home.

"We don't have umbrellas," Alla says looking up at the grey sky.

"It's okay," Ken laughs, raising his hands to the heavy mist that is starting to fall.

We ring the bell and two pretty young women in headscarves open a window one story above us and lean out inquisitively and ask, "Who are you?"

"I'm an American professor and these are my students," I say smiling while Alla translates. "I've come to ask if the family would be willing to speak to me about Ayat?"

"Her parents are not at home," they say, smiling back and looking intrigued to see an American professor with two young men around their age.

"Who are you?" I ask, still smiling.

"We are Ayat's sister and sister-in-law," one answers. Both young women seem excited by the prospect of company but they say, "We cannot invite you in without the permission of Ayat's father."

"It's okay. We'll wait," I answer.

"It could be a long time," one of them calls out in resonant tones.

"That's okay," I say.

The young women withdraw, closing the window behind them.

"Looks like we are out of luck on this one," Ken says, shrugging his shoulders and turning to leave.

"Wait," I say. Ken and Alla look at me as if I'm crazy but I intuit that we are not out of luck. We stand together in the rain and begin to get soaked.

In a few moments the young women open the window again and look down on us.

"It's raining!" one says.

"Yes, it is! It's cold out here," I say smiling warmly.

"Wait, just one minute!" one of them calls to us, "We are coming to let you in," and again the window closes.

Arabic hospitality has triumphed! I smile in victory at Ken who laughs incredulously as the young women come down, open the door and invite us into their home.

Inside, we leave our shoes on pieces of cardboard that cover the stone floor near the doorway and follow the young women up a flight of stone stairs to a brightly lit living room with overstuffed chairs, sofas, lamps, a thick rug and coffee table. The young women seat us on a sofa on one side of the room and take seats on two armchairs across the room, beneath the window they had just been leaning out of talking to us.

"Would you like some tea?" one offers.

"Sure," I say, and Ken and Alla add, "Sounds great!"

The young women go to make us tea and when they come back serve it on the table between us.

"We can't give you any information until Ayat's father comes home," one reminds us.

"So if you cannot speak about Ayat without her father being here, can we tell you about us and maybe you can tell us a little bit about you?" I ask. "How is life in Palestine?"

The two women look at each and burst out in giggles and then begin to talk. I decide not to ask their names as I don't want to make them uncomfortable and I am really grateful that we've been allowed into the house to wait for Ayat's father. I also don't take notes at first or press them about Ayat as I want to respect their deference to Ayat's father's wishes for privacy.

I tell them about my project, with Alla translating. I explain that I am recently interested in the female "martyrs" and that I also interviewed Arin Ahmed in Israeli prison. They know Arin and confirm that it was her traumatic grief over Jad's assassination that spurred her to volunteer for a suicide mission.

"We know other girls as well in the Hasharon prison," one of the young women tells us. "It's really difficult for them."

"We know a girl, Amila," the other adds. "The Israelis took her pregnant and she gave birth in prison. The baby is still with her in prison at one and a half years old. [The Israelis] wanted to take the baby out of prison but she preferred it."

"I got scared from the Israelis in all ways," the other says. "For example they came here while we were sleeping. I had just given birth to my daughter and they put all of us out in the rain." On a day like today I can imagine how awful that would be, standing outside in the cold and rain for hours at a time with a newborn who is sensitive to temperature changes and therefore more at risk for hypothermia.

As we chat more I learn that Ayat's sister-in-law is from Jenin and is married with three boys and a girl. The other young woman is Samhah, Ayat's sister. Both of their husbands were arrested and imprisoned by the Israelis but were finally released in an exchange brokered with Hezbollah. Like Hamid, who we met in Birzeit University, they were "open check prisoners" held with no charges. One was imprisoned for a year and a half, the other for six months, released and then arrested again for six months.

"How was it here when the Israelis came in April, 2002?" I ask, referring to the massive Israeli *Operation Defensive Shield* actions occurring just before Ayat made her operation, when entire refugee camps and towns were surrounded by Israeli soldiers trying to route out Palestinian militants.

"I'm afraid when they come to the camp," Samhah says in present tense as she relives the memory, a sign of trauma. "They come in numbers. They wear camouflage paint and olive leaves on their heads. I was watching them when they searched the other houses, but when they came here I hid in the bathroom! They are cowards but their weapons are scary. They locked us all in one room and we couldn't go to the bathroom!"

"Did the soldiers return after Ayat went on her operation?" I ask.

"They came to destroy the house two or three times!" Samhah answers, her eyes wide with terror referring to the Israeli's response to Ayat's suicide mission. "They took my brothers away in order to destroy our house but the UN objected to the house destruction."

"Our husbands were arrested at that time!" Ayat's sister-in-law explains. "[The Israeli soldiers] brought explosives and were ready to destroy our home, but then they saw that it will destroy all the neighborhood." Indeed, their home is part of a row of homes built in a continuous line with shared walls.

"The soldiers often came though," she adds. "'Get ready in one half hour we will destroy your house,' they said. Every time they came to the camp, we would wear our clothes and get ready to evacuate our house. When they destroyed others houses they usually warned us that they will come to ours next. We lived in constant terror!"

"The first time they came to destroy the house I was pregnant in the third month," Samhah says. "I lost the baby from fear!"

"The next pregnancy she returned here from her mother-in-law, and I watched her carefully," Ayat's sister-in-law explains, gazing protectively at Samhah. I'm touched by the obvious love between them.

"The house of my husband was destroyed," Samhah explains, indicating why she moved back to her family home. "The brother of my husband was a shaheed. This house they tried to destroy four times," she continues. "It's just recently we brought our furniture back here. For three years we didn't live here. We expected it to be destroyed."

"How did your children deal with it?" I ask.

"During this period of time, the children woke up a lot, peed on themselves at night," Samhah answers. "I had to get a psychologist. My children got bad grades. The whole family was affected." I wonder later where she found a psychologist in the West Bank, although the Birzeit faculty did tell me there was one operating for some time in Bethlehem until the checkpoints finally made it impossible for her to continue.

Ayat's parents return and when the women explain that they have guests, they don't seem alarmed. Perhaps they have given us a good introduction.

"Marhaba! Welcome!" Ayat's mother, Khadra, greets us warmly. We introduce ourselves as she sinks tiredly into an overstuffed armchair. Khadra's grey hair peeks out at her forehead from beneath a large pink scarf wrapped over her head and pinned under her chin. It's long corners flow down over her shoulders and chest. She is heavy set and dressed in a burgundy velvet abaya with embroidery on the arms.

"Hello, welcome," Mohammed, Ayat's father says and takes a seat on the side of the room between the young women and us. He is a strong looking older man, also grey haired and sporting a distinguished grey moustache. He is wearing blue dress pants, a checkered blue and white button down cotton shirt with a blue cable knit cardigan buttoned over it.

Ayat's parents are interested to learn about us as well and they readily agree to the interview.

"How many children do you have?" I ask, starting out easily.

"We have four sons and seven girls," Khadra announces proudly. "All my sons are married and have kids and live with me."

"You seem like a very warm and nurturing mother," I comment.

"Yes, with Ayat, I kept her by my side," Khadra nods. Then she changes the subject to Mohammad Durrah, the little boy killed in Gaza. "Mohammad Durrah was murdered, but the media flipped the picture to look like the Israelis are innocent."

I see she is worried that I am part of the media and will craft her story to my end.

"I'm not a journalist, I'm a university professor," I remind her.

Khadra settles back in to the interview, resuming her role as a mother.

"I kiss the children when they come home with a star on their heads," she tells us. The star she is referring to is a Palestinian tradition. Lacking stickers, teachers reward their young students' good behavior and academic success at school by drawing in ballpoint ink a star on their foreheads so that when they return home everyone can see that they have excelled in school that day.

"Can you tell me about Ayat?" I ask to steer her back on topic.

"It was a big shock, a girl going for martyrdom," Khadra answers.

"Do you know why she did it?" I ask.

"The occupation. That was Ayat's aim to make the world look at her case," she says meaning the Palestinian perspective. "Ayat was frustrated by the political conferences held in behalf of Palestine that accomplished little. 'Look, what they are doing, it's not effective,' She would say."

"Did you know she was going to do it?"

"I wish I knew," her mother says. "That day she was completely normal. She went to school and took her exam. I saw it. She got good marks. Her aim was to become a journalist. She wanted to publish the Palestinian case to the world. She was engaged, about to get married. Everything was set up. She was eighteen years old. He didn't know."

Ayat's mother shows us pictures of her daughter in a shrine of sorts, on a table and hanging on the walls. Ayat was a very pretty girl, slim with soft brown eyes, a full-lipped smile and creamy complexion. In her pictures she wears a soft red lipstick, her head covered in a soft black and white woven checkered keffiyeh tied artfully around her face with the ends tucked into her black abaya. She looks like a nice girl. There are no posters from the group that sent her, only sentimental pictures of her that have been lovingly placed in hand embroidered frames. There is

even a wooden sailing ship that bears different pictures of Ayat on each of
the sails. I wonder if the symbolism is that she is being borne to paradise
upon it.

"Did you talk to her sender?" I ask.

"We don't want to talk to her sender. She wanted to do it. No one
forced her to go," Khadra answers, "I don't know and didn't try to know.
I don't want to open a closed book. It's painful for the mind."

I nod. She is probably wise in that regard—Ayat was not forced to carry
out her mission and her handler when caught even explained that he had
offered Ayat the convenient exit strategy of throwing her bomb rather than
her wearing it into the crowded grocery market but she had been adamant
about going as a "martyr".

Ayat's handler was Ibrahim Sarahne, a Palestinian also living in the
Dehaishe refugee camp. He was approached by the al Aqsa Martyrs
Brigade to help select targets inside Israel and drive bombers to them. He
was asked to lead Ayat's mission because he drove an Israeli registered
taxi and therefore could move freely in and out of Israel. He knew which
public areas were most crowded and where a suicide operative could
achieve the highest lethality, leading to the identification of a busy grocery
store in Jerusalem as her target. Sarahne evaded Israeli security by carrying forged identity papers identifying him as an Israeli Arab who lived in
Jerusalem. His wife, Irina Polchik, also had forged documents identifying her as an Israeli Jew. Together, they had also driven Arin Ahmed on
her aborted mission and played a role in two additional successful suicide
bombings

After Arin Ahmed turned back from her attack and was subsequently
arrested, she made statements during her interrogation that led to Sarahne's
arrest. From his prison cell in Israel he told journalists that his motivation for participating in terror attacks was "pure force" - that he wanted to
demonstrate that just as the Israelis forces could cross into the West Bank
and Gaza at will to kill and injure Palestinians, so too could Palestinians
breach Israeli security.[173] Sarahne bragged, "Palestinians can get into Israel
any time they want, without any problem, if there's a closure or not."[174]
And when he recalled hearing the ambulances and sirens responding to
Ayat's attack, confirming that he had succeeded in assisting a successful
mission, he said, "I can't describe the feeling of pure joy that I felt in my
heart."[175]

While Sarahne's motivations were rooted in his experiences as a Palestinian living under occupation in a refugee camp, his wife's involvement
is more complicated. Ukrainian born and a Christian married to a Palestinian, she told journalist Barbara Victor, "I felt no compunction about
killing civilians including women and children. They were part of the
army that killed Palestinian civilians." Those sentiments probably came
to her after marrying a Palestinian and living with him under occupation;
however, she referred to her own personal motives as well, "Personally I
hated [the Israelis] because they discriminated against me. They only let
me into Israel because I lied and said my mother was Jewish. If I hadn't
(lied), I would have been stuck in Ukraine without any hope of a better
life."[176] I have heard bitter statements from other Russian-born Jews who
immigrated to Israel only to be shocked at the discrimination they feel,
but this is the first that I heard of one whose hatred grew to proportions
enough to want to kill the Israelis who granted her access into the country
in the first place.

Other operatives were also involved in Ayat's mission. Someone from
the al Aqsa Martyrs Brigade prepared the bomb and placed it in the black
bag she was given. These operatives also video taped her ahead of time
and disguised Ayat to look like an Israeli girl by dressing her in western
style clothing and styling her hair appropriately.

Interestingly, before Ayat exploded herself, either she (as Victor
reports)[177] or Mousa Sarahne (who the Israeli Ministry of Defense claims
was in the car with Ibrahim)[178] approached two elderly Arab women who
were close to the supermarket and warned them of the expected attack.[179]
The women fled and saved themselves before she exploded herself.

"Can you tell me what you think motivated Ayat to volunteer herself
for her mission?" I ask.

Her father, Mohammed nods. "Ayat was very upset about the shooting
of our neighbor. He was holding his child in his arms inside his home when
an [Israeli] sniper shot him dead. He was shot in the head. The child was
one year old. The ambulance could not come because there was shooting
[at that time] and they had to take an indirect route."

This story is confirmed in Victor's book in which she interviewed Jamil
Qassas, a leader of the al Aqsa Martyrs Brigade in Bethlehem and brother
of the victim. According to Qassas, Ayat was visiting his sister at their
house when the Israeli sniper fired shots through the window hitting his
brother and Ayat was deeply affected by it. "'Ayat got hysterical,' Qassas

recalled to Victor. 'I picked up my brother who was bleeding very badly and ran with him in my arms toward the nearest hospital. Ayat ran with me, sobbing and screaming.' ... 'My brother died in my arms, and Ayat collapsed on the street. At the funeral, Ayat came up to me and said that the death of my brother had changed everything for her. She believed it was a sign from Allah that she had to do something to make her father and the others understand that any contact with the Jews only ended in bloodshed. I knew then that she was destined for great things. She had too much emotion and hatred inside her to just sit quietly while our people were being massacred like that.[180]

Less than a month after the shooting, Ayat volunteered for her mission.

Meanwhile, the Israeli invasion of Palestinian refugee camps was still in full force.

"The Israelis stayed seven days," Mohammed says. "Then they returned again on April first and invaded the camp again. They invaded the Nativity Church in Bethlehem where it's forbidden to kill. It's a city of peace, they are not allowed to kill, but they killed lots of people inside," Mohammed recounts. He fails to explain that at that time the Palestinian militants used the church as a place to hide out.

"It was very terrifying," Samhah explains of the first invasion, her eyes wide with terror. "The snipers were searching every room with their lasers (attached to their sharp shooter rifles). Anything that moved, it was dead."

"Even a doctor here, Dr. Noman, went to help the injured and they killed him," Mohammed adds. "All the medical group—they shot them, they shot the ambulances."

Samhah has begun to shake with terror, likely reliving the memories in a highly aroused bodily state.

"They had aircraft and snipers on the high buildings," Mohammed continues. "Their lasers would cross our windows. You see it and you feel terror."

"We all hid in the corner, twenty people lived in one room for seven days," Khadra explains.

I shake my head.

"Also, later, for fifty days they came. We make our food during this time. Old people can eat anything, but little ones need milk. Someone who got sick or has diabetes, it is very hard for him to get medications. Some died in childbirth," Khadra recounts. "My daughter gave birth and her baby died during the invasions of the camp."

"Every home here has their own story," Mohammed says referring to the tragedies that occurred during the blockade. "The occupation destroyed [Ayat's] dream, destroyed houses, trees, animals, rocks, even our dreams."

"What other things affected Ayat?" I ask.

"During the March eighth invasion they martyred our neighbor with his boy, Issa," Mohammed says. "There were two assassinations by rockets—our neighbors Siad and Jad [Arin Ahmed's boyfriend] were killed."

"Were they her friends?" I ask.

"Friends to her brother. We all know each other," Mohammed explains.

"Everyone was terrified [during that time]," Samhah recounts.

But Mohammed says, "Ayat was completely normal. She would pray and fast and read her Koran."

Khadra says that Ayat's video reflected how she wanted to move the world and shame the Arabs. "'The whole Arab nations couldn't stand before you,' Ayat said. 'But a girl could,'" Khadra recalls.

Later I learn that Ayat appeared in her martyr's video with her head wrapped in a black-and-white checked keffiyeh and her face made up attractively. She chided the Arab leaders reading from a statement she had prepared beforehand: "I say to the Arab leaders, 'Stop sleeping. Stop failing to fulfill your duty. Shame on the Arab armies who are sitting and watching the girls of Palestine fighting while they are asleep.'"[181]

"How did you learn about her operation?" I ask.

"From TV," Khadra recalls. "I went straight to the hospital. Her sisters and brothers went to the hospital. The whole thing came as a huge shock! I took medication, they gave her brother and sister medication."

"I thank Allah I was patient," Mohammed says. "People came [to the house] and you have to be a man in this situation and hold everyone else. Not one drop of tears fell but from inside I was totally torn up." Mohammed's face collapses as he recalls this time period and he begins to cry.

"We're proud of her and we respect her beliefs and we respect everybody's beliefs and we value *everyone's* blood," Mohammed told reports the morning after her act, adding. "I respect her convictions but I don't like the spilling of any blood." He explained that he had no idea about Ayat's plans and expressed genuine sympathy for the mother of Rachel Levy, the Israeli girl killed by Ayat. But like most Palestinians who have mixed emotions about terrorism directed against Israeli civilians, and as a bereaved father, he wouldn't condemn her act.[182] "No one does this and asks for permission from their father or mother," he said at that time. "I would rather die a hundred deaths than see the death of my child."[183]

Now as I watch tears spilling down his cheeks, I know the words he said after Ayat's death were straight from his heart.

"We have not received the body till now," Khadra states with fatigue in her voice. She is referring to the Israeli policy of refusing to return the corpses of suicide bombers and terrorist operatives preventing their proper Islamic burial.[184] "No obituary was made. Different people came to the house. After three days Israelis came, at the same time as the invasion of the Nativity Church. They took her two brothers and said they will destroy our house. They came not one time, but many times here to destroy it."

"The people came and took our furniture out when the Israeli's came. Our house was emptied," Mohammed recalls sadly. "I was fired from my work with no pension, no severance pay. I worked for a construction company in Israel for fifteen years."

Victor's account of this case emphasizes that Ayat bombed herself partly because her father's working for the Israeli construction firm during the blockade was causing him to be viewed badly in his community—akin to a collaborator. Collaborators in Palestine are often murdered. While many Palestinians in the camp had lost their jobs working in Israel during the second Intifada, Mohammed had continued working with the Israelis and worse yet was involved with construction in the ever-expanding Israeli settlements that were encroaching on Palestinian land. Both Ayat's brother and her sender told Victor about the anger in the camp over Mohammed's work, and Ayat's brother recalled to Victor that the leaders of the al Aqsa Martyrs Brigade had delivered an ultimatum to Mohammed to quit his job or face dire consequences.[185] Victor concluded that Ayat saved her family by becoming a "martyr", though it would be ironic if Ayat killed herself because her father wouldn't quit his job, since he ultimately lost his job because of her act.

I ask Mohammed if he remembers giving his interview to Victor and knows that her book that profiles Ayat is now published.

"I never saw her!" Mohammed says, surprising me because he is quoted in it. He continues, his voice filled with anger and disgust. "We never sat together. It's a book of lies. She wrote that we were exiled from our society and neighbors and that is why Ayat made her operation. She wrote lies about many of the girls. I laughed out loud when I read her book!" Mohammed continues shaking his head and spitting out his words.

"How could any educated person write such lies? It's really a shame [she is] a writer because writers hold the letter of honesty and truth."

"I'm sorry," I say, shocked now to hear two people claiming that Victor got it wrong. "I will try to write the truth." The truth though, I realize is complicated and not so easy to arrive at.

"How did you happen to read it?" I ask, curious if Victor's book is available in Arabic.

"An Irish guy had the book. I can read in English," Mohammed explains. "I felt it's all lies, every paragraph!"

"Truth will prevail," Khadra says calmly.

It's possible that Ayat did chose her mission in part to save her father and family's position in their community. Certainly his work with the Israeli company constructing new settlements while the others were unemployed was creating an untenable situation. And it's understandable that her father would be aghast at the suggestion that his stubbornness and refusal to detach from the Israelis at that time of high tension could have cost him his daughter's life. I can see that I cannot press him on this point.

"The world should know," Mohammed continues, "we don't hate the Israelis or the Jews. We hate the hate. We feel very sorry when anyone gets injured, when there is one drop of blood [shed]. We have feelings: crying, dreaming, laughing. [The Israelis] think we are a people empty of emotions. We don't like to see a woman crying. We want all people in happiness."

"I miss her," Samhah says. "We were like twins. We looked alike. We spent all our time together. I always dream of Ayat. I dream she is living and with us, still around us. We talk and hang out as it used to be."

I feel so sad hearing these words. I've always treasured my sister and I can imagine Samah's pain. We thank the family and leave telling them tomorrow we will be speaking to Wafa Idris's family.

"Give Mabrook our best regards," Khadra says as we stand to leave. I promise to do so and ask Khadra and Mohammed if I can photograph them. They agree and touchingly Mohammed picks up one of the many gifts they have been given honoring Ayat. He holds it near his heart as I photograph him.

I realize the entrance of Palestinian females into suicide terrorism raises some interesting points about why terrorist groups chose to use them. Females definitely garner more media attention for the group's cause as audiences are fascinated with the violence of women. And females are much better at eluding security because female modesty is generally respected.

We often search for reasons to negate a woman's violent urges—that she was coerced, that her society was so oppressive that she was desperate to die, that someone compromised her sexually, raped or impregnated her—so as a matter of honor she must die rather than reveal the damage to her and her family's reputation, etc. However the truth is far more likely that on an individual level, female terrorists, just like their male counterparts inside conflict zones reach their tolerance for the amount of violence they can witness before they desire to strike back while also exiting this life.

Ayat's story and the many events that led her to her fate seem to prove this. A friend of the Akhras family explained to a journalist that Ayat had reached her tipping point in response to multiple traumas and that her response to all the violence she had witnessed was likely gender neutral."[The violence of the occupation] bred in us *all* feelings of despair and revenge. And that is what a suicide bomber is: a mixture of despair and resistance. You don't have to be a man to feel that. You don't have to be a woman. You can be a boy or a girl."[186]

CHAPTER 36

Wafa Idris - the First Female Palestinian Suicide Bomber

After speaking to Ayat's family, we take a taxi minibus back to Ramallah and I stop in the city center and buy a brown knit slip-on head and neck covering in case I need it in Gaza where we will head after our interview the next day with the family of Wafa Idris, the first Palestinian female bomber. We all go back to Alla's house, where Jamilah joins us for dinner. We wind down with some wine, and after a few drinks, Ken slips into Alla's room where my things are and retrieves the scarf. He returns with it on and slouches in a chair, glass of wine in hand. He begins speaking to us in a falsetto voice until we look up and notice him. We all double over laughing.

"I'll produce this picture someday in the future," I laugh as I snap a photo of him.

Before bed, I read what Barbara Victor has written in her book Army of Roses about Wafa Idris, and the next morning we set out for the al Am'ari refugee camp nearby, just south of Ramallah.

The story of twenty-seven year old Wafa Idris is now well known throughout Palestine and the Arab world. As soon as she accomplished her act, a flood of celebration occurred and she was highly venerated as the first Palestinian woman to willingly "martyr" herself for the cause. Dispatched on January 27, 2002 by the Fatah Tanzim, Wafa made her way from the West Bank into Israel, entered a shoe shop in Jerusalem where she browsed around for a bit and upon exiting, blew up the twenty-two pound bomb that she carried in a black handbag that had been prepared ahead of time for her. The explosion killed Wafa, an elderly man and injured ninety others.[187] And it unleashed a new horror upon Israelis: that young innocent Palestinian girls are also capable of terror acts.

At first it was unclear if Wafa had actually been sent as a "shahida" or if her instructions had been only to place the bomb and detonate it from afar but something had gone wrong. The controversy over that continues to this day, although Wafa allegedly told friends in her camp that she was going to Jerusalem and would not be returning.[188] Her sending group also did not at first claim responsibility, perhaps fearing a public outcry over using a woman as a suicide operative. But in the days that followed, the huge public outpouring of support within Palestine and throughout the Arab world for Wafa's "martyrdom" changed that. Wafa had inaugurated the day of Palestinian women as shadidas, and soon many more were to follow.

It's a short drive to the al Am'ari camp. We find the Idris's cement house nestled between a row of similar homes on a dusty and rocky road. Their cheap white metal door swings open and Wafa's brother, Khalid, greets us, wearing jeans and a blue zip-up jean jacket over a collared knit sport shirt. Khalid takes us inside to a sparsely furnished room with grey cement walls and cheaply-floored tiles and introduces us to Wafa's mother, Malbrook, his wife Mervit and his female cousin, Sharehon.

Malbrook, who I've read about ahead of time, is only in her fifties, but already looks elderly. Dressed in a long abaya and a headscarf, she is seated on a twin bed pushed against the bare wall with pillows behind her back. Her feet jut out over the edge. Khalid seats Ken and Alla on a sofa beside me, while Mervit and Sharehon sit at the end of the twin bed on another small sofa. Khalid pulls up a plastic chair.

Mervit, Khalid's wife, wears a long abaya and full head covering like Malbrook, but Sharehon, his cousin is dressed in a turtleneck and jacket with her hair uncovered and pulled back into a clip. She wears pretty gold hoop earrings and has her eyebrows plucked into striking arches. None of the women are wearing makeup, although the two younger ones have clear beautiful skin and smile kindly. Their three young children, two boys and a girl, play rambunctiously around us as I explain my project, telling them we have just come from the home of Ayat al Akhras and that Ayat's mother sends her greetings to Malbrook. Malbrook smiles warmly and they all agree to participate. I can see that Malbrook is very anxious, so I commence gently.

"How are you feeling today?" I ask her kindly.

"Since Wafa passed, I have had so many operations on my eyes and my gall bladder," she answers. Khalid explains that his mother's health has been failing and I can see we must be careful, as she is still heavily bereaved. I decide to ease her in and start with Khalid.

"Can you tell us what Wafa was like?" I ask.

"She used to be strong and never afraid of anything," Khalid begins. "She went to demonstrations and threw rocks at the Israelis soldiers."

"Do you know the things that affected her?" I ask.

"She saw many people martyred in front of her eyes. Some lost their eyes from rubber bullets [shot by the Israeli army]," Khalid answers. "In the refugee camp we are all like brothers. Two hundred and fifty thousand people live here,[189] the second biggest camp in the West Bank. Many got martyred from our camp – all in the second Intifada. And there are one hundred and twenty [political] prisoners from here, forty with life sentences [in Israeli prisons]."

Khalid walks across the room and takes a laminated poster from the wall. I notice that there is also a giant photographic poster of Wafa that covers half the wall from floor to ceiling. Al Aqsa mosque with its gleaming gold dome is in the background and Wafa at age fourteen stands in the foreground, a black and white Palestinian woven checked keffiyeh folded and tied around her head and another wrapped over her black shirt. She looks very serious, but pretty. Near her shoulder there is the emblem of the group that sent her, displaying two hands holding weapons in the air. Arabic script across the poster proclaims her "martyrdom" act.

Khalid comes back to me and points to the poster he's now holding, which consists of cameo shots of the "martyrs" from the camp.

"These are all the martyrs from our camp during the first and second Intifada," he says pointing out different ones. "See here is a baby girl. This one is a four-year-old girl. Here is a nine-year-old girl. They hit them by firing from aircraft around the school at the beginning of the invasion. That was four months after Wafa [went on her mission]. Fifty to sixty people here are handicapped from injuries--these all just in one camp."

"This is the home we lived in," Malbrook says, beginning to feel comfortable. "They made a lot of damage to it many times and destroyed everything inside. They used to get us out of our house in the rain and the cold."

I am confused so Khalid explains, "They cannot dynamite our home because it's in a row of homes and structurally that would destroy the neighbors as well so they keep coming back and shooting up the insides and destroying the furniture."

He describes a recent incident in which a soldier came to wreak havoc on their house, in retaliation for Wafa's suicide mission.

"'Come on destroy it!'" Khalid recalls telling the Israeli captain.

'Set me free and I'll destroy it whenever I want,' the Israeli answered. But they didn't," Khalid recalls. "We sat on the corner of the street. Afterward they arrested my brother, Khalil."

Khalid again challenged the soldier to decimate the house."'Come on!' I told them. 'It's better than this repeated terror.'

'I'll do it whenever I want,' the captain said, 'It depends on my mood.'"

Instead, they arrested Khalid's younger brother, Sultan.

Barbara Victor, who visited the Idris home in 2002, one week after Wafa's mission, witnessed the ransacking that occurred the first time the soldiers were there.

"There were bullet holes in the walls, drawers had been tossed, beds turned upside down, and slashed cushions strewn around the floor of the living room," she wrote.[190]

"They used to get all the kids and little girls out on the street in the cold and rain, with no mercy, no sympathy at one, two and three a.m." Malbrook continues, recalling the numerous times the Israeli soldiers returned in anger to ransack their home. She says they now invade with camoflauge painted faces, and are even more terrifying.

"What kind of damage do they cause?" I ask.

"You see our doors and windows are all new," Khalid says sweeping his arm to point out the new items in the room.

I note that their place looks very sparse—it's the first home I've seen that seems like cement and tile only, no warm carpets, very few personal items and cheap plastic lawn chairs stacked on top of each other in the corner, waiting perhaps for guests.

"We have some new furniture," he points to the sofas we are seated on. "I'm afraid to buy more. They have destroyed the furniture of this house four or five times."

"How?" I ask.

"They stab the furniture with knives," Khalid explains.

Wafa's brother, Khalil, according to Barbara Victor, was Wafa's entrée to Fatah and the Tanzim organization. Shortly after Wafa's terror act, Victor interviewed Khalil and the rest of the Idris family. According to Victor, Khalil said he proposed Wafa as a Tanzim shahida, talked them into making her the first female suicide bomber and then led her across the checkpoint to her attack destination in Jerusalem.[191]

Victor states that Khalil, who she interviewed twice, at first admitted recruiting her for Fatah, then retracted his story the next day, apparently due to pressure from Fatah leadership.[192] They did not want to claim responsibility for sending a female bomber—until Wafa's terror act became so highly acclaimed.

I ask more about Khalil's record of arrest and imprisonment, and Khalid says that he was jailed in 1985 and locked up for eight years.

"What was he imprisoned for?" I ask.

"Resisting the IDF," Khalid explains. "He was arrested once before that also. The charges are usually the same for Palestinians. You can go to the archives or talk to lawyers who defend prisoners to learn this. They usually say that they threatened an Israelis soldier's life, they arrest and then make charges against them. Khalil was released in 1992 or 1993, and after that locked up again for six months, and again after Wafa's operation for six months."

"How old were all of you when Khalil was arrested the first time?" I ask.

Wafa was ten or eleven years old, I was close to fifteen," Khalid answers. "Khalil was fifteen and did not even have an ID yet.

"They came here at night around two or three a.m. to take him. They entered [our] room and took him away. At the beginning we had only one room—Wafa, me and Sultan."

"They came dressed for combat," Malbrook says, "and surrounded the house. Two or three soldiers came inside." That was in 1985.

"Are you afraid when they come now after Wafa's action?" I ask.

"The soldier tied my hands and beat me," Khalid answers. "This was between three and six thirty a.m. and it was just because I said, 'It's too cold for the children to come out. My mother is a pretty old woman. She can't handle it.'" Khalid's face contorts and he folds his arms in distress.

"Once when they came to destroy the house," Khalid recalls, "there were eighty people taken out of their homes, little children, all our neighbors. They put us all in the room of a neighbor. It's all revenge behavior."

"Did your family receive money from Fatah or others?" I ask.

"No!" Khalid answers aghast. But then he explains honestly, "What happened with us when they destroyed the house was there used to be a union of workers from the PA. They came and rebuilt the house."

"Who comes to replace the windows and doors each time the Israelis return?" I ask.

"A committee of the PA—Public Works," Khalid answers. "But they don't replace the furniture. We replace it ourselves. When they destroyed the first furniture we bought very simple furniture because they destroy everything. They don't leave anything behind. The door used to be an iron door but they exploded it. When they did this we took our clothes outside with us to save them. They got soaked. They treat us with no mercy. And it's not only my house, but all my brothers' homes! We had another picture of Wafa on the wall, larger than that one," he says indicating the huge face of Wafa filling their wall. "They shot up the picture with twelve bullet holes. This is a new one."

"Wafa did the operation," Khalid says. "After they chase her brothers and relatives. But we have nothing to do with it."

"Khalil was involved in Wafa's mission?" I ask, explaining that Barbara Victor claimed in her book that Khalil admitted to her introducing Wafa to the Fatah Tanzim as a potential "martyr".

"It's not right," Malbrook says crossing her arms over her chest, while Khalid shakes his head violently. "Wafa did it."

"Poor Wafa was a completely sensitive person," Khalid says. "If me or my brother knew, you think we would have let her go and do it?" His voice raises in anguish. "We already sacrificed Khalil in jail and we don't want to lose anyone else! Khalil wasted most of his life in jail. The last six months he spent in jail with no charges! It's just their tyranny!"

"I'm confused," I say. "Barbara Victor claimed Khalil admitted to her that he was involved in sending Wafa."

"Do you think someone knows his sister is going to go and bomb herself and does nothing?" Khalid asks.

There is actually one Palestinian mother who urged her son to go as a bomber. She is an aberration among Palestinian mothers of boys who went as bombers, but she does exist. And there are cases among the Chechens where men have sent their wives and sisters—all willingly—to become "martyrs". So no, I don't believe that a brother will always protect his sister. Things can become complicated in many ways in crowded living situations where female honor is paramount—and a sister being sexually compromised is a problem in Palestinian culture. An illicit affair, out of wedlock pregnancy, incest—many things can create the circumstance where a brother might like to "extinguish" his sister. But I don't say these things to Khalid now as he is already upset.

Khalid looks at me intently and speaks in a serious voice that emphasizes that he really wants me to understand.

"Her brother *did not* send her. There was an arrangement inside the Red Crescent. She asked to get in an operation. She worked with the ambulances to carry the wounded. Now we know the one who sent her. He was arrested by the Palestinian intelligence. He's from Nablus or Tolkerim. We were told about him three days after her operation. They called and told us. Khalil did not send her, no way! When Khalil found out he went to the Red Crescent and started beating the guy himself!

"'I sent her in order to place the explosives and return back,' her sender told Khalil. We don't know exactly what was her intention. Others say she got scared of being discovered and blew herself up."

"If I knew she was going to do it," Malbrook says. " I would have prevented it. She's my *only* daughter!"

"She's the only daughter. We won't let her go for free!" Khalid adds. I see they are both genuine in their despair.

"Why do you think she did it?" I ask, deciding to let the sending part of the situation rest for a bit. Clearly they don't believe or do not want to admit that Khalil had anything to do with it.

"She worked at the Red Crescent," Malbrook explains. "She saw people's intestines falling out of them, the Israeli soldiers attacking and beating people to death."

I learn that Wafa volunteered on Fridays, and in Palestine, Fridays are the days when fiery mosque sermons are delivered and demonstrations occur, with many ending in violent altercations with the Israeli army. She also traveled to Jenin, Bethlehem and Jerusalem to give first aid when battles happened.

"She was shot twice herself while wearing the uniform of the Red Crescent," Malbrook adds.

"She was shot?" I ask.

"Yes, once in the shoulder and once in the thigh and she was beaten by Israeli soldiers three times," Khalid answers.

"Once she was in an ambulance with a wounded man," Mervit explains. "He was shot in the head. Wafa was holding his head in her hands and she was not supposed to move at all so he can live, but because of the closures at the checkpoints he passed out. Then the ambulance moved over rough terrain and Wafa could not keep his skull held closed and as the ambulance went over a bump, his brains fell into her hands," Mervit says, her face gone pale. Alla gasps as he translates, and we all recoil in horror.

"She used to come home very tired and cried after working," Wafa's cousin says. "Her hands were yellow from blood and they would shake from fear."

"Imagine her sensitive gender," Khalid says. "Imagine when she sees all these things happening and go and have a look at the hospital. Go and see all the wounded! Israelis prevent treatment and we get bad treatment as well. Handicaps occur as a result. The IDF used to prevent ambulances to the wounded. Enjoy watching these wounded bodies dying. The IDF shoots little kids!"

As Khalid speaks I notice that his eight-year-old nephew begins to rock and become dissociative as he talks. It's not good for him to hear these things recounted. It's too personally threatening.

"This is not defense as the Israelis claim," Khalid continues. "This is terrorism! Look at these little children martyred! These are terrorists, shooting from aircraft, hitting our ambulances!"

"The Jews themselves will never make peace with us. I wish for you to come here and live the things happening on our land so you can understand."

I don't comment and redirect the conversation back to Wafa and the circumstances of her life.

"Wafa was married?" I ask.

"Yes," Khalid answers. "She used to be married to my cousin, but they divorced because she could not bear children. Until now, he wants her. Wafa loved him, too."

In conservative Palestinian culture, marriage is in large part for establishing a family and the desire for many children is customary. A barren wife can hardly create a family, and so, under pressure from his parents, Wafa's husband disintegrated their union and found another woman to marry and bear children, though it sounds like his love for her continued.

"Wafa did not have any psychological problems," Khalid states, his voice firm and a bit belligerent, indicating he has read accounts that describe Wafa as depressed and grieving after the divorce. Barbara Victor argued that the desperation of a barren woman was the main reason that Wafa bombed herself. "Put aside that idea," Khalid insists. "She was completely mentally healthy."

"Her husband never had a fight with her over the infertility," Malbrook adds, "but his parents did. She was very happy when she graduated and happy to be married."

"She was pregnant once?" I ask to confirm the stillbirth I read about in Victor's chapter on Wafa.

"Yes, but while in the seventh or eight month the baby died," Khalid explains. "She stayed eight years with no children. If you say the reason why, it was the doctors themselves. Our lives have a lack of medicines and good hospitals."

I nod. A woman who carried a baby to seven months is hardly infertile, but a stillbirth handled incorrectly could result in an infection leading to permanent infertility.

I decide to return again to Victor's claims, explaining to Khalid and Malbrook that in Victor's book she claimed that Khalil was involved in sending Wafa as a suicide bomber and that others said to Victor that Wafa felt that she was essentially useless to the family, one more mouth to feed, and a burden. They stare at me, uncomprehendingly, as I stumble along with what feels almost like accusations. Uncomfortable, I pull the book out of my bag and ask them if they remember speaking with Victor. They nod.

"I want you to hear for yourself what she wrote about your family because these are not my words, but hers," I say. I read a passage slowly as Alla follows along translating. The family becomes incensed as I read, so I don't go far.

"She's not allowed to put *anything* in her book!" Khalid rises from his chair and shouts angrily. "Like for example, that Khalil was supposed to do the [suicide] operation. It's completely false!"

"Completely untrue!" Malbrook stares, a look of shock registering on her face.

"It's lies!" Khalid shouts.

I feel as though they may throw me out of their house, they are so angry. I turn to Alla and his face confirms my fear.

"I'm just reading to you what she wrote," I say. "It's not *my* words! If she is wrong please correct the record." I hastily throw the book back into my bag as though that will somehow remove her offensive record. "I'm here to hear the truth. Please tell me so I can write another book and hope-fully tell the truth of what happened to Wafa."

They see the sincerity in my face and hear the care in my voice, and they calm down a bit. I breathe a sigh of relief and catch Alla's eyes. He, too, is regaining himself from the tense moments.

Khalid sits down again but gestures agitatedly. "I don't know how you think, but as an Arab the most valuable person to himself is his brother and his sister. For example, I have four children. Let them die, but let nothing happen to my brother." I flinch as he says this looking at the children, but he continues. "I can get another son, but my brother—I cannot get another. As Arabs we have different thoughts. If I have any problem, I cannot go to my children, but to my brother. What can my son do? But my brother, [yes].And to lose my sister it's not a simple thing." Khalid's voice fades in sadness and defeat.

Khalid and I discuss Barbara Victor: that she did come to the house, that he remembers her. I tell them that it seems to me that she is arguing that women who go as bombers all have some deep difficulty in their life that makes death attractive (here, divorce and infertility) and that they also they find equality only in death.

"I think it's a stupid argument,but I'm not an honest researcher if I don't ask you about what Victor said she discovered here in her interviews with you," I explain gently, saddened to be causing them so much pain by repeating her words to them.

"I don't respect Barbara," Khalid says. "She made a very bad reputation for us. I might not allow any other journalist in my house."

"The worst thing ever to happen," Mervit says, "she killed herself over infertility!" The two sisters begin to laugh hilariously, rocking on the sofa with laughter.

"Where did she get these ideas?" the cousin asks incredulously.

"After her divorce she can live with her brothers' families and live peacefully," Khalid says reflecting their shared lifestyle. "There are ten children between us. She had *ten children* around her! She's not in need. The son of my brother in my house is completely as my child. I don't make any distinctions. *She had children!*"

The children are still running about and suddenly I get it. Palestinians live communally and there is often little distinction between cousins who usually refer to each other as brother and sister, although, of course, each knows who his mother is. I nod my understanding.

"Was Wafa a burden to the family?" I ask, to correct another part of Victor's record.

"No!" the family shouts simultaneously.

"I am completely mad from these lies," Malbrook shrieks. "I wish Barbara could never have the chance to piss!"

When Alla translates this, I burst into giggles. The family is clearly pleased to see me laugh.

"Khalil had a taxi company when Wafa went on her operation," Khalid explains, his voice tired and pained. "I had two taxi cars. My little brother has one for him. My older brother had the al Hadon taxi company. We had a lot of money at that time. We had ten horses. Imagine how much they need care and feeding. I have more than two hundred canary birds. I used to feed all of these animals and not Wafa?" Khalid asks angrily. "I had my mother at my place for fourteen years. Does that mean I don't feed her?"

"I swear to Allah," Malbrook says. "A food issue, we never brought to anyone. Send this message to Barbara: tell her she's a liar and a disgrace!"

"Dare her to come back here and speak what she wrote in her book to them!" Mervit says gesturing angrily to his family.

"In the future all Palestinian houses are closed to her," Khalid adds. "I would ask our court to sue Barbara!"

Khalid wants to further dispute Victor's claim about Wafa's suicide.

"No one goes to bomb himself easily!" he says. "The courage, you cannot find in all the people. It is something that Allah gives the person. To kill oneself in jihad is allowed. In all religions people are allowed to fight against an occupier for freedom. It's not just Muslims, but Jews and Christians as well."

I nod.

"Do you think anyone pressured her to go?" I ask.

"No!" Khalid shouts. "These things are completely sensitive!" meaning a person volunteers him or herself out of his or her own sensitivity, or anguish, for the country. "There is no pressure to go!"

This I realize is mostly true. In the second Intifada there are so many volunteers for suicide missions, that senders have no need to coerce potential recruits. The Israelis, however, claim that some women are coerced by illicit affairs and one woman in particular, Reem Riyashi from Gaza, is claimed to have been sent willingly when her husband discovered she was having an affair and was impregnated by her Hamas operative lover, but Palestinians, even those involved in the operations, generally say these are false claims made by Israelis to dishonor the women who gave their lives to the cause.[193]

I look back to Wafa's poster. "How did you learn of her mission?" I ask.

"From our brother. The Palestinian intelligence told us they had her martyr tape and we heard it on the radio, and Bethlehem broadcasting showed the tape."

After two or three days, Khalid says the Palestinian intelligence came to officially inform them.

"'It was an operation on Jaffa Street,' they said explaining she was not a missing person, but a dead one. 'Don't search for her. Open an obituary house for her.'

"It took us a few days to tell our mother. It was a big shock for all of us."

"After she made the operation," Khalid continues, "for the first ten to fifteen days we did not live in the area. This was because the Israeli soldiers came for three days and destroyed the area here. If we were caught at that time we may have been killed straight out. I went to stay with the family of my wife, my brothers to friends, and my mother to her sister's house."

In fleeing their home, the Idris family arranged to open another home to receive the crowds of wellwishers for Wafa's obituary.

"Are there many Americans who came here?"

"Yes some came and cried with me," Malbrook answers. "The Israeli press came also. Most were simple people, like me."

"Yes,' Khalid agrees, "We don't have any problem with Israeli citizens. The problem for us is the Army. They threaten, kill, and butcher us and call themselves defense."

"We still don't have the body," Malbrook states, identifying a serious issue of contention for the Palestinians as Islam dictates a certain type of religious burial within a short time frame after death. Malbrook begins to weep.

"I will speak some. My mother is maybe too upset," Khalid says taking over. "There is an area on the way to Jericho, where the Israelis bury all the martyrs as punishment and torture for the family.[194] This area is very well guarded by Israelis. I have a lot of Arab lawyers who went to ask for the corpse of Wafa. We don't care about the corpse really. Her soul went to Allah."

When Wafa's family returned to their home after fleeing it, the Israelis invade their camp, surrounding it and curfews were enforced for twenty-one days.

"[At that time] No one had the courage to leave," Malbrook explains. "They had snipers on the tops of buildings. At night they threw rocks in the windows."

"We had warnings—we will invade so you can evacuate, so you can get out in time," Khalid says.

But the reality was that the Israelis had already encircled the camp, and if they tried to flee to their relatives' homes or elsewhere, sudden military action surrounded them.

"Three times they invaded this area – all were after Wafa," Khalid continues. "The first was for three days, the second for twelve days and the third was for twenty-two days. At that time, they would gather all the men who were above fifteen-years-old in a school here and keep them the whole day.

"After gathering all the males, they took the women out of the houses," Khalid continues. They used to steal things from the houses as well. They stole three hundred shekels from my brother's house when they took his wife out."

"Some of the soldiers were making fun of us and pointed their guns at us," Mervit recalls. "When we saw soldiers with black paint on their faces we got really scared of them. Our house is made of hollow cement blocks and they destroyed the walls with a sledge hammer."

"How did you protect the children?" I asked, wondering how they withstood the stress.

"The children cried and were really scared," Khalid explains. "When they see their father beaten, hatred grows inside."

As we speak the little boy brings his toy weapon and Khalid comments on this as well, "Look at our childhood. With his pocket money he buys black tape to cover a piece of wood. He carries a gun instead of dreaming of what to be or buying a notebook."

It's clear all through the West Bank children are reenacting in posttraumatic play what they see and hear about each day. This kind of play can help them to come to terms with things that disturb them, but it can also encourage them to identify with violent solutions.

The boy stands with the gun directly in front of the floor to ceiling picture of Wafa. He looks so young and vulnerable posed in front of her giant "martyr" poster.

"Can I photograph him?" I ask reaching for the camera in my purse.

Khalid nods and I quickly snap the photo. His sister or cousin joins him and I take both of their pictures. They look so small and forlorn in front of the giant poster of Wafa. The boy suddenly becomes shy and runs to his uncle and I take his picture as he nestles in his uncle's arms and then put my camera away to resume our conversation.

"Tell Barbara this is me in my work clothes," Khalid says, a bit embarrassed that he is not dressed up for the photo. I laugh that they think I have a direct line of communication to her.

"You miss Wafa?" I ask, nodding to the poster.

Khalid nods and Malbrook answers, "She doesn't ever leave my mind."

It seems the family is exhausted so we finish our interview and I thank Wafa's family and say goodbye.

I returned home to Alla's house that afternoon and later tried to contact Victor and even to find the editor of her book. I was curious if she had a bad translator and if Victor would still insist the families had told her what she reported after I shared my experiences, but I never managed to make contact.

Victor's book is bent on emphasizing the personal life and emotional difficulties of the first Palestinian female bombers and suggests that their decisions to go as bombers is the result of the plight of Muslim women, their desire to win equality in Palestinian society in death - if not in life. Victor focuses on and blames Arab society, Islamic culture, and the exploitation and manipulation these women faced at the hands of their male operators. By making these arguments Victor ignores and downplays the reality of the Palestinian nationalist struggle. She ignores the posttraumatic stress that these women face from living under Israeli occupation—the death, wounds, and horrors that each of these women personally witnessed and also learned about over television. Victor also ignores the widespread anger and support for suicide terrorism in Palestinian society in its offer of an honorable exit from real suffering under Israeli occupation and an instant entry to a better life in paradise.

Victor may be right that the female bombers are fighting for equal rights, but their fight is not one about gender rights within their own society. Instead it's about equal rights to be equipped by sending groups to express their despair, anger and desire for revenge against the Israeli occupiers. Wafa was the first to open this door and Darine and Ayat followed after her as I believe, not under coercion or because their personal problems were so insurmountable, but because they were angry and in despair about what they were experiencing under occupation.

Chapter 37

Entering Gaza

The day after interviewing the family of Wafa Idris, Ken, Alla and I walk to the city center to try to leave for Gaza, the other part of Palestine that is separated from the West Bank by Israel proper. It's Ken's dream to go there, but I don't think it's going to work.

"You know you have to wear an abaya there," Alla says as we walk along.

"You think so?" I ask. Here in the West Bank more than half the girls wear headscarves, but below the neck most of the young ones are dressed in Western clothes - many wearing tight form-fitting sweaters and body-hugging jeans. It's a bit of a contradiction about the purpose of hidjab, which is modesty. Islamic women are instructed to hide their beauty, including their curves and hair, from men outside their family but here among the youth, those who cover mostly hide only their hair.

"What does it look like? Is it a black get up?" Ken asks puffing on his cigarette and laughing as we both imagine the possibility of a black burka.

"No, it's not black! They come in many colors. It's a dress that zips up the front and it sometimes has a hood. It covers you from head to toe," Alla says smirking. "I'll show you one when we walk past the stores in the center." He pauses and then adds with a smirk, "We call it a sack of shit."

Alla is not conservative and likes to make fun of the more traditional practices pertaining to female modesty, and he and Ken talk about girls as we walk toward the now familiar bus stop. There, Alla shows us the mini-bus to take us back to the checkpoint, and we say our goodbyes.

After a fifteen-minute ride, the bus from Ramallah spits us out into the rocky parking lot of the Kalandia checkpoint. We disembark and follow the other Palestinians through the dust and rocks, splitting company as Ken joins the male line and I queue into the female line. Both are long and it's already hot under the morning sun. The lines move slowly until we reach a shaded area under a corrugated tin roof where we wait to show our identity documents to the Israeli soldiers manning the checkpoint.

I'm dressed like many of the professional Palestinian women – wearing a high-cut knit top covered by a long sleeve button-up jacket that falls well over my hips, worn over long pants with flat shoes. I'm carrying a soft fabric bag in one hand that has my change of clothes and research notes in it and a large purse over my other shoulder. As my turn comes, I approach the female Israeli soldier sitting on a stool with her automatic rifle draped over her shoulder.

"Halt!" she shouts out sharply in Hebrew as I walk toward her. I don't speak any Hebrew so I think she is irritated that I'm walking slowly. I speed up.

"Halt!" she shouts again in Hebrew, this time jumping to her feet, automatic rifle in hand. I am confused. There is still about twenty feet between us, and I am looking her right in the face and cannot decipher what's wrong. A bit sleepy and sluggish after standing under the hot sun for so long, I still think I am moving too slow for her and move even quicker toward her while trying to interpret from her incomprehensible language and facial expression what is going on. Suddenly she jerks her gun into a ready position and points it right at me.

I gasp and freeze in my tracks.

"Halt!" she screams, still speaking Hebrew. I see now that her eyes are fixated on the soft fabric bag I am carrying and that she thinks that I am a Palestinian about to explode myself.

"It's only clothes!" I say, as I comprehend her terror. "I'm American!"

Understanding that I am speaking English and hearing me call myself an American, she calms and lowers her gun, and as she does, my terror turns to outrage.

"You should learn how to say 'stop' in more than one language!" I shout. "You think Arabs can understand Hebrew? That anyone but Israelis knows what you are saying? This is a checkpoint for Palestinians! How could I possibly know you wanted me to stop?"

I see that she understands. She looks upset too.

"Sorry," she mumbles in a thick Israeli accent and gestures with her gun for me to keep moving. I am so furious I want to keep screaming at her but her gun holds all the power—I have none. I numbly follow her command and walk sullenly past her with my bag and my life, out through the checkpoint, where I meet Ken, who is leaning on a chain link fence, smoking a cigarette.

"So how's it going, Speckie?" he asks, looking at my ashen face.

"I almost got shot," I say, my hands shaking and my voice burning with anger as I tell him what just occurred.

"So she thought your pajama bag was a bomb," Ken shrugs. "You can't blame her for wanting to take you out before you exploded and killed her! Fuck, these soldiers are just kids. They want to live!" He laughs cynically, flicking his cigarette into the dirt as we walk through the cyclone-fenced alleyway and exit the checkpoint.

In the dusty parking lot we find another minibus that stops nearby our hostel in East Jerusalem. There we pick up the things we left behind before going into the West Bank. I stuff my bag into my small rolling suitcase and Ken retrieves his backpack. Then we go back out into the hot sun and pick up another taxi, this time to take us to the Erez crossing into Gaza.

"We won't get into Gaza," I tell Ken as we speed along the highway in the direction of Ashkelon, a large city south of Tel Aviv and close to Israel's border with Gaza.

"Why not? I speak Hebrew. I'll talk our way in," Ken says with his mischievous blue eyes sparkling.

"I told you, I asked all the NGOs before we came. The UN and Dr. Sarraj at the Gaza Community Mental Health Programme all said that even with an official invitation from the UN mission we can't get in," I answer.

"We won't know if we don't try," Ken argues.

"We should have kept interviewing with Alla," I tell Ken. "We were getting traction with him."

Ken rolls his eyes and we both laugh, hoping against hope that we will break the odds and get into Gaza somehow. We have no definite plan if we do get in and no idea where we will stay. I have only the phone number of one of the higher-up Hamas militant leaders from a Palestinian graduate student in Belgium and the promise of interviews with him and his cadres if I get in.

I obtained this phone number months before in Brussels after I had attended a few Palestinian events at our university and met the Palestinian student leaders involved in political activism in Brussels. They introduced me to graduate students from Gaza, and one of them, an engineering major named Farid, invited me to his office and showed me pictures of the area on his computer. He then moved cautiously to pictures of targeted assassinations of his "brothers", one involving the aerial bombing of his entire home, while watching my reaction carefully as he revealed more and more about his family and their obvious militant activism, which I realized later was a test of sorts to determine how trustworthy I was.

"Your brothers are leaders in Hamas?" I calmly asked, studying his face as well for a reaction.

"Yes, my whole family is heavily into Hamas, but me no," Farid answered.

"Your brothers must be highly placed if the Israelis are trying to kill them with missiles," I pointed out.

"Yes, it's true," Farid answered, watching me cautiously.

"And you?" I asked.

"I am working on my Ph.D.," Farid answered, smiling warmly. "I'm the only intellectual of the family."

He seemed genuine, the studious misfit of a militant Hamas family.

"I'd like to interview them—do you think they would agree?" I asked. "If I can get into Gaza, can you set up a meeting for me? I won't ask them anything operational. I just like to understand what motivates them and how they think. I will try to enter Gaza at the end of my next trip on the fifth of April."

"Yes, I will tell them about you," Farid answered, deciding to trust me. "I'll text you their telephone number after I speak with them. As soon as you get into Gaza—if you do—you should call them."

Now, en route to Gaza, their telephone number in hand, I am seriously doubting we will make it in. Hamas has its strongholds in the West Bank, but in Gaza, Hamas rules, and the Israelis make frequent incursions to take out militant hotbeds and disrupt their terrorist plots. The Israelis currently have Gaza locked down pretty tightly.

After about an hour we arrive to a small Israeli village outside of Ashkelon where the taxi pulls over to the side of the road. Ken and the taxi driver converse in Hebrew.

"We have to get out here and take one of those taxis over there to the checkpoint," Ken explains, pointing to a taxi stand. "He doesn't go any further than this." We pay the driver and continue in another taxi for about fifteen minutes. When we disembark, we are in a flat rural area with green fields bordering the road. There are two armed Israeli sentinels ahead, guarding the Erez entrance from Israel into Gaza.

"Shalom!" Ken calls as we approach. Ken offers cigarettes to the soldiers and explains that we would like to enter Gaza.

"Who are you, and why do you want to go into Gaza?" the soldier asks in English, realizing I do not speak Hebrew and Ken is not Israeli.

"I'm an American professor from Belgium, a Holocaust researcher," I say. "This is Ken, my student. We've been in Jerusalem and Ken's tired. It's a tough topic. Today we have a day off and I let him decide what to do. He's crazy—he wants to see Gaza! I told him it's impossible, but he insisted we try. So here we are."

"I know Israel from when I lived here for a year abroad, when I studied at Hebrew U," Ken explains, pausing to draw deeply on his cigarette. "I know the beaches in Tel Aviv are great, so I'd just like to go and see if they have beaches in Gaza too and who hangs out there." Ken snorts with laughter at that thought, throwing his cigarette stub down on the crushed rocks and stubbing it out with his shoe.

The soldier laughs along with him and then looks from my face to Ken's, evaluating us cautiously.

"Give me your passports," he says. We hand them over and he looks carefully through both of them.

"Okay," he says handing them back to us. "I don't know why you want to go into Gaza, but go ahead," he adds as he waves us forward toward the checkpoint.

I'm in disbelief as we walk past the soldiers along a blacktop path toward what looks like a small glass airport terminal building. Inside, people are seated on a row of orange plastic chairs and some Israeli soldiers in khaki uniforms man a large counter, while others pace about vigilantly watching everyone.

"Let's keep moving," I say. We walk briskly and silently through the terminal, and amazingly no one stops us. Exiting the glass terminal, we are discharged into a massive long concrete and corrugated steel corridor covered with a green plastic roof that filters the bright sun into a surreal light. The passageway is wide enough for a corridor of people to walk shoulder to shoulder and reminds me of a cattle shoot. But there is no one here, just Ken and I. We are alone inside the Erez crossing into Gaza.

"I can't believe it!" I say to Ken excitedly.

"Geez, that was too easy!" Ken answers.

"I think they must have microphones in here," I whisper, looking around us. Sure enough, there are cameras mounted on the walls every twenty feet or so. The corridor turns ahead, so we aren't sure what lies around the corner, and I keep thinking someone will come and tell us we cannot continue onward, but it doesn't happen. Finally we see bright sunlight up ahead.

"Wait, I need a picture of this," I say pulling my camera from my purse as I run ahead of Ken and turn to snap his picture. We exit the corridor into a rock and dirt area and a buzz of activity. We walk onward, still not sure we are in Gaza until a Palestinian taxi driver approaches and asks if we want a ride.

"Sure," I answer and we climb into his dusty taxi, dumping the suitcase into the trunk.

"Gaza City," Ken instructs.

I fumble in my purse searching for the phone numbers of Farid's brothers and begin to get excited that we have the promise of interviews with highly-placed Hamas militants. As the taxi travels along the flat land leading to the city, I call and explain to Farid's brother that I have successfully entered Gaza.

"Okay, Anna," Farid's brother says. "Farid told us about you. We will send someone to pick you up around four p.m. to bring you to us. Can we call you then to decide where it will be?" I agree and hang up the phone. It's only noon now. Farid's brother is being extremely careful, perhaps concerned that I may be under surveillance by the Israelis or would reveal a prearranged pick-up point to them, somehow allowing them to follow us. He's a wanted man and surely on their targeted assassination list. I won't learn where or who will pick me up until the very last moments.

In the meantime, Ken has been talking in broken Arabic with the taxi driver about a good place to stay in Gaza City—somewhere safe near the beach. We agree on a hotel where foreign journalists often stay.

We enter the hustle and bustle of the teeming Arabic city. At first the homes and shops are mostly one- and two-story cement block structures, the roads are dusty and crowded, and the cars are mostly older models sprinkled with a few Mercedes and BMWs. Women in their long colorful abayas and headscarves browse the fruit and vegetable stands and haggle with vendors of pots and pans, hardware, and all sorts of other items that line the streets, as the green domes of mosques and minarets rise above them. It is completely different from the West Bank—no young girls here dressed in tight fitting western clothes or going without headscarves. Many of the men are wearing Arabic shirts, pants and sandals as well. Everyone on the street looks poor.

As our taxi weaves in and out of the traffic and slowly makes its way to the city center along the coast, the buildings become taller – six and eight floor cement block structures with a few taller buildings interspersed among them. As we enter the fancy hotel district there are tall palm trees and greenery, and no street vendors, but even here the Palestinians on the street still appear poor. The driver drops us off at our cement-block hotel and we go to the front desk to check in. We've agreed beforehand that we feel safer staying in the same room together so I ask for one room with two twin beds. The hotelier does not ask if we are relatives, perhaps assuming that Ken is my son. Ken and I go up to the room, and I tell Ken I'd like to take a quick shower and freshen up before heading onward.

"Okay, I'll go check out the beach," he says, leaving me alone in the room.

"It's no good; rocky and no one on it," he reports a half-hour later as we prepare to leave. "But I think there are swimmers and a beach farther south."

"Where should we go?" I ask. "We have three hours to burn."

"I don't know, let's just have a look around," Ken answers as we drop our key at the hotel desk and pick up a tourist map of the city.

"There's Gaza Islamic University not far from here," Ken points out.

"Okay let's walk in that direction."

It's about a half hour walk along busy streets. I snap pictures of the sights as Ken gazes around.

"It's a hell hole," he comments as we both take in the bullet-riddled and grafittied walls of the city. It's a great deal poorer and much worse than the West Bank and far more conservative.

"Are you Americans?" a young man asks as he suddenly lopes up behind us. "I heard you speaking English. I'm an English major!" he explains, a big smile on his face.

"I'm American and he's Irish," I answer, smiling back.

"Wow I can't believe it! Foreigners in Gaza! Welcome!" he says. "My name is Mohammed. Call me Moh."

We introduce ourselves and talk a bit. It becomes clear that Mohammed wants to practice his English and would like to show us around. We smile and agree.

"We are on our way to the Islamic University," I explain.

"Sure," Moh answers, "But I think we should stop in here first," he indicates a store nearby. He leads us in and I'm dazzled by the array of beautiful fabrics on display. It doesn't occur to me that they are all heads-carves and that he wants me to buy one.

"If I'm going to show you around the Islamic University I think you need one of these," he admits.

"But I don't wear hidjab, Moh," I answer. "I'm Christian, not Muslim. I don't need a headscarf."

"Yes but here you are the only one without it," Mo explains. "It's not necessary for you, but it's very conservative at the University, I don't think they will let you in without it."

I understand, and we pick out a pink one together. My hair is already up in a hairclip so Moh and the store clerk quickly and expertly wrap the scarf around my head and neck, using small stickpins to fasten it in place on the sides and front.

"There, now you are ready to go," Moh says satisfied with his work. "You look beautiful!"

I smile, feeling strangely odd wrapped up in a headscarf. I've never worn one before and notice it muffles the sounds a bit and interferes with my peripheral vision, but it also feels surprisingly comforting—warm and safe around my head.

We walk the remaining blocks to the university asking Moh about life in Gaza. We begin to trust that meeting him was indeed random, that he hasn't been following us, doesn't seem to be a collaborator with the Israelis, and realizing that his English is really good, I tell him about my research project.

"Moh, we have an interview with some Hamas guys this afternoon at four. I don't know if they have a translator, but if you want, you can help us while we are here—today and for the next two days to make interviews with families of 'martyrs' and extremists. We need help in getting intro-ductions and translating. I'd pay you of course," I explain.

"Oh you don't have to pay me anything!" Moh answers his eyes spar-kling with excitement. "I'm just so happy to meet foreigners and be able to speak in English!" Then pausing to think about my request, "I think I could find people for you to interview, but not until tomorrow. I'd have to make some phone calls."

We spend the next hours walking around the Islamic University campus listening to Moh's description of life at the university and in Gaza itself. We finally sit down on a grassy area waiting for our meeting with the mili-tant Hamas leadership. We've texted back and forth with Farid's brother at this point and they know where we are and have agreed it's a good pick-up point. Around four p.m. a Palestinian man who looks to be in his late twenties arrives.

"Are you Dr. Speckhard?" he asks in very broken English. "I'm Jamal. I've come to take you to your meeting."

"Yes," I answer and introduce Ken and Moh. When I ask if they have a translator and suggest that Moh could help, they switch to Arabic briefly and discuss that possibility.

"We have a translator with us," Jamal tells Moh in Arabic. Moh tells us in English that Jamal does not trust him. As they continue, I see Jamal trying to intimidate Moh, indicating with his steely eyes that he should leave.

"Okay," I say, "we have your number, Moh. We'll call you tonight when we finish. Let's plan to meet tomorrow. If you can arrange interviews for us tomorrow, that would be great." Ken, Jamal and I walk to his car leaving Moh behind. I feel a bit like we've kicked a puppy from the look on Moh's face, but I also understand that Jamal and the others are fugitives and many have already been assassinated by Israeli missiles when the Israelis somehow learn their location. They don't trust anyone they don't already know—or who has been vouched for by someone they do know.

"Make sure you call me when you finish!" Moh calls out anxiously as we walk away, and I think to myself, Maybe it's good someone, even this totally new acquaintance, has witnessed us vanishing into Jamal's car – in case we don't return.

Jamal drives us for about a half hour through Gaza City into an area we haven't seen yet. Dusk is falling. Jamal points out a broken Israeli tank track that is hanging in a city square, proudly telling us in broken English that the Hamas militants broke it with a mine.

As we drive deeper into the city, I am aware that we have taken a very big risk trusting Farid, the Belgian graduate student, for his introduction to his family and the Hamas leadership in Gaza, and we are now deepening our risk by going with Jamal to an undisclosed location. As far as I know, Hamas has not taken any American or foreign hostages in Gaza recently, but I certainly don't want to be the first.

"I have no idea where we are," I say turning to Ken with a feigned smile, "and no idea how to get back out of this area. I hope we'll be safe."

Ken nods looking nervous. "Fuck, we'd never find our way back on our own from here!"

Eventually Jamal parks the car, and we get out and enter a large building. It seems to be a warehouse. An elevator takes us up four or five floors and opens into a hallway and from there into a large open diwan.

"Hello! Marahaba! Welcome!" a small group of men gather and welcomes us. An older woman emerges from the group dressed in an abaya and headscarf and says in Arabic, that is translated by one of the younger men, "I am the mother of Farid, welcome!"

I have insisted that Farid send something to his mother because he has told me that it's been seven years since he's been allowed by the Israelis to reenter Gaza to see his family. He's sent a Belgian chocolate bar and a two-line note that I forced him to write. He had protested that he talks to her on the phone often, but imagining a mother missing her son, I insisted on a letter in his own hand. I wanted her to feel that she received something he had touched.

"I have a letter from your son, a very *short* letter," I say smiling and pulling the Belgian chocolates and folded letter written in Arabic from my purse and handing it to her. She begins to cry as she opens the letter and reads the two lines for everyone to hear. It reads "Dear Mom, Dr. Anne is a nice woman; please take care of her. I miss you very much. Farid." I smile and put my hand on my heart in the Arabic way of expressing warm sentiments and tell her, "I have a son as well."

Then the men usher us into their diwan to sit. Looking about, I see there are eight men with us, all bearded. One of them, Farid's father, is elderly but still spry and another, Farid's brother, a huge man, wears a revolver in a harness strapped to his hip.

I explain my project to them, and one of the men begins translating for me. I ask them if they would be willing to tell me about themselves. I don't get a chance to ask them for false names as they begin speaking immediately so I simply record their comments without attaching names, using only descriptions of the speakers.

"Maybe we can start with your fighting with Israel. Can you explain it to me?" I ask.

"It's jihad," Farid's brother, the big burly man with the revolver explains. "Palestine is an Islamic land. We are ordered to fight Jews, not because they're Jews, but because they occupy our land."

"A lot of Palestinians died who didn't do anything against the occupation," another jumps in. "They died without doing anything."

"I've just come from the West Bank," I tell them, "and I spoke to the families of Wafa Idris and Ayat al Akhras. Do you agree with their actions—with suicide operations?"

"My brother was ista shaheed [a suicide operative]," Farid's brother says. "The only solution is to fight this way. There is no balance in the power between us. We don't have tanks or Apache helicopters. This is brute force. We have only simple weapons. We only have Kalashnikovs."

"The Israelis always fight us with Apaches and F-16s," the other earlier speaker adds. "The only way to fight them is to make an explosion with our bodies."

"The world media presents us as terrorists," Farid's brother adds. "If someone attacks you, you may not get revenge on one of them?"

I nod listening, although I personally think the idea of revenge just perpetuates a cycle of violence. In the last year, Hamas has sent missiles into the bordering area of Israel, terrorizing the local population without killing anyone. They have also been responsible for sending suicide operatives into Israel and to checkpoints controlled by the Israelis. Their suicide missions kill scores and now many Israelis opt to avoid crowded places, busses, nightclubs and other places where suicide operatives frequently strike. And that has resulted in Israel tightening the passage from Gaza into Israel and the building of the wall or what the Israelis call the "security fence". Israel has also retaliated via targeted missile assassinations and making many incursions into Gaza with tanks and helicopters to disrupt terrorist and militant cells, unfortunately also killing innocent civilians, women and children in these security raids.

"There was a one-year-old girl killed by the Israeli forces," Farid's father tells us. "And another little girl from school—the Israelis killed her with a bullet in her neck."

"The Israelis say to the world that they want only one man, but they actually kill children and women. Sheik Salah Shehada is a good example," the slim one says, referring to the Israeli targeted assassination of Palestinian leader Sheik Shehada by a laser-guided, one-ton bomb that was dropped on his home in Gaza City in July 2002 while he and other Palestinian leaders were trying to negotiate a unilateral cease-fire that would be active across both the West Bank and Gaza. The bomb killed fourteen other people who were present, nine children among them.[195]

"Farid showed me the home of your brother, after it was destroyed by a missile," I say, recalling how utterly destroyed it looked after the targeted assassination of their relative.

"Their operation was done without any warning," he answers. "It happened at prayer time, at night. No one expects his house to be destroyed over his head. A lot of innocent children were frightened. Any person who sees this scene will have reasons to fight the Israelis. Our religion says don't kill civilians, except if someone kills your civilians. Then you may do an eye for an eye."

"I built that house and paid a lot of money," Farid's father says. "The Israelis destroyed it. Thanks to Allah my sons were not in it when it happened. But I spent all of my money in the construction of that house. I had eight children. When a father says to his sons, 'I built a house,' and in one moment the Israelis destroyed it, what do you expect me to do?" He looks at me, his eyes blazing. "I want revenge for this!"

"It is natural to resist and defend your people," the slimmer one adds. "When these young women like Wafa go and give their lives, people name it suicide, but really it is just a factor of weapons. We have little else to fight with," the slim one explains.

"The real problem is that the mass media shows us as terrorists," Farid's brother says. "Anyone with a small gun," he says tapping the pistol holstered to his hip, "he is a terrorist, but the Apache and tanks are just weapons."

Farid's brother has a point. State-sponsored military actions are rarely, if ever, referred to as terrorism by western nations. This is because western states, including Israel, officially claim that they do not aim directly at civilians with the intention of causing mass terror. However the Israelis, and we in the United States also, carry out calculated military strikes well aware that in many cases these actions will kill and wound many, if not *more*, civilians than actual militants.

As I interview terrorists, I am learning that they, like these Hamas militants, see military actions with high collateral damage as state-sponsored terrorism, no different than their own actions of intentionally targeting civilians. If confronted on this point, they simply argue that they lack the means to carry out surgically precise military strikes so they must equip suicide bombers to go to their targets and that they prefer to target military targets, but when they need to have a high impact on their enemy they will target civilians as well to equalize forces.

"Are you a fighter?" I ask Farid's brother.

"Yes, I am a mujahedeen," he answers, using the Islamic word for the defender of Islam, Islamic people and lands. "Everyday I am guarding our borders and ready for any invasion against their tanks."

"What can you do against tanks?" I ask.

"We try to be inventive," Farid's brother explains. "With the tanks that come into Gaza, we developed a mine to break the tread."

"Yes, I saw the broken tank tread; your driver showed it to us" I say. Farid's brother looks proud—he must believe that they are like David bringing down the sword-wielding Goliath with only a stone from his slingshot and the help of Allah.

"You are a fugitive," I say, "On their hit list?"

Farid's brother nods solemnly. "Yes. I am ready to present my soul to Allah," he answers, apparently accepting the inevitability that the Israelis will eventually locate him.

"Do you think they can find you?" I ask.

"I never sleep in the same place. I move to another place each night," Farid's brother answers, echoing the strategy of Zakaria Zubeidi.

"It is our time to pray," Farid's brother announces and all the men rise and begin moving to the next room. "Please wait for us here while we pray." Ken and I sit until the men return and invite us to dine with them. We join them in a large dining area and take a stool at a small table to a meal of roasted chickens, hummus, tabouli and an Arabic salad placed neatly on colorful ceramic plates.

The women are not present and I soon understand that they are sequestered behind a swinging door to another part of the kitchen where the cooking area must be. From time to time the women call out that more food is ready, and one of the men gets up to receive it from a woman handing it over from inside the door. They probably don't come out to serve because Ken is present or they are not all family members, so the women must stay separate.

I realize that it's unusual that I would sit alone with the men, but there is no alternative offered so I make myself comfortable with them. We all eat heartily in silence, until Farid's brother comfortably breaks it.

"Why do you wear the hidjab?" he asks.

"Out of respect for you." I answer.

"Are you Muslim?" he asks, as he takes a bite of his chicken raising it to his mouth with his massive hands.

"No, I am Christian," I answer. "But I wanted to respect your ways."

"You were right to do so," Farid's brother comments. The other men nod and grunt their approval, and I am glad that I took Moh's advice.

"Did you consider in coming here that we could take you hostage?" Farid's brother asks putting his chicken down momentarily, his gaze weighing on me heavily. The room becomes silent again with this question, and I feel that all at once these men are considering this possibility as they observe our total vulnerability. We are deep inside the city in an unknown location and no one knows where we are but them. I feel unexpectedly that everyone suddenly is cast into a decision moment, one that *they* have considered beforehand, and that I now have to handle swiftly and correctly in a way that heads off a negative course of action.

"Yes, I did consider that," I say slowly while I deliberately look Farid's brother fearlessly and straight in the eye. I refuse to allow myself to feel the terror rising inside me. I push fear totally out of my voice and posture, dissociating it completely and answer calmly. "But I decided to trust you because I wanted to learn the truth from you."

"You were right to trust us," Farid's brother says breaking the sudden tension and I feel in his words a promise that he won't violate. He goes back to eating his chicken. The strain in the room dissipates as suddenly as it arose, and the men nod and murmur their approval to this answer. We finish the meal in silence.

When the meal is finished we return to the diwan and speak some more but the interview is essentially finished. Farid's father tells us, "It wasn't always like this. We used to go back and forth between Gaza and Israel. I worked in Tel Aviv for years. That's why I know Hebrew. And many of the Israelis came here too. It's a real pity that it's come to this."

My Israeli friend Reuven Paz has told me the same thing many times, that not so many years ago Israelis would drive to Gaza to get their cars repaired at less cost and that the relations were far less strained than they are now.

"We don't hate the Jews," Farid's father states. "We just want the occupation to end." I decide not to bring up the Hamas charter that speaks about drinking the blood of Jews and driving them into the sea, as he appears sincere in his words.

"We don't have any argument with the Americans either," Farid's brother adds. "We saw 9-11 as a crime and we don't follow Osama bin Ladin."

"You don't blame Americans for supporting Israel?" I ask.

"No our argument is with Israel only," he answers. I find it surprising that they do not hold Americans culpable for supporting and even giving weapons to Israel, unlike the al Qaeda leadership who came to believe that the American government's support of their corrupt and cruel dictators was a good reason to attack Americans.

We get up to leave, thanking them for agreeing to meet and sharing their meal with us. Farid's mother comes to say goodbye and kisses me warmly on the cheeks. We exit with Jamal again through the warehouse elevator and return to the car. It's dark now, and Ken and I think in silence about what was all discussed, particularly taking us hostage, as we drive back through the darkness to our hotel.

A year later in 2006, Hamas won a resounding victory in the Palestinian elections, both in the West Bank and Gaza. Prior to the elections, al Qaeda leadership had warned Hamas not to take part in the elections and publicly mocked them in extremist Internet forums for believing that any Western power would ever allow them to rule if they did win. They were right. Immediately following their sweeping victory, the U.S. and EU refused to support the people's electoral choice, saying that Hamas had to recognize Israel and disavow violence. Perhaps because Hamas did not receive Western support after legitimately winning the election, some groups in Gaza turned to al Qaeda and AQ operatives did manage to infiltrate some of the groups inside Gaza. The Army of Islam was one of them.

Two years after our interview, in March 2007, Alan Johnston, a BBC reporter who had faithfully reported on the human rights situation in Gaza for years, was taken hostage and held captive for one hundred and fourteen days by the Army of Islam. Johnston spent a grueling three months of his four-month captivity in Gaza in a shuttered room, chained, threatened, reported as killed, and convinced he was going to be put to death.[196]

The Hamas leadership was aghast and reportedly threatened to hunt the Army of Islam operatives down if they did not release Johnston. Eventually the Hamas government who headed the Gazan security forces arrested two members of a clan with close ties to the Army of Islam. They revealed information about Johnston's whereabouts, leading to his eventual release into the Hamas leadership's hands.[197] During the months Alan Johnston was held hostage I listened to BBC daily, hoping and praying for his release. I thought often of my time in Gaza and the West Bank, thankful that I had not arrived there at a time when I too could have suffered his fate.

CHAPTER 38

Tayseer and Naji al Ajrami - The "Martyr" Brothers of Jabaliya

The next day we meet Mohammed for breakfast in the dining room of our hotel, a stately but cheaply decorated hall overlooking the seaside.

"Have some food," we encourage Mohammed, but he is excited and ready to go.

"I've arranged for you to meet the widow of Tayseer al Ajrami," Mohammed tells us. "Tayseer and his brother both martyred themselves and his widow agreed to give us an interview."

Tayseer al Ajrami was equipped and sent as a suicide bomber by Hamas at age twenty-six. Tayseer detonated himself at the guard booth of the Erez Crossing that separates Israel from the Gaza Strip—the same crossing that Ken and I just passed through to get here. Tayseer had formerly been employed in Israel as a laborer and crossed the checkpoint daily. He had evidently scoped out the weak points in the tight Israeli security procedures because when he approached the guard booth he lifted his bomb up to the small rectangular slit and only then self-detonated. The blast tore his head and upper body from his torso and injured the two Israeli border police behind their security barrier.[198]

Four months later, Tayseer's twenty-year-old brother, Naji, followed in his footsteps by attempting to explode himself within an Israeli settlement in Gaza. Naji is unique among suicide bombers because he equipped himself for his mission due to Hamas's policy of never sending more than one son from a family.

We leave the hotel with Mohammed, handing our room key to the front desk as we exit and find a taxi on the street outside. Mohammed gives directions and tells us, "We are heading north of Gaza City to the Jabaliya Refugee Camp."

As we travel through the crowded streets of Gaza City I reflect on this narrow strip of desert only about thirty miles long and five miles wide. In 2005, Israeli forces control forty-two percent of the territory of Gaza Strip which is used for their military bases, buffer zones and bypass roads that have been built to protect the seven thousand Israeli settlers who make up only about 0.5 percent of Gaza's population and who live in twenty-one settlements here. That means that the majority of the population - the 1.2 million Palestinians are packed into only fifty-eight percent of Gaza territory, making it the sixth most densely populated place on Earth.[199]

Many Palestinians hate the Israeli settlers who enjoy all of the advantages most Gazans can only dream of: living in beautiful homes, using modern roads and enjoying luxury. Most Palestinians in Gaza are impoverished, with more than half living below the poverty line on approximately two hundred dollars per month. And due to the closing of the Erez checkpoint since the beginning of the second Intifada, unemployment ranges above sixty percent.[200]

One third of Palestinians in Gaza live in UNRWA (United Nations Relief and Works Agency) refugee camps, including the Jabaliya camp that we are about to visit is one of them. Established in 1948, the camp originally provided temporary shelter in United Nations tents to thirty-five thousand Palestinian Arabs seeking safe refuge from the war in Palestine but it has since grown to a population of ninety three thousand (reported in 2006)[201] becoming the largest refugee camp in Palestine. Squeezed into one and a quarter square kilometers, the Jabaliya Camp is very poor and overcrowded and considered a particular hotbed of Hamas fanaticism and a place of misery. The First Intifada in December 1987 started in Jabalya, and in this second Intifada the camp has been subject to some of the most intense violence in the Israeli-Palestinian conflict, with Israeli tanks and troops often invading the camp to try to rout out militant leaders.

As our taxi winds down the narrow and dusty streets of the camp I exclaim, "This is the most pitiable camp we have visited yet! Look at those children playing in the dust – there's nothing here for them."

"You see the goats?" Ken laughs. Indeed there are three small goats tied to a lonely tree where children play in the rocks surrounding it.

The grey two-and-three story cement block structures of the camp are packed together, separated by narrow streets and alleys lined with billboards of "martyrs" and graffitied with what looks like extremist slogans and artwork signifying the various militant groups.

I notice some sandbags on the streets and Mohammed explains, "Those are there to keep the Israeli tanks from moving down these streets in case they invade."

"You think there will be an invasion here?" I ask.

"The way Hamas keeps firing missiles into Israel and with all the suicide bombings, it's likely only a matter of time," Ken states.

"They often make raids here and sometimes there are tanks," Mohammed adds, fear flashing in his eyes.

Indeed, in 2005, patience on both sides is running out. During the second Intifada, Hamas unrelentingly sent suicide bombers into Israel, sometimes causing massive deaths and injuries. They continue to aim their missiles into Israeli territory over their border to severely harass the local Israeli population, also causing several deaths. Already the Israeli government has been discussing withdrawing from Gaza as the security costs are too high to sustain, and the Israelis will unilaterally pull out of Gaza three months after this visit. But when they do exit (three months from now), what could have been a major move for peace building quickly failed as Israelis readily built new settlements in more favorable territory, continuing to encroach into the West Bank and areas to the east of Jerusalem, effectively encircling it and ending reasonable hopes for a shared capital between Palestine and Israel. Enraged, Palestinians thus continue to fuel their militant movements while Israelis claim they gave up all their Gaza settlements and therefore the Palestinians should be more reasonable. In less than three years from our visit, Gaza and the Jabaliya camp will become subject to the Israeli Operation Cast Lead invasion of January 2008 characterized by heavy artillery firing, aerial bombing and an all-out tank and military invasion resulting in the destruction of many homes, schools, hospitals and infrastructure. Now, however, the population is only wary of the potential of a large-scale invasion.

When we arrive at the al Ajrami home, Mohammed knocks on the cheap metal door and two young women in abayas and headscarves greet and usher us into their small flat. We take off our dusty shoes and follow them into a small bare room with grey cement walls and a rug. Colorfully covered sleeping mats serve as the only furniture. Beyond the room that we have been invited into, Mohammed explains to us, there are two other rooms making up the entire apartment that is inhabited by the sixteen other people who comprise the extended al Ajrami family.

The women motion for us to take a seat on one of the mats and they sit across the small room facing us. Three small children play while a baby crawls about among them. One of the women introduces herself as the widow of Tayseer al Ajrami and the other as his seventeen-year-old cousin.

I take out a box of Belgian chocolates, open it and offer it around ,wishing I had more to offer. The women smile and take a chocolate gratefully as I explain my study through Mohammed's translation, gain their permission for the interview and begin by asking if they can tell us what Tayseer was like.

"He was a very committed person," Tayseer's wife tells us. "He worked as a tailor in Israel."

"He blew himself up from the oppression," Tayseer's cousin adds, referring to the closure of the checkpoints between Gaza and Israel, hindering his ability to work.

"He read the Koran a lot and was detached from the family," Tayseer's wife explains referring to the larger extended family that all live together in their flat. "But I was surprised when it happened. I didn't think he would do this."

"You didn't know he would go?" I ask.

The women both sadly shake their heads no, though they describe some warning signs.

"He was hoping to wake up with seventy-two angels around him," Tayseer's wife says of his desire to transition into a better afterlife. "He started to feel this way one year before. During that year he said things like telling his mother, 'If I'm killed or something happens to me don't be sad.' He was very sensitive about all the deaths shown on TV. They upset him."

"Have the Israeli soldiers tried to destroy your home?" I ask wondering how things work in Gaza after a suicide bomber attacks.

"Not yet but they can destroy our home anytime," Tayseer's wife says, wide-eyed. "We wait for it. No one can say when. But maybe not now."

"When did Tayseer do his operation?" I ask.

"It was Ramadan, November 26, 2001, a Monday."

"How did you learn of it?"

"It was reported on television and also the Hamas sender came and told us."

"How did you feel?" I ask.

"It's unbelievable I can't describe it." Tayseer's wife gives a pained smile. "I just collapsed! He had just asked me to fix some favorite food he likes to eat."

"But after we learned, we were proud!" Tayseer's cousin adds.

Tayseer's wife nods. "Yes, after the shock, I was proud."

Looking at her children underfoot I wonder what else she feels knowing her husband willingly left her in this position and how she copes as a widowed mother.

"How many children do you have?" I ask.

"I have three boys and one girl," Tayseer's widow answers.

"Were you afraid to be left alone?" I ask.

"At first I was afraid," she answers, "but people here are used to it. Another of our relatives who is also a martyr [suicide bomber] left seven children behind."

"How do you support yourselves?" I ask.

"Hamas gives us money from the Islamic Association for what our husbands would have earned," Tayseer's wife explains.

So there is a type of "life insurance" that is provided by the terror sponsoring organizations, I note.

"Every three months they give us seven hundred dollars. It helps, but when he worked he brought more home. He used to bring seventeen hundred shekels [four hundred dollars] a month before the second Intifada, but after that the owner of the place he worked at, as a tailor, didn't keep hiring him. There is no work for us now."

Tayseer's wife pauses. "I don't feel fear but something missing," she says, her face screwed up in an expression of grief.

"How did you tell the children?" I ask.

"When your family is killed, its for Allah," Tayseer's cousin explains.

"At the beginning it was very horrible for them," their mother says, "but now they got used to it. Children here generally don't sleep well and have problems."

"The leaders of Hamas visit us even now to give us and the children spiritual support," Tayseer's cousin explains.

"Yes, they check us frequently," his wife agrees. "Other [political] movements don't care about their martyrs after. They are just killed and forgotten. But these ones don't forget. They bring sweets and toys for the children, visit frequently and at festivals their names are read. This makes us very proud. Now [the children] are enrolled in the Hamas school and take social cars to school. For the poor and martyr children these services are free."

"Do you know why Tayseer did this operation?" I ask.

"He didn't do this because he lost his job," Tayseer's cousin states perhaps fearing that I think he wanted the Hamas money for his family. "He did it for his people. Someone has to stop this. He made a good salary. He didn't need this money or benefit."

However Tayseer had just been working odd jobs since he was laid off so he must have needed money, but Tayseer's wife clarifies what she perceived to be his primary motivations.

"He wanted to be a martyr for about one year, first of all for the sake of Allah. He and his brother loved to be martyrs."

"These people are spiritually very elevated, it's hard to understand," his cousin adds. "Every house in Palestine has a martyr. All of them have a reason," Tayseer's cousin explains. "The people here don't *have* to hate Jewish people. Before the Intifada it was normal, everyone got along. But now when you see [the violence and closures], you feel you have to do something!"

"We don't have tanks, guns anything to fight back with. You have your body and you must do something. You're dead anyway..." Her expression becomes blank. "Our family members – one was killed by helicopter gunfire in an operation, another was killed when a tank came and crushed him during the invasion six months ago. He was only twenty years old! So you understand our motivation? Ninety-nine percent of our people are depressed. Even if you say I am normal, we are not thinking about normal life. We think about tanks and feel constantly insecure. Ask to see a normal child!"

This is something I am definitely seeing throughout Palestine: family members claim that the "martyr" was psychologically healthy when it is looking like in truth that the majority, if not all, Palestinians appear to be deeply traumatized by the violence they have witnessed in their national conflict with Israel.

One of the older aunts of the family has joined us while Tayseer's cousin was speaking and we are introduced. She joins in the conversation saying, "All the children are affected."

"When women see a body, a piece of a body . . ." Tayseer's cousin's speech drifts off, her face contorting in horror.

"When I saw my first person shot in the neck on TV, I felt horrible," Tayseer's wife says. But now she's seen much worse. "Sometimes you see a rocket hit a person in front of your eyes and you just collapse. We watch them put the injured with their [detached] body parts in an ambulance. Elsewhere people try to run away [when there is an attack], but here people group together and try to help each other."

"You begin to feel numb to it?" I ask.

"No we are human, not animals," Tayseer's cousin answers. "You still feel it. Most people think Palestinians are very violent people but when they see with their own eyes they understand. You generally see people very sad if their relative exploded but here people also decide to be proud."

"Did your husband say goodbye before he left?" I ask Tayseer's wife.

"At about nine p.m., at night, he started looking at people, looking at their faces: his children, his mother, me," she answers with pain etched on her face.

"He was psychologically faraway?" I ask.

"Yes, you feel like he is next to you, but his mind is not with you," Tayseer's cousin answers.

"Did he seem happier?" I ask, wondering if he also experienced euphoria pre-mission.

"One day before," Tayseer's wife answers, "he came home from work, and he played an Islamic tape and started to dance with the children. On the day he went, his father said, 'Wow, you seem to be very happy!' Tayseer told his brother,' I have my wife and children.' Then he added, 'There is only one thing missing. I want to blow myself up.' Only I paid attention to this."

"He left a will or a video?" I ask.

"Yes," his cousin answers. "On the tape he is very happy, like before marriage or going on a vacation. He said, 'My dear wife, I just want you to be happy. Please don't be sad for me.'" Tayseer's wife wipes a tear from her cheek.

Can you tell me about Naji as well?" I ask after pausing for some minutes as Tayseer's wife recomposes herself.

"Tayseer's brother, Naji, also went as a martyr," Tayseer's wife explains. "Naji was always checking to be a martyr and we knew it. He was in Hamas. We expected him to be a ista shaheed for Hamas, but not Tayseer. We thought Tayseer will be a martyr (killed in action) but not a bomber. But after four months he took a bomb."

"Naji was married for only seven months," his cousin explains. "Their little boy," she gestures to the boy who has been crawling around playing between us as they talk, "his mother was pregnant with him."

"Hamas will not take two brothers to go as martyrs and because Tayseer had already gone, Naji had to equip himself. It's their policy," she explains. "Naji's wife knew he will go to do something. He told his wife he will go. They took her gold jewelry and sold it to get the materials to make his bomb. His [pregnant] wife helped him to strap the bomb onto his body. He went to buy it and did it all himself, but he is still considered now a martyr for Hamas because he is a member."

"How do you think his wife could do this?" I ask.

"She knew he really wanted to be a martyr," his cousin explains. "We all knew this."

Did you also know that Naji was going on a mission?"

"No, he didn't tell me," she says, shaking her head sadly. "If he had, I would not have kept silent. I would have told his father to stop him! It's a great honor, but a great loss too."

This is the first time I have heard of a suicide bomber working without the support of a sending group.

"Where is his wife?" I ask.

"She is married for the second time so we keep the baby—his baby—with us." Tayseer's cousin explains.

"What was Naji like before he activated?" I ask.

"In the four months before, he grew his beard very long," Tayseer's wife recalls, "but three days before he shaved it."

Likely he was growing his beard long as an expression of his devotion to Islam but shaved it before his operation to pass more easily to his target, an Israeli settlement that he attempted to penetrate.

"He attacked the Dugit settlement in March 2002," she continues, mentioning a nearby Israeli settlement in the northern tip of the Gaza Strip by the Mediterranean Sea.

"What happened?" I ask.

"Naji went to the settlement at three a.m.," his cousin tells us, "but soldiers who saw he was trying to enter shot him before he could detonate himself." She frowns and excuses his mission "failure" because of his lack of help from a sending group. Tayseer on the other hand "succeeded" in his mission as his cousin recalls, though he too had difficulties in waiting for the Palestinians to clear the checkpoint before he could bomb it.

We end the interview thanking the women for sharing with us and leave the dusty camp taking another taxi back to Gaza City and our hotel.

Much later after leaving their home, I find additional interviews given by Tayseer and Naji's mother confirming the boys' deep wish to end their lives as "martyrs". Nine months after Naji's death, his mother explained on Palestinian TV, "Before I went on my pilgrimage [to Mecca], Naji put his hand on my head, and said: 'Mother, pray for me to become a Shaheed, or it will be your sin, and I won't forgive you until Judgment Day.'" She went on to explain, "During [the ceremonies] in Mecca and Medina, since it was entrusted to me, I prayed for him, saying: 'Praise Allah, my children asked for Shahada [Martyrdom].' It's better than other ways to die, and anyway we will die."[202]

For me these words are the resigned acceptance of a mother to her militant son's probable fate as a fighter in the battle for independence with Israel. And the fact that the Palestinian Authority arranged for her interview along with other mothers of "martyrs" shows that the PA uses its media outlets and authority to glorify suicide operations by honoring the parents of those who have carried out such acts. By doing so, the PA actively contributes to the Palestinian "cult of martyrdom" by creating a supportive social environment for promoting suicide terrorism.

Naji and Tayseer's mother gave an additional interview in April 2005, published on the Amila magazine website of Qatar. She said: "Naji told me he wanted... to carry out a Martyrdom-seeking operation, but he didn't mention exactly when he would blow himself up. His Martyrdom was... the most beautiful present for Mother's Day."[203]

Although parents of "martyrs" make these kinds of statements publicly celebrating the "martyrdom" of their sons and daughters, I find in my interviews that the real truth is more complicated. To another journalist, Michael Cabbage, Naji's mother spoke in 2002 of her privately held feelings. He wrote that Naji's and Tayseer's mother "tearfully insists she knew nothing of her sons' plans and would have tried to stop them if she had. But now that they are gone, she considers them shaheeds, martyrs in the struggle against Israel." Naji's mother described her grief this way, "I feel they are not dead but alive with God in paradise . . . I am proud of them, and I see them every day. They are never away from my eyes."[204]

• • •

After the Jabalya Refugee Camp we return back to our hotel and Mohammed hangs out with us for a while. "You don't have to stay in a hotel," Mohammed says, inviting us to stay in his family home. We demure but as he departs Moh insists, "Tomorrow night you come home with me. My mother is a good cook."

"Okay," Ken and I laugh giving in. "We'll join you tomorrow night after our interviews."

Ken and Moh shake hands, and as soon as Mohammed is out the door, Ken says, "I don't know about you, but I could use a beer."

"You think there's any alcohol in Gaza?" I ask, smiling at the thought of easing my stress with a glass of wine.

"There's got to be," Ken answers. "Let's go for dinner and ask the waiter to bring out whatever they've got hiding behind the counter."

In the hotel dining hall we ask the waiter if we can have a glass of wine or a beer, but he shakes his head and answers, "There's no alcohol served here." Even when Ken persists asking if there is a way to hide it, he answers, "No, we don't serve any alcohol."

A group of foreign journalists with their Palestinian crew are seated at a nearby table and we go over to introduce ourselves.

"You don't happen to know any place where we can get a glass of wine in Gaza?" I ask.

"You used to be able to get served at the United Nations bar but Hamas has closed that down for about a month now," one of the foreign journalists tell us. "It's just down the street. You could go and check if it's reopened."

These correspondents have been covering the second Intifada for the past few years and as we chat with them, they fill us in on the skirmishes and larger battles with the Israeli Army that occur nearly daily in Gaza. One of the Palestinians on the crew shows me a picture he took of a dead child draped in the arms of his father, whose face is stricken with both horror and sorrow as he runs with the boy from what looks like a street fight.

"He was killed by a stray Israeli bullet in a skirmish in Rafah," the photographer tells us. From the photograph, Rafah doesn't look like a very safe place to be going—but it's exactly where we'll be tomorrow for interviews.

"How do you manage to stay safe?" I ask.

"We wear bullet proof jackets and helmets," the photographer tells me, "but we still get overwhelmed by the tear gas. It's very dangerous."

Feeling both intimidated and horrified, walking down to the UN club sounds even more enticing. Ken and I finish our dinner and stroll over in the direction of the UN headquarters. When we arrive we see the UN bar is indeed closed down with a large sign lettered in Arabic sealing the doorway.

"Bummer," I say disappointed but not surprised and we walk back to the hotel to sit in one of the community rooms overlooking the now darkened beach.

"Hey I forgot I have these," Ken says reaching into his pocket. "You want a Strepsil? I think they have alcohol in them," he says handing me a cough drop while he reads the print on the box. "Yeah they do!" he says as he pops one into his mouth smiling widely.

Laughing, I take one too and we begin to joke about how many Strepsils we'd have to eat before we'd have the same effect as a glass or two of wine. We continue to eat the Strepsils joking and laughing about how inebriated we are becoming, when in fact they have no effect at all, except to make us laugh hilariously after a very heavy week of interviewing. When the box is empty we merrily agree neither of us should have a sore throat for the next week after eating the whole box and we turn in for the night, emotionally exhausted but rested from the laughter.

CHAPTER 39

Reem Riyashi

The next night, we stay with Moh at his home in Khan Yunis, which is another Hamas stronghold and a point from where the militants launch Qassam rockets into southern Israel, most aimed at the Israeli city of Sderot. In 2004, militants here sent eighty rockets and mortar shells into the Israeli Gush Katif settlement and ambushed civilians on the settler road, in one case using sniper fire to force an Israeli woman with her four daughters off the road. The woman and her daughters were then shot to death at close range. The Israelis retaliated in August 2001 and October 2002 with helicopter attacks that killed several civilians, wounded hundreds and destroyed many civilian buildings within the vicinity. On December 16, 2004, the Israel Defense Forces also raided Khan Yunis with armored bulldozers and tanks, bulldozing buildings that had been used by militants as sniping posts and mortar bases to shoot at Israeli settlements and soldiers.

Before we arrive at Moh's home, we drive to Rafah for an interview. Rafah at the very southernmost tip of Gaza is an area, I realize, that is completely different than any other Palestinian town we have visited. Among the rubble and destroyed buildings are yellow Fatah, black jihad, and green Hamas flags and banners flying everywhere, illuminated by bright lights. Gigantic billboards depict proud now dead Palestinians holding assault rifles, the al Aqsa mosque and often the white bearded Sheik Yassin floating behind them.

"That one is of the brothers, Tayseer and Naji, from Jabaliya," Moh points out. I recognize the picture that we saw in their home when we interviewed Tayseer's widow.

"We're early for our interview," Moh says. "I want to show you the border between Gaza and Egypt." We snake through suburban streets of two-story cement block buildings, some surrounded by cement walls and low green palms. Most of the garden walls are heavily covered in graffiti. We ask Moh to translate what they say. He explains that one claims a "martyrs" victory here or there, another proclaims the militant group, and so on.[205]

As we approach the border, rubble is everywhere. Many buildings are half destroyed, others completely. Approximately a year ago, in May 2004, the Israelis made a major incursion into Rafah and after a battle with the local Palestinians, bulldozed two hundred and ninety-eight buildings in an effort to stop the underground smuggling of Qassam rockets via tunnels from Egypt to Gaza. According to Human Rights Watch, the bulldozing occurred during regular nighttime raids and with little or no warning, displacing more than sixteen thousand people (ten percent of Rafah's population). Some of the fifteen hundred destroyed homes were built over the smuggling tunnels, but Human Rights Watch claimed that others were not,and that the Israelis violated international law in order to expand a "buffer zone" at the border that is currently up to three hundred meters wide.[206]

We approach the buffer zone now. In the distance we see a barrier fence with barbed wire across it, dotted every forty feet or so by a raised Israeli guard post – similar to what one would see on a prison perimeter.

"Can you go back and forth between Egypt via the Rafah checkpoint?" I ask Moh.

"No, not freely," he answers. "The Israelis control it. It's closed most of the time."

"Let's get out of the car and look around," Ken suggests.

We get out and walk along the perimeter of the "no mans land" between the high-rise cement buildings and the first row of barbed wire. We are probably in range of the guard posts and therefore the Israeli soldier's assault rifles, but I am not too worried given there are others outside here, children mainly, playing in the garbage and rubble. The sun is slowly setting, giving the whole area an even bleaker feel.

Moh has struck up a conversation with some locals who are curious about us.

"See that building over there," Moh points. "The Israelis destroyed it and this man says it housed four hundred Palestinians."

The right half of the building is destroyed, exposing its innards. The concrete floors that remain sag toward the earth and look like they could all suddenly collapse like a house of cards.

"They bombed it with one of their planes," the man says referring to the Israeli incursion a year earlier. "And some people were killed in the house.

There was no warning. And tanks and bulldozers arrived here. There was no time to think."

"Why did they destroy it?" I ask.

"The Israelis said Hamas was smuggling weapons in through tunnels underneath it," the man explains.

"Sad," I say.

"Well, were there any tunnels underneath?" Ken asks.

"Yes," the man answers.

Ken shakes his head and laughs cynically. "These guys probably have tunnels all through this rubble and new ones opening up as we speak!" I realize he's probably right. Later news reports confirm this in part, including film clips of reporters going down into the tunnels and showing how the militants ride on roller boards to operate a smuggling operation that brings food, supplies and weapons from Egypt into the embargoed Gaza Strip.

A circulating van with a loud speaker and banners drives by.

"They are saying that the settlers are going to destroy the al Aqsa mosque on the tenth of April and all Palestinians must mobilize," Moh explains.

"Is it true?" I ask, doubting that there is any such plan, though we have been disconnected from any news sources since we got here.

"The people here say it is," Moh answers.

When we arrive back at Moh's house, his family is all home now, and his father, mother, and sisters greet us enthusiastically, even though his father is still dressed in laborer's clothes and looks tired from a long day of work.

Moh shows me his sister's room, where I will stay, and invites Ken to sleep in the other twin bed in his room. Then he takes us up to the still unfinished third and fourth floors of their home, explaining that this is where he'll live after he marries. We step out on the rooftop terrace and look at the bright stars in the now black night sky. It's a beautiful place, and I imagine Moh has a very good life for someone living in Gaza.

We return downstairs for a tasty meal of leftover Palestinian food. Moh's mother has a grant from World Vision and runs a small shop selling handcrafted items from the women of the area. She presents me a red and white fluffy hand-woven wool purse as a gift, and I give her a box of chocolates. We retire to our rooms, which are very cold, but soon Moh's mother knocks softly on my door. She and his sisters enter and sit on my bed. Moh's mother pulls the covers back and gestures for me to slip out. Then plugging in a hair dryer she lifts the covers up and blows hot air inside the sheets and then gestures for me to climb back in. It's an ingenious bed-warming technique and toasty warm.

"Thanks!" I say laughing and they all giggle as they leave me in peace to fall sleep.

In the morning we take a taxi back to our hotel and have a late breakfast while Moh attends his classes.

"He's crazy," Ken says of Moh. "Last night he waited till we switched off the lights to go to sleep and then he asked me to tell him all about sex!"

"Really?" I say, smiling and leaning forward to hear the details.

"Yes, and he didn't know a damn thing about it! He wanted me to tell him how it all works. I mean really, the details of intercourse and everything—like a kid. And he wanted me to explain how you know when it's over, when it's finished!"

We laugh that a young man Moh's age could be so unenlightened about the basic facts of life as Ken continues to relay the late night conversation.

"And his father is a total asshole, beats them all," Ken says.

"What do you mean?" I ask.

"He beats Moh regularly with a belt and a chain! He gets drunk, comes home and chains Moh to a chair and then beats the hell out of him. And he beat his sister so badly that she escaped by marrying the first guy she could find and now her husband beats her just as badly. Moh said their father drags his sisters around the kitchen by their hair, beating them."

I feel sick thinking of it. Last night Moh's father had sat quietly in a chair when we met him, engaging only minimally in conversation about our research. He looked like an exhausted laborer but friendly enough. My mind drifts back to my virulent colleague that accused me and Khapta of not believing his claims that the root of all terrorism is family violence and chastised us for missing these things in our interviews. Khapta had reacted by saying that many Chechen terrorists arose from loving families and that many other forms of violence can drive a normal healthy person to join a terrorist movement. Of course, when my colleague sent me piles of research articles on violence in Arab families, including ubiquitous rates of sodomy particularly in the Gulf states, I had to acknowledge that children often reenact what they have lived at home, later directing their violence unto others.

In this case I see I totally missed it, but Moh, unlike what my colleague claims, doesn't seem to have a violent bone in his body. He's made it very clear to us that he is afraid of Hamas and doesn't want anything to do with the militant movements. Of course, I realize that all victims of abuse do not become abusers or dangerous themselves.

"You can't tell him I told you any of this," Ken continues, suddenly anxious that I will try to intervene to help Moh. "He made me swear not to tell you."

I nod, but when Moh arrives and Ken later excuses himself to use the toilet, I immediately say, "Moh, Ken told me your father is really violent and beats you all the time."

Moh's eyebrows rise in panic and he pushes his chair back. "I told Ken not to tell you!" he exclaims, eyes wide with fear.

"Yes, I know," I answer calmly. "He told me not to say anything, but Moh, Ken told me precisely because he cares about you and he knew I wouldn't be able to keep silent. It sounds like your father is dangerous and could seriously injure you. You don't deserve that! I'd like to help you if I can."

Moh has turned his gaze downward and his head is bowed. It's clear he's really ashamed and afraid to say more.

"Moh, I'd like to help you if I can," I repeat. "You are an adult man now, but what you told Ken is terrible. It's child abuse when you were younger and now its assault, and in either case it's dead wrong."

"You don't know Islam. You don't understand that in Gaza we honor our parents," Moh says quietly, staring at the floor.

"I know, Moh. Christians believe the same. It's really important to honor our parents," I say. "But you don't have to suffer abuse to honor him."

"There's nothing you can do," Moh says lifting his head, his lips firm in an impassive expression, "but thank you for caring." He smiles shyly and glances over across the room where Ken is now returning. I decide to drop it for now, but inside I feel like a tiger.

According to plan, Ken, Moh and I head out of the hotel to try to meet and interview the family members of Reem Riyashi, a twenty-two year old mother of two small children from Gaza City who bombed herself at the Erez checkpoint on January 14, 2004. Moh is not sure if we can get the interview and doesn't know how to reach Reem's relatives by phone, but he has the address of the family-owned store, so we head there to hope-fully make contact.

"You know it won't be easy. They may refuse," Moh warns us. "There is a lot of controversy surrounding her case and they have tried to keep it really private."

"All we can do is try," I say as our taxi snakes through the crowded streets of Gaza City to the outskirts where we find the Riyashi's shop. There, we introduce ourselves, I explain my study and say, "I'd like to speak to some of her family members. Do you think that would be possi-ble?"

"You have to ask the family spokesman," the relative at the counter tells us. "No one is allowed to give an interview about Reem unless he agrees." He gives us the name, phone number and address of the family spokesman. We find him, and though he is sympathetic and understanding, he refuses the interview.

"The family is all still very sad about Reem, and we are very sensitive about talking about it. I'm sorry but it won't be possible."

Disappointed, we depart and later when I return home I read news reports of her action. According to the IDF, Reem successfully thwarted security procedures at the Erez checkpoint by pretending to be crippled. She claimed to have plates in her legs that would set off the metal detec-tors and requested a body search instead. When taken to the private area for her check, she detonated her two-kilogram bomb. The explosion killed four Israelis (two soldiers, a policeman and a civilian security worker) and wounded an additional seven Israelis and four Palestinians. Reem and her Hamas senders took full advantage of this instance of Israeli decency to kill as many Israelis as possible.[207]

At the time of her action, Reem was a mother of two children: three-year-old son Obedia and eighteen-month-old daughter Duha. Reem was the eighth Palestinian female suicide bomber, the second to leave little children behind and the first female bomber sent by Hamas. Following the attack of Darine Abu Aisha, Sheikh Yassin, the spiritual leader of Hamas, had withdrawn his objection to using women in such actions and switched instead to lavish praise of their involvement. He applauded Reem's attack as well and urged other women to volunteer while warning the Israelis to expect even more female bombers.

Reem's family, wealthy Gazans, did not support her action.

"I denounce her attack ... I support peace," Yusuf Awad, Reem's broth-er-in-law announced at her obituary. "We don't accept women doing such things. She has two children. It is not right."[208]

The conservative population of Gaza was also aghast and widely criti-cized Hamas for deploying a mother and releasing photos of her in combat gear, posing with weapons alongside her children. In one picture, her baby son is clutching what looks like a mortar shell. Hamas protested that the pictures revealed the depth of despair of Palestinian women and their strong desire to defeat the occupation.[209]

Reem's attack struck further terror into the Israeli military and civilian population. The Erez checkpoint was closed for several days, prohibiting four thousand Palestinian laborers from reaching their jobs in the Israeli industrial zone.

Hamas and the al Aqsa Martyrs Brigade, who jointly claimed respon-sibility for Reem's attack, cited the weeks of incursions into West Bank cities during the Israeli *Operation Defensive Shield* as the reason she was sent on her mission. Reem, according to their propaganda claims, wanted to retaliate for the twenty-five Palestinians who had been killed at that time.[210]

In her "martyr's" video, Riyashi is filmed wearing combat fatigues and brandishing an automatic rifle with a rocket-propelled grenade. She announces that since age thirteen she dreamed of turning "my body into deadly shrapnel against the Zionists."

"I always wanted to be the first woman to carry out a martyrdom opera-tion," Reem continues, "where parts of my body can fly all over . . . God has given me two children. I love them [with] a kind of love that only God knows, but my love to meet God is stronger still.[211]

"We should expect that more female martyr warriors will do this," Abu Jihad, a Hamas official announced at Reem's obituary. "[It] is allowed in Islam because Hamas saw that it is no longer easy to send a male warrior to attack [the Israelis]. This year will see a large number of women joining in the attacks."[212]

The case of Reem Riyashi turned out not to be as straightforward as it first appeared. When Palestinian security officials in Gaza and Israeli internal-security experts studied her case, they claimed that Riyashi had been caught in an affair with a senior Hamas commander prior to her action. Adultery in her society could be punished by death, but according to their reports, Reem's husband and the senior Hamas commander allegedly came to terms by deciding that Reem could clear the slate by becoming a "martyr".[213]

When I asked Israeli security officials about this rumor, one told me he was privy to internal Israeli security reports that revealed Reem's deceased body was discovered to be pregnant. Knowing that there is often a desire to discredit the nationalistic or otherwise potentially legitimate reasons for the actions of suicide bombers and to disparage their motives by replacing them with scandalous ones, I also asked my colleague Yoram Schweitzer what he knew of the case from his prison interviews with Hamas senior operatives. Schweitzer confirmed that there was controversy over Reem among the imprisoned Hamas leaders and that one Hamas senior operative had shared that he was deeply offended by what had occurred in her case.[214]

Adding to the shame surrounding Reem's death, I learned that in 2007, three years after Reem bombed herself, al Aqsa TV, the official station of the Palestinian unity government (led by Hamas), began airing a two-minute fictionalized dramatization of Reem's four-year-old daughter following in her mother's footsteps. The two-minute video was shown between programs, with Duha Riyashi (played by a child actress) singing to her mother, Reem, as she dresses for a suicide bombing. "Mommy, what are you carrying in your arms instead of me?" sings Duha. The next day, Duha learns that her mother was carrying a bomb and exploded herself killing four Israelis. As Duha mourns, she finds a leftover stick of dynamite near her mother's bedside table. She picks it up and sings, "My love will not be words. I will follow Mummy in her steps."[215]

While sociological and political concerns in Palestine, such as occupation, refugee status, violence on both sides, constricted movement, and poverty, along with instances of coercion, all combine to motivate Palestinian women to become suicide bombers, the modeling that occurs in television programs like this one are also powerful tools for instilling in young girls the idea that it is not only acceptable to murder others with one's own death, but also that it is heroic.

Even more chilling than their depiction in the video is that Reem's actual children were involved in such propaganda ploys. While interviewed on al Aqsa TV in 2007, Duha was encouraged to recite a poem in which she declared, "Reem, you are a fire bomb. Your children and submachine gun are your motto."[216]

By 2007 eighty-eight Palestinian women had attempted to become suicide bombers—the cult of martyrdom, now including women as well, was in full swing.

CHAPTER **40**

Exiting Gaza

After attempting to speak with Reem Riyashi's family, Ken and I prepare to leave Gaza. We say goodbye to Moh and pay for his translation and guide services.

"Thank you Moh," I tell him. "We were so lucky to have met you!"

"I have some gifts," Moh says, handing me a porcelain candle holder depicting Jerusalem with Mary and the infant Jesus. "I remember you are Christian," Moh says. He gives Ken a Gaza t-shirt. "I hope these things will help you not to forget us. You've got to come back here." Moh's voice catches in his throat.

"I'm not sure we'll ever get back, Moh," I say, "but we'll try."

"I brought you these too," Moh adds, pulling a stack of computer discs from his backpack. "They explain Islam, and they're in English." There are so many, it looks like they must cover the entire Koran.

"Thank you Moh," I say, knowing that his gesture to educate us about Islam means he really cares—he wants us to have what he believes is the "true" answer. We give Moh warm hugs and then hail a taxi to return to the checkpoint back into Israel.

Our flights leave early tomorrow morning and I have arranged for us to have dinner upon our return in Tel Aviv with my Israeli counter-terrorism colleague Reuven Paz. It's still early afternoon when we arrive at the checkpoint. Everything goes routinely until we get to the passport control.

"Have a seat, over there," The Israeli border agent says as she gestures to the orange plastic chairs lining the glass walls of the border crossing. She retains our passports. "Someone will be with you in a moment."

"Is there a problem?" I ask.

"Have a seat," she repeats. Questions are not welcome.

"What do you think is up?" I ask Ken as we sit.

"I don't know, but it doesn't look good," Ken says, glancing around.

After about fifteen minutes, a college-age border policewoman wearing a khaki uniform comes over. "Where you have been in Gaza and who have you met here?" she asks in heavily accented English.

"At the hotel, looking around Gaza City," Ken answers.

She sweeps her wavy light brown hair from her face and looks down at the paper she is holding.

"We have information that you have been talking to Palestinian militants. We are not accusing you of anything, but we want you to know that frequently such people have used foreigners like yourselves to carry messages and money. Who have you met with while in Gaza?"

"No one. We just walked around and had a look at Gaza City," Ken says. I nod. Neither of us wants to admit to our research in fears of getting shut down.

"We know you have met with Palestinian militants," she continues.

"No, no one," Ken repeats. I shake my head as well.

"Stay here please."

She leaves and we wait about an hour and a half, noticing that there are many other foreigners, mostly Westerners, also waiting to be given permission to reenter Israel. After some time, we strike up a conversation with a young couple near us.

"We're Americans—missionaries," the blonde wife dressed in beige Capri pants and a button down cotton shirt tells us. "We have four young children and live in Gaza City in the north. This happens every time we try to cross. They usually keep us for four or five hours."

"You've got to be kidding!" I say. The terminal is air-conditioned but it's not a place I want to sit all day.

"What is it like living in Gaza City?" I ask.

"Awful," she answers. "There have been so many Israeli invasions in the last years, you wouldn't believe it. Our area doesn't get invaded that often but we hear the tanks and mortars, and a couple of months ago we could see the tracers right outside our windows. It was terrifying!"

"Wow. How did your kids deal with it?" I ask.

"We kept them inside and away from the windows," she answers. "The Israelis fly their F-16's low over Gaza City all the time too. It's really scary here."

After another hour the border guard returns. She still has her paper and I notice her hands shake as she reads from it. "We have information that you have met with Palestinian militants," she says trying to sound stern. "Who you have met with and where have you stayed in Gaza?"

"We stayed at the hotel," I say, feeling sympathy for how rattled she is.

"Who did you talk to at the hotel?" she asks.

"No one," I answer, looking at Ken as we both shrug our shoulders at the question. "We talked to the guy at the hotel desk and to the waiter who served us our meals."

"What did you talk to them about?" she asks.

"What was on the menu and if we could get a glass of wine," I say.

"Where did you go in Gaza City?" she asks.

"We walked around the city and went and looked at the Islamic University."

"Who did you talk to there?" she asks.

"No one," I answer.

"Did you go anywhere else in Gaza?" she asks.

"No," I answer shaking my head wondering what she would say if I told her we just returned from the Rafah refugee camp.

"Look, we know you have met with some militants in Gaza," she says consulting her paper once again. "Who have you met with in Gaza?"

"I am a Holocaust researcher," I say, smiling kindly. "I'm American and Ken is Irish. We both love Israel and have no interest in harming your country. There is nothing to worry about with us."

She persists. "You spent three days in Gaza. Who did you meet with and where did you go?" she insists.

"We just looked around and we haven't met with anyone," I repeat.

Frustrated she departs again. We sit for another two hours and the conversation repeats again. Finally after about six hours of playing cat and mouse I approach the woman who is holding our passports.

"How much longer do you think we will be stuck here?" I ask while trying to keep my voice as pleasant as possible. "I have a dinner date in Tel Aviv and I need to let my dinner partner know if I am not going to make it," I say tapping my Blackberry.

"Who are you meeting in Israel?" she says, looking pointedly at my phone. I realize immediately I have made a tactical error—she can take my phone from me and search all my recent calls. I'm actually surprised they haven't taken it yet. Usually in a search, they require I move it away from myself first thing in case I use it to detonate my suitcase somehow.

"An Israeli friend," I answer.

"You have friends in Israel?" she asks, her interest suddenly piqued.

"Yes, many," I answer.

"Tell me their names and phone numbers," she demands, casting her gaze once again on my phone. I realize she can discover it whether I admit it to her or not.

"His name is Reuven Paz, and he used to work for the Shabak," I say, trying to intimidate her by mentioning Reuven's former position in the Israeli intelligence service.

"Give me his phone number," she insists as she writes Reuven's name on her pad.

"I don't know it by heart," I say but she stares at my phone. Of course she can look him up, so I give in, scroll through my phone and give Reuven's number to her.

"You can go and sit down again," she says.

"Will I make my dinner date?" I ask.

"I don't know," she answers. "You should sit down now."

"I think I just blew it," I say, returning to tell Ken what has just happened. I dial Reuven to explain as well, surprised that the Israelis have allowed me to keep my phone and that I've gotten through to him first.

"Reuven," I say "Ken and I are stuck at the Gaza crossing. We've been here six hours and they keep questioning us. I told them I have to meet you soon, and they took your number so I'm sure they will call you shortly. I'm not asking you to lie but I'm sticking to my story—that I am a Holocaust researcher and have just been looking around. I haven't told them anything and I don't know how long they are going to hold me, so I may miss our dinner."

"That's no good," Reuven answers. "They are really tough at the Gaza border. I can't lie to my own country," he muses. "Let me think what to say."

In a little while Reuven calls me back. "You will be out of there soon. I told them you are married to an American Ambassador and not a threat to Israel. I also told them the truth, Anne. I told them about your Holocaust *and* your terrorism research. They'll let you go soon," he promises. "Call me when you are through."

The border policewoman returns again, still holding her paper. It takes even more this time as she sits down to question us. "We have information you have met with Palestinians militants," she begins once again but this time I cut her off.

"We have met with people from Hamas and from the Palestinian Islamic Jihad," I say. Her eyes widen in shock. "Look, I know my colleague Reuven told you about my terrorism research. I'm sorry for not telling you about it at first, but I didn't want any problems," I explain. "We have been in Gaza City, Jabaliya Refugee Camp, Khan Yunis and Rafah."

Her eyes get huge and she takes a sharp breath. "Who have you been talking to?"

"Families of suicide bombers," I answer.

"Suicide bombers?" she gasps. "Who are these suicide bombers and where are they now?" I realize she thinks we have talked to people who are thinking of launching an attack.

"No!" I say. "We've talked to the families of already dead suicide bombers."

"Who are these suicide bombers and where are they now?" she repeats, obviously convinced she might be able to thwart an attack if she gets the information from us urgently. I explain again slowly and patiently until she understands. We then review the entire trip. I don't tell her the names of the people I've interviewed. "They are all known to your security services and they are all dead." Satisfied, she gets up this time and consults excitedly with the senior police guards behind the counter. We wait a few more hours, exchanging calls with Reuven. "I'm not sure we are going to get out of here," I tell him.

"Don't worry the checkpoint closes soon," Reuven says. "They'll let you go then because they won't want to hassle with you," he says. I imagine them hauling us off to some jail, but it turns out Reuven is right. When the border police begin shutting the crossing down and even switching the lights off a guard finally comes to say, "You can leave now."

I feel that what she has really said is "Good riddance, don't come back," and that they have held us the last two hours, if not more, just to punish us. Looking at the wall clock I say to Ken, "Eight hours at the checkpoint. That's our new record." We laugh and shake our heads as we exit and walk to the taxis to find one to take us to Tel Aviv.

By the time we get to dinner with Reuven, he's been waiting a long time as well and everyone is tired. We talk for a few hours over our Mediterranean meal telling Reuven our impressions of Gaza and then Ken and I return to our usual youth hostel in Tel Aviv. This time I'm greeted with a toothless smile by the immigrant Romanian woman who was there the previous time. As she smiles warmly I recall that her front teeth are missing from her Israeli husband beating her. I wonder if she lives here, perhaps cleans the place in return for a bed and the security of escaping her husband. In any case it's nice to have a warm welcome as I push my small suitcase under the bed and flop down on the bed. Our plane is leaving in a few hours, in the early morning, and I have just a few hours to sleep.

The next morning, Ken and I join the long lines for the security check in, and Ken removes the yellow papers the Israelis placed into our passports at the Gaza crossing.

"No sense alerting them to where we've been," he says, crumpling and thrusting them deep into his jeans pocket.

"You don't think they will know?" I ask.

"Not anymore," he answers.

I laugh and we continue forward. When it's our turn to be questioned we remain calm and tell our usual story of having stayed in Jerusalem, enjoyed the sights, went to the museum, etc. It works and we pass onward.

Our luggage goes through the electronic search, and we are waved onward to get our boarding passes without a body check. Everything goes well until we arrive at passport control. When I hand our passports over, the guard takes an exorbitant amount of time studying them. Suddenly a serious looking Israeli officer steps up beside us saying, "Please come with me."

"You've been in Gaza?" the border agent asks as our suitcases are brought aside and emptied in front of us. I watch helplessly as they pull everything out of my wallet, purse, briefcase, makeup and toiletry bags for further search into their plastic bins, destroying any order there once was. Ken and I are separated and escorted into booths where our clothes are searched, our bodies patted down and our shoes and my brassiere taken away to be x-rayed.

When we return from the body search, Ken and I sit and watch the guards minutely search our possessions, opening each cosmetic to sniff, squeeze or poke. Bored we drink sugary cappuccinos out of a vending machine placed nearby.

"You can repack your things now," the agent finally says. I do it hurriedly though the wall clock indicates we have long passed the boarding time for our plane.

"You are traveling on your diplomatic passport or your tourist one?" the agent asks holding up my two passports.

"On the tourist one," I say, tired of the numerous explanations. "My husband is a U.S. Ambassador and I need the other passport to reenter Belgium where we live. It has my visa for living there."

"You know it's illegal to travel with two passports," he says.

I stare at him blankly, knowing I am following the law as best I can. I have actually made a point of not using my diplomatic passport to enter Israel, as I don't want to represent that I am on any official business, but I do need it to reenter Belgium. "I am traveling in Israel on the tourist passport," I repeat. Suddenly, all the sugar and caffeine takes its toll, and I begin to feel lightheaded.

"Excuse me," I say letting myself down to the floor suddenly. "I'm sorry but I have to get horizontal or I'm going to pass out."

"Should I call an ambulance?" The border guard asks alarmed by my sudden change of condition.

"No! I have a blood sugar problem," I explain. "It's been hours here with no food and just sugary coffee. Let me rest a minute so I don't faint," I explain as I lay horizontal on the floor. "Please don't call an ambulance. I think I just need to eat something."

One of the guards goes and gets a small sandwich for me while I lie on the floor, my head spinning. I sit up gingerly to eat the sandwich and slowly begin to feel normal again.

When I recover, I laugh with Ken at how stupid I feel. We are seated again still waiting. "Looks like we've missed our plane," I comment. Ken nods.

After about an hour a senior agent comes and tell us that we have missed our flight and that they will take us to the ticketing agent to rebook it for tomorrow. "We are putting you in a hotel in Tel Aviv. You are our guests," they explain. "You can take your lunch and evening meal in the hotel restaurant as well." I look at Ken with raised eyebrows. No one has interrogated us here, and I suspect the generous treatment is out of respect for my husband's diplomatic status. We thank them and go talk to the Brussels Airline representative who rebooks our flights for the same time the next day. The agents walk us to the exit and tell us, "Tomorrow just come right up to the agents and let them know you are here," she explains. "They'll want to search your things again so please come early."

"A free day on the beach, compliments of the State of Israel!" Ken says as we walk out into the hot sunshine. We laugh and get into a taxi, discussing that there must be some marker in our records now as a result of entering Gaza. I call my husband and explain what has happened.

"There's been some flat footers here," he says grimly. "I think you'll have some explaining to do to the embassy." I don't understand at first but Dan makes it clear he doesn't want to discuss it on the phone. "Enjoy your time on the beach. I'll tell you tomorrow when you're home," he says.

When I get home the next day I understand he's had an early morning visit from the embassy security personnel who were concerned after getting an irate call from the Israelis.

"The Israelis called our embassy burning mad. I guess when they saw your diplomatic passport, they thought you were an undisclosed CIA agent, that our embassy was running you in Gaza without telling them," Dan explains. "Of course the embassy told them that wasn't the case, but then our security guys came here wanting to know why you were in Gaza talking to Hamas. They thought you'd turned into Patty Hearst and were joining the militants," Dan says shaking his head. "They want you to come in and explain what you are doing."

I had something similar happen years earlier when my research in Belarus was stymied after the U.S. State Department recalled our entire family from Belarus as a result of a diplomatic dispute when the Belarusians took over our home. I made the mistake of letting my husband tell the State Department that I was making plans to travel independently back on a research trip during our fourteen months recall period. The State Department forbid me to go.

"Are they giving that order to me as an employee of the US government or as a private citizen who draws no salary and is pursuing her own academic career free of the State Department?" I asked my husband angrily at the time. "Certainly they're not giving a 'no travel' order to a private citizen?"

This backed them down, but the State Department officials made it clear to Dan that if he valued his career he should personally block me from traveling back to Belarus to complete my research until the diplomatic dispute was settled. The resolution took over a year and caused me to lose my funding and research project. I had learned my lesson the hard way—to keep my academic affairs totally separate from the State Department—and I was not about to repeat that experience now.

"I think I'll delay on that," I answer. When I do in fact go into the embassy to meet Dean Shear, our regional security officer, I hand him a stack of my published studies on terrorism.

"We're amazed at what you've been able to do," Dean tells me, taking the papers gratefully, "but we're concerned about your safety—as you know, it's our job to keep diplomats and their families safe."

"I'm concerned as well," I admit, "but Dean, my work has nothing to do with our diplomatic posting in Belgium, and I do my best to make sure that what I do and the situations I put myself into are not more dangerous than driving in Belgian traffic. You drive here too, no?"

Dean smiles and agrees driving in Brussels equals taking your life in your hands. "But these people are militants; they could see you as a high value target and kidnap you," he says.

"Yes, they could," I say. "But as far as I know there have been no kidnappings of Americans by Palestinian groups to date. "Do you know anything that I don't?"

Dean shakes his head but continues, "We'd like you to at least tell us where you're going and let us warn you if we have any [intelligence] traffic beforehand that indicates if someone may be thinking of kidnapping you. Then we can warn you not to go—that is if they are expecting you and know ahead of time you are coming."

"I don't usually announce my plans too far in advance," I explain, "and if I tell you I'm going to travel to Palestine again for instance, wouldn't you just get on the phone to your Israeli counterparts and then I'd get blocked from entering or I'd get a tail on me? It doesn't sound like it would be very helpful to my research. In fact, it would effectively shut me down."

Dean and I go back and forth until we agree that I will tell him immediately before departure to dangerous places. He will then check the intelligence traffic but will not alert his intelligence officer counterparts of my arrival in their countries. And if he says I should not go, I agree to trust him and understand that he cannot divulge intelligence information that would explain his decision.

As I get up to go, Dean says, " I was doing my master's thesis on security issues, but I got discouraged and didn't finish my degree."

"What?" I ask, immensely bothered he didn't finish his higher education because of lack of confidence. "I'm a professor and you're going to finish that thesis. I'll help you," I promise as we part.

Anne Speckhard

And I did just that. We kept in frequent touch, meeting for lunches and communicating via e-mail as Dean finished his thesis—while Dean kept light oversight over my safety. In the end, Dean had his Master's Degree in hand and I managed to escape the State Department getting in the way of my research. The Israelis, however, were solidly on to me after our trip to Gaza, and I would soon find that all future trips into Israel were going to be marked by their suspicion that I might be a Palestinian terrorist sympathizer, which of course I am not.

CHAPTER 41

Gay in Gaza

Like many of our translators and guides, Moh (our translator from Gaza) begins writing e-mails and texts to us as soon as we pass out of Gaza. He will keep up a correspondence with both Ken and I for six years, sharing his life with us long after we leave. Since I know his "secret" of being a victim of family abuse, I bring it out into the open in our emails in an effort to help him deal with and break the cycle. Perhaps as a result of that honest approach, Moh's emails are often filled with despair, discussing both the society-wide desperation in Gaza that worsens after Israel institutes a blockade beginning in June 2007 (following the Hamas elections) and how he sees his personal situation with his violently abusive father as hopeless and inescapable. As the months pass and Moh shares his life with me, I realize that I am becoming an emotional lifeline for him. I also find that I learn as much from his letters about what it is like to live in Gaza as I did from going there. Often I begin to feel the same helplessness and despair in trying to think how to help him. Like the other traumatized people I have encountered in my work, Moh has a huge backlog of unprocessed anger, hurt, grief, shock and fear.

"I'm dying slowly Anne," one of Moh's first letters begins. "My heart became a huge black box that I'm trying to open but can't. I think that my mind is shutting down. People think that I'm happy, but inside it's dark and cold or even burning."

At first, Moh writes to me mostly about his family situation. He knows that I want to protect him from his father's violence and help him to find a way to escape it, but he is also so steeped in the trapped mentality that victims of domestic abuse develop that he sees no way out.

"Anne, for how long do you think I will live?" Moh asks in June of 2005. "I'm very tired very much. Do you think that I'm useless or sick?"

"It's not you, but the circumstances you live in that are sick," I write back. "You are simply a victim of prolonged and intense traumas and with help you can get healthy one day."

On the day of the unilateral Israeli withdrawal from Gaza, Moh writes with joy.

"Hi Anne! We're so happy today—there are no checkpoints!" "We can go wherever, anytime. I wish you were here to see how much that people are happy. I love you, Anne. You are a good human!"

Moh's happiness is short-lived, however, with anger, depression and exhaustion always setting in.

A year later, I reenter Israel.

"Are you in?" Moh texts desperately when I arrive. "Are you at the airport? Or a checkpoint on the way to the WB?"

"I'm at the airport, detained and not sure if I will even be allowed to enter Israel, much less the West Bank," I answer before the Israeli soldier assigned to guard me notices me texting and confiscates my phone.

Hours later when my phone is returned to me, I see Moh's response. "You see how they are treating you? They want no one to know anything. I'm so sorry that I can do nothing. I wish I could do anything for you, but I can't. They feel happy when they see people suffering or when they humiliate humans. Be strong and cool. Love you, Moh."

While I don't agree that the Israelis are intentionally mistreating me— they have dire security concerns and have every right to be concerned about anyone that repeatedly enters Palestine—I appreciate his concern.

"Hi, are you in the WB yet? Why don't you come here to Gaza? You are so close but so far away," he begs. Unfortunately, I know my chances of being allowed back into Gaza are close to zero now that Israeli security knows about my research.

Hamas militants raid Israel in June of 2006, crossing through an underground tunnel near the Kerem Shalom border where they infiltrate an army post. In the ensuing attack, two Palestinian militants and two IDF soldiers are killed, three others wounded, and nineteen-year-old Gilad Shalit is captured and taken into Gaza to be held for five long years. When the Red Cross tries to arrange visits to Gilad Shalit, Hamas refuses and the Ezzedeen al Qassam Brigades, the Popular Resistance Committee, and a previously unknown Palestinian group calling itself the Army of Islam release a statement offering information on Shalit only if Israel agrees to release all female Palestinian prisoners and all Palestinians under the age of eighteen, who have been held without charges and tried without the right of defense. Israelis, who mainly base their sense of security on the strength of their military, are crazed with anger that one of their own has been taken captive and invade Gaza in search of Shalit.

"Are you okay?" I write, anxious as I follow events on the news.

"I'm so worried," Moh answers. "They're going to invade my village. I hope that nothing bad will happen but at the same time, I know that they will kill and destroy and arrest many innocent people. Please pray for us, Anne. Thanks for caring and asking about me. Love, Mohammad."

"What's happening?" I ask.

"Sonic bombs, nasty smell of bombs, F-16's Merkava tanks, Apache and Cobra helicopters. Rockets, no electricity, no water, crowded sheltering, civilians and children and the well of destruction," Moh writes a day later. "But I believe God will help me to stay safe."

My queries of "Are you okay?" fall into a black hole, met with no reply, and I begin to worry that I won't know, and perhaps might never learn, if Moh is killed in the conflict. Finally I hear from him.

"I'm fine, thanks Anne," Moh writes. "I hope that all will end soon. There is no electricity—they destroyed the main generators. And they like to amuse us every night with sonic bombs. Thanks to God that I'm still breathing."

July comes and Moh writes, "It's your independence day—congratulations! I hope that one day we will have a real one. Say hi to all Americans, especially Grannies Against the War in Iraq. Don't say hi to people like Bush. Have a nice day full of fireworks, cookies, joy and happiness!"

Eighteen days pass until his next e-mail.

"…The IDF were in my village for four days, killed two civilians and arrested more than seventy people. I wish to stop all of that [violence] around the world. Life is so nice and important and it's not any ones decision to finish it, only God should do that, and am sure that He will be fair."

His next is less hopeful.

"I feel dead. Again and again, I can't scream. I can't shout or cry. The amount of anger inside me is just inside. I can't release it. I thought writing will help, but it didn't. Am just clicking and pressing small dumb things that transfer what I feel in one way or another to you. Electronic signals are not the real feelings, Anne. My heart is so tired. I don't know what to do, what to say.

"I want someone to hug me, someone to feel sorry for me, someone to make me happy. I have no one to do that here. I am living in the worst place in the world, with the worst parents ever and I feel angry—so angry that the Iranians can make a nuke using my anger, Anne. Anne, please tell me what to do? I feel like I am choking inside, like I can hardly breathe. Yours, Moh."

From that distance and receiving only sporadic e-mails and texts, I can't be sure what's going on. Is he suicidal? Having manic responses to the excruciating emotional pain? I encourage him to try to get help from Dr. Sarraj's mental health clinic but I know that they are overwhelmed with requests for service, plus Moh has no money and in his culture its unacceptable to seek help from a psychiatrist. I continue to write to him, encouraging him, giving him feedback on PTSD, telling him that many of his reactions are normal responses to the very abnormal and deeply painful, stressful and terrifying events surrounding him. I worry he will disappear one day—killed by his father, a faction in Gaza, or by Israelis. I don't know how else to help him but to keep listening and keep writing.

"I want to leave home but I can't," he continues on September 8th. "I tried to find a job and I failed. Now [my parents] are threatening to kick me out. I feel like I have no feelings, like my heart really wants to scream, shout, fight and cry but somehow my body keeps stopping it, but not on purpose,"

Moh is describing a typical dissociative phenomenon in which a person cannot feel their own emotions because they are too overwhelming. I realize that I might be the only "safe" place where Moh can really say what is happening to him and that at the keyboard, he is at least opening himself up a little.

On September 21, 2006, Moh writes to ask what I think about the Pope's speech, in which he quoted a fourteenth century Byzantine emperor that led some to conclude that he saw Islam as "evil and inhuman". The interpretation sparks violent Muslim demonstrations and culminates in the murder of a Somali nun and the kidnapping and beheading of an Assyrian priest in Iraq.[217]

"To be honest with you, the Pope, bin Ladin, Bush and Blair are all bad people; they did nothing good—all bad. They are supposed to solve problems, but they are not doing so at all," Moh writes, seemingly disappointed with authority figures of the world who likely symbolize his parents and who according to his perspective, do not care about his plight nor do anything to lessen it.

In his letters, Moh often writes, "there is something I can never tell you" and hints that his "dark secret" would result in total and utter rejection. For some reason I intuit that Moh is gay, and knowing that homosexuality is not only socially unacceptable, but can be grounds for being murdered in Gaza, I write to him again and again, saying that I am quite sure I know his secret and that it is really okay, that it is nothing he should feel shame over—even as a religious person he must accept who he is and that he must trust first and foremost that he is loved by God, no matter what others may say.

A year and a half after we left Gaza, Moh finally admits it.

"Anne.... This is the hardest e-mail I ever written in my whole life. Remember when I told you before that I have a little secret that no one knows about at all? I am so confused that I tried to write you many times about it, but it wasn't easy at all and still isn't. I never told that to any one. I never trusted anyone about that. You may hate me. I tried to deny the real fact—that I am gay, but that's me anyway.

"I am not normal at all, Anne. I feel so ashamed of myself, telling you that, but you are the only one that I trust. I am totally alone in this world.

"The other thing is that I left Islamic University, Anne. I couldn't complete there. I was trying to find a job and many times I didn't attend lectures, and I have bad grades. The problem is that they will send my grades to my Dad. I don't want him to know; I am living in hell nowadays, afraid, so afraid. My father, he never cared about my life and now, I can even be killed.

"Anne, please help me, and I will totally understand if you don't want to help me, but it's my life between your hands. Please don't tell anyone Anne, please."

I resolve that as long as Moh needs me I will write to him and do everything in my power to help him. I know that his understanding of Islam and of the conservative believers surrounding him cause him to condemn himself for his sexual orientation, and I explain to him from a psychodynamic point of view how sexual orientation is formed in one's development; that many things--abuse, genetics, hormones--can set a person on a homosexual path. And I encourage him to believe in a God that loves him no matter what.

"It's a matter of time, he will know, I must leave home," Mo writes about his father shortly after his admission of being gay. "Yesterday he beat my sister so badly with a leather belt. He is becoming more aggressive. I don't have much money. I am thinking to sell my cell [phone] and my hearing device." Moh has had a hearing aid since losing his hearing in one ear after a particularly violent beating from his father. "I can't hear very well without it, but need I cash. I ask God to help me, but also should help myself. Please tell me what to do. I don't know what I could do without you."

I encourage Moh to get out of Gaza and claim asylum in some other country. I desperately want to send him money but I have little to send at the time and no way to send it. I also fear the Israelis, who have added me to their security list out of concern that I might unwittingly or out of pity help some Palestinian militants by passing money or messages. I am quite sure Moh has no militant streak in him but how can one ever know for sure? If I send money that aids militants, I might end up in Israeli prison, arrested upon reentering Israel.

I also encourage Moh to consider claiming asylum in Israel, but he fears the Israelis would not accept him and instead use his admission of homosexuality to blackmail him into working as a collaborator, so he stays home and continues to be beaten by his father.

"Moh, I've seen your father and I've seen you and even though you may not feel like it, you've grown up and you are now bigger than him. All it takes is grabbing his arm and telling him, 'No! You won't beat me or my sisters anymore.'"

It takes over a year of coaching him to say it firmly but with respect. Finally, he works up a little courage.

"I told my sister and Mom that I will try and stop [Dad]. They think that he can't be stopped and the worst is that they believe it's like a diabetic— his sickness can't be stopped but you can live with it. [My mom] wants to live that way, my sister too. If I tried to stop him no one will support me. In Islam you MUST obey your parents. But they mistake the concept and can't change it."

"Moh, your mother is a victim of abuse as well," I write back. "Try to understand that. She doesn't see any escape either, so she cannot understand that you are beginning to see how to stop him. Try to love her and support her as much as you can and not take personally what she says when it comes to your father. His abuse has made your whole family sick. Try to understand and heal yourself by making him stop in a nonviolent way. All the main religions tell us to honor our parents. That's why you must be firm but respectful when you let him know you won't be allowing him to beat any of you anymore."

Asylum as a real option finally comes through.

"Anne, guess what? I'm going to NORWAY!" Moh writes at the end of October 2006. "I am traveling there in February 2007. It's a program that I applied to sometime ago. I am so, so happy!" I encourage Mo to immediately apply for asylum once in Norway, claiming that to be gay in Gaza is like carrying a death sentence. Mo writes many letters during that time dreaming about what it will be like to get of Gaza, mixed with some guilt about leaving his mother and sisters behind in the hands of his abusive father. But gradually the difficulties and complicated process of getting a passport and a visa and arranging travel out of Gaza began to dawn on him.

"Hey, I have a passport now," Moh writes in November of 2006 but he still has to get a visa and the Norwegian embassy does not appear to have a consulate in Gaza. "I found the official website of the Norwegian embassy in Ramallah but it's impossible to leave Gaza right now," he writes. Then a bit later he texts, "I called [the Norwegian Embassy] in the West Bank and they have a hidden office in Gaza. I am heading there now. They want bank insurance of about $3,000 and a paper saying that I'm returning home and a paper from my university and 200 NIS [Israeli currency equaling approximately fifty US dollars]. Oh my God!"

Moh does not get his Norwegian visa nor does the conference offer him the travel support he needed. "I am shocked! I am out of order! I still can't imagine what is happening to me," Moh writes upon learning of these two denials. "Why me? I beg you! I really beg you if there are any NGO's or something like that to help? I'll die here. Am really not exaggerating Anne. I have nothing to say." He sinks deeper into depression as the months file by, but he still searches for refuge. "The Chilean embassy wants a paper that says I am working,"Moh writes in January of 2007. "Things would be much easier with such a paper, don't know if you can help me with it or not. They also want over $3,000 in my account. The [Rafah] checkpoint with Egypt is opened today and tomorrow, then who knows? Problem is that if I go to Egypt I'll need cash and I don't have much. Tell me what do you think Anne?"

I have no idea what to advise him. Running to Egypt as a gay refugee with no cash seems ill advised.

"I went to the Egyptian embassy asking them for a visa to Egypt," Moh writes a few days after. "They refused it Anne. As I told you before, it's impossible. Now I have no hope, not anymore Anne."

"Hey there, you want to hear something funny?" Moh writes in February 2007. "Ok, about the appeal that I sent to the Norwegian embassy. I called them two days ago to ask them about it, and guess what? They told me that this would take eight MONTHS! Can you believe this? I don't know, but do you think that they are right? I mean how it would take eight months in the time that they supposed to answer me? Well, viva democratic stupid Europe, Anne, and I mean it, that's not fair at allllllllll!"

"Anne," Moh texts hysterically in May of 2007 after witnessing a violent altercation with militants, "I swear to God that some militants shot a guy in the leg in front of my eyes. I was in the car behind him. Then they came to my [taxi] and asked me about my ID. I couldn't even talk or breathe. Two women and a little girl were in my car. I need to talk because I can't handle it. Please call me. It's my birthday gift and I will never forget it. So happy birthday to me."

I normally never called Moh as I didn't trust the phone calls to go through and I don't like talking when the phone can die at any moment, and the Israelis are likely listening, but after reading his text, I phone him immediately and am amazed that the call goes through. Moh is hysterical and cries as he incoherently tells me that masked gunmen who were stopping cars on the road and searching for someone they thought had betrayed them, stopped his car also and nearly killed him.

Later in May 2007, Moh texts me about his father. "I hate him! I hate him! I hate him! Anne, I beg you to help me ASAP. I want this man to die lonely with no money or house and no one beside him. Pardon my language but I'm boiling and steaming because of him. He is a motherfucker, a bastard, an asshole, a trash pan, and old shoes, smelly old underwear. He is shit. I hate him more than anything. It is 1:15 a.m. and he can't stop making problems. I wish I could kill him."

I send my usual responses to try to calm himself, to nonviolently prevent his father from harming the rest of the family and to continue searching for a job and a way out. But Gaza was and still is a prison.

"In my world I don't have my own world," Moh writes at the end of May 2007. "I don't have a word in my so-called world. In my world, joy is sad. He killed the happiness that I've never had. In my world, there is pain. There are eyes that are always red. In my heart there is a knife, made of evil, made of sorrow. In my life, life is lifeless. In my dream, visions are helpless. In my dreams, in my mind, there is a wish not to be famous, not to be rich, only to be loved."

In early summer of 2007, I attend a counter-terrorism conference where John Ging, director of the UNRWA operations in Gaza, is one of the speakers. John discusses the difficulties ordinary Palestinians face since the Hamas election victories and the Israelis blockade of Gaza, citing shortages of food supplies and concerns about the population.

On a break I introduce myself and ask John if I could send money back with him to help my former guide and translator, assuring him that as far as I know, Moh is not a part of any militant group and that I am really worried about him. John agrees and I empty my wallet. Unfortunately I am carrying only about three hundred dollars in cash so it isn't much, but at least I send something.

"I'm sending you some cash through Mr. John Ging, director of the UNRWA in Gaza," I text. "Can't stand to think of you not being able to get food. I'm ashamed it isn't more after all you did for us when we were in Gaza but it's all I have at the moment."

"You paid for my help many times Anne," Moh writes back. "You listened to me in the time when my own family never tried to understand me. You believed in my abilities. You gave me your trust and friendship for free. I am the one who should pay you back. I'll be grateful forever. I am speechless. I don't know what to say. With all love and respect, Moh."

I keep encouraging Moh to get empowered with a job so he can free himself from his violent father. I suggest offering his services to foreign journalists and write him a general letter of introduction and recommendation from our time together that he can carry and use as needed.

In July, Mo writes again, "Oh my God. Eye contact happened between a French girl and me. She kept smiling when she looked at me, finally she asked me to join them and her two British friends from BBC. We spoke four or five minutes, but they have translators, but the Palestinian producer took my phone number. He told me that if he needs any help he'll call me and he gave me his card. I hope to get a small job soon! Thanks to Allah that I have a friend like you! Love and respect, Moh."

"I saw Mr. John Ging on TV today," Mo writes a few days later. "He didn't call me, hope that I didn't misunderstand your messages. Lots of love, Moh."

"You have to go and introduce yourself in his office," I write. "He has the money for you." Moh finds the idea of presenting himself to the head of the UN mission in Gaza an intimidating task but he finally carries it out and receives the cash.

"Hi Anne, I really want to thank you again for the extra money which I never expected to have. And by the way, I'll do my best to keep it and not to spend it; because it's not just money—it's money you have your fingerprints on. That is money that you should give to your research or family but you gave it to me, although I don't deserve it. Thank you indeed. Anne."

Mo's elation with receiving a gift is sadly short-lived. Gaza in 2007 is a big pit of despair and the situation is worsening each day. I know that my letters are helping, but I often feel I am pouring words into a deep bottomless well and Moh is trapped at the bottom of it with no way out.

I encourage Moh to try to write about himself, thinking that maybe if he could anonymously pen his autobiography as a gay in Gaza and aim it for a western audience, then he could get asylum abroad in that way. I tell him his letters to me are compelling and offer to help him, but Moh begins to write self consciously, getting mired in politics and stifling his raw pain. Only one excerpt shines:

> As readers, you have the full right to wonder why am I going to talk about myself, because in fact there is no me, and I never had space to talk about me, and I never had my own entity as a human being.
>
> When I was a little kid, I had and still have the same central dream: to leave my father's house, to live alone, or at least with people that I love and people that love me. I did nothing in my life, and do you know why?? Simply because I don't have one. I don't have my own life. I have that man called my father ruining my life, turning it upside down. For me he is not more than a DNA match for me.
>
> Imagine yourself, a Palestinian gay guy, living with the worst family ever, living in Gaza strip, and you are going to marry your father's niece only to keep properties and lands inside the family. A sixteen-year-old nice girl named Fatima[1] . She has a serious problem with her thyroid gland, because her mother (which is my aunt), was married to her cousin, and now it is my turn to do that.[218] People, I'm gay, and I can't do that. I cannot do that at all. And I can't make the life of this child [bride] more miserable, and that kills me all the time.

1 A pseudonym

432

I'm lonely, living a double life, trying so hard to hide the real me, trying to hide my real identity and my real sexual orientation. I'm afraid to lose my humanity, and to lose my own me. I'm very tired, really tired and all that I want is a life, my life, my own life, a life to live in peace..

Well, while I'm writing this, I have a very big dark blue painful circle around my eyes. Hehehe, my so-called father smashed me like a punishing bag and spit in my face because I was watching a TV show called *So You Think You Can Dance*. But it is ok, because I never experienced a week without being beaten like a punishing [sic] bag.

To be surrounded with hundreds or thousands of people and to still feel lonely is not funny. To live in a house that is supposed to be your house but in fact is not, is really painful. To cry alone in the nights as a way to have fun instead of going to the bar or go shopping is really killing. To see your friends with their parents having fun, and to see your friends that you are supposed to be graduated with are finished and you are standing still will make your heart bleed. To see your own sister marrying a man only for one reason—to escape—is not that simple. And to be married to a sixteen-year-old girl, this will be the real disaster because you will crush two innocent lives. And as a tradition here, the mother of the groom and the bride will wait for me on the wedding night to see the white sheet of the bed full of blood after deflowering her. Please, people, please help me.

Signature,

A semi-human being waiting to be a full human.

I encourage him to write more in this vein. Maybe because he doesn't feel he is a real person and because he can't tell who he really is, in his community, Moh can't sustain writing in this way about himself. As chapters of militant-sounding diatribes pile up, I slowly stop encouraging him to capture his story as a means of escape.

"I want to propose a toast," Moh writes at the end of June 2007. "For me, as the groom, and for my future wife, Fatima, and for my mother who took us in her car, happy about us, and for the shame and disgrace that will follow me as the weak stud and for the children which will never be born, and for being the one who helped my so-called father to keep his lands inside his family. A toast of joy and ever after fake happiness—a toast of a man with no dignity or ability to deflower his future wife."

Meanwhile, Moh has begun to communicate with others on gay Internet forums, where he distinguishes himself from the many other Mohammeds as "Moh the Gazan". He befriends gays in Europe, telling them of his predicament. Many offer to help and finally it looks like Moh may be able to escape when a Dutch Palestinian friend he meets on the Internet invites him to the Netherlands.

But again, no visa is granted.

Moh and I lose touch for a while when a family tragedy hits for me at the same time that I am immersed and overwhelmed with designing the detainee rehabilitation program for Iraq. Moh has reached out to others by now and keeps writing to all of them, and to me sporadically.

The Israeli invasion of Gaza (Operation Cast Lead) occurs in the last week of December 2008 when Israel announces that it is fed up with the Qassam rocket attacks into Israel. During a three week heavy air and ground strike, Israeli forces attack Hamas-held government buildings, police stations and devastate the densely-populated Gaza City, Khan Younis and Rafah. When the invasion ends, more than a thousand Palestinians are killed. Thirteen Israelis are dead.

At our embassy home in Greece, where we are now living, I switch between watching al Jazeera English, following their live coverage from inside Gaza City, and CNN, who mainly covers the invasion from the Israeli side. For the first time I begin to see what the Palestinians often claim: CNN doesn't seem to capture hardly any of the devastation I am watching live on the al Jazeera English channel. For Moh, however it's the aftermath that brings him a job as a guide and handler, covering the devastation. And ironically the war that demolishes Gaza ultimately leads to his freedom.

Finally on February11, 2009 Moh gets the news he has been waiting for.

"Hello Anne, How are you doing?" Moh writes. "I hope that the situation in Greece is much calmer now. Well I just want to update you with my news. I have all my papers set to travel to Spain, and I already have a job there. I'm a part of a documentary about Gaza and the job will be translating the tapes and so on. And they even told me that if plan A doesn't work, which is moving to Spain, then plan B will be a formal invitation for some conferences in Greece and work with the Greek photo journalist that I told you about. All what I'm waiting for now is the Egyptian Authorities to inform the Spanish Embassy in Cairo that I can use the Rafah terminal as a passage to the Spanish Embassy, where I will take the visa and the nearest plane to Spain and that's it. Or at least it should be that easy. Wish me luck. Loads of hugs, Moh the Gazan."

I waited on pins and needles until Moh writes again:

"Hello Anne. At last, I'm in SPAIN! I arrived here a week ago, and it's so strange for me to come here. I met the immigration lawyer today and she asked me if I could have a reference from people that I have worked with, so I don't know if you mind be one of my references?"

Of course I agree and write him the best letter I can, along with any advice I can come up with for making a winning asylum case in Spain.

Unfortunately the heavy baggage that Moh carries with him out of Gaza continues to haunt him. In June of 2009, he writes from safety,

"Anne, I want to ask you about something. After I came here, I mean after almost a month and a half, I started to experience some strange, scary, horrific nightmares about the war in Gaza—dead bodies and even much worse than the war itself. Alberto, the Spanish journalist who was with me in Gaza during the war, told me that a psychiatrist told him that we might experience this after four or six months after the war, and I forgot the name of it. Could you please provide me with more information about it? It's really bad. I mean now I almost see one nightmare every week. And I wake up scared, shaking and sweating and I even feel like I was really running for ten kilometers . . . I don't know if I'm going to see more of these nightmares, also I don't know if its going to go another direction, if there are stages or things like that. . . Hope to hear soon from you. Many hugs. Moh the Gazan."

Moh, like most survivors of insidious, horrific and ongoing traumas, was dissociative —blanked out, emotionally deadened, feeling like he survived half dead—while the traumas were going on. But when he got out to safety, the dissociation rolled away like a thick blanket of fog, revealing the jagged cliffs and deep valleys of PTSD, including Technicolor full-sensory relivings in the daytime and in the dead of night. I tell him about PTSD, that he is just in the first stages of it and what he must do to heal.

In August of 2009, Moh's mother calls to talk with him and tries to put his father on the phone. Moh refuses and that same day his father is killed in a motorbike accident.

"Hey Anne," Moh writes, "just want to tell you that my father died in an accident. I have a mixture of feelings. Tell me what should I feel? I mean, normally in my case, what line of feelings I should be experiencing because I just don't know."

I normalize his numb feelings and encourage him to let go of the anger and the hate and just grieve for his father and what he never was for Moh.

Two years later in October 2011 when I check in on him, Moh admits that he is still struggling with a lifetime of trauma and PTSD, including survivor guilt for having gotten out of Gaza when his family did not, as well as struggling with the social condemnation of homosexuality.

"I am still in Spain but I am not ok. Looking for a job, and feeling guilty to be here while my family is there. I am literally fighting to survive and having strange thoughts. I have many discussions between me and myself. I am trying to control things, but I can't. I am thinking a lot of well, *Just jump and end things*. I am a loser, I am! Useless, helpless, and well, a sinner maybe! Better not to talk about that," he writes, immediately shutting down the guilty and posttraumatic thoughts even as he voices them on paper.

Moh's letters dripping with pain and his arduous search for an escape out of Gaza help me understand on a whole other level what it is to live inside a conflict zone with violence and desperation. I see how those living with multiple private and political traumas and no hope to escape the overwhelming psychic pain, sometimes choose the only way they can: volunteering for suicide missions. And the fact that Moh was gay in Gaza gave me a rare insight into what it is like have to hide one's real self and to live in daily fear of being found out and the violent end that would bring.

CHAPTER 42

Return to Jenin

It's January 2006 and I'm on my way into Jenin, again. The last time we went it was daylight; now we go at night, perhaps tempting fate. But when I interviewed Zakaria Zubeidi in March 2005, he spoke so openly and deeply about himself and the "martyrs" he sends for al Aqsa Martyr's Brigade that I have been wanting to meet with him again to learn more.

According to the Israeli actions, he has a short expiration date—they are targeting him for assassination—so it's important I take this opportunity.

Yousef and I are with Ahmed and Abdul, two doctors we met when we came to Hebron earlier in the day, and a young woman, Najila, who they have arranged to come with us. Aside from meeting them earlier in the day, they are virtual strangers and I worry that the doctors may be aiding the militants. They look a lot like the Hamas militants we met in Gaza—rough cut with beards.[219]

It's raining and the road out of Hebron is backed up from the check-point. We wait as the cars crawl slowly forward and when we reach the checkpoint, we are told that with Palestinian plates we are not allowed to take a direct route into Israel proper, so we head out along the side roads through Bethlehem.

After about a half hour, we crest a hilltop and Ahmed points out a field.

"That's where the shepherds saw the sky open, to hear angels singing about the birth of Jesus," he says.

We stop at Abdul's house to pick up his seven-year-old son who will go with us to Jenin. In a half hour we reach the next checkpoint, outside of Ramallah. We have to get out of the jeep, and so we huddle outside around a grill, devouring hot chicken pita sandwiches sold by a vendor there. When we are cleared to cross we pile back in the jeep, and I share some Belgian chocolates that I brought from home.

"These are delicious!" Najila says as she takes another. "I can't stop eating them!

"Yes, they are dangerous!" I agree and take another as well.

We discuss our strategy for meeting Zubeidi. "Without a local guide, we can't know where he is," Yousef states.

"I think if we walk around the camp and let it be known we are in town and want to interview him, someone will know where he is and word will get back to him," I say. "He has many informants. I think they'll remember me from last time."

We speed along the highway and don't hit another checkpoint until we come to the outskirts of Jenin. The Israelis stand under bright lights with their automatic rifles, and our driver stops and gets out with Ahmed, but they are afraid to approach without permission. The two Palestinians stand helpless, smoking in front of the jeep, conferring on what to do. They return to the car frustrated, preparing to leave.

"The road's closed. The soldiers won't talk to us."

"Let me try," I say as I climb out from the back of the jeep taking along our open box of Guylian chocolates.

"Hello, I'm American," I call out in my friendliest voice as I advance alongside the waist high cement barriers. "Is it okay if I approach?"

I'm aware that the box of chocolates and my purse bumping alongside me can be mistaken for explosives or a weapon and I walk slowly, making all my movements predictable.

Silence.

They see me. I know that.

I've gotten used to this. As long as they think I'm a Palestinian or with Palestinians, I am a non-person. I don't exist.

"Hello, I'm American," I repeat walking steadily forward. "I have some chocolates here," I say holding the box out in plain view. "They're Belgian, but I'm American." I'm watching to see if they will raise their rifles, if they doubt the box is really chocolates.

I can see their faces now.

"Would you like a chocolate?"

They're dressed in camouflage, black boots and helmets. The younger boy's eyes light up, eyeing the chocolates.

"No thank you," his superior answers, firmly. The younger soldier immediately assumes a stern stance, averting his eyes from the chocolates that he clearly wants.

I remember the airport, how after being detained in security upon arrival I once in a gesture of good will offered the security team one of the sealed boxes of chocolates I had carried in with me for interviews and they refused. Afterwards my Israeli friend Yoram scoffed when I said that I was disappointed that they didn't accept my gift. He explained that someone once disguised explosives as chocolates and tried to board an El Al flight. I guess mine could be poisoned. Unfortunately for Israelis, harsh experiences often teach bitter lessons.

Are you sure?" I ask holding them out. The young soldier can't control his face. His eyes answer affirmatively, but his partner again sternly refuses.

We've established contact at least, and they see my American passport clutched in my other hand. "We'd like to go to Jenin," I say.

"No, the road is blocked," the senior soldier declares with a thick Hebrew accent.

"Are you sure you can't let us pass? I'm an American psychologist, traveling with two doctors and two students. We came from Hebron and they want to visit their clinic here."

"No. The road is closed."

"Is there another road we can take then?"

"No ma'am, all the roads to Jenin are closed."

"Oh. . . Does that mean there's an action in Jenin tonight?" I ask.

"Not necessarily," the senior soldier answers. The young soldier looks as if he was going to say something different.

"I guess it's dangerous for me to go if there's an action going on," I probe hoping to glean something, anything, about the situation in Jenin.

"Yes, it can be dangerous for you," the senior soldier answers.

I see I am blocked and it would be dangerous to continue. I thank them warmly, say goodbye and hop back into the jeep. Everyone is anxious to hear the news.

"All the roads are blocked. Jenin is closed," I report, laughing when I share the bit about the younger soldier who wanted the chocolates but was forbidden by his superior. We begin to nervously devour them as we consider what to do.

The driver turns the jeep around. I assume we are going back to Ramallah. In some ways I'm relieved. Last trip, Jamilah had telephoned the family of Hanadi Jaradat, to see if she could arrange an interview for us. Jaradat, a young trainee lawyer from Jenin and a mother of young children blew herself up in a restaurant in Haifa killing twenty-one and wounding sixty more. Her family had refused an interview, and Jamilah was glad.

"Anything can happen in Jenin," Jamilah had said even though she had taken us their once. "It's an outlaw town. Everyone is afraid to go there."

I was probably stupid to try to interview Zubeidi again, I tell myself. *He's a wanted criminal and the Israelis are in Jenin now. Who knows, maybe they are going to kill him tonight.*

Suddenly our driver swerves the jeep off the road into a ditch and climbs up a steep incline into a boulder-strewn field.

"What's going on?" I ask Ahmed, alarmed.

"We're going to Jenin," he answers matter-of-factly.

Now off-road, the jeep is struggling, its wheels spinning in mud. The driver guns it to make it up the next steep mound.

"But it's all locked down!" I protest, hanging on to the seat in front of me.

"The roads are closed, but they didn't say we couldn't use the fields," the doctor answers as the jeep dives down a short ravine and takes the other side of a steep incline. The driver turns his lights off for a minute and slows the car as though listening for someone.

"What's he doing? Why does he turn his lights out?" I ask, remembering how the driver who took us to Beit Fourik did the same. "Will the Israelis shoot our tires if they catch us in this field?" I ask.

The doctor's voice is calm. "No Anna, we do it all the time," he answers. "It's the only way into Jenin. I drove through this field nearly every month last year to visit my clinic. It's why I brought the jeep. "

"But why does he turn the lights out?" I insist.

"He can see better that way," Ahmed answers. That's clearly not true, but I am too speechless to reply.

I see a truck approaching us, and I can't believe it! There are more vehicles than just ours traversing the field! Yousef and I exchange glances as the jeep lurches from side to side.

"It's always with you that I get into these troubles!" Yousef cries, fear filling his voice as well. "It took me a whole year to calm down from when we went into Nablus!"

Our eyes lock remembering. This is just like last time—no one explains, no one asks if we want to risk our lives this way. I begin to silently pray for safety.

"Pray, Yousef. It's all we can do!" I tell him, trying to sound calm.

He nods and I know he's praying just as hard as me.

The jeep slides in the mud. The driver accelerates, but it's slippery and the tires spin. Suddenly they catch on something, and we lurch ahead.

"Don't let them shoot at us!" I pray. "Don't let them see us. Don't let them be in this area tonight."

Everyone but Ahmed looks scared. He is *too* calm—maybe dissociatively calm.

I search my mind wondering if there is anything I can do to decrease the danger. Maybe if I start texting on my phone the Israelis will know I'm here. Maybe if I keep it up, they will triangulate on my position and know exactly where I am and hopefully not touch where I go. I wonder, *How smart are the Israelis? Do they even care if I stay alive? Maybe I am an irritant and they would just as soon have me dead, seeing that I'm on my way traveling illegally into Jenin about to interview their sworn enemies.* Maybe to them I am just another Rachel Corrie, the American human rights activists who stood in front of a bulldozer in Gaza to try to stop the Israelis from destroying homes. The bulldozer kept on its course, running over and killing her.[220] The Israelis claimed she was killed unintentionally. *How about me? Could they "accidentally" kill me if I'm enough trouble to them?* I keep a firm grip on the seat in front of me and try to calm the panic rising inside.

I keep passing Najila the chocolates, and she pops them into her mouth eagerly thanking me each time. I am good at calming others, and they need me to be composed, so I pull myself together as best I can.

Finally the jeep tumbles down a rocky incline back onto a gravel road in the outskirts of Jenin. Ahmed signals the driver to pull over at a building.

"We're are getting out here, Anna," Ahmed says as he and the others disembark leaving me, Yousef and Najila in the truck. "The driver will take you to your hotel in Jenin. They are expecting you. He'll pick you up again here, tomorrow morning at eleven. Najila knows this address. Good luck with your interviews."

"Okay," I say, "Goodbye!" a bit speechless that we have been so suddenly left on our own.

We carry on to the hotel and the Jenin refugee camp. The "camp" is comprised of two-to four-story stone buildings, housing sixteen thousand Palestinian refugees from the Carmel region of Haifa and the Carmel mountains, areas that are now in Israel proper.[221] The camp came under Palestinian control in the mid-1990s and during the second Intifada has been the subject of intensive violence. In 2002, as we heard in our first trip to Jenin, the camp was encircled by the Israeli army and declared a closed military area. The Israeli army held the camp in a ten-day blockade while it fought the militants. They finally withdrew after killing at least fifty-two Palestinians, up to half civilians, but being unsuccessful in routing the militants out. Now in 2006, Jenin refugee camp is still an area filled with militants and undergoes many Israeli incursions.

Our hotel in Jenin where the driver drops us is on a roundabout named after the electrician Yahya Ayyash,a famous Palestinian bomb maker. We get out of the jeep and get our bearings as it drives off.

"Take my picture under the street sign," Yousef says, and I do—with mixed emotions.

We check in to our hotel and scandalize the owner when we say, "We'd like to take a large room together, two big beds or three twins."

"I cannot allow unmarried men and women to stay in the same room," the owner protests.

"We want him with us," I say indicating Yousef, "to feel safe. Don't you have a suite or something that would work?" I argue.

"There's no need to have the young man in your room. Jenin is calm and quite safe," the owner explains, but we insist.

He finds a compromise: a suite with a bed in the anteroom and two twin beds in the bedroom. "The women stay in the bedroom, you in the ante-room," he tells Yousef. "And be careful not to be seen," he warns. "It's very conservative here. I could get in trouble. And I'll have to bill you for two rooms. Otherwise I can have problems with the religious authorities for allowing you in one room."

"What do you think, should we still go for interviews or is everyone too tired?" I ask after we eat a small snack.

"I'm totally wired," Yousef answers.

Najila nods.

"Okay then, let's go!" I say. After risking our lives to get here it seems stupid to not try to go get some interviews. We agree to head out to the camp on foot, about fifteen blocks away.

It's quiet as we walk along the widely paved boulevards underneath the moon and palm trees. Many of the homes here are behind tall fences with Mediterranean style gates. The air is balmy and the scent of jasmine is in the air. I think to myself that the only way we'd know we were in Palestine is that there are posters everywhere for "martyrs" and radical groups and the occasional Palestinian graffiti spray-painted on the walls.

It's ten p.m. when we reach the refugee camp, and everything is shut down except for a barbershop where the lights burn brightly. There are men inside getting their hair cut and some younger ones are hanging about outside under the yellow glow of the lights. "You think we should ask them if they know where Zubeidi is?" I ask.

"No," Yousef answers. "They are just kids."

We walk a bit further up the steep road. The teenage boys catcall to Najila and me as we pass. I don't understand what they are saying but it's clearly something sexual in nature. I am not bothered by it, but Najila is clearly ruffled. She doesn't wear a headscarf and I wonder if she could incur their wrath by being without one. As a foreigner I'm fine uncovered, I think.

They begin to taunt, "There are Israelis are up there. They say don't go up there, they are shooting." We don't hear shooting, so we ignore them and carry on.

The camp is set on a hillside. We walk up the winding alleys between the old houses and the new, which were rebuilt after the entire midsection of the camp was destroyed in the 2000 Jenin "Massacre" as the Palestinians call it.[222] I see a familiar stairwell and am quite sure it's the ambush site the fighters had shown us as the one used for the urban warfare that took place during *Operation Defensive Shield*. As we near the top of the hill we stop and take it all in: the narrow stone streets and stone buildings and stars overhead, the mountainside down to the valley below.

"That's the town of Jenin and her sister town below," Yousef explains. All their lights are twinkling in the clear night sky.

"It's really romantic here," I say to Yousef and Najila. "We could be in the old part of Rome you know." They are surprised to have the beauty pointed out, given that we are in a Palestinian refugee camp currently undergoing an Israeli raid, but we all agree that it's a lovely evening as we continue silently up the hill, the clicking of my kitten heels on the paving stones the only sound of our progress.

We emerge back onto the main line up the hill and see a lone store lit up and decide to go in. There are three men inside. "We heard there is an action going on?" Yousef asks in Arabic.

"Yes, the Israelis are on the hilltop," one of the slimmer, dark men answers.

"No one is out?" I ask with Yousef translating.

"They shoot before asking questions," the men explain.

I ask Yousef, "Do you think we should tell these men why we are here?"

"No!" Yousef says emphatically and Najila agrees. "They are dangerous men," "Better to steer clear of them."

I wonder who is more dangerous than Zubeidi, but I know killers of all kinds can be found here: terrorists, criminals, and religious zealots.

We leave the store and continue up the hill and just as we do we suddenly hear the roar and whine of Israeli jeeps. Yousef and Najila immediately react and instinctively fall back into the shadows. Confused, I quickly follow their lead and fade with them into the dark cover of a space between two buildings. Suddenly we see four armored Israeli humvees race up the mountainside, two of them with their back doors gaping open. It looks as if they are ready to grab and arrest anyone, throw them inside and roar off back down the mountainside.

"Better keep clear of them," I say, and we veer off to the right, one street below where the jeeps turned, to try to learn what is going on while keeping a safe distance.

"How did you know it was Israelis coming?" I ask as we continue along the gravel road in the darkness. There are no street lamps alongside this road.

"I know every sound of all their vehicles," Yousef says. "After living through two Intifadas, I can identify any airplane, any helicopter, the whine of a humvee, a tank, or a simple car."

"It's something you learn the hard way," Najila explains, "and you never forget."

Clinging to the left of the hillside are rows and rows of two- and three-story stone houses, some lit up but all quiet. On our right the road falls off into a small cliff of rocks piled up along the steep hillside. There are no sounds but our feet crunching in the gravel of the road as we walk along.

Suddenly, I hear a whisper calling us.

"Someone is calling us from that window," I say to Najila and Yousef. "What's he saying?"

"There's Israelis in the house next door," Yousef says.

"What are they doing?" I ask.

Yousef asks him, but he doesn't know anything other that they've been there since morning. We walk faster now to pass the site.

Najila suddenly remembers she has a friend of a friend in Jenin. She phones and asks what is going on.

"The Israelis have been in the camp for three days," she says. "It's an action related to anticipated trouble over the elections and they are here to keep it from happening, or so they say. They've taken over four houses and threw the occupants out."

"Okay, so they already have their position secured. There shouldn't be any shooting in that case," I say.

Yousef nods.

"Maybe then we can go back closer?"

We agree and turn back up the serpentine gravel road doubling back to where we have been. We discuss what to do next but our words are interrupted by the sudden roar of Israeli jeeps speeding down the winding road headed right towards us.

I look around. There's no place to run, nowhere to hide, no place to back off the edge of the gravel road, only a steep incline of rocks below. We wait, frozen on the edge of the road, as four jeeps roar past. Surely they see us in their headlights but they don't slow down or change their trajectory in the least to make way for us as they catapult down the pitch-black road. I feel terror ripping through my body, as though one by one, they have generously spared my life—but just barely. And then I feel it: the overwhelming anger and humiliation and the desire to strike back surging up inside of me. I've heard from Palestinians a thousand times how their anger exploded inside and hurtled them into becoming rock throwers, and now, suddenly, I find this urge bubbling up inside of me!

It's not foreign any more, I realize. It's not me, the American, studying *them* anymore. I am them. It's so human to feel this way. But I'm also shocked and sobered by it and want to laugh and cry at the same time. Is this what it is to be a Palestinian living in the occupied territories? Is this what turns ordinary people into violent beings, into terrorists? I tell Yousef how I feel, and he says, "Of course you feel this way. We all do. Now you understand what we feel every day of our lives."

We carry on up the hill and cross beneath the house again with the Israelis occupying it. The man calls softly to us again, "Come here! The Israelis are in the next house."

We tell him we would like to interview one of the families whose home was overtaken.

"Yes, I know them, I will arrange it. Come quickly, the door is open below."

We climb up the rocky paths between the gardens to his house, wondering where the Israelis are and if they see us. He opens his door hurriedly and ushers us in, "Quickly," he says. "They'll shoot if they see you!"

We enter his home into a tiled hallway and follow him upstairs through a darkened kitchen and into a foyer with a brightly lit living room on the left. Oriental carpets are tastefully covering the floor and we all become acutely aware of our muddy shoes. We begin to take them off, but he says, "Come, come in, don't worry about that."

"But we are muddy!" I say.

"Ignore the dirt. It's nothing," he says. "Usually the Israelis take my house. But this time they didn't and I'm so glad. They trash it when they take it." He ushers us into the living room and we perch on his sofas, still nervous about our shoes. Our host offers tea, but we decline, anxious not to trouble him.

"How many times have the Israelis taken over your house?" I ask.

"Ten or eleven times," he says. "They like it because it's a good lookout, but this time they took our neighbor's home."

"Can we speak with them?" I ask.

Our host nods and picks up his phone to call. When he finishes he tell us that the displaced neighbors agree to give us an interview. "You must be careful," he says. "The soldiers could shoot if they see you outside." We discuss how to climb a bit further up the hill to where they are staying in a house overlooking their own home.

We chat a bit more and I like our host, so as we stand in his upstairs foyer again about to depart, I decide to trust and ask, "Do you know Zubei-di?"

He's a bit put off by the question and dodges it. "I know *of* him," he answers.

I decide to play along and hand him my business card. "If you can, will you pass him this card," I say. "Tell him his American psychologist came to make a home visit." I laugh lightheartedly as I watch how he takes it in while trying to size me up. "He knows me," I add.

"Okay if I *can* pass it to him, I will," our host assures me.

I imagine that he, like a lot of the camp residents, knows exactly where Zubeidi is tonight, but I don't challenge him on that. He opens the door and points our way up the hill through the gardens.

We pick our way along the path. Another door peeks open hesitatingly and a crescent of light shines out. "Psst, over here," the owner calls and we hurry over. "You can cut through our house, go up the stairs and through the next garden," the men inside explain with concern. "Watch out. There are Israeli snipers everywhere." I wonder if it's true and when we exit the house at its top, we are much further up the hill from where we started on the road below. I scan the rooftops. I cannot spot any snipers in the darkness, but in case they have us in their sights I talk calmly in a regular voice and laugh to my translators. I want them to hear us and hear that we are unafraid and calm, speaking in normal voices, not trying to sneak up on them.

We walk slowly up the next garden path and as we scramble over a small rock wall I think to myself,How vain I was to dress like this to come to Jenin Refugee Camp? What am I doing here with a briefcase and in boots with kitten heels? There's no way to change now, so I throw my briefcase over the low garden wall and clamber over the rocks. We cross over a courtyard and approach the house we were directed to.

We knock and the door cracks ever so much.

"Who is there?" a male voice inside asks. They are scared and I wonder if they will let us in.

Yousef explains who we are, that we just called moments ago. A few more minutes pass as we stand locked outside, dangerously exposed to the snipers. I look over at the house next door. Now I can see them. Israeli soldiers stand in all the windows each holding an automatic at the ready. One stands on the rooftop. Finally the door where we are waiting slowly eases open and a middle-aged man in faded clothing allows us in. A grandmother, her daughter and a young boy are inside and greet us in the living room lined with Arabic style sofas. We introduce ourselves and they readily agree to an interview. "We want the world to know what happens here," the younger woman says.

We sit on the couches and discuss with the grandmother what has occurred. It turns out that this is not the first time the family home has been occupied by Israeli soldiers. Distraught and wringing her hands, she tells us, "We are four families, three generations of us living together in one house. Last time when they took over our house, all of us were herded into one room. Then they came and stayed fifteen days. We had to ask to use the toilet. We had no mattresses. We took all our clothes from the closet to sleep on. We had to take permission from the soldiers to get food from the kitchen. When we ran out of food the soldiers said we couldn't go out, but after some days they let us go for food."

Yousef explains to me that the woman is distraught and confusing time periods. The Israelis have overtaken their home many times, including twice this week.

"What happened this week?" I ask, trying to help her to focus on this recent turn of events.

"The first time they came at five a.m. on Friday," the grandmother recounts. "They ordered us all outside. We were all shaking. It was a couple of hours while they searched the house.

"We regret building our house now, so high on the hill. The soldiers like this location," she explains. "In the 2002 invasion, we anticipated that they will come to our house. So we left and locked the door. At that time they broke in and wrecked our toilets, everything. They shot randomly through the house and destroyed all the windows."

"And this time, what happened on Friday after they put you out of your house? Were you allowed to reenter?" I ask..

The woman nods. "But the soldiers stayed for two days and put everybody in one room. There were sixteen people in one room. My husband is seventy-five years old and sick. When the soldiers came, he got really sick and had to go to the hospital. He is there now. I am afraid these are his last days."

After two days the soldiers left but then returned again on Tuesday at one-thirty in the morning. The family decided it was better to leave the house than try to live in one room as they had in the past and came to stay here with their neighbors.

"Tomorrow it's our holy day, Eid," the grandmother says. "It's one of the most important holy days in the Muslim calendar following the month of Ramadan and our family will not be able to celebrate!"

"What do you normally do for Eid?" I ask.

"We cook a big meal," she says, "but even if they leave, I am afraid to go home now. Last time they dumped out all the drawers, everything was on the floor. It was a huge mess."

"The soldiers have already consumed two tanks of our water. Right now we depend on rainwater from a cistern on the roof, but we saw that one of the soldiers urinated and defecated on the roof near where we collect the rainwater. I am praying it doesn't rain and get into the pipelines, making it dirty and unusable."

As the old woman talks, I watch her grandson. He is eleven years old, quiet and serious, listening in rapt attention to her.

The younger woman, the boy's mother, tells us about her son trying to fix it. "Ghassan got upset when he saw our mother crying over the cistern so he went outside and removed the hose connecting the rooftop water collection area to the main cistern. At least that way the pollution remains on the roof and doesn't enter the water system. But he could have been shot doing it!"

I look at the boy and imagine how much courage it must have taken to approach the house. "You did that?" I ask.

He nods, smiling shyly as his grandmother snuggles him close to her on the sofa.

"Weren't you afraid of being shot?" I ask. He nods his head yes.

"He did it because his mother mentioned that she would go out and clean it," Ghassan's father tells us. "He didn't want her in danger so he did it himself. And he managed to take the pipe out so it's no longer connected to the rooftop."

The whole family beams.

"How is Ghassan?" I ask his parents. "Is he doing okay, sleeping okay?"

The mother answers learning over to hug Ghassan, "All of us, we feel anxious."

Then suddenly, his grandmother rummages through some of her things and holds up a colorful turquoise, orange and black checked abaya and says, "Look here, there is a bullet hole in my dress! The Israelis did this when they were here." We all gape as she shows us a round singed hole that looks like a bullet went right through part of her dress, luckily missing her.

The father of Ghassan who has been pacing in the front room for the last minutes has now opened the door that he was loathe to open when we arrived. Together with him, Najila, Yousef and I go to stand on their balcony overlooking the Israelis occupying his home. In the darkness I pick out the Israelis: one in the kitchen window, one in the foyer, one on the front porch, two on the roof. They are all helmeted with Kevlar flack vests and carrying automatic rifles. I wave from the balcony at one of them trying to appear as much as possible like a stupid American. I want them to clearly differentiate me from the Palestinians.

Suddenly the four Israeli jeeps we saw earlier arrive again. "Look they are packing out," Yousef says.

"Let's go and talk to them," I say beginning to walk cautiously down the steps through the garden and to the driveway of the house. Yousef and Najila follow me, made confident by my American sense of entitlement.

We enter their driveway and the four jeeps are there, surrounded by ten or so Israeli soldiers. We walk slowly up to them and they seem amazed to see us.

"Hi!" I say, greeting them as though things are totally normal. "Are you leaving?"

"Who *are* you?" they ask in amazement as I gaze about me.

"I am an American researcher," I answer.

"How did you get in here?" they ask.

"We just walked in, no problems," I answer, looking from face to face. Then suddenly it hits me. They are all baby faced: they are boy soldiers who hardly look like they shave.

"How old are you?" I ask gasping a bit with the realization. They seem to catch my sense of maternal concern for them and answer respectfully as though speaking to their mother, going one by one stating their ages: nineteen, twenty, twenty-one, eighteen and so on.

I am touched by how young they seem for carrying such heavy responsibilities.

"You must be scared here?" I ask.

"Yes, we can't wait to get out!" one of the young men answers as the others nod in agreement. There is no hint of wanting to appear macho.

"Can I see the house?" I ask.

Entranced, I think, by the fact that I have suddenly appeared out of nowhere speaking English and obviously care about their welfare, and perhaps also thinking that I'm a US embassy or United Nations (UN) official that they should afford observation privileges too, they answer without hesitation.

"Sure, come this way."

With Yousef and Najila following close behind me, we walk carefully along the driveway past the jeeps, making sure we are on the visible side of them to the entry and into the house. It's only when we are on the front steps that one of the soldiers calls out – their collective trance suddenly broken.

"Who are you?"

"I'm an American," I answer and don't bother to explain about my Palestinian students. They accept it and let us pass. I am amazed what a little confidence and being an American can accomplish.

"Are you from the UN?" one of them asks as we enter the house.

"No, I'm a university professor, a researcher of terrorism," I answer. "We just interviewed the people up the hill—the family that lives here— and they are afraid you are trashing their house," I say, looking around at the furniture turned on end to barricade the windows that have had their glass frames removed. "It looks like you haven't done much damage though. Things are okay?"

"Yes ma'am," they answer clearly pleased that they can account for leaving the house in somewhat good order.

"You are going to put the windows back in their frames before you leave, no?"

"Yes ma'am," they answer.

"There's a little boy in the house up the hill who lives here. I worry you may see him again as a terrorist in some years if you keep on this way."

"Yes that's a problem," the oldest of the young soldiers admits. "It's the hard part of our job."

Then he adds gently, "You need to leave now, ma'am." But even he seems like he won't argue with me if I give him a hard time. I don't and leave bidding them good luck.

After we leave and walk back out the driveway to the home where we made the interview, Yousef speaks excitedly to me, "I can't believe we could be here and walk up to them and talk to them as simple as that. I didn't think we could do that!" He is suddenly empowered. Najila is the same, visibly charged. Standing alongside me they have become super-powers walking in on an Israeli action and checking it over, suddenly transforming themselves from powerless victims to overseers, supervising the soldiers who usually terrify them.

We walk back to the courtyard near the first home and I call to the father who is watching us, "Your house is okay. They are leaving now and they will put the windows back before they leave. There is no damage."

I notice he comes out to the courtyard now too, bravely, forgetting his earlier fear. The door of the house that gave us safe passage suddenly opens too and the man there comes out as well. They no longer fear Israeli snipers all about. Other neighbors open their doors as well. I feel like I have melted a temporary freeze in the heart of Jenin. I am happy to have given them this feeling of empowerment, but I find later I will pay for it at the airport with the Israelis, who figure out that it was me and are not happy that I came to Jenin.

We walk back down the hill talking of our adventure and Yousef and Najila comment on how young and vulnerable the soldiers seemed when they talked to us.

"You showed me another side of my own country that I've never seen before tonight," Najila says.

I am touched as well by all that we witnessed tonight—especially the young soldiers' fear and desire to go back to Israel. As we walk down the hill I feel again transported elsewhere, the inky black sky alight with stars.

Tucked into our twin beds that night, Najila talks to me about her family, telling me how violent they are and that her father once tried to strangle her, that he nearly killed her. She lives away from them now, defying Islamic traditions, and her brother is angry about it. But she is obstinate.

"You are right to protect yourself," I tell her. "But you have to find a way to work through your anger." She disagrees, saying the anger helps her. I think again of my colleague[223] who is so convinced that terrorism, springs from the roots of childhood violence. Najila has been a victim of domestic violence but, like Moh, I doubt very much she will ever become a terrorist: her education, ability to speak English and her ties with foreigners seems to protect her. On the other hand, the little boy we saw tonight—even if his family was never violent to him—what will he conclude after he has repeatedly witnessed Israeli soldiers in helmets, flak jackets and automatic rifles force his family out of their home? Will he come to believe violence is the answer, even if it is aimed at innocent civilians?

I go to sleep with such questions on my mind. In the morning we check out of the hotel and meet back at the drop off point returning again with the doctors in their jeep, this time taking the road, back to Ramallah.

Chapter 43

Getting Shut Down

My next trip to Palestine in January 2006 is scheduled just two weeks after going into Jenin with Yousef, Najila and the two doctors. Yousef was very happy that I looked him up again last time and to have been paid (generously) and tells me that he's anxious to work together again, so we plan for him to translate for me again. Meanwhile to keep costs down during the conference in Israel that I'll be attending first, I've accepted an offer to stay with my friend Gil at his place in Herzliya.

Earlier, Gil made it clear to me that he'd be happy to get intimately involved saying, "Your husband can't expect you to remain chaste at home like a medieval woman while he's working for a year in Iraq," but I answered that much as I value his friendship, I'm a loyal wife and not interested in having an affair with anyone.

Just before the trip, I reconfirm his status with his current girlfriend.

"Is it still good for me to stay with you in two weeks?" I ask.

"Yes I'm looking forward to it!" Gil answers warmly.

"And you understand its just friends?" I add, to be sure I'm not sending any mixed signals.

Gil laughs. "I have two beds. Don't worry!"

My misadventures on this trip begin not with Gil, however, but at the airport in Brussels where I am still living at the time with the children while my husband is away. Used to arriving one hour before departure, as is customary for international flights in Europe, I arrive as usual to find the El Al flight attendant anxious to greet me. When I show him my passport he seems to know who I am and nods to who I later understand are two Mossad agents standing off to the side. They walk over and beckon, "Can you come with us please?"

I nod and pull my small suitcase as they lead me behind the El Al counter and into a search area similar to the one in the Israeli airport. *Oh no!* I think to myself, groaning inwardly. *They want to search me and all my things here in Brussels before even taking off for Israe*l! The agents ask me to open my briefcase and suitcase and take off my boots, and I watch helplessly as they quickly begin dumping the contents of every pocket and crevice of my purse, my wallet, my briefcase and suitcase into a big bin as they begin their intensive search process. I know the drill and try to stay calm, but I get upset when one picks up my laptop and mobile phone and begins walking out of the room.

"Excuse, me!" I call out. "That's my laptop. I have all my life on there!"

"He'll bring them right back" is all the answer I get.

I'm escorted into a cubicle where two of the female guards carefully search me and all of my clothes, requiring me to take my brassiere off so that it can go through the x-ray machine as they pat, probe and smooth their hands along my clothes, body and into my hair. When it's returned, I put myself back together and begin to pick up the jumble of my things and repack.

"Look, you arrived late for this flight," one of the Mossad agent tells me as I try to make order of my things, "and we don't want to put your laptop and mobile phone on this flight, so you have a choice. You can fly now and we'll send your computer and mobile phone on the next flight after this one or you can wait and miss your flight."

I argue that, for one, I wasn't late, but they inform me that El Al insists their passengers arrive 2-3 hours prior to departure. And so I plead my bigger case.

"I can't leave my computer here! It's got all my work on it, and I need it for the conference!" I protest. "And my phone! How can I call my friend in the airport when I arrive?"

"Your things will be fine, we'll pack them well and put them on the next flight. You're friend will find you—and there are pay phones in the airport," the agent answers. "You have to board now if you are going on this flight," he adds urgently.

Knowing that Gil will be waiting for me on the other end and I can't call him now, I decide to trust them and board the plane. Gil meets me as planned, despite not being able to text me. When I tell him what has happened he's outraged that an invited guest from an allied nation attending an Israeli counter-terrorism conference has had her personal computer and phone taken.

"I can't believe they did that to you!" he says. "There must be something you can do."

"You worked in the Shin Bet," I say, "Is there anyone from your past life that you can call on my behalf? I really don't like being stripped of my computer – it's got all my work on it." Gil shakes his head as though that's an unwelcome idea. "They have all the power, I think the only thing you could do is contact the newspapers and try to embarrass them."

"That's hardly a tact I want to take," I answer, so we pass on to other subjects including how his girlfriend is and whether he is also coming to the Israel Defense College conference that week. He's not, and though he's renowned outside of Israel, he regrets not feeling as appreciated at home.

When we arrive at Gil's place he shows me around and I'm dumbstruck to realize he's got one large bedroom with one king size bed. "Where do you want me to sleep?" I ask anxiously, worried that I've gotten myself in a bad situation.

"You can sleep here," Gil says, pointing to his bed. After a short moment he adds, "I'll sleep on the sofa in the living room – it folds out into a bed." I groan to myself and think, *I am sooo stupid*!

That night we walk a few blocks down the street to meet Gil's girl-friend, Amy, who prepares dinner for us in her spacious townhouse, and I exclaim over a tall tree filled with avocados.

"I have them everyday," Amy says as she serves our salad richly garnished with ripe avocados picked from that very tree. Later over dinner she remarks about my staying with Gil in his small condo. "I don't know why he doesn't just come over here and let you have the run of his place alone," she says, clearly not pleased by the arrangement. I blush unsure how to answer, as I don't want to get caught between them. And I also don't want to leave her with the wrong impression as I think Gil is clear now that I have no intent of sharing his bed with him. I think, *Best to just act friendly and supportive as this must be really uncomfortable for her too.*

"Anne already had problems with the authorities," Gil answers for both us after an awkward silence, explaining how the Mossad has my computer. "I think she shouldn't stay alone, who knows what they may do next?" *Maybe he's right*! I think. *I certainly don't want to be harassed in the middle of the night by some goons who want to intimidate me*!

When we return to Gil's house, he checks e-mails while I get ready for bed and then closing the door between us I bid him a chaste goodnight. It isn't a good night however, as I feel almost as if Gil's desire is a powerful force seeping along the floor, across the living room, under the door and up onto the bed where I'm sleeping. It feels palatable. I toss and turn until I fall into a disturbed sleep. In the morning when we wake, Gil acts perfectly normal and has a nice breakfast prepared for us. After he drops me to the Israel Defense College for the conference, he promises to pick me up after our group meal in the evening.

"Amy and I are going to a play in Tel Aviv so I'll pick you up around nine p.m. You may have to wait a little bit after your dinner, is that okay?"

It is and we part with a friendly goodbye.

The conference goes well although I keep worrying since my laptop has not arrived on the next two flights from Belgium. My phone, curiously, has been returned already.

"How am I going to give my presentation? I ask Pini, our police host at the college. "Can you do anything to help as I will need it for my Power-Point?"

"Why exactly did they take your computer?" he inquires, his brow knit in confusion over why one of the Israel Defense College guest speakers would have this happen.

"It's a long story," I say and explain to him about my trips into the West Bank and Gaza interviewing terrorists as I watch his eyes go wide.

"Okay, I see," he says backing off, "You got on the wrong side of the Mossad. Don't worry they'll have it delivered here—probably tomorrow."

"Is there anyone you can call?"

Pini shakes his head as if to imply no one messes with the Mossad! I get the same reaction from Yoram who is usually more than helpful. No one wants to be associated with this, I realize. They are all afraid of their intelligence agency.

My trip gets further complicated when the conference dinner ends, Gil does not show to pick me up and doesn't answer his phone or texts either.

"He didn't give you the key to his place?" Pini asks.

"No he said he'd pick me up just after nine," I reply. "I don't know what's gone wrong. Maybe the play lasted longer. You should go home Pini," I say. "I'm fine waiting here alone." Pini refuses to go and as the hours tick by and Gil still fails to show up or answer the phone, Pini gets increasingly concerned. During this time I end up telling Pini my worry: Amy is upset and they are delayed by a fight.

"But I'm not interested in having an affair with him." I say, "He knows that and I really tried to let Amy know as well!"

"You don't understand Middle Eastern men at all, do you?" Pini asks, shaking his head. And then as more time wears on, he becomes irate. "This is crazy. You shouldn't stay there with this going on," Pini finally says. "You've got to get a hotel! He's placed you in a really uncomfortable situation!"

"Yes, but wouldn't that just make things worse at this point?" I ask, "To walk out on him after he's been hospitable to me? He hasn't done anything wrong really—he hasn't crossed any lines."

"But he's left you sitting here for over two hours in the dark!" Pini answers.

Pini has taken over calling Gil from his mobile in order for me to bypass the international charges every time Gil's answer machine picks up. And everytime it does, Pini leaves what sounds to me like rude messages in Hebrew.

"Don't insult him!" I beg, but I can see that Pini is furious in my behalf and he convinces me to no longer stay in this self-conscious position and to check into the hotel in Tel Aviv where the others are staying. Finally Gil picks up his phone and says he is almost there—no explanation as to what went wrong. I tell him, "Gil, I'm sorry but I think it's best I move to the conference hotel."

"You don't need to do that," Gil protests.

"It's okay Gil," I answer, having already practiced what I'll say with Pini. "I really appreciate your hospitality, but I don't want to cause you problems. I think my staying with you is causing tension between you and Amy."

"No! There's no problem." Gil protests but I remain adamant. When Gil arrives he looks sheepishly embarrassed and Amy acts friendly as though all is normal. Pini explains that he will follow behind and that he will take me to the hotel. I jump into Pini's car.

Inside Gil's home, Amy quickly gathers my belongings, moving briskly about the bedroom and bathroom picking up my possessions and putting them in my suitcase faster than I can keep up. Within minutes I'm all packed and standing outside Gil's house.

"I'll call you tomorrow," he says as I give him a friendly kiss on the cheek and leave.

"I had my police lights on the whole way to his house," Pini admits on the way to Tel Aviv. "That will teach him!" he says. I laugh ruefully, feeling sorry for Gil who got himself caught between two women.

My computer still doesn't show up for the next four days, causing Pini to reschedule my presentation. In the meantime Pini and his group take us to Jerusalem to visit the police headquarters. Pini points out the cameras set up all over the old city and then takes us to the police monitoring room to show us how their system works.

"Here you see a Palestinian stabbing a police officer at the Damascus Gate," Pini says pointing to one of the monitors as he plays a rerun of one of the security tapes. We watch in horror as a Palestinian militant runs up to an Israeli policeman directing traffic, suddenly stabbing him repeatedly in the torso. "We have also caught ordinary criminals with these cameras and even rounded up a molester of young girls," Pini explains.

Following that demonstration we go to the Israeli Special Forces training area and watch demonstrations of "snatch" operations.

"This scene depicts a typical Palestinian village," Pini says pointing out some soldiers dressed as Palestinians at an outdoor café. "You don't see the soldiers but you will in a minute," he adds. We watch as an Army jeep pulls up to the scene and four camouflaged soldiers suddenly drop from the tree overhead, grab one of the "Palestinians" and throw him in the jeep as it squeals out. One of the soldiers who didn't manage to secure his position in the jeep rolls out the back as it drives off. I can't help but remark that he'd be unlikely to survive "over there".

One of the younger women in our group, Maria, is a student of martial arts and challenges the men of the Special Forces unit. "Would you be willing to let me try to attack and you show me how you would defend?" she asks.

"None of us want to hurt you ma'am," one of them says as they all suddenly become shy.

"Oh you won't," she says preparing her stance until one of them steps up to "fight" her. When she "attacks" he briskly counters by picking her up and throwing her high up in the air and then holding her perpendicularly above his head like a trophy while everyone bursts into laughter. He continues holding her there seemingly effortlessly for a few moments—a remarkable feat given she is tall and muscularly built. When he lets her down we return to the hotel talking animatedly about the day's adventures.

On the morning of my rescheduled talk, I finally receive my laptop, but without its cord.

"Pini, they are trying to harass me!" I complain, convinced it was not an oversight. He phones them, and the cord arrives literally a half-hour before my talk.

"I called and asked some of my colleagues what's going," Pini tells me at lunch. "They told me that collaborators in the West Bank and Gaza have talked to the Mossad about you, probably making up stories that are untrue about you bringing messages and money from sympathizers and militants in Europe to the Palestinians there."

"That's ridiculous!" I say. "I've been cleared by the US government, I'm married to a U.S. Ambassador and I'm aiding terrorists? That's crazy!"

"We are paying the collaborators. They have to come up with something for all that money so they make stories up," Pini explains. I suddenly lose my appetite.

The next day when the conference ends, Pini offers to drive me to Jerusalem but I have to go to my embassy in Tel Aviv first to discuss with them what has happened.

"I'll take you there and wait for you," Pini offers, as curious as I am to learn what the U.S. embassy will tell me. I check in through the security gate, arguing to keep my computer with me.

"I brought it here specifically so our guys can have a look at it," I explain to the Marines at the guard post who finally allow me to bring it inside.

"Can you tell if it's been copied?" I ask the political officer as we chat about my situation in the consul offices that overlook the Mediterranean Sea.

"I'll have our security guys have a look," he says taking my laptop from me and handing it off. "There's nothing to be done about the search. It happens to us too all the time. We complain but they keep detaining our staff and going through our things at the airport."

"Our guys can't tell if they copied it," he adds when the computer is returned, "but they say it's definitely been scanned in the last few days, so their guess is that they probably copied the entire hard disk. And they say that although they can't find it, that your laptop very likely now has a Trojan horse."

"A Trojan horse?" I ask.

"It's undetectable but inside the computer. It sends them copies of all your files probably every two weeks via the Internet. So if you don't want your work to be under their surveillance, our guys recommend that you get a new computer. But if you copy your disk on this one over to a new computer the Trojan horse will likely come right along with it."

"Can they get rid of it?" I ask.

"No," he says shaking his head. "We learned these techniques *from* the Israelis; they are the best in the world."

"So I'm basically screwed?" I say.

"Yes," the officer answers laughing.

"At least they are allies," I joke, "but I'd prefer to give them my work in a more finished form." I exit, thanking the embassy officer for his help. *Crap*! I think as I walk back out to Pini. *I store my raw interviews on my computer, and while I don't ask about or record operational details I don't like that they can now piece together all of my work —what I would choose to share and what I would not*!

I rejoin Pini and tell him my news.

"You still want to go to Jerusalem?" he asks knowing that I plan to head out to Palestine from there.

"Yes," I say.

"You're not really going to the West Bank, are you?" Pini asks incredulously as we head up the hills toward Jerusalem with his blue police car lights flashing.

"Yes, Hamas just won the elections," I answer. "It's a historic time. My translator is ready and I've got good contacts to work with. So yes, I'm still going."

"But the Mossad is really upset with you," Pini says. "Aren't you worried about that?"

"Why should I be?" I ask. "I am not doing anything wrong. I'm a professor doing my research, nothing more."

"But you have to see things from their point of view," Pini argues. "You told lies at the airport—that makes you a liar in their book."

"Pini, I don't like lying," I answer. "It's against every grain in my character, but even my friend—the one who worked in the Israeli intelligence—told me I could not tell the truth at Ben Gurion about my plans to enter the West Bank or Gaza if I want to get into Israel. He told me it was necessary. The same with the US State Department website—it basically hints at the same thing. And my embassy contact here laughed when I told them I don't admit my plans at the airport and said, "Of course!". Everyone who wants to go in to Palestine cannot admit it. Your country gives me no choice on that!"

"Okay, that lie [of omission] is no big deal," Pini says. "Just like that you go over and talk to terrorists—no big deal. But you go over repeatedly. And you pass on roads [in Palestine] that they have trouble passing on, and you go from camp to camp and even pass between the West Bank and Gaza. You even go into the prison here. And you do it all under the radar."

I nod listening quietly, mesmerized by the way he's constructing my story.

"And you come from Belgium, where you have contacts that tell you who to meet in Gaza," Pini continues. "And Belgians love Palestinians and hate us. And you give money to—"

"To pay translators!" I cut him off, fed up with his insinuations.

"And you stay in their homes!" he adds.

"I have no choice, Pini," I protest. "If I want to interview them, I can't get back across the checkpoints unless I stay in their villages overnight and leave the next day."

"And you socialize with them, and *like* them to a point," he continues. "Okay, it's all fine and honest, no?" he asks.

I nod, a bit sickened by his characterization of my activities.

"But then add in that one third of the collaborators are lying," he says. "And we all know that, but it doesn't matter because five or six of them say: 'She gave me or him money,' 'She sleeps with me or him,' or 'She passes information and resources.' Are you getting sick yet?" he asks, turning to me.

"I am. It's a totally sickening portrayal of my perfectly respectable research activities," I spit out, with some venom in my voice.

"Look," Pini continues, "it's only a matter of time. The collaborators enhance their reputations, their pay and their prestige if they get you caught. You are innocent one hundred percent—I know that—but it doesn't matter. They will plant on you unknowingly something dangerous—a microscopic message on your clothes, in your luggage, anywhere—and let the Israelis know. Then you go to the airport, smile nicely, cooperate and they find it. You protest saying, 'I didn't agree to carry that; I know nothing about it and you get arrested.'"

"That's crazy, Pini!" I say.

"No it's real!" he argues back. "You are innocent, but you get arrested and you spend two weeks in interrogation with Shabbak. You will never be the same person after this. You then spend six months in trial and all you can say for yourself is, 'I am honest, good, naive, sweet…I'm a researcher, I have done nothing!'

"'But you lied at the airport,' they answer. 'Why should we believe you now?'

"You tell them who told you to do that. It can be the highest level Israeli advice not to tell the truth at the airport. You tell them, 'My embassy supports me.' You show your publications, your work.

"'No, sorry my dear,' they say. 'We have many like you that go over there. They have lovers, collaborate, and pass money and messages. We have five to ten witnesses that you did *all* of this. And you want us to believe you? By the way, is your Israeli admitting that he told you to lie at the airport or has he disappeared?' they ask. 'Isn't this the same guy who told you to stay at his house and then surprised you that there was only one bed? Or you sleep with him too? Is that how you get secrets to tell your lovers over there? Your husband is gone no?'"

"Pini!" I cry out. "This is outrageous! I am a university professor, nothing more! Our countries are allies! My husband is a high level diplomat! I've never done anything —nothing—wrong! I've never slept with anyone here and I've never passed messages, money, nothing! They can accuse me all they want, they can plant messages and money and anything else they want on me but I am *not* guilty of anything—except that I was forced into not admitting where I am going at the airport in order to even do my research. And by the way it's excellent research. Your country could benefit if they asked me to help them understand the mentality of their enemies."

"But you see my point," Pini answers. "Of course you are innocent. That is plain to see, but when they add it all up, the way I just did, you will be arrested."

"I don't think so Pini," I say, shaking my head but inside feeling shook up.

"Do you know what our interrogation is like?" Pini asks. "If you go in there, it's a minimum of two weeks and you will not come out the same person."

"I'm sure I'd come out with PTSD! But I'd turn around and write about it and I would do so with no holds barred. Up to now I have never written one negative word about Israel, and I've never written up any of my research for newspapers or anywhere that it can be cast in a sensational light. But if I ended up like you are saying, I would write about it everywhere and I would not stop writing until I did my utmost to embarrass your country."

"And what about your husband?" Pini asks. "Wouldn't it embarrass him to have his wife arrested? Wouldn't he have trouble with the State Department?"

"No, I don't think so," I tell Pini thoughtfully. "I think it might be just the opposite and play well for him. The embassy is aware of the situation here."

"You can't go!" Pini's voice is filled with frustration. "The stakes are too high! They are going to arrest you!" he repeats mournfully.

"Well Pini," I answer resolutely, "I know who I am, and if they want to lower themselves to that level I guess then I'll be arrested. I'll deal with that if it comes, but in the meantime I'm continuing my research."

"You can't go back over there again!" Pini repeats slamming his hand on the steering wheel. "You have to understand these people have no sense of humor. And now they have your computer with a Trojan horse planted inside and for sure they read everything you write—every e-mail! They know everything you do. They listen to your phone. And right now *they want to catch you*! They would love to make a scandal to divert attention from their spy sitting right now in U.S. prison," Pini says referring to the recent arrest of an American arrested for spying for the Israelis, an event that created ire in Washington.[224]

"I don't believe Israelis are this evil," I answer.

"I do," Pini answers chillingly. "And even if they are not, the collaborators among Palestinians are and they will plant things on you just to make money."

"That's disgusting," I say, "But if it happens I'll deal with it honestly. I know who I am," I repeat.

"What about your children? You have children and their father is in Iraq. If you go to interrogation, who will take care of the kids?" he asks in a wheedling voice.

I feel it suddenly—his words hitting me in my soft spot, just like a hard punch to the gut—and I fold over, collapsing, gasping for air.

"Fuck you, Pini!" I say when I catch my breath. Hot, angry tears spill over the rims of my eyes, burning down my cheeks. "Fuck you!" I repeat softly. "Turn the car around. You win. I'm not going."

Silent and yielding in his demeanor Pini pulls the car over into a roadside café.

"Can I buy you lunch first?" he asks kindly. Tears are streaming down my face.

"Sure, might as well have a nice lunch if my research is fucked over," I answer with a sniffle. "Oh fuck this!" I repeat. "This shouldn't be that hard!"

Pini and I go inside and order a Middle Eastern lunch, dropping the subject of my imminent arrest if I don't comply, and speak about other topics. But as we head back to the hotel I begin to wonder, *Did someone in the security organs put him up to this, tell him to threaten me and scare me into not going? Or is this his wild imagination and confabulated view of how things could go? Or is it simply a realistic impression made by a seasoned police officer that obviously likes and cares about me?* There's no point in asking. If the Mossad put him up to it, he'd never admit it.

We arrive back in Tel Aviv as the sun is setting. Pini heads home telling me I'm welcome anytime to bring my family and come stay with him in his village bordering on the Negev and promises to escort me in the airport early the next morning.

"You don't have to do that Pini," I say. "I'm used to their drill and it doesn't bother me anymore."

"No," he answers. "You don't have to go through that again. I'll come with you and take you through."

I know he hasn't meant to be cruel today and that it's just the harsh world we live in that prompted all his comments, and I give him a hug. At the hotel I go for a walk along the beach as the sun sets. It's too cold for a swim—otherwise I'd gladly dive in to wash all the stress off. Back in the room, I watch in frustration as the Hamas landslide victory is reported from Ramallah.

"I should be in the West Bank tomorrow getting interviews," I tell my husband when he calls from Iraq.

"Just get up in the morning and go," he says. ""Don't let them intimidate you!"

"I can't do that to our children," I answer through tears. "They got me where it hurts. It's not fair to have you in Iraq and me end up in interrogation."

Dan keeps insisting that I go, but my mind is made up. If there is one thing I am, it's loyal to him, to the kids. Being a good mother has always been extremely important to me. So far I've judged the danger of my trips tolerable, but now as Pini has pointed out, the stakes are too high.

"Okay you go back in the day I come home," Dan answers.

"Alright," I say. "I hope they're listening right now because I'm not going to quit my research. I'll be back—just not tomorrow." When we hang up the phone I lay on the bed and cry myself to sleep, exhausted with the worry of raising a family alone for two years while he serves in Iraq, exhausted with chasing my own career and exhausted with the emotional ups and downs of chasing terrorists.

Early the next morning Pini picks me up and we go to the airport. He obviously has knowledge only of how an Israeli travels out of Israel, so I show him how the system works for foreigners: there is a different line to enter if things are normal, but in my case, I must locate airport security and turn myself in if I want to make my flight on time.

"No, you don't have to do that," Pini says. "Let me go and talk to them, stay here in this line." I wait and watch as he goes to speak with the security guards who respond by making telephone calls. I know this will trigger the Shin Bet guy to appear along with more security guards, which is exactly what happens. They are all jumpy as usual and when Pini points me out they look ready to pounce.

"They want you to come over there," Pini says when he returns, pointing to the group that has assembled for me.

I do, pulling my rollie behind me, ready for the drill. To Pini's amazement, one of the guards stops me before I get the whole way there and asks me to abandon my rollie. I do and walk a ways away from it. Then he asks me to set my shoulder bag and mobile phone aside as well and walk three or four meters away.

"It's so I don't detonate my bag," I explain to Pini, who is watching in amazement.

"No!" he says in disbelief, looking to the guards who remain tense and stern.

"Yes," I answer cynically "And this is just the beginning. I think we are in for the full drill now. You should go home, Pini. It takes a long time, and you don't need to worry about me. I'm used to this and I'm fine."

Pini, however, is not about to leave and asks if he can accompany me to the search area. At first they block him from entering, but somehow he talks his way in and they allow him to stand off to the side, near the entrance. From there he watches – while they ask me to open my bags and then begin rifling through them: emptying the contents, opening, sniffing, and touching every item. They take me into a curtained off area where I take my brassiere off and they carry it away for x-ray and do the full-body pat and search. I go through it subdued, joking a bit with the Israelis and trying not to get upset, looking from time to time to gauge Pini's reaction. He's upset. When they finish with me they let me repack and take my bags, except for my pillow, phone and perfume,which they pack up in a box to send home to me on the next plane. Evidently they cannot be sure these items cannot be detonated from the plane so I cannot take them on the same flight.

"I can't believe it!" Pini says angrily, his fists clenching as he accompanies me to passport control, the agents following close behind. "They do this to you every time you come here?"

"Yes," I say laughing at his amazement. "And I don't mind it that much, and I still love your country."

"And I told them you were our guest and hadn't left Israel," Pini says.

"As you said, Pini," I answer, "someone could have planted something on me. And I want the security guys to find it if they have—for all of our safety!"

Pini shakes his head, dejected.

"The world we live in rots when good people get treated this way, doesn't it?" I ask, smiling kindly.

"Yes, it does," he answers and smiles back. I give him a kiss as I pass to the plane, thanking him for all his care and hospitality in Israel. He laughs and we promise to meet again, hopefully soon, and under better circumstances.

CHAPTER 44

Security Risk

In my work studying terrorism I find that people in many ways perceive me as a clandestine operative—or worse! Most of my European colleagues who attend the security conferences where we all give talks think I work for the CIA, and eventually I begin to understand that most of them work for their security apparatuses. The terrorists, extremists, radical supporters, etc. who I interview also often suspect me of working for the police or CIA. This fantasy is furthered during the time when Victoria Plame, a retired U. S. Ambassador's wife, is outed for working as a spy. [225] And when I'm doing my interviews in the UK and a news article breaks revealing that the CIA has it's biggest undercover operation, observing and spying on Muslim extremists in the UK who they fear may be targeting their activities at U. S. citizens, I think to myself, *Great, now for sure I'm a spy*! Pini later tells me that he checked me out with the Mossad, who say that I'm trusted as a professional friend in Israel yet am still considered a security risk because I live in Belgium, have research relationships with members of Hamas in Belgium and Hezbollah in Lebanon and hold interviews in the West Bank and Gaza. So I find myself misperceived in many arenas and I understand from rumblings even before the time with Pini that my research in Gaza and the West Bank may be shut down.

The first occurs on a trip home from an Najah, the university in Nablus known as a hotbed for terrorism. An Najah had the bad taste to hold an art exhibition in which the aftermath of the August 2001 Sbarro Pizzeria suicide bombing in Jerusalem was restaged. To enter the exhibition, one had to either walk across an Israeli or American flag into the re-imagined pizzeria after the blast, where exploded furniture, bloodied Israeli body parts and the head of Sharon leaking blood from his mouth were all horrifically depicted as the results of glorified "martyrdom". Ken and I went to an Najah in Spring of 2005 hoping to talk to those who support and are active in terrorism but found the university student body hard to penetrate.

There, Ken picked up an Najah materials and stupidly kept them in his suitcase for our return home. Ken had also absent-mindedly thrown his toothpaste into the bag with the contraband papers—a liquid/gel that will surely trigger a search. Later when we are exiting Israel, the security guards promptly ask him to open his bag inside the airport.

A guard goes through his clothes and other items until she finds the toothpaste. "Good job," I cynically quip to Ken as he and I wait to see how much further she'll search. Next she pulls out the Arabic books. "What are these?" she asks obviously alarmed to see Arabic text. "They're children's books. I picked them up in East Jerusalem," Ken explains. "I'm trying to learn Arabic. "

"He's very good with languages," I jump in. "He knows Hebrew already from his year at Hebrew U and now he'd like to learn Arabic. " The young woman smiles as Ken says something in Hebrew to her, but her face quickly turns from a smile to alarm as she discovers and pulls out the an Najah papers. Swiftly she turns to her colleagues, chattering rapidly in Hebrew. They also register looks of alarm and disgust when they see the an Najah seal on the university papers.

"Where are these from?" a security officer asks as he approaches from behind. Other officers quickly encircle us as Ken answers honestly this time, "They are from an Najah in Nablus. We were there two days ago. "

"And *what* were you doing *there*?" the officer asks.

"Ken is not a security risk," I say jumping in. "He lived here for a year and loves Israel, and I'm married to a U. S. Ambassador. We are researchers and neither of us is a risk to your country. "

"You are married to a U. S. Ambassador!" the security guard repeats, surprise registering on his face and suddenly backing down. I think, *Good we're out of trouble*, but in truth it's only just beginning. "Are you traveling on a diplomatic passport?" the officer asks recovering himself.

"No," I say, "but I have it with me to get back into Belgium. "

"Can I have it please, and the other also?" he asks and taking them disappears. In a short while he returns saying, "Come with me please. " We follow him and have the full Israeli search.

As my research activities become known to the Israelis I find myself being searched each time I enter and exit and one time becomes a humorous exit at the security checkpoint when the female guards become intensely interested in my underwear. Wearing the new "gel" bra from Victoria's Secret, I hadn't given any thought to it as a potential security hazard. As

I go through the body search however, the female Israeli soldiers request my bra and take it away as usual, presumably to hand search and x-ray. When she gives it back and I put my clothes back on she returns and sheepishly asks, "I'm sorry we need your bra again. " As they take it away the second time, I try to imagine what is going on while I fervently hope I won't have to travel bra-less back to Belgium.

"Where did you get that bra? It has gel pads!" the young female soldiers excitedly ask when they return my bra the second time.

"It's the new one from Victoria's Secret!" I tell them as they gush in a completely unmilitary style.

"Israeli girls here would love to be able to buy a bra like that!" Laughing I dress myself again, glad to be able to wear it flying home.

That incident was humorous but when I fly in to take part as a speaker for a NATO sponsored bio-terrorism conference held in Ein Gedi in June of 2005, hoping to spend some days afterward with Ken in the West Bank collecting more interviews, I find the security services far less light-hearted. Ken and I have agreed to fly in together, but he will go ahead to the West Bank to hang out with Alla, our guide, while I go on to participate in the conference. The plan is for me to join them afterward to do interviews together.

But things don't work out that way. On the way into Israel, I get through the security with only the search, but Ken is taken for further questioning.

"Where is my student?" I ask before leaving the intensive search area. "He'll come shortly," they assure me and tell me to pass through the remainder of the passport control to retrieve my suitcase, which has now been circulating on the luggage belt for over an hour. I do and then look for a place to sit. There are no chairs, no benches, nothing. Clearly the entry part of the airport is not meant for loitering, but I can't leave Ken. So I stand near the guy renting luggage carriages, and eventually he feels sorry for me and offers me his plastic chair while he goes around the airport retrieving carriages.

From that vantage point I watch as hundreds of American Jews pour into Israel sporting orange t-shorts printed with the words "Jews don't evict Jews. " These Americans are here to hunker down in the Gaza settlements in camaraderie with the settlers, anticipating passive resistance to the order for the Israeli settlers to be evicted from Gaza. I notice that they are for the most part loud, pushy and obnoxious and appear entitled, like they own the place. They make me feel embarrassed to be American and

I wonder how the mainstream Israelis feel about them interfering now in the already-tense political situation with the Gazan settlers.

I wait for Ken for another three hours during which I repeatedly ask the border guards manning the security entrance if they know when he will emerge. When I explain that he was taken for questioning and has been gone for over two hours, one of them gets an alarmed look. "Oh we don't have anything to do with *them*!" she says, referring to the Mossad. "That's not a good sign," she adds ominously and looking nervous, refuses to discuss it further.

Ken finally emerges white-faced and shaken by his experience but also refuses to discuss it while in the airport or in the taxi to our hostel. All he will say is, "I met Sami—from the Mossad. "

When we check into our youth hostel the usually friendly staff acts suspicious and questions us about our plans. They don't seem to believe me when I say I'm going to Ein Gedi for a NATO conference. They linger in the lobby after offering us coffee apparently trying to overhear our conversation. Ken still won't tell me what happened at the airport and suggests we leave our belongings in our rooms and head out to the beach. There with the wind blowing full blast, he finally trusts that he won't be overheard and opens up.

"They want you to quit your research in Palestine," he says, obviously debating what to share and what to withhold.

"Tell me everything," I say.

"They threatened to beat me up if I go over to the West Bank again!" he divulges, distressed.

"What?" I say, outraged.

"They said if they find out I'm helping any of the Palestinian terrorists, they have plenty of collaborators over there who will be happy to beat me up," he explains.

"That's a bit different," I say. "It's not like you've ever helped a terrorist or plan to!"

"Yeah, but they want us to stop," Ken continues. "They said, 'Tell your professor to take her research elsewhere. She doesn't need to come here anymore. '"

"So they are threatening *me* too?" I ask.

"No, they were very careful *not* to threaten *you*," Ken explains. "And they went crazy when they understood that I speak Hebrew! They didn't know that!"

"Geez, their intel is pretty bad then," I say. "Given that you spent a year at Hebrew U and dated an Israeli girl, you would think that would show up in your profile!"

"Yeah, this guy Sami—he's definitely from the Mossad," Ken continues. "When they were talking, he saw that I understood and he yelled to them, 'Stop talking! He understands Hebrew!'" We both laugh at that.

"When I understood he was Mossad, I asked him if I could work for him," Ken adds smiling for the first time.

"No you didn't!" I say, imagining Ken's eager face volunteering to be a spy for the Mossad. "He didn't agree, did he?"

"No, he wasn't interested," Ken answers, clearly disappointed, although intensely proud of having undergone a true interrogation.

After some silence walking on the beach Ken adds the kicker. "They aren't going to let me back in Israel if I go over again," he says referring to the West Bank—a serious punishment for someone with many friends and a love for Israel. We walk along kicking sand and discuss how to respond to this threat.

"Let's call Reuven," I say. "He worked with them—he knows how they think. "

The guys in the hostel are still hanging around when we get back, so I go out to the street to call Reuven.

"Sounds to me like you've raised their concerns and it might be best to give it a rest for awhile and not go over this trip," Reuven answers. "Where were you planning to go?"

Is he part of this as well? I wonder.

"Jenin," I say offhandedly, although in reality we have no specific plans for Jenin or anywhere else. Our trips aren't like that—we usually ask our guides to help us find good leads and then we follow them until they tap out and begin again with new ones. It's probably good for our security not to have a definite plan where we will go—less vulnerability of being kidnapped or surveilled.

"They've had a couple of operations against Zubeidi recently, maybe they are trying to catch him these days and don't want you getting caught up in it," Reuven offers. He's right that if there's something going on we'd be best to avoid it. Ken and I discuss our options and decide that he'll come instead with me to the conference and we can forgo a trip into Palestine this time. I don't want him to get blocked for travel back to Israel, which is a very real possibility and I surely don't want him getting beat up. Neither one of us is sure what helping Palestinians means. Does taking our guide out drinking qualify?

So Ken continues on with me to the NATO conference and while he offers to sleep out on the grass I tell him he can stay in my room with me, which starts rumors that we're sleeping together. We leave Israel from that trip disappointed but well rested, having had the days we planned to spend in the West Bank traded in for beach days in Tel Aviv.

In 2012 when I ask Ken by e-mail what he remembers of his time with "Sami" he writes me a long answer—probably the best writing I've ever seen from him:

> We were waiting at the airport trying to enter for the NATO conference. We were always waiting [in security] so there was nothing new to this. We chatted to a few people and then began to go over our work. Two people entered the waiting area. One was a smaller guy with a clean-shaven head and a rough face. The other was a taller, younger, rather non-descript young man in his late twenties. I don't remember exactly what was said, but the gist of it was that I had to go with them. I complied and as I put my reading material away to go with them, Sami asked me to bring it with me. You immediately stepped in and said, "No." There was some back and forth and I left all the reading material with you.
>
> I walked towards the men, empty-handed to follow them out. A hand was placed on my left shoulder as I walked out the door, an uncomfortable maneuver nestled between brotherly and forceful. I was now property of Sami, my craggy-faced friend. I followed Sami out and another guard joined us. I remember him because he had bright orange hair, almost like a typical Irish guy. There was about ten seconds of small talk with me, joking about the Irish football [soccer] fans who had just run amok in Tel Aviv as we made our way to Sami's office. Then Sami said something to the tune of, "And now the games are over. No more laughing and no more "joking." My first thought was simply to comply, but my second one was, "Well, I'm not much use to

you if I can't laugh and joke. I'm not much good for anything else!" I obviously didn't say anything of the sort.

We came to a stairwell and there Sami opened his palm to indicate that I go in front of him. It was then that I noticed how small he was. While a whole foot separated us, ironically making him more Leprechaun than I was, he seemed to embody that peculiar parallel of being both small in stature yet large in presence. *Fascinating*, I thought to myself. *Who is this guy*? I had no idea that the little guy walking behind me as we went up that staircase was the one who would make me feel as small and insignificant as I had ever felt in all my life.

As I was going up the stairs I noticed there was a fire extinguisher on the wall but the signs around it were in Thai. *Weird*. We entered Sami's office and I sat down. Both Sami and the young man left me there and went somewhere else for maybe ten minutes but it felt like a lot longer. There was a camera on the upper wall to my left pointing at me. I looked around the office. There was nothing there. No notes, no computer that I can remember, no books, no nothing. Just a desk, a picture or two on the wall of something patriotic and a sign on the desk in a picture frame from the airport security services. I think there was a couch to my left under the camera.

Then they came in and the young man asked if I'd like a coffee. The Israelis make exceptional coffee so I obliged. He asked what type. I said Turkish coffee—an Israeli staple. Then he left and Sami informed me that this was his office and clutching the picture frame with the Israeli airport security picture in it, he said that this was who he worked for. Bear in mind I spent the last ten minutes looking at this bleak office and there was no way he worked here. So I asked him, since this was his office, why he didn't have any photos of his family? Not a great way to begin. . . I don't even think he answered the question.

He began to ask me what I was doing here and I answered in the plural. He quickly stopped me and said he wasn't inquiring about "my friend". He was only asking about me. I didn't remember your diplomatic status and just noted that as my second 'weird' observation. I told him I was there for the NATO conference on bio and nuclear terrorism. Funny, I remember him saying he had studied a lot on nuclear and bio terrorism. I frankly told him that I was there more for the soc/psych side of it: how people will react, how to contain humans to save lives, etc. I think it was at this point that the young man came in with the coffee. Perfectly brewed. *Brilliant, my twentieth of the day*!

I don't think we spent too long talking about the conference because Sami took the conversation to the Palestinians. I think it began by him asking my point of view on the whole Israel/Palestinian situation. I don't remember exactly what I said, but it was apolitical. Sami kept on pushing, as if I had something to reveal. Then the passport thing came up. I had two Irish passports (which they found by doing a more thorough search of my bag while I was either with Sami or waiting for him in his 'office'). But I had a very reasonable explanation for this: I booked the plane ticket using the older passport but it only had a few months left on it and Israel requires you to have at least six months. So I took it with me in case customs checked my ticket with my passport number, which they didn't. And then it dawned on me where he was going with this. "You lost your passport X time ago in Ramallah," Sami said. "We think you sold it to get Arabs across the checkpoints to bomb Israelis.

Actually, it wasn't so direct; he didn't accuse me as such, but he laid the facts bare. To me, this was an insult. He basically accused me (in a tactful, roundabout way) of aiding and abetting terrorism. I explained to him how it happened, that I would never do such a thing. But he shrugged me off saying in that typical belittling Israeli way, things like, "I know your kind. You come from pretty little human rightsy Europe with all your big ideals. You think the Arabs are nice little innocent people being bombarded by us for no reason at all. We are the bad guys and you, you people come here and we let you in, and you get hurt and killed, like that stupid American who laid down in front of the Army bulldozers and was flattened[226] or those stupid journalists who get killed in crossfire. . . " and on he went. He hit me right where it hurt—and it's a very small target—he accused me of being one hundred percent anti-Israeli.

He was right—the games were over. I raised my voice and told him again I would never do such a thing and then I told him in Hebrew. That was the first time I saw the younger man move. Sami turned to him. "You guys didn't know that I lived here for a year?" I shouted at them. Sami came back with, "Of course we knew that! What do you think we are?" etc. I knew I had to ride this wave so I kept going on, "How can you accuse me of assisting terrorists in terrorist actions when you didn't even know that I lived here and that I speak Hebrew!" I remember there was a calmness. Maybe it was just me, but I remember just looking at him and feeling hurt,like even though I don't know Sami, but to accuse me of being like every other Irish guy who comes to Israel and is blindly pro Palestinian (without doing proper research on the topic, just favoring the stereotype) hurt me. Silence. I remember looking at him. And him looking back. But that was a scary face and I didn't have the balls to hold the stare. I picked up my coffee, still almost full, and I noticed my hand was shaking. I was having a physical reaction and felt like a traitor—even though I wasn't at all. Horrible, truly horrible feeling. That feeling is the worst feeling I have ever felt. Even though I had no reason to be loyal to a country I never pledged allegiance to.

I don't know how long the silence lasted but Sami began to say something and I was looking down at my shoes feeling in the dumps. What would my Israeli friends say if they thought I had assisted in killing their people? "LOOK AT ME WHEN I'M TALKING TO YOU!" Sami shouted at me. I knew that as soon as I looked up he would see how vulnerable I was, how hurt I was. I tried to control my face as I lifted my head but I think I was either blushing or all the blood had gone from my face. Couldn't control it.

The questioning continued. Stuff along the lines of, "The conference doesn't begin for a few days, why are you early?" I told him that I wanted to see some friends in Jerusalem. "And?" he asked. "Are you planning on doing anything else?"

"Maybe I'll go into the West Bank for some interviews," I answered. It was such a stupid thing to say, I know, but I felt like I had to appease him somehow. As if telling him something I really shouldn't wouldn't make me such a bad guy after all. Stupid. But, he knew all about it. "Who are you going to meet?" etc. but I didn't know names. I told him I never really worked on a plan. And then the questions turned to why? Why would I want to talk to these people? I told him I just didn't understand how somebody could blow themselves up. I wanted to understand what it takes for somebody to do that.

Without realizing it, what I was saying was: "How bad do you Israelis have to make it for these guys, for them to go and do this?" I remember Sami raising his voice and me trying to retort. And then I began to rationalize. I said something along the lines of, "Look, you as an Israeli citizen cannot really go into the West Bank and ask these people why or really look at the dynamics. Only somebody who is impartial can do that. That's why they'll talk to us. " And Sami blew up. I don't remember exactly what he said but I do remember him jumping out of his seat and pointing his finger in my face and bellowing things at me. He had a huge golden ring on one of his fingers with a big blue Star of David on it and it was in my face. My eyes watered up.

He continued bellowing for a short while and sat back down again. "I can and do go in there whenever I want. I know all the people there. There's nothing, NOTHING you can teach or show me from doing this. NO MORE LIES. Do you know what we can do to you? Do you?" I just looked at him blankly. And here's what he said, or some derivative there-of: "We'll put a blindfold over you, take away your passport, your stupid Irish embassy won't know ANYTHING and we'll keep you and find out what your really doing here. " Now, at this point I had perked up. He wasn't shouting, he was sitting down and I felt so much better because the shouting had stopped. I thought to myself, "WOW, I'd love to do that! What an experience that would be!" Sami was pointing to the corner of the room, as an example of where I would be forced to sit with my blindfold. I didn't know what to say, it was alluring for me, so I said something like, "Really, you'd keep me in your office!"

I remember me starting the next phase of the conversation. I reassured him that I was not a threat to the State of Israel and that I had the country's best interests at heart—which I did. He laughed and so did the other guy. Sami said things along the lines of, "You don't know what it is to sacrifice for a country. You haven't lost friends. Your family didn't go through the Holocaust," etc. etc. etc. Then he spoke about the West Bank. He said I should not go there, under any circumstance. "If you do, I will find out. It's like a spider web and I will find out. If you go, you will no longer be welcome in Israel. " He said that somebody took a picture of me when I was there. He mentioned the place, next to some Belgian funded building or farm. I remembered it. And funny, I remember a young boy snapping a photo of me with his camera phone.

"The guy who took the photo gave it to us. " I quizzed him on it (day or night, wearing a baseball cap, etc.) but he said he didn't know the details. Then he told me that the guy who gave the photo to Israel told them that I was also having sex with goats. "You think these people are your friends; THEY'RE NOT. " He began to talk in Hebrew to the younger guy and I tried my best to listen in. When they finished I said, "I didn't understand" and Sami said I wasn't supposed to.

And then everything changed. He asked me what I knew about the Bible. I said I didn't know much. He told me that he has grandchildren and how much he loves them, how he wants them to have a much better life than he ever had. He said he was known in his village as a great storyteller and children came from all around to hear him. "Even this guy," he said, pointing at the young man who gave a shy smile. "Would you like to learn?" "Yes," I said. And off he went. For well over an hour. Maybe two hours. I wasn't really listening to him; I was just gawking at him. *What is going on here*? I remember thinking. I was completely off kilter. But it was a hell of a lot better than him shouting at me so I just continued gawking. The other guy really enjoyed the stories. Sami stopped when he got tired. I sat there for the whole biblical duration like an obedient schoolboy. It was calming and maybe that was the point, to calm me down before seeing you.

Before leaving he said, "Don't go to the West Bank. Repeat it. "

"I won't go to the West Bank. "

"You don't speak Hebrew. Repeat it. "

"I don't speak Hebrew. "

And right before leaving he said, "You know, this isn't Spielberg. " This is a funny remark because a few years later (or sometime later) Spielberg came out with the movie Munich. The younger man escorted me out. And there in the stairwell was the Thai sign again. I asked the younger man, "Why is this in Thai?"

"Weird," he said, "I've never noticed it before. "

I was led downstairs where I waited for a bit in a communal hall. An Englishman was next to me, mid-forties. "Are you stuck here as well?"

"Yep, security and all that you know," I answered. He showed me his passport. The poor bastard had flown from Tehran to Cyprus to Tel Aviv and had no idea the countries weren't the best of friends. We spoke for a bit then Sami came to see both of us. I don't remember what he said but he took me aside and said, "You remind me a lot of myself when I was your age. Now, you know where not to go!" And that was that. We entered Israel.

Reflecting on how he felt about it Ken adds, "Part of me really wanted to enter—just to see what would happen. And part of me thought, *If I enter and Sami finds out, I'll never be allowed back in*. And it dawned on me that I may not be allowed in anyway. Haven't been back since. "

I continue my research until January of 2006 when Pini indirectly threatens me. Then in September of 2006, I join members of the NATO research task group that I chair on *Psychosocial, Cultural and Organizational Aspects of Terrorism* for a NATO Advanced Research Workshop in Eilat, Israel hosted by Boaz Ganor, Katharina Von Knop and colleagues from the ITC, a prestigious Israeli think tank dealing with counter-terrorism. It was then that I understand that I still remain on an Israeli security list.

When I arrive at the airport I'm stopped at passport control, questioned and searched. I'm so used to it that it hardly registers and I don't notice until the next day when I'm taking an internal flight from Tel Aviv to Eilat that my suitcases now carry small red-alert security stickers. When the security officials see them, they immediately become alarmed, and I'm taken to the side for a more thorough search. And a female colleague from the UK that I've just met is taken along with me.

"She's just a colleague," I protest. "We don't even know each other. We just met over breakfast at the hotel. Please leave her out of this," I beg, knowing that Latifa, a young immigrant descent woman coming in from London, who has admitted to me at breakfast that she was violently attacked in a store just after entering Israel, will not handle the security search well. "Please!" I say leaning in to lower my voice as I plead with the soldiers. "She was violently attacked in a store yesterday in Israel, and I promise you she will fall apart if you take her to be searched. Don't make her take her clothing off at least, okay? And I promise you I just met her this morning—she's basically a stranger to me!" Unfortunately they don't budge and each of us is led in separate directions to have our luggage and bodies searched.

The soldiers return after some time, I dress myself and ask about Latifa. As predicted, she got hysterical and is crying. I pack up my luggage and we are reunited as the soldiers take us to sit at a table where they can observe us. "You missed this flight," they explain, "but there's another one in two hours. " During that two hours I sit with Latifa and listen to her rant about Israel. I tell her they have to treat everyone with any taint of suspicion as a possible threat, given how many times and how lethally Israel has been attacked by terrorists. "Try to see it from their perspective," I say, but she is furious. And I think, *How ironic that I, the person on their security list, is spending two hours defending Israeli security practices to an influential UK citizen who is offended by them and providing her with posttraumatic counseling for being attacked in their country and then humiliated at their airport!*

Eventually we are allowed to board the next plane to Eilat where we take part in the NATO conference *Hypermedia Seduction for Terrorist Recruitment.* Fortunately the organizers recognize the beauty of the place and allow us late afternoons on the beach and our evenings free. I swim in the warm Red Sea while looking over to Aqaba, where an oversize Jordanian flag waves, signaling to the vacationing Israelis that their territory extends only so far. On the other shores we see Saudi and Egypt, a reminder how vulnerable and surrounded Israel really is.

During the conference my European colleagues, Latifa, Berto, Thalia and Bernard, get upset by the anti-Palestinian and anti-Arab statements made by their Israeli colleagues, some of them quite bigoted, and they all feel uncomfortable about the intrusive security personnel they sense observing them. On the breaks they ask among themselves, "Have you noticed anything strange in your room? I think the Israelis were looking in my computer when I was at the beach—it was put back in the safe differently than I put it in," and so on. I don't notice anything in my room, but if the Israelis inserted their "Trojan horse" inside my computer earlier when they took it from me, they'd hardly need to physically hack into it anymore. And I'm pretty used to intrusive Israeli security so I just laugh and tell them, "This is Israel!"

One of the conference participants, Paul Roberts,[1] an ex-CIA operative, and I fall in together during the five day conference and begin a rhythm of swimming and walking along the beach and while doing so develop a friendship. It's fascinating to look into an ex- CIA operative's experience, and I'm surprised by how much he reveals about his former secret life. Paul easily agrees when I propose taking one of our nights to go to Taba, the Egyptian city on the other side of Eilat's borders. *With him, I should feel safe*, I think.

Exiting the taxi to the small border control station at the Israeli border I warn Paul, "I should let you know that because of my travel in the West Bank and Gaza the Israelis have put me on some kind of security list. I want to be sure I can return without a hassle and I don't want you to get involved if I get hassled, okay?"

"I'm not worried about that," Paul says. When we pass through the security point I stop to ask the soldiers, "Listen, I'm a researcher and frequently get stopped at your checkpoints. We are going to dinner and returning late and I don't want to go if I'm going to be held up here for hours coming back. Can you check your security list before I go and assure me all is okay?" I ask.

The soldier, an older portly gentleman laughs and says, "As long as you come back with shekels to spend in Israel you'll be welcomed!"

"No, please check my name on your list," I say, handing him my passport, "Please make sure and tell me if you will be here at midnight when we return. "

The jovial soldier laughs again and says, "Yes, I'll be here. Trust me, all the Israelis go to Taba to gamble and I'll let you back in. Just bring your shekels back with you!"

Paul and I pass through the Israeli border control and then the Egyptian one and from there take another taxi to Taba. Taba is similar to Eilat, with many resorts and high- rise hotels situated on the beaches of the Red Sea. We pick one and are about to enter through the security when Paul hesitates. "I have my knife," he says bending to unstrap it from his leg. "Maybe I'll just leave it here in the bushes," he says. Alarmed that he's carrying a knife and not liking the idea of him leaving it in the bushes—it somehow seems dangerous to do—I open my small handbag and tell him to drop it inside, "Give it to me. Guards never search women well," I say. I snap his knife shut inside my small handbag and walk toward the security

---

1 A pseudonym

guards. There is an electronic gate so I put my handbag down on the table beside it as I go through with Paul passing along behind while I engage the guard in conversation about how lovely Taba is. Happy to talk with a Western woman he doesn't notice when I slip my hand behind me and pick up my small clutch again without it passing through the sensors. I flip it open for him to glance inside and ask him about the hotel restaurant as I slip my lipstick out to reapply and snap the purse shut. He smiles failing to notice Paul's knife on the bottom or that it's not been scanned.

Laughing Paul and I proceed to the restaurant and find a table out on the beach while I ask, "Why are you carrying a knife?" He doesn't have a good answer but I suppose he doesn't feel entirely safe here in Egypt. The moon is full and shines down on the sea as we order our meal and drink wine talking about his experiences recruiting local informers for the agency and my work interviewing terrorists. At some point after a few glasses of wine and a lot of sharing, we walk along the beach. I've already been wondering to myself what Paul's interest in me is and if he has been sent to try to recruit me to work for the agency. I've realized for some time that they are probably interested in my work and could use someone like me, but frankly I've never been interested to work for a security organization, especially the CIA. It would violate my values to "trick" people into opening up to me and imperil themselves and loved ones by doing so.

The conversation turns intensely personal as we begin discussing family. After I say something about my sister, Paul remarks, "She's a schizophrenic, isn't she?" And my blood suddenly turns to ice.

"What did you say?" I ask staring into his eyes as my mind races ahead. *What does this man know about me? Has he read some CIA file on me?* I ask myself as my mind races trying to decide who he is and what he really wants. *Has he's been sent here to recruit me? If so, he's just blown his cover completely because NO ONE could know this information except someone who has read her file, and mine—if there is one*!

"She's a schizophrenic," Paul repeats. "You told me that earlier," he continues without averting his eyes. *He's good, really good.* He think he's recovered but he hasn't, because NO ONE knows this information and I would never have referred to my sister as a schizophrenic! In fact it's a diagnosis she once received temporarily from a psychiatrist that I thought was daft and I called him up to ream him out about it. Perhaps it still shows up on some medical file. *How does he know this information? No one knows this*!

I think as I nod and answer, "Oh, I didn't realize I said that. She's not really a schizophrenic but some doctor thought she was one once," I say, my blood still icy cold, my mind racing as I try to act as though everything is fine. *He's still in the Agency! He's here to recruit me*! I shouldn't really be frightened by it but I am.

Paul and I continue our conversation, with me steering it far from the CIA and from anything personal about me as we make our way back to the Arab checkpoint. In the taxi, I hand him back his knife.

" I don't think I can get it through the border control," I say and he slips it into his side pants pocket saying, " I can—watch and see. " At the border, I pass through first and again try to engage the soldiers in conversation as I watch nervously as Paul sets off the metal detector. He takes some change out of his pocket and passes through again and repeats this four more times taking various small metal items out of various pockets as he exhausts the soldier's patience. "I guess I'm getting old and forgetful," he says smiling genuinely at the soldier who waves him through after the fourth pass. I smile thinking, *He sure knows the tricks of his trade*!

When we arrive at the Israeli checkpoint my name must come up on a list again because the soldier who we present our passports to takes me aside to take a seat in an adjacent area and Paul, against my protestations, follows. "I'm going to be here for hours Paul," I tell him. "You should go. No sense sitting here bored!" Paul refuses to leave, and I ask the soldiers where the portly one is that assured us we could return easily. I tell him that we have an early morning flight to catch and cannot afford delays. The older one is gone, and this one is doing his job and refuses to answer any questions. We sit for a few hours talking and laughing about the microphones that are probably recording all we say when finally the soldiers call me.

"Off to the search," I say to Paul without realizing I've failed to explain this part to him.

The female soldier takes me along with a female colleague into an area with a table and bench and pulls a curtain around us while Paul becomes infuriated standing on the other side. "You can't search her!" he yells from beyond the curtain. "She's the wife of a U. S. Ambassador! You'll create a diplomatic incident with the US government!" he shouts. "You have no right!" Meanwhile I cannot understand why Paul is so upset so I call back to him from inside the curtain, "Everything's fine, Paul! Don't worry! Calm down!" When I emerge they take the highly agitated and fuming Paul into the same area and I sit waiting. As they pull the curtain shut around him, I quip, "Bend over!"

And Paul who still doesn't understand it's not a full body cavity search quips back, "Well I've been working for the government all my life so I'm used to that!" Then he goes silent. When he emerges he's composed, having realized it's not bodily invasive, and we are passed through passport control and catch a taxi where we laugh heartily over his misperception and upset. "Thanks for throwing a fit in my behalf!" I say laughing. Paul explains that the Israelis found his knife and were angry about that as well.

The next day the conference participants meet in the morning for breakfast and a few of us, including Paul, take a last swim at the beach before packing up to meet out at the bus taking our group to the Eilat airport. When we board the bus, Paul initially takes his seat by me but when we are all asked to hand our passports up to the front he pats his pocket and suddenly panics, "I must have left my passport in the safe!" he says and takes his bag, running back into the hotel to retrieve it. And he doesn't return before the bus takes off. "What about Paul?" everyone asks but the conference organizers insist we need to get to the airport and not miss our flight taking us back to Tel Aviv.

At the terminal I keep a watch out for Paul wondering what could have happened and eventually he texts me explaining that his passport has gone missing. He thinks it fell out when we were exiting the cab the night before or the Israelis took it from his safe while we were out swimming, but he's only going to be able to fly to Tel Aviv and then he'll have to go to the US Embassy to get a new one. "Reminds me of when I was rolled in Saint Petersburg," he texts, and I recall him telling me how the KGB followed him and stole his documents on a trip into the Soviet Union some years back while he was still active in the CIA. I'm confused why the Mossad would take Paul's passport and wonder if there is much more going on than I'm aware of, but I soon find I have my own troubles to contend with. [227] When I pass through the last security check to enter the plane an Israeli soldier takes my passport while saying, "Come with me please. " My European NATO colleagues already fed up with Israeli security and angered that they prevented me from traveling with the group *into* Eilat, start to protest.

"Don't make a fuss!" I say and give them each a hug goodbye before departing with the soldier, tears inexplicably filling my eyes. I generally hate goodbyes and it feels a lot like abandonment to have them all board the plane leaving me behind. I quickly pull myself together realizing I'm probably confusing being abandoned too many times as a child (my mother died when I was young) with what's happening now. I sit waiting while I watch the clock tick away. *Damn! I'm going to miss my flight again*! I go to argue with the soldiers a few times about not wanting to miss my flight but they give away nothing and tell me to sit down again. Minutes before my plane is to depart, they suddenly release me and I race to the counter where the agent tells me I better run, indicating the direction.

I run to the end of the corridor but once there, I see that there are six gates and none have English signs. There is no one about but a Russian cleaning lady. I ask her in English what gate is going to Tel Aviv. She stares at me uncomprehending until I realize *she's Russian*! And I quickly ask my question in Russian.

"There," she answers in Russian, pointing to one of the six exits and I run through the doorway with my briefcase in hand only to find I've been spit out onto the tarmac where there is a line of airplanes ready to depart! Not knowing what to do and with the exit door having already shut and locked behind me I run toward the closest plane until I notice there, farther out on the tarmac, is the one holding all my colleagues and they are waving anxiously to me through the windows! I run to them, completely frantic that a plane will plow through me or the police will arrest me for running across the surely forbidden tarmac. The door is still open and a stewardess meets me halfway down the steps grabbing my arm and hustling me on to the plane as they shut the door behind me.

Thalia and Bernard say, "We threw a fit and refused to fly if they didn't let you board and fly with us!" I smile and gush out a baffled "Thank you!" as I take my seat and stare out the window when, just as before, tears of distress stream down my face. *Damn Israelis! Don't let them see you cry! They're punishing you for going to Taba! Better get ready for more in Tel Aviv*!

True to course when we land in Tel Aviv, I'm separated again from my colleagues and I get the search going home as well, but nothing more than that.

Later back in Brussels, I am approached by two other former CIA operatives. Susan,[1] a very beautiful blonde scientist I've met at various counter-terrorism conferences, suddenly upon my return takes a renewed

---

1 A pseudonym

interest in me and invites me to lunch a few times, where she divulges that she has worked as contractor agent, going into high-level scientific meetings with our allies and reporting back to the Agency about what she learns. When I tell her about meeting Paul in Israel and wondering if he was trying to recruit me she responds, "Paul Roberts! He was a very high level operative, Anne. He's probably still working for them. Haven't you received any training as the wife of a U. S. diplomat in understanding when someone is trying to groom you for clandestine recruitment? I would think that would be standard training before you go overseas?" I shake my head as she goes on about how all the international espionage agencies try to recruit diplomats and their family members and how we should be trained to recognize and repel it. Likewise when she admits to her clandestine activities it seems she now works for the Mossad, although she doesn't outright say so, and it also seems she is trying to interest me to join in, asking me things like, "Would you ever agree to go to a meeting and write up a psychological profile of someone you met there?"

As Susan keeps inviting me to lunches and talking the spy life up, I can't help but wonder if she is working with Paul who is now e-mailing me all the time and seems to know more about my family, especially my husband, than he lets on. I begin to wonder if he has access to the e-mails going between my husband and I as Daniel currently serves as Deputy Ambassador in Iraq. Then Susan arranges a lunch between Janey, a retired CIA operative, and herself, telling me that Janey really wants to meet me. I wonder why, but say nothing until at the lunch I bring up Paul and say it seems he knows things about me that he couldn't possibly know unless he had access to things an ordinary person wouldn't know. This brings about a chilled silence in some ways confirming all of my fears but Janey quickly recovers saying, "Oh that's not possible. He's retired, Anne. " I think, *Yeah, my foot he is*!

Having no idea how to handle the swirl of intrigue around me, I call a trusted friend on the phone and tell her that I think the CIA is interested in recruiting me but that they haven't come straight out and said it, which makes me feel very off balance. I repeat this a few times that I have no interest in working for them, even saying I hope they are listening and will leave me alone. And amazingly both Susan and Janey fall immediately out of contact and Paul keeps writing to me, but I think it's motivated from true friendship and nothing more.

I return to Israel a few more times, once to take my daughter's Godmother, Elisabeth, on the Ethiopian Orthodox version of a Hage trip—the trip to Mecca that Muslims are required to do once in a lifetime if their resources permit and that some Orthodox Christians take to Jerusalem. I also take her not only to Jerusalem, but also to the Kinneret (Sea of Galilee), the claimed baptismal site of Jesus along the Jordan River, the Dead Sea and Bethlehem. Going to Bethlehem means we cross over to the West Bank via Palestinian taxi, which ends with another search at the airport upon exiting Israel. I tell Elisabeth to take her distance from and pretend she doesn't know me when we go through the Ben Gurion airport security checks, but she is nervous to be alone and insists that she'll stay with me.

Elisabeth, a stately older woman, also gets the full body and luggage search right along with me, and becomes enraged at the humiliation of it vowing never to return to Israel. Again, as with Latifa, I try to explain to her how many times Israel has been attacked and that it's necessary for them to be cautious, but she refuses to forgive them for submitting her to such an indignity.

Perhaps finally my name seems to be removed from the Israeli security list when over a period of years I do not return for any more Palestinian field research, as my last trip into Israel in 2009 to help a U. S. embassy colleague with a legal suit she was pursuing was completely uneventful. Going through the normal airport procedures I almost feel sad, like some rite of passage into and out of Israel was absent. I guess there's always next time as well as other places to get hassled!

Birzeit Universit - Painting of the wall, 2004

Ramallah- Boys playing "Checkpoint", 2004

Beit Fourik - Destroyed home, 2004

Beit Fourik - Grandfather and Grandaughter in destroyed home, 2004

Beit Fourik - Grandfather in destroyed home, 2004

Jericho - Hamdi Quran in prison, 2004

Jericho - Ahmed Sa'adat in prison, 2004

Nablus - Darine Abu Aisha's sister showing Darine's scrapbook, 2005

Nablus - Darine Abu Aisha's mother holding her diploma, 2005

Nablus - Darine Abu Aisha's scrapbook, 2005

Bethlehem - A shrine of Ayat al Akhras in her family's home, 2005

Bethlehem - Father of Ayat al Akhras, 2005

Hebron - Fadi Ziad al Fahudi's little sister wearing a Hamas head-band, 2005

Hebron - Fadi Ziad al Fahudi's "Martyr" picture, 2005

Niece and nephew of Wafa Idris playing in front of her mural,
2004

Nephew and brother of Wafa Idris playing with toy gun, 2004

Mother of Wafa Idris, 2005

Mother of Ayat al Akhras, 2005

Iraq - Me in Camp Victory, 2006

Iraq - Rohan Gunaratana, Ustaz Mohammed and me in Camp Victory, 2006

Iraq - Rohan and me in Camp Victory, 2006

Ramallah - Ken fooling around with my headscarf, 2005

Gaza - Ken entering Gaza (with me), 2005

CHAPTER 45

Sidi Moumen and the Casablanca Bombers

It's May 2005 and I'm in a plane on the tarmac in Brussels, Belgium where I live about to take off for Casablanca, Morocco. I'm buckling in when I hear a man screaming in the back of the plane. I don't understand what he's saying but he's clearly in distress. He screams in both French and Arabic throughout the safety presentation and I stop the stewardess as she passes by, "If you don't mind my asking, is there something wrong with that man in the back—the guy who is screaming? I'm a psychologist and would be happy to help if you need assistance," I offer.

"Oh, he's a rejected asylum case, or an illegal immigrant who has committed some criminal act!" she explains. "They always scream until we get in the air! Their lawyers tell them to scream. He should settle down after we take off—when he realizes it's too late."

"Wow!" I comment. "I've never heard anything like it! What if he *doesn't* stop?"

"Then we turn back," she answers matter-of-factly. "We get these on a lot of our Africa flights. We're used to it," she smiles kindly, "but thanks so much for your offer to help."

Later when I use the bathroom, I see him dark eyed and subdued now, sitting in the back seat, silent but his eyes still wide with terror as he sits between two Belgian police agents to whom he is handcuffed. Knowing that Morocco has a tough prison system that still uses torture I wonder what he will face upon landing.

My colleague Dr. Mokhtar Benabdallaoui, a friend and university professor at Hassan II University, comes to pick me up at the airport. He has offered to help me to try to make interviews in Sidi Moumen,[228] and I'm staying with his family in Casablanca. We met earlier at a counterterrorism conference and corresponded for some time by e-mail, though during the U.S. attack of Fallujah in Iraq, Mokhtar said that he could barely write to me because he was so angry at Americans for what he saw as their mistreatment of Iraqis. Sometimes I think that I am Mokhtar's project: the

American he is determined to educate about the plight of Palestinians and how Arabs see America's actions in the world.

The scenery is beautiful between the airport and Mokhtar's apartment in downtown Casablanca. We pass through a grove of pine trees along the highway and I comment on how lovely it is.

"You wouldn't say that if you knew what happens there inside that forest," Mokhtar answers. "That's our prison and your country just sent a group of prisoners picked up by U.S. forces to be interrogated there. They are probably hanging from the ceiling and being beaten right now as we speak," he says bitterly. Staring at the grove of trees that a moment earlier had looked so peaceful, I realize that there are secrets and suffering locked inside their depths that may never be told.[229]

When we arrive at Mokhtar's apartment we take off our shoes and his wife, Sadjida, a beautiful Syrian born woman who speaks no English, ushers us inside. She's extremely hospitable, showing me to their younger son's room where I will stay. She appears excited to speak, through translation, to this exotic foreign guest.

"Where will the little one sleep?" I ask upon entering their son's room, realizing they have given me their only spare room.

"Oh, he likes to jump in our bed," Mokhtar answers, "or he'll sleep out here." He points out that their living room is completely lined along its walls with built in sofas lavishly upholstered in rich blue fabric. "See, we can have many guests here!" Mokhtar pats the sumptuous sofa cushions.

Their bathroom has an Arabic style toilet that one squats over with a small hose for washing in lieu of toilet paper and I hope I don't have the same challenges—and wet pants—that I had in Beit Fourik, Palestine. I settle my things in and we have a nice meal together that Sadjida has obviously fussed quite a bit over to make for us.

The next day, I attempt to dress modestly in a midi length dress with a long coat over it. I ask Mokhtar if my outfit is modest enough, and he eyes my bare legs poking out under the midi-skirt and laughs heartily, "Not with those bare legs sticking out." But we proceed and Mokhtar insists we start by going to the U.S. embassy in Rabat where he has a friend. He wants to be sure we'll be covered if the authorities get upset over my research.

I'm here to interview the friends and family of eleven of the twelve suicide bombers who exploded themselves at four separate locations on May 16, 2003. The young men from twenty to twenty-three years old, self detonated at two restaurants, in the doorway of the five star Hotel Farah where forty Jewish guests were staying, at a Jewish community center and the last one insensibly exploded himself alone in a Jewish cemetery killing only himself. In total the group killed thirty-three victims and injured another one hundred. And by May of 2004, in a gross overreaction, the government had arrested over two thousand Islamists in connection with the attacks. This opportunistic move was perhaps intended to completely snuff out the emerging Salafi-led Islamist movement in Morocco—a movement thus far more associated with non-violent political change than terrorism.

As we drive from Casablanca to Rabat, I notice many billboards in the shape of a hand. Mokhtar explains that the hand is a common symbol in the Middle East and the billboards are part of the popular "Don't touch my country campaign", which were sponsored by an NGO after the attacks as means of trying to solidify social support against terrorist groups and their ideologies.

We meet with Mokhtar's friend who works as a local hire in the embassy and tells us that we need to be careful going into the slum. "Right now is a sensitive time," he warns. "Many journalists are asking about the bombings because it's the anniversary." He tells us it's okay to try to do the research and doesn't think I'll be arrested for attempting interviews in the slum but warns that I may be hassled by the police.

Mokhtar, like many middle class Moroccans struggles to provide for his family and holds two jobs (working both as a professor and as a commentator reviewing books on a popular television show), so he is not available to go with me into the slums in the following days. Instead after an Arabic breakfast with his family we drive into the university and Mokhtar sends me off with a female student, Makda, whose family lives there. Makda and I take a taxi to the edge of slum where she shows me into her family's shanty town house. It's made of concrete blocks with a corrugated metal roof and does not have running water, electricity or a telephone. The floor is cheap linoleum and I think it may be spread out over bare earth. The entire house has two rooms and is ramshackle. Makda's mother and father are home and greet us warmly, offering us a lamb stew for lunch.

I feel guilty to accept but know that in their culture, it will be more of an insult not to eat so we sit on the floor together to dine with Makda's parents and younger siblings gathered around. They are dressed in clean but worn clothes and have bare feet.

After a short time, Makda's contacts arrive and she introduces me to them, having already explained to me that they are adherents of the militant jihadi ideology, which is close to that al Qaeda promulgates. They also live in the slum. We sit on blankets on the floor in one of the rooms while Makda attempts to translate. It turns out that she has only a limited vocabulary and has a very hard time translating and they are also reticent to share much more than that they support the militant jihadi ideas. They are uncomfortable with my American clothes, and during our interview one of them asks me if I can cover the bottoms of my bare legs, as it's distracting for him.

When I meet Mokhtar at the end of the day I feel frustrated but I also don't want to be too demanding given his situation so when he asks, I tell him it went well.

"You think Makda can introduce me to the friends of the actual bombers?" I ask. Sajida is meanwhile again filling the dining table in the center of the room with a delicious home-cooked meal for us. I've offered to help but she won't have it.

"To tell you the truth, Anne," Mokhtar explains, "I'm surprised you even got into the slum at all today! I didn't think the authorities would let you go in. I guess Makda lives only on the edge of it, but they watch everything in the slum nowadays and I thought they would stop you. Maybe it's because of your husband's position that they stayed away. Usually no one gets longer than ten minutes to make interviews in the slum —even journalists—before the police come and tell them to leave." I file the information away but don't let it deter me.

We sit at the table and Sadjida serves everyone plates of savory lamb, rice and vegetables. Condi Rice appears on the television and Sadjida comments excitedly in Arabic to her husband. He translates telling me that Sadjida is much more extremist than he. Sadjida is very upset about the U.S. led coalition invasion of Iraq and she simply *hates* Condi Rice. "She calls her the cockroach," Mokhtar explains, and I burst out laughing.

"What is your opinion of why Jordanians and Syrians go as bombers to attack the U.S. forces in Iraq?" I ask Sadjida, knowing that in only a month my husband will be posted there as the head of the U.S. reconstruction office (IRMO) and could fall prey to such an attack from one of her citizens.

"It's very simple," Sajida answers with her husband translating. "It's resistance against a foreign occupier. I agree with them completely!"

Mokhtar apologizes but I ask him to let her speak freely. I want to hear the truth.

"Would you go if you had the chance?" I ask, curious to hear how strongly she feels.

"*Me?*" she answers. "I don't have such courage! And I have a child and responsibilities here," she says, waving her hand over the table laden with food and looking around her home as if to demonstrate that all would fall apart if she departed. Given how hard I've seen her working the past few days, that's probably true. "But yes, I agree with them and I'd give money! I'd give any material support I could! You must understand that for me the Arabic people are all the same people. What happens to Iraqis also happens to me!" Indeed many in the Middle East must share her views as in these first years of the U.S. led invasion in Iraq, hundreds of Saudis, Syrians, Jordanians, Moroccans and even European militant jihadis have streamed across the borders into Iraq as "foreign fighters", many ready to "martyr" themselves in suicide actions against the U.S. led forces.

Mokhtar apologizes again and tells me that he views his wife's bluntness as inhospitable, violating his Arab views of how to treat a guest. I reassure him that I am grateful for her honesty and for the opportunity to learn how others see the actions of my country—and that I am also not a big supporter of the invasion. We continue our dinner and Mokhtar insists on opening a bottle of red wine at the end of it despite that many Muslims don't drink.

"I don't follow those rules," he explains telling me how he also talked his wife out of wearing her headscarf. We drink together while I beg him to give me another student to go back into the slums with—one who is a real translator and who is not afraid.

"I think I can find the friends of the actual bombers myself if I have a good translator along with me," I insist. "Just give me a good student from the English department, okay?" He nods and makes a phone call to his colleague on the English faculty to set it up.

As the evening progresses, we discuss politics in Morocco, and Mokhtar explains to me that religion is a very powerful force for creating political change in Arabic countries. "When freedom of expression is so lacking and government repression is so strong and there is no possibility to speak against it safely," Mokhtar explains, "there is one way that exists that not even the government can speak against and that way is religion. Then religious expression for the purposes of political discourse on behalf of promoting social justice can be a very powerful medium. Because no one, not even the government, can go against the Koran!"

Indeed Islamists such as those following in the footsteps of the Muslim Brotherhood who attempt to solve modern political problems by referencing Muslim texts have been in recent years finding a high resonance for their message among Arabs. These populations are tired of corrupt and repressive political regimes, and these regimes in turn fear the ability of such opposition groups to use Islam as a rallying call for change. This is perhaps why the Moroccan government used the Casablanca bombings as an excuse to quickly round up, arrest and jail thousands of Islamists who likely had nothing to do with the attacks. Mokhtar remains optimistic about social change in his country and even supports the Islamists opposition groups.

"I think we can have democracy here," Mokhtar says. "But the democracy Arabs make will be our version of it, not a Western version." Indeed if the Islamists are allowed to run for government here and in other Arab countries, they will likely win and take power, we both agree, and we finish our supper discussing what that would likely look like. Islamists who agree to a democratic form of government may outwardly adhere to democratic forms but that they are unlikely to allow freedom of speech that conservative Muslims may find offensive; their version of human rights may favor collective versus individual rights; and an independent judiciary and equal social, economic and political rights for all elements of society may be missing in an Islamist democracy. "But I don't think they will vote in Sharia law here," Mokhtar states.

That night after supper Mokhtar takes us for a drive to preview the slum more closely. He has an old Mercedes and I feel uncomfortable going there in such a nice car but he assures me, "We won't drive inside. We'll just circle it."

As we drive along the edge of the shantytown, I see that it consists of a jumbled mass of shacks constructed of whatever building materials were available.

"In winter there is no heat," Mokhtar says. "And there is cold rain and it leaks between those roofs," he says pointing to the corrugated metal held in place by stones atop the mishmash construction of homes. "And in summer it's deadly hot and the stench of the garbage here becomes overwhelming.

"The families can have six or seven children and they all sleep in one room," Mokhtar explains. "Of course they witness sexual acts. For sons, their mother is sexualized, they sleep close to their sisters and in teen years their sex drive is strong but the only choices are to engage in homosexuality or incest."*He may be right*, I think to myself, *but in truth close sleeping quarters define most of the developing world and that doesn't necessarily translate to sexualized mothers and incest.*

At the far end of a dirt field, there are large public sinks with running water serving the shanty homes that don't have water. Mokhtar calls this the agora, and we see women collecting water in large jugs and colorful buckets that they lug away and others leaning over communal sinks doing the washing.

"Do they have communal toilets here?" I ask, but neither Mokhtar nor his wife know for sure.

Some young boys play soccer nearby on a litter strewn dirt patch and swirls of red dust fly up encircling their heads.

"Imagine the condition they come home in, to homes with no running water," Mokhtar remarks. Along the roadside we see multiple small packs of older teenage boys hanging out. They are all dressed nicely and are well groomed but look bored. These are the unemployed of Sidi Moumen, Mokhtar explains.

I notice the girls wear colorful floor length robes: Moroccan style abayas that zip up the front and have triangular shaped hoods that fall down their backs. Some wear headscarves and some tie them creatively so the fringe of their scarves falls in seductive patterns along their foreheads and necks. They form a graceful presence walking through the ghetto in twos or threes, unchaperoned but never alone. As I gaze out the window observing all this poverty, I feel guilty sitting in a Mercedes.

• • •

"You shouldn't have dressed like that," Mokhtar says the next day as we drive in his car across town to the university. Now I am in a turquoise Moroccan style long cotton tunic that falls to my knees worn over a pair of matching trousers. My chest, arms and legs are all fully covered. And I've put my hair back and up in a bun and I'm even wearing Moroccan leather slippers. I bought the whole outfit after spending the day with Makda. "You don't have to wear our clothes!" Mokhtar insists. "Women are free here!"

It's true and Mokhtar should know—his mother is a leading feminist and together, they can take credit for having fought for the rights for women have to initiate divorce in Morocco and retain property that other Arab and Maghreb people do not. And now he is offended that I have chosen to dress in the traditional Moroccan style of dress.

"Yesterday the guy I interviewed asked me to cover my bare legs with a blanket," I explain. "I'm just trying to get it right."

When we arrive at the university, Mokhtar introduces me to my translator for the day: Abdul, a bright faced intelligent looking young man. "I want to go into the slum and try to find the friends of the Casablanca bombers and interview them," I say after introductions are made. "I'm not afraid to go into the slum, are you?" I ask.

"No, I'm not," he answers smiling warmly. I like him already.

"Good. Are my clothes okay?" I ask, indicating my Moroccan style dress. He nods. "And it's okay for you and I to go there together? It's appropriate?"

"Yes," Abdul nods.

"Okay, let's go!" I say. But when we get to the street I realize I have not changed money yet so we cannot hail a taxi. Abdul tells me the banks aren't open so early so it's better if we go to his home nearby—he has some cash and he'll finance our taxis until later in the day when I can change money and repay him. We walk a few blocks to his house and once inside I see that his family of six live in a two-room cement block unit that has barely any furniture. Although he's obviously poor, Abdul digs his cash out from under a pile of clothing and leads us back out to the street where we find a taxi to take us to Sidi Moumen.

When we arrive, Abdul and I get out of the taxi and walk across the garbage-strewn field that separates the Sidi Moumen slum from the busy street. It is only May, but the stench from rotting garbage is already strong. At the far end of the field is the "agora" of yesterday—the large public sinks with running water serving the shanty homes that don't have water. Some people are there collecting water from a communal spigot and others are washing themselves and doing laundry in the large sinks. We pass over the sandy rubble and I stop in our tracks facing the blocks of shantytown ahead of us. Colorful freshly washed clothes hang on lines strung above some of the corrugated metal roofs drying in the hot sun and satellite dishes dot the horizon above many of the homes. *They even have satellite TV here?* I think to myself.

"Are you scared to go into the slum?" I ask Abdul again as we are still paused before the entrance to the slum.

"No," he answers, looking me in the eyes. "Are you?"

"No," I answer. It's totally intimidating though and once we are inside I suppose we could disappear without a trace, but I'm curiously unafraid, drawing courage from Abdul's confidence as well. As we approach the rows of shacks we see that there is a barbershop on one side with some young men hanging about outside.

I explain to Abdul how I like to work: that I just go up to people and ask them directly about what I am working on and see how they respond. "It's kind of strange, but seems to work," I tell him. "And one person leads to the next until I finally get the interviews I want." Abdul looks a bit anxious with this but agrees to try it.

On the corner of the slum we see a handsome young boy maybe seventeen or eighteen hanging out. I tell Abdul, "Let's go and talk with him." This boy nervously admits he knew one of the bombers. He explains how his friend suddenly turned ultra conservative and religious, giving up drugs and girls while our informant tells us a bit shamefacedly that he continues to struggle with drugs. Indeed, he seems under the haze of drugs even now and appears deeply despairing. He becomes upset telling us so we thank him and move on.

Abdul and I then turn inward and begin to walk through the slum. I don't feel ready to approach anyone else. The last interaction left a very sad impression on me and I need time to process it. I also want to focus my attention on the slum as we enter deeper inside. It's lunchtime and women are cleaning their homes. The cloth doors that hang down over the openings to their shanty homes are pulled to the side while they sweep debris out to the hardened mud alleyways that separate the homes. I am amazed at how even here the Arabic tradition of keeping a clean home is respected. These women are not drugged, addicted and irresponsible women, but rather prideful and hardworking despite their circumstances.

We walk quietly along the alleyways observing everything. Outside some of the homes, men sit in chairs they have placed outside, smoking, or playing games in small groups. Small children run in and out of the doorways and older children ride run-down bikes or play in small groups. Every once in a while we pass a very small shop that sells groceries. Outside the shops teenage boys listlessly hang about. As we pass each doorway, I look into the eyes of those who glance at us and greet them with a friendly 'Salaam Aleikum', watching their responses. Even though I am wearing Moroccan clothes, I'm clearly from somewhere else, but there is no hostility except maybe questioning looks from the teenagers hanging around at the shops.

We arrive at a big market on one edge of the slum. Abdul asks if we should turn back as there are many people gathered there. There is warning in his eyes, but I push ahead determined to see everything. We walk up and down the two rows of vendors selling raw unrefrigerated meats with flies buzzing about and many foods I cannot identify, little plastic toys and the cheapest plastic kitchen wares I have ever seen, though I can see they are valued here by how the slum dwellers pick them up and admire them without purchasing.

I buy a fresh orange juice for Abdul and I, and we smile to each other drinking it. *Even here there are some pleasures*! I think sipping it under the hot sun. We turn around taking another twisted alleyway back again through the slum and when we circle back to the sinks, I turn to Abdul.

"Your going to think I'm crazy but I'm setting up my office here," I say. He looks at me like, *Yes you are crazy*, but I continue. "This rock here will be my office, let's sit down. You watch," I explain. "Someone will come and it will be just who we need to talk to." I have this peaceful feeling that I sometimes get. I feel this place strongly now, its rhythms and it's mood, and although I'm sure it can change rapidly and I only feel a small part of it, something inside tells me this is the place to wait, that I'll soon meet the person I need to interview. I don't know why, but I am sure of it. So I sit on the rock in the hot sun waiting.

"It's a pretty strong sun here," Abdul says, doubt lacing his voice.

"I know, it won't be long," I say. And I am right. It's a strange thing to have these intuitions but I have grown to trust them. I've taken my disposable camera out of my purse and started snapping pictures of the homes and the small children playing around when a well-dressed good-looking young man walks up to me.

"Why don't you take my picture?" he asks.

I laugh and say, "Okay, who are you?" and snap his picture.

"*Who* are *you*?" he asks in return and I tell him that I am a psychology professor from Belgium, come to learn about the boys who were the Casablanca bombers.

"I knew them," he says. "They lived on my street." Voila! My intuition has worked and we are ready to roll!

"Well, that's who I came to meet!" I say with a big smile. "Will you give me an interview about them?" I ask picking up my tablet from my "office" rock.

"Sure, but not here," he says. "It's too hot out here in the full sun. Let's go over there under the shade," he indicates a shanty house that has a corrugated plastic overhang. The young man, Jamal[1] , pulls a small stool over for me to sit on and together we take seats in the shade of the overhang with Abdul ready to translate. As Jamal begins to fill me in on the lives of the suicide bombers, a small crowd of young men who have become interested in what we are discussing surrounds us. Some of them also knew the bombers and add comments as well. Two or three of these young men are Jamal's friends and were also neighbors of the bombers and they seem the best informed. When some comments are made that are wrong according to Jamal, small arguments occur. I scribble feverishly in my notebook trying to keep up and sort through what Jamal and his friends say is the truth versus rumor.

As I'm taking notes, a hush falls over the crowd and the interpreter suddenly turns to ask me a question that someone in the crowd has put forward.

"They want to know who you are and where you're from," Abdul says his face suddenly a cloud of anxiety. I've faced this many times before and I know what they are thinking, so I decide to address it head on.

"CIA and Mossad!" I say looking deadpan at Abdul and knowing these two words will need no interpretation. Abdul gasps, his face a mask of horror and I crack up laughing while telling him to go ahead and translate it. "It's what they think anyway!" I say laughing heartily. But as I do I suddenly realize how small the space has become. My back is against the shanty wall and there is a crowd of at least thirty young men pressing in to be part of this "interview". *I guess they could rip me apart and be done with me*, I think to myself but I still don't regret having addressed their suspicion. Abdul looks terrified. But my laughter works—the tension disappears and we continue.

But now it's Jamal's turn to get upset. "They are telling you all wrong!" he complains, tiring of arguing with those who he says are just making things up. "Come over here," he says getting up to walk away, taking his two friends, Bashir and Yousef who also lived near the bombers with him.

---

1 All the Moroccans interviewed in this chapter have been given pseudonyms along with the translator.

Abdul and I follow him behind a large oriental carpet someone has hung up to clean near their hovel. Jamal has taken my stool and puts it down between the carpet and the wall and he and his friends surround me again inside the small two foot space. Others from the group have followed and try to wedge into the small space as well to hear what they are telling me but the young men block them from entering and they speak softly. I ask why they are concerned.

"There are informers [to the police],and we could get in trouble for talking about the bombers. We don't want the others to hear what we are telling you," he explains.

Jamal goes on to explain that the boys on his block were all drafted to their mission by a recruiter inside the slum but that another man from Fez was the real person in charge. "He organized everything," Jamal says. "Our friends were like us before they got involved with the recruiter. They did drugs and slept with girls, but after they met him they completely changed. He took them to the mosque and taught them and they started praying and going all the time to the mosque." I write notes again, but Jamal is still suspicious of the boys trying to poke their heads in and listen.

"There are too many informants here," Jamal suddenly says. Irritated he adds, "Come, we'll go to *my* house." Again we follow Jamal, a small crowd trailing behind through the slums until we arrive at Jamal's shanty house. Allowing only Bashir and Yousef to come inside with us, Jamal leads us into the narrow house,we file through a small kitchen and into a narrow bedroom. I suddenly realize, *That's the entire house*.

"Sit here," Jamal says, indicating the only bed. Abdul and I obey and perch on the twin bed, while the three young men bring kitchen chairs and gather close around. Jamal goes quickly to the kitchen and comes back with a tray filled with five glasses of soft drinks. I feel impressed that even in his poverty he is a good host.

"Listen, we won't have much time to tell you about them, before someone interrupts," Jamal says in a conspiratorial voice. His friends nod. "Let's go through them one by one," he says and together the boys start reciting the names of each of the eleven bombers who came from their shantytown.

"Rachid was twenty-nine and his cousin was almost twenty-two. They were both butchers," Bashir tell us. "Rachid did not blow himself up," he adds, explaining that Rachid panicked at the last minute. "He's in prison now."

"Mohammed was never religious before, but about a year before the bombings he grew a beard and started going to mosque. He used to download and watch jihadi films," Yousef explains.

Hamid was my friend but he wouldn't spend time with me anymore because I still slept with girls," Jamal explains. "He became very religious and a distance came between us. He demanded me to change and wanted to stay close with me, but I wanted distance because I still wanted to sleep with girls."

Adil and Abdelfattah also became very religious in the year before," Bashir says.By my count we have discussed seven of the bombers and they continue to pour out small details about each of them, emphasizing that they all withdrew from their previous lives, showed outward signs of becoming more serious Muslims in their change of dress and by growing beards. They all also became strictly observant in their religious practices: praying, eschewing drugs and premarital sex, turning off the television, *and* they all regularly downloaded and studied jihadi propaganda films from the Internet. Evidently their recruiter was teaching them that Islam could offer them a new cleansed life but was also preparing them to take on one shortened by "martyrdom".

As I am recording what they say in my notebook, Jamal's mother suddenly arrives home from work. When she sees me sitting on the bed taking notes she mistakes me for a journalist. "You have to go!" she exclaims her face wrought with anxiety. "I'm very sorry, it's against all our Arab customs of hospitality to ask you to leave, but I cannot have you here in the house! Just a few months ago our neighbor's son was arrested for speaking to a journalist!" she cries. "You have to leave *now*!"

Seeing the terror on her face, I immediately put my pen down and begin to gather my things saying, "Oh I'm sorry. I'm a mother too, and I wouldn't want anything to happen to your family as a result of my visit. I'm a research professor by the way, not a journalist."

Jamal argues with his mother but she is adamant, pleading with her eyes for me to leave despite his protests. I tell Jamal we must leave and then as we reach his door I ask the young men, "Isn't there somewhere I can take you where we can sit down and talk quietly? A café or something?" They all shake their heads and one asks, "In the slum you mean? No, there's nothing here."

"How about outside the slum? Somewhere we could sit down and have something to eat?" I ask. The young men consider for a moment as though it is an entirely otherworld "out there" and then say, "Yes, there is one place."

Before leaving the home, one of them goes out to the street to check if there are any "informers" or police watching and when the coast is clear we set off together.

The young men take us to a café that specializes in roasted chicken. But strangely, when we arrive they insist, "We'll sit outside here while you get something to eat." I stare at them in consternation and then laugh understanding that they think I am hungry and need to eat, but they won't accompany me because they cannot afford anything. "No, you are missing the whole point! I'm inviting you to be my guests so that we can talk. Please let's all go together. I am paying for everything!"

The boys shyly agree and we go upstairs in the restaurant where we have the upper floor to ourselves. We order a large roasted chicken dish and drinks for everyone. When it arrives the waitress places the platter of chicken in the center of the table and everyone begins to eat with their hands. I follow along and take handfuls as we continue talking. One of the young men looks at me incredulously and asks, "Where did you learn to eat with your hands? Are you married to a Moroccan man?"

I laugh and tell him no but that I've been plenty of places where people eat with their hands and that I love to eat communally, remarking that the chicken here is great. Everyone wolfs down the food as I continue to ask them about their lives in the slum.

"You said the bombers stopped seeing girls," I ask. "Do you all have girlfriends here?" I ask.

"No, none of the girls here will date us," Jamal says forlornly. "Without jobs what can we offer them? The only girls that will go with us are prostitutes."

My eyes widen. "You pay prostitute instead of have girlfriends?" I ask. "You have money for that?"

"Yes," Bashir says explaining that in the slum there are some girls that will agree to have sex with them for very small amounts of money—some for as little as ten cents.

"We want to have girlfriends," Jamal says, "but it's impossible without a job."

"You can't get jobs anywhere?" I ask.

"No one will hire us," Yousef explains. "They see on our identity cards that our address is Sidi Moumen and they assume right away that we are on drugs or will steal from them."

"My only hope is to go to Spain and join my cousin," Jamal says.

"You can get to Spain?" I ask.

"Yes—illegally," he answers. "I almost made it once. I stowed away on a ship, hiding in one of the boxes, but the guards found me and took me off. My mother is saving the money to send me [illegally]. It costs over a thousand Euros to pay someone to take me in a ship, but if I get there I can live with my cousin in Madrid and he'll get me an [illegal] job. Then I'll work and save up to bring my mother over." Jamal smiles at the thought of it, telling me his mother is a seamstress and makes very little money. The first money she was able to save went to buy a sewing machine to work from home. I have the feeling that Jamal's dream will take a long time to materialize.

"Why are you wearing Moroccan dress?" Bashir suddenly asks me.

"I wore it out of respect to fit in with your customs," I answer.

"It's good you did," Bashir says, nodding respectfully. "Otherwise we would have had to [sexually] harass you!"

I smile but inside am quite shocked at his frankness. *I guess Mokhtar was wrong on that one* -I think to myself, glad I missed being harassed.

Yousef wants to smoke and asks Abdul to ask me if it's okay if he orders a cigarette from the waitress. "Yes of course," I answer. "Order whatever you want." With my coaxing, all of the young men shyly order cigarettes that the waitress produces one by one. I've never seen cigarettes sold individually and it makes an impression on me – that something we take so for granted is a big treat here sold singly and so highly valued.

"You said that your friends downloaded a lot of jihadi movies from the Internet," I say. "Have any of you ever watched these kind of films?" I ask. They clam up, so I add, "I have and when I did I have to say I was shaking afterwards from the horrible scenes they showed!" I show them shaking hands to emphasize my point.

That opens them up and Jamal answers, "I only watched a few but when the police came to our friends homes they took everything away and we saw how many CDs they actually had!" Jamal gestures and shows a pile of about three feet (or one meter) high.

"I don't know how they could watch all those jihadi films and not get crazy!" Bashir adds. "That must have been hours and hours of films that they downloaded from the Internet!" The young men go on to explain that the recruiter convinced their friends to become more devout and in doing so they cleaned up their lives, got off of drugs and forswore illicit sex so that they could be good Muslims. Then after watching so many jihadi films he convinced them that the best way to ensure attaining paradise was to "martyr" themselves. While they cannot be sure that is what happened, from the outward signs they viewed, it seems accurate.

"Are there many al Qaeda type materials around here that you can get easily besides on the Internet?" I ask.

"They sell jihadi cds everywhere here," Yousef says. "They used to all be about Chechnya but now that the war in Iraq started there are many about striking the U.S. forces in Iraq. You can get them anywhere in Casa."

We have spent about three hours with these young men now and Abdul reminds me that we have an appointment with the wives and sisters of the Salafi prisoners who were rounded up after the bombings. We are supposed to be at their association's headquarters soon and need to leave. I turn to the young men explaining that I need to leave and ask if we could continue talking a few hours from now.

"Don't come back here in the night," Bashir says. "Why?" I ask. "We'll be different people! You don't want to see us at night," he answers looking sad to disappoint me. I sense his strong sense of shame and also a protective desire towards me as he explains, "At night we all do drugs! Don't come back here at night!"

Abdul leaves the table to go and pay the bill, again using his own money, and when he does Yousef leans close to me and says quietly in a mixture of French and broken English, "I was so angry when I found out they went to bomb themselves and didn't tell me beforehand."

"You would have tried to stop them?" I say.

"*No!*" He answers totally surprising me. "*I was angry that they didn't take me with them!*" he adds gazing sadly into my eyes.

I gasp. "Why?"

"You see our lives," he answers. And then I understand it all. They have so little to live for and just maybe he could have "gloriously" exited to something better.

As we ready to leave, I see out the window that there is a cash machine across the street. I point it out to Abdul and tell him that we should visit it so that I can get the cash to pay him for his time and also repay the expenses he has covered. Then I excuse myself to the ladies room.

When I return I am carrying my purse tucked under my arm. Our informants are still here and I notice that something has dramatically changed in the dynamic between us. "They want you to give them money to buy some bottles of alcohol," Abdul says, his face and voice serious. And I see all of the young men eyeing my purse aggressively now. I realize it would be simple for them to push me over, take it and run and I momentarily feel that they are all quite strongly weighing that option.

"No, I never pay for interviews," I answer without really thinking. "That might corrupt the process!" I look kindly but firmly at all of them. "And I don't want to buy alcohol for you. I like you too much to do that!" I add with great care in my voice. Abdul translates and I think between the two of us genuinely caring about them, the young men suddenly transform again before our eyes, all of their aggression suddenly disappears to be replaced by kind expressions of gratitude on both sides for the lunch and the interview.

"Thank you so much for all you shared," I tell them warmly as we say our goodbyes and they file down the stairs ahead of us and walk down the block fading back into the slums. As they do I wonder what will happen to them. Abdul and I go to the cash machine discussing what just happened and he agrees that they seemed about ready to take my purse and run.

After experiencing the slum myself and talking with these friends of the bombers and hearing the pain and desperation of their stunted lives caught in poverty and unemployment, I begin to understand. By no fault of their own other than place of birth, they are sentenced to dull lives where they have few good choices. They can be petty criminals, drug addicts, frequenters of prostitutes, stowaways or other negative identities that all end badly and have few, to no good paths in life. Of course it's not just poverty and desperation. It took a terrorist recruiter and an attractive ideology to convince the "martyrs"that exploding themselves is an instant gateway to paradise and there may even have been the rumored threats (reported in the press) made to convince those with doubts to go forward with their plan once it was hatched. Once again, the lethal cocktail of terrorism had been at work.

Each of these young men I've talked to today—and the bombers they told me about—were facing lives that are completely blocked with frustrated aspirations on all fronts. Even though education, as they told me,is provided by the state, it will not lead to jobs as long as they are slum dwellers, and without jobs they have no chance of normal sex lives or marriage and only a bleak endless future of nothingness. And all lack any positive means of escape from overwhelming despair and psychic pain. Instead, each found his own negative means of escape: drugs, prostitutes and hopes of clandestine illegal migration while the bombers found theirs in "martyrdom".

CHAPTER 46

Arriving to Beslan

It's August 2005, and I'm on my way to the small town of Beslan in North Ossetia, one of the autonomous republics in the North Caucasus region of the Russian Federation where just one year ago Chechen-sponsored terrorists took over a school taking one thousand hostages—the majority of them children. The hostage-takers quickly rigged bombs through out the building and announced they were willing to "martyr" themselves and kill the hostages if their demands for the Russian forces to withdraw from Chechnya and allow it to become an independent republic were not met. The three-day siege ended when Russian forces stormed the building. Tragically three hundred thirty-three hostages were killed in the shoot-out,more than half of them children.[230]

The hostage-takers, twenty-nine men and three women, were mostly Chechen or Ingush and were organized and dispatched by Shamil Basayev, the Chechen militant rebel leader who claimed they came from his Riyadus Salikhin or "martyr battalion". On the one year anniversary of the event I am on my way to interview the survivors of the siege about what they endured and to learn more about this new form of suicide terrorism: hostage-taking with the will to die. Like the Moscow hostages I previously interviewed, the Beslan hostages spent forty-eight hours in close proximity with the terrorists, conversing with and observing them.

While preparing for the trip to Beslan, a little town tucked away in the North Caucasus, not far from Chechnya, I find it's not only off the beaten path—it's a place the Russian authorities prefer you not to go. When I apply for a visa, the Russian service center is unusually helpful, promising me that it's quite simple to go to Russia. But when I list my final destination as Vladikavkaz, the capital of North Ossetia and the main city near to the village of Beslan, the cordial, welcoming and helpful e-mails suddenly turn cold. I receive the following letter:

Dear Anne Speckhard,

Please note that The Northern Caucasus is a region of a strict passport control and in order to visit it you need not only a Russian visa but a special authorization from the local authorities. As you undoubtedly know, this is not at all a place for tourism.

We regret to cancel your application and we strongly recommend that you obtain an invitation from a local company in Vladikavkaz.

Thank you for using Visa Help Center!

Best regards,

Customer Service Team

Undaunted, I continue with my plans, more prudently listing only Moscow on my next visa application. I have diplomatic friends in the Russian embassy that help me with obtaining the visa, and since I told one of them months ago exactly where I plan to go, I decide not to remind them of my final destination now in case it is deal breaker for the visa. At the Russian embassy I also don't reveal my ultimate travel plans and just accept my visa a bit guiltily and book a plane ticket for Moscow. Once in Moscow, I will hopefully board a plane onward to Vladikavkaz, and go from there to the small town of Beslan.

Before leaving, I try to call Dima, one of the Russian psychiatrists who treated hostages after the Beslan siege and whom I know from my counter-terrorism work with NATO-Russia. Dima has offered us housing in Vladikavkaz and to help us make contacts for interviews in exchange for funding to fly three psychiatrists to Beslan to continue their research with the hostages—money they haven't been able to get from their own government. Now with help from a colleague's research grant I can deliver.

But it doesn't turn out so simple. The one surviving hostage-taker, Vladimir Khodov, is currently on trial in Beslan, and the town is an uproar blaming Moscow for the many hostages who were killed when the Russian forces stormed the school. The authorities might not welcome a psychiatry team arriving on the scene right now. And besides that, I'm having trouble reaching Dima by phone; I repeatedly reach his wife, but she seems convinced that I am his lover and slams the phone down on me each time. I only get through when Seda Akhmedova, my Chechen colleague who is living with me in Brussels at the time, calls and speaks quickly in Russian, explaining I am a professor trying to reach her husband. When I finally get Dima on the phone, he demurs.

"Anna, I cannot go with you to Beslan right now because of politics," he says, "but when you come to Moscow I will give you all the contacts you need, but not over the phone. Call me when you arrive to Moscow and we'll meet before you go to Vladikavkaz."

I agree and fly to Moscow, where I meet my British colleague, Ces Moore. A year ago Ces was in the Caucasus trying to talk to Chechen terrorists and warlords when his plane emergency landed in Vladikavkaz to an uproar of press coverage. Unable to speak Russian he only understood from the TV monitor that two planes had exploded while his was in the air – both having taken off from the same Moscow airport and blown up by female "Black Widows", suicide bombers posing as passengers. Then, only hours after he left Vladikavkaz to return from his trip there, he learned that he had been driven to the airport along the same road that the hostage-taking terrorists were taking to get to Beslan where they overtook the school. Ces hasn't returned to Vladikavkaz since and is nervous about doing so. He's offered to pay my way on this trip and wants to tag along on my interviews so that he can travel with another colleague. He has both a driver and interpreter in Beslan who covered the school siege and promises that they will be available to help us contact the surviving hostages.

Because we are both a bit nervous about the FSB, the Russian security services, Ces and I opt to share a hotel room with twin beds even though we don't know each other that well. My thinking is I'd rather trust that he's a gentleman than trust the Russian FSB or some criminal element to get a key from the hotel desk and make a surprise visit in the middle of the night. Ces proves to be extremely nervous—he's got a bit of trauma responses from his last trip—and he stays up reading late into the night, long after I drift off to sleep in the adjacent twin bed.

We have one day in Moscow before our internal flight to Vladikavkaz and Ces insists that we use it to go to register at his embassy. He's worried that he could be kidnapped or arrested and feels he must tell his embassy where he is traveling. I have a completely opposite response. I don't want my embassy to have any idea I'm in town or much less catch wind of the fact that I'm heading off to the Caucasus for research interviews the next day. I've had enough run-ins with the U.S. State Department and with diplomatic security trying to dictate to me where I can and cannot go, given my marriage to a State Department official. I prefer to be independent of my husband's career and abide by the "don't ask, don't tell policy".

"You know telling your embassy about our plans to fly to Vladikavkaz tomorrow is basically announcing it to the Russians," I say, chiding Ces about his insistence on reporting in to his embassy. "I'm sure the Russians have microphones in all the offices of the UK officials and it won't be a secret anymore after we report in."

Ces insists we carry on and we meet a lowly visa officer who agrees to see him. As he announces our plans and motives I am a bit reassured by knowing that if the Russian security services have become interested in us they now know exactly who we are and what we are up to and hopefully realize we are timid researchers instead of suspecting us as bold spies.

"As a representative of the UK government I have to warn you against going to this area," the UK visa officer intones in an official voice. "We cannot forbid you, but we warn you against it. You may get arrested or kidnapped and there is not much we can do to help you."

Ces looks terrified and I jump in to ask out of morbid curiosity, "What *would* you be able to do to help out if Ces disappears or something else bad happens?" The officer sheepishly admits that the only real assistance he can offer is to ship Ces's body back to the UK if he is discovered dead, visit him in hospital and assist him in a med-evac if he is discovered gravely injured or ill, or make sure that he is receiving the same treatment as any other Russian citizen in jail if he is imprisoned. To this reply, I laugh aloud, much to Ces's annoyance.

"Okay Ces, have you heard enough?" I then say, urging our departure. Ces however insists on filling out the emergency contact forms should any of these tragedies befall him. I consider if doing the same at my embassy is wise but decide there's no need —I have three children and a husband who will send someone to start looking for me if I don't return! We leave the embassy with me laughing, and Ces looking white as a sheet.

Our next stop is the BBC Moscow. Ces has a journalist contact there, Damian Grammaticas, who reported the siege as it unfolded—and still hasn't recovered from it. He tells us he has only a short time to talk but ends up speaking to us for two hours, drawing comfort from sharing.

Damian draws us a crude map of the little town of Beslan, explaining where the school is located, how the terrorists ran toward it from the train tracks and assaulted it and where he stood reporting during the siege. He gives us contact names to interview and marks their houses on his map as well. We leave with warm wishes, promising to let him know how it goes.

Next, I call Dima as agreed, and his wife again slams the phone down on me. I call once more and try to explain my way past her, but I cannot speak in Russian fast or well enough to assure her that I am not one of his lovers. After she hangs up twice, I realize that tomorrow we will fly to Beslan, and like most of the other places where I've done research, we are on our own.

Ces and I grab dinner and then head back to the hotel. Again Ces has trouble falling asleep. He's terrified that Vladikavkaz is filled with criminals, that we could be kidnapped by Chechen rebels or arrested by the FSB and that the plane could go down with another Black Widow's suicide bomb. I listen to his fears, but I feel peaceful about it. I would actually like to interview Shamil Basayev so I fantasize that if I fell into the Chechen's hands, I would insist to be taken to him and that my Russian would hold up to the challenge. I fall asleep easily, hoping for the best.

In the morning we go to the airport and purchase our tickets in cash, hoping no one notices that we lack the appropriate visas and permission to travel out of Moscow. We've agreed if they turn us away here, we'll go to the train station and board the two-day train to Vladikavkaz, but all goes well. Tickets in hand, we are sent to luggage control where all our hand and checked luggage is weighed and we pay some sort of tax. I walk through security and am shocked to see my entire skeleton on the computer monitor as I pass by—I've just received a total body x-ray! I walk away dismayed that a woman of child bearing age could be given a full body x-ray without any questions like, "Ma'am, you don't happen to be pregnant, do you? Or would you like something to cover your ovaries with while we expose your body to a dose of radiation?" *Welcome to the former USSR!* I think laughing to myself as we go forward to boarding the old Soviet plane.

The ex-Soviet plane is dilapidated. The seats fold completely forward, and people have haphazardly placed luggage everywhere on the floor and covering empty seats. We take our seats and Ces puts in his earphones, switches on loud music, closes his eyes and tries to block it all out. I, on the other hand, relish the post-Soviet culture and the opportunity to practice my Russian.

The flight is uneventful, and when we land in Vladikavkaz, I'm thrilled that we've made it into the Caucasus! But as we deplane, I realize it's not so simple. We face another checkpoint: internal passport control. The federal police are checking everyone coming off the plane and asking about their business. Everyone with a foreign passport is asked to step aside. When we are approached, I tell the police, in Russian, that we are tourists, come to see the mountains and beauty of the Caucasus and are here to see friends of Ces. The officer looks suspicious, eyeing Ces in his black jogging suit and unshaven beard. Suddenly I realize Ces could be mistaken for a returned Chechen refugee living in the UK! I begin to talk faster, adding more details about our visit to "friends" and hope it will work. The officer gets distracted by a young blonde Latvian woman who is anxious to pass and waves us through.

As we wait for our luggage to arrive on the jerkily moving old conveyer belt, I notice that every exit is heavily controlled. When exiting with our baggage, another officer checks our passports and asks our business. When I repeat our story about tourism and meeting friends he nods and lets us out of the airport, where the sky overhead is blue and sunny.

Madina, our translator who Ces knows well from his last trip, and her uncle Volodya are there. They greet us like old friends and take us to their old fashioned Russian Lada. Volodya is former military and reminds me exactly of my well-loved driver, Vanya, an ex-Soviet submariner who drove for me in Belarus. They are so similar that I feel immediately in good hands and good company. Madina's English is great and Volodya is friendly and communicative in Russian.

Vladikavkaz is not more than twenty minutes away by car. As we drive, I'm exhilarated and don't realize that Ces is re-experiencing the terror of his previous trip. We arrive into Vladikavkaz, a typical Soviet town with some old architecture. We check into our hotel, which is not too bad as far as former Soviet hotels go, and then go for a walk about the town with Madina and Volodya. When we sit at a modern café for dinner, Ces is nervous and doesn't want us to speak English, fearing that we are being watched or will stand out from the crowd and could be abducted. I laugh thinking I can easily switch to Russian if he prefers.

I ask Madina about her experience covering the Beslan siege. She whitens and begins to shake as she recalls translating for a reporter who pulled her toward the shooting instead of running from it when the first bomb went off.

"He was asking me to translate, while bullets were being fired all around us," she recalls. "Our forces were shooting from two sides at each other and we were in the middle of it! They were screaming at each other not to shoot and he was screaming at me to translate while he pulled me by the hand deeper into the shooting! I finally just lost it and started swearing at him and said, 'If you want to die, okay, but I don't!' He let me go then and we ran back to my uncle's car. I'm amazed I lived!"

Madina's mother is a psychiatrist and worked with the victims after the siege. Madina tells us her mother was deeply disturbed by the work but kept with it because she felt grateful that her daughter had been lucky enough to survive. Interested to talk with her, Madina calls and invites her mother to join us. Though she tells us about the hostages, she warns about talking to them saying, "This work changes you, you can't hear these stories and not be changed! They are too horrible!"

I wonder about my ability to bear it. Trauma psychologists are trained and know that their skill lies in their ability to not turn away from the pain, but this event involved hundreds of victims—children, mothers and fathers shot, burned and killed in their school by brutal terrorists. Tomorrow I am going to talk to many parents who lost their children. It won't be easy and Madina's mother might be right - taking in this pain will change me. When it's time to sleep, I go to bed sobered and say small prayers hoping I can do this work without turning away, without flinching in the face of horror.

CHAPTER 47

Three Beautiful Boys from Beslan

Every school year in Russia starts with a celebration, the Letnika. Freshly scrubbed boys and girls dressed in their finest clothes, accompanied by parents and grandparents and trailing younger siblings, come to the schoolyard laden with flowers to celebrate the annual Day of Knowledge. It is a joyful reunion of the teachers and children, a time for singing and dancing and reciting poetry. But as summer draws to a close in 2005, children and parents all over Russia are apprehensive because of what happened last year in Beslan. And many Beslan children are not sure they will attend this celebration. Some say they wish to wait a week or two beyond the opening days of school before returning– even though a new shiny school replete with slides, towers and beautiful equipment stands waiting to welcome them back. The horrors of last year are still too fresh.

Our first day begins with cold calls. Since Dima, my psychiatrist contact, didn't come through and Madina's phone calls to her contacts also don't pan out, we have no real contacts. So we take the BBC correspondent's advice and go to the homes he pointed out to us on his crudely drawn map while in Moscow. No one is home at those houses, so we begin to walk around the town and ask men on the streets about who might be willing to speak with us. A few of the men point us to a home where a boy lives who survived the siege. We go to that home and ask for an interview. The parents, Sveta and Vadeem, size us up and call their fourteen-year-old son, Alan to their living room and ask if he will talk to us. He agrees and takes a seat on the couch while we gather in seats around him. Alan's parents sit down as well, listening cautiously on the periphery while I explain my study and Alan begins his story and Madina translates.

Sensitive to the possibility of causing harm by asking anyone about this siege, especially children, I try very hard to respect his boundaries and ask about what he can and is willing to talk about, leaving alone what he seems not to want to touch.

"I had a new white t-shirt and jeans," Alan begins. "It was just me and my two sisters [both who died in the siege], one sister was my twin. Mama didn't go because we decided we were old enough to go without her. We [also] decided we were old enough to go without bringing flowers [for the teachers] as the little kids do.

"Everyone stood in lines outside [in the schoolyard] and my classmates and I were [also] in line. The teacher started talking on the microphone and as she made her speech I turned my head and saw them running toward us: some were bald, some with beards, some with hats—they were with automatics! At first I thought it was a play, a game made on purpose to entertain us. The terrorists came from behind me. One shot into the air and another screamed, 'Allahu Akbar!'

"At first we ran to escape in different directions. All the students were trying to run to different classrooms. The terrorists came to find us and assembled everyone in the gym. I tried to run. We were taught at school if there is a fire and we hear three rings, we must run to the emergency exits. I knew one. I ran to it, but the door was locked with a chain.[231] I couldn't escape there. I ran to another classroom after that and there were many people there. But one of the terrorists came after us and made us all go to the gym. Our neighbor, Vadeem jumped one of the terrorists and tried to fight with him but the terrorists shot him in his hand. I saw there was blood and then I understood it was *real*, and I felt horror!"

The terrorists stripped everyone of their mobile phones and very quickly strung up their bombs all around the gym. At first they gave water to all and snacks to the youngest children, but Alan[1] says there was no fresh air and it was very difficult to breath.

"Our school goes from the first to the eleventh grade. At first they agreed to release the little ones, even the fourth, fifth and sixth graders. The school [principal] made a list of all classes. They were saying that below seventh grade will go out, but then they left that plan," Alan says, disappointment registering in his eyes as he remembers.

"Alan, how did you feel during those moments?" I gently ask. "You must have been terrified."

"At first I was terrified," he says nodding, "then I was calm." He seems to go into a bit of a dissociative trance, which is probably how he calmed himself in the original event. It's clear that he prefers not to discuss his feelings so I don't probe further and let him stick with the facts of the story.

---

1 A pseudonym

"Then, what happened?"

"They stopped giving water," he says, his face a mask of horror. "At first they were letting us go to the restroom, but we were accompanied. They let five people go at a time but always with one of their men, even the girls. Some were going just to get water."

These terrorists evidently learned from their compatriots' experiences in the Moscow Dubrovka Theater siege of 2002. There, the terrorists let their hostages go to the restroom unaccompanied and two girls escaped out of the restroom windows. The terrorists fired on the girls, but snipers outside gave protective fire and the girls escaped. This time the terrorists were taking no chances.

"People started talking and saying it was bombs the terrorists were stringing up," Alan recalls. "They were fast, organized and not speaking. Some terrorists said, 'We will blow the place up!' Others said, 'We will blow all of you up! Nobody cares about you!' They also said, 'While we are here, we are not going to blow you up.'" Alan falls silent remembering.

"How do you handle these memories?" I ask gently. "Do you suffer nightmares or are you sometimes afraid to go to school?"

He answers with a shrug. "I don't think about it often. No nightmares. I've been to school." He's young but he already emulates the Caucasus tough guy, pretending it doesn't touch him although he's still a boy and his parents drop in and out of the room to check on him, hovering at times with concern.

Alan eagerly resumes his story, seeming to enjoy recounting it for me as long as I don't press on his emotional responses. "The first night it was raining, they broke the upper parts of windows and the rain came in and it was good!"

Two neighbor boys, Anton and Edik, who were also in the siege, have heard there is a psychologist interviewing Alan. They enter the room and take seats on the couch alongside him, keen to add bits and pieces of what happened.

"We were standing together, Alan and I," Edik recalls excitedly. "We were all in the schoolyard. We heard shots or explosions. We thought it was toy bombs,then they appeared! They broke the windows to the school and made us climb through. "The schoolyard is shaped like a pocket or a u shape, and they closed the open end so we couldn't escape. They had us all in the gymnasium in less than a half hour. One of them was hanging bombs on the walls. They were saying, 'If [the Russian forces] start storming us, we will blow us all up!'"

"Do you recall other things the terrorists said or if they fought among themselves?" I ask the boys.

"They told us, 'We bought you all for 20,000 rubles!'" Anton recalls. While these boys also avoid direct discussion of their emotions, they show them indirectly. They look completely horrified by this terrible fact: that the terrorists had bribed their way through all the checkpoints out of Chechnya, across North Ossetia, to the Beslan school and were telling their hostages that they had essentially been "sold" by their own people for so little money.

"They were pushing all the people inside [the gymnasium] and people were screaming and shouting," Edik continues. "They said, 'We will kill this one if you don't stop screaming.' [But] there were too many people upset, and they didn't stop screaming. A bald colonel with a beard killed the first man, Betrovov—shot him in the neck. Later his two children died as well." Edik falls silent momentarily and all the boys look at me wide-eyed.

"How do you cope with this?" I ask. "Do you have thoughts about it, nightmares, trouble going to school or other troubles?"

Edik shrugs. "Then it was horrible, but not now. I think it's not going to happen again. I only think of it sometimes, almost never."

"So you've pushed your memories of it far away?" I ask.

They all nod in agreement, glad to think of it that way.

"After, I was in shock," Alan explains. "I just didn't feel anything." I think about how this echoes so many of the suicide bombers stories, how their traumatic experiences led them to this state of cold emotional numbness, what some of the Palestinians referred to as being the "living dead". These boys have had a strong taste of the same, yet they have remained very humanly warm as far as I can tell, but maybe they too can't allow themselves access to certain emotions, to get too close to things that bring up the emotional pain that they have numbed inside. Trauma victims often go throughout their lives trying to deaden the pain of memories too excruciating to remember but too difficult to bury completely.

"What happened at night? How did you sleep?" I ask referring to the siege.

"We slept on the floor maybe five minutes, not more," Anton explains.

"What happened the next day?"

The boys say they can't remember anything. This has got to be disso-ciative amnesia, as the adults later tell us that the second and third day were the most horrible—that children were passing out from thirst and hunger and that the terrorists became vicious. These boys either passed out or more likely have blotted it from their minds.

"You were fainting, losing your consciousness," Alan's father says as he lingers on the edge of the room. Although he was not in the siege, he may know from the others who were or from his son's own reports after-wards.

"I couldn't sit or stand anymore," Alan suddenly recalls. "I was pacing back and forth. I wanted to stand at the window but a boy and a girl were already there. They told us the water is poisoned but we drank it the second day too. They didn't know we were drinking when we went to the bathroom. My throat was parched."

Meanwhile, the director of the school begged to have the youngest released. Anton recalls, "Now and then she left the gym. She was stand-ing up and coming to talk to the terrorists."

"What about the female terrorists? Did you see them?" I ask.

This sparks a fierce discussion among the boys as to whether there were two or three female bombers. They think there were three: two in dressed in long black abayas and one in grey. They know the most about the two who sat near them.

"They were wearing bomb belts," Alan says. "You could only see their eyes. They didn't say anything to us, but they spoke in Chechen to each other. They would walk out from time to time."

According to hostage reports, the female bombers were said to have been aghast that the group had taken so many children hostage—that they did not know ahead of time that their target was a school and had been told they were going to overtake the local FSB command post. According to those hostages who overhead the arguments between the male and female hostage-takers, the women were told they could 'martyr themselves now' if they wished and after that detonations were heard in the courtyard. The female terrorists were not seen again. It's unclear if they detonated them-selves or were shot by their cadres.[232]

"Even now when we go to the canteen, there is blood. Their flesh is there!" Alan recounts.

Edik continues telling us how the terrorists put blame on the police, saying, "These are your forces who are shooting [at you] from tanks."

The terrorists made calls on their mobile phones to others outside the school. Alan recalls after they spoke to someone, they announced, "Your president [Putin] says that nobody needs you!"

"We all started to cry!" Alan says. Later many other hostages tell us of the hysteria that ensued when everyone began screaming and crying in hopeless anguish.

The boys say that the terrorists then began to shoot into the air, as a method of crowd control. As the crowd remembered the bombs rigged overhead, they quickly silenced themselves.

"What were the hostages screaming?" I ask.

"One boy, Albert, was screaming and crying to let us go!" Alan says. He is fourteen like us. Others cried out to be able to join their families or to be with their mothers. In the beginning they put us in groups, rows of people, and ordered us to stay there and not to move. We were also not allowed to look at the terrorists." Alan recalls, "A neighbor boy was always looking at them. One of the terrorists pointed his pistol at this boy's head and asked him, 'Are you going to remember me forever?' The boy tried to move the gun from his head and put his head on his hands and screamed, 'No! No! I don't want to remember you!'"

The boys remember how the adult male hostages were taken to be shot. "Timsov—he was taken out and shot," Anton recalls. "They thought maybe he could resist." They discuss among themselves and recall, "Salagov and Bologov also."

"How many men were shot?" I ask, horrified to ask children such a question.

"Maybe ten," Edik estimates. "They were taken to the Russian language office and shot there. You can see it on the wall."

Later when I walk through the school and I see that there are still, a year later, bloodstains on the wall of this room where the men were executed. I am sure the terrorists chose this room purposefully as the place for executions—the place where the Russian language is imposed upon its territorial subjects.

"They were ordering men to kneel in front of the terrorists but they refused," Edik recalls of the events they witnessed inside the gymnasium. "Zarosov knelt and he lived. He was obeying them and closing windows."

I feel sickened thinking this is such a cycle of violence. So often the Chechen refugees tell stories of how the Russian soldiers made villagers come out of their homes and how they were humiliated and made to kneel before being shot. Now the terrorists have the upper hand and turn these actions upon their captives.

"Did they have a television?" I ask, as hostage-takers frequently watch the news to learn what the other side knows and is doing in response to their operation.

"Yes, there was a television," Edik explains. "They brought the TV set from one classroom."

"They were asking how to view their video," Alan says, explaining that the terrorists did not use the TV to watch the news but to check on the quality of their own filming. "They had cameras to connect to the television and they were trying to find out who knows how to do that. They filmed the whole time. One terrorist was holding a bomb." Terrorists generally film their actions to play back to their constituencies as ways of drumming up social support and more recruits, to impress funders and to release to the other side's public in order to spread the effect of their terror act beyond just their immediate victims.

"What were they wearing?" I ask.

"They had military uniforms," Alan answers, "camouflage ones. One man had a sports suit, another was in a black t-shirt and camouflage pants. Some wore long shirts, Arabic style, and others had military vests with grenades."

"What else do you remember about the terrorists?" I ask. The boys recall the mundane but necessary things of life—even that the terrorists had brought toothpaste and toothbrushes. Funny to think that terrorists who are willing to die to kill still worry about brushing their teeth, although I have found that this is a frequently bizarre occurrence when it comes to suicide terrorists. I think of the Palestinian boy who agreed to carry a bomb into Israel to become a martyr but told his senders he had to wait a week until after he finished his college exams.   Death by martyrdom is often like this: the living "martyrs" go on living normally on one plane, while on another they are agreeing to take their own lives and appear a bit confused about interrupting their daily tasks and duties.

"One was reading the Koran," Edik recalls.

"They ate, but not in front of us," Anton adds.

Alan's mother ducks her head into the room. She is holding a bunch of flowers she has gathered from her garden. She tells Madina in Russian that she is going briefly to the graveyard, as she does daily, to lay flowers on her two daughters' graves. The boys seem undaunted by this display of grief—it's a daily occurrence in their homes—so we carry on.

"What type of weapons did the terrorists have?" I ask. "Did everyone have the same?"

"They all had weapons: automatic rifles and hand grenades," Alan recalls. "The women had a pistol in one hand and in the other hand the trigger button for the self-bombs."

"Can you tell me about the bomb belts?" I ask.

"Their triggers had two wires that went to the belt," Alan states. Apparently the woman had to connect the wires because Alan explains, "The women would play with the button, pushing it." I imagine how awful that had been to watch.

"Do you think they came to die?" I ask.

"Yes, they even said so," Alan tells us. "They said, 'We came here to die. If we die, you are going to die with us.'"

Alan explains that after some time passed, the terrorists allowed some of the hostages to move within the gymnasium and find their families.

"What else did you observe about the terrorists?" I ask.

"Two men stood on a pedal at the entrance to the gym," Edik recalls. "Every two hours they changed. They had to stand on it all the time or it would explode."

I ask them if they know what happened in the final conflagration—what set off the first explosion that triggered the shoot-out between terrorists and Federal forces. There is a great deal of controversy over whether it was caused by a Russian sniper's gunfire, Russian tank fire, a terrorist taking a shot at the ceiling or the accidental detonation of a terrorist's bomb. Whatever started it, immediately after, the Russian forces stormed the school using a great deal of military force, including incendiary missiles which many believe made the school's roof catch on fire and caused many more deaths. The boys honestly don't know but feel it was unintended by the terrorists.

"It was a surprise to these guys [meaning the terrorists]," Alan remarks.

"What did you do when all the bombs started going off and the shooting began?" I ask.

"I heard the explosion," Edik recalls. "I thought someone threw a grenade. Then I looked up the ceiling and saw it was not that. Tamelok said [to me], 'Let's run away from here.'"

"I saw people running and decided to run," Alan adds.

"I couldn't really see," Edik explains. "It was misty, like dust falling and a piece of ceiling fell on my face."

"I remember, just before, I tried to sit on the window," Alan recalls, "but they didn't allow me. There was a low bench between two windows and I leaned my head on one woman's back. [Then] I heard the explosion. Then it was all white from this window. I remember everything was grey and there was huge tension between my ears. I saw people running to the window. I ran too, but as soon as I reached the window, I heard the second explosion. I fell down and someone stepped on my back and jumped out of the window. Then I did the same and ran. I kept on running in the direction others ran —to a little cabin with a billiards tables. I lay on the table and there was water there. I laid and drank water. There were others there too. The terrorists were shooting on top of this roof. Then the people broke the windows [that faced away from the school] of this cabin and escaped toward the ambulances and I was taken to the hospital."

"When the first explosion happened," Anton explains," I ran to the schoolyard with the others. I can't remember how I was running, but my feet were running. There is a little shop. We were taken there and then to ambulances."

"I ran to the billiard cabin too," Edik recalls. "They opened the windows and told us, 'Jump out and run to where our people are,' but I could not. I was too weak. One man took me in his hands and passed me to another local man through the window. That man carried me to the OMAN [the Russian Special Forces]."

As I gaze into the open faces of these young boys, I am overcome with emotion listening to them. They are one year older than my son at home. And just like my son, Alan had two sisters—but his were killed in the shootout. These boys are so ordinary in their innocent boyishness. It's hard to take in this story and comprehend it's real—they tell it like it's a movie they saw. There is very little visible emotion in any of them except boyish excitement of telling an adventure tale. I wonder how they have constructed their psychological defenses to the emotional pain of all they endured. I am about to cry listening but I push my emotions to the side as well.

"I'm curious," I ask, "how do you cope with all you've been through? Did you talk to psychologists? If you did, did it help?"

"I talked to two psychologists," Alan answers, "but I didn't like it. The psychologist asked me to draw something and I drew a bench. The psychologist asked me, 'Who can sit on the bench?' It's a stupid question!" he says with derision in his voice."

We will hear later from one of the teachers that *too many* psychologists descended upon the town after the siege, some to help, many to pursue their research interests and *all of them* asked the children to draw, a standard way of eliciting emotions from children who are reticent to put their feelings into words. The teacher we talk to soon will tell us that now, none of the children will draw—they hate it because they understand it can be a trick to get past their defenses.

Evidently at the time when he was asked to draw, Alan was being cooperative and he was trying to tell the psychologist his story by drawing an *empty bench*—the one he had been sitting at where people were killed when the final explosion occurred—but he was doing it slowly, carefully telling her symbolically about his grief and emptiness, but the psychologist moved too fast, asking him to explain and also didn't seem to get his message. When the explosion blew a hole in the wall and Alan ran away through it, the bench remained behind empty of its former occupants, as did his two sisters who he did not think to and probably could not have saved. The empty bench is a terrible story trapped inside of him, but it is not one that Alan is ready yet to tell and is perhaps a story he will keep trapped inside for his entire life.

I am happy at least that he has opened up today and he has found out that some psychologists let you keep your defenses, let you tell only what you are ready to tell. I feel good that I have made him safe talking about such a difficult subject, but my heart aches for his pain.

"If the psychologists don't help much, what does help?" I ask.

"We talk in our families," Edik answers.

"Does it help?" I ask.

"No, it doesn't help," he answers honestly.

"What happens when you talk with your families?" I ask.

"If I talk to my Mom she cries," Edik explains. "It's better not to talk to her. And Papa starts cursing the terrorists!"

I smile understanding how they have the added burden to protect their parents, too. Child survivors need their parents to stay "put together" and when their pain causes Mom to cry and Dad to begin cursing, children quickly learn it's better to keep their parents psychologically available and keep their pain locked inside.

I ask Alan if he can talk to his parents and how they respond.

"My mother cries," Alan answers. "That's why I don't talk to her. I don't tell Papa either. Everyone is angry!"

"I didn't tell anyone," Anton agrees. "I don't tell my mother. I don't say anything. I met the school psychologists and I was offered choices about going to school. I also went to Moscow [with some children who were sent for rehabilitation] and I was asked to draw a tree and I played the rabbit game."

I don't ask him to elaborate and instead ask the boys, "Will you go to the new school when it opens [in a few days]? Will you go to celebrate the Letnika this year?"

"I am going to wait," Edik says sadly.

"What if something happens again?" Alan asks anxiety filling his voice. "I don't know if I will go."

Alan's parents have returned from the graveyard and his mother comes to the living room now inviting us to the kitchen for food she's prepared.

I see this is a good place to end and I'm glad that I've allowed the boys to tell their traumatic story in a way that paced it according to what they can handle—while keeping my own emotions out of the mix. My questions and clinical demeanor, I am sure, helped them to focus and stay with a horror that they probably often try to avoid and they clearly have no one safe to discuss it with. Each time a trauma survivor tells his story and manages his emotions in the retelling, the story takes on more and more coherence and the horror increasingly finds a safe place to reside in the mind. It stops being the terror that intrudes unbidden and finds a resting place much like a grave, a place in the mind that one can return to for grieving and remembering, but a place left in peace. I can see these boys have many things they avoided talking about today, particularly their emotions and the likelihood that they suffer from survivor guilt, but they managed to tell a great deal and held themselves together doing it. And I saw that reliving it along with them helped them to feel their own self-respect, as they honored the fact that they had survived unspeakable horrors while others had not.

Now in thinking about the upcoming Letnika, they have touched a fear that they can't avoid. I don't want them to open it too much but to just address it and try to give them a bit more peace in a sense of safety for the future.

"You know," I tell them "I came here to make interviews to learn about the terrorists and the hostages and how they coped because I do think there will be *other* hostage-takings in *other places*. There are many terrorists in the world and this has opened a door to a new type of violence. But I am also *more than one hundred percent sure that nothing like this will ever again happen in Beslan!*" I can see that they respect me and they are very attentive when I tell them this. They know I am a foreigner—an American professor—and they think I know a lot.

They listen intently as I repeat "It may happen *elsewhere*, that is a real possibility as long as terrorists are active, but *not here!*" I emphasize that point. "Your police, your parents, the authorities here are too alert to let that happen! No one could possibly penetrate your town! *Somewhere else yes*, where they aren't watching everything, aren't on the alert, maybe— *but not here!*"

The boys nod solemnly, silently listening, mesmerized by my words. They do know that there is another school in Russia where only days ago the police found bombs inside the school, but they take my assurance that their school and their town should be safe.

We discuss a bit more about going to school. Given their anxieties about attending in the first week—when their posttraumatic recall will likely be the highest and destabilize them, I tell them I don't think it's bad to miss the first week of school and to go when they are ready.

"There's no sense in going back if you are just getting all kinds of bad memories and feeling afraid," I say as Alan's parents listen. "Nothing bad is going to happen at school, but if you feel the need to rest the first week and avoid it, it's probably fine. You are smart boys so you can catch up easily. You can go the second week when you will feel comfortable again," I add to strongly suggest that *when they do return, at their chosen time*, they will feel completely confident.

The boys nod and I turn to Alan's parents and tell them what great kids these are, that I am sure they will all be fine in time, but that it's good to be gentle with them as they return to school on the anniversary of the siege.

Alan's parents agree, happy to hear that a psychologist supports their son pacing his re-entry according to his needs.

"It's true," Alan's father nods, "He's smart and he'll do fine if he only misses the beginning days. He doesn't need to go through all that again and remember it all. Better to take it easy and enter in a week. Why go back and be afraid?"

Alan's mother, Sveta, invites us to come and eat something and we thank the boys for sharing with us and follow her outside across a courtyard garden, where flowers are blooming and fresh laundry hangs on the line, into her kitchen. As we walk behind Sveta I suddenly feel the deepest feeling of shame thinking, *I am not sure I was right to come here. Am I a vulture preying on these people's pain to get a story? Both her daughters died! Mine are alive!* I look at her slim frail figure and think, *We are both mothers, we both have sons nearly the same age, but she has been robbed of her daughters and her son lives with trauma*! I hope to God I can say something that will help her, that I haven't come here *only to take*.

Sveta gestures for us to sit at her white-enameled kitchen table as she puts plates in front of us and offers us each a potato pancake. Ces begins to refuse and I look at him severely reprimanding him in English, "Ces you cannot refuse to eat right now. I know you have food allergies but that would be the *worst insult* to refuse. You must eat!"

Ces takes his cue, stops protesting, and she gives him a large portion of pancake on his plate. She gives me the same and I think, - *Okay forget the low carb diet, it's time to eat for work*! I thank her for the food and eat it heartily telling her what a great cook she is, how kind she is too feed us, and that I am so very sorry about her loss. I ask her about her daughters and she looks at me as if to ask, *Are you sure you want to hear*?

I don't avert my eyes to her pain, telling her by my demeanor, *Yes, I'm ready to hear it*, although in truth I would like to get up and run from the room. It's so awful to see the pain already on her face before she has said anything. I feel tears welling up in my eyes. She gets up silently from the table and brings two pictures—the last school pictures of her daughters. She puts them on the table in front of her and I feel completely devastated looking at them. I just shake my head and let the tears come.

"They are beautiful," I say tenderly shaking my head. "So beautiful. I'm so sorry. How old were they?"

"Thirteen and fourteen," she answers.

"What happened?" I ask.

And she begins to tell, with the pictures there in front of her. As I listen I am captivated by this image: a pretty, thin housewife—a mother—in a worn cotton dress, with a full-length apron tied around herself, a scarf tied fifties-style at the back of her hair, leaning on the table as we talk, her bosom reaching toward the pictures of her daughters who she can never reach again. It's heartbreaking even without her words attached.

"My daughters kissed me and my mother-in-law that morning," Sveta says remembering. She recounts how her children had felt so grown-up that they had wanted to go without their parents that year.

"How are you doing?" I ask. "How do you cope, especially with the anniversary approaching?" I ask.

"I can't sleep!" she says.

"Do you have nightmares?" I ask.

She nods her head, "Yes, I had them for some time." I can see she wants to talk about it, if I am willing to listen—which I am. Now I have to find my courage to hear it without flinching, without turning away.

"What are your nightmares about?" I ask, knowing this will likely be the key to the things that are still unresolved, the questions that can't be put to rest.

Sveta looks me in the eyes, her eyes burning with sadness. "I think of our girls running and being shot in the back. The neighbor's daughter was nine. They ran together. That girl saw Alena, our daughter, getting shot in the back. The terrorist shut his eyes and was shooting his automatic. That girl and her mother went to the States [for treatment]. She lost her eye."

"How do you get beyond this memory?" I ask.

"In my mind I struggle," Sveta replies. "If I had been there they would have survived. I feel this strongly." These words are so common in trauma survivors, especially bereaved parents—the feeling that they could have somehow prevented the tragedy if they had only been there. Psychologists call it survival guilt—the guilt of those who survived when others did not.

"For two weeks before she told me, 'I don't want to go to school,'" Sveta recalls explaining how her daughter eerily had some kind of premonition of trouble and did not want to go to school. "She begged me, 'Maybe you could take me to the polyclinic for an excuse. I can't go.'"

Strangely more than one mother will tell us this story—that their children felt something was wrong.

"Again that first day she said, 'Mama please, I don't want to go!'" Sveta continues. "She talked to her sister saying, 'Amina, how much I don't want to go, let's not go!' I gave them little candies to comfort them. The night before when they were in bed I told my daughter, 'But you haven't seen your friends for three months! You can see them!' Alena and Amina went together."

It's clear in the pain written across her face that Sveta so regrets not listening to her daughter's fears.

"It was never before that she said, 'I don't want to go to school.' It hurts me inside—*why didn't I let her stay?* It's very difficult for me! I just keep blaming myself!"

We discuss how children and adults too, sometimes do have an uncanny feeling for the future, but that as mothers, if we took all our children's fears and trepidations seriously our children might never go to school, and that she only acted as a good mother to encourage her daughter to rise above her fears and go. No one could have known what was going to happen there, and Sveta must stop blaming herself. She nods, glad to hear another mother say it was only normal to send her daughters to school, despite the premonition.

"You must blame the terrorists for your daughters' deaths, not yourself," I say hoping to help her unhook from her posttraumatic survivor's guilt. "You were supportive and nurturing in the best way you knew to be at the time."

Amina's father has been silent up to now, alone in our group with his pain, but he begins to feel safe enough to touch it, to speak about it.

"As a father I can't stop the pictures in my mind," he says. "I always think if I could have done something." This too is normal in a trauma survivor. Having constant intrusive thoughts of the horrible thing that has happened is the body's way of continually bringing the subject to mind until the person finally deals with the tough emotions and then can finally put the subject to peace.

"What do you keep seeing?" I ask gently.

"How my daughter was shot!" he answers, pain contorting his face. "How she fell, how no one could take her and save her at that moment!"

Sveta gets up to make eggs and serves us more food, while Vadeem gets out glasses and pours us some homemade cherry liqueur and vodka for himself and Ces. We drink together in the Russian tradition to ease the pain of such sad conversation while Vadeem tells us about his children. I recognize this behavior from my time living in Belarus—so typical in the former Soviet Union to use vodka as a way of accessing feelings and finding the words and communion with others to speak about deep emotional pain.

"They were great students," he recalls. "Alan was not as good in school and his twin sister helped him always. If they fought, she would take her math studies into the bathroom to prevent him from looking at it, and he would cry, 'Tell this fool to give me some help!' but we would tell him not to fight with his sister if he wants her to help him."

We laugh together at this sweet memory as we sip our liqueur and Vadeem continues to drink his vodka. He tells us he tried never to hit his children and to raise them right and that his mother who stayed home with the children helped too.

"Yes, my mother raised them right," he recalls sadly, "But my mother died within one month of this, of a heart attack." Vadeem stands up from the table, overcome with grief and walks away. After composing himself, he sits down for another vodka.

"We have cheap leaders," he complains. "If they were strong, this would never have happened! They only care about their own selves, their own pockets—our authorities here and Putin, they are all the same in this." He continues, "If Dzasokhov, our former President [of North Ossetia][233] had entered the school [to negotiate] it wouldn't have happened, but he did not. The terrorists asked him to come. If he died there he would have had more honor." Indeed later I learn that President Dzasokhov was ordered by Russian President Putin's officials to refrain from heeding the terrorists call to come to the school to negotiate and Dzasokhov was later blamed by his own people for not doing enough. Likewise, many well-known Russian figures had volunteered to go inside, remaining as hostages in exchange for the release of the children, but before any of their offers could be put into effect the Russian forces had attacked the school.

"What can help us?" Vadeem asks pouring more liqueur and vodka. "We go to the cemetery each day and stay there for some time."

After passing a bit longer together, we get up to leave, thanking them profusely for sharing their torn up lives and stories with us. I hug Sveta close before we leave, wishing I could give her more than just my genuine care to heal her pain.

CHAPTER 48

Someone Sold You

Our next interview is with a woman named Luda[1] . She was held hostage with her five- year-old daughter, a first grader who now suffers from posttraumatic stress.

"She is afraid to go back to school again," her mother explains. "When she comes to some new place she asks to look around for grenades! How will it be at school? After the siege, her character changed completely. She is afraid of every little noise and doesn't understand that they are not dangerous. She has regular nightmares, and lately she is becoming aggressive and begins to cry and is very nervous!"

Luda also has posttraumatic symptoms and enduring medical problems. "My blood pressure is high, I can't walk well and I don't sleep much—three hours maximum! And I always see it [like] I am looking at some movie," she states, referring to her posttraumatic recall. "Some psychologist in Salzburg gave me medicine. I was taking pills till now. But nothing helps to survive such horror. No medicine can help me!"

Luda was inside the school when the terrorists appeared. "From the railroad side an athletic, well-built boy came, wearing black," she recalls. "Men were running to us. When they reached us [inside the school], they took off their masks and were shooting in the air and screaming, 'Shut up!' But when pupils began to run they began to shoot around as well. Then, I lost my daughter! I was running to find my daughter and they were shooting in the corridor. I saw her and her classmates leaning against a wall. I took their hands and ran down the corridor to the toilet on the right where I thought there would be windows. There were two doors and I locked them, but there were no windows.

"When we were locked inside, the terrorists put gas under the door. We couldn't breath and something happened with our eyes. I [turned on] the

---

1 The first part of this interview is exclusively with Sveta Cherdzhemova, but another woman who had a son and daughter in the siege joined the interview part way through and it became confused in parts of the transcript who is saying what, so I have combined these two women into one under the pseudonym Luda.

water and put it on the children. Then one of the terrorists broke open the door and forced me out into the corridor. The terrorists threw me to the wall and cried, 'Where is the sports hall?' I said that I didn't know and I understood they would put us under threat. They put the older boy to the wall and put an automatic on his neck, saying they will shoot him if we don't tell them. So I had to indicate the door behind me.

"Then they broke open the doors [to the gym] and began to push the people inside. When those who were pushing us into the hall saw the other terrorists in beards and gowns running from the canteen, they begin to embrace each other and spoke in Ingush or Chechen. I understood that those who came from the canteen had been waiting for them and when they greeted each other they both were very glad.

"'Go over there and take seats!' they told us. And they forced people to break the windows with their hands to jump into the gym. They were shooting at them. They did it in panic. One of the terrorists came and put his automatic gun to one of our [male] PE teacher's neck to force him to the floor. He fell on his knees as the terrorist shot him. Blood ran all over. It streamed over our legs. Children were shouting and crying. I hid my daughter's head between my legs!

"The terrorist shouted that they will kill everyone in that way. The terrorist ordered the older boys to carry his body back and forth so everyone can see the blood and understand.

"In only forty minutes they were completely ready. They put the bombs everywhere, every three meters—they were shaped like a brick bound tightly with heavy tape. One was over my head all three days. Where there were more people they hung more bombs.

"While they were doing that, we heard the sound of breaking wood. We could hear everything as they brought things from place to place and heard breaking floors elsewhere. They were bringing in supplies [that they had hidden beforehand]. All had been prepared beforehand; they just needed to put us in the gym.

"The first day those near the toilet were allowed, but our side was not allowed to go. I managed to hold myself, but my daughter peed herself. First day I didn't even want to go to the toilet! I was so nervous! On the second day, the children had yellow lips from dehydration. A lot of children were sitting with open eyes but looked as if they were sleeping and a lot of people began acting strangely.

"On the second day when Aushev[234] [the former Ingush President] came, the terrorists who were without masks put them back on [to conceal their identities]. And later when the man who shot the PE teacher the first day called the others to lunch, he called their names: Ali and Sefolo. Then those two became very angry, shouted at him and put him to the corridor. I think it was because he called their real names.

"After Aushev left, 'They were shouting at us, 'Nobody cares about you, not your president, not your God, not even Saint George! Pray to Allah! You should, because we came to die! We don't care!

"I was praying. They took crosses from the necks of our children. I took my daughters and put it in my pocket. I wrapped it around her hand and kissed her hand.

"At first they walked around and took all the Ossetian men upstairs and shot them. There was a man, Ayman, from Vladi. He hid facing me, but in the evening they saw him and also took him out. They also took younger boys to do something. When these boys returned they looked very tired. When they took Ayman I thought they would kill him. They beat him, but he returned alive. One of his eyes was black and one was out."

Of the female terrorists, Luda recalls seeing two of them and that on the first day they spoke to the hostages in good Russian with no accent, indicating a high level of education.

"She was singing her prayers in her own language. She said, 'Only Allah can help you. When we all die we will be with Allah and only he can help us.' I understood then that we are all surely meant to die. She prayed with her hands in the air, crying and singing for twenty minutes. After that she asked—or forced—everybody to clap. The children where afraid and clapped," Luda recalls. "She was from the Caucasus—dark skin and eyes. She was not a villager. She was in a black hadjib tied around her face and all but her eyes were covered, and she wore a black robe. But she had tennis shoes and sport pants! And she had a pistol and the "martyr's" belt—there were wires coming from it.

"After Aushev left [on the second day], it all became worse. They became aggressive. The director of the school was saying, 'Something is going wrong. Be silent.' We sat at night as well. No one could sleep. We sat like sardines in a can. During the second night they were shooting the walls of the gym from inside. They left the lights on all the time. From the first day they said, 'If your forces cut the electricity, we will shoot all of you.'"

Luda recalls the end, "The first explosion was in the corner. It got dark and dusty so we couldn't see for two minutes. The second explosion was above my head. I felt a wave from behind as if my head was cut of from my body. I was thrown from the wave and then fell to the floor. My back and head were burning. I saw my daughter was under me. After that I was thrown back again.

"Then, I saw children were jumping from a window. I don't know how I did it, but I stood up. The windows were very high—the bottom of them was level with my eyes at least. I couldn't hear anything but I could see that the terrorist snipers on the roof were shooting children. I wanted to throw my children through the window, but I could not climb up myself. I don't know how I climbed up with two children and threw us out.

"Outside, I saw people running in the direction of the police—there was a small garage there. The entire crowd ran there. One boy was shot in his head. They were shooting our backs but we ran and hid in those garages. They saw us where we were hiding and kept shooting at us from the roof. They shouted to each other in Russian with an Ingush accent, 'Shoot them, don't let them go!' Then I climbed from that garage and saw ordinary Ossetians who came shouting to me. I showed that I have two children. One of them came shooting [at the terrorists] as he ran and took my daughter; the second man took my son. I was running after to protect their backs with my body. Someone took me—I couldn't run any farther. Then some stranger put us in their car and took us to the hospital. To this day, I cannot hear from the right side.

"I understood the depth of [the terrorists'] evil afterward when I saw all the dead and I asked God not to not to forgive them! The mothers who were not there cannot understand how awful it was inside! For me the most horrible is why they came to kill children?

"Now I am losing my eyesight; I have a bad kidney, high blood pressure! Every treatment is useless! No one cares! But God has already helped me. My children and I are alive! It is better to heal then to keep asking. I take herbs to calm myself and try to treat my soul, but I cannot recover my soul. This can't just disappear. I was on fire! I am brave, but those who lost their relatives, it makes me ask, 'Why are we alive and they are not?'

"But it is not only [the terrorists]. Someone let them in here [to pass from Chechnya to Beslan] and they had help. They told us, 'Someone sold you.' One of them was shaking his hand saying, 'We gave so many green dollars for you. How do you feel about the person who sold you?'"

We finish the interview drinking some tea together and then go out to the car to hear more from Volodoya who has been musing about these things as well.

"Who is behind these terror acts?" he asks rhetorically. "It's from the Taliban. After the Afghan war against the Russians, there were many children left without parents whom the Taliban gathered and taught them to hate Russians and Americans. Then in 2000, the fighters who came out of Afghanistan went to Chechnya. Terrorism is the child born of U.S. and Soviet power."

While I don't agree that global militant jihadi terrorism can be blamed on the U.S., it is true that even terrorism that is confined to one region has many global roots, and when there are shifts in power, what happens in one place has strong effects in others. Here in Beslan, for instance, we have seen the long-term repercussions of the global militant jihad, a miscreant child born and raised in Afghanistan perhaps from unknown parents.

CHAPTER 49

Larisa - the Hero of Beslan

Madina tells us that she has arranged our next interview with another survivor of the Beslan siege, Larisa Kudzieva. It's already early evening when we arrive to her small apartment.

Larisa meets us at the door and invites us into her ex-Soviet style living room. It's furnished warmly with upholstered furniture and a large patterned oriental rug hanging on one of the walls. Larisa is a strikingly attractive woman, tall, dark haired and slim, and smiles as she indicates chairs for us to sit on. She pulls one up close for herself, tilting her head to the side to look at us. It's then I notice that she is hiding the right side of her face behind her long dark hair and has arranged the seating so we see only the left side of her face.

"Madina told me you were in the siege last year?" I say, after explaining to her through Madina who we are and what my study is about.

We learn that in a quirk of fate, Larisa only decided at the last moment to go to the Letnika celebrations. Her husband had died just months before and still grieving, she had sent her children to go along without her. The plan was for Larisa's college-age daughter, Madina, to drop her brother Zoar, at his first day of school and then carry on to her Institute, but when Larisa saw them out her kitchen window buying their flowers for Zoar's teacher, she suddenly relented.

"When I saw them out the window, I felt bad—like someone kicked me. 'I'll go with you!' I called to them. I quickly combed my hair and joined them," Larisa recalls.

"When we arrived in the schoolyard all the mothers were already there with flowers and all nicely dressed, gathering for a photo. I didn't go in the photo because I was in black [still in mourning for my husband]."

"The morning of the first day started the same for everyone, bright and beautiful like a holiday," she recalls remembering how abruptly things changed and that when the siege began she tried to use her cell phone to call for help.

"Actually it was impossible to call anyone," she explains. "I tried to call out right at the time when they took us hostages but the network was jammed."

We are already familiar with how the siege played out so I ask Larisa for information specifically about the terrorists.

"Do you know how many terrorist there were?"

"At first there were ten men and two women [terrorists] in the gymnasium but then they were changing places. Many more of them—more than twelve—sat in the corridor and also they had a sniper on the second floor. They say there were thirty-two [terrorists], but it seemed to me like forty or more."

Larisa remembers her first encounter with the terrorist called Abdullah, whose real name was Vladimir Khodov, an Ossetian who speaking in Russian rather than his native Ossetic did not let on to the hostages who he was or where he was from.[235]

"Abdullah came up to me [early in the siege] and told me to stop speaking to a man near me who was wounded," Larisa recalls telling us about how the man next to her had been gravely wounded in his hand, perhaps the same man that the three boys had told us about who had been shot in his hand when he attempted to resist the hostage takers.

"He was seated with his [young] son close to him," Larisa recalls. "He was trying to stop his bleeding while trying to pull his son closer. I asked my daughter, a medical student, what to do. His blood was spurting out! My daughter tried to help, but the bullet had hit an artery and it was impossible to stop his bleeding. His shirt and pants were soaked in blood.

"'We need a doctor!' I screamed. 'Give us some bandages and water!' Probably one of them got tired of my screaming, because one of the terrorists came and shouted at me to shut up and leave the man to die alone. My hands were already all bloody, and sweat and blood covered my face but I did not leave him. 'Stand up! Stand up! Come with me!' he yelled at me with his gun. But the wounded man grabbed my shirt and said, 'Don't go with him!'

"'We'll survive,' I told the dying man. Then the terrorist shoved me with his gun and kicked me on my back toward the corner of the gymnasium where they had already executed some persons.

'Go to the corner,' he ordered.

'Which one?' I asked. In one there were mobiles [phones] piled up and the corpse of a man already shot by the terrorists.

'Get on your knees!' He yelled very loudly, for all to hear.

'I will not!' I answered him.

'Get on your knees!' he yelled again. And he put his gun to my fore-head.

'Why are you making this theater performance between women and children?' I asked him as I took the gun from my forehead. 'By the way, your children are resting in our rehabilitation centers and your wives give birth in our maternity hospitals!'

'No! Those are Kadyrov's bastards!' he said [referring to the chief mufti of Chechnya who became the Russian backed president of Chechnya in 2003.][236] 'And you know what the Ossetians are doing to us!' he said.

Larisa didn't finish her argument with her would-be executioner because Abdullah ran up to them interrupting their dispute.

"'What's going on?' Abdullah shouted.

'He is going to shoot me only because I asked for bandages for the bleeding wounded man!' I told him.

'There is nothing for you!' Abdullah then shouted at me. 'Just go back there and shut up!' I saw that Abdullah's hand was already in bandag-es. The militiamen surrounding the school [after the siege started] had wounded him.

'Could you give a piece of your bandage?' I asked him.

'Are you crazy?!!' He screamed at me. 'How is it that you don't under-stand that there is nothing for you! Go and shut up!'

"That is how I met Abdullah," Larisa reflects, resting from her story for a moment. Then she continues with another memory about him.

"At one moment Abdullah ran into hall shouting, 'Who sent a SMS [text message] from here?' They had already taken all our phones away. But we still had mine. After my husband died last year," Larisa explains, "my daughter [Madina] was keeping her father's mobile as a memento. 'Madina, don't give it up,' I had told her [when they were taking all the phones] and I put it in my brassiere.

'We will search everyone,' they announced, 'and who we find with a mobile [telephone] will be shot and ten more [hostages as well].'

They sent the women terrorists to search and they started searching in the training equipment area, very close to us. The women [terrorists] were searching the women hostages. When I saw them approaching us, I leaned over the wounded man on my knees and I let my phone fall down to the floor and I put it beneath him saying:

'You don't have to stand up.' Then I stood up and they came to search us. My daughter did not know and there was such terror in her eyes.

'It's not here,' I told Madina in Ossetic as the terrorist woman searched me.

'What about him?' the terrorist said looking at the wounded man.

'Can't you see he can do nothing?' I told her and she left him alone. After she left, I took the phone and put it back in my bra.

"[As he was bleeding to death] the wounded man wanted to find his two daughters," Larisa resumes. I was trying to calm him and asked, 'Tell me their names.' The man was in a very bad state. He told me and at that moment all the people were screaming and shouting and then the terrorists shot their guns and yelled, 'Shut up! Silent!' Everyone was terrified and suddenly became silent. In the silence, I yelled, 'Madina! Zarina! Your father is dying here! Come here!'"

The terrorist who had just threatened to kill Larisa came running back to her.

"'Didn't you get it?!' He shouted at me. 'Just shut up!'

'Can't you see what state he is in? He's looking for his daughters!' I answered him.

'Now you will understand!' he shouted at me and he called the female terrorist to come. He told her to watch me, and that if I spoke again she should shoot me, and ten others [hostages] after me! She stood with her pistol pointing at me, one and a half meters from my head. She stood like this, rearranging her tired arm for a half hour!"

We both fall silent reflecting on this.

"The women [terrorists] took orders from the men?" I ask after a few moments.

"Yes," Larisa states nodding her head solemnly.

"It sounds like you spoke to some of them," I say. "Can you tell me about them?"

"There is a notion of fear—fear that makes you frozen and makes you just sit and look down and think, Oh my God they can kill me!" Larisa explains, thinking back to her feelings about the terrorists. "But when you make yourself think more normal, you realize [the terrorists] are not so very different then you, brought up not so very far from you. Their ages were around thirties. It makes you ask yourself, What makes them come here? Maybe it's some insane bravery to make them do what they did, to take hostages, women and children," she muses.

"You can try to contact them and ask, 'Are we going to stay long here? How old are you? What's your name? Do your parents know you are here? What did you get paid to come here?'

"'I am not here for money!' one terrorist answered," Larisa says, shifting totally into her memory of one of her conversations with the terrorists in which she asked these very questions. "'I am a warrior, a mujahedeen of Allah!'

"'Do you live poorly?' I asked him.

"'No,' he told me. 'I have one sister and six brothers. My brothers live in Russia. We're not here for money, but because of the idea of liberty for Chechnya.' I understand from his comment that the fact that his brothers all worked in Moscow means that they most likely could send money home.

"I heard that Abdullah was an Ossetian. Did he speak with you more?" I ask.

"Abdullah was his war name [nom de guerre]," Larisa explains. "Only after the siege we learned that he was born in Elkhotovo [in North Ossetia]; his stepfather married his mother only after he was born. There is no open Islamic group where he lived, but somehow he joined [the terrorists] under the influence of a secret movement. No one among the hostages knew he was from there. All the hostages who stood far from him were speaking badly in Ossetic of him—fucker and so on—and he was sitting and showing no signs of understanding. Even when he sat very nearby, he didn't even raise an eyebrow. But on the third of September when the explosion occurred he was standing in the corridor. Those hostages who were still alive in the gym tried to get to the canteen to escape and he screamed in Ossetic [to the hostages] 'Everyone here, come this way!' So the women thought as they moved through the haze of the explosions and smoke that he was an Ossetian rescuer, but it was not so. He was taking them further [into the school] and they perished."

"In what language did you speak to him before this?" I ask.

"In Russian," Larisa recalls. "I spoke in Russian to all of them as they were speaking Russian to each other," Larisa explains. Indeed as it turns out the terrorists were mainly from Ingushetia and Chechnya but there was one Georgian and possibly an Arab among them as well.

"Could you tell what ethnicities they were?" I ask.

"The first one [who was going to shoot me] was perhaps Ingush or Chechen probably, since he referred to Kadyrov's bastards," Larisa answers. "One of them sounded Chechen. I don't know his name. After some time he brought me two liters of water." Given that the hostages were not allowed to get food or water after the first day, this was a live-saving gift.

"When did that happen?" I ask.

"I was trying to help the wounded guy, tearing up a t-shirt to make bandages for him and I was helping the mothers and babies. He could see I was all in blood. He saw what I was doing and he brought me water. In some time he brought me [more] - a bucket of water and plastic glasses. He had his two dirty fingers in the water and it was a cleaning bucket. He gave it to me.

'I'm not going to drink this water!' I told him.

The women sitting behind me said 'Drink! Drink!' just to make him calm.

'I'm not going to drink this!' I said.

'As you like,' he answered me.

"When they took the wounded man's [corpse] his son was left with me," Larisa continues, reentering the memory. "I was just staring in space. Then that terrorist came back to me.

"'Why do you stare at me?' he shouted. 'You want to remember me?' He had his automatic rifle pointed at me.

"I put my finger on his gun [to push it away] and I tried to pull him lower to me. He leaned back saying, 'Hey! What are you doing?'

'Don't worry,' I said. 'I just wanted to explain why I looked at you.' He leaned in and I told him, 'I don't even think where I am looking or at who.'"

Larisa stares off into space as she recalls this and I wait a few moments for her to return from her dissociative trance.

"He would have shot you?" I ask.

"No, I don't think so. But there was already a corpse there. I don't know."

"You spoke to the terrorists, even the one that wanted to shoot you, without fear and as a human being retaining your dignity," I reflect. "It sounds to me as though they responded to that. It made them act human as well, and they probably felt shame afterwards when the man died." Larisa nods.

"What do you know about the female terrorists?"

"On the second day there were two Chechen female suicide terrorists," Larisa recalls. "I heard that they agreed among themselves in some class-room [to die] and that the women blew themselves up. A man sitting in the corridor overheard and told this [after the siege]. I didn't know at the time.

After the two female terrorists exploded themselves the terrorists must have been upset about their female cadres' complaints about the moral-ity of their mission because Larisa recalls, "Abdullah came to me on the second day and asked if I have my passport.

'Why do I need to carry it?' I answered. 'I was not going to customs [on the day of the Letnika celebration].' He asked me to come out of the crowd. He took me in some hall. There were two male terrorists standing there.

'Are you Ingush?' Abdullah asked me. 'What was your last name before marriage? How many kids do you have there [in the gymnasium]?'

'I have three,' I told him. 'I have my son and daughter and that's [dead] man's son as my own.'

'Put your children out,' he said. 'And you can join us. If you have any other relatives here, we can let them go and all you have to do is put on hidjab, a [suicide] belt and become one of us and stay with us.'

Larisa thinks her black mourning dress led them to believe she might be Muslim.

"Where are your women?' I asked them and I thought, He can force me to join them even without my agreement!

"'I am not a Muslim!' I said. 'I probably cannot help you because you are here from an idea [that I don't share]. Maybe I can spoil it for you?'

'How?' he asked.

"Do I have some time to think it over?' I asked.

'Yes, you do,' he answered. 'Go and think.' Then Abdullah and these two men asked me to go and sit at my place.

When I took my place the other women wanted to know what had happened. I told them and they immediately said:

'Do it! Do it! Maybe they will release us too!'

"I was completely lost," Larisa recalls, "but I thought, God please help me that he never returns [for an answer]. And he didn't return to me again the second day.

In my opinion, Abdullah and the other terrorists approached Larisa with a suicide belt because he recognized the heroism in her and was ashamed;

they wished to be what she was—truly self-sacrificial and brave—and by asking her to join them they hoped maybe some of her courage and good heartedness would confer to them. I know from my research with Khapta that most Chechens who join the "jihad" have seen terrible atrocities: their family members and loved ones have been killed, kidnapped, tortured and mistreated. They search for an answer on how to repel their oppressors and those that join the militant jihad become highly ideologically moti-vated, indeed fanatical, in their belief in the militant jihadi ideology and all it represents in terms of fighting back with terrorism. It seems to them the only thing that can save them from their despair, and they honestly believe they are serving Allah and defending the innocents among their own society through "martyrdom" missions. And they are not cowards. It takes courage, faith and real character—even if the terror acts they are sacrificing themselves to carry out are in reality, pure and simple acts of evil. And here in Beslan, those who aspired to be heroic were confronted with someone who really was: Larisa, who stood up to them from the start, risking her life to save the hurt and the oppressed. She won the terrorists trust and became a caretaker over many, probably fulfilling their image of an ideal woman and becoming their confidante once their women had either "martyred" themselves or been executed.

"Abdullah also told me," Larisa continues smiling as she recalls his words, 'Ossetian girls are very beautiful.' He was joking and said, 'I will gather the most beautiful and take them to hidjab.'[237]

'No! You won't take as old as I am!' I answered him.

'You call yourself old?' he asked me.

'This is my [eighteen year old] daughter,' I told him. He could not believe it!

'The two planes that were exploded were operations made by our sisters,' he told me. 'And the Russian metro bombs by our sisters. Our group has very long arms and can reach very far,' he said. 'Only praying will save you! You just have to pray! There is no one needing you. Just sit and pray!'

'Are you praying? You are warriors of Allah—are you praying?' I asked him.

'Yes, we are,' he said and he turned to the guy behind him to get a little green Koran commentary written in Russian that he handed to me.

'This is the first time I see any part of the Koran,' I told him. This was the third day [of the siege]." Larisa reflects for a moment and then continues, "As real Muslims they must remove their shoes to pray. They washed their faces, hands and feet and had a little prayer carpet. But they had military boots to untie and they did not do so!"

'You can find it in no religion at all that you can kill anyone next to you—small children!' I told them.

'We are the right religion and the more we kill of the wrong religion, the more right we have to be in paradise!' they answered me.

'Of course, I understand, for you it's awful,' I said. 'Your situation is terrible but you don't have to move that here to us!'"

"I heard also about a terrorist named Ali," I say. "Did you speak with him also?"

"Ali was the person who was making negotiations, calling himself their press secretary," Larisa answers, nodding.[238]

"'It's not your real name is it?' I asked him.

'I see you are a wise woman,' he said.

'Just answer me,' I answered.

'No,' Ali told me. 'I don't need a name. I have no one to call me by my name. The Russian air strikes, their bombs killed my village. All my family were killed—my wife and five children,' he told me. 'Now I'm Ali. I'm wearing this uniform ten years!' He was twenty-eight or twenty-nine. He had a short beard with a few days growth, I saw when he was without his mask," she recalls.

"He must have been eighteen or nineteen when he joined the rebels," I reflect.

Larisa nods and continues, "Then he said, 'By the way you look just like my wife. Even twins are not as alike as you are!' I didn't answer but realized I should make us much profit out of this as I could for the lives of my children.

"'I saw you when you were praying,' he said. 'You can't imagine the situation we have. What its like for us.'

'How can we be responsible from only what is shown on TV?' I asked him.[239]

'There are things that no one knows are happening there—bad that no one knows,' he said.

Larisa falls silent for a few moments rethinking her conversations with these bearers of death.

"You could see his face at that time?" I ask.

"Yes," she recalls, "He was without his mask. When they took their masks off it was so scary! We were thinking, [now that they showed us their faces]we are not going to get out of here!" Indeed after some time and realizing that they were probably going to die inside the school, the terrorists gave up trying to hide their identities.

"How were they dressed?" I ask.

"He was wearing a black t-shirt and camouflage vest with grenades hanging off it. He had a short automatic rifle and a pistol in a holster on the side and he wore military boots. Some of the others were dressed like him. Abdullah had military shoes and pants but also short grey pants."

I ask her about the timeline of events.

"After the first day some mothers came to their children inside the school. It was impossible to leave [the school but the mothers came inside]," Larisa tells us.

"How many did this?" I ask amazed at their courage.

"Less than five," Larisa recalls. "At the end of the first day they were already strictly controlling this. When they stopped letting people drink and go to the toilet, it was the second day. When it was such a bad situation, I called Ali's name. I raised a finger and he nodded his head yes. I took so many [to the bathroom]. I had that privilege."

"Do you know why they restricted the water?" I ask.

"They broke the [water] tap just in one place and said that the water is poisoned. They also said that our people turned off the water," Larisa explains. But it seems from all I've read and heard from the hostages that the terrorists withheld water, even from the children, as a means to pressure the Russians to give into their demands.

"Our question [always] was, 'When will you release us?'" Larisa continues.

"'When the last federal soldier leaves Chechnya,' Ali answered us," Larisa recalls. And she explains that the terrorists became infuriated when the Russian news announced that they were holding only three hundred and fifty-four hostages when they believed they held over twelve hundred.

"'So we will make you that number,' Ali threatened in response to the news report. I think twelve hundred people were there. We were very crowded."

"What was your impression—that he expected to die in this operation?" I ask.

"They expected to die, but also they hoped for a negotiation and [some] success in their mission because on the second day at lunchtime he came to sit by me and he was throwing his automatic [rifle] from hand to hand. He was very nervous and was not watching the hostages as usual. Instead he was looking at the floor.

"Actually, that day Ali left—the second day, at night," Larisa recalls. "I think that Ali left when they opened a 'green' road for someone," she says referring to safe passage that he was offered for going to negotiations. "When Aushev took some [hostages] out at four p.m., and when it became dark, I think that's when Ali left.[240]

Larisa recalls that Ali was in negotiations and became very concerned about the arrival of the Russian Special Forces—it looked like Putin was ordering the school to be stormed and he desperately wanted to avert that.

"'Your people are trying to storm the school,' Ali said. 'A tank just moved to the corner.'

Later when he was taking his turn sitting with his feet on the pedal of the bomb, I came and talked to him again, asking:

'What will happen to us?' Then I heard a noise in his throat and asked, 'Are you singing?'

'No I am crying,' he answered."

Ali's negotiations with the Russians had hit a wall. Putin who had in the first days promised not to storm the school was not interested to give any concessions to the terrorists and was apparently signaling that he was willing to risk all the hostages dying. "[Putin's people] said I have a day and a half to do as I wish until you'll die,"Ali told Larisa. Evidently Ali was extremely troubled by the idea of all the hostages dying.

"At that moment everyone [around him] was shivering and I began shivering as well. My teeth were chattering [with fear]. I went back to my seat. Everyone there questioned me, but I didn't want to answer," Larisa recalls.

"Do you think they thought that somehow they could negotiate their way out of this?"

"No," Larisa answers referring to this turn of events. "In their rucksacks it was clear that they expected to stay a long time, but they were planning to die."

"What was in their rucksacks?" I ask.

"They had two rucksacks near the training equipment in the gymnasium. Before the first and second explosions people ran to this small room where it was cooler. From one rucksack I saw there was a carton of candies. I saw that there was a lot there: condensed milk, figs, coffee, calorie-rich foods. They had a coffee pot for boiled coffee. There were three pockets and in the pockets were razors, shampoo, body wash, after-shave lotion, toilet water," Larisa recalls.

So they had enough food to last for a long time, I note. The Russian press, usually highly unreliable reporting facts about Chechen terrorists, had reported that after the siege, narcotics with syringes were found in the rucksacks of the terrorists and that they had been injecting themselves. I ask Larisa if she saw any evidence of this.[241]

"No," she says shaking her head emphatically. "Abdullah had the bandages on his broken bone and Larissa Mametova, one of our doctors for the ambulance service told him, 'Let me give you an injection.'

'No,' he answered her refusing medication. 'I have aspirin and Tampelgen [an anti-pain and analgesic medication].' So she told him to take two Tampelgen."

"What about rapes?" I ask, another thing of which the Russian press had accused the terrorists.

"I heard a lot of stories in the newspapers, but they are not true," Larisa says. "They didn't beat any of the women. They were killing men and threw them out of the window. The terrorists took men to the second floor and demanded them to kneel down before they shot them. That was their favorite phrase: 'Go and kneel down!' Only on the third day they let the people take the corpses from the ground."

"How did they manage to sleep while guarding the hostages?" I ask.

"They took turns sleeping for three to four hours at a time,"she answers.

Larisa reflects again quietly and then suddenly smiles impishly. "On the third day when Ibrahim was sitting in the corridor and the children wanted to go to the toilet, he wouldn't allow it," Larisa says. "I saw an empty bottle of mineral water and noticed that the sticker on it was Ingush. I grabbed it and passed it to the children saying, 'Hey, who is the fastest to fill this bottle [with urine]?' Then they gave it back to me. I closed it and rolled it to him. He didn't notice and later he started to lift it and push open the cap.

'Hey don't!' I called to him. 'Can't you see what it is?'" Larisa laughs, recalling her prank.

"I went to the bathroom then to wet some cloths [for the children] and said to them: 'I will bring you water.' But he saw and said, 'You go and you drink.'

'I'm not going to drink; my children want to drink," I told him and then I went and took just a sip. I wet the cloths,' and when I came out he warned me to wipe off the drop of water left on my lips from drinking before I returned to the gym so that the other terrorists would not realize that he let me drink water.

When I was passing he also gave me a little caramel mocha candy.

'Give me two more,' I said.

'You can have only one,' he answered.

'I have three children," I told him. When I returned I threw the wet cloths to women and the candy I cut it in three pieces inside my mouth and called my children to come close. I told them, 'I will give you a candy; now don't dare to tell anyone! Let Mommy kiss you.' Then I kissed each of them on his lips and passed them the candy."

Larisa reflects on what motivated the terrorists to come to her town. "Maybe during all these years of war the Chechen teenagers have a vacuum in their heads and are filling it with Wahhabi ideas, and they begin to believe that the only believers are in Chechnya and there are only unrighteous people outside the borders to fight against.

"They were asking, 'Why hasn't Ossetia taken Islam when all our neighbors take it,' and they said, 'In the future all the world will be Muslim, and Islam will be the only one religion.'

"How their brains were filled to believe that this will be?" she asks herself. "But this is not Islam. This is something different—to kill.

"The terrorists told the hostages, 'If you accept Allah as your God and that no one is above him, your souls will be saved on the third day.'

'You will release us on the third day?' the people asked.

'No, you will go to paradise,' the terrorists answered."

Then, when the third day arrived without food, water and use of the toilet, Larisa recalls everyone crowded together. "It was unbearable to live, impossible to breathe, and psychologically, all the people were very tense. If [the terrorists] had said, 'In fifteen minutes this will all be finished', I was in such an awful state, I won't ask or care how!"

The final conflagration and shoot-out began first with what most investigators attribute to a Russian sharp-shooter taking out a terrorist who stood on the pressure-held pedal bomb—when he was killed, the bomb was activated and set off a chain reaction. In my interviews, however, I find that each of the hostages has their own theory of why and how the final explosions happened and no one seems to know the real truth. In those moments just before the conflagration, Larisa was busy trying to help the children.

"I was trying to take as many children to the training room as I could. Some mother had just given me another child and I was saying to the child, 'Mama is coming.' At that moment, I had just straightened my body, and the bomb exploded. I flew into the air and landed in all the dust. There was a ringing in my ears. Ibrahim [one of the terrorists] had been sitting on a red chair and he was still there. He fell over me. I thought, All the walls are falling down—we're exploding now! I felt the dust falling on us, and the shock from the explosion. I thought, Where are my children? I had been taking others [to that room] and then I opened the door, and I was so afraid to look out into the hall to see that all the people there were killed but thanks to God they were alive!

"Then I saw Ibrahim looking for his automatic and I screamed at him, 'What are you doing? Blowing us up?!'

'It's not us!' he shouted back at me. 'It's yours who are killing you!'

"Some men and women ran into the training room. In fifteen seconds the second explosion occurred and the shooting started.

"We were maybe ten or twelve hostages. I gathered all the children there. The cold air was there. It was nearly impossible to breathe! Some women were asking to come into the training room. Ibrahim came from the corridor and I told them, 'Don't look at him. Come and breathe, take turns [going inside for the cool air].' They looked so awful with bloody lips! Then I saw all the candies and sweets. I started to pass out all the candies.

"Probably we sat for forty to forty-five minutes there while there was constant shooting. There was a little corridor between the training room and the gym hall. Ibrahim was sitting facing the sports hall. I decided to find out what was happening there. When he saw me [coming] he shouted, 'Go back! Go back!'"

Ibrahim soon returned to the room.

"'Go and take the people out,' he said. 'The ceiling is burning.'

'No, if you want to go, then leave us,' I answered.

'You don't understand, the roof is burning!' he told me. 'The ceiling will fall on you!'

'Where is it burning?' I asked. 'It's normal!' Then he took me to the sports hall and I saw pieces [of the burning ceiling] dropping. The people there were very weak and wounded. I shouted, 'Who can move, come!' Some people stood up. I took another person's son in my arms. In the other hand I had Saramot, the boy of the man who died. My daughter was holding my sleeve and my son was holding onto my neck like a monkey. Ibrahim was rushing us through a hole [in the wall]. Afraid to fall, I stepped on a woman with no head! My shoulder touched her and I started falling down, then I heard Ibrahim screaming,'Hurry! Hurry!'

"He hid us in the classroom of the physical education teacher, and Ibrahim stood there with the people behind him. Constantine [an elder hostage] attacked him and grabbed Ibrahim's gun from behind, but Ibrahim was much younger and stronger. They wrestled for the gun and Ibrahim suddenly let go, so Constantine fell to the floor! Then Ibrahim took out his pistol and shot Constantine four times right in front of us! I had seen this woman without her head and now this! I got hysterical and started shouting at him, 'What did you do? What? Do you understand you killed an old man?'

"He turned to my direction with the gun and I thought,Now he will kill me too! I was with my back against the wall and his pistol was aimed at my baby's spine. I was looking in the terrorist's eyes and I turned my son from him, trying to hide him.

"He understood and put his pistol away, picked up his automatic again and controlled himself and again began moving the ten of us. Two or three of the people were from the older grades and a woman was screaming. It was then that Abdullah called in Ossetic, 'Come this way! We are here!'

"The women thought it was their savior and they ran to him. He was standing at the exit of the sports hall. He screamed in Ossetic to trick the hostages!" Larisa recalls.

"The terrorists then pushed us to the canteen. When I saw him again he was with a new terrorist I had not seen before. 'Are you Ossetian?' I asked when I reached him, but he made a signal to zip my mouth. I said, 'Whoever you are, Ossetian or you just speak Ossetic, you have always been a bastard and always will be one!'

"'Hurry! Go further! Go further!' They shouted at us. They wanted us as human shields. Our forces were shooting through the windows and the terrorists inside the kitchen were shooting back at them. We were made to lie on the floor in between the shooting zones. They also made two women stand at the window and wave the curtain calling out, 'There are live children here!' Our forces were careful and shooting above us, they knew we are on the floor. The terrorists were shooting weapons, tubes [hand held rocket launchers] held on their shoulders and the noise was unbearable.

"Then three Spetsnaz [Russian Special Forces] came in through the window. We were hiding ourselves on the floor.'Where are they?' they asked as they stepped over us. We silently directed them by pointing to the kitchen.

"At that moment Ibrahim jumped out—hell take him. He was going to shoot in front of himself but noticed the Spetsnaz on his right. First he shot bullets [from his automatic] and then he took out two grenades. He threw them one and a half meters from us.

"There was an explosion. Then silence, when you can't hear anything. Then I heard the clinking sound of glasses. I didn't feel any pain but I felt something heavy over my face and arm. I didn't lose consciousness. In the silence I thought,This is how it is to die!

"My son was in my arms, and I was covering my daughter's face with this arm," Larisa explains, lifting her reconstructed arm to show us. "It was all shattered. And Zadat was on the floor near Madina. Then the after-blast from my face flew to my son's face. He understood I was wounded and he began to cry. I turned my face from him to hide it with my hand. I lay there wounded like that for twenty minutes before we were saved. In that time period I lost consciousness.

"'Run! Run!' the soldiers told Madina when they came inside.

'No, she's still alive. Take her!' Madina told them pointing to me.

Other witnesses to the siege, including Madina the journalist, tell us about the chaos that ensued outside the school—that the Ossetian men with their rifles, who had been kept at a distance outside a police cordon, were firing, as were the Special Forces and the terrorists. Hostages tell us "that bullets were flying from three different directions and it was complete chaos" and that "it was total pandemonium" as the children and parents were running and trying to escape from the burning school. An incendiary missile from a tank was also fired by the military and it is later proven that it must have been the main cause of the roof of the school burning so voraciously.

Larisa came again to consciousness again inside the school. "I tried to wipe my face with both hands, but only one moved. I tried to stand.

A Spetsnaz standing above me said, 'Wait! Wait, girl, they will bring a stretcher soon. Wait!'

"It's so silly, but at that moment I was so happy that he called me 'girl' at age forty-one!'"

Larisa says a self-organized group of Ossetians saw that the ambulances were overwhelmed and drove their own cars to the school, serving as makeshift ambulances to ferry the wounded away to the hospital in ones and twos. She was driven in one of these cars.

"I asked the driver, 'What is your name?'

'Sergei.'

'I will never forget your name!' I told him. I didn't answer his question about my name because I closed my eyes then again and lost consciousness. Much later I couldn't find him to thank him. I asked about him but no one knew who he was.'"

At the hospital, Larisa was in and out of consciousness and underwent three emergency operations.

"In the morning when I came to, Dr. Torlova, the doctor who was operating and the rest of the doctors were all looking at me.

'What date is your birthday?' she asked. I thought it's a test and I told my birth date.

'From now your birthday is the fourth of September!' she said. After the operation I was in a deep coma—in agony—and they thought I was dead. They had already washed my body for the morgue but I regained life.

'You will definitely live one hundred years!' the doctor told me.

'Where are my children?' I asked them.

'Everything is fine with your children,' they said. 'But we must send you abroad for treatment.'

"I refused saying, 'I am not going farther then Moscow!' I thought they are not telling me the truth [about my children]."

Indeed in the former Soviet Union, doctors today still do not always tell cancer patients the truth about their diagnoses to avoid depressing them, and they may well have held the news from Larisa if her children had been killed.

"I talked to my children by telephone, and then agreed [to be medically evacuated to Moscow]. There were no wounds on my son. Madina was shot in the shoulder. But when the grenade went off, my arm protected her face. I had twelve shrapnel in my hand and face. Another teacher lying near me had her head toward the terrorists and mine was behind her. Her legs were blown off and she died.

Many hours have passed as we have been listening and Larisa invites us into her kitchen for tea.

"These three days were like hell," Larisa continues. "Small children can't understand. 'What do you mean there is no water? Okay let's go to the shop. You can buy me some Coke and Sprite'; 'Why don't we go home?'.

"Children don't understand what a terrorist is and what it means to be a hostage. We lied to the children that the bus will be coming soon. We told them fairy tales and told them it's better for you to sleep. I remember that the other boy [of the killed man], started calling me Mama. Zoar my son became jealous and they both started crying. I told my son, 'Zaramok, you have such a name as a great warrior! He wouldn't cry!'

As she takes the teakettle to put on the flame, Larisa glances at her reconstructed hand saying, "I thought I'd never use this hand again. The bones were shattered. Five pins and three screws held it together, and the pain was so big that I was under anesthesia. For six weeks I wore [the hand brace]."

Larisa blames the Russian central government for not acting in a way that protected the hostages better.

"It would have been better not to irritate the terrorists and give them the image of hope," she states. "They had to make the terrorists believe and trust the authorities and at that moment start a plan to save us. Instead the terrorists were put in a position that told them that they are not significant and Moscow's important people are not even willing to talk to them. That's why [it blew apart]."

"I can't forget Ali's words" Larisa says recalling how he dejectedly told her, "'Russia doesn't have any notion of terrorists and hostages. They gave me a day and a half.'" Larisa says shaking her head sadly. "Now since this event my life is divided in two. I have a life before it and a life after. The question I face: there are so many who were slow [to rescue us] and all those who lie in the graveyard. Why am I alive?

"In the first days everyone looked for who is guilty. Everyone blaming. They would say, 'He escaped and didn't save my children.'

"Above me lives my neighbor," Larisa explains. "She didn't get to the school—she was late. Her daughter, eleven-years-old in the fifth grade, went and her son in the eleventh grade. They were shot in their backs. When the mother saw us afterwards, she blamed everyone. She asked my daughter, Madina, 'If you saw my daughter why didn't you save her?' When I was in the hospital, my mother-in-law explained to this woman that I saved my own children."

We discuss the sadness everyone carries to this day.

"Does your faith help you cope?" I ask.

"I got baptized in Moscow," Larisa says nodding. "I feel so sad for all those who died. It was in the siege, when I began to believe. I was desperately praying, asking for help, to save me, and my children. I always had the thought that there is no way we entered this siege and there is no escape. Before, I only believed in God in a 'Thank God!' sense, but I never went to church. In the canteen is where I began to understand and believe in God."

Larisa says she will take her son to school again this year.

"The new school is built so close to the old one. Isn't it awful?" she says.

"It's hard to return?" I ask, knowing that of course it is.

"Yes," she nods. "For the survivors it's very awful! Last year on the third of September I was carried out of the school. And I was only able to return to it on the twentieth of June [when she was released from the hospital]! I made myself go with no tears. I returned to all the places and all the corners and I finally comprehended what had occurred.

"When I was in the hospital in Moscow I had no emotions until the tenth of October [a full month after the event]. Then I burst into tears and I was very emotional for about a week."

"Something triggered this?" I ask.

"It was nothing special," she answers. "I woke up at two or three a.m. and just started crying as if someone had kicked me. The memories came [flooding] back. In Moscow, the psychologists visited us in our rooms. She saw I was in tears and said, 'Even strong people can cry.' She talked with me for three or four hours and my head got to the right state and then I was able to regulate my emotions. It took me another four days of crying and then I felt much better."

"All the time my questions were: 'Why did all this happen? Why did it finish this way? And was there something—anything—that could have been done to avoid so many funerals?' How to answer [these questions]?

The only thing I realized when I asked myself is that in this life the only person that can help you is yourself."

"How about the psychologist?" I ask, horrified to think she came to this alienated conclusion.

"Yes, she helped," Larisa nods. "The psychologist said to me that it's very good to cry, that crying and discussing my emotions are a way out of this [physical] pain and digestive problems. And my children help," Larisa says, smiling at her physically unscathed daughter who enters the room to join us for tea, hugging her mother as she passes her in the tiny kitchen.

As Larisa turns to take the teacups from her cupboard and put them on the table her hair still covers half her face. I ask her if she will show me her face and gingerly, afraid to see our reaction she pulls her hair back revealing a missing cheekbone and gaping eyeball not properly set in its socket. It's frightening, but with tears in my eyes, I tell her, "You are truly the most beautiful woman I have ever met!"

We drink our tea together; then thank Larisa for sharing her story with us and leave down her stairway silenced by the weight of it.

CHAPTER 50

Jumping to Freedom - Aslan

After leaving Larisa's we head back to our hotel. I ask Madina if we can take her and her uncle to dinner but she begs off.

"That last interview was so sad; I think I just need to go home and cry. I'll meet you tomorrow in the breakfast bar." She points out the restaurant for breakfast in the morning, and Ces insists that we pick up food and eat our evening meal in our hotel room. He's convinced that if we sit openly in a restaurant we'll attract attention to ourselves as foreigners and may disappear.

"If it's the terrorists who take us, we can insist to be taken to Basayev and then we'll get a great interview!" I joke. "And if it's the FSB, I think they'll think twice about messing with a diplomat's wife."

"That's fine for you," Ces answers, "but I just have no such protection!" I acquiesce, although I'd love to be surrounded by Russian speakers and enjoy the live music so frequent in former Soviet restaurants.

When we enter the hotel I see that our clerk is still suffering from the heavy allergy symptoms she had when we checked in; she's coughing, sneezing and blowing her nose and looks totally miserable. "Wait here!" I tell her and run upstairs to bring her some American allergy medication. I return and tell her the instructions for taking it while wondering if my do-good actions could end in my being imprisoned if she keels over from some strange side effect. She takes the medicine gratefully, and Ces and I head up to our room on the second floor.

After eating our meal sequestered in our room, we turn in. Ces reads again late into the night unable to fall easily asleep, whilst I totally exhausted—emotionally far more than physically—fall into the sleep of the dead.

The next morning as we make our way to breakfast the hotel clerk runs up to me to thank me for the good night's sleep.

"You saved me from my grave!" she says. I laugh thinking how often medicines sold in the former Soviet Union are counterfeit. I run back to our room to retrieve the entire box for her and warn her not to take more than the recommended dose.

Madina is supposed to join us for breakfast, but as we sit down I remark, "She not going to join us today. It was too much for her last night and she's going to quit," I say, fully convinced of my sudden intuition. Ces argues that Madina is very reliable. "She may be reliable, but she's emotionally blown away and she's going to quit today," I insist as we eat our strange but deliciously prepared eggs, fried in a combination of herbs and tomato sauce.

Madina arrives late and when she sits down she refuses a meal, stammering through a prepared speech about how she cannot carry on translating for us—that it's just too painful especially after she herself almost died reporting on the siege last year.

"It's okay, we understand," I reassure her, a bit surprised myself by the accuracy of my intuition. She assures us that she has already arranged a new translator, Zarina, for us, and that her Uncle Volodya, will continue on as our driver. We agree, kissing her and thanking her for all she's already done for us.

Zarina joins us and we head out to our next interview with Aslan, a prominent village businessman who was held hostage inside the school with his children. He was the only one among the men slated-to-be-executed that managed to live to tell about it.

Aslan has invited us to his office for the interview. We arrive with Zarina and wait in reception until his receptionist takes us back into his spacious office furnished with a desk and modern aluminum and black leather. Aslan rises from his seat behind his desk, greets us with handshakes, and invites us to sit. He pulls a chair alongside us while Zarina explains my study and the purpose of our visit.

Aslan tells us that each year in the Letnika, one young schoolgirl is chosen for the honor of ringing the school bell to start the year. As a businessman who had given a lot of charity to the school, Aslan's daughter had been selected to ring the bell. Aslan, his wife, baby and mother-in-law all excitedly gathered at the Letnika to watch his daughter carry out her honored role.

"My daughter was sitting on an older boy's shoulders," Aslan explains. "I had an operator and a journalist standing near me because I wanted that picture – of her ringing the bell – on the first page of the newspapers!" he recalls smiling proudly as he recalls her moment of glory.

Then his face contorts in pain. "When I saw the terrorists coming and shouting orders, I picked up my daughter and gathered her with my mother-in-law into the gymnasium as they demanded. At first we couldn't understand or believe it. If I could understand how it would end or what is going to happen we could fight them, but we had no idea."

Aslan knows we have already heard the descriptions of what went on in the gym and moves ahead to tell us about when the terrorists gathered all the strong men, who were able to resist, to be executed.

"I was the first [of the men] taken out of the crowd. My daughter was on my side and other some girl who died [later in the siege]. The terrorists saw me and pointed at me to stand up. My daughter clung to me and didn't want to let me go but I put her down. Her mama was holding our little baby. There were fifteen of us men taken out of the gymnasium to the corridor. There one of the terrorists held a pistol to my head.

'You are with the police!' he shouted at me. I was standing and my children were sitting not far from this area, and I was horrified thinking, *If they see me killed right in front of their eyes*!"

Alsan recalls that the gunman was Khodov, who he claims is a famous kidnapper of unknown nationality and an orphan.[242] Vladimir Khodov, nicknamed Abdullah, was from nearby Elkhotovo although as Larisa told us, he kept his Ossetian identity hidden until the end of the siege.[243] Khodov eventually backed down and ordered the men to take seats in the corridor -awaiting what they presumed would soon be their executions.

"We sat in the corridor for four hours," Aslan continues. "They didn't talk to us during that time. Then around four or five in the evening they took us in different directions to different locations. They took me, and some others upstairs to the second floor. It was the Colonel himself who took us," Aslan says referring to the bald leader among the terrorists."When he was leading us to the classroom he said, 'Your authorities, your government thinks that we are joking.'

"I thought, *It's just words*! Then you can imagine the reaction we had when we entered the classroom and saw the men that we had just saw a few moments before, lying there—dead!"

The Colonel told Aslan and the remaining men to throw the corpses out the window and left us with the other terrorist.

"When I opened the window I felt the smell of life!" Aslan says. "We threw three corpses out. Then I felt sick. I thought, *I will throw up*! They had done some awful things to them."

"What did they do?" I ask.

"I cannot tell women such a horrible thing," he says averting his eyes, but I reassure him that I want to hear the truth of what happened, no matter how gruesome.

Aslan looks again at me and Zarina to be sure, and seeing that I am resolute, explains with a scowl, "They were just big strong men, but when we got there - some had no heads, legs, and hands. They had shot them until their body parts fell apart."

I nod silently. Aslan repeats that he told the terrorist he felt sick and was allowed a minute to rest before throwing the rest of the bodies out.

"To my colleague I said [in Ossetic] 'Let's jump though the window,'" Aslan continues. "Meanwhile the terrorist was recharging his Kalashnikov with bullets. I told my colleague this idea three times but he just answered, 'How?' Then I ran suddenly and jumped out the window. I fell on the corpses – they broke my fall and probably saved my life. I began crawling to get away. The terrorists shot at my back. I ran to a car near the school and crawled under it. When our forces saw that one of the hostages had jumped out the window, they shot a tear gas grenade [for cover]. It made a good fog. I ran to them. They took me to the hospital."

Aslan rises from his chair and goes to a glass. He opens some cognac and hands out small glasses, pouring shots for all of us. We all drink a round of cognac with him as I ask, a bit afraid to hear the answer:

"What happened to your family?"

"My mother-in-law stayed in the gymnasium with my daughter." Aslan's face clouds over in pain again. "She died when she was protecting children running from bullets shot in their backs."

He pours cognac again and raises his glass to me, "Let's make a toast that you visit us next time for good reasons instead of these!"

We down another round of shots. I'm feeling the alcohol but would not have dared to refuse his toast. In Russia to fail to bottoms-up to a toast signals that you don't agree with it. Knowing their traditions, I add my own raising the glass he has already refilled to him, "And that we can always protect our families!" I say as our eyes meet with sadness.

We drink another round of shots and I can feel already how this way of dealing with pain works on some level – it both opens up the pain to being able to talk about it *and* dulls it while creating a warm camaraderie.

"Your daughter?" I ask returning to our interview. "How did she cope psychologically with all of this?"

"Since then my daughter was educated at home," Aslan explains. "When she was invited to open up the replacement school, she cried and refused to go. We took a picture with Luskhov[244] and begged her to go. I thought she was okay but she was too afraid. Before this she was very brave girl and never afraid."

"It was terrible to bear the loss of her grandmother," Aslan adds. "Our baby girl was a year and a half then and she also was always crying for her grandmother."

"Have the journalists caused any problems for you?" I ask.

"People ask such stupid questions!" Aslan answers angrily, explaining that after the siege journalists frequently asked him why the men did not resist the terrorists – when in fact they had no idea what was happening and no time to organize themselves before they were overtaken by them.

"It's better to live in another country!" he says, cynically telling us he would move away from where this was allowed to happen if he could. "But not to the U.S.," he adds, "Americans call [the Chechens] rebels, not terrorists!"

I smile over that, then he adds, "The journalist asked me such stupid things: 'Were you happy when you learned you are alive?' and 'When you crawled to our people what did they tell you?'" Aslan shakes his head at the perversity of such questions.

"I wonder what do you think is the best advice for a situation like this?" I ask.

"Attack them immediately," Aslan answers with no hesitation. "We shouldn't have given them a chance. Do like the Israelis and refuse to negotiate with them. That is the policy that might have helped. If our forces had attacked at once they can't arrange themselves that quickly. We would have lost less. We lost two hundred and fifty people waiting three days before the storm - maybe we would lose five hundred if they waited longer. We could fight with the rescuers, instead of sitting and waiting for our deaths."

It's interesting to hear his perspective as most of the other hostages are angry over the storm, feeling it caused so many deaths – but Aslan is also one of the only surviving men of fighting age, and he alone had to endure being asked why the men did *not* immediately resist the terrorists. Perhaps that, more than anything, forms his views now.

Aslan continues, "The terrorists said, 'You won't have problems with us. The problem for you is your government. If they storm, they will kill us - and it will be worse for you.'

"What about the female terrorists—did you see them?" I ask.

"There were two women with bitten fingernails," Aslan recalls. "They were very young, sixteen or seventeen years old. They didn't speak. They only passed by. They spoke in Chechen or Ingush sometimes. I was a witness to one of their conversations. When the terrorists took us to board over the windows early on in the siege, I heard the women arguing in Russian with the male terrorists, that there are children here. Later on I think they killed them. Or they killed themselves. We never saw them again."

"And you – how did you cope after the siege?" I ask him.

"For the first six months I couldn't fall asleep – unless I drank two hundred grams [of vodka]," Aslan says. "But now it's okay."

"You had nightmares during that time?" I ask.

"Yes, I had many terrible dreams," Aslan recounts. "About why it happened and what could I have done? I slept alone during that time period because I had such terrible dreams. Once I dreamed I pulled off one of their masks!"

"What helped you?" I ask.

"I needed a psychologist at that moment and one came and helped me," Aslan recalls speaking about a broadcast that spoke to him. "In Moscow there is famous Georgian psychologist—I can't remember his name. He said that God said you were left alive and God helped you for a reason. You have a purpose."

I smile and ask him, "Do you know your purpose now?"

Aslan nods smiling back. "Yes, to help my family!"

"It also helps to work," he adds. "At first my business partners in Moscow and everybody supported me a lot. Friends arrived here to support me, my wife helped and the children helped us. Every day until January we talked about it.

And mostly our children helped us. When I put them to sleep I tell them fairytales. I constructed many fairytales for them, with *big* heroes," he says smiling broadly. Then more seriously he adds, "If my family didn't survive I don't know how I would behave."

"You needed the heroes too?" I reflect.

"I dream to die in such a way - protecting my children," Aslan states.

We drink a bit more cognac as Aslan moves the conversation to milder topics. We discuss the beauty of North Ossetia and the mountains surrounding us. Aslan suddenly decides that he must show us "his mountains" and proposes to take us on a picnic to the foot of Mount Elbrus, the tallest mountain in Europe located not far from Beslan. I smile at the idea as I grew up as a small girl in the summers near the Rocky Mountains in Colorado, and I'm beginning to realize some beauty might be a lovely respite from all the pain we've been hearing. He makes us promise to go with him on a picnic in the mountains two days from now. We part fondly with Aslan with promises to meet again in a few days time, a promise that somehow feels so comforting after listening to how he almost died.

CHAPTER 51

Encounters with the FSB

The next morning after our breakfast, Ces and I walk back up to our hotel room to get our briefcases and other things for the day. As we walk up the wooden steps to the second floor we pass by a group of men in black suits coming down the stairs and I hear them making a remark—something about a woman. I sense that they are speaking about me and I think they are FSB. I keep my head down as we walk up the steps hoping that the clothes I selected specifically to mimic the ex-Soviet styles of the region do indeed blend in and that they don't notice that I am a foreigner. They pass us by with no incident and I say nothing to Ces, so as not to worry him anymore than he already is.

Feeling alarmed, I go through my things checking to see if any of them have been disturbed—common FSB behavior. Nothing appears to be out of place, and we descend again into the lobby. The hotel clerk still so grateful for the allergy medicine, runs to me and begins warning me in Russian that the authorities are looking for us, but before she can finish, I see them looking menacingly as they stand in the doorway of the lobby, blocking our departure. Not wanting her to get in any trouble, I tell her thanks and head forward into the inevitable.

"Documents please," one of them says sternly, repeating the phrase that always precedes trouble with Russian authorities, as he steps forward to block our exit from the hotel. Ces is confused but I tell him, "These are FSB agents and they need our passports. Please stay calm, Ces; I will handle it." Distressed, he rifles through his things for his passport and I also produce mine. Now all four agents are surrounding us and one of them asks as he scrutinizes our passports, "Why are you here?"

"I am an American psychologist, and he is a researcher from the UK," I tell them in Russian. "We are here to learn from the hostages of Beslan about how to help psychologically in situations like this. It's so very sad, isn't it?" I say.

"We are being very strict with travelers here at this time," the agent answers.

"Yes, it's a very sensitive time," I agree. "The hostages are worried that the event can be repeated, and the journalists can be quite aggressive. We are leaving in three more days although first we are going to see Mount Elbrus. It's very beautiful here."

Volodya is concerned that we have not arrived to his car and has parked it and enters the lobby. His former military bearing adds a level of credibility, and I'm thankful to him for coming to stand with us as we are being questioned.

The FSB agent sizes us up, deliberating about what to do. After a moment of thought he hands our documents back, allowing us to pass. I thank him and practically running, we spill out of the lobby and jump into Volodya's car, me laughing and Ces ready to pee his pants.

"Don't worry," I tell Ces. "They have to do their jobs and they were just checking in on us. I think it's as much a warning as a check—they don't want us causing them any trouble with investigating their failures and we won't. So we should be okay." Volodya agrees, and together we calm Ces down.

For the next two days, we continue with our interviews, most of them repeating what we have learned already, and each day the sadness becomes even more unbearable, especially when we hear about the many failures of the military, Special Forces, FSB and local authorities in rescuing the hostages.

"The terrorists said that no one cares about us," one of the hostages, Zemphera, tells us. "And now I see that even now—no one does. The women [in the Beslan mothers group] are right," she concludes adding sadly, "It's the system we have! I still cannot believe that people were burning and that the ambulances were not ready and the fire trucks came with no water!

"Our forces that came to save,killed us. The Alpha forces saved many but they came late, only forty minutes into the attack and only fifty of them—why? Another one hundred of them were in the banya [Russian sauna] and training—why?"

Volodya, who was assisting his journalist niece Madina as her driver during the siege, feels the same.

"They were not ready for this operation—no plan," Volodya tells us. He explains that when the first explosion occurred the Russian Special Forces that had been sent were inexplicably unprepared to storm the school. "Two batteries of Alpha [Special Forces] came on the corner where I was parked. They were counting and dropping their weapons and helmets [as they assembled] because they were nowhere ready to attack. And forty minutes went by [after the explosion] from when Alpha approached this corner!" He shakes his head in disgust. "There *were* Ossetians who wanted to solve it themselves," he says, referring to the many men who had come out armed with their rifles surrounding the school since the siege had begun.

"I saw the first girl and first man appear after the first explosion—it was about ten minutes after the hostages began to run out. There were rumors that some of the terrorists left the school and were among them," Volodya adds. I nod, understanding if Kuliyev laid down his arms and tried to hide among the hostages, it may be possible that some of the other terrorists also ran and escaped alongside the hostages.

"Panic started," Volodya recalls. "Shooting began and everybody tried to run away, men and women. But some women refused to leave because their children were still inside. The police that were here [Volodya indicates where his car was parked and where he sat witnessing the events] didn't get any closer. And the journalists didn't run away when the shooting began."

Volodya said Madina was among them, urged onward toward the school and gunfire by the journalist she was translating for, while he stood by, angered and watching helplessly from a distance.

"We saw the first man carrying a girl out. She was fifteen or sixteen years old in a white blouse and black shirt [the school uniform]. She had short hair and her head was bleeding. She was very thin. All the correspondents ran to take pictures and make interviews but she was unable to answer. She was in shock and wounded. Then came a man, thirty years old; he was also wounded. He could not even stand. It was very hot and the ambulances were not there yet. Then came little children. They began to bring more children, and men were screaming, 'What I saw! What I saw!'[1] And we understood there are a lot of them killed. The journalists and other men were screaming, 'Where is an ambulance? Where is an ambulance?' But none came, so some men decided to take them to hospital by themselves. After that there was a lack of private cars. More men came with cars and started driving people home or to hospital. Then children also

1 Perhaps this translates more accurately "The horror! The horror!"

ran to the garage. Only after forty minutes the ambulances came. And for fifteen minutes we carried children ourselves!" Volodya says. He is a tough man, but the horror of it all shows on his face and creeps into his voice as he recounts all that he witnessed.

Many of the failures are indeed questionable. How could the fire trucks not be filled with water, and the ambulances and Special Forces not on the ready after the hostages had already spent two full days locked in the school with bombs surrounding them? It seems like it has to be willful negligence or something even more sinister.

Later between interviews Volodya tells me about his time serving in the military and how corrupt the Russian soldiers are, especially those who served in the war against the Chechens. He says the soldiers commonly sold their arms—and even their tanks—to the Chechens to get cash that they pocketed in return.

"I wish I had sold a tank to them when I was in the Army," he says in a cynical voice.

I gasp. "You're joking, right?"

"No, Anna," he answers. "After all I've seen, I wish I had done it. I could use the money to have a dacha [summer cottage] somewhere in the mountains and forget all that goes on here. What would one more tank have meant in this corrupt war with the Chechens?"

I shake my head, unsure if he really means it or not. He doesn't seem like someone who could bend his principles so completely. But I also understand that he and many others here have had their fill of corruption. Maybe for them, after a time it just doesn't make sense anymore to follow rules that no one else bothers to follow or enforce.

Regarding the widespread corruption of the Russian soldiers and other forces serving in Chechnya, Chechen colleagues have also told me too many stories of how the Russian forces take bribes from the rebels and terrorists to leave terrorist-ridden territory alone. Then having to show some action and results, these soldiers bomb innocent villages and arrest blameless young men who are tortured into confessing crimes they haven't committed. It's a dirty war and polluted with politics concerning oil, power and corruption. And now militant jihadi ideas have poured into Chechnya in recent years from the Middle East, and it seems to have exhausted everyone in this region.

That night when we return to our hotel and after hearing so much pain all week, I cannot bear to eat a sequestered dinner of carryout food again.

The live music playing out on the veranda drifts through our windows along with the balmy night air and I know I will feel much better there. I tell Ces who is planning to hole up again in our hotel room, "Listen, the authorities obviously know we are here and if they want to kidnap us, they'll haul us right out of our room! I'm going down to the hotel restaurant. You can join me if you want, or come later if you change your mind," I say. Ces refuses, shaking his head at "my foolhardiness" and I head out to the restaurant.

I've shed my professional attire and put on a festive summer dress to cast off the sad mood, and I smile as I feel the balmy air and see the moon shining down on the restaurant veranda. The hostess seats me at table facing the musicians, playing sad Russian ballads interspersed with lively dance music—all tunes that I recognize. After ordering a glass of wine and beginning in on my appetizer, I begin to feel much better. Another diner seeing me alone invites me to dance and throwing caution to the wind, I get up and dance with him, drawing comfort from the music and the joy of dancing. After a couple of dances, I sit down making clear to him I'm not interested in taking it any further, and I eat my next course with another glass of wine. But before I can finish my meal, the pain suddenly sears into my mind again and I find myself completely overwhelmed with tears. The night is too beautiful, and the sad ballads must hit a chord inside—I know the Russian words and they are tragic, echoing all the pain we've been listening to. Russia has the saddest history and now after all the stories of dead, burned and shot children and their bereaved parents, my tears burst through the dam I've been trying hold them behind. Quickly wiping away the tears that won't stop, I push back my chair, lay money on the table and flee back to our hotel room.

There I find Ces who takes fright when he sees my face. "What happened?" he asks, alarm and concern crossing his face.

"I just can't take it!" I tell him, literally collapsing to the floor in sobs. "It's too painful. I can't take it anymore—all these children and their bereaved parents, it's too horrible!"

Ces puts his arms around me and clucks comfortingly as I sob and blubber through my pain. I'm totally embarrassed by my outburst and at the same time completely unable to control it. "I think it was the music and the moon and the complete normalcy of it in contrast to all we are hearing!" I sputter out in between sobs.

After recovering myself, I join Ces in reading magazines late into the night until I'm calm enough to sleep and face more interviews the next day.

After two nights in our hotel, we have to move the next day to another one because ours room is needed for other guests. Ces is glad to move after our FSB visit and Zarina helps him to arrange for a room in our new hotel on the main square of Vladikavkaz, while I take the opportunity to go check out the shops. I like the Russian jewelry made of semi-precious stones mined from the surrounding mountains and get engrossed in purchasing some necklaces for myself, and my two daughters as they finalize the hotel arrangements. When I return after about a half hour of shopping, Zarina is absent and Ces is in a panic.

"Where were you?" he asks in an accusatory voice. "I have Zarina and Volodya searching all over town for you!"

Realizing he cannot let his fear of kidnapping go, I try to calmly explain that I can speak Russian and that all of this is very familiar to me—the little shops and the town square—and that I don't share his fears. "I'm not going to disappear on you Ces!" I protest. "It was only a half hour I was gone!" Zarina returns and she also seems unconcerned and admires my new purchases while Ces fumes.

At night when we return to our hotel, Ces and I have a good laugh; looking around the deluxe room Ces has procured for us. It's totally uphol-stered–walls and ceiling–in thick burgundy velvet, and there are crystal chandeliers hanging from the ceiling of the bedroom and spacious ante-room. The chandeliers are classy but the velvet walls looks like it's a room for high government officials and their prostitutes.

"I hope the beds are clean," I joke. Ultimately, we agree the important thing is that it has two beds and is comfortable, though I don't like that there is a door to an adjoining room that is locked on that side but there is no key or way to lock it from *our* side – a perfect set-up for the FSB or anyone else to have easy access to our room. I, for one, know the dirty tricks security agencies in the former Soviet Union liked to play on our diplomats. In Minsk where Daniel and I lived when he served as US Ambassador to Belarus, the security services there – still called the KGB - would frequently enter our diplomats' apartments while they were at work. The agents would smoke a cigarette, discarding the butt and ashes on a plate they put in a prominent place or urinate into the toilet and leave it unflushed. They would also leave a window open, all to send a message to the returned diplomat that his home security had been breached and there was little he could do about it.

Knowing they may enter our room, I remind myself to keep everything I don't want them reading on my person at all times. And at night I check the adjoining room's door before heading to bed to make sure it's closed tightly. Perhaps because this is on my mind when I fall asleep and wake some hours later in the middle of the night to see a beam of white light flashing on the floor near me, my mind jars into wide-awake panic mode. I immediately think, *Oh my God someone is in our room crawling along the floor by my bed with a flashlight! Have they sent someone to come in our room at night while we are here? Would they sink that low to intimidate us?*

"Ces! Ces!" I cry out in as controlled a voice as I can muster "Ces!" I call out again as he wakes from his light snoring and answers me with a sleepy "What is it?"

"Ces, wake up please! I don't want to scare you," I say, "but I don't think we are alone in this room. I think someone is here with us!"

That jars Ces wide awake as he sits up in his bed. The light switches are far away on the wall so I say, "I'm going to stand up now and go switch on the light, please help me if I need it." Then I swing my legs off my bed, terrified of what I might run into, stand up in the pitch-blackness and make my way to the light switch.

When I switch the lights on the glittering crystal chandelier is blinding and the burgundy velvet walls look surreal. Ces is sitting up in his bed in his pajamas, rubbing his eyes and I go to the cabinet and pick up a champagne glass to use as a weapon if I need it. Holding it menacingly, I begin checking the anteroom, the bathroom and the lock on our outer door. Then I walk up to the door separating our rooms and try it, terrified that it has been unlocked and will swing open revealing whoever is lurking there. But it's still locked from the other side. There's no intruder in the room.

Ces and I sit up and discuss what it was and what to do. I know I saw a light flickering by my bed and there is no good explanation. We discuss if it could have been my phone flickering on and off in the darkness. Maybe—the electricity here is spotty and that could account for it but it seemed more like a flashlight to me. Unable to explain it, we decide it had to be my phone and we uneasily switch the lights off again, this time leaving the bathroom one on. There's no choice but to go anxiously back to sleep.

The next morning is sunny and bright. We forget all about the last night's terrors as we head off to take our holiday with Aslan to the mountains. He's packed a fine picnic including homemade cherry cognac and vodka. Sitting by a mountain stream in view of the snowy Mount Elbrus and her sister mountains, we laugh and share toasts and good food together, forgetting the reasons that brought us here and enjoying the human camaraderie that exists all around the world between decent people.

On the way home from the neighboring republic of Karbardino-Bulkaria we pass the road to the airport that Ces remembers the terrorists took and perhaps more eerily, we stop in Nalchik[245] for me to use the restroom. It is a terrible place with a Soviet style bathroom – a hole in the floor – filled to capacity with garbage and excrement, and after fulfilling my call I run from it. A month later when we've left Beslan behind, we hear on the news: a subgroup of the newly-formed terrorist/militant group, the Caucasian Front - uniting Chechen and other militant jihadis from the neighboring Muslim republics - stormed Nalchik only days after we were there - taking hostages and causing a shoot-out with the police and FSB![246] Ces has narrowly escaped another terrorist happening in the area and vows he will never return! I laugh and think, *We were protected! It happened after we left!*

CHAPTER 52

The Beslan Terrorists

W hen all the numbers were tallied, the Beslan hostages totaled eleven hundred twenty. Of these, four hundred and seventy were left wounded and three hundred and thirty – mostly children—were killed. There were thirty-two hostage-takers with the number of females established at either two or three depending upon the source.[247]

Zemphera has an interesting take on the politics of the siege. "Putin wanted and needed the terrorists' deaths for his power," she says. "After this terror act he enacted his vertical," she says referring to Putin's dismantling of democracy, in which he transformed the government into a vertical system of appointments from his office downward, consolidating his presidential power.[248]

Zemphera, however, doesn't think the terrorists came to die. She recalls how Kuliyev, the only terrorist left standing after the shoot out, stopped fighting during the storm, changed his clothes and hid among the hostages in an effort to escape. Zemphera remembers that when the Special Forces were alerted to his identity by hostages who recognized him as a hostage-taker and discovered him still alive hiding among them, he screamed, 'Don't kill me, I'm ours [nasha in Russian].I want to live! I didn't kill anyone!'"

But, the terrorists were also clear in their "martyrdom" statements— "victory or Paradise"—and the women came wearing bomb belts clearly ready to self-detonate. They plotted out their actions ahead of time and came with the express purpose of mass hostage-taking to gain media attention to their cause and to try to force the issue of an independent Chechnya with the Russian government. Perhaps these terrorists hoped for a negotiated settlement to force the Russians out of Chechnya, but surely they must have realized that kind of victory was a very remote possibility with the Putin government.

"When there is such fanaticism," Aslan told us, "the connection of fanaticism and religion [causes them to] think in a different way. When

Russia attacked Chechnya some years ago and killed their children, the Russians never thought that they would come back and revenge here like this," Aslan added. "Afghanistan—it came from this," he explained. "It is politics and business."

That the origins of this assault come in part from Afghanistan is correct. When the exultant mujahedeen who had just won a victory in Afghanistan against one of the world's superpowers were intoxicated with their victory and looking for their next cause, many of them turned to Chechnya's plight with Russia, going there to support their next "jihad" for occupied Muslim lands. During the years when the Afghan veterans made their way into Chechnya, the Chechen rebel fighters transitioned from secessionist guerilla fighters to militant jihadis taking on the "martyrdom" ideology and suicide terrorism as one of their most lethal tools.[249] And after suffering so much at the hands of the Russians, they brought the ideology of "martyrs" and holy warriors that had first formed in Afghanistan and began striking at the heart of Russia with numerous suicide attacks in Moscow. When funds became too limited to send terrorists a long distance – to Moscow or Saint Petersburg (Putin's hometown) as Basayev desired,[250] they came to take children hostage here in Beslan. The Chechen terrorists' goal was to bring the world's attention to what Russia was doing to their children and the people of Chechnya during their two wars of independence, but the ideology they followed had already been formed during the "jihad" in Afghanistan.[251]

Aslan observed one point of humanity he noticed in the terrorists. "They felt sorry for their killing. They were apologizing to God each time they killed someone - I noticed that. When I heard shots [executions] they took their Korans and began praying."

After hearing about the terrorists from their hostages, I wanted to know what made these men and women come to Beslan and why they decided to target children. Their sender Chechen warlord and terrorist leader Shamil Basayev gave some explanations in his public statements and demands during and in the aftermath of the siege.

In one statement he mocked Putin's appeal for international support for Beslan, reminding readers that Putin "forgets . . . that 'Chechnya is Russia's internal affair'", the statement Putin had repeatedly used to repel international journalists and those making international calls for investigations of human rights violations in Chechnya.

Basayev obviously feels bad about the children's deaths saying, "What happened in Beslan is a terrible tragedy," but he blames Putin, rather than his own actions, for the massacre claiming, "The Kremlin killed or wounded 1,000 children and adults by ordering the storming of the school to satisfy [Putin's] imperial ambitions and to keep his job." And as terrorists often do, he points to the overreaction by the Russian forces to the terrorists' action, casting blame Putin's way and calls for an international investigation of what actually occurred at Beslan.

In the same statement Basayev goes on to detail the demands of the hostage-takers during the siege and argues that they are freedom fighters, stating that his side remains willing to peacefully negotiate for a free independent Chechnya while downplaying that his group just killed over three hundred children.

"We regret what happened in Beslan," Basayev claims. But he quickly balances his regret by asking, "Officially, over 40,000 of our children have been killed and tens of thousands mutilated. Is anyone saying anything about that?" And in a press interview he confesses, "I admit, I'm a bad guy, a bandit, a terrorist ... but what would you call [the Russians]? . . . If they are the keepers of constitutional order, if they are anti-terrorists, then I spit on all these agreements and nice words."[252]

And like most terrorists who blame the governments and its citizens that they feel justified to attack, Basayev concludes, "Responsibility is with the whole Russian nation, which through its silent approval gives a 'yes' [its consent]. This is simply a war declared by Putin five years ago . . .They are fighting us without any rules with the direct connivance of the whole world. We are not bound by any commitments and we will fight as we know how and in accordance with our rules..." These are chilling words from a terrorist who had earlier said he would stop at nothing—that he would use weapons of mass destruction if he had access to them.[253] Basayev signs off as the emir of the Riyad alSalikhin Martyrs Brigade and vows to fight on to Chechen independence.[254] Like many terrorists who see themselves as freedom fighters Basayev obviously believes that using terrorism and striking at civilians is justified given his contention that the civilians had put the government in place that was harming his constituency. Terrorists often see things this way.

Khapta, my research colleague in Chechnya, busy continuing our project of constructing psychological autopsies of the Chechen terrorists, became very curious when I had told her that I was going to Beslan to interview the hostages. In response, she specifically sought out interviews with those who knew the Beslan terrorists in order to complement my research from the other side.

Her work did indeed shed additional light on the inter-ethnic struggles that often underlie motivations for terrorism. In this case it turned out that the Ingush terrorists, who made up a fifth of the total Beslan terrorists,[255] had personal motivations to return to North Ossetia. They had a score to settle from twelve years earlier when the mixed ethnic border towns that they lived in had been overtaken by Ossetians who committed ethnic cleansing, raping and slaughtering mothers and children and driving the surviving Ingush villagers away over the mountains into Ingushetia and Chechnya.

So when these Ingush terrorists (who as boys had been violently forced out of their homes in North Ossetia) returned to Beslan under the banner of Shamil Basayev's Martyr's Brigade and took mothers and children hostage in demand for independence in Chechnya, they felt justified. And Chechen independence was not *their* only cause: they had also returned for revenge.

Busana, the cousin of a twenty-five year-old unmarried male terrorist, talks with Khapta about how the Ossetian-Ingush conflict motivated her Ingush relative to participate in the Beslan hostage taking.

"The Ossetians raped his sister!" Busana says, referring to her cousin. "She was married and lived on another street. [When the Ossetians were attacking the Ingush in the village] she tried to come to us, hoping that the Ossetians wouldn't touch her because she was pregnant. But the Ossetians seized her from the street."

They brought her to the place where they had gathered the men and other women.

"Then the Ossetians raped our women, forcing our men to watch," Busana tells Khapta. "In that time we hid in our cellar and were terrified to go outside. We didn't know what had happened with our cousin. Our street was fired on with artillery shells. At night we decided to escape from Ossetia. We gathered our children. Her brother, my [male] cousin [who later went as a terrorist to Beslan] was thirteen at that time. We took some food and we escaped to the mountains. We—four families, about twenty persons—were afraid to go on the roads because the Ossetian checkpoints were there.

"We decided to go to Ingushetia through the mountains. It was very cold and snow lay on the ground. We traveled on foot the whole day and stopped only to eat. We hoped that by the next night we would be in Ingushetia. But it was hard to go through the mountains, especially for the children, because of snow and frost. They were tired and cried often.

"We had to overnight in the mountains. We couldn't make fires because there was no firewood and the branches of the trees that we broke off wouldn't burn. Our food ran out and we didn't know what to do. Then our boys found a cave and we went there.

"It was dark and I was afraid to sleep, because then I would freeze. But some of us fell asleep. In the morning some couldn't stand up or move their legs due to the cold. We pounded the legs of the children so that they could stand up. There was an old woman with us – she fell asleep during the night. In the morning she was dead! We couldn't take her with us so we left her in that cave.

"Then we went further and on the evening of the second day we reached the village. The villagers met us and brought us to their homes. They warmed and fed us. We told them that we had left the old woman [dead] in the cave. Men from that village, with our boys, went and brought her body and buried her in their village.

"Then we went to Ingushetia, to our relatives. They sheltered us. There we learned about what happened with our cousin. When her brother heard about it, he didn't go outside from their home for many days. He said that he should revenge for her. We told him that he is only a boy, that we have men who will revenge for her and for our other women. After some time he stopped talking about it, but he didn't stop thinking about it."

Indeed twelve years later when Basayev offered him the opportunity to return to Ossetia as a "martyr" to take part in the Beslan terror act against the Russian government on behalf of Chechen independence, this young man, no longer a powerless and traumatized boy, found what he had been waiting for. And whether it involved hurting women and children, or not - he was ready to die for his cause.

When asked how she felt about the terrorist attack in Beslan, Busana echoes Basayev's sentiments. "I understand that they shouldn't take over the school—children are not guilty in anything. But our children and our women were also not guilty in anything. But what they did with us! And why has no one done anything in response to it —even up to now? We can't return to our house in Ossetia, the house built by our grandfather—they don't allow us to live in it!

"And I have a chronic disease of my kidneys after that trip through the mountains. All these years I have headaches and insomnia. I cannot think about anything good, only bad thoughts come to my head. I know this is depression! But what should I do with it? They destroyed our life. And why, after what they did to us, are people really surprised that terror acts happen?"

Indeed, historically the colonial powers and empires, including Russia quite often consciously drew national borders to the nations and republics that they created with the wave of a pen, forcing ethnic groups together in order to more easily divide and conquer. But when colonial empires and unions disintegrated in North Ossetia and elsewhere in the early nineties, the nations that were drawn in this manner had many ethnic and religious problems to work through regarding who should live where, who should have access to services and who deserves to control the resources. When these contrived unions between peoples and groups falter, the aftermath is far-reaching, igniting sparks of hatred that are fueled both in the present by current day militant jihadi ideology and from power politics of the past.

Fatima, the sister of another thirty-year-old male Ingush terrorist who, although married with two small children, went to Beslan, recalls to Khapta similar motivations for his taking part in the terror act.

"My brother was a sportsman and participated in sport competitions. But after what happened in Ossetia he was changed very much. He and our elder brother were hostages of the Osssetians for three days, and they forced our brothers to watch while they raped our women. My brothers were released and they survived, but many people disappeared or were killed in those days. Our uncle was taken by the Ossetians at that time and disappeared.

"After we fled to Grozny, the Chechen war of independence began after two years. We fled again and lived in Ingushetia [as refugees] for about one year. Then in 1996 we came back to Grozny and in 1999 the war began again and we went again to Ingushetia [fleeing the carpet bombing of Grozny with hundreds of thousands of other refugees].

"In that time my brother began to visit a Wahhabist mosque. Then the wahhabists were not well known in Ingushetia—no one knew much about them. The special Wahhabist books [promoting "martyrdom", Takfiri ideas and militant jihad] were distributed there and they agitated among the worshippers too.

"Then in 2000 someone informed the militia that the Wahhabists gathered in that mosque. Militia workers came to the mosque and found arms there. They arrested everyone who was in the mosque at that time. Our relatives managed to release my brother through a bribe [to the authorities].

"Our brother promised not to return to that mosque. The mosque was closed after that event, but he probably met with Wahhabists in another place. And then they took over the school in Beslan." Upon reflection, the cruelties of these hostage-takers actions begin to make more sense. These are men who as young boys witnessed mass rape of their women and slaughter of their men by the Ossetians. Revenge must have been high in their own minds when they were inside the Beslan school.

When Khapta asks another respondent, Tahir,whose family was also subject to the ethnic cleansing and who lost their home and family members,how she feels about Beslan she states, "Now when I remember all that happened with us more than ten years ago, I am indignant. Though I understand that children shouldn't suffer from it. They were not in the world when it happened to us. But I cannot accuse those who took over the school either. I understand my brother and my cousin, but I don't know how they became involved to go there—no one knows that!"

At the time when Beslan occurred, the Chechen brand of militant jihadi ideology (referred to there by the Russian authorities as Wahhabism) was spreading throughout the region. And while the Chechen conflict was beginning to cool down, many more uprisings with militant jihadi rebels began occurring throughout the Caucasus involving Ingushetia especially. In May of 2005, Basayev announced the newly-formed and activated Caucasian Front, the wider militant jihadi rebel militant and terrorist movement of the region (a part of which attacked in Nalchik shortly after our departure from Beslan in September of 2005).

Not all the hostage-takers were Ingush. Those who were Chechen had their own personal reasons for going. Madina tells Khapta about her two male Chechen cousins, aged eighteen and thirty, who went to Beslan.

"The elder had a wife and children, the younger was unmarried," Madina recalls. And no one in our family knew they were going to participate in the school takeover. Our elder cousin lived in Ingushetia with his parents. He had participated with the Chechen rebel fighters and was a fugitive and as a result was afraid to live in Chechnya. His younger brother was not connected with the rebel fighters and lived with his sister's family in Grozny. But his parents feared that he would be arrested because of his elder brother, a common move by the authorities to make the elder brother surrender. So the younger brother went to Ingushetia to live with his father and elder brother. "Probably he went to Beslan from Ingushetia," Madina explains. "His elder sister with whom he lived in Grozny said so. At first we didn't believe that our younger cousin participated in the [Beslan] terror act, but then one of our relatives saw the list of terrorists who were killed in the Beslan school takeover and both brothers were on it."

Regarding their motivations, Madina explains that the elder brother participated in the first war as a fighter and "then he became a Wahhabist and also participated in the second war. That's why he was a fugitve." Madina says his parents were against his joining the rebels and later transitioning to the "jihad" with the others, and that the entire family, particularly the men, suffered as a result.

"The past five years all of our relatives lived in fear," Madina says. "Our men were interrogated [by the authorities] often because of him. At night the soldiers raided our house and they watched our family members because they knew that he visited his house sometime.

"I think he understood that his situation was desperate, he couldn't be hidden all his life—that's why he participated in the [Beslan] terror act," Madina says. Her words echo many other interviews Khapta and I collected from Chechens in which we learned that those who were fugitives are often willing to become "martyrs" because the alternative of being captured, brutally tortured and killed appears far worse.

Havaa, the mother of one of the Chechen female terrorists named Belita, a twenty-seven year old who worked with her mother selling items in the local markets, tells Khapta that her daughter never married because she took care of her invalid father. "I couldn't do it because I had to earn money to feed my family. After my husband died in 2003 Belita began to trade on the market with me," Havaa explains.

Havaa learned from police inspectors who arrived at her house to search and interrogate that her daughter had participated in the Beslan hostage-taking and perished there. Havaa explains how Belita would travel to Baku (the capital of neighboring Azerbaijan) to buy clothes and other things that Havaa, then sold in their local Chechen markets.

"Every two or three months she went with her friends," Havaa recalls. "We lived together in Grozny in a rented apartment near the market, because it was difficult to go home [through the many military checkpoints] every day.

"It was on August twenty-second when I saw my daughter last time. In the early morning of that day she and her friends went to Khasav-Yurt, to go from there to Baku. My daughter took twenty thousand rubles with her and my elder daughter had given her money also to buy her some clothes as well. We wanted to bring new school things for the September first celebrations," Havaa recalls, explaining that the beginning of school year celebrations are a time when everyone is buying nice things to wear.

"Then after two or three days I heard on the TV news that two friends of my daughter exploded themselves on airplanes! And after some days the Beslan school was taken over. I didn't know anything about my daughter [being there]. Usually when she went to buy goods, she returned after three days. But in that time she didn't come back."

When Khapta asks why she thinks that Belita participated, Havaa is without an answer—other than denial. "I don't think that she participated in that terror act!" she claims. "Maybe someone forced her, I don't know! My daughter never would go there if she knew! She had a careful and quiet character. I didn't see her corpse! No one told me officially that she was dead. Inspectors came to us, then journalists, all of them asked about her. They said that she was in Beslan with Roza Nogaev. But she *really went to Bakuwith the Nogaev sisters and Sazita!*" her mother insists. "They were her friends."

Often one is highly influenced and similar to one's friends and Belita's friends were bad news and serious about becoming "martyrs". Of the two Nogaev sisters who were to travel to Baku with her, twenty-seven year old Aminat blew herself up on a Moscow bound plane and twenty-four year old Roza went to Beslan. Sazita, Havaa's other friend blew herself up on the second plane explosion in that same month, before Beslan.

Khapta's interview with the brother of the Nogaev sisters reveals a similar level of familial shock and disbelief over the involvement and terrorist deaths of his sisters, Aminat and Roza.[256] "I don't know exactly what happened," he tells Khapta. "It was said that Aminat was blown up on a plane and Roza disappeared with her too, and on TV it was announced that she was blown up near the subway station in Moscow. But there isn't any proof of it. Since that day when it was declared about the explosions of planes we didn't know anything about them."

Later it came out that Roza was in Beslan. "I didn't believe it at first," her brother continues. "I thought they would return home soon. I thought maybe they went to Stavropol region to our relatives. I phoned everywhere and asked everyone, but no one knew anything about them. Then someone from the Special Services came to us and took all their picture albums, papers, and cassettes."

When Khapta asks about their possible motivations their brother says he doesn't know. Their brother compares the girls' economic challenges and deprivations in Grozny to the rest of their post conflict society normalizing their poverty. "We lived like everyone else," he says. "We didn't have any special problems. Both of them traded in the market. They earned well and bought all the things that they needed. There were no other [better] jobs therefore I didn't protest. They went for their supplies to Dagestan or Pyatigorsk, but they returned the same or the next day. In that time they went to Khasav-Yurt and didn't return. Maybe they were deceived or involved in [planning] it. I don't know."

But we do know that these two sisters suffered heavy traumatic losses from the Russian oppression, as their other brother was arrested in the [Russian] checks in 2000 and never seen again. According to her brother, Aminat suffered deeply from this occurrence.

"She couldn't eat anything for a long time," he says. "She told us, 'Maybe they don't give him any food,' and she couldn't eat because of this. She believed that our brother is alive, but she said maybe he was tortured."

All of the family became more religious in response to his disappearance, the girls moving slowly into fanaticism and seeking out the Wahhabists. "Both of them began to pray after it," their brother recalls.

Khapta spoke also to the aunt of the fourth girl, Sazita, about her suicide act of blowing a plane out of the air. "I didn't know that she was going to do it," her aunt recalls. "She told me she was going to go to Khasav-Yurt to buy clothes for trading. She traded on the market with me. I traded for many years and taught her this business."

Sazita was divorced fifteen years before the war began, according to her aunt, and returned to her parental home. "It was very hard for her," her aunt recalls of the divorce that occurred because "her husband didn't give her a son. Then he married with another woman and they had children. But

Sazita became lonely. There weren't any jobs in her village. So she asked me to help her to begin her own business."

When asked how and why she could participate in a suicide terror act, her aunt answers, "It is a difficult question. Though during the last years she changed very much. I didn't like her environment, her friends. And her brother influenced her very much. Her brother was a Sharia [Islamic] judge before the second war. He was killed in August of 1999 during Basayev's campaign to Dagestan. All her friends were Wahhabists. They lived together on a flat here near the market. I told her, 'Live with me. Why do you need that flat?' But she wanted to live with them. I told her mother [my sister] that it would finish very badly, but she didn't do anything about it. Sazita had a good income. I don't know why she made it!"

"Was it related at all to her brother's death? Did she speak of him much?" Khapta asks.

"Yes, she recollected him often," Sazita's aunt answers. "She would say, 'He died in jihad. He is in paradise and we should envy him, that life is a heavy burden. She dressed in hidjab after his death. I threatened to stop any relations with her if she didn't remove this masquerade. She removed it after some time, but not because I said so, but because it became dangerous," her aunt recalls, referring to the authorities cracking down on the Wahhabists in Chechnya.

In regard to her friendship with the other terrorist girls, her aunt recalls, "They were younger than her but they had the same interests. They were Wahhabists, too. They all worked in the markets and they began to trade together. In that time they went together and one friend Maryam [Taburova][257] was with them, too. Sazita had many pictures with these friends in hidjab and with their index fingers lifted upwards" she recalls, referring to the jihadi practice of pointing one finger skyward to indicate 'Allah is one'. "After her death, all these pictures were take by security service workers," her aunt recalls.

The girls were all suffering from life inside a conflict zone, living under the heavy occupation of Russian forces in Chechnya and all but one was traumatically bereaved, having lost a close family member to the conflict. One was infertile and divorced as a result, but from her aunt's recollection it sounds as if she had adjusted herself (for fifteen years) to that sad reality and was activated to terrorism by the traumatic death of her brother, similar to the response of infertile and divorced Wafa Idris who became overwhelmed with all the violence of the Israeli occupation. The girls also had ties to the Wahabbi extremists and certainly there was a contagion effect operating among these girls who all activated in the same time period.

Khapta's sister, Seda,also a trauma psychologist who had come to live with me in Brussels,had already told me horrific stories about the ethnic cleansing in North Ossetia and while visiting Beslan, I had asked many people about Seda's stories, but they all either appeared oblivious or denied them with some look of upset, telling me that they were just that—only stories. I had begun to wonder if Seda, a war and trauma victim herself, had exaggerated to me, but after reading these interviews from Khapta, I am again shocked and I begin to see this as a repressed part of ex-Soviet history that played a very big part in the brutality that took place at Beslan. Even though I am loath to hear it again, I force myself to go and ask Seda to tell me once more what happened there, to explain.

"They forced the women to the streets," Seda repeats, wide-eyed as she recalls the terror. "They made their men come and watch. First they slit open the bellies of the pregnant women and took out their fetuses, throwing them to the pigs to eat. And they ripped off the clothes of the remaining women and raped them. And when they finished they took their knives and sliced off their breasts."

Dumbfounded by the brutality I ask her, "How could they do it? Mass rape and ethnic cleansing. I know it happens, but slicing off their breasts? It's beyond bestial! Why would they do this?"

"Maybe so they could not feed their babies after they were born," Seda replies,her eyes weary with the task of telling me again such a traumatic history.

"And you are sure this is true?" I ask again.

"Anne, I saw it myself," Seda tells me. "First when they came out of North Ossetia to Ingushetia, it was broadcast on the news in Chechnya and we saw the pictures of them—their breasts were cut off. And then when we were [war] refugees in Ingushetia, I met some of these women and I asked them about it as well. I saw their chests, Anne. It's true."

As with many things that Seda has shared with me, things that she witnessed first hand in Chechnya during the wars and now from Ingushetia, I have no reply. I only feel sickened inside with the horror and realization that humanity is capable of such depths of depravity. And it seems to cycle around and around again trying to find an outlet and some means of healing, unfortunately repeating the violence instead of addressing it correctly with truth, justice and reconciliation. I wonder as long as these types of things occur, if there can ever be an end to terrorism.

CHAPTER 53

The Jihad in Belgium

When I first moved to Brussels in 2000, I noticed that white Belgians (of European descent) often speak in a very derogatory manner about their "Moroccans" citizens, who they very clearly don't like and my students at the university often tell me stories of how the second generation Belgians of Moroccan immigrant descent are often blocked from going out to night-clubs, renting apartments in certain areas of town, getting good jobs, etc. while the white Belgians complain that they don't integrate well! For me, it is reminiscent of the discrimination blacks in the U.S. faced before the civil rights movement,but I give it little thought—until I learn more.

When 9-11 occurs in 2001, diplomats working in Belgium become alarmed about their safety. Their workplaces at the U.S. Embassy, NATO Headquarters, etc. are suddenly cordoned off with military barriers and barbed wire, and they have to walk past phalanxes of guards toting machine guns to enter their work places. Likewise while anthrax scares are plaguing Washington, particularly Capitol Hill, envelopes of white powder begin arriving at overseas U.S. embassies as well, including the U.S. Embassy Belgium. A whole portion of the embassy near the mail-room is quarantined in plastic sheeting to prevent contagion and exposed personnel are given prophylactic doses of antibiotic until our particular white powder packet of "anthrax" is discovered to be a fake.

In addition, right after 9-11, al Qaeda puts out rumors that their next targeted hit will occur in just one month—in October of 2001—at NATO headquarters, located on the outskirts of Brussels. To deal with the anxiety that all of these events cause, I am called in by the U.S. embassy to lead seminars with diplomats and family members about staying calm in the suddenly looming face of terrorism. But I find my job complicated by the fact that the embassy's regional security officer (RSO), who usually addresses the groups in the same meetings with me, spends his time point-ing out to our American community that Brussels is a city with twenty percent Muslims of immigrant descent—many of them of Moroccan descent—and that some of these have recently been arrested as they had been plotting to bomb U.S. embassy Paris.

"You shouldn't get into a taxi alone at night with a Moroccan driver," the RSO warns, agitating my audience further, while my jaw drops at his blatantly bigoted statements intermixed with real stories of Belgian Moroccans' plots to American security.

When I take the time to examine it further, even meeting with members of our diplomatic security team, I learn that much like in London, the militant jihad in Belgium has been brewing among those of immigrant descent for quite some time and that there are multiple festering hotbed of extremists in Belgium, with many thwarted plots occurring —often aimed at Americans! In 2005, I decide that it is time for me to add to my terrorism studies an investigation of extremists in my own backyard and to look more closely at the militant jihad in Belgium.

So in October of 2005, I am sitting with two of my informants, twenty-four years old Sami and Jamal, in a café talking as we wait for an appointment with Ali, a second generation Moroccan Belgian whose cousin became so radicalized that he recently volunteered to fight jihad in Afghanistan. As we wait I ask Jamal and Sami about life as Belgian Moroccans, both of their parents came to Belgium from Morocco to work in the mines.

"I hear that Moroccans can't go to clubs here. Is it true?" I ask referring to what I've been told by my students about Moroccans systematically denied entrance to nightclubs. I add that I found it so hard to believe that I had actually gone to witness it and indeed found it to be true.

""What is difficult," Jamal explains, "is that we can't go to the clubs eighty percent of the time. A lot of people are frustrated by that. They want to go and party with other people. And many people become angry when they are turned away and go home to their own neighborhood and smash things."

I ask Jamal why they don't smash things in the neighborhoods of the people who discriminate against them, but he just shrugs his shoulders.

"Why do you think Moroccans are turned away at the clubs here?" I ask.

"They [the owners] think people won't feel safe if there are many Moroccans in the club, or they think we don't spend money," Jamal answers. "It's a big pity! We try to act like Belgians and they tell us, 'No go back to your own culture.' We have to be more fashionable and more educated than them to get in!"

"How is it that they can discriminate this way and get away with it? It's against the law isn't it?" I ask.

"They can say he's not well dressed, or we knew him [as a trouble-maker] from before," Jamal explains.

"Will the person turned away from a club be vulnerable to becoming radicalized?" I ask.

"Yes we have radicals, but here it is different," Jamal explains. "I come with a friend who knows the bouncer and I can get in, but if I want to go out with *all* my friends, it's impossible. I can't go out clubbing with the guys from my community."

"What about these small gangs of Moroccans that roam the streets on weekends?" I ask, referring to the many roving bands of "Moroccan" boys I often see out at night in the city center wandering from bar to bar, knowing they won't be admitted anywhere, and harassing European girls in frustration.

"They are the guys who couldn't get into clubs," Jamal explains. "They say okay, 'Let's annoy people! We can't enter, let's annoy the people who can.'"

"They are angry then?" I ask.

"Yes," Jamal answers. "It's really deep. One time get rejected, okay. But over and over again, you start to wonder, *What am I doing in this country?* We say I'm Belgian, but when I want to go out and act like a Belgian I can't!"

"Are *you* angry about it?" I ask.

"If you become angry, you become blind," Jamal answers.

"Do the Moroccan girls here club?" I ask deciding to switch the topic as we wait for Ali to arrive.

"Yes some of our girls go out to R & B clubs," Sami answers.

"Their parents allow them?"

"No, they say they are going to sleep at a girlfriend's home," Sami explains laughing. "If their parents find out, there will be violence. In our community everyone knows each other, so they can't be open about it."

"Everything is about reputation," Jamal explains. "If it's found out she goes to clubs, it's like she's a whore."

"How is dating in your community? Is it possible with Moroccan girls?" I ask.

"You can't be with her in the center [of Brussels]," Jamal says. "You have to find very far away places to be together —Antwerp for example [a city about forty minutes north of Brussels]. You can't be seen hand in hand. It's all hidden."

"If you are caught with a girl,it's either violence or you have to get married," Jamal explains. "It's easier to date across cultures, to date [white] Belgian girls. You only have to get past if her family minds that she is dating a Moroccan and their expectations, and you have to explain I don't eat pork."

Others have told me that many of the parents of the second-generation Moroccan descent girls ensure their daughters' virginity by taking them to a doctor who places a surgical stitch inside their vaginal wall to prevent intercourse until they get married when the stitch is removed. Some young women get around this by visiting the doctor themselves having it removed for premarital relations and then re-stitched when it's time to prove their virginity. Others resort to anal sex, but in the main, I've learned that many of the Moroccan immigrant descent girls are strictly controlled by their families.

"Here [Moroccan origin] people are more conservative," Sami adds. "More so here than in Morocco. Here people are scared to lose their roots, so they hang on to the old ways. Some have two wives," Sami continues. "One here and one back there and they like the one back there the best because she doesn't ask for anything and is happy with whatever he can give her."

"How do you see [white] Belgians?" I ask.

"They are very different," Jamal says. "They are hard workers. They don't smile like we do."

"What are your other problems in life here?"

"There are problems to find a job," Sami answers. "Problems if you speak French only. You need Dutch fluently to find a job."

"Which nationality do you consider yourself?" I ask.

"I'm Belgian. I was born here," Jamal say. "I have both Belgian and Moroccan passports. But in Morocco people say, 'Go away, Belgian guy!' Here they tell me, 'Go away, Moroccan!' We lack identity."

"The [white] converts are easier to get along with," Jamal continues. "They want to be like us. It's group dynamics—he wants to prove himself.

A Moroccan will do the same to belong. They look up to us, because we are different than they are. We take more risks. We are aggressive. They want to be like us a bit."

I understand now that wanting to fit in with the tougher immigrants can be some of the power that pushes those who convert after exposure to extremist militant jihadi groups.

"What do you see as the reasons for Moroccans becoming radicalized in Belgium?" I ask.

"Discrimination," Jamal says. "The person who becomes radicalized— maybe he's watching TV doing nothing, thinking I'm here doing nothing. This country doesn't need me and another does."

"The person who is radicalizing others comes to the simple person and says, 'This world is not that important,'" Sami adds. "He says, 'I'm going to save you. You don't need your life here. You just need your life after.' It's like he sells a product."

"And how do you feel about the US?" I ask.

"The U.S. is like Caesar: it has an empire," Jamal answers. "It's like David and Goliath. The U.S. is always in other people's business. If the U.S. used it's power in another way everyone could be happy, but it's very hypocritical."

At that point twenty-six year old Ali arrives and we explain my study explaining also that Jamal and Sami have just been telling us what life is like living as a Belgian "Moroccan". The four of us sit drinking sweet tea prepared in the Moroccan style with the fresh green mint leaves floating in our glass teacups.

Ali starts by telling us that he graduated with an undergraduate law degree but like many educated second generation Belgians of Moroccan descent, he could only find work as a taxi driver. Ali hopes that when he finishes his graduate studies that will change but tells me that he is glad he has now the security of driving a taxi.

When I ask him about the situation in the nightclubs he answers, "I don't try to go to the clubs often because it's difficult to enter." I ask how he feels when he's turned away. Ali answers, "Angry! It's like a tension inside, I ask myself 'Who is the doorkeeper to say to me *Don't enter*?' He has the power to make me feel that I am less. Who do I have to be to enter? Only important people can enter? We [Moroccans] always have to prove who we are to enter, to be respected."

"When you are angry, what do you do with it?" I ask.

"I don't ask why. I just leave and go home. I have to find a way to forget. There's no use to go to clubs in general. I'm sure I'll be refused. Belgian culture is not open to other people. It's a type of racism. It's in their genes," Ali says.

"Do you *feel* Belgian?" I ask.

"I have two passports, but I think I'm more Belgian because *I was born here*. I go to Morocco, and the more we go, the more I don't want to go back. I don't enjoy it. From the beginning my parents wanted to see their parents, but now I know the world is big and I prefer to travel elsewhere."

I ask Ali if he knows any extremists and what he sees as the reasons for radicalization among second generation Belgians of Moroccan descent.

"I have radical friends," he tells me. "They do it because of discrimination. Some people take some sentences out of religion and make what they want out of it. But it's true the Palestinians are persecuted," he quickly says, confirming a widespread view here among Moroccan descent Belgians, as well as many European descent Belgians that they feel sympathy for the plight of Palestinians. "The people who become radicalized here are not well educated, poor, excluded, and have no prospects." Sami and Jamal, nod in agreement. "They don't know the Koran. Everything they know from the Koran is in French. The person radicalizing them can change the [translations from the original Arabic] Koran as they like and they won't know it! They don't know their own religion. They don't know Arabic, and they can't judge it for themselves. It's a natural defense—if attacked from every side, feeling angry and upset—to become radicalized," Ali explains. "If his mindset is, 'I feel persecuted,' each one finds his own interpretation. He has a feeling of desperation and can do anything. It's one of the reasons people fall into radicalization."

"But there is also the problem of the media," Ali states pointing out how the media since 9-11 portrays Muslims as extremists. "The media likes exaggeration and shocking stories. They make it as though all Muslims are public enemy number one."

"One of my cousins here, the same age as me, wanted to go to Afghanistan on jihad to strike the U.S. forces there," Ali admits. "He wanted to show that he is an Islamic hero but he did not have enough courage to actually go," Ali states.

"What do you think motivated him to think that would make him a hero?" I ask.

"A person doesn't go to jihad to be a hero. It's a human feeling: sympathy. It's to help others who have a problem," Ali explains, confirming what I am coming to learn is a central operating force among non-conflict zone militant jihadis—those in Europe and elsewhere. Terrorist groups, their recruiters, instigators and propagandists find a way to impart a feeling of secondary traumatization and identification with the pain of those Muslims suffering *inside* conflict zones upon young impressionable Muslims from non-conflict zones. Militant jihadi recruiters use these pictures, films and stories to direct the emotional reactions of those viewing them into terrorist supporting responses.

"When the U.S. goes to invade another country for instance," Ali continues. "Or when we see a country with oil invaded and that it only take ten minutes for the other countries to come and help [the U.S.], but another [country] with nothing is just given a small bag of rice in time of trouble,then we go and strike," Ali says angrily referring to how Belgians among his community view the U.S. invasion of Iraq as wrong and how they then justify militant jiahdi counter-attacks against the U.S. led coalition forces.

"So part of joining the militant jihad is seeking justice?" I ask.

"Yes," Ali answers. "People are not crazy to go and strike the first and best army of the world [the U.S. forces] without a reason. There is something behind that."

I ask why Ali's cousin responded to the provocations of the U.S. invasions of Iraq and Afghanistan by wanting to join the militant jihad, but Ali was immune.

"My cousin didn't understand religion well. I knew more. He took one sentence and ran with it—like jihad for him is a way of life," Ali answers.

"Are there problems in your cousin's family?" I ask suspecting that there was also some private pain he wished to escape.

Jamal explains that his cousin was a lost child in his family. "We have big families," he says. "It's good to have big families but there are downsides too. Lost people can occur. At around age ten or so all the [Moroccan immigrant descent] kids are on the street and all the families mix—the good families and the bad families, and some kids can get lost with bad friends. It can happen this way," he says referring to his cousin.

"When I studied law I thought I understood but I had a lot more to learn. My cousin is the same," Ali adds and then getting more honest he admits, "He had a lot of problems at home, stealing, drugs. When he entered religion all his problems stopped. It was a good thing for him. Now he has a sense of life. He's got his equilibrium and he avoids the bad. He had bad friends earlier."

While Islam and the militant jihadi ideology saved him from his problems it also almost cost him his life. I am learning that in non-conflict zones when secondary traumatization and identifying with the victims of violence *inside* a conflict zone occurs, it can be an especially powerful elixir for those youth lost in criminal and drug-ridden lives. Called out of drugs, crime and broken families into a brotherhood of extremists who care about the larger "Muslim family", the strict religious rules form a structure in which to leave behind drugs and criminal activities and to build clean habits and good living until the new "substitute family" calls upon them to go deeper into jihad. Lost youth are rehabilitated and transformed by their extremist "brothers" but instead of becoming truly healthy they go on to embrace the roles of Islamic "hero" and become "martyrs" for the cause. Thankfully, Ali's cousin didn't go that far—his fear and perhaps his more clear thinking family members held him back.

As we finish our interview, Ali looks at my notes and he tells me, "I worry you will create stereotypes [of European Muslim as extremists and terrorists]. In Belgium we [of Moroccan descent] are already guilty of stealing, drugs and criminality," Ali cynically explains, "and now they add terrorism to our profiles—it's the cherry on the cake. It's a very good c.v. you know!"

I assure him that I will be fair and stick to his words. Ali nods adding, "I don't believe Osama [bin Ladin] is real. He is a creation of the U.S. Or if he's real he worked for the CIA before." I smile. And thank him.

The next night I stop in at my friend Hamid Sebaly's house and have dinner with he and his wife Jenny. Hamid is a part of the Christian Lebanese diaspora in Belgium but he has many Arab Muslim friends. One of them, a Sunni Iraqi, stops by when our supper is finished. Hamid tells me ahead of time that his friend may not greet me because he is so angry about all the destruction and Iraqi deaths occurring as a result of the U.S. led invasion of Iraq and because he knows my husband is serving there. When his friend arrives, I greet him shyly not looking for a response and then go to sit in front of the television to allow them to talk without worrying about me. The television is on an Arabic station and I watch it mesmerized. It's showing a jihadi video of an Iraqi extremist group in which the narrator is claiming that the U.S. forces are misreporting their actions and were attacked quite heavily by this group. It shows footage of the U.S. attack, the Iraqi militant and civilian victims who died in it, and then the revenge attack by this group—all accompanied by rousing Islamic songs and verses from the Koran. I am sickened when they show the Iraqi civilian victims—collateral damage in the U.S. attack—and I understand their desire for and exultation in the revenge they have extracted.

Hamid noticing that I am watching in Arabic suddenly calls out, "Anne, the channel switcher is right on the coffee table—you can watch in English or French!" I answer that I am completely hypnotized by this film and can understand a lot of it without knowing much Arabic! And I am amazed that this kind of thing is being beamed into a normal Belgian home! *How easily a vulnerable marginalized Muslim can be convinced to join the militant jihad with films like these*! I think as I am reminded of all the potential disgruntled second generation Moroccan Belgians rejected from nightclubs and possibly sitting home at night angrily watching such broadcasts.

Rejoining Hamid at the table when his guest leaves, he tells me that his guest was also moved by the film. "Even being a secular Baathist, he told me that he was proud to see that film!" Hamid shares with me.

A few days later Jamal introduces me to three students: Nabil, Hassan and Kamal.[1] We meet them at the main campus of the Free University of Brussels where they are all studying. Choosing a table in the back of the cafeteria where no one is around we introduce ourselves, order coffees and I explain my study. Jamal has already told me that Nabil used to be part of a militant jihadi group affiliated with al Qaeda. Nabil appears intelligent and serious and tells us that he is married with two children and working on his Masters degree. Hasan and Kamal, each of second generation Moroccan immigrant descent are working on their undergraduate degrees. After explaining my study to the young men I tell Nabil, "Jamal has already told me that you were part of an extremist group. Could we start with you? Can you tell me about yourself, maybe starting with your childhood and then moving to how you became involved?"

"I'm not Moroccan," Nabil begins. "I was born in Rwanda during the conflicts and my mother couldn't raise me there so I was adopted by a Belgian couple. I grew up black in a totally white Belgian community." When he became a teenager Nabil started searching for his African roots and found an affinity with the Moroccan Belgians, who were brown

---

1 A pseudonym

skinned and of African descent like himself. They introduced him to Islam and he converted at age fifteen.

"Like a typical convert, I took Islam much more seriously than my friends," Nabil explains, "I was always searching for the truth so eventually I gravitated to the extremists and I found a Wahhabi teacher," Nabil recalls. "I wanted to have Islam in its purest form. I prayed five times a day, I followed all the rules, and even though I was a young man full of hormones, I didn't look at women." I ask him how that went. "It was very hard actually. I finally got to the point where I was praying all the time and just had to stay inside the home because it was too hard to go out. If I went out I saw [uncovered] women and I couldn't stop myself from looking at them." I smile imagining his struggle.

Reflecting on how he endeavored to stay on the "true" path as his teachers were presenting it, Nabil explains, "If you say to yourself this thing is God's will, you have to do it. It's simple. If you can't read the Koran in Arabic and your teachers tell you that you cannot understand [the original language] and you have to do it. I tried very sincerely to do so. I followed everything, the prayer schedule, eating and way of drinking all in the *Sunnah [the sayings and practices of the Prophet]*. But there are also ideas about jihad."

In his later teens Nabil became a regular at an extremist militant mosque in Brussels. "They were very active," Nabil recalls, "and from there many went to fight jihad. I knew people who went to Afghanistan as [suicide] bombers, the people who killed General Massoud."[258]

"To get the connections to go on jihad here in Brussels is no problem," Nabil explains. "At age nineteen I was ready to go and fight for my brother Palestinians. I didn't know politics but I had an idea we had some Muslim community, our brothers that we must defend."

Nabil's journey to jihad deepened at age nineteen when he married a local Belgian girl of Moroccan descent and went to Casablanca with her where he fell further under the extremist influence, studying at a radical mosque there and watching a daily diet of al Manar, the television station affiliated with Hezbollah from Lebanon that regularly beams a beacon of hatred about its neighbor to the south: Israel.

"When I watched al Manar, they have a way to mix religion and politics," Nabil recalls telling us how the graphic images of Palestinian suffering caused a level of traumatization that moved him to action. "What I saw on the television was two Israeli soldiers taking big stones and breaking

596

the bones of a Palestinian man, breaking his arm bones, his shoulders, all the bones in his hands, all the bones in his feet, his ribs, smashing them with a big rock. I'm sure they killed him or left him to die. I couldn't understand all of the Arabic but I didn't need language to understand—it was all there in the pictures. Imagine people see that in the morning, get breakfast and see that on their television? When you see that you feel there is a unity of Muslim people. I decided to go there [to become a fighter]. I was completely crazy! I had a wife and baby but I thought I would go anyway."

"You wanted to become a suicide bomber?" I ask.

"No, my group did not agree with suicide bombing," he says (although General Massoud was killed by a suicide operation so some of his group in Belgium obviously did). "I wanted to get a gun and go and shoot as many Israelis as possible until I was killed," Nabil explains, drawing a fine line between being an "active shooter" intending to die shooting as opposed to being a suicide bomber intentionally exploding himself to kill others.

"So you were ready to kill and to die for your beliefs?" I ask.

"At that time I was a believing radical. For a radical you can kill and die for God, no problem. I can die or be killed at any time," Nabil explains.

"What stopped you?" I ask.

"I was planning to go and had no problem sacrificing myself, but right before I was to leave I had a dream," Nabil answers and explains that his dream symbolically showed him that it was wrong to go and kill others. Many extremists, particularly those I interview in Europe tell me that they come to points of doubt while engaged in terrorist groups, moments when they realize it's wrong to enact terrorism, to kill others, or explode themselves in the case of a suicide bombing. However, their doubts don't automatically end their relationship with the extremist group. Doubts are only the precursors of a possible disengagement from terror cells and a possible process of deradicalizing from their violent influence and ideology. And while some disengage they may retain their extremists beliefs and remain vulnerable to reengage in the future.

"How did you get out from the influence of your group?" I ask.

"The problem is you see all the people, politics, everything through the Koran and it's your perspective," Nabil explains. "I was completely lost. It's very difficult to question what is being taught if one does not learn Arabic."

Nabil explains that upon his return to Belgium he began to question the validity of his militant jihadi teachers but that they always told him, "You don't know Arabic. The Koran you are reading is a translation in French, but only the Koran in Arabic is the true words of Allah. What you are reading is not correct." His teachers pointing out that he could not verify the original texts himself quenched every doubt Nabil voiced—until Nabil began to study Arabic. And once he could read in Arabic the Koran and Hadiths for himself, he no longer believed what the extremists had taught him.

Looking back at how close he came to "martyring" himself Nabil reflects, "The difference between me and the others [who remain in the extremist groups] is my [Arabic and religious] studies."

"If anyone comes to us speaking Arabic, if he is from Saudi we roll out the red carpet for him." Nabil adds bitterly, "He can be a used car salesman for all we know but we hang on his every word about the Koran as though he is some great teacher!" This starts a heated discussion at the table with Kamal and Hassan agreeing with him. "That is what happened to me," Nabil states. "I thought my teachers knew the Koran better than me so I believed every word they taught me."

As we talk more I ask the young men about Moroccan child-rearing customs. I've talked to many second generation immigrants of Moroccan descent and I get the feeling that their families are more violent than is normal among Europeans, that beating one's wife and kids as a form of discipline is considered normal, but no one has been willing to open up about it yet. I still recall, Lloyd deMause's words about child abuse being a necessary precursor to being able to enact terrorist violence and wish to know how much domestic violence opens the doors in this population to consider political violence an acceptable choice.

"How are the children raised in your community? How are they disciplined?" I ask. As soon as I do I notice Kamal and Hassan go silent as all the others have before them, but Nabil answers openly, "There is a lot of family violence. There was none in my family because they were [European] Belgians and they didn't believe in hitting their children, but I always saw a lot of violence in my Moroccan friend's homes."

"Who disciplines the children and how?" I ask and Nabil's honesty opens a floodgate. "It's the mothers," Kamal says and Hassan adds, "They beat you with anything they can find: a belt, a brush, a slipper, anything that is at hand."

"And these beatings are only from the mothers or the fathers too?" I ask.

"It's the mothers who do the discipline at home," Kamal explains. "If the fathers are violent its to their wife—not the children."

"And the mothers are also very hysterical," Hassan says. "You have to understand -for us, our mothers are everything. They do all the cooking, the cleaning, we have large families and they raise all the children while our fathers are away at work. They love us very much but if we do something wrong they get hysterical and say that we are hurting their health or killing them!" We have a good laugh over that but as I go back over the violence, it's clear hitting, even beating, are considered appropriate child rearing practices. And it's likely that if one grows up with violence as the norm, the suggestion by an extremist group to use it to solve political problems may be much more easily accepted.

I ask Nabil if he could introduce me to any extremists he knows that still attend that mosque.

"Most of them don't trust me anymore," Nabil says. "They call me Takfir—a traitor to Islam." But then he admits that he has a few friends who are serious in the militant jihadi groups. "How about them?" I ask.

Nabil shakes his head, "No, I can tell you four reasons why they would never accept meeting you," he says.

"Go ahead," I answer and he tells me, "You are American, Christian, white, and a woman—look how you dress."

"I can cover," I answer blushing slightly even though I am dressed conservatively as it is, but he repeats, "No, they would never agree."

Then after thanking them we get ready to leave and Nabil suddenly asks me, "You are a psychologist right?" I answer yes and he continues, "Can I ask you a personal question about my family?"

"Yes of course," I reply putting my things back down on the table. Hassan and Kamal discretely excuse themselves and Nabil goes on to explain a situation in his marriage in which his wife, who was raised in what he explains as a typical Moroccan family—beaten and witnessing domestic violence, is now reacting in fear to him. "She is always afraid of me, if I move suddenly she flinches and she fears that I will hit our two sons," he says. "She is jumpy all the time around me and protective of them when there is no need to be." That's an easy question so I explain while asking him many questions to verify that I am correct that she is probably getting posttraumatic flashbacks when he does things that remind her of her father and that to heal the situation he needs to be extra gentle and aware of what he is doing that triggers posttraumatic recall so that together they can address it by he trying to do less of what triggers her and she working through the traumas that it makes her recall. When we finish about an hour later and gather our things again, Nabil suddenly says to me as he is rising to go, "I can help you talk to the people from the mosque I used to attend. My wife and I both still know people there. Let me make some phone calls. I'll tell them that they can trust you." Smiling we say goodbye and I think to myself contrary to the Russian proverb, *I guess sometimes good deeds do go unpunished*!

A week later I arrange to meet with Dyab Abou Jahjah, the leader of the Arab European League, a group that claims to represent the interests of Belgians of Arab descent. Abou Jahjah, an immigrant from Lebanon, is often seen by European Belgians as a violent agitator of Moroccan descent Belgians and was credited with instigating many of the Antwerp riots that occurred after a schoolteacher was killed there. I am curious how he became radicalized and what he believes are the solutions for Belgians of Arab descent.

Dyab and I meet in an elegant restaurant in Brussels where I've invited him as my guest for dinner and he arrives clean shaven, wearing his hair oiled back and wearing a smartly cut pair of black trousers, fancy leather shoes, a knit shirt and form fitting black leather jacket. As we order and begin our first course of a creamy pumpkin soup, Dyab tells me of how he first got involved in Belgian politics. At the time he was being courted by white Belgian parliamentarians to stand for the party while simultaneously facing a lot of personal discrimination as an Arab immigrant in Belgian society.

"I became sick of being called a 'white monkey'," Dyab explains. "The bouncers at the nightclubs [in Antwerp] wouldn't let us in because we're Arabs. Skinheads roamed through our neighborhoods looking for fights. And at that time I was deeply involved for a few years in Belgian politics but I understood that the leadership liked me and would promote me to a high office as a token Muslim only. They weren't interested in any of our platforms about fighting racism, discrimination, or in promoting fair employment practices. I was just supposed to shut up and be their token Muslim. Finally I got fed up with this and together with my colleague we decided we had to go out on our own and begin a movement that would speak to the concerns of the Islamic community here in Belgium. Somebody had to fight back."

Abou Jahjah recalls his first efforts in Antwerp at organizing Belgians of the second generation Arab immigrant community, "At first we organized in coffee shops. We went to the lowest level of society and met with the people there who were smoking hashish and we talked to them about unemployment, discrimination,the things that run their lives. We began to organize. Okay, at first we were violent," he admits. "We went and challenged the bouncers at nightclubs. If they didn't let us in we kept moving forward until they took the first swing, then we hit back of course. We were always arrested, but we didn't get charges against us because we hadn't started the fights. We went looking for the skinheads and we fought with them. We gained our credibility [among the Belgian Moroccans] in these ways, but in time we moved away from these tactics. Instead we started working for political changes. We complained to the Antwerp police that they called us 'white monkeys', that they practiced a higher level of brutality in our communities. We encouraged our guys to go out and observe them whenever they were active in our neighborhoods," Dyab explains telling me about how he organized a group of "observers", inspired by the actions of Malcolm X, to film the police actions in their communities—police that are in the majority affiliated with the anti-immigrant Vlams Belang movement.[259]

Dyab gave an instruction to the group to dress up in black, which was seen as an intimidating move among the white Flemish communities. "We had no idea this would so incite the Flemish community, make them so angry," Dyab explains. "Yes our guys dressed in black, but not to intimidate the police, but because we told our observers to dress up nicely. This is how Arab men like to dress. We look good in black!" he says, laughing at the misunderstanding.

Echoing the same mindset so frequently expressed in terrorist ideologies, Abou Jahjah admits that the alienating and marginalizing experiences he had in Belgium as an outsider Muslim ultimately led to his own radicalization process and that as a result of this victimization he was not at first opposed to using violence as a means of self-defense.

"Do you still agree violence is the answer?" I ask.

"No, we are committed to the political process for working out tensions between host and immigrant communities," Dyab says. That is an important difference between his group and others who follow the militant jihadi ideology.

In 2006 when I visit some of the Arab European League's workers in Antwerp after the Danish cartoon controversy over the depiction of the Prophet Muhammad, Dyab's workers tell me how they fought back, organizing mostly nonviolent demonstrations. They also put up their own cartoons on their website—one a scandalizing depiction of Anne Frank in bed with Adolph Hitler—made to try to demonstrate their view that some things are too sacred to be subjected to free speech.

Just as I am about to go deeper with Nabil's contacts I stop my interviews in Belgium based on a tip from a friend warning me that there is about to be a sting operation rounding up many of the extremists in Belgium involved with militant jihadi terror cells. However as I continue to watch Belgium and return to interviews two years later, speaking with over a hundred Belgian Moroccans in Brussels and Antwerp, it's clear that the second generation Muslim immigrants, especially the Moroccans, have a hard time integrating both because many reject mainstream Belgian values, their families do not allow the girls to date across cultures and because both genders often find themselves rejected from mainstream Belgian society. I learn that unlike the conflict zones such as Palestine, Iraq, Chechnya, etc. the widespread traumatization (as a result of armed conflict) that occurs is not an issue, but culture gaps, alienation, marginalization and negative self-identity from discrimination, ethnic hatred, and self-hatred (over both feeling rejected and failing to reach idealized moral standards, etc.) abound in this population that live amongst militant jihadi ideologies and terrorist instigators that promote taking on a positive self identity vis a vis hatred for the host culture. And when young people especially feel an overwhelming sense of not belonging, there is a vulnerability to extremist ideologies and groups that offer adventure, identity and belonging that is based on hatred and violence.

CHAPTER 54

Muriel Degauque - the First Female European Muslim Convert Suicide Bomber

How females get involved in terrorism varies from group to group. In the anarchist and nationalist terrorist groups of the twentieth century, women, especially in Europe, played central and even leadership roles, but in the Islamic groups I've been studying women are often sidelined. Al Qaeda leader Zawahiri, for instance, encouraged women to stay home, raise their families and indoctrinate their children, leaving the operational roles to the men. And while the Chechens used women as suicide terrorists from the start, none played leadership roles. Palestinian, Iraqi, Pakistani and Afghani terror groups only resorted to using females when their male operatives were getting blocked from crossing checkpoints and women could more easily carry bombs strapped to their bodies, and again none of the women terrorists ever entered leadership roles.

Despite never making it to the tops of their organizations, the roles that are open to women in the militant jihad are many and varied. First there are the instigators: women who become committed to the militant jihad, but blocked from active combat and "martyr" roles, decide instead and let it be known that they will only marry a young man who intends to die a "martyr". Thus they use their youth and beauty to encourage their men to go and commit acts of terrorist violence and as a widow of such they gain social status and prestige within their groups. Or like the Belgian Moroccan Malika Aroud who *was* widowed when her husband bombed himself to kill General Massoud, they may live on to instigate even more men to take up arms by writing blogs and websites that encourage them to take part in the militant jihad. Others, following al Qaeda leader Ayman Zawahari's advice, stay at home and raise their children to follow the AQ ideology and still others become fundraisers, messengers or money couriers. And despite the top al Qaeda leadership being opposed, some of these women manage to get themselves sent as "martyrs" on suicide missions.

Muriel Degauque, a thirty-seven year old Belgian convert to Islam was one of these. On November 9th of 2005, al Qaeda inaugurated her as their first "white" western woman in Europe to become a successful suicide terrorist. Muriel went to Iraq with her Belgian Moroccan immigrant descent husband and attacked an American convoy by driving her bomb-filled car into it. Her explosion sent a chill through Europe and was a shocking wake-up call to Belgians.

At this time, my Belgian interviews are still on hold, and Belgian authorities have been monitoring the group Muriel Degauque's husband, Issam Goris, was running in which he was clandestinely recruiting volunteers for Abu Musab al Zarqawi's AQ affiliated terrorist group in Iraq. They intercept a call in which they learn that he and his wife are already in Iraq. The Belgian intelligence alerts the U.S. and Iraqi government that a Belgian couple is in the country with intent to carry out attacks, but they are too late. Muriel Degauque has jumped ahead and carries out her mission. The Belgian police swing into full force, making multiple arrests of anyone they have evidence could be involved. And all of my leads to the serious extremists in Belgium that I had been hoping to interview dry up, immediately too frightened to talk to me or anyone else.

Completely fascinated with the story of Muriel and free now to resume my interviews, I head out days after learning of her attack to the small town of Charleroi to join the droves of journalists descending upon her family in hopes of learning what drove this European descent Belgian woman first to convert to Islam, and then to become radicalized to the extent that she would go to Iraq to explode herself. As I drive the half hour from Brussels to Charleroi with Muriel's parents' address in hand, I struggle with a mixture of strong curiosity and deep shame at disturbing her bereaved family. I've brought my daughter, Jessica, a fluent French speaker along as my interpreter, hoping that working with my daughter might soften our request for an interview.

Charleroi is located in Wallonia, the French speaking part of Belgium and the fifth largest municipality in Belgium. Originally thriving upon the steel and coal industry whose factories mostly shut down in the 1950's, Charleroi experienced some of the highest rates of unemployment for all of Europe during the 1980's and 1990's, when Muriel was growing up. As Jessica and I pull into town it appears typical to me, perhaps poorer than some, but still with a European charm.

Muriel, I know from speaking to a few of the journalists who have already made this trek, is the second of two siblings. As a teenager, Muriel witnessed her only brother, Jean-Paul, die on his twenty-fourth birthday in a motorcycle accident when another car sideswiped him. According to most, this was the turning point for Muriel.

Neighbors remember Muriel as a lovely child who grew into a troubled teenager who did drugs and dropped out of school at age sixteen. Andrea Dorange, a neighbor recalls, "When Jean-Paul died, she completely changed. She was always sad and she told me that it was unfair that her brother had died and that she should have died in his place." Another reporter who interviewed one of the close friend's of Muriel's mother tells me that this haunting thought plaguing Muriel came from her mother, Liliane, who according to her neighbor was so distraught when Muriel brought news of her beloved son's death that she said to her daughter, "It should have been you!" The death of her brother and these words—if they were indeed said by her mother—seem to have broken Muriel as her life went seriously off track from then on.

Muriel worked in a local bakery and a café but was known for frequent absences and what many said was drug abuse. Her mother reported that she worked haphazardly and took state unemployment benefits. In her early twenties Muriel married a Turkish man whose parents worked in the area, conferring Belgian citizenship on him and together they moved to Brussels. At that time Muriel is reported to have taken Islam and donned a headscarf.[260] The marriage may have been of convenience as they divorced not long after and Muriel then met an Algerian man and deepened her commitment to Islam, after which she married Issam Goris, a Belgian of Moroccan origin (on his mother's side), beginning a whole new life.

In 2000 when they married, Goris was already known to Belgian authorities as a radical Islamist and was being watched by the police. Goris took Muriel to Morocco where she learned Arabic and studied the Koran. They returned in 2002 with Muriel wearing a full Saudi style burka, complete with nikab (face covering), shocking her family and former Charleroi friends.

Yet many reported that Muriel appeared to be happy. However, her parents found Goris difficult, as he insisted on men and women eating separately and "there could be no question of turning on the TV or opening a beer."[261] Liliane recalls that Muriel grew distant and did not visit her mother even when she was hospitalized and that the last time the couple

visited, "We told them that we had had enough of them trying to indoctrinate us." Goris was apparently making more money than the unemployment both he and his wife collected, as he chauffeured Muriel to family
visits in an elegant white Mercedes.

When my daughter Jessica and I locate the Deguaque family home in
Charleroi, it's already late afternoon and getting dark.

"How do you feel about this?" I ask Jessica before we get out of the car.

"It's really sad, but maybe you can help them?" she says, and I am
pleased to be reminded that as a trauma psychologist I at least have something to offer this family. That is if they agree to speak to me. "Remember
to tell them I'm not a journalist, but a psychologist," I tell Jessica, "and
that I'm your mother." We go together to the door and press the bell, both
of us feeling the heavy grief of the situation. We exchange a glance as
the door opens and Muriel's father asks us through the screen door if we
are journalists. In soft-spoken French, Jessica addresses Muriel's father,
a crane driver by profession, apologizing for disturbing him in his grief
while explaining that I'm a psychologist and have interviewed many families of young people who died in suicide operations and wondered if he
might be willing to speak with us. Muriel's father looks with the saddest
eyes at Jessica, drinking up her young innocence and seems to want to
throw his arms around her and weep and then his gaze turns from her to
me. *Mother and daughter*, his face seems to say—something his family no
longer has. He stares at us for a few moments and seems to want to invite
us in, but then his eyes filling with tears he tells Jessica, "No there have
been too many journalists ringing our bell asking for interviews. I can't
speak about it now. I'm too tired. Maybe later, another time." Jessica and
I both cover our hearts and nod to him in expressions of solidarity and
respect for his grief and Jessica wishes him well as we leave mortified that
we have even disturbed him at this terrible moment.

"I feel so ashamed!" I say when we are back in the car.

"Yeah, Mom, but did you see how he looked at us?" she asks as we
discuss the words written on his face. Maybe he felt some sense of care
from us—I hope so. From there we go to sit in one of the local cafes to
have a snack and to get a feel for this depressed town Muriel grew up in.
No one there wants to talk about her either and we end the day with no
interview.

Later I find where Muriel lived as married Muslim woman in Brussels
and go there as well. It's an apartment on Rue de Mérode in the heart of a

crowded and rundown immigrant quarter near Gare du Midi, the main railway station. It's Friday and we arrive when the local "garage" mosque, a home used as a mosque, is just finishing afternoon prayers. Belgians dressed in Moroccan traditional clothes spill out onto the street along with a few black burqa and nikab clad women. We try to talk to some of those who exit the mosque but none are interested to discuss the case. I know from journalists who did manage to interview her neighbors that living there, Muriel was known to them as an extremely polite unobtrusive woman. One shopkeeper remembers her and tells me that she shopped daily in his tiny shop for food and household items. "She was always wearing a black burqa, black leather gloves and her face covering," he tells me, "but always very polite. She bought mint for her tea here most days." Other neighbors told journalists that piles of shoes would be in the hallway when many people gathered in their apartment to pray.[262] While they knew she was very religious, no one seemed to have any idea that she was an extremist or plotting to explode herself in Iraq.

In August of 2005 Goris and Deguaque left Brussels for the Middle East. According to journalists they didn't tell her parents they were leaving. "Their landlord believed they were heading to Kenya and a local cafe owner recalled Goris 'said goodbye and that they were going to Morocco, to Meknes, where he apparently came from."[263] Muriel's mother hearing only once from her daughter when she called, seems to have known something was wrong. She recalled to one journalist, "The last time I spoke to my daughter on the telephone was a month ago. She told me she was in Syria." Liliane recalled repeatedly trying to call her daughter's phone but only getting voice mail. Muriel's mother even phoned her on the day of her suicide operation at ten thirty p.m.—too late to stop her.[264]

"I had a bad feeling when I was watching the news on television and they were talking about a Belgian [suicide bomber]," Liliane told a journalist. Muriel's parents learned the truth when police officers arrived on their doorstep at six a.m. the next morning after news of their daughter's suicide bombing had been broken at Baquba, thirty miles northeast of Baghdad. Liliane knocked on her best friend's door in tears. "I've lost my daughter," she wept. "I now have no children!"[265]

After Muriel's mission, American soldiers with the aide of Belgian intelligence discovered her husband's hiding place where he was holed up with explosives plotting to suicide and kill the soldiers looking for him.

Goris however was killed in the ensuing gunfight without being able to self-detonate or harm anyone else.

When I look at Muriel Deguaque's psycho-social history and try to reconstruct what happened with her I see again the lethal cocktail of suicide terrorism: a vulnerable individual exposed to a group that is willing and able to equip her for violence; an ideology that met her psychological needs of cleansing her survivor guilt, offering her instant admission to paradise, where she may hope to reunite with her brother, and that gave her the courage and social support to carry out her act.

While no mother learning of the traumatic death of a child can be held fully responsible for words spoken in shocked grief, they apparently stayed with Muriel and were finally reenacted years later when she chose to nearly replicate her brother's manner of traumatic death—sideswiping her car into a much heavier and stronger target. On an individual level Muriel was working through posttraumatic stress, survivor guilt and complicated mourning. Her first response to her trauma had been turning to drugs and failing to function, but when she was led into the militant jihadi interpretation of Islam, she found a way to overcome her guilt and a group who helped her retain that feeling of being okay with herself—as long as she kept deepening her commitment to their cause and finally gave her life to it.[266]

In regard to the social support that Muriel experienced, it seems to have come from narrowing her life into a tight group of like-minded individuals. Wearing a burka and nikab she cut herself off from most social interactions except those within her "in" group. While many in Belgium, as well as around the world, were upset about the U.S. invasion in Iraq and satellite television and Internet images showed graphic photos of Iraqis suffering, Muriel likely was more exposed than most by living in the Muslim quarters of Brussels among Arabic speakers. And as a trauma victim herself, she likely found herself over-identifying with and angered by the Iraqi suffering. Participating in home-centered extremist meetings, she probably found that agreeing to try to fight the U.S. invaders was viewed as heroic among her cadres and that she had all the support she needed to gain courage to carry out the mission that I believe was, on some subconscious level, the ultimate expression of a blend of remorse, self hatred, identification with the pain of other victims who had lost loved ones unfairly, and a desperate attempt at self-redemption.

The arrests that ensued following Muriel's suicide operation led to fears that her mission was not an isolated incident. A Belgian couple of Moroccan origin was reportedly arrested before they headed on a similar journey of death. And another Belgian of Moroccan descent, Mohamed Reha, arrested earlier in November, told police there were several wives of imprisoned Islamic extremists who were prepared to go on suicide missions, and others with them.[267] Apparently there was a considerable net of Belgian operatives all aiming at sending both men and women from Belgium to act as suicide terrorists in Iraq and perhaps elsewhere.

When asked to comment on the case, Claude Moniquet from the Brussels-based European Strategic Intelligence and Security Centre stated that Muriel Degauque could become a "model" for other fanatical young women to follow.[268] Indeed, in March of 2012 the French newspaper le Figaro reports about the case of a young Parisian lawyer who like Muriel was radicalized by her partner and abandoned her job to move to Cairo. According to French journalist Malbrunot, the young woman told her mother before leaving that her heroine was Muriel Degauque. Thus far there is no indication she has taken the final steps to emulate Muriel, but perhaps some like her will.[269]

There must have been delight among the ranks of al Qaeda leaders when a white Belgian woman who wouldn't be likely to raise suspicions as she passed through checkpoints, traveled into Iraq on one of their missions knowing that her successful suicide act would send a shiver of terror throughout all of the Western world. If white Belgian females are now acting in behalf of al Qaeda, all of Europe and even Americans have to ask: Is anyone safe from their attacks?

Indeed in succeeding years al Qaeda has threatened to raise a force of "white" European suicide bombers. And evidence recently discovered in captured documents has indicated that AQ groups in Pakistan have successfully lured white European descent converts, who are much less likely to be suspected of involvement in terrorism, to their training camps where they were taught explosives and clandestine communication techniques and further indoctrinated into the AQ ideology.[270] While drone strikes in 2012 may have killed many of the leaders of AQ we have yet to see what lies in store from these secret operatives who may now be returned and living as sleeper cells inside Europe, and who with the visa waivers open to most European countries to be able to travel freely to the United States as well.

CHAPTER 55

Hamid and the Militant Jihad in Antwerp

At seventeen, Hamid would have given his life for Osama Bin Laden. Now, sitting on the modern beige sofas in the living room of his contemporary Antwerp apartment, the bearded young Belgian, sporting a traditional ankle length robe, cap and sandals, serves us coffee and cookies. Hamid is of Moroccan descent but with his lighter hair could easily pass for a "white" Belgian, and not, as is the case, a jihadist who learned his trade at night in the forests of western Europe and then pulled himself back from the brink of extremist violence.

How we happen to be sitting with him now in the Spring of 2008 in the cool quiet of his "diwan," the segregated living space of the traditional Muslim home, deep in conversation and undisturbed by a wife and child who are unseen but presumably engaged within the traditional architecture of their own lives, is a story that begins and ends beyond these walls.

Antwerp, one of the largest cities in Belgium and a vibrant business center, relies on a workforce that is nearly twenty percent Muslim, the majority of whom hail from North Africa and Turkey This wave of immigration began during a boom period during the seventies when Belgium invited temporary laborers to come work in the coal mines and manufacturing industry. It is doubtful the Belgian government expected that these "guest workers" would stay and settle in, dramatically altering the social fabric of the country. But they did, and they became Belgian citizens who were allowed under the Family Reunification Act to invite their spouses and other extended family members. Over time these couples gave birth to immigrant descent second generation "Moroccans" and the trend of bringing more immigrants continues to the present.

Antwerp's history with Moroccan immigration in particular has been turbulent. The majority from Morocco came from the North as uneducated illiterate workers who are now segregated to the poorer areas of town where incidents of racist violence drudge up cultural antagonisms. Six years ago, in November of 2002, Mohamed Achrak, a public school teacher and Belgian of Moroccan origins, was shot by a Flemish Belgian man in what appeared to many Belgians of Moroccan descent to be a racist murder. Thousands of Moroccan Belgians poured out onto the streets of Antwerp to protest the way the criminal justice system handled his crime. When the city authorities claimed the Flemish man to be mentally disabled and the case was dismissed, few Moroccan Belgians believed the explanation and marched to raise their voices against racist violence. The police did little to calm the situation. Riots broke out among the immigrant youth of Antwerp, ending with violent clashes and over two hundred arrests.

To make matters worse the Antwerp police were heavily infiltrated by members of the Vlams Blok (Flemish Block), an anti-immigrant political organization that had been convicted by the Belgian courts authorities in 2002 for "incitement to hate and discrimination". In an attempt to clean up their image, the Vlams Blok renamed itself Vlams Belang (Flemish Interest) but the group continues to have a strong presence in the Antwerp police department. It also has a strong following in Antwerp among the Flemish people who promote a racially "clean" society and fight for adhering to the traditional "Belgian" ways with popular slogans such as "Adapt or Get Out". A small minority of disenchanted and disenfranchised Belgian Muslims, instead chose a third way.

Hamid was seventeen when Mohamed Achrak was murdered. Smart, capable and enraged he was propelled, like others from the second generation of European Muslim immigrants, into militant jihadi extremism.

Educated in the accessible and affordable Belgian university system, many of the Muslim children of this generation have come up against racial and ethnic barriers they believed their intelligence and good grades would have erased. Expecting to transcend their parents' struggles for good jobs, good housing and the other privileges reserved for "white" Belgians, they graduate instead to a rude awakening of bitterness and hopelessness. My twenty-year-old guide Tayseer, who is studying business at the Free University of Brussels and also a second-generation immigrant of Moroccan descent, makes this frustration clear.

"When I graduate university," he told me angrily, "I will leave Belgium. I'll go and live in Qatar or some other Muslim country where I am welcomed. Here I can never belong. I will always be a Moroccan Muslim and hated."

Interviews with such youth reveal that they encounter daily discrimination and many speak of insults and humiliations when they were turned away from work with comments like: "No Belgians would want to see a Moroccan face at the front desk,"; "Our customers would not feel comfortable dealing with you,"; "We cannot offer you a professional job [despite your college diploma] but there are job openings for cleaning the toilets [or alternatively janitorial jobs]." The bite of this discrimination extends to the home, public square and nightclubs. Frequently landlords make clear to their "white" tenants that they will not accept sub-leases with "Moroccan" Belgians and turn "Moroccans" away, telling them the leases have already been filled. And as I have already witnessed, bouncers in the night clubbing scene routinely turn away "Moroccan" youth telling them the club is full, turning around in the space of minutes to admit "white" Belgian youth. One young man recalls being told, 'Go home Moroccan' yet he had a Belgian passport. This wholesale rejection of Moroccan youth into the clubs leads to "gangs" of young Belgian men of North African descent angrily roaming the streets on weekend nights. Just a few months before today, I asked a Belgian government official how this kind of discrimination could be happening on a systematic basis. His answer was equally shocking, "We'll you know the Moroccans cause nearly all the problems in the nightclubs."

There's nothing like routine rejection for breeding complex emotions, including anger and hatred. As one French youth of immigrant descent told a Paris reporter, the first time you are rejected from a nightclub you accept it, "but after two or three times, you go home carrying a bag of hatred on your shoulders." (Astier, 2005). Similarly a young Belgian of Moroccan descent explains to me, "Many people become angry when they are turned away and go home to their own neighborhood and smash things. It's really deep."

One young man of Moroccan descent remarked to me about his understanding of the immigrant culture in the United States, "…there I can become an American, but here no. My parents came here fifty years ago and still I am not accepted." Pointing to his face and skin color he states, "I can never be a Belgian."

It's no surprise many "Moroccan" youth report feeling they have to fundamentally strip themselves of their Muslim identity and customs in order to succeed among "white" Belgians. One young woman in Antwerp said in an interview with me that she was told she would have to remove her headscarf to obtain employment, and another young man was told, "I could never hire you with that name, my customers wouldn't like to be served by a 'Jamal'.

Hamid was radicalized by an al Qaeda recruiter operating out of an Internet cafe. Like many Muslims in Europe who become extremists, he started out as a believer with little knowledge of the fundamentals of Islamic beliefs and practices and could not read the Koran in its original Arabic. This, as well as his emotional volatility over civil disturbances, made him an easy target for a recruiter who could tell him that his views and practice of Islam were incorrect and who claimed to interpret the Koran for him. At the start of our interview it was obvious by his dress and beard that Hamid had dedicated himself to the Salafi way; attempting through dress and beliefs to follow the original teachings and to emulate the original customs of the Prophet Muhammad. In more ways than one clothes communicate a series of stories and traditions and Hamid's militant jihadi story begins when he rededicated himself to Islam, taking on a much more conservative form than he had been born into and becoming what many in Europe refer to as a "revert".

Though Tayseer and I have not seen her, it's likely that his wife also follows the Salafi ways in her dress: wearing an all black robe including a headscarf, black gloves and perhaps even a nikab that covers her face in public. These women are not commonplace but we have seen them in Antwerp, looking like black ravens crossing the modern city streets.

Unfortunately for the nonviolent Salafi believers, their style of dress has been strongly associated with extremist groups. Muriel Degauque as we have learned donned the same black robes and nikab after she took on militant jihadi extremist views. Likewise arrests in 2004 and since in the small village of Maaseik, not far from Antwerp, uncovered an international terrorist cell linked across Europe and back into an al Qaeda affiliate group (the GICM) operating inside Morocco. Many of the adherents of that group dressed in a similar style drawing alarm from local residents. Sadly for Salafis their beliefs and traditions of going back to the original teachings and practices of the Prophet Muhammad have been hijacked by extremists inside Belgium and beyond, breeding distrust in the general population.[271]

Hamid appears at present as a peaceful but conservative believer, far removed from extremist ideas. I begin the interview by telling Hamid a bit about myself and my research, including my work in the slums of Casablanca and interviewing the friends of the suicide bombers there. I find that it helps a lot for him to trust me that I have been inside the slums of Morocco, especially since many Moroccans don't dare to tread in those areas. I tell him a bit about what I learned there and I find Hamid understands the young hopeless Moroccan.

"In Morocco the ones that go as bombers are still young and on drugs," he says. "You don't see the [religious] ones with beards. They have no knowledge in Islam. Just take the ones who already say 'We are dead.' They want to leave the slum and take a short cut to paradise. [Their recruiters] tell them that the Prophet Muhammad told his followers that of all the seventy-two Muslim groups, most are not on the right path. Only one is. They say we are the ones."

Hamid explains how these recruiters work on them psychologically. "They tell them 'If you do a big sin, you are kafir (non Muslim);[272] if you drink alcohol, if you go with a girl, and so on, you are kafir'. But for those who are 'true believers,' the recruiters give them permission to kill and take from the rest. They say, 'You are allowed to kill [the kafir], allowed to take their money. We are in a country that is at war. And those people in Holland and Spain, all their women and their men, their blood is ours, their money is ours.' These people take the Koran and make their own interpretation."

Hamid is describing the practice of declaring other Muslims "Takfir" – asserting that they are apostates and can be killed. This practice originated in the early years of Islam and was first practiced by the Khawarij, who declared other Muslims as unbelievers that could be killed, often for political reasons. These practices were eventually abandoned and condemned as non-Islamic, although when the early Muslims who were only nominally practicing Islam but calling themselves Muslims were facing Mongol invasions, Takfir practices resurfaced again. At that time, the great Islamic scholar Ibn Taymiyyah declared that it was not only acceptable but obligatory for Muslims to fight with and kill the Mongol Tartars invaders that had converted to Islam but were not following Shariah law. However earlier and subsequent teachings in Islam always emphasized the need for Muslims to respect each other, to avoid fighting amongst themselves, and that it is prohibited for one Muslim to kill another. Now modern day Islamic extremists such as al Qaeda adherents have resurrected these old teachings on Takfir and apply them in modern day circumstances to justify attempts to overthrow Muslim dictators (despite the Koran urging restraint with regard to corrupt Muslim leaders) and also to justify their violent attacks where other Muslims are killed. The Muslims who practice making or declaring others as "Takfir" are themselves referred to as "Takfiris".

Hamid and I discuss the poverty and hopelessness that I witnessed in the slums of Casablanca and how it made the job of the militant jihadi instigators pedaling a false form of Islam simple for motivating the young men there to become suicide bombers. As we discuss this I reflect that while the prevalent view just after 9-11 was that terrorists spring up amidst poverty and illiteracy which was the case for the Moroccan bombers in terms of poverty but not illiteracy, a closer examination of the 9-11 bombers actually revealed that this theory didn't hold water when applied to them. The 9-11 bombers, the majority Saudi, came from relative privilege vis a vis their counterparts and were well educated,as were many of the Palestinian suicide bombers I have studied. Indeed as some counter-terrorism experts began to realize the holes in the prevailing theory regarding poverty and illiteracy being motivating factors for terrorism, some quipped that raising literacy rates in Islamic countries might be a risk factor for more, rather then less extremism! Why those from more affluent backgrounds get involved in terrorism is debatable and is likely multi-causal. It can be anger at the injustice of their societies, identification with the masses, increased knowledge of and sensitivity over corrupt government practices, frustrated aspirations when a good education leads to a dead end, or as former CIA Operations Officer Marc Sageman argues it can be the "gang of guys" philosophy: if one becomes an extremist, the others follow.[273] In my opinion, there is no one size fits all theory of terrorism. But as I listen to Hamid, we are in agreement that the hopelessness of poverty and drug addiction played an important part in terms of the Moroccan bombers' vulnerability to their acceptance of the extremist ideology.

The conversation moves to the European sphere and Hamid becomes upset speaking how recruiters here justify violence against unbelievers and how they manipulate others to accept their justifications, resulting in the London metro and the Madrid train bombings. Hamid is agitated; his voice becomes excited and angry as he explains how militant jihadi recruiters manipulate young minds the world over saying, "… this is wrong. This is *not* how the Prophet lived. He used violence for real defense when the Muslims were attacked, but if they made peace, he stopped."

Referring to the current crisis in Iraq, Hamid expresses his frustration over Takfiris who denounce each other and kill those they denounce. "In

Iraq they kill barbers just because they shave beards! They kill those who they say are not Muslim, professors in the universities and so on! Some extremists even brand their parents as apostates telling them, 'You are not Muslims.'"

As we discuss these ideas I reflect that while the riots in Antwerp have calmed, the conflicts and unease between the immigrant Muslim and Flemish community here continue. And as we learned from the Lebanese immigrant Dyab Abou Jahjah who formed the controversial Arab Europe-an League (AEL),many disgruntled Muslims have been mobilized model-ing their fight against Belgian racism after the "By any Means Necessary" strategies of Malcolm X. In Antwerp, Abou Jahjah and his AEL are often credited for fomenting street riots and violent clashes with the police. But this is not the only path that disgruntled Belgian Muslims have open to them. Others like Hamid found the militant jihad.

Hamid's road to violent extremism started, interestingly enough, at the Internet café. He was checking his e-mail and talking with friends when someone he didn't know asked if he'd yet seen a particular movie on the Internet. He hadn't, so they looked at it together. It was about attacks against Islamic people in various parts of the world.

"I was crying," Hamid recalls after seeing it. "It was about the situation of the Muslim ummah. It showed babies dying in Palestine, women, old people, victims of the Iraq boycott, victims of Iran, Afghanistan, Sudan, Somalia, Chechnya, then our lack of responses—that no one was doing anything. It showed Osama bin Ladin saying 'If no one takes action, I will.' There was a training camp, and I knew then that I would give my life for Osama bin Ladin."

Hamid said the recruiter began immediately to appeal to him on many levels: to his sense of duty, tender-heartedness for the victims and anger at what had happened to them. Hamid recalls how the recruiter manipulated his thoughts and emotions.

"He said we must prepare ourselves. He spoke about Bosnia and Serbia that they were Europeans and neighbors too, but killed each other. He said we are neighbors here and it can happen here as well-that one day they can decide to kill *all* of us."

Hamid says the recruiters work one-on-one at first and usually in public places, like Mosques, Internet cafes, and places where there are a lot of young people.

"It deepens by friendship. Everyone knows each other in our communities. If a [Muslim] stranger introduces himself you can always find a connection, 'Oh you are his friend! There are one hundred thousand Muslims in Belgium and we are all interconnected."

Hamid explains that many recruiters use the tactic of exposure to a video packed with emotional graphic images of despair and a call to heroism. They watch their recruit and see how he responds. If they get an emotional response, they know they can take him further.

"They make the call for a non-believing Muslim to 'revert' to Islam," Hamid says, explaining how the first moves are to present the Salafi ways to the new initiate, the first invitation being simply to walk away from the Islam one was born into and step into what is presented as a more authentic form. I"The first step is someone begins to wear the thobe, to start a beard, to make friends. It gives them courage," Hamid recounts. Indeed in these subtle first moves the recruiter has already asserted himself as an "expert" on Islam and positioned himself as able to dominate and steer his new recruit from this point onward and he has also driven at least a small wedge and distanced the recruit from his family and previous community of believers. All of this empowers the recruiter in taking charge over his initiate as he continues in recruitment and instigatation to terrorism.

Hamid's recruiter convinced him to take the next step in joining the militant jihad by constantly impressing upon him that Muslims must be prepared to defend themselves, reminding him repeatedly of what had happened in Bosnia: that the Muslim women had been raped and the men killed. Once convinced of the need to prepare for self-defense, Hamid agreed to come to physical training with the recruiter and his indoctrinates to prepare and it continued from there.

"First it was just physical training—one hour a night. Then I came to the training camp where we [expanded to military training], running, training, we used b-b guns, had target practice and sometimes we split ourselves into two attack groups and trained against each other". Their leader let them train on how to handle an AK-47. "We were very excited to use the AK-47. They let us train with one but not shoot it. If you don't shoot it correctly it will break your shoulder. It is the gun used by snipers. You have to hold it ten centimeters from your eye to protect yourself from the back fire." The leaders fanned their trainees' excitement by telling them, "Maybe we will go to the Czech Republic and use real weapons."

"We went to train in the forest at night," Hamid continues. "We started at eleven p.m. and went until three or four a.m. We can't go in day. [The police] will catch you if you do.

"The last time we were training we were divided into teams, and we were shooting at each other. A brother and I saw a house, dark and in the middle of the forest so we thought it was empty. We climbed up on the roof to ambush the others, but we didn't realize that there were people living inside. The people called the police, and they arrived and began searching for us with searchlights. Some of us ran away, but me and two others climbed high up in some trees to hide. There were three of us in the trees, all of us with beards and I was in my Pakistani clothes. If they had caught us for sure they would have said we were a sleeper cell in Belgium." The image of Hamid in robes hidden up in the trees with the Belgian police searching with flashlights below them makes me laugh heartily.

"What can you tell me about the organization of the training camps and the recruiters?" I ask.

"They have a leader. First you meet the smaller ones. They are a bit older, twenty-six to thirty years old," Hamid explains. "The main leader is forty to forty-five years old." Taking great pains to make sure Hamid knows I am not interested to learn the man's identity, I ask him what his nationality is. "He is a Chechen," Hamid says. "He has jihadi contacts with Austria and Spain. He's a teacher at a public secondary school, he teaches religion! He holds a Belgian passport."

Since 2008, seven to ten thousand[274] Chechens displaced by the wars in Chechnya have gone to live in Belgium,[275] with at least two thousand of them granted political asylum in 2003.[276] This man, whose identity I do not want to know(I don't want to endanger either Hamid or myself by asking too many operational details) is one of these—a Chechen who was granted Belgian citizenship. And in Belgium, children in all public schools are offered religious education that they choose according to their creed, and this person is evidently using the goodwill of his asylum status and his *state funded position* to influence and recruit young Belgian Muslims into the militant jihad! I shake my head in disbelief tempted to ask more about him, but I don't dare.

"Is the training camp only militant?" I ask.

"No it's Islamic as well," Hamid says. "They use tapes and lessons." He tells me the lessons are in Arabic and Berber,the dialect from the North of Morocco where most Moroccan immigrants to Belgium come from.

"They know tactics of intelligence," Hamid explains how the group protects itself from police detection. "They take their sim cards and batteries from their mobile phones before they begin (teaching) so no one can listen in."

As time went on Hamid committed himself fully and decided he wanted to get into the action and join the jihad as a fighter. Hamid set his sights on Chechnya, the most likely place at the time to go to fight.

"I started training in Ramadan and was with them nine to ten months," Hamid recalls as I think how quickly he went from a disgruntled Belgian Muslim with real grievances to an activated al Qaeda sponsored mujahadeen. Luckily Hamid got out before he activated as a violent jihadist. He tells me that when he was about to leave to Chechnya he decided it was his duty to tell his mother, to ask for her blessing for his mission in the likely case that he died there. "My mother knew. I told her, 'I need your agreement. I want to go to Chechnya, what is your answer?' She said, 'No, are you crazy. It's only a war for politics.'"

Without her permission Hamid's sense of honor in going to fight jihad was dented. Once she knew his plan she told his father who decided to stop him. Hamid recalls how his father came searching for him, convinced that his son was already on his way out of Belgium.

"I went with my friends to see a movie. My father thought I had already left for Chechnya. He became crazy and phoned me. My phone was dead so I didn't receive his calls. He found me in the movie theater. My father was beside himself and asked, 'Where are those people [sending you to fight jihad]? If you go, I will become crazy.'" Amusingly Hamid and his friends had been viewing Harry Potter!

His father's show of emotion got to Hamid. Already he had begun to have doubts about the leaders, but they crystallized during this period. "Usama my friend said, 'Don't go to those people. They are not good, they have another end [death].' I realized also as time went on that people like them killed others in London, Madrid, Amman, Saudi. They are all innocent people, why?"

Beginning to doubt his trainers, Hamid began to seek answers from others outside the group more knowledgeable in the Koran than himself who also knew Arabic to explain, and as he did he began to find out that what the jihadi leaders were preaching was not necessarily Islamic. Hamid began to question the leaders.

"I started to discuss with them, to argue with what they say. Now they hate me!" Hamid, like any others who questioned the leadership, was isolated and branded as an apostate. "My friend who stayed with them said to me, 'You are not Muslim, you are a collaborator with kafir (unbelievers).'" Later Hamid's friend also had doubts and left as well.

"I changed completely after this," Hamid recalls. He says he works now to try to talk others in Antwerp out of having responded to the call to militant jihad. "You see the people who follow them. They are young, eighteen and nineteen year olds. Most are rascals and thugs, small criminals, petty thieves, the ones who are breaking into cars."

I ask Hamid if this man is still active in the community and Hamid says he is.

"I know he collects money (from the participants). Fifty euros a person, from every person, twenty-five from students. The money goes to support the mujahadeen in Chechnya or Iraq. They also collect donations in Muslim-owned groceries, little stores, bakeries and butcheries. There is a small collection jar for coins. It says on the jar that it is collected to help the orphans, but it is not for orphans. It's for the fighters and for the jihadis in Europe. I spoke to some of the halal butchers and told them they are Takfiris who are collecting this money and that it's not for orphans. That's why they hate me."

"How do you feel about knowing this man is still recruiting young people?" I ask.

"I spoke with a (Muslim) brother about him. This man speaks Arabic well and here people see him as a scholar. They name him Ustad (which is a title of respect in Arabic for a scholar or a musician). My brother tells me, 'You must call the police.' My brother wants to turn him in because he feels pity for the young."

It's obvious Hamid is torn and uncomfortable about following this advice to turn someone from his Muslim community into the police. But he also says that he is not afraid of his former militant jihadi leader. "He must fear me," Hamid says.

Hamid has tried to confront the leader of the group that continues to operate in his community, but it is to no avail. He explains, "If you go to discuss with him he becomes very angry. He says you are collaborator to those who killed our sisters in Bosnia and those who sell our Muslims in Iraq."

Now Hamid has formed a group of like-minded Muslims who study the Koran and they try to save their neighbors and younger kids who have been sucked into the militant jihad. Hamid and the others see themselves so strongly in these kids—they are symbolically saving themselves by working without pay to tirelessly fight what almost destroyed them.

He explains how difficult it is for him, after going through his own transformation first into the militant jihad and now back out of it, to convince the others to come out. "Now they say, 'First you are Bin Laden, now you have changed channels.'" He explains that it's hard to be trusted and that there is suspicion that he has become a police informant, government collaborator or is in alliance with Americans.

Hamid laughs at the idea of being considered sympathetic to Americans. He doesn't trust them himself. But paranoia over who might be a collaborator is only one of the confusions about militant jihadi activities in his community. Those who fought in what many believed were legitimate jihads (i.e. Afghanistan, Bosnia, etc.) are seen as heroes in his Muslim enclave in Antwerp. Hamid explains, "Many went from Saudi to Afghanistan to fight against the Russians and they won. But after they fought between themselves and the scholars told them, 'Now, you must go back to your country, back to Europe, Tunisia, etc. But many stayed in Afghanistan and for those that did, they brainwashed them to believe that if we free Afghanistan we can go further, that the Saudi leaders are not Islamic, that they should start a jihad again," Hamid explains referring to how the Afghani jihad veterans looked for their next places to fight jihad: in Chechnya to overthrow Russian rule, in Saudi to overthrow what they saw as the apostate Kingdom, and now in Belgium, the Netherlands, Spain, the UK, etc.

Hamid uses the term brainwashing, a term I don't care for. For me it seems that recruiters are not so much brainwashing as adept at using *already existing vulnerabilities and societal forces and at manipulating emotions* to pull people into accepting their ideological beliefs, but underneath it all, it's a voluntary process and the recruit has already accepted beliefs that support a lot of what the recruiter tells him and also has his own motivations and needs for following the process. Al Suri, the al Qaeda strategist, actually argued for this slippery slope method of bringing huge numbers into the AQ fold to support the militant jihad ideologically and to only later draw militants from among their ranks.[277] I see this already beginning for entire communities of Muslims in Europe, first with ideologically building a society-wide foundation that the suicide bombing of Israelis by Palestinians is morally based, then that suicide bombing in Iraq and Afghanistan is defensive, then that militant jihadi acts can and should be used in Europe as well. When enough are convinced, it is time for uprising, al Suri argues. It seems to me this incremental slide propelled by his existing beliefs is exactly what happened to Hamid. And until he learned how to interpret Islam and its scriptures correctly he was vulnerable to being drawn into violent extremism.

"Young people tell me 'It's jihad. We must do jihad.'" Hamid explains. "I tell them everything has conditions: before we pray we must wash ritually; when we pray we must point to Mecca, to the qibla. The same is true when dealing with the leader of a Muslim country and making decisions about war. As Muslims we can only go to war when we have enough power. If we don't have an AK 47, if we have no guns we cannot go. Also we have strict rules about war, we don't kill women, old men, kill or hurt people inside churches, or damage and kill trees. Jihad also has conditions. If you fulfill the conditions of jihad, then you can go. But you cannot go and kill without a leader." Hamid is referring to an Islamic emir with legitimate authority, which doesn't exist in Belgium. The young people Hamid tries to reach answer, 'Osama bin Ladin is our leader.'" But Hamid asks them back, "Who made *him* an Islamic leader? He studied economics, not Islam!" Hamid explains, "Then they are silent."

As I listen to Hamid I doubt that pointing out logical contradictions is enough to pull the most vulnerable back from the brink. They have taken on the mindset of militant jihad not because it's logically coherent, but because it appeals to their emotional needs. They live in a hostile community where a lot of their neighbors are highly prejudiced, where it's hard to get jobs and the police don't like Moroccan immigrants; they don't feel protected and they don't see good opportunities for their future. Many of them lack a sense of dignity and have strong doubts about their ability to flourish in Belgium. When a recruiter offers them better and argues convincingly that Muslims the world over are being downtrodden, the offer resonates. It's only slowly that they begin to accept the violent parts of the answer for their own communities, and most have acted violently only outside the country—joining the "jihad" in Chechnya, Iraq, and elsewhere. But when a spark like the killing of a Moroccan teacher in Antwerp by a Flemish Belgium happens, their dedication is tested. When provoked, it's unclear what they may be willing to endorse for actions at home inside Belgium and inside Europe, and this is the serious aspect of the matter. Hamid knows some of the others I have interviewed earlier and he says that they are still involved in militant jihad and only gave me superficial interviews, confirming what I already suspected: they are far closer to al Qaeda than they admitted to me.

CHAPTER 56

Muhammad - the Fiery American in London

It's October 2006, and I'm in London to interview extremists and followers of the militant jihad. Ken lives in London now, having completed his Masters degree at SOAS, and he's arranged for us to hear Muhammad Dawud, a fiery Muslim who often preaches at Speakers' Corner in Hyde Park, and have lunch with him. Dawud, a tall, imposing bearded black man, wearing an ornate white thobe and skull cap with a decorated cape that flows behind him arrives flanked by four of his followers. He strides up to and mounts a small platform to address the mixed group of young Muslim men of immigrant descent and "white" British middle-aged people that assemble around him.

Up to recently when London finally began cracking down on extremist preaching and passed laws against inciting terrorism, speakers like Dawud were common in London mosques and outdoor areas, and Dawud's diatribe against the west is nothing compared to his predecessors. Abu Qatada, once described as Osama bin Ladin's right hand man in Europe, preached the militant jihadi ideology openly in London along with Abu Hamza, who both lived in the UK and collected state funds after claiming asylum.[278] These two are credited with radicalizing Richard Reid, the infamous "shoe bomber" who tried to down a US bound plane by igniting his shoe while in flight. They are also credited with sending dozens of extremists to train in militant jihadi camps in Pakistan and Afghanistan, for raising funds and recruiting for violent extremism.[279] According to a senior government security official speaking in 2012, extremist preachers in London have now mostly gone underground, spreading their messages of hate during secret meetings in private homes, rather than openly in mosques and universities as they did in the past.[280] It's 2006 now and some are still preaching their violent ideology out in the open, but Ken who has frequently come to the Speakers Corner tells me that Duwad is not one of them. But today we are in for a surprise.

According to my colleague Dr. David Mandel, a social psychologist, inciters to terrorism are a unique category of individuals involved in the terrorism trajectory who are poorly understood and understudied. They may never carry out an act of violence, yet they are important catalysts for aggression. Instigators, according to Mandel, legitimize collective violence, giving moral authority for individuals to participate directly in it, and they also often shape bystanders' reactions to these events and establish the social parameters for depersonalization and stigma.[281] I'm here to learn more of how this phenomenon occurs.

"Don't invade our countries!" Duwad shouts, explaining, "When Western countries invade Muslim countries you're going to have a problem! It's called jihad. I have love for you and I have respect for you, but once you invade my Muslim brothers, that's a different story automatically. What are you there for? As tourists? Or to steal their oil and natural resources?. . . When you come as a pirate, you will only see the sword! Democracy? You come into our countries to implement the laws of men to govern mankind? No. We have our own law. It's called Sharia—Islamic divine law. So don't invade our countries in the first place on the pretexts of lies, talking about how well you're building up homes and bridges after you have destroyed them."

As he goes on confidently orating about Islam, jihad and democracy, the young Muslims listening to him seem to be enamored by his charisma, while the "white" British listeners react negatively to the word "jihad" and some angrily heckle him. For those who have genuine questions, Dawud listens carefully before giving a small speech tying his answers to Islamic scriptures.

Many ask when jihad is acceptable and Dawud tells them it's appropriate to fight jihad to defend one's country and that "martyrdom" is glorified in Islam. I recall a recent event in Baghdad—a suicide bomber approached soldiers who were giving out candies to children and exploded himself, killing all the children who had gathered. A soldier who was present but uninjured later told me that he couldn't get over the cold-hearted murder of so many innocent children. I ask Dawud his opinion.

"It was justified," he answers completely shocking many of us listening. "And I will tell you why. The parents of those children should never have let their children approach the soldiers or receive candies from them. When the soldiers gave those Iraqi children candies they knew that the children would tell them who is around the corners and where the danger is, and surrounded by children they thought they were keeping themselves safe. The bomber had the right to explode himself killing them all and Allah will take him as a martyr to paradise!"

Murmurs breaks out and some of the "white" British listeners begin shouting at Dawud and arguing with him, some even shove forward. "What about on the subway here? Are suicide bombers justified to act here?" someone in the crowd asks.

"Yes they are," Dawud answers carefully adding, "If this country is attacking Muslims then we must defend our people, but only in that case."

I turn to Ken with raised eyebrows. Before we arrived, Ken had told me that Muhammad is fiery but never crosses the line. I guess we got lucky today as he seems to be speaking his mind quite freely at present. Indeed I'm surprised, as he could be arrested for his last statement.

Dawud keeps lecturing but seems to understand he's gone too far, while his hecklers shove and push to get to him. One in particular reaches his "pulpit" and begins to jeer at him. Dawud is practiced at this and does a combination of studiously ignoring and occasionally asking him to polite- ly desist, but the heckler continues shoving himself forward and at one point Dawud becomes enraged when the heckler jabs at his massive chest and Dawud shouts back angrily, pulling himself up tall as he steps down from his pulpit into the man's space. I wonder if a fight will ensue, but Dawud's followers quickly interpose themselves between the heckler and Dawud, and he steps back up on his pulpit and continues to preach.

When he finishes, Dawud walks regally away with his entourage surrounding him. We wait the few hours until our appointed time to meet him at the East London Mosque. There we introduce ourselves, and Dawud smiles, recognizing me as the person who asked the question about Iraqi children and the suicide bomber. First he gives us a tour of the mosque, obviously proud of it and his work there, before we set out to lunch in a nearby halal cafe he has chosen. We sit in a booth and order our meals while I take out my notebook, explain my study to him, and ask him to tell us about himself starting with where he was born and how he grew up.

"I was born in London in 1958," Muhammad begins. "My mother was Jamaican British and my father American so I have UK citizenship but I was raised in the States." When he says that a lot becomes clear for me— his accent is not British and he's got some of that anger that slavery and disenfranchisement often lodges in the hearts of poor African American men.

"My father moved our family to the Bronx when I was two years old," Muhammad explains.

"It was rough when you were growing up?" I ask.

"Yes, but I was a good kid and I studied hard. I went to Howard University," he tells us proudly of the Washington, D.C. University founded for black students. "I couldn't stay in school though. My financial aid was cut and I didn't have enough money to pay the tuition so I had to drop out. Then I fell into crime, petty larceny."

"You were angry?" I ask.

He nods, rubbing his head through his skullcap. "I got caught and sent to jail, and in jail I found Islam."

"You were Christian before this?" I ask and he nods, telling us about his fundamentalist mother taking him regularly to church as a boy. "So you know the Bible and Christian teachings well?" I ask and he nods again smiling. Muhammad spent seven years in the federal penitentiary and under the tutelage of the Muslim prisoners there turned his life around. He emerged from prison as a Muslim, and after serving his parole left for Saudi Arabia where ironically he attended university on a full scholarship.

Muhammad tells us that he also lived in Morocco and Syria and spent some time fighting "jihad" in Bosnia and elsewhere. "Did you also fight in Afghanistan?" I ask, but he demures saying, "I can't answer that." However his body language clearly indicates that he's proud of having fought there, too.

When I ask Muhammad again if he believes suicide attacks inside the UK are justified, he says that he does not, clearly contradicting some of what he said earlier in the park but I decide not to challenge him and just see where the conversation goes. I'm intrigued that he grew up in America and saw the civil rights movement firsthand. When I ask him if he admires Martin Luther King, Junior he becomes excited and says that he does.

"You know he believed in nonviolence?" I say and Muhammad nods. "Have you ever thought what it would be like here if someone like Martin Luther King rose up and led the European Muslims to stand up against discrimination and to be all they can be?" I ask. He clearly hasn't, but as we talk more Muhammad warms to the topic and we discuss it in detail. In recent weeks I've been talking to funding sources both in the U.S. and UK (Home Office) about running street programs for European and UK Muslims to prevent radicalization and to attempt to "deradicalize" those who have become radicalized. One of the thoughts I've had is that if leaders like Dawud could be turned from their flirtations with violent extremism and trained in the methods of civil disobedience that Martin Luther King, Jr. and Gandhi followed, they might become extremely important leaders of change among vulnerable groups of Muslim youth, addressing both their sense of marginalization and disenfranchisement and empowering them to create societal change through nonviolent means.

"If you really believed in nonviolence, you could become a leader like that," I tell Muhammad. "I see that you have a charisma with your followers." We discuss this idea more and I tell him that I also have a vision of someone from within the Muslim community creating a "Muslim Peace Corps". I ask him if he is familiar with the Peace Corps which was started in his youth in the U.S. and what he thinks of the idea of Muslims from the West being equipped to go out to help their Muslim ummah through charitable acts of teaching, building and carrying out aid projects. "This is the real jihad," I say, "and could save a lot of young people from signing up for senseless acts of terrorism!" Muhammad nods enthusiastically.

As we talk I can see that I am reaching a man who lived through Martin Luther King's rallies and who could potentially be trained to be a real leader for peace. But he also lived through Malcolm X, a whole lot of discrimination in his upbringing and is on the fringe of the militant jihad perhaps ready to tip into serious extremist violence. I wonder, *Can someone like him be brought back from the edge to do truly good work?* And while I'd love to find out, I have no funds to train him or equip such missions.

As we finish our meal I realize Dawud has caught some of my enthusiasm and he thinks I can make these things a reality. *Maybe he thinks I'm from the Agency and will now open up a briefcase full of cash to hand over to him!* I think to myself as I pay the bill for lunch offering him the boxed up leftovers that he quickly accepts. He seems hungry to me and I feel awkward that I have no more to offer

"I would be interested to lead such things," he tells us. "But I can't stay working here unless I can get a visa for my wife and children," he adds. We discuss that for a bit and I realize that he is deeply torn by his desire to follow his faith and "call" to preach with its scanty financial support and the fact that he has left his wife and children in the care of his father-in-law at present. He's clearly ashamed and tells us, "I am going to take us all to Syria if we don't get visas."

Two years later Ken is in Damascus and by chance runs into Duwad and his family. "They couldn't get into the UK and he got a position teaching in a Syrian university and was able to bring his wife and family over," Ken recalls in 2012.

Now in 2012 with the uprisings in Syria including some infiltration from al Qaeda there I can only guess what Duwad, a trained and experienced jihadi, is doing. I hope that he and his family are safe and that if he's joined the opposition, he hasn't also become a dedicated terrorist.

According to the UK Director General of the Office for Security and Counter Terrorism Charles Farr, others like Duwad continue to incite for terrorism under the radar in London and other cities in the UK, evidenced in the continued arrests for thwarted terrorists plots. According to a private Home Office survey carried out between April 2009 and March 2010, three percent of Muslims thought it was 'always' or 'often right' to use violent extremism in Britain to protest against things they judged to be very unfair or unjust and twelve percent of UK Muslims thought violent extremism was 'always/often right' or 'sometimes right, sometimes wrong', compared with fifteen per cent of Hindus and six percent of Christians.[282] Clearly what al Qaeda leader al Suri argued for is present in a small minority of Muslims in the UK and those who incite to militant jihadi violence here have already malleable material to work with.

CHAPTER 57

London Gangs - Sulaiyman

It's Spring 2008, and I am in London trying to interview people as close to the militant jihad as I can find. Latifa, a former journalist, has agreed to introduce me to her contacts, and we head off to lunch in central London to meet Sulaiyman, a Jamaican third generation immigrant who grew up in London. Sulaiyman trained as a social worker is now a gang specialist and works with young gang kids from South London who have been indoctrinated and trained in militant jihadi training camps inside the UK. Most of the kids he works with have parents who are on drugs, in prison, or simply neglectful.

Sulaiyman is just back from a vacation in Cuba and our interview has started out a bit off course as he is more interested in discussing Cuban ladies than violent extremism in south London.

"I don't pay for sex," Sulaiyman explains after ordering our meals in a Lebanese restaurant, recounting what he said to the two "hot" Cuban nurses who begged him to take them for a night of clubbing and sex.

As usual I decide it's worth listening to what an interviewee has to say, even if it's way off the beaten track. It will serve to get to know him better and build rapport. We spend about an hour listening over a meal of kebab, pita and hummus. We've come to this restaurant because Sulaiyman wants to be sure the meat is "halal"—that the animal has been killed and the meat prepared in the way the Koran prescribes, so that it is acceptable for Muslims to eat. Meanwhile he is practically salivating at his descriptions of the Cuban women and their eagerness for illicit, paid sex.

"Did you give in?" I ask, curious about his character, and Sulaiyman insists he didn't.

"Well it's not 'haram' [forbidden]," Latifa pipes up. "You're Shia. You just had to make a muta marriage."

Latifa is referring to the Shia practice of allowing temporary marriages. According to the Shia, the Prophet Muhammad's decree to his soldiers, who were far away from their women, allowing them to make sexual relationships for a period of three days time in exchange for goods, is still valid today. Sunni Muslims disagree, saying the Prophet made this provision only for the specific times of war and that his decree was later revoked. In either case, "muta" marriage is considered by devout Shia as a serious matter, with the children of such marriages treated like any other children of marriage, and it is only acceptable in unusual circumstances and is not something that should be profaned into simple prostitution.

Sulaiyman laughs and gets into a heated discussion of Islam with Latifa, telling her that he follows his religion faithfully. Latifa, also Muslim, is not strict in her practices and has already ordered two glasses of wine. She has also exited a few times during our conversation to have a cigarette and she may be snorting coke as well as she seems agitated and keeps rubbing her running nose nervously each time she returns.

"They used to always be able to find me in the bar at my last job during breaks," Latifa snorts in laughter as she orders her third glass of wine, "but it was no problem because I have really high tolerance."

"That's what *all* alcoholics say," Sulaiyman answers cynically, as he struggles to keep his kebab sandwich from falling apart as he munches at it.

As they debate, I think about the concept of unofficial marriages in which the parties retain their independence but are "marriages" none the less, set up mostly for the convenient, but legal, sexual gratification of the two parties. I consider it in relation to Western society where many men who profess to be serious Christians have multiple serial marriages and many also have affairs. It seems to me each society struggles to handle issues of marriage, monogamy, protecting children, and how to allow for such inevitabilities as divorce, unfaithfulness, etc. and perhaps this is no different.

"You said you are married right?" I ask Sulaiyman.

"Yes," he answers, "with a small child, and another older one from a previous marriage."

I frown. "You think being with a Cuban woman would be a good Islamic thing to do, when you are married and all?"

"I don't know, I didn't think it was right when I was there, but now I'm wondering if I was correct or not." He pauses thoughtfully, obviously regretting the lost hedonistic pleasures. "I have an appointment to go and discuss it with my imam. I want to know if it's forbidden or not. If it's not, I sure missed out on a lot of good times."

I feel slightly sickened wondering why he doesn't see that the oppression of women who are desperate enough to sell themselves to foreigners for cash is a pitiful thing, no matter what his imam says. But I recognize that when we get down to it, men around the world are often lustful, and women have everywhere and in everyplace sold themselves to men, and religion has often failed to protect either of the sexes from degrading themselves. It's just another twisted part of humanity.

I begin to steer our discussion to the issue at hand although it's clear to me that Sulaiyman would prefer to stay on the topic of the hot Cuban ladies.

With no sense of irony, Sulaiyman gets straight to the point when I ask him about his current work with young London extremists. He tells us first about his previous job as a social worker assisting 16-18 year old kids in a poor area of London.

"My job was to prepare the kids for adulthood, to sort their medical and health needs, to help protect their sexual health, to look after their education and training, and so on," he explains. "It was a holistic approach. Then I found out the home I was working for was deep in corruption. They were billing for kids they have had never seen, making money off these kids."

Sulaiyman reported the corruption to the local government, only to be stunned to learn that local officials were deeply involved. He was fired, and the social work home went on functioning and billing for kids they didn't serve.

This was two years ago and in the meantime Sulaiyman has begun his own organization in which he and a few others work with three to four hundred kids. Of these teens, a sizeable portion has been exposed to militant jihadi-type training and indoctrination, and some of them have even been taken to training camps inside the UK. I ask Sulaiyman about the teens who have become militant jihadi extremists.

"I thought it was a joke the first time I heard it from one of the kids." Sulaiyman says. "I didn't believe that happened inside the UK. But they proselytize these kids and take them to training camps, and we try to get them back by talking to them one-on-one. We talk to them about what they feel about themselves and society, and we challenge what they've been told."

Suliayman has worked intensively with fifteen teens that went to such training camps during the years of 2006-2008. From these gang members,

Suliayman learned about what goes on inside the camps, including that at times, there were up to two hundred teens present.

"Some [teens] said they went for a weekend, some went for one week, others two weeks. Others repeat and go back more than once," he explains.

"Once at a camp can they leave freely?" I ask when he makes reference to one asking to leave.

"Yes they can request to leave," he answers. "They are driven home. I know this for sure because one told me he left because it was too cold."

"The camp's in Wales or West Yorkshire and it's [been functioning] over the last two years. They are taken there in a van and they camp in fields or the forest in tents. There they teach them small arms fire and to convert replicas to real guns; they give them lectures on Palestine, Kashmir, Iraq, and Afghanistan etc. And because these kids are already in gangs, they tell them the difference now is if they died in gang war they would go straight to hell, but if they become true Muslims and die for Allah they will get all the rewards of martyrdom. They explain to the kids that they are fighting for an ideology against Christian enslavement and Western imperialism. Some of the kids are white converts, some are Muslim reverts. They tell the kids, 'You can go back to sell drugs, rob banks, rob post offices, even within your own community, because the UK is a kafir [infidel] country.'"

Suliayman explains how the training camps send indoctrinated leaders back into the gangs and how as a result, the gang kids convert en masse to a superficial form of Islam that justifies their continued criminality.

"They are told, 'You can rob anyone, even Muslims because if you rob a Muslim, Allah will repay him,'" Suliayman explains. Many of the South London gangs have taken on a Muslim identity as a result of the training camps.

"There is a certain cache to being Muslim," Latifa agrees, as she keeps nervously rubbing her dripping nose after briefly exiting again. "Many [also] convert to Islam in prison and go back out to the gangs. They are older when they return and they convert the others. Of course it's not a proper form of Islam."

The names of many of the gangs even reflect this.

"We now have the Gypset Taliban," Suliayman explains, "the majority are Somali, black kids; we have the Thornton Heath Taliban—Jamaican and Somali kids and in the Myatts Field Estate and the area they control is known as Baghdad."

When Suliayman explains, I recall how the Scotland Yard imams[who are discussed in Chapter Sixty-three] didn't want me to take a taxi alone from their private offices in Brixton (London), calling the area around them "Little Beirut" and complaining that it was an active conflict zone. I reflect on my research of those who are driven to terrorism by experiences in conflict zones and those who come to their ideology along another pathway in non-conflict zones. I've always conceptualized Europe as a non-conflict zone but here I am listening to what sounds like and is even defined by the participants as a "state of war"! *Maybe conflict zone motivations are active here in these contexts too*, I think, listening to Suliayman describe what the gang-controlled neighborhoods of South London are like.

A day earlier Abdul Azeem, a youth worker from the Brixton Mosque, Lambeth part of town, had told me similar stories of how the gangs in the poor areas of London have become heavily influenced by Islam and that some are now referred to as the "Muslim boys",whose criminality is totally sanctioned by the militant jihadi ideologues who explain to the kids that, according to Islamic definitions, they are living in a state of war *inside* the UK, and that to steal and take the booties of war are justified Islamic actions.

These teachings of the extremists come from Islamic teachings about "dar al harb," which is defined in Islam as 'the state of war or chaos', where Islamic governments do not reign. In dar al harb the inhabitants are not Muslims and according to Islam have no rights in relation to Muslims. Indeed, according to the scholar Yusuf al Qaradawi, an inhabitant of dar al-harb does not even have the right to live. Al Qaradawi states, "It has been determined by Islamic law that the blood and property of people of Dar al Harb (the Domain of Disbelief where the battle for the domination of Islam should be waged) is not protected."[283]   Likewise Dr. Sheikh Ali Gomaa, speaking of Israelis traveling out of their country as harbis, states that, "...it is permitted to kill him, because he is a Harbi and the Harbi spreads corruption throughout the face of the earth."[284]

Among the gangs that have taken on an extremist militant jihadi identity there are newly instituted codes of conduct that follow the extremist teachings.

As Suliayman sips his iced tea, he explains that when extremist Muslim gang members confront non-Muslims, they make threats such as, "We've got a gun to rob or to shoot you. You've got a choice. You can convert

now and live, or you can die. We are still going to rob you so you decide."
Obviously many conversions occur. According to ancient Islamic practices when a "harbi" wants to enter the territory of Islam (dar al Islam),
he needs a safe conduct pass called an *aman*. Suliayman tells us how a
similar practice has been adopted among the converted gang members.

"You cannot go across post codes in many areas of poorer London
due to the conflicts between gangs," he says. "For instance if you want to
travel from SW9 to SW24 and you confront another gang, the only thing
that may protect you is if you can say, 'Salaam alekium, I'm Muslim.' In
that case they may let you off, otherwise you will get stabbed." Likewise
Suliayman explains, "If you are a Muslim you don't get bullied at school.
You get respected. There is a lot of protection in it. Often at least one
person in a family converts and this protects the entire family."

Latifa exits again for the third time and I think to myself, *There is no
way she is going to the bathroom that many times—and it really seems she
is snorting coke*!

"We've got the Krips and the Bloods now," Suliayman explains. They
name themselves by the color of their garbage bins. In Larewishim the
bins are blue so they become the Bluewishim Krips. In Brixton we have
the Bloods, the Bloodset. They wear all red. There are seven or eight
groups of them. Seventy percent of these kids are Muslim and all of them
are exposed to extremism—to DVDs about making attacks in Iraq, lectures
and sermons about why you can steal from kafirs and so on."

Suliayman is describing the Koran's instructions for collecting booty
during times of war: a certain percentage of the spoils can be kept by
the warrior but that an amount must also go back to support the Muslim
cause. In this case, these rules are being applied to the present day with
the warfare inside the UK between the newly converted Muslim gang
members and the infidel UK citizenry, and the greater Muslim cause of
the war between al Qaeda and the British in Afghanistan and elsewhere.

As we order ice creams for dessert, Suliayman describes to Latifa and
I what the kids learn in the camp.

"They learn how to make Molotov cocktails, to make a basic hand
explosive, to strip a gun, what the rules for collecting booty during war
are; and they play war games." They are being taught their "Islamic duty,"
Suliayman explains sarcastically, "that they are at war. They are allowed
to sell drugs to kafir, rob banks, rob bookies, and to rob drug dealers.

According to their leaders, this money will be used to help the citizens of Afghanistan and to fight the British."

According to Suliayman, the kids are told at the conclusion of their training, "Sometime in the future you will be called upon to give your life for Allah, to be martyred," and with this statement they are returned back to their communities, encouraged in their criminality as gang members who no longer fear death because Paradise and all its rewards await the mujahedeen who dies in battle for Allah. And worst of all, in the future they are ready to be tapped for an even greater mission than damaging the UK through crime and collecting the booties of war. They may be called to duty for a "martyrdom" mission.

Of the fifteen kids that Suliayman has pulled away from the militant jihadi trainings, six are girls—nearly half!

"When it comes to gang life the girls are worse than the boys," Suliayman tells us as Latifa nervously fidgets in her seat. I wonder if she is going to exit yet again. "They rob just the same. There is an all-girls gang from Stockwell. Even the boys are scared of that group."

"All of these kids live in a world with no adults. They are androgynous—they dress the same, in jeans and hoodies. When the girls get into Islam they don't need to change much," Suliayman explains. "They already wear shapeless clothes, the more covered they are the safer they are. So they just add a hidjab (headscarf)."

It's a protection for the girls to be Muslim. "In South London the boys are always grabbing them up and touching them," Suliayman says. "The DNS gang is the worst. They go around and stop the girls on the street, feeling her up. Then they take her phone and get her phone number and address from it and tell her, 'We are coming to your house two nights from now for sex. Bring another girl or we'll kill you.' It's for group sex (gang rape basically). They film it on their phones and put it on You Tube. If she says 'no' they immediately slash her. You can see all kinds of girls with slash marks on their faces or necks. If she's a Muslim (in a headscarf), they won't do it."

In addition to the protection it provides, Suliayman explains that conversions are also a way to assert ones identity. "It's a rebellious thing to be Islamic. It's considered the anti-thesis of Christianity, like being a punk rocker. The baggie, hip hop look fits right into the Muslim style."

When Suliayman counsels the kids, he finds that they are more into the leader than into Islam itself. He finds that when he challenges the messages they have accepted, the gang kids becomes upset and complain, "You are rubbishing that guy, he changed my life." They can admit that the messages they learned are flawed, but the person to whom they have attached themselves is too important to lose. He has become "a very emotional persona for them, and they are attaching to him like a father figure," Suliayman says.

"There are a lot of these kids that don't have a strong paternal presence," Suliayman explains. "Then someone with a full beard, fire in his eyes and passion comes along saying, 'You are fantastic. You are great, maybe you were a sinner before, but now all of you can become mujahedeen. In the eyes of Allah, you have become Ali, the young fighter for Islam.' This represents a form of masculinity for them."

Hamid in Belgium basically had said the same, "I would have died for Osama bin Ladin." And Omar, the young boy in Chechnya who was searching for male role models to believe in—men who could fight and protect him and his family said the same to Khapta. The extremist message it seems is accepted by some because the *message bearer* has become a protector, nurturer, father figure or male role model and filled a gaping hole in the life of his protégé.

I am curious about Suliayman's methods and ask him to tell me about how he was able to "rescue" the fifteen kids he has taken out of extremism.

"I challenge them about what they have learned," Suliayman answers. "Kafir for instance, who is kafir? Many of these kids are converts, so I tell them, 'Okay we are in a state of war and you can kill and rob from kafir. So who is kafir? Your Dad? Your Mum? Your brother? I am going to kill your Mum tonight. She is kafir."

"No you're not; I'll kill you," The gang kid answers.

"Okay, not your Mum, but someone else's Mum then," Suliayman answers.

He also attacks them on their newfound Muslim self-identity.

"So you're 'Mr. Big Guy'. 'Mr. I want to kill everyone'. But you are a disgrace to Islam! Did you get up for morning prayers today? You didn't? Show me a notable Muslim who is lazy like you. You are a soldier? Do you know at West Point they have a cadet who comes in with white gloves and checks if you have cleaned, if you are disciplined, trained, and you call *him* a kafir! Look at you."

Suliayman shames them about their sinful habits, about using cannabis (what they call zoot), about failing to fast during Ramadan and about having unprotected sex with multiple partners.

"Are you married to any of those girls you are sleeping with?" he asks.

"Show me in the Koran where it shows me to be like you and then I'll be like you tomorrow," he challenges, "but I'm following the Koran."

All of Suliayman's points are about their failing to follow the most basic principles of Islam: of keeping the prayers, the fast, and living clean. But his challenge is not intellectual or religious only. In fact Suliayman is Shia and would be discredited by many extremists for that alone. It seems his success comes from not only confining himself to a religious challenge but coupling his disgust with genuine care for them.

"I tell them, I think you are a beautiful person, but there is this fucking ignorance in your brain," Suliayman says. "Me, you, and your ignorance are at war. I declare war on your fucking ignorance! You are a disgrace to Islam! You are a failure as a Muslim! To save a life is more notable than to take one. Where do you see yourself five years from now, brother? Do you provide for your mother, for the girl you are sleeping with?

"What you do as a Muslim is important," he challenges them. "You want to fight a war? But you are not even a practicing Muslim. How can you be a mujahadeen living how you live?"

He also talks to them about anger.

"Anger is like steam inside a kettle," he tells them. "It can dissipate or it can whistle out of the kettle if the lid is on or it can be used in another way. It can be used, like a steam powered locomotive, focused and with direction powering a gigantic train forward on its tracks to get to a destination decided upon ahead of time. It took your mother nine months to create you, to carry you inside her, and *you* put yourself in a position to be shot and dead *in an instant*!"

As a mother of three, this touches me deeply. He tells me it touches the kids as well, as most of the kids love their drug-addicted and neglectful mothers, despite their failures. It is probably due to this hunger for love and a real mentor—and for a male father figure—that the kids respond to him and drop the AQ affiliated leader who has been "selling" them death, albeit painting it as a glorious doorway into an afterlife in Paradise.

We finish our ice cream and I reach for the bill as Suliayman recounts that he argues with the kids and when they cannot stand up to him, he tells them to take him to their teacher so he can argue *for* them, speaking back to the one filling them with extremist lies. Surprisingly the leader of the training camps lives right in South London, openly working in a butcher shop. I ask Suliayman to tell me about him without telling me details. I honestly don't want to know who he is or where he lives and works because I would feel obligated to phone the police immediately. Suliayman is guarded, but he sees I truly don't want to know his identity, only how he works and why.

"He's from Kashmir," Suliayman explains. I ask if he is afraid of this extremist recruiter. "No I'm not afraid of him. I think he's afraid of me, because I know about him and I can turn him in."

Suliayman recounts how he went to the butcher shop with some of the kids he is protecting to confront him.

"What is this shit you are teaching our kids?" Suliayman asked. "If you've got a problem in your own country, that's one thing, but I'll be damned if I'll let you spoil the lives of these kids."

The Kashmiri butcher answered Suliayman peacefully asking back, "What is your problem with it?"

Unlike Belgium where Hamid told us that when they confront the militant jihadi instigators and try to pull their recruits away they find themselves thrown against walls and threatened in reverse, Suliayman explains, "I think he was afraid I could call the police."

I don't know Suliayman well enough yet and I sense asking him why he doesn't call the police would be too confrontational at this point. Obviously he does not trust the authorities and has been burned by them himself. Perhaps he believes it will do no good, or that the repercussions of doing so are too strong.

I am frankly amazed by Suliayman's courage and dedication working with the gang kids trying to enrich their lives and protect them from extremism. Suliayman recounts an interaction where a gang member put a knife to his gut telling him, "Give me your money or I'll kill you."

"You say you'll kill me and I feel your knife," Suliayman responded, "but you better go ahead and plunge it in, okay? Do it now, because if you don't I'm going to take that fucking knife away from you and hurt you with it. You better hurry up and do what you say you are going to do."

The gangster cowed by Suliayman's bravado withdrew his knife saying, "I'm sorry man, sorry. I just needed some money."

"How did you deal with the terror of almost being knifed?" I ask.

"I wasn't afraid of the knife, or of dying, but what scared me shitless is what he said afterward," Suliayman says. "He said, 'You know the thing is, if I stabbed you, I don't mind. I go to prison. My life means fucking nothing and no one will cry for me. But if I stabbed you and kill you, then I know that your family is crying over you. That gives me pleasure. I would go to prison happy, knowing that someone at least would know what I feel. If you kill *me*, no one would cry. I'm just another dead nigger.'"

For me these words echo some of what we found in Palestine, that the bombers know their "martyrdom" actions make no real difference in the struggle against Israel. But they are still willing to "martyr" themselves to escape from their own pain, to hearten their fellow citizens and to express the community-wide outrage and emotional pain over the losses they have felt, and *to make others feel their pain.*

I wonder if the kid is an addict and wanted money for drugs, but Suliayman explains that after he put his knife down and spoke his angry words, the boy started to cry and said, "I love you man." Suliayman responded, "I love you too, but why did you pull that knife on me?" The boy explained that his mother was in prison for selling drugs and he needed the money because his Mom was coming out for a one-day pass and he wanted it to be a special day. I imagine the child inside this gangster thug, a small boy who just wants one day to be right, to be perfect between he and his mother, and he was willing to risk his life, and even to take a life, to make it so.

Although I was fighting disgust over Suliyaman's potential dalliance with the destitute and desperate Cuban prostitutes at the beginning of our conversation, now I am so impressed. Suliayman is already doing what I have been pitching to the UK Home Office to fund—an Islamic and psychological program of one-on-one outreach of those on the street infected by militant jihadi extremism just as I had designed for the prisons in Iraq[discussed in Chapters Fifty-eight to Sixty-nine].

"I'm from the slums just like them," he says sadly. "My Mum had five kids, my father left when I was three."

"How did you make it?" I ask.

"There was this Jewish white guy and his [gay] partner who lived in our neighborhood," Suliayman explains. "He loved black boys so we were always invited to their house and we would hang out there. The gay Jewish guy used to cut my hair and run his hands over my face and tell me, 'You've got fantastic cheekbones. Your skin is so soft.' He would cut my hair."

"He was trying to seduce you?" I ask.

"Yes probably, but I didn't realize it then."

"This must have been very powerful for you to have someone touching you and caring about you," I comment.

"Yes it was," Suliayman answers. "And he was the one who made me realize that I was smart. He said it to me one day when he was cutting my hair, he ran his hands over my face and said, 'You're fairly smart, you know.'"

As Suliayman recalls, it is that one statement that saved him. Seeing himself positively in the eyes of another person who he respected changed everything. It was then Suliayman realized he could be someone -that he had the way out.

Suliayman had a "looking glass" experience, what sociologists refer to as the social mirroring of self. All of Suliayman's previous experiences had told him he was garbage, nothing, a "throw away" ghetto kid. But the care and nurture of another man, even one trying to seduce him, suddenly filled a hole left by his absent father. And this man's words told Suliayman something that he could resonate inside as truth: he is smart and someone else had finally seen it and affirmed it. Suliayman said he began studying at that point. And now, perhaps because he was rescued out of the street life by the care of another person, he feels obliged to pass it on, even at great personal risk to himself.

I congratulate Suliayman on carrying out a program that can turn the battle for hearts and minds in the UK. He admits that he has success in his work but no sponsor.

"I'm unemployed," he tells us. "I'm 42. I put my unemployment money into the charity. I live with an elderly woman who helps me and together we feed the kids."

After meetings all week long with UK government officials in which we have been discussing million dollar budgets to put such a program together I feel shame. Here is a man that is already doing it and doing it well with nothing but his own barely nurtured intellect and the care in his heart for street kids. And Suliayman explains that he has trained others so his effect is multiplied.

"Now they are teaching other kids this is wrong."[285]

CHAPTER 58

A Deradicalization Program in Iraq

It's Halloween, 2006. I've accepted an invitation to participate in a U.S. Department of Defense sponsored conference titled "Countering Ideological Support for Terrorism", held at an Air Force facility in San Antonio, Texas. I've flown in from Belgium, where I'm still living with the kids while Daniel is now serving at the U.S. Embassy in Iraq, and I'm strangely feeling like a bit of a foreigner here in the U.S. I look around the tables that have been organized into a huge square and see that the seventy or so participants seem to be all Americans, many of them military.

In the center of the square, John Rendon, the contractor who has been hired to chair the conference, asks us to go around the room and say in one word our impressions on some aspect of terrorism. He enters each descriptor onto a big-screen computer display. I shift in my chair, bored and bit frustrated at the level of the discussion thinking, *Who cares what a bunch of military guys and Americans who have probably never even traveled out of country free-associate with the word terrorism? Is that going to get us any useful answers on how to fight it effectively?*

When the participants are allowed more than one word for their remarks I notice that most seem to have little grasp of the real issues at hand. They stick to catchphrases assuming all terrorism is related to Islam and don't seem to have any idea of the frustrated aspirations, imprisonment, torture, killings, and other types of violence that would-be terrorists from Muslim countries often endure and witness within conflict zones—violence that has to do with their corrupt and hardened regimes, not with Islam per se. And no one harkens to the blocked opportunities, oppression, social marginalization and discrimination that others face in non-conflict zones. While there is no justification for terrorism, it's also true that Muslims don't just become militant jihadis over nothing; and it's not Islam that is the main contributor to terrorism, but rather the living and social conditions of many of those who become attracted to the militant jihadi ideology. And while the militant jihad builds upon and interprets widely held

Islamic teachings taking the believer onto a violent vector, ultimately there is plenty of terrorism carried out by non-Muslims both worldwide and inside the U.S. as well.

Despite only playing the free association game and making a few cogent comments during these exercises, my reputation as someone who actually interviews terrorists has apparently caught some high-level attention. One of the military participants approaches me at a break as I'm filling my coffee cup.

"Excuse me Doctor," the handsome middle-aged man in uniform says, smiling warmly. "My boss sent me over to ask if he could grab you for a few minutes."

"That's a pretty funny way to be addressing a woman," I say, raising my eyebrows and bursting into laughter. "Who's your boss?"

The boss it turns out is a very fit Special Forces colonel who is introduced and jumps right to the point.

"Do you know about deradicalization programs for terrorists in prisons?" he asks.

"Yes, of course," I answer, "The Saudis probably have the best program at present, but there are many such efforts."

We begin to discuss the situation in Iraq, which I am well aware of because my husband is on his second year in Iraq, serving first as the head of the reconstruction in Iraq (IRMO) and now as the Deputy Chief of Mission to the U.S. Embassy. I know that the U.S. government is in a difficult position when it comes to prisons run by the U.S. led military coalition. The prisons hold over twenty thousand detainees suspected of terrorism or anti-coalition violent activities, but all of them are being held without convictions—some for over three years now.

The UN and other human rights groups argue that without convictions, the detainees are being held against international law and must be released. But the inability to convict these prisoners is due to the fact that the military troops were not well trained to collect forensic evidence on the battle-field at the time of their arrest as proof of the detainees' crimes. And now the U.S. military is reluctant to release individuals it reasonably believes have tried to lay bombs, run guns or otherwise plot or carry out violence against U.S. led coalition troops or the government of Iraq and who they believe still constitute dangerous security threats. Thus the U.S. prisons in Iraq are bursting at the seams and it is our military that is responsible for finding a solution to releasing the prisoners without jeopardizing the safety of the Iraqi population, the government of Iraq and the coalition forces.

In 2006, deradicalization programs are still fairly new and mostly confined to prison settings. And as I know too well from my own research, radicalization into the militant jihadi groups occurs in many places, among friends, family members, in Internet cafes, mosques and community centers—basically anywhere that impressionable people gather and instigators can reach them. But when the context for radicalization is prison, the audience for extremist instigators is literally captive. There are well known cases of prisoners who went in as common criminals and emerged as militant jihadis.

The Jordanian Abu Musab Zarkawi, for example, the current leader (in 2006) of al Qaeda in Iraq, went into Jordanian prison as a thug and after prolonged prison exposure to militant jihadi ideologues emerged as a dedicated terrorist fighter, or what he would proudly call a "mujahedeen". Zarkawi went on to execute dozens of terrorist attacks, including brutally beheading American and British captives.

As the chair of the NATO Psycho-Social, Cultural and Organizational aspects of Terrorism Research Task Group, I know that many countries are getting on board with prison-based deradicalization programs, even the UK, who had one of their own (Richard Reid, the "shoe bomber") who converted to Islam in a UK prison and then later radicalized.[286]

"All of the programs to date rely on differing methods of Islamic challenge—that is, bringing in imams to engage with the prisoners while challenging violent extremist beliefs and providing re-education in more moderate interpretations of Islam. It is a new and largely untested area of research and treatment," I tell the colonel.

The colonel nods. "The U.S. Department of Defense wants to make a deradicalization program in Iraq. Would you be willing to help?"

"Yes, of course," I answer.

"Are you willing to go to Iraq?"

I hesitate; a pregnant silence fills the air.

When my husband first accepted his assignment to Iraq, I asked him if he could help get me into the prisons there to interview terrorists and failed suicide bombers. Dan's answer was a firm no. Now, I talk to my husband nearly every day by phone and like all the rest of the world who watch the daily news, I am well aware of the danger on the ground. Recently there has been a spate of suicide bombers, and mortar is regularly being fired into the "green" or international zone (IZ). Land transport is by far the most dangerous because it's subject to land mines and IEDs, but lately the insurgents have been using rifles and surface to air missiles bringing down helicopters.

"I'm sure I could help you get into the prisons," Daniel had answered at the time, "but Iraq is too dangerous for both of us to be there at the same time. You are doing a good job researching in other parts of the world. It's bad enough for our kids to have one parent in Iraq, and you are not exactly going to the safest parts of the world for your research. Why should we push it? You have plenty to do."

Dan's words, along with news images of the carnage in Iraq run through my mind as I consider the colonel's question. Why would *anyone* want to go there? Yet, something pulls at my insides. This is an amazing opportunity and a huge challenge that could make a difference worldwide. If the U.S. military is willing to develop a "deradicalization" program for over twenty thousand prisoners inside a conflict zone, then they better get it right. Because no matter what they do, sooner or later the detainees are going to win their freedom. And if they are still violent militants when let loose, they will be targeting Americans—maybe even me and my family.[287] This is a venture that could change the outcome of the war and perhaps change the outcome of the militant jihadi movement worldwide. It's too important to say no, despite my fears of going to Iraq.

"Well I guess if I went I wouldn't have to trouble you for a place to stay," I say smiling. "I could stay with my lover."

The colonel and his aide stare at me uncomprehending.

"My husband is serving there!" I add, laughing at their shocked looks. "I can stay with him."

"He's in the military?" they ask.

"No, he's a diplomat," I answer, glad they were not aware of and influenced by his position but asked for my help solely on my own merits. "The Deputy Ambassador to Iraq."

They ask me to come to Iraq to discuss possibilities with the top military staff who runs the prisons and determine if a prison deradicalization program of the scope they are considering is even feasible.

"We'd fly you to Baghdad a month from now," the colonel states. "We'll arrange all your travel and lodging."

"Okay," I nod, thinking quickly, "but I have two requirements. I don't want to talk only to the U.S. military. I want to interview at least twenty security detainees, the more hardcore and committed to the militant jihadi ideology the better. I need to know how committed they are to violence and how amenable they are to treatment before I can tell you the best way to proceed, if at all. And once we are working in the prisons in Camp Bucca [in the south of Iraq] as well as Camp Cropper, I want to travel only by air. No land transport—airplanes and helicopters for me. I don't want to get blown up trying to help you," I say, realizing that while air transport is still dangerous, it is the safest of my options.

The colonel looks delighted. "Don't worry, ma'am we'll keep you safe."

I smile, and we shake hands as he leaves me to discuss logistics more thoroughly with his aide.

When I get back to Brussels, it's a waiting game while the Department of Defense prepares for my travel into Iraq, giving me plenty of time for reflection. Anything can happen and I am well aware I can go to never return. I have thoughts of getting my arms or legs blown off in an IED attack. I imagine being disfigured for life, or both my husband and I being killed in some mass killing action, leaving our children orphans. I wonder, *Is it fair to our children for both of us to be in Iraq at the same time?* Each night, I wrestle with these thoughts before drifting off to sleep and again in the morning before waking, struggling to commit to courage and banish fear.

I keep in mind that the U.S. military is on a short timeline and has only one shot at getting it right before they can be forced by world opinion and international law to begin releasing detainees—whether rehabilitated or not. I have unique insights to help make such a program successful. And knowing I will be helping to make sure things are done well and ethically is a historic opportunity and may make a huge difference keeps me going. I can guide the U.S. military in developing an ethical and compassionate program creatively using Islam and psychology to move the detainees to renounce terrorism before releasing them back into society. I will be working to secure my children's future if we get it right.

Interestingly, as I find psychological coping mechanisms to calm myself, I begin to understand on another level how suicide bombers feel: turning to faith and intellect for calm, while blocking out my fears in order to commit and move forward.

My travel plans materialize in late November 2006, and I fly first to Jordan. By coincidence, the trip falls on the same dates when I was already scheduled as a speaker at a NATO-sponsored conference in Amman, Jordan. My birthday is at the same time, and though I have already made my husband promise he will leave Iraq and to come to Amman for my birthday, I decide not to tell him that I'm scheduled to go onward to Baghdad immediately afterwards. At his level, his phone is surely tapped and I prefer that fewer people know I'm coming or know that I'm connected to him. I don't want to become a valuable kidnap or kill target as a result of being married to a high level diplomat—especially since most of the kidnap victims of al Qaeda in Iraq end up beheaded. Likewise I don't want to take *his* fears on board. I want to stay in the calm, committed center I have created for myself to face my fears and aim to surprise him after our Amman reunion simply by showing up in Baghdad.

It turns out that he is the one full of surprises. His boss, U.S. Ambassador to Iraq Zalmay Khalizad, is very demanding and rarely lets Dan go. So, once obtaining permission to leave Iraq, he has decided to carry on traveling from Jordan and go home to the kids in Brussels right after my birthday, expecting that I will also join him in Brussels when the conference ends. When we meet in Amman we discuss his "surprise" plans over my birthday dinner and I laugh at the irony of it.

"Well I have a surprise of my own!" I tell him as we sit between candlelight. "I'm not returning to Brussels after this conference. I'm going into Baghdad on Sunday, and I planned to surprise you there! But I guess the surprise is on me!"

The embassy and military staff are required to use military flights from Amman to Baghdad that fly at random times for security reasons and that use only the military side of the airport. Bureaucracy is always slow, and my travel orders are only being cut as I am en route, and I find there is no opening on the military flights.

"Would you be willing to fly commercial into Baghdad?" my military contact asks. "It's more of a risk but the only way to get there on time." Already committed, I agree, knowing that there is no coalition security or random flight patterns on the commercial side of the airport.

At the Amman airport, I go through two light security checks. *I could have two grenades hidden in my bra like the Palestinian hijacker, Laila Khalid, and they would never know it!* I think. Clearly the Jordanians don't expect women to be terrorists and are hesitant to search them.

Sitting in the pre-boarding area of the commercial flight, I notice that there is only one other woman about to board. She is Arab and in a headscarf. I also notice that most of the men waiting to board are U.S. contractors, dressed in jeans or khakis, wear mirror sunglasses, and all have a swaggering, cowboy bravado. I wonder how many of them work for Blackwater? They talk loudly to each other and laugh nervously, as though trying to dispel their fears. Ten or eleven Arab men are there, looking openly fearful. Their clothes and shoes look worn; they seem poor, but they must have enough money for traveling. I think that chances are most of the contractors are going to the Green Zone whereas the Arab passengers, who I assume are Iraqis, are likely to be passing out into the Red Zones. I notice one in particular sweating profusely. He keeps nervously clasping his hands and seems distraught. I wonder, *Do their grave and nervous faces reflect what they will soon face when they reenter Baghdad?*

When our flight is called we all descend an escalator and walk outside to board a bus going to the plane. The nervous Arab is still sweating profusely. Suddenly two armed Jordanian policemen board the bus and speak sternly to him in Arabic, motioning for him to de-board. He steals a glance at his companion who silently motions for him to leave his bag behind while the police haul him off the bus. I watch as his companion now steps close to the bag, which no one else has noticed. Clearly the man is a suspect of some sort, and now his bag is still with us—left behind to be taken on the plane! The nervousness and profuse sweating is classic behavior for a suicide bomber. I wonder if I am reading into it all or if there is serious danger. I am unsure what to do.

I watch as we pull up to the airplane and the second man picks up the bag naturally as if it were his own and walks toward the plane. *Should I try to tell the Jordanian soldiers guarding our way as we board the plane?* I look anxiously at them but they don't appear to speak English. The soldiers are heavily armed with semiautomatics. I am nearing the steps of the plane and think, *Maybe I shouldn't board? But I am already out on the tarmac. How can I fail to board with all of these soldiers flanking us on either side? What will happen if I refuse to board?* My thoughts are racing but I decide to go ahead as I have no idea who to approach or how—no one here speaks English. I have prayed and thought a lot about this trip and I have put myself in God's hands. I force myself to trust.

I take my seat by the window, and see the Arab man carrying his nervous companion's bag coming down the aisle. He stares at me and starts to take the seat next to me but an American comes behind him and indicates that the seat is his. I feel a cold fear prickling along my spine.

Has he noticed that I was watching him? What is going on? I turn to my traveling companion and ask if he has noticed anything strange. He hasn't so I explain what I have seen. He is alarmed as well, which makes me feel calmer, like I am not imagining it all. As we discuss what to do, the first man who had been taken by the police suddenly boards the plane. We conclude that if the police have let him board he must check out, it must be okay. I relax hoping this really is the case and wonder then why the second Arab tried to sit by me, but conclude he's seen me watching him and being a conservative Arab, has taken my watching him as sexual interest!

The plane takes off and I'm on my way. We leave behind the city of Amman, fly over an ancient castle of Jordan, and I watch as the sands of Jordan melt into the deserts of Iraq. It is about a two-hour flight and I am glued to the window, fascinated by the swirls of sand, palm trees, herd of camels traversing the desert and the occasional small city below. My travel companion admits to me that he works in the Red Zone and is a contractor working on influence strategies. He is interested in my interviewing work and how I get access to terrorists. He tells me his team has lost seven men in the past couple of years, all killed in duty in Iraq. I ask him how he and his team remain resilient.

I've been warned about the corkscrew landing that the planes use to stay inside the security perimeter provided by the military and to avoid being blown out of the air by surface to air missiles, or even shot at by rifles. As our plane begins its downward spiral, I watch mesmerized out the window. Below on one side are the far reaches of the city of Baghdad with its traditional Arabic two- and three-story block homes and flat rooftops that serve as living spaces. On the other side of our circular descent is Saddam's former palace, a complex with lakes and a mosque surrounded by stone walls. The palace has now become Camp Victory, the U.S. military compound where I will soon arrive.

After we land, a bus rattles up to our plane. It's an old airport, cement walls and cheap white tile floors and fluorescent lights above. There are at least six lines for passport control. The Iraqis go to one side and I get in line with the contractors. One of them is a nervous young man who tells me that he is newly married and has never been in Iraq. He will soon be getting in a nonmilitary car and traveling out into the Red Zone. He speaks no Arabic and neither do his traveling partners. I tell him, "Don't worry, you will be okay," and give him my number if he needs help from the embassy.

I don't have a visa or a common access card and my military orders are supposed to be delivered to me by someone waiting for me on the other side of passport control, so I am pulled out of the line and taken to an administrative office where three Iraqi men, all in military uniforms, start asking me many questions in Arabic and broken English. The only thing I can understand is that they are very much enjoying having a woman in their office and that they want me to pay a large sum of money to enter Iraq. I wonder how long to put up with it. I am also a bit irritated that we are wasting valuable time. I only have six days on the ground to interview prisoners.

Finally I decide to show them my diplomatic passport, though I'm not traveling on diplomatic orders. It gets their attention and they decide to let me pass. Raheema who is holding my order meets me on the other side of passport control. Raheema is an American of Iraqi descent, part of Saddam's diaspora, and works for the U.S. military advising on cultural affairs. She is wearing a white short sleeve crew neck button-down knit shirt and khakis with army boots. She is civilian support staff but looks like military to me. I later learn my kitten heels, pant suit and matching briefcase look strangely feminine in a warzone to her.

Raheema takes me to collect my bag from the baggage carousel and we move quickly through customs where we are joined by the Colonel's military aide who is carrying an M-16. I swallow seeing it and resolve to stay calm. We walk out the doors of the airport into a multiple-story cement parking lot—the same one that all of the Arabs who had flown into the airport are also using. I feel a sense of fear welling inside me as cars squeal by driving faster than necessary. It's clear this is not an area secured by the U.S. military and no one wants to linger long here. We climb into an American vehicle and drive out onto the common airport road, where there have been many IED attacks. I see that my agreement with the military not to travel outside the secured areas by ground transport in Iraq is already up in smoke.

We chat as we drive and I find that Raheema is a complex, multifaceted and deep woman. I like her instantly. I am relieved to find that Camp Victory is only a short drive, but I'm anxious as we approach the first checkpoint, where there have been many suicide attacks and even mistaken friendly fire shootings. The guards are serious and well armed. Once inside the secure area, our truck bounces along a rough dirt road and passes through a series of armed checkpoints to enter what was once

Saddam's former compound. A marvelous complex of small sandstone palaces dotted along artificially created lakes, it is strikingly beautiful. Raheema explains to me that Saddam kept his palaces hidden by the tall walls that surrounded it and that no one understood why the Tigris River lost some of it's volume, since all of the water in these lakes had been diverted from it.

The grandeur of the palaces is presently disturbed by the military presence, and yet there is still a breathtaking expanse of glittering blue water. Across the lake are more palaces of differing shapes and beyond them a beautiful blue domed mosque. Passing by a six-foot high barricade of sandbags, we enter the building and briefly meet Karen Himmelheber, the sergeant who has made all the arrangements for me to come to Iraq. I hand her a brown bag of two or three contraband Belgian beers that I've smuggled in for her to enjoy on a rare moment of leisure and she gives me a wink as it quickly disappears from sight. Then she gives me a short briefing while Raheema goes off to pray (she is Muslim). Then we meet General John Gardner, the head of Task Force 134, who has the command at that time of all the detainees in Iraq and the vision to begin a detainee deradicalization program here with them. We shuffle back out into the jeep and are driven to yet another building.

This time the aide parks our jeep in an unfinished parking lot formed of small stones piled about a foot deep and I learn quickly why the army boots are useful as I struggle to make my way through the piled up stones in the low heels I wore in an effort to look professional. From the parking lot we cross a narrow cement footbridge the spans across the lake to another palace that looks almost as if it's floating in the water. It's the Generals' headquarters now. As we walk across it we discuss mortar attacks.

"Do you get them often here," I ask.

"We get our fair share of rockets, ma'am," the aide answers. "We had one hit this bridge last month."

"What do we do if there's incoming?" I ask.

"If it's out here on this bridge, you just hit the ground ma'am," the aide says. "You don't get much notice, there's a whistling sound, you hit the ground and hope it's not coming for you." Later I see that there are two-to-four person, U-shaped concrete shelters placed all around the camp.

Inside General Gardner's headquarters, we meet up with a longtime colleague Rohan Gunaratna and his colleague Ustaz Mohammed, an imam who has worked in a prison rehabilitation program for the Singaporean group of would-be suicide bombers. Rohan, a Sri Lankan born terrorism specialist worked on global terrorism with two decades of experience in interviewing detainees in the U.S., Iraq, Afghanistan, Pakistan, Philippines, etc.

Rohan's book <u>Inside Al Qaeda</u>, published in 2002, was one of the first books written on the subject and he is a walking encyclopedia of facts about all the major players in al Qaeda. I've been to Rohan's counterterrorism center in Singapore and it's impressive. I see that Rohan is very interested to promote rehabilitation, including deradicalization, and to set up this program for the military.

Ustaz Mohammed seems like a good guy, soft spoken with a kind-smile. He is from Singapore but was educated in al Azhar, Egypt's premier Islamic university for imams.

I know that Rohan and the International Centre for Political Violence and Terrorism Research in Singapore served as an advisor to the U.S. government on terrorist rehabilitation, so I'm not surprised to see him here. While he is very cordial and seems personally happy to see me, he does not seem pleased to share the briefing platform. I listen humbly to his remarks because in reality I don't think anyone has a good clue yet how to approach the Iraqi detainees to "deradicalize" them. As my good friend, Reuven Paz in Israel wrote, "It is likely naïve to think that we *can* do it".

We sit with ten intelligence and prison officials, all dressed in military. General Gardner gives us a brief detail and tells us that two-thirds of those taken prisoner by the military are released by their capturing unit but even then, the prison is receiving fifty to sixty detainees a night and that the detainees often misrepresent themselves, so it's hard to know who they really are. He estimates that eighty-five percent of the detainees are Sunni and another fifteen percent are Shia, and that the hardcore militant jihadis (all Sunni) make up at most fifteen percent of the prisoners.

The military is aware of jihadi recruitment activity inside the prison and has tried various schemes of moving detainees around to break up their networks and isolate the leaders. No matter how much they move them, they find that there are still instigators and propagandists active among the detainees and that moving them sometimes just spreads their reach farther into new populations of detainees. General Gardner is worried that the prison population keeps growing and that radicalization inside the prison is also on the increase. Likewise the intelligence experts admit to us that they have a very hard time distinguishing who are the violent extremists among the detainees, even to tell who is Shia or Sunni, because the detainees lie both for deception purposes and out of fear of being attacked within the prison.

General Gardner is clear that a detainee who reverts to violence for self-defense is not his worry but he does not want to release prisoners who are still ideologically committed to the insurgency and to carrying out acts of terrorism.

Without any more information, Rohan and Ustaz Mohammed launch into what I quickly realize is a "sales pitch" to set up a program similar to what they have running in Singapore. There, Ustaz Mohammed and the other imams meet with the prisoners regularly and discuss Islam, challenging the militants on their violent jihadi beliefs while befriending them at the same time. They also work with the wives of the prisoners. There are sixteen they have worked with and the results so far are very positive.

As I listen about the Singaporean deradicalization program, I think the prisoners they are working with are far different than what we are facing here in Iraq. In Singapore the young men who were arrested are a small isolated group and they do not have blood on their hands. They plotted to blow up the U.S. embassy in Singapore among other local targets, but they did not kill anyone before they were arrested. They also have not lived in a violent conflict zone and when they are released from their prison program, it is into the very controlled Singaporean society where they can remain under surveillance and are required to report back for further counseling.

By contrast, the Iraqi prisoners very likely have blood on their hands, have witnessed numerous violent traumas and death and even before the war have lived under the violent legacy of Saddam. Despite this Rohan and Ustaz Mohammed seem convinced that they can transfer their know-how into designing a similar program for use in Iraq.

Rohan tells General Gardner that he can compile an individualized program for the military's use in Iraq. He also promises that he can also staff the program with Iraqi imams. I am impressed but also skeptical. It seems that they have come here to sell something and that they are pitching their program as an answer, even before any of us have talked to any of the detainees imprisoned here. I'm a hands-on practitioner and I want to know exactly what we are dealing with before I can venture to say what might work here, and I tell the General so when he asks my opinion.

"General, I'm a psychologist. We are trained to listen first. I want to interview as many detainees as I can and after I listen to them I will give you my views of what you can possibly achieve and how to do it. So let me get back to you after I speak with the detainees." He agrees to meet again tomorrow after we have had time to make some interviews.

CHAPTER 59

Inside Camp Cropper

Rohan and Mohammed already have interviews set up, so we agree to see these prisoners together tonight in nearby Camp Cropper where the Baghdad-based U.S. prison is located. We pile back into the jeep and travel around the lake and through a series of armed checkpoints leading into Camp Cropper, where the majority of the hardcore Takfiri prisoners are held. As we drive down a dirt road through the final checkpoint I see that the prison complex is completely surrounded by cyclone fencing topped with barbwire.

We enter a lobby where we are asked by a U.S. military guard to surrender our computers, mobile phones and cameras.

"I'll just listen silently, unless you let me know I can participate, okay?" I tell Rohan, wanting to acknowledge his graciousness in sharing his interviews with me.

I duck into the prison restroom, and slip on my long black abaya, pull my hair back underneath a thick pink headband and wrap myself up in a long black scarf effectively transforming myself from a western professional woman into a Saudi-style researcher. When I emerge Rohan laughs, Ustaz Mohammed smiles approvingly, and the American guards look horrified as though I've suddenly become the enemy. Sensing the respect in Mohammed's eyes—the only Muslim present—I think I've made the right decision - to cover.

The military guard escorts us from the reception area down a long tunnel of cyclone fencing to the last checkpoint entering the prison. There the guard asks us to don protective eyewear. "The prisoners often throw stones, ma'am," the soldier says. "You need to protect your eyes."

I haven't yet been issued any protective eyewear, so I put on my sunglasses, and Rohan and Mohammed do the same. Inside the prison courtyard, there are pens of men, ranging in age from teenagers upwards to elderly men, on all sides.

According to UN regulations, the prisoners in U.S. custody are housed communally rather than individually. All of them are wearing orange and yellow prison uniforms, and most have plastic sandals but some walk barefoot. Some have their prayer mats out, others are eating a meal. Living out under the sun they are all sun tanned and many look fatigued by the heat and imprisonment. Raheema, our interpreter greets some of them through the fence and a few call out to her. I sense no hostility from them, only dull curiosity as we pass.

When we enter the interrogation building within the prison territory, I notice that the American interrogation staff and guards don't seem happy to have us entering their territory. They look at us uneasily—even guiltily—as we walk down a long hall, passing a holding room filled with detainees. The holding room door has a small window with bars and it smells powerfully of the detainees' sweat and fear. I see that the detainees inside are standing up waiting to be called and they call out to us anxiously in Arabic as we pass. We are led past their cell and turn a corner into another hallway lined with interrogations rooms. Our guide chooses one of them and we enter.

The room is small and square with no windows. There is a shabby wooden desk in the center with a cheap plastic and metal office chair situated on either side, and a few more plastic chairs scattered on the periphery. A surveillance camera in the corner of the room, near the ceiling, stares down at us. A guard armed with a stun gun takes his post as we enter, standing by the side of the desk.

It's all wrong for creating any kind of rapport with our prisoners.

"Do you mind if I do a quick rearrange on the set up here?" I ask Rohan. He nods and I push the desk into one corner of the room, then take the chairs and arrange them into a half circle. I ask the soldier with his stun gun to sit or stand farther back by the desk in the corner in a less noticeable place. Then we take our seats and I leave the chair next to me open for our detainee. The way I have set it up my chair faces the entrance, Rohan and Mohammed are seated facing the detainee, and Raheema our interpreter takes the end chair. We are ready.

Soon a detainee shuffles into the room, his hands held high and crossed over behind his head, a guard prodding him from behind. He is in his late twenties, and his face looks drawn with fear as though he is expecting to be interrogated once again.

As he enters the room I see his surprise and confusion when he sees me sitting in a headscarf and black burka opposite him. From my perspective, it looks as if his transference reaction is immediate—his body and face suddenly relax and he looks infused with hope. Perhaps he sees "Mom" or some other Arab female relative in me that he trusts. I feel it strongly and smile kindly to him but do not speak, although I notice that he keeps looking at me as though he expects protection from me and is trying to understand how I fit in with the others.

Rohan motions for him to take his seat as the soldier who brought him leaves and closes the interrogation room door behind him.

Rohan doesn't introduce himself or us, doesn't explain our purpose and doesn't ask the prisoner for permission to interview him. I realize Rohan is not approaching this as an academic or an American, peppering the prisoner with questions about why he is in prison, what terror group he worked for, etc. It's clear the prisoner is terrified and confused and I want to interrupt but it's not my interview.

"Who are you?" the prisoner finally cries out after telling Rohan his name, denying his guilt for any crimes he has been accused of and doing his best to answer all the questions Rohan has thrown at him. "Why am I here?"

"We are academics helping the military," Rohan says waving his hand to introduce Mohammed and myself, "But we are not military people." I finally speak up.

"I am an American university professor," I say in a soft voice with Raheema translating. "We came here to learn how the detainees are doing. This is not an interrogation."

Rohan, however, continues firing his questions, asking where the prisoner was arrested, why and how long he has been in prison, what his charges are and what extremist group he is affiliated with. He doesn't get much in terms of answers as the detainee clearly wants us to believe he is innocent and wrongly detained. I feel very sorry listening to the interchange.

"I'm twenty-two. I've been here sixty days," the prisoner explains. "My brother is the cause of my being here. He was helping the mujahedeen. They got my brother, then me, then my other brother. Me and my older brother are together. Only my one brother is involved."

"What group is he in?" Rohan demands.

"I don't know, he left one year ago," the prisoner answers. This goes on for some time but Rohan gets nowhere. The detainee is either innocent as he protests or he has been interrogated so many times before that this is just one more time to deny knowing anything. As he finishes, Rohan looks to Mohammed and me, asking if we have additional questions.

"You understand English, yes?" I ask having noticed how he seemed to get the questions before Raheema translated them.

The prisoner nods answering, "I studied in university to be an English teacher."

"I wonder if we could help you to pursue your goal?" I smile and ask, "What do you need?"

"I want a dictionary," he answers with a mixture of surprise and sullenness in his voice.

I nod telling him we will pass the request onward. "We came to learn how to reach the extremist prisoners," I explain to him. "I understand you are not one of them, but we want to know how to help those like your brother who joined the mujahedeen, and prevent others from being recruited inside this prison. Can you tell us how many men are in your compound and if you see some getting recruited?" I ask.

"One hundred and fifty," he answers adding, "The person who respects himself does not get involved."

"But some do?" I probe.

"Yes, there are always problems here," he admits.

"Where is your older brother?" I ask. "Is he okay?"

"He is in another prison," he answers. "He's fine."

"Can you tell us a bit about your compound?" I ask. "Do you see people getting indoctrinated here in the prison?"

"We are a mix of where we were arrested, but all Sunnis," he explains. "No one [here] opens up to the others. Each one holds everything inside. No one knows what the other has done."

"Do you have much sympathy for al Qaeda and groups like that?" Mohmammed asks, glancing at me as we have already agreed between us this is an important area to investigate.

"Al Qaeda are not mujahedeen," the detainee answers. "The mujahedeen don't kill the innocent."

"But your brother agrees with them?" I ask.

"My brother? I don't know." The detainee laughs cynically. "He's in your hands. I can't tell. He never convinced me. I didn't have any connection with them. I used to advise him and say this is not good for you, but my brother got persuaded."

"He saw terrible things?" I ask.

"Yes," the detainee answers, suddenly frowning deeply. "Many people in my family were killed by Shia. It's not Americans. It's from Iran." We go on to discuss the sectarian fighting in Iraq and his brother's involvement in fighting the Shia.

"How do you feel about being detained by Americans?" I ask.

"My feelings are hurt," he admits, his voice petulant and full of emotion. "I missed my university graduation because I'm here. But we have no problems with Americans."

"Do you know how your family is doing while you are here?" I ask.

"My wife is all alone," he answers, rubbing his brow. "I am worried about her because the situation is troublesome. She doesn't work. My mother is employed as an elementary teacher, but the school is closed. She had four sons but only one is at home and he is only fourteen. There is no man with them. I want to go home."

"You want to revenge for being locked up?" I ask, trying to pry out any feelings he may be hiding about aggression toward the U.S. coalition forces.

"No, I will not take revenge because the Americans are trying. The investigator [here] promised me I have nothing [no evidence for charges]. I want to know my future," he says, referring to the indefiniteness of his detainment and lack of charges against him.

Rohan signals that he wants to move on so we end the interview, thank the prisoner and call the guards to come and take him away. When the guard enters the detainee who has now told us his name and identifying number puts his arms up again and his hands behind his head as the guards lead him out of the room and down the hall while we wait for the next detainee to arrive.

"Doesn't look like a real guilty guy to me," I say looking to Rohan and Mohammed for their views.

"I think his brother is involved, but he got caught up in a sweep," Rohan agrees and Mohammed nods as well as the next prisoner is brought to the door, his hands also raised behind his head. Rohan motions for him to be seated in the empty chair, and I notice again how the detainee seems to feel comforted by my Muslim appearance.

"I was in Bucca first and then transferred here. They accused me of being involved in a terrorist act," the prisoner explains. "They told me the transfer bus [from Camp Cropper to Bucca] was the 'happy bus' but it was not," he says referring to the bus that takes detainees to their release sites outside of the prison. "I'm here." He looks resigned to his fate.

Rohan, Ustaz Mohammed and I interview this detainee as well but nothing comes of it. He is just another "light-weight" this time someone involved with a Yemeni who perhaps was a foreign fighter. Rohan dismisses him as well and when he leaves Mohammed and I take the opportunity to confront Rohan on his interrogation style.

"I think they have all been interrogated more than once," I tell Rohan. "I don't think we are going to learn anything more on operational details than what they have already admitted to the military," I say. "You might want to ease up on that."

"Yes! I thought we want to know how they think, what motivates them," Mohammed adds, glancing at me for support.

"I think we also need to introduce ourselves and why we are here," I say. "They look so scared. They think we are here to interrogate them so when you come on heavy handed and don't introduce us, it just reinforces their fear."

Rohan goes noticeably lighter than before. The only interesting thing this prisoner has to say is that a ten-year-old had been admitted to his compound today.

After a brief interview, we dismiss this one as well, shaking our heads over how none of these prisoners seem to fit the "deradicalization" program we have been asked to come develop for the military.

"I have been here for two months and two days," the next detainee tells us after seating himself in the chair beside me. "I was at home and picked up by the Iraqi police. They said, 'We take you for questions.' The Iraqis hurt me and tortured me with electricity. They blindfolded me and tied my hands behind me. I was afraid. They beat me with a [rubber] hose. They fractured my leg. They hurt me a lot. They hit my head. They cursed me. They tortured me for five hours to try to get me to confess, but I can't confess to anything I haven't done! I fainted and lost consciousness finally [and woke up in U.S. custody]. Maybe they gave me to the U.S.

forces or the Americans saw and came and took me, I don't know." He shows us an open wound on his leg.

"How long did you stay in Iraqi custody?" Rohan asks.

"They kept me for one day," he answers. "Then they gave me to the Americans."

"Where were you when they arrested you?" Rohan asks.

"I came home and found my Mom sick," he answers. "I wanted to take her to the doctor but they came and took me and my neighbors. My neighbors were released but they accused me that I have weapons. I don't have any. I have to pay rent for the house. I don't have time for anything [militant]. I could only work for food and medicine for my Mom," he explains.

Indeed, terrorists do not often come from terribly poor families because they are too busy trying to make ends meet—unless they are sons or daughters given to the movement by parents unable to feed and raise them.

"Now I'm here and I don't know what is happening to my family," the detainee continues. "I'm guilty of nothing."

"Is your family okay?" I ask.

"My father is disabled," he answers. "My mother is old and I have five sisters. I am the only [male who supports and protects them]. I have a younger brother—five years old! I'm the only one who works," he answers.

"Do you have nightmares or flashbacks of what happened to you when you were arrested?" I ask.

"I have nightmares all the time," he answers, looking into my eyes. "I keep hearing my Mom calling asking me, 'Why did you leave us? Why did you leave us with no food?' When I was arrested she was there and she became hysterical and fainted on the ground. I can't forget my Mom!" His eyes widen with terror and fill with tears.

"Have you been able to call them from prison to let her know you are alive?" I ask.

"There is no phone at home," he says as the tears overflow down his cheeks. He wipes them clumsily away with his suntanned hands adding, "They are in Fallujah!" Fallujah is the area of the heaviest insurgency and fighting inside Iraq—a place where he cannot even be sure they are alive, much less with electricity or phone services.

I hand him a tissue, and we sit silently as he cries unabashedly.

"I want to go home and take care of my mother and get food for her," he says, wiping away the tears that keep falling. "I can't sleep! I can't eat! Now I imagine that they are hungry and cannot sleep."

"In your mind, you are now back at that time when you were arrested?" I ask understanding he is in a posttraumatic flashback as we are speaking.

"Yes!" he nods, grimacing in deep pain. "I see her now [collapsed] in front of my feet!"

"She thought you would be killed?" I ask.

"Yes! It was the Iraqis who took me. She knew what they would do to me!" he answers.

"I can't eat when they don't have food!" he adds.

I speak gently with him for a few minutes, Raheema translating also in a gentle voice. "You have to eat, even if you don't know if they have food," I say. "Listen I'm a mother too and you must listen to me. Your mother needs you to return from this prison strong, not weak. You must ask the doctor here to look at your leg, and you must eat. You understand me?" I say, in my most firm but loving motherly voice.

"Yes," he answers tears still falling but a small smile forming on his face.

Raheema then gives him a small lecture as well. When we dismiss him, she tells us that she told him he must be a good Muslim and pray regularly and repeated what I had said about eating and getting his leg taken care of. I smile warmly at her when she explains this, understanding she will be a perfect translator to work with as she is working from her heart as well.

When we finish, the guards escort us back down the hallway where the detainees we have not spoken with yet still wait inside the large holding cell. They won't be called tonight and they are upset. They have been uninformed and worrying anxiously for hours that they are about to be interrogated. They call out to us in Arabic as we walk past but none of us understands their words, although the despair and anger in their voices is unmistakable. *Someone should have explained and set this up better*, I think to myself.

Before we get into the waiting car, I duck back into the restroom and change back into my street clothes. All of us are exhausted as we pull up to one of the former palaces of Saddam that has now been converted into a military hotel. I am so anticipating a nice hot shower and the double bed my military contact promised me when I originally thought Daniel would somehow be able to join me for one of the nights I was to be in Camp Victory.

When I check in, however, the clerk tells the bellboy to help me with my suitcase and he takes me back out of the palace across the street and up to a container that has been converted into temporary military barracks. When he opens its door and switches on the light I'm shocked to see the occupants, who have been rudely awakened, are female soldiers sleeping in bunk beds.

"You can take any empty bunk," the bellboy tells me as he turns away to leave, but I take my suitcase and follow him back out the door, switching off the light behind me.

"There must be some mistake," I tell the clerk at the check-in desk. "I was promised a room with a double bed by the soldier who arranged my billeting," I say. "And I need a shower after this long day of travel!"

"There are no empty beds in the hotel," the clerk answers. "The communal shower is just down the road from the barracks."

"But I haven't brought pajamas or a bathrobe," I protest. "I was expecting to meet my husband here and have my own private room and bathroom. That's what I was told."

Distressed by my situation, Rohan offers me his pajamas and bed in the "hotel" but the clerk explains that he also does not have a private room and no females are allowed to sleep in the communal male rooms. But at least he has the hotel bathroom! I ask for a towel at least and am handed one as I dejectedly make my way back to the barracks across the road.

Outside the container door in the cold and darkness, I fumble around in my belongings to find a workout outfit that I luckily carried along that I can sleep in. I dig out my toiletries bag and make my way down to the bathroom. Back in the barracks, I switch on the light just long enough to locate an empty bunk and switch it off again as I find my way in the dark to an empty upper bunk, push a chair over to climb up onto it and try to fall asleep. *This really sucks! I wonder if we will have any incoming tonight?* I think as I lay on the bunk. *This container wouldn't hold up against any mortar. I guess it's a crapshoot until morning.* Sleep finally pulls me under and all my fears fade into oblivion.

CHAPTER 60

Meeting the Trio

The next day we continue our interviews and then meet again with General Gardner and his staff.

"The detainees we've seen don't seem to need a deradicalization program," we tell the General. "They seem like bit players just picked up in sweeps but not ideologically indoctrinated—at least not yet," Rohan explains. "They could probably even now be safely released."

"We also wouldn't want to expose any of them to a full program because it would just be introducing them to the militant jihadi ideas," I add and the General nods. A discussion ensues in which the military advisors admit that they often don't even know the religious affiliation of their inmates, much less if they are violent extremists or simply minor operators or even innocent civilians picked up in sweeps, because the detainees tend to lie so much out of fear of their captors and especially terror of the other inmates.

"I've collected all the deradicalization programs in existence," Rohan tells the General. "And I'm sure we can fine tune one for you." I frown. *There are no prison deradicalization programs that I've ever heard of in the world that are dealing with detainees held in an active conflict zone with prisoners that have blood on their hands like these hardcore detainees have.*

"General Gardner," I say. "I don't think Islamic challenge programs alone are going to be effective here. I would enact a treatment plan that is at least half-day psychological as well. I say this because of all the detainees we've talked to so far, and all of my work interviewing terrorists that come from active conflict zones, have trauma and revenge as primary motivators. To get to the heart of these matters, we need to do more than just show them that Islam does not in fact support their violent ideologies. We need to get at why they adopted these ideologies in the first place and try to redirect their passions and motivations into some other nonviolent stream that will serve their existing, and hopefully changing, motivations.

I'd be happy to help you develop that side of things alongside of what Rohan and Ustaz Mohammed can bring."

"You think we need psychologists?" Colonel Vinzeni[1] asks, clearly horrified. "Isn't this all about Islam?"

"Yes," I answer, realizing that while he may be a battle-hardened soldier, he is afraid of my ilk. I also correct him. "It's not just about Islam. No one joins the militant jihad without strong psychological reasons for doing so."

Colonel Vinzeni nods distastefully, but General Gardner agrees with me and together we begin to hammer out the actual logistics–how to achieve separating the hardcore from the moderates, offering different approaches depending upon how ideologically indoctrinated they have become, and the necessity of operating in small groups of ten since we have so many detainees. It is also important that once detainees commit to take part in the rehabilitation program, they are housed apart from the others to prevent threats and retaliations against them or their families by those still in the movement. Our meeting with the General adjourns with an agreement to talk further after we interview some more detainees.

As we leave the room I joke with Colonel Kato[2] about my dashed expectations of having a hotel room in Saddam's former palace only to find I've ended up in the trailer barracks without even a nightie.

"I'd like one of those orange prison outfits," I say joking. "They would make good pajamas!"

"You issue her a pair of them," Colonel Kato says smiling as he turns to his aide but then stops. "No wait, that's no good. You could get shot running to the latrine—the guards might think we have an escaped prisoner!"

In the meantime Karen has arranged for us to meet some of the hardcore prisoners, the type our program would address, and we go into the "high value" part of the prison to meet three Salafi trained imams that we later will call the "trio". They were deeply involved as members of al Qaeda, producing Internet-based materials glorifying the jihad in Iraq, but have recently renounced their membership. To avoid suspicion, the "trio" serves their days as normal prisoners mixed among the others, but at night they come to an office and write materials to help the military in their fight against extremist ideology.

---

1 A pseudonym

2 A pseudonym

Rohan, who is a walking encyclopedia of knowledge about the militant jihadi and al Qaeda actors around the world, wants to ask them about the Islamic sheiks that were leading the AQ movement in Iraq: what their beliefs were and how they were influenced over time in instigating for certain types of violence. I also want to learn how these three think in general, what made them join al Qaeda in Iraq, what they were getting out of it psychologically and how they came to renounce it now while in prison.

Karen walks with us through the dark to the high-value prison where we are met by Tom, the interrogator responsible for turning these three prisoners away from al Qaeda. Tom is a tall man with a charming smile and I can see how he could win someone's trust.

Tom explains that allowing us in to talk to them is highly unusual as none of us have clearances—Rohan and Mohammed are not Americans and my clearance is still pending. Tom hands us legal forms to sign saying we will not disclose what we are about to hear, but I demure on signing it for multiple reasons: one, it's too dark to read the forms and two, I came here with an agreement to interview the detainees and to be able to write about them, and I don't want to be placed in the position of having to ask permission of the military to write about it later. After some discussion, Karen and Tom agree that General Gardner wants us to meet these high-value prisoners and even without our signatures, the guard is instructed to unlock the gates. We are led along a crushed stone lined path down to another set of buildings and meet the trio inside.

I'm in my black burka and headscarf as before, and Rohan and Mohammed are dressed in khakis and polo shirts. I'm surprised to see the prisoners are also in street clothes and their "cell" looks like a comfortable office.

"They spend every evening here until one or two in the morning working for us," Tom explains.

Ali rises to greet us. He is tall and smiles with a large dimple appearing on his cheek and sparkly eyes as he greets us. Wathiq is also tall, slimmer, very dark and strikingly handsome. They appear to be in their early thirties and Mahmoud, who greets us last, is the older of the three appearing to be a portly fifty-year-old man. Ali is clearly their leader and they defer to him as we take our seats in the large room. Rohan begins to question them about the religious teachings of al Qaeda in Iraq.

Just this month Abu Musab al Zarqawi, the leader of al Qaeda in Iraq was killed by an American bomb dropped on his safe house. Zarqawi, a Jordanian, had begun as a criminal thug but after studying under the extremist al Masri in prison had emerged as a dedicated militant jihadi and killer. Zarqawi then ran a paramilitary training camp in Afghanistan and in 2004 pledged his group's allegiance to al Qaeda, making him the emir of al Qaeda in Iraq.[288] When Zarkawi was active in Iraq he fell under the influence of Sheikh Abd al Aziz[1] , an Iraqi Islamic scholar under whom these three prisoners were studying. A year ago, in 2005, Zarqawi declared war on the Shia in Iraq, naming them a high-priority enemy along with the occupation forces. Rohan is very interested to learn who was influencing the changes in Zarqawi's militant thinking, as he had significantly scaled down in the last year on car bombings, beheadings of hostages and other attacks on civilians during the Iraq war.

"Zarkawi met Abd al Aziz in 2004 in Fallujah," Ali explains to Rohan. "I was studying with the Sheik and many people said good things about me and the al Qaeda in Iraq leaders wanted to meet me as well.

Ali tells Rohan how Zarqawi and his followers began to go strongly down the Takfiri path, declaring all Shia and many others as infidels and claimed that slaughtering them by any means was deemed acceptable within their Islamic beliefs.

Sheik Abd al Aziz, the men explain, did not agree and persuaded Zarqawi, that his strategy of declaring others infidels, following Takfiri practices of conducting suicide bombings among civilians and especially his beheadings of hostages were not at all Islamic.

As the trio explain how Zarqawi was positively influenced by Abd al Aziz's teachings we see first hand how the charismatic teachers of religion become so powerful.

"Sheik al Aziz is my sheik and *I love him!*" Mahmoud explains, his eyes shining. "All who know him say he's a genius and he knows Islamic teachings. When he presented his thoughts, what moved you the most was the *way* he spoke."

"The books of the first scholars are in our old language," Ali jumps in. It's hard to explain the meanings of the words, and when you study an old book [with him] he relates it all to life now. *He opens light in the darkness and it's so great!*"

"Before Zarqawi was killed, he asked that we print Abd al Aziz's book on Takfiri teaching and the way to defend the state," Wathiq explains.

---

1 A pseudonym

"It asked, '*Why* are you fighting?'" Ali says and explains how the Sheik taught that the Koran and hadiths forbid fighting an overwhelming powerful enemy when there is no hope of winning, a teaching that could convince the al Qaeda inspired insurgents to lay down their arms.

"9-11 was, of course, not jihad," Ali explains. "[The Twin Towers] is a civilian building, not a military one, and the result is that it brought the enemy to us and our families were struck. Zarqawi agreed with this analysis at the end."

"According to Abd al Aziz," Wathiq adds, "you never kill women and children. It must be army against army. Sometimes you can break the rules if it's the *only* way to save the people."

" And no one is allowed to bomb himself," Ali says.

"My wife is Shia," Mahmoud tells us and Ali tells us his mother was Shia. "Zarqawi did not hate all Shia," Mahmoud explains, "but many in al Qaeda did."

The trio are discussing the differences between traditional "orthodox" Islam which follows the original teachings of the Prophet Muhammad and his Companions, and the first three generations of followers who knew the Prophet,and the al Qaeda ideology which is essentially Takfiri. The difference is that those who believe the original teachings of the Prophet and his Companions and follow the Koran and the Hadiths, which are stories of the Prophet and his life and sayings, refer to themselves as Salafi Muslims, or in Saudi Arabia, Wahabbi Muslims. Among these is a small subset that also follow Takfiri ideologies believing that they can declare other Muslims infidels and kill them. Unfortunately there is a lot of confusion about these labels because al Qaeda leaders declare themselves to be "true" followers of Salafi Islam whereas mainstream Salafis explain that the AQ practice of declaring other Muslims as infidels is Takfir and is generally not accepted by most Muslims—Salafi or otherwise—as a legitimate practice and therefore AQ members are not following the Salafi path. Yet terrorism experts who study al Qaeda often refer to AQ members as global Salafi Jihadis!

"Takfir is the person who adopts the thought that 'All who disagree with me are infidels' and he then wants to kill them," Ali explains. "Takfir is an extreme form of Wahabbist Islam".

"Salafi refers to the companions [of Muhammad], their followers and their followers—three generations [after the Prophet]," Ali continues and explains al Aziz followed the Salafi way of understanding Islam.

"He prevented us from taking any money [for teaching Islam]," Ali says. "If you take one cent all your rewards [in Paradise] are negated. He had three children and one wife and they lived [very humbly] in one room with only a shower and a kitchen."

As they speak, their obvious love for Allah shines through, as well as their reverence and love of their teacher. I reflect about how the U.S. coalition invasion must have engendered in many Iraqis—even those who wanted to be rid of Saddam—feelings of national pride and a desire to defend their own country. These guys seemed to have joined al Qaeda at a time when they believed that fighting to get the invader out was the right thing to do as long as al Qaeda leaders did not veer off their view of correct Islamic practices. On some level most Americans agree with freedom fighters, or those who stand up for their own liberty when their country has been invaded by a foreign force. And most Americans can also understand someone using their faith to guide and bolster their choices about which actions are acceptable and which are not in risking one's own life and defending one's country. Indeed, their teacher seems to have adhered to values about protecting civilians and defending their homeland that many Westerners would agree with.

"I saw a big change in him," Wathiq states of Zarqawi. "He was going to poison Sadr city at the end of 2005 [where the Shia militias were located], but Sheik Abd al Aziz talked him out of it and told him he can kill only Shia that were going to JAM [a militant Shia group] or otherwise supporting what they believed were Iranian led groups.[289] He also stopped using car bombs unless the road was totally clear of civilians. He came to understand that he will be held responsible and answer to Allah for all civilian and accidental deaths. Abd al Aziz taught him that to create change among the other leaders of al Qaeda in Iraq, who are all Takfiri, that 'you must change – you must be a better fighter and a higher leader' yourself, and the rest will follow."

On that note, Abd al Aziz changed Zarkawi's views on beheadings calling them "'not in Islam,'" Mahmoud says, pointing out, "Zarkawi carried out beheadings in 2005, but stopped in 2006 after meeting with Fadl al Aziz."

"Sheik Abd al Aziz asked me to join Qaeda" Ali explains. "He wanted us to influence Qaeda. [He thought] they are very dangerous. He said, we have to join and control them." Evidently the Sheik believed that he and his imams could change al Qaeda in Iraq from the inside.

Unfortunately it sounds like Sheik Abd al Aziz had managed to convince only Zarqawi to change, but after Zarqawi was killed in an American attack just this month, the new leadership of AQ in Iraq are even worse, adhering even more strongly to Takfiri beliefs. I shake my head listening to the irony of it.

"I was asked to stop those who were going to Takfiri ways," Sheik Mahmoud explains and we continue to discuss the trio's attempts to influence lesser players in al Qaeda in Iraq while joining their movement.

"How were you arrested?" I ask when we exhaust that topic. "Was it violent?"

"The American [soldiers] kicked me very hard and I couldn't sit afterward," Mahmoud complains. "They took my wife for forty-three days and my two daughters. They stole everything in my house."

Indeed after speaking to some of the security guys at the US embassy in Baghdad and to a soldier I know in Brussels who served two tours in Iraq,[290] I know this may be a true statement—some U.S. soldiers unfortunately looted jewelry and cash from homes where they made arrests.

"You think maybe the soldiers who arrested you were worried that you had a bomb strapped on?" I ask. "You are a heavyset guy and many AQ guys blow themselves up instead of submitting to arrest. Maybe they didn't know what was hiding under your robes?"

"I was in shorts and a tank top!" Mahmoud protests. "They could see everything on my body! They came over the garden wall and they beat me! I sent my young son to the house to protect him and I got on my knees. They yelled at me, 'Fucker, don't move!'"

It's clear to see that Mahmoud is still angry about it and feels the U.S. soldiers beat him unnecessarily.

"I was also beaten," Wathiq admits, "but more from ear to ear."

The trio has been imprisoned for six months, and now after turning away from al Qaeda have volunteered to write up some of their ideas about Islam for the military to fight AQ in Iraq. On nights like this they come here to write for Colonel Kato who visits them often.

"What made you begin to cooperate with the Americans?" I ask.

"The way I was captured," Mahmoud states, shaking his head angrily, "for three days I would not talk. I thought about my daughters and my wife and my son."

"It's not easy to talk in open in this place," Mahmoud continues. "It took me five months [to open up]. The first interrogators were very hard.

In the first days I asked, 'Give me something for my head wound.' All my body is blue, my head is bleeding but he won't help me so I don't help anybody."

When I ask why he opened up to Tom, Mahmoud explains, "Because he was *human*. The first thing he asked was about my head wound and told me he would take me to the prison doctor. Then I wanted to tell him all.

"I open my chest to you," Mahmoud says, looking up with admiration to Tom. "He gave me respect. I trust him. I tell him, 'I'm not a fighter,' I tell him all.

After listening for a few hours to these three speak I explain a little about why we are here and ask them if they would be willing to help with our prison initiative - if they believe they could turn others away from al Qaeda and the other extremist groups in Iraq.

"We already have," Ali tells me. "There was an Algerian here. He had been in al Qaeda for years and killed more than thirteen people with his own hands. I talked with him everyday and made him understand what he was doing was not Islamic. But it was very hard for him to accept because then he became terrified he was going to go to hell for what he had done."

That is one of the toughest problems actually in potentially deradicalizing a militant jihadi. The ideology fits so well with the needs of a traumatized and lost person, giving him an outlet for his anger, justification and assistance for his violence and an immediate meaning to both his life and death. Giving up the ideology can return the person to a state of powerless despair and hopelessness and deep guilt if he's committed crimes. When we challenge those beliefs, we have to find something that also imparts a sense of purpose and self-righteousness to replace what we are taking apart.

"I think you guys could really help us," I tell the trio. "In fact, I've been wondering when I would meet guys like you. I knew there must be educated imams who are passionate and understand how the AQ ideology fits troubled people and how to offer them a viable Islamic alternative. I think you have the teachings and charisma to do just that!"

"We would love to work with you!" Ali states enthusiastically. "You can keep us right here locked up in this prison," he continues. "We can make our same propaganda materials we were making for them, but now against them and broadcast on the Internet, the radio or television. We can teach the detainees. We can write materials. We can do whatever it takes, and we don't even need to be on the outside to do it."

I nod, warmed inside with having found imans who might just fit the bill exactly for what we need.

It's late so we part warmly with wishes to meet again in better circumstances. The next day before Rohan leaves, I bring up the subject to General Gardner.

"If we go forward with this program," I say, "I'd suggest using these three imams we met last night. I think they could play a very powerful role in our initiative. They have the charisma, the knowledge and the experience to reach even the hardcore."

The General is open to the idea, but I can see that there are strong reservations in the room—these three were inside al Qaeda after all. To me that is the strongest reason *to* use them, but I can understand the caution on the part of the military.

CHAPTER 61

My Cropper Interviews

Rohan and Mohammed depart Baghdad after a final meeting with General Gardner in the morning and I continue with my own detainee interviews with Raheema. I instruct Raheema that from here on in we will follow accepted human subjects protocols, which means we will explain to the detainees who we are, our purpose for the interview, that we have no power over determining their release and that we must obtain their informed consent to give an interview. No more intimidation or interrogation tactics! Raheema smiles happily, and I can see that we are going to do well together.

The interviews we do are interesting, but more of the same. Nearly all of the prisoners refer to their arrests by American soldiers as brutal—with beatings, and some also refer to rough treatment during interrogations. They all reference how hard it is to be imprisoned, separated, as one states, "from our homes, our wives, our children, our work,"while, he continues, "I don't even know what I am accused of." Some of the detainees have been in the prison for over three years without charges, and many of the young men had just been married or their marriage plans were disrupted—and frequently, the girl they had hoped to marry was married off to some other man in their absence.

Likewise, many complain about the juveniles and elderly who are in prison who don't seem to be guilty. One prisoner tells us, "There's a blind guy—he's eighty, a retarded man, crippled people." Indeed, one of our interviews turns out to be with an elderly man who was arrested with his two adult sons during a sweep immediately after an IED exploded. He and his sons run a phone store and somehow fell under serious suspicion. The man doesn't seem to have any ideological commitment to militant jihad or insurgency and his hand tremors are so bad that I can't imagine him being a danger for firing a rifle or planting a bomb. His case prompts me to later ask the head of the prison if she knows if he has been medically evaluated for Parkinson's and is receiving appropriate medication. Seemingly irritated with the question she answers that she will check into it.

Another tells us that the Americans arrested him for having a fake ID and suspect he is a terrorist, but even Raheema agrees that in sectarian-torn Iraq this is common practice. No one wants to arrive at an extremist checkpoint having only a Sunni or Shia document—one needs to be prepared to fake it if stopped by the other side.

Most of the detainees seem highly traumatized by the things they have witnessed during the recent conflicts. One tells us about a sectarian murder in his neighborhood saying, "It was the first time I saw someone shot. My psychological factors are not right. I cry at night all of a sudden. I see [the murder] every time I am silent."

One of the detainees tells us that his compound is filled with Takfiris and says that they are actively recruiting inside the prison and hold Sharia courts and beat up anyone they think is collaborating with the prison officials. "Everyone is scared, terrified of them. They teach who is an infidel and who is not, how to kill the police. Sometimes I pray at home, but *here* I am forced. They will slaughter me [if I don't]. Don't you remember the guys killed in Bucca and Abu Ghraib? A lot were killed. They choked them to death. Terrorism and jihad—that's all they talk about and they teach the new ones."

Disturbingly, another one tells us, "The American have hurt me a lot. I will say it strongly. They beat me up. What did I do? Did I burn the twin towers? They threw water on me and they electrocuted me on the back of my neck. Now when I lay my head on the pillow I get dizzy."

These comments prompt me to tell General Gardner in a later briefing, "I think we have a lot of prisoners with posttraumatic responses to the circumstances of their arrests and some of what has gone on during their imprisonment. For the moderates we might want to figure out how to incorporate an explanation and perhaps even an apology of sorts for any mistreatment they have suffered. There is no sense sending them home angry with us over how they have been treated here."

The General points out that the soldiers in the field are in tough circumstances and often have hair trigger violent reactions when they are arresting people who may be suicidal terrorists but nods his agreement to finding a way to neutralize the prisoners' anger at the U.S. forces before releasing them.

When I ask Karen again to see more of the hardcore detainees, she accompanies me to the prison and has a heated discussion with one of the military intelligence officers who is apparently controlling who I see and don't see. I don't think I am meant to overhear his comments, but he basically tells her that if he gives me interviews with the hardcore, he will have alerted them that he knows who they are and will thereby blow his covert surveillance of them. He doesn't want them to understand that they are being observed or that there are informants. Karen insists he find a way to give me some more serious detainees to interview, but nothing really changes. I am frustrated—the whole point of my visit is to learn enough to create a treatment program of the hardcore and thus, a situation where the military won't need to do as much surveillance.

Karen's intervention does however lead to one more interesting interview with a Saudi "foreign fighter" named Aziz,[1] who is locked up among the high-value detainees where the trio are also housed. Aziz is introduced to me by his interrogator, who I think wants to rattle him before our interview by reading out his "crime" of having been observed in a video at a gathering in Fallujah with Zarkawi, the leader of al Qaeda in Iraq. The interrogator states that Aziz is accused of having come to Saudi to join al Qaeda. I have no way to ascertain if this is true, because Aziz doesn't want to discuss this accusation, as undoubtedly our interview is being observed and recorded and anything he admits to can be used to convict him. I don't press it and Aziz insists that in fact he came to Iraq in 2004 to buy land.

When the interrogator leaves and we begin our interview, I can see that Aziz is terrified of me. I've been silent up to this point, and I realize he probably assumes since I'm dressed in a Saudi-style burka that I've come from Saudi—perhaps to take him back with me. When I explain to him that I am an American professor and that I am not military and, given his level of fear, add that I don't work for the CIA either, Aziz seems to relax a bit and agrees to discuss his arrest and prison experience.

In regard to his arrest Aziz recalls, "[The American soldiers] hit me and broke four of my ribs. I cannot tell you why they hit me. If I have struggled in any way, they have the right—or if I was caught with a weapon, but when they caught me I had a flashlight. That's all I had in my pocket and I had it because I knew the electricity [in Fallujah] was cut off."

He says during his first interrogation with the American soldiers, "They hit me with their fists, boots, the butt of their rifles and broke glass over

---

1 A pseudonym

my head. I said, 'This is American democracy?' They answered, 'This is *not* democracy. They beat me for forty-five minutes." He continues, "In another [American-run] detention center I was beaten all day."

If he is telling the truth—which he seems to be, judging by his sincere demeanor—he was beaten during his prison transfer, too.

"I think I was taken to the airport," he recalls. "I was taken in a Hummer. [At that time] *I wished I was an animal* in Europe or the U.S.—I would have been treated better than I was in that Hummer. It did not have any seats and there are a lot of pieces of iron and pieces of equipment. They threw me on top of these things and two others caught with me were thrown on top of me. Then they stepped on our heads until we reached the compound."

"You were scared?" I ask.

"How would you feel with a soldier's boot on your head?" he asks sneering cynically. "Let me tell you something. In Saudi if someone looks at us eye to eye or in a demeaning way it can cause a fight, so think when a soldier's boot is on my head. What is the feeling?"

"I was taken to three different places after being beaten," he continues. "The treatment there was worse and then it got better. It's very bad treatment here. I have told the Americans you are holding innocent people who have done nothing. Some have diabetes, high blood pressure, and other illnesses. Is this American democracy? Human values? They give more rights to animals than to us."

I nod. "How is Cropper now? Does anyone hit you?"

He says no but recalls his interrogation in Cropper two years previously. "If I ask an [American] soldier, 'Excuse me I need a toothbrush. I am Muslim and I have to wash.' [The soldier] is sitting with his arms extended behind his head and his legs crossed and says an arrogant 'No!' But it's his duty to give it to me. Once when I needed to use the restroom, he started mocking me and said, 'Pee on yourself!' He wouldn't open the door until I finished the interrogation period. [During it] I had plastic bands tying my hands behind me while he hit me. They have no value for the human being."

"I have been here two years. I spent seven months alone in a cell. It was light [there] sometimes. After two months they gave me books to read."

"How do you cope in prison?" I ask.

"I remember my life before, going to Pizza Hut and to fast food and driving my car around fast and having fun."

"How do you feel about Americans?" I ask.

"I never hated Americans before. I saw them all the time in Saudi— their military and Aramco [the Saudi oil company that employs many Americans]. My hate is not toward the American people but the government and what they did to me. It's because of the leaders. America will become old history."

As Raheema and I exit our interviews, we happen across a transfer of detainees from one group cell to the next. All the detainees dressed in yellow are squatting on the ground with their arms held up behind their heads. It looks like a very difficult position to maintain and I feel concern walking by. The soldiers are yelling at the detainees in English and some of them don't understand. One in particular doesn't respond seemingly not understanding a command. We watch helplessly as the soldier comes up to him with his rifle and forces him down to his knees next to the fence. Raheema wants to continue on, but I want to watch the scene to its conclusion. A gate is opened, and the humiliated and totally cowed detainees are ordered inside the next cage. I leave that day to return to Belgium with a heavy heart, concerned about how to design a rehabilitation program that can work.

CHAPTER 62

Designing the Program

It's June 2007, seven months after consulting at Camp Cropper with General Gardner and his military staff in Iraq. I'm on the train from Brussels to Paris, the first leg of my journey back into Iraq. Now, Rohan, Ustaz Mohammed and I have all three been hired by the military *through* a contractor.

During this first phase, my job is to design, write, help pilot test the program, and hopefully by next August, I will have a pivotal role in running it en masse for all twenty-three thousand adult and eight hundred juvenile detainees. I have made it clear to the military that I can't go live in Iraq, as Dan's already living there and our children need one parent on hand, so I've agreed to come and go for a week every month to supervise the people I help select and train to run it.

As the train nears Charles de Gaulle airport, it suddenly pulls to a stop on the tracks and an announcement is made that there is a suspicious bag found near the terminal that has to be removed before we can carry on. Knowing that Algerian terrorist have previously blown up bombs placed on French train tracks I think, *Well I guess I don't have to go all the way to Iraq to get blown to smithereens; it can happen right here in my backyard!* Somehow I find that comforting – that all the danger I imagine is lurking in the war zone of Iraq and perhaps going to bring me harm, is not so different than the dangers of everyday life living in Europe!

When the tracks clear and I get to the plane I find my seat companion enroute to Amman to be a lovely surprise. She's a twenty-something Afghan American girl named Atia, about to begin her new job as a CNN producer in Baghdad. Looking at her flawless skin and bright blue Afghan eyes, I wonder, *My God does she know what she is getting herself into?* Yet as we wait for our plane to take off, Atia tells me about how her family narrowly escaped the Soviet invasion of Afghanistan while her mother was eight months pregnant with her.

"Babies directly experience their mother's stress levels that late in pregnancy through the neurotransmitters and blood hormones," I comment.

"Yes, it's true," Atia says, nodding. "My mother always reminds me that I was born with a tiny strand of white hair amidst all the black!" As Atia tells her story of escape, I think about all the children that don't get out, and how they live with the stress of war and destruction surrounding them all their lives, never knowing anything else. I wonder –what fate has in store for Atia. She has escaped so much already - what adventures will she go on and what good will she do? When she shares with me about her reporting from Afghanistan over the last year she seems unaffected but tells me instead she was deeply shaken by the recent madman shooting and killing of college students at Virginia Tech, in the US.

"It shattered your sense of the predictable and secure in the U.S. where you expect it to be safe?" I ask.

"Yes," she nods. "It's okay that it's dangerous elsewhere, but not at home." I've heard that from many soldiers too who can face everything that happens in Iraq but can't bear to hear about violent shootings back in the U.S. As I look at Atia flying into to produce the news for CNN from Baghdad, the mother in me wants to tell her to return immediately on the first flight back– that it's way too dangerous and traumatizing for a girl her age!

I spend the night in Amman and meet briefly with Princess Aisha, a friend now and colleague who serves as an expert on the NATO counter-terrorism group that I am chairing.

"Let me know if I can help you in any way," Princess Aisha offers after I explain the rehabilitation program to her and the hope that our military will be able to release thousands of detainees in the coming months without the risk of them turning back as jihadis, or even fleeing to Jordan to create troubles here.

In the lounge waiting for my plane I take the opportunity to talk to some of the Americans working as contractors in Iraq. I'm a collaborator on a NATO studying resilience reactions of our troops and civilian workers in high-threat security zones such as Iraq, and I want to use this chance to learn from them how they are coping. I ask them what their biggest challenges are and how they are dealing with them. Some of the Blackwater guys I talk to are totally non-reflective. One tells me that he drives a truck that clears and secures the streets before the high level military or diplomats arrive for meetings in Baghdad. They've already had one IED pierce their armor and blow his colleagues hand off. "It's hard clearing the streets now that we can't run people over anymore," he complains. I stare at him shocked that he has said that so nonchalantly and ask him how they cope now with the new rules. "We throw frozen water bottles at them. They hurt so that usually works," he explains.

Another tells me that he's lost eight of his co-workers, all of them killed by IED's or snipers, and he does seem genuinely troubled by this. A woman I speak with on the bus taking us to our plane tells me that she has been propositioned numerous times by married and divorcing men and that "everyone comes [to Iraq] to escape something. Everyone has problems." From the diplomats I know who volunteered to do a tour in Iraq at least in the early years, I'd have to agree with this assessment—many are running from their personal lives.

When my plane lands in Baghdad, Rick[1], one of four of the contractor's men on the ground, meets me and we head back to Camp Victory. As we exit the car, the C-ram goes off, creating whistles and explosions in the air. Rick freezes in place, startled with his arms out at his sides, and I look stupidly to him for guidance.

"Is it mortar?" I ask alarmed. "Should we be hitting the ground?"

Staring in the direction of the explosions, Rick hesitates and then answers, "No, I think it's just the C-ram. I'm not sure, but I think it's over now." Rick then explains to me that the C-ram is a defensive weapon that targets incoming mortar, exploding it while it's still in the air. *Welcome to Iraq!* I think as shaken, we walk together down a dirt and cement alleyway to the trailer which has been designated the contractor's headquarters. Inside I meet Jim, Susan and Dr. Tahir.

Steve, who is not present, is the head guy for this contractor in Iraq and oversees many programs. He's hired Jim, a bit of a fumbling, middle-aged heavyset man to head our program. Jim manages to tell me in less than a half hour that he's three times divorced and a recovering alcoholic and glad to be in the dry zone of Iraq to carry out this program. With a top-secret clearance and trained in defense intelligence,Rick is Jim's right hand. Dr. Tahir is a Shia psychiatrist from the Iraqi diaspora, brought in from the UK as a bilingual and cultural consultant to the program. Susan is responsible for running data and logistics as the program unfolds.

---

1 Nearly all of the contractors and military staff except for General Stone and General Gardner are referred to in these sections with pseudonyms including Jim, Susan, Rick, Dr. Tahir, Dr. Fadl, etc.

We get down to work discussing what General Gardner had asked for in the original consultations. I lay out my recommendations: carrying the program out in groups of ten detainees or less, running six weeks at a time, and using a combination of Islamic challenge and psychological counseling to build upon and surpass all of the existing deradicalization programs currently in existence.

When I finish laying out the design aspects, I point out that Rohan and Ustaz Mohammed have agreed to write the Islamic challenge portion of the program and that they will locate and hire all the Sunni imans for it. Jim is responsible for locating and hiring the psychological staff and wants my help. The imams and psychologists will be hired from the pool of local and diaspora Iraqis so that there won't be any failures to understand the Iraqi experience and culture.

While we wait for their inputs I go ahead writing the psychological part of the program. Everyone seems impressed with my plans, and Jim tells me that I'm in charge for design and will retain the full copyright of all my materials. As I sit down and begin writing, Jim keeps interrupting all of our work telling adolescent sex jokes and filling us in with the details of his private life. Then he says, "The military leadership has all changed. And Colonel Kato hates us."

I look up and listen as he speaks, understanding how the military would find him difficult to respect. He's an ex-Marine but now plump, tends to pepper all his conversations with Alcoholics Anonymous one liners and seems a bit incompetent. The next day when we meet with Colonel Kato at his headquarters, I see that the Colonel has lost all patience for Jim and I jump in to handle discussion of the program.

"Great job with the Colonel!" Jim tells me as we head back to our trailer. Rick seconds the congratulations but as we continue to work together I notice that things on this team are not going to be easy. Jim sees himself as the "boss" and while he needs me to design the program, he won't give me access to details I need to know to be able to do it well. For instance when I tell him that I can begin recruiting psychologists, he won't share with me their pay scale.

"That's proprietary information," he informs me. "You recruit them and then have them contact me."

"But how can I recruit someone out of an existing job in Jordan, if I can't give them some idea of what we are paying?" I ask.

Jim holds firm. Rick is the same when it comes to detainee decisions. He seems to love the "secret" and intelligence aspects of the work and does not want to divulge how we are going to work with the prison authorities to select and sort detainees for our groups.

"But how can I be confident that I will have only hardcore believers in a group that I've designed to go over the extremist beliefs?" I ask. "I don't plan to introduce that in the moderates groups." Rick stonewalls, telling me that it will be his decision with the prison authorities. And I begin to feel exasperated.

On the day Jim does set me up for interviews, he sends me with Dr. Tahir as my translator. Dr. Tahir has already admitted to me that he knows nothing about posttraumatic stress disorder, and when he arrives to go with me to the prison he is wearing a red baseball cap and reflector sunglasses, completely obscuring his face.

"You're coming dressed like that?" I ask him.

"Yes, I'm Shia and these bastard terrorists are all Sunni," he states. "I don't want any of them to recognize me."

"Dr. Tahir," I say. "You can't come like that. You can't translate wearing mirror sunglasses! How in the world will they know if you are listening well or understand them if they can't see your eyes?"

"But if they recognize me it's dangerous for my extended family who still live here!" he explains.

"Okay, if it's dangerous for you and you are afraid, you shouldn't come," I tell him. "But you cannot go like that. I'll ask Jim for another translator."

Probably realizing there is no translator in the budget, Dr. Tahir relents and takes off his cap and sunglasses. "Just don't tell them my name or that I'm Shia," he says.

Our interviews turn out much the same as before: loads of trauma, many seemingly innocent or hardly committed to ideological violence and nothing new from what I learned before. Once with the prisoners, Dr. Tahir actually warms to the task and does a good job. I can tell he is touched by all they have to say and no longer as afraid.

When Dr. Tahir and I exit the interrogation section of the prison the American guards are clearly not pleased to see us. It's late and they have a "transfer" going on. There are about two hundred yellow clad prisoners, blindfolded and shackled together by chains, lined up single file waiting in the corridors, probably getting ready to board a bus and then a plane to

Camp Bucca. As I look around me it seems the guards feel ashamed and the detainees are terrified of what will come next. A human odor surrounding the detainees fills the air around us and I feel sickened as I realize it is the smell of fear.

CHAPTER 63

Pulling the Program Together

On my third day in Camp Victory my husband calls to say he's arranged to pick me up the next day for a two-day overnight with him in the Green (International) Zone where he is working. I've already cleared this with the contractor and to their advantage Dan tells me, "General Stone is coming here tomorrow night. I'll try to arrange a dinner so you can meet him." General Stone has recently replaced General Gardner as head of the program. "I'll call you sometime between nine and ten tomorrow. I'm not going to say anything about coming to get you when I call tomorrow because I don't want to leak that information in case someone tries to shoot us down. But that will be your signal to go out to the helo pad and wait for me. And I don't want us to ride in the same helicopter so you get in the one I'm not in." He signs off, leaving me in total suspense.

I've never ridden in a helicopter, and I haven't been to the Green Zone yet either. The next day after Dan phones, I stand out on the landing strip waiting for him to arrive. After some time I spot two Blackhawks flying in at the height of utility poles. They are cruising low for security, a method that makes them hard to spot and be fired upon. The first helicopter lands and two of the four Blackwater guards, former Special-Forces guys, jump out. They are wearing camouflage uniforms, helmets and toting guns and wave to me to approach. I see Dan waving to me and pointing to the helo I'm to get in as I run to them, again in a suit and kitten heels pulling my wheelie behind me. The rotors are still running so as I approach the wind gusts makes it hard to continue but the two guards reach out and pull me close as they place a bullet proof vest over my head strap it on. Another puts a helmet on my head,as they quickly lift me into the helo and throw my bag in, while I clutch my briefcase (holding my laptop computer) close to my body. In lightening speed they strap me into the center and take their seats on either side of me as the helo begins to lift off.

I thought I'd be terrified but find that being airborne is a wonderful feeling, the gentle lifting completely different than taking off in an airplane and I'm surrounded by four testosterone filled guys—two of which are half hanging outside the helicopter's open doors, their rifles pointed downward as they scan the territory below. Oddly, I feel completely safe as I watch in fascination as we fly low across Baghdad from Camp Victory to the Green Zone. The helicopter lets down gently, and just as quickly as we embarked, we disembark. I'm again hustled across the tarmac, this time to waiting armored vehicles. Dan takes me to see his trailer, pointing out an alleyway where one trailer has been completely burned by mortar. He tells me this particular strip has been named "death alley" because the insurgents have figured out that it's a commonly used pathway from Saddam's former palace, where Dan has his office, and how to target it with mortar. Dan's trailer has never been mortared but he did come home one day to find a hole in his ceiling with the bullet laying in the toilet—probably from celebratory fire—and a mortar came through his bathroom window at work causing the security guys to brick it over. I shake my head, thankful that he's never been hurt.

Dan introduces me to the regional security officers at the embassy and leaves me to discuss with them their understanding of the different violent groups active in Iraq, including al Qaeda. I am taken into their operations room where I meet some of the surveillance operatives, one with tattoos covering his arms and neck who tells me:

"You know these guys—their religion teaches them to kill." I nod wearily, tired of running into provincial Americans working here in Iraq who assume that all the Iraqis who fight against an occupation force are somehow religiously-oriented brainwashed fanatical zealots. Of course those type do exist, but the socio-political forces that have unleashed the current violence here are a lot more obvious and less simple than just blaming Islam.

Later that evening, Daniel and I meet with General Stone and two of his aides for dinner. We have an animated discussion about his hopes and my vision for the detainee rehabilitation program and I'm quite sure I win his confidence. Given that Colonel Kato later admits to me over e-mail that he really doesn't like or trust in the competence of the TRS staff – the contractor they have hired to do this job – and how I have been brought on as well, a view I share, I feel good that both Colonel Kato and General Stone at least seem to trust me to do a good job for them.

The two days spent with Dan fly by and I am grateful to have gotten a brief window of his life in the IZ as I depart again by helicopter back to Camp Victory. This time on the ride back I think about what the security guys have shared with me including that recently the terrorists have hidden in the weeds along the Tigris River and successfully shot down our military helicopters as they passed by. Now, I lend my eyes to the armed soldiers leaning out of the helo, carefully scanning the terrain below along with them.

When I return to work at Camp Victory, I find that Ustaz Mohammed and Rohan have supported the program from Singapore despite several obstacles, however we still don't have the materials in hand that we need for a substantial Islamic challenge program. Given that situation, I sit Jim down and explain that we must consider other options in that case.[1]

Upon finishing up my preliminary work in Iraq, I return to Brussels to finish writing the program. There, I receive confirmation that we are going to move ahead pursuing other options, and I volunteer to travel to London to talk to the Scotland Yard imams, a group called Siraat and a few others, all Salafi imams who have been working with extremists prisoners in the UK. That takes some convincing—as being Muslims, they are not supporters of the war in Iraq.

"Listen," I tell the Siraat team—all imams working inside the UK prisons in our face-to-face meeting. "I am not a supporter of the war in Iraq either. I think it was a big mistake, but that's already a done deal. We now have a war-torn country with a lot of Iraqis signing up for al Qaeda. There are twenty-three thousand detainees held by the US forces and eight hundred young boys in our prisons! If you care about the Iraqis, try to focus on them. The U.S. military has taken a big step in agreeing to put together a deradicalization program and this is really a once in a lifetime chance to help the U.S. military to get it right—versus make an even worse mess in Iraq. If you really care about the Muslim ummah, please will you help us? I promise you I will make sure the detainees in our program are not tortured, mistreated or in any other way mishandled. That's of paramount importance to me as well! And you have a possibility to do good here. Please, I can't do it without you!"

This leads to a long discussion of their Salafi-based methods of meeting convicts in prison and challenging their Islamic beliefs, showing how their method of evaluating scriptures related to the militant jihad could be used in our program in Iraq[291] and how it would dovetail with my psychological plans.

---

1 Refer to endnote 315

"It's not going to be as clean as simply convincing them that they don't have an Islamic basis for the actions and beliefs they have signed up to," I point out. "You already know how to make them realize that there is no solid Hadith to base their claims on or that their interpretation of the Koran is incorrect," I explain. "But they took that interpretation on for a reason. They are angry, or hurt, want revenge or they simply want the foreign occupier out, and they have already committed and acted. Some have blood on their hands—it's serious. We are going to have to provide a psychological basis for their recovery as well to help them work through anger, grief, trauma and all the emotions that got them to sign up for this ideology and these groups to begin with. It's a two-pronged approach."

The London imams, who I've been told have come out of a life of serious drug abuse to become Muslims men of service, easily understand that there are always psycho-social reasons for taking on a violent ideology and agree that a combination of both Islamic challenge and psychological approaches will be most useful. After hours of talking it through the London based Siraat team of imams become enthusiastic about the project and agree to seek permission from their government to temporarily suspend their own work and receive payment from our military (via our contractor) to work on our program. Leaving their offices in Brixton, I feel confident that we will now have a real Islamic training manual to work with that fits with what I am writing for the psychologists.

Meanwhile, Jim and Rick begin collecting resumes of imams and psychologists from inside Iraq and the Iraqi diaspora for us to review. I keep trying to steer the contractors into hiring conservative Salafi imams and into seeing if the "trio", the three Salafi imams I met in prison in November, can be released from prison to work with us because those with actual al Qaeda experience and who are from the Salafi tradition of Islam will have the most credibility with the Sunni extremists prisoners. Rick and Jim, however, don't seem to grasp this concept and keep sending me resumes of Shia imams threatening to hire them. Arguments break out among us as I keep reminding Jim and Rick that the al Qaeda extremists in Iraq have named the Shia as one of their primary enemies and that our Sunni extremist prisoners will never take a Shia imam seriously. Jim and Rick reply that they are under pressure from the military to get all the staff positions for our pilot test of the program up and hired. I insist that hiring staff that won't work will just lead to program failure.

While I try to keep things cordial with the contracting staff, I can see that my goals of an excellent program fall counter to the contractor's goals of checking off boxes including hurriedly hiring staff—even if they are substandard or totally useless—because this is essentially a money-making business for them and more staff hired equates to more profit.

As all of this is going on, Khapta, my Chechen colleague, e-mails to tell me that she is applying for jobs to work in the Red Zone of Iraq as a trauma psychologist and wants to list me as a reference.

"Are you crazy?" I e-mail her back. "What kind of person moves from Chechnya to Iraq? It's not safe, you will be killed!"

"You know that I am a Muslim," Khapta replies, reminding me that Muslims think the day of their death is foreordained. "I believe that God has numbered my days. So yes, I know it's dangerous, but I am going. The people of Iraq need me."

"Okay," I write, "I'll be glad to be your reference, but let me see if I can hire you to our program instead. Then at least you'll be safe inside the base."

Khapta is quickly hired and begins to turn out weekly lesson plans for our manual. And I am happy when Colonel Kato and Rick write with the news that the military and agency have both cleared the "trio" and they will soon be released as prisoners from Camp Cropper. As free men, they have agreed to join our team. Ali, the most educated in Islam of the three, will, according to Colonel Kato, be able to head our Islamic counseling team. Jim also hires my student Ken, who has now graduated with a Master's degree in Middle Eastern Studies, to come and assist full time on the ground.

The psychologists are still proving problematic to find, as most who apply try to pitch their own idea of an entire program and are not interested to join a program being put together for what the military actually wants to do. But all the same, as the weeks fly by into July, the program is coming together bit by bit.

CHAPTER 64

Arriving to Camp Bucca

It's July now and the pilot test of the entire program is scheduled to take place in Camp Bucca, in the south of Iraq by Basra. I'm dismayed to learn that we won't be working in Cropper instead, near Baghdad. It's especially dangerous in Basra—nearly all the local staff that work for the provincial reconstruction team (PRT) there have been attacked, some killed and only one courageously continues to work for the embassy outpost there.

Jim and I continue to argue over the staff he is hiring. He hired Shia counseling staff over my objections, but at least the imams are Sunni. Jim then writes to tell me that the military has long ago forgotten their promise to me regarding air travel in Iraq and that he wants me to join them in their move by convoy to Camp Bucca. I tell him that traveling in a military convoy to Camp Bucca is a no-go for me and when he gets extremely upset by my refusal and doesn't seem to be able to find a solution, I e-mail directly to General Stone reminding him that the military promised me air travel inside Iraq.

Leah and Jessica, now both college kids, are ending their last days living at home, and Danny, our son, is going to Helsinki with a friend. I have everyone's tickets purchased, suitcases packed, passports and money ready when I learn that General Stone will fly me down with him to Camp Bucca but only if I move my departure date up. Tears roll down my cheeks as I prepare dinner that evening. *I thought I had four days and now it's only two! There are only two more dinners with all the kids still living at home and then I board a plane.* My kids laugh at me, hug me and say, "Don't worry Mom we had to grow up sometime! We'll be back!" I smile through tears and laugh with them.

Khapta calls and laughs when I unload all my worries about the inexperienced students Jim has hired as the counselors.

"I was worried you had hired all psychiatrists," she confides. "You know psychiatrists are very inflexible." I laugh, grateful to her for helping me see that it could be worse and remembering how egotistical some of the psychiatrists were in wanting their own programs and probably would have been problematic.

"Don't worry, Anne. You know when we were in the tent camps in Ingushetia," Khapta recalls, referring to her work in the neighboring republic where thousands of Chechen refugees fled during the war in 1999. "We didn't even have a table to eat lunch on. They gave me four students that I had taught in university, just out of their Bachelor's degrees in psychology with *no* clinical experience and I took them and trained them. They were so eager to learn, they cared so much, they worked not ten-hour days but twelve and fourteen and they learned everything! Now they are respected psychologists in Chechnya. We will do the same in Iraq."

I'm smiling again and sleep peacefully until the next day, which becomes a blur of packing and preparing for everyone's travel including my own, then another short sleep and up in the early morning to the train to Paris where I'll catch a flight to Jordan and then continue on into Iraq. On the train reading the newspaper, I am amazed to see that police have just discovered two car bombs rigged with huge canisters of gasoline and nails in downtown London. And I've just been there twice! Again I think to myself, *Maybe I won't get killed in Iraq. Maybe it's London where I'll bite the dust!*

Dan meets me at Baghdad International Airport to briefly say hi before I continue on to Camp Bucca. He is distracted with many worries and we don't really connect. When General Stone and his entourage arrive they discuss the latest Iraqi politics and Dan soon has to leave.

Concerned about the lack of armored plates in the flak jacket I've been issued, I ask General Stone if I can get a real one. He asks his staff but no one is able to find one for me.

"It would be really heavy for you anyway," the General says trying to make light of my lack of protection. There are problems with the arrival of our plane so we sit waiting hours before taking off. General Stone and I sit quietly talking. He surprises me telling me his mother started one of the first nudist camps in California! I laugh and he begins to seem a lot more human to me.

It's after ten p.m. when we finally get the go ahead to fly, and after about an hour we land at the Ali al Salem air base in Kuwait, just on the other side of the Iraqi border, and are taken in military vehicles across the airport tarmac to board Blackhawk helicopters. We put on our flak jackets and helmets and the military handler helps me climb in and straps me into a complex seat belt. He hands me some fire gloves and safety glasses to wear.

"What are these for?" I ask.

"If the helo catches fire, you'll want eye protection, ma'am, and you'll want to be able to use your hands." I nod and take them setting them inside my briefcase—I don't think we are going to burn. If anything bad is going to happen its much more likely we'll be shot out of the sky, but I don't want to focus on fear so I focus instead on the exhilaration of a vertical take off as we ascend and head back toward Iraq.

When we approach, General Stone points out the camp. Surrounded by desert on all sides, it's a blazing inferno of lights and barbed wire. As we swoop in closer I see that there's row after row of prison yards, each one brightly illuminated by gigantic halogen lights. There are tall guard towers posted about every twenty meters or so alongside the prison walls, which are surrounded by desert on all sides.

Our helicopter lands, and we are picked up by the prison staff and taken for a tour around the camp in military jeeps. We see that the outer prison wall is made up of tall cylinders of sand piled one next to the other with rolls of razor wire running along the top. On the inside there is another perimeter of cyclone fencing. When we drive by gaps in the sandbags, we catch glimpses of hundreds of prisoners wearing orange and yellow prison outfits, encircled like animals inside the enclosures.

"Why aren't they sleeping?" I ask.

"It's the heat, ma'am," one of the aides answers. "They come alive at night, sleep in the heat." As we near the complex I stare in fascination at the thousands of Iraqi men—20,000 in total on these grounds.

Our guide points out new construction of more prison barracks explaining, "Here is where we had prisoners housed in tents until just recently."

"Why did some have tents?" I ask.

"Some of the prisoners rioted and set fire to their barracks," he answers. "They burned up everything so we had to put them in tents for a few months. The tents were rough on them because they were without air conditioning." He turns to the General. "They are all back to barracks now, sir."

I try to imagine being held prisoner in a tent with no air conditioning in the hot Iraqi summer. It regularly gets over one hundred degrees here. I wonder how frustrated and angry the prisoners must have been to set fire to their own barracks and how they did it in the first place.

We drive into the military side of the camp. We are dropped off on a boardwalk with military tents on both sides. General Stone says good-night and goes with his aides to his quarters, and I'm taken past rows and rows of long tents with large window air conditioner units attached at one end. These tents house the military guards, contractors and staff working at Camp Bucca. At my level, I've been rated to be bunked in a "pod" so I continue on down a boardwalk to the "upscale" side of the military camp near the forward operating base headquarters, known to insiders as the FOB.

Jim comes out to greet me warmly and takes me to my pod, which looks a bit like a small plastic tool shed with a wall unit air conditioner sticking out the backside. Jim gives me my key, points out that the outdoor port-o-potties about a block away and says that for shower and toilet facili-ties, I need to walk about five blocks down one of the main "avenues". After Jim leaves, I slip inside and switch on the bright overhead fluo-rescent lights. The pod is sparsely furnished with a steel bed frame that someone has thoughtfully made up with a military issue sheet, pillowcase, pillow and topped with a military camouflage sleeping bag. There is also a tall military locker, a small metal desk and folding chair and a wall unit air conditioner hanging near the ceiling on the opposite end of the room. The locker has a very thin layer of red dust covering it—the ubiquitous red dust of Iraq. There is a window near the door, but upon inspection I see that the window has been sealed and covered over, probably to protect the occu-pant from shrapnel. I sigh and think, *This is home for the next two weeks!*

I hang up my things, lay out my toiletries and trying to get my bearings. A previous occupant has installed a few plastic stickup hooks to the wall, so I hang my bathrobe on one and a small four-inch round cosmetic mirror on another. I realize looking around that it will be the only mirror I'll have for my stay. I pull out my laptop and charger and plug it into the wall, along with my mobile telephone, which has no signal. I feel disconnected from the rest of the world.

As I walk toward the showers and my feet crunch along the stone walk-way which helps keep fine sand from blowing about the camp, my thoughts drift to the Holocaust prisoners interviewed earlier in my career. Maybe the razor and barbed wire returns me to thoughts of their ghetto. I know that even in the best of circumstances, losing one's freedom and living in prison is nearly always a terrible experience, and after our interviews in Camp Cropper I know that some of these prisoners are likely innocent, picked up on vague suspicions or on wide sweeps. As I stare at the orange clad prisoners I feel the weight of what our program may achieve and it inspires me to work hard to make it a success.

I continue crunching along the stone path to the showers where I wash my hair and scrub the desert sand from my body. At the sinks I meet some other military women who introduce themselves. When I tell them I am a psychologist working with the detainees one of them says, "Why do *they* get a psychologist? We need one desperately!" She doesn't laugh and I realize she is dead serious about the need for support serving in this place.

I smile at her in the mirror answering. "You can talk to me anytime!"

Back in my pod, the air conditioner is pouring out a stream of warm air and with the door closed it's unbelievably hot. I'm sweating so much I can't sleep. The mattress has a plastic cover under the sheet so finally I pour water all over the bed and lie down in it, knowing it's the only way to keep cool. I drift off into an exhausted sleep only to wake up a few hours later after all the water has evaporated and repeat, which I do until morning.

The next day, everyone congregates in the contractor's office, set up in the newly refurbished FOB building with two computers and two desks. I've come to work and begin the training but just like when I had come to Camp Cropper, Jim appears more interested chewing the fat than getting to work. Rick works at computer, Susan is sitting off to the side looking frustrated, and Ken, dressed in his contractor issue khakis and helmet, lounges in an office chair looking like a boy that is thrilled to be in a war zone.

Dr. Tahir, the contractor's psychiatrist arrives and declares, "I don't trust these former AQ guys at all. They are listening to jihadi music all the time and when they pray, two of them get behind their leader. That means he is the emir, and you only get to be an emir if you have killed a lot of Shia! I don't believe they have left al Qaeda. They are probably going to use our program to recruit more members."

"Dr. Tahir, why would they come and work *here for us* if they are still in al Qaeda?" I ask with a smile and a tone of voice that is poking fun at him. "It doesn't make any sense. They are trying to talk the hardcore *out* of being involved in AQ, *not* recruit them."

"That's what *they say*," Dr. Tahir continues, "But how do we know that's what they are really doing unless someone listens in? They are going to be alone with the detainees right?"

I still want to laugh but I realize the rest of the room has already joined in his conspiratorial and warped sense of fear.

"Listen Dr. Tahir," I say firmly now. "I am absolutely positive they have changed. They joined AQ at the beginning of our invasion because they wanted to defend their country from outside attack, and it's normal to want to defend one's country." Reason may help him out of his fearful stance. "But with the beheadings and terror acts among civilians they understood that AQ went too far. At this point they don't believe that AQ is following the Koran. These are very religious guys and if they think something is not Islamic they won't have anything to do with it."

"Well they could still be active in AQ," Rick suddenly chimes in. "How do we know what they are saying in their classes? They could be recruiting in their classes, while we think they are talking against AQ."

"Okay," I concede. "Why don't we arrange to have them monitored randomly from time to time. Ken is free and his Arabic is getting better. He can drop in on their classes." I nod at him, lounging playing with his helmet like a young boy. Ken sits up and nods assent. "

"I think we should watch them at night, too," Dr. Tahir adds, upping the fear factor. "Who is to say they won't slit our throats while we're sleeping?"

"Come on!" I say. Realizing that his fear has infected the entire group, I get suddenly dead serious and a bit angry. "Listen guys, these three were thoroughly checked out by the Agency and by military intelligence. They have been in prison and cooperating with us for over nine months now. I don't think that everyone, especially the best security personnel in the world, would have been so completely fooled. They are super religious and they have given their word to work with us and left their families behind in danger to do that. They are dedicated to this program. We can count on them. Anyway, Dr. Tahir, how would they get a knife in here if they were going to kill you in your sleep? They can't even have their telephones!"

Jim looks up from his computer shaking his head and says, "Don't get me started. Don't even ask me what I think about Islam." Then he mutters loud enough for us all to hear, "Some things are from the devil…"

I gasp shocked that he could be working on this program and say such a thing but I have no time to respond as Susan chimes in a sour tone, "I don't see why we would want to work with anyone who has been an active member of al Qaeda."

"Susan, they are our best resource," I explain. "They have the credibility to say to the other extremists, 'I was deep into it, I thought it was the right thing to do, but now I realize it was wrong, that what AQ is teaching is against the Koran, against Islam.' That is a very powerful message. We should be thanking them for risking their lives and their families' lives to help us."

I ask where the "trio" is and am told that they don't have badges yet and can't leave their tent, and even if they could, they are not allowed into the FOB. *Oh great,* I think, *they are freed from prison but essentially on "tent arrest"*!

Back in the office, Jim continues to waste time telling adolescent anecdotes about growing up Catholic and his repressed sexuality as a boy. It gets a bit raunchy and I try to ignore him while I review the final chapters from the London imams. The Internet connection is very bad here and downloads take forever. I spend the rest of the day putting our manual together, while Ken and Dr. Tahir mill about inefficiently.

At one point the office empties except for Susan. I ask her how she is doing and she suddenly releases a torrent of anger.

"I'm so frustrated," she says. "I'm thinking about quitting. I can't take it with these two jokers anymore, the constant storytelling, lack of management and wasting time day after day. They ask me to track all the statistics but everything else they hold close and won't let me do anything, so day after day I watch as they just spin their wheels. I'm going crazy with this."

She's nailed it completely. Rick likes working with secret intelligence and doesn't like to share anything even things he could. But Rick at least does the majority of the work, allowing Jim to keep up a façade of running an efficient operation.

Rick and Jim return from their meeting with the military and Jim anxiously tells us, "They want us to start the training as soon as possible."

"I'm ready," I say. " We can begin immediately – but you need to figure out how to print the manuals since you insisted I come here before they were final and now they need to be printed and assembled." For appearances sake, Rick and Jim rushed the trio and me down to Camp Bucca before they were actually ready to activate. It means the trio has been sitting for days steaming in their tent, angry that they are separated from their families in Baghdad while they do nothing productive, and I have arrived with a manual that still needs to be assembled and printed.

Jim however is inept as ever and I find he has not yet set up the printers. When he does, he finds he doesn't have the necessary printer cables. He doesn't want to admit this to the military, however, for fear of looking inept and it takes him a while to finally go to the FOB for supplies.

Back in my pod, I spend another night pouring water over my sheets every few hours to be able to sleep through the unbearable heat.

CHAPTER 65

Training Day One

In the morning we start our training. With Ken's help, I arrange the tables in the VIP dining hall into a circle. The trainees arrive, including the trio—Ali, Mahmoud and Wathiq. We greet each other warmly and with excitement after so many months of waiting.

"It was really weird to come back here [to Camp Bucca] as a free man," Ali laughs and says before the others arrive. "One of the guards recognized me and said, 'Welcome to the other side!'"

The others soon join and everyone is seated. Major Thompson who has been cynical about the program and especially the need for anything psychological comes in at the last minute and announces, "I would like to observe if you don't mind."

I nod my assent, feeling I don't really have a choice. He takes a seat behind our circle looking out of place among us, in his camouflage uniform and army boots.

"If you sit in on our training," I go and tell him quietly, "I may pull you into one of the role plays."

He smiles but crosses his arms and I have the feeling he is refusing before I even invite him. Rick also arrives a bit later to sit in. It's not easy to feel free with observers but I soon forget them.

To start, I turn to my group of five psychologist and four imams, all Iraqis. I introduce myself and the program and explain the group includes both imams and psychologists because we both need to understand the other's content.

I ask everyone to introduce themselves by first names only because I know that there are concerns about security among all of the participants. No one trusts the others not to leak their identity back out into Iraqi society, as their families can come under attack from the militants still on the outside.

The trio starts, followed by a few others on the Islamic side.

"I'm Abdul Sittar, I came to work here because I have been in prison myself under Saddam and I was tortured many times," he says softly. "I know what it's like to be in prison and have hate in your soul. I want to help because I know the detainees will eventually be released and we have to help them to give up fighting and killing each other."

Abdul Sittar is from the Muslim Brotherhood (MB), the world's oldest and one of the largest Islamist movements that combines political activism with Islamic charity work.[292] Officially the group shuns violence but has in the past housed a paramilitary wing and carried out bombings, massacres and political assassinations. Westerners have often been suspicious of the Muslim Brotherhood's stated commitment to democratic principles while simultaneously promoting Sharia law. Important for our group is the fact that al Qaeda directly opposes the Muslim Brotherhood for it's support of democratic elections as opposed to militant jihad. As Abdul Sittar introduces himself, I look anxiously at the trio to see their reaction. They appear fine with him.

The psychologists are a more motley group. To confront al Qaeda-inspired extremists, we needed Sunni psychologists and psychiatrists, but most with any experience have already fled to the Gulf where they and their families are safe and where they can be employed for much more than we can offer them. Those that remain are overworked, as nearly the entire country has been traumatized, first by years of Saddam's horror and now by the U.S. led invasion. By the time we were recruiting for this program, there were only sixty psychiatrists left in all of Iraq and psychologists were also nearly nonexistent, leaving us to hire mostly Shia Master's level graduates.

Omar, a short squat young man eager to begin his first professional job, introduces himself.

"I'm Omar. I've just completed my masters in psychology from Baghdad University. I want to get my Ph.D. but it's not possible to go there now, at least not for anyone who is Sunni."

Taha, an older gentleman with graying hair is a former military psychologist, is past retirement.

"I'm Taha," he says. "I served in the military as a psychologist and trained soldiers in the Military Institute."

"Taha, are you Sunni or Shia?" I ask curious to how the extremists will respond to someone from Saddam's military.

"Shia," he answers and then abruptly stops speaking, while Dr. Tahir interrupts him and has a whispered side conversation with him in Arabic. Taha turns back to me and abruptly changes his mind answering, "I am Sunni."

"Taha, didn't you start to say you are Shia?" I ask.

"No, I am Sunni," he answers emphatically, looking over to Dr. Tahir for confirmation. I suspect it's a lie. Dr. Tahir, who is Shia, knows that I did not want to use Shia staff for this program and it's been an ongoing argument between us, but I don't want to challenge him now in front of everyone so I pass on to Samir.

Jim has warned me that the next psychologist, Samir, is deaf. I cannot believe he has hired a deaf psychologist for our program and when I ask Samir, who is in his early thirties to introduce himself, he looks confused, leans forward, and puts his hand to his ear to hear better. Omar leans over and tells him to introduce himself. Samir's smile is kind and reveals teeth with gold fillings.

"I'm Samir," he says in soft tones. "I have a Masters in Psychology." Samir also has no clinical experience and is Shia.

Madi, also Shia and in his late twenties, says, "I'm from Basra and have a Masters degree," He has some clinical experience, but not much.

The last psychologist, who has informal experience counseling teenagers as an imam, is Shafik. He is a crossover for our group as he has been trained as an imam as well. Shafik looks the most western of the group in jeans and a button-down collared cotton shirt.

Confidence brims in his voice as he says, "I grew up here but we left to the UK when I was in university. I attended the same high school as Saddam's sons so I knew them *too* well." He rolls his eyes. "I'm very glad we got rid of them and I'm here to rebuild my country."

Given the lack of experience, I keep things simple, teach the basics and give them a lot of practice and supervision.

"We have three programs we will be learning to implement," I tell them. "The first is a six week program called 'Redirect from the Militant Jihad'. It is for those who have a strong ideological commitment to violence, something we estimate for about twenty percent of the detainees. The second group is three weeks long and called 'Psych Lite'. It's for the moderates—the majority of the detainees—those who got involved in violence but have no real ideological commitment to it. The third program is six weeks and is called the 'Juvenile Protect Program'. It is for the detainees under eighteen, of which we have eight hundred at present. Their group will involve school and sports as well."

I explain the objectives of each of the programs and how success will be evaluated.

"One psychologist and one imam will be assigned to the same twenty detainees. Because of the huge numbers, the detainees are going to be divided into groups of ten for daily group sessions. We will run sessions separately in groups of ten, but switch groups halfway through the day so each imam and psychologists will see the same twenty detainees each day. The idea is that we work closely together—if a religious issue arises in the psychological groups, you can confer with the imam and make sure it gets addressed or vice versa. Any detainees that need individual sessions will get them at the end of the day.

"Each detainee will be invited to take part in the program through an individual interview with the psychologist and the imam," I explain. "Our program is one hundred percent voluntary. We must get an informed consent, which means we explain thoroughly what the program entails, any harm that could come from participating and the possible benefits of participation. The rewards are simple: it can accelerate their release from prison. But we must explain that they should not agree to join unless they actively participate. They are totally free to refuse. Once they enter our program, the detainees will be separated from all the other detainees into a new living space. That's so that they can't be beaten or intimidated by their previous cellmates for cooperating in the program. No other prisoners but those inside their group will have access to them or know what they are doing or saying in our program.

I stress that we must protect everyone that goes through our program so we have to explain the risks as well. "Inside a prison, they may be filmed or recorded by the prison authorities and we have no control over that," I say turning to indicate the corners of the room. "Even in this room there may be hidden cameras." Everyone begins scanning the room for cameras and I continue, "That is not our business, if they are filmed or not. But we have the duty to warn them that it is not in their best interest to admit to crimes for which someone in the prison can be recording their admission and could, in turn, hand them over to the Iraqi criminal justice system.

"It's very important that you understand," I explain, "We don't work for the prison authorities and we have no interest in discovering the detain-ee's crimes except to the extent it helps them to rehabilitate and be able to leave prison as soon as possible. We are not here to collect information, to help the interrogators or to put anyone who is guilty permanently behind bars. Our goal is simple and limited to deradicalization and rehabilitation. Deradicalization means that through our program we get the detainee to a point where he relinquishes any and all commitment to violence against the U.S. military, the government of Iraq and across sects. That means that they don't endorse violence as an appropriate or moral choice. Rehabilitation means that we have worked with them enough to have built a strong alternative response to violence in reaction to the conflict zone they inevitably will be released back into. Everything else related to their crimes, other than how they need to heal, has nothing to do with us."

One of my biggest concerns about this program is that it operates ethically. "I'm sure you are all aware of the prison abuses in Guantanamo and elsewhere, including here in Iraq," I explain, "but our program cannot be like that. We cannot have anything to do with mistreatment, beatings, so-called "soft torture", violence, coercion, or anything else that is unethical."

I've lectured for a long time and now I want to get down to brass tacks - to see now how my team performs, how well they are equipped to carry out these tasks. I set up our first role-play, asking Ali to be the hardcore detainee, Omar the psychologist.

"Listen guys, we are going to start work practicing on the 'hardcore,' those heavily indoctrinated into the al Qaeda or Takfiri ideology. They are going to be the toughest. They likely joined due to real traumas and grievances and are not happy about being in prison, about the US presence in Iraq or about being invited to take part in a deradicalization program. Some of them have training in how to evade interrogation and create false impressions of themselves and they may be actively recruiting and running cells inside the prison."

Omar looks at me tentatively and then begins in role, "I'm here to invite you to take part in a program for the detainees. It's a psychological and Islamic counseling program."

Ali interrupts him suddenly, roaring out his words contemptuously, "Islamic counseling! I don't need any religious counseling! Who is going to counsel me? A Shia? You?"

Omar just about jumps out of his seat and looks at me frightened, I signal for him to continue. "No I'm a psychologist; there are imams for the Islamic counseling. This is…"

Ali jumps in again shouting, "You are Shia! You are a Shia traitor working for the Americans!"

Omar's eyes widen with fear. He looks at me pleadingly but I don't rescue him. He turns back to Ali, "No, I'm not Shia, I'm Sunni," he stutters out.

"But you are a traitor working for the Americans, a traitor to your country! You work for the invaders!" Ali taunts him.

Omar looks at me again his eyes begging me to help, but I just smile and say to the group, "This is how it's going to be, guys. They are tough and you have to be prepared." I turn to Omar and tell him, "Continue."

"I'm not a traitor!" Omar says.

"Yes you are!" Ali continues to shout. "How much are the Americans paying you to betray your country, you Shia pig?"

"I'm Sunni!" Omar pleads.

"Shia or Sunni, you are still a traitor. How much do they pay you to betray us?" Ali asks sneering at him.

I interrupt and say, "Omar, do you see you have lost control of the intake? The power has shifted totally over to Ali now who is asking *you* questions and you are answering instead of vice versa." Omar nods. "And do you see that you have gotten sucked into his reality now? Your job is to explain the program to him, get an informed consent if he agrees to participate and do an intake interview. It doesn't matter if you are a traitor." Then I ask him softly, "Are you a traitor, Omar?"

Omar shakes his head and answers emphatically, "No!!!"

"Are you sure?" I ask again softly.

"Yes, I'm sure." Omar answers. "Good," I say, "Then we don't need to deal with that. He can call you anything he wants, but *you* know who you are." I turn to the group. "This is going to be rough. The detainees, especially the Takfiri, are going to shout at you, spit at you, call you names and try to make you doubt yourself. They are going to call you a traitor and the enemy and for them, *you are the enemy*! You have to be ready for this and not let it deflect you from your task. Your job is to get through to them that it's best for them to participate and to bring them through to the intake interview where you will begin to build rapport." I smile and turn back to Omar whose confidence has returned.

But Ali does not even let him restart. "Where do you live? Are you from Baghdad? Because I'm going to find out your name and find out where your family lives and I'm going to have their throats slit—every last one of them. Then you'll find out what it is to be a traitor to your country and to your religion!" he roars.

"I'm here to explain a program to you," Omar says, his eyes wide with terror.

"I don't want your program, you Shia traitor, scum!" Ali shouts.

Omar looks at me again for help. "Tell him that it can help him get out of prison faster," I coach. Omar repeats this and suddenly he has Ali listening to him.

After some time of repeating these role-plays with the others, everyone suddenly has an idea of what they are in for.

"Listen I want to see pictures beforehand of those who you are putting in my group," Taha says. "I trained many of them in the military academy and I don't want to work with anyone who knows me. It's not safe for my family."

Taha's comment sparks a discussion about safety and how to deal with real threats.

"Listen guys, you are free to use a fake name if you want," I say. "But if you do use a pseudonym, I want you to honestly tell the detainees, 'This is a fake name and I am using it because I don't feel safe with you.'"

After lunch, I hand manuals out to the team that include lesson plans for each day of our six-week program. Everyone looks at them skeptically and finally Omar breaks the awkward silence.

"Can we get these in Arabic?" he asks. "None of us read well in English."

Oh geez, I think, *the staff was all supposed to be fluent in English*! That was a requirement we had made for hiring, but here we are facing reality and no time to lose!

I turn to Rick and ask, "Rick can we get these translated to Arabic, printed and back to them fast?"

Rick shifts in his seat and says, "I don't know about that."

"Maybe Dr. Tahir can do it?" I offer. They have to be able to read their manuals and I know Dr. Tahir has nothing to do.

"Okay we'll try," Rick says, squirming uncomfortably in his seat.

"Great!" I answer and we continue on with the training. I don't realize that Rick feels very cornered in this interaction because the contractor is not responsible for translating the manual and unless Dr. Tahir does it, it's additional cost, which will embarrass him in front of his boss or Major

Thompson, who he will have to go to asking for the additional funds. With all the arguments we have already had over Jim and Rick trying to hire Shia and over the psychologists Jim hired being unskilled and also mostly Shia, I have no idea that asking for the needs of our team to be met efficiently is only the beginning of more miscommunications about what the contractors can and should do to make our effort a success.

CHAPTER 66

The Training Life as a Contractor in Camp Bucca

The next day in training I'm a bit surprised by an outburst by Mahmoud.

"You are not who you say you are," he says, confronting me.

"Why do you say that?" I ask.

"The first time you came to us you were wearing a head scarf," he says.

"Yes, Mahmoud, I did that for respect. We were in another setting and I thought it might be difficult for you to speak with me if I didn't wear it, but we are here now and it's hot and I am not a Muslim. I told you the first time I met you that I am a Christian and I wore the scarf out of respect for you."

Mahmoud is not happy but he doesn't argue anymore. I feel badly that he feels tricked, but I'm also satisfied with my answer. I was never dishonest with him. By lunch, things are smoothed over and Mahmoud is not angry anymore.

General Stone is only planning on staying in Camp Bucca for few days so when he sees me in the mess hall, he warns me that he is not certain he will come back for me in two weeks when I am slated to leave. I have insisted from the start that I will not take ground travel, which means I might be stranded in Camp Bucca. When I say I'll risk it he asks, "Are you sure?" It's a weird feeling to know I could end up stranded here for weeks, but I trust General Stone will honor their commitment and come back for me, although I understand it may be later than I planned.

We continue to meet in the VIP dining room of the mess hall, working around the hours when it's being used for meals. Otherwise, I work in the contractor's office with Jim, Rick, Ken, Susan and Dr. Tahir. They are really pleased that the training is going well although I find out that Rick is upset with me.

"You really embarrassed me in the training asking for the manuals in Arabic," Rick says, his eyes flashing with anger. "It's not in our contract to provide materials in Arabic, and it can get expensive."

The last thing I wanted to do was embarrass him so I apologize profuse-ly, but also say, "What should we do Rick? They are not going to learn the material if they can't even read it, and none of us anticipated that it would be so hard to get good staff that is fluent in English."

Rick accepts my apology and says, "At least they can *speak* English!"

We laugh and I add, "At least they are not all deaf too," which just makes us laugh more.

After the second night of poor air conditioning, I ask Jim about it and he says he will put in a work order but that the camp maintenance guys typically take a week or so to come. After enduring three more nights of sleeping by pouring water onto my sheets, I mention it to Ken and he takes a look. While messing around with it, the front pops off and both of us are amazed to see a solid block of ice adhering to the air conditioner. We turn it off and when I return that night it's easy to chip away the remaining ice and wipe up the water that has collected on the floor. Then I flip it back on and blessedly have full-blast air conditioning. I am reminded of my friends in Belarus who used to tell me that when you are used to having nothing, the smallest things can become such incredible pleasures!

The next day I that a small refrigerator has arrived in the PX. I buy it immediately and ask Ken if he and the guys will help me carry it to my pod. I load it up with juices and a few yogurts from the mess and the remaining beer that I haven't given away and think, "Life is definitely looking up."

In the first days of being at the camp I learn that no one on our team, except for Dr. Tahir and Ken, has their phones, which still haven't passed security. Given we are in a conflict zone and everyone except Shafik has wives and children back in Baghdad I think it's appalling. Madi asks me if I can help him call home to check on his three-year-old. I want to give him my phone but I know if I do there can be problems. I talk to Jim about it but get the usual stonewalling.

Then a couple of nights later I learn that not only can the trio not leave their tents without an escort, they need to be accompanied by Ken or Dr. Tahir to take them to the porta-potties and showers. I argue with Jim and finally get all their phones busted loose and permission for the trio to use the johns and the showers without an escort.

When I talk to my husband and tell him how it is in Camp Bucca and how I feel like I'm in a high testosterone zone with so many men and so few women around, he warns, "You know that some of our military guys are in gangs. You shouldn't walk in the dark alone, Anne. Just because you are on a base doesn't mean it's safe."

Dan has already told me that when women come to the IZ they suddenly feel glamorous with so much male attention. I've noticed that too. Just being a woman walking into the mess hall causes many male heads to turn. Camp culture is interesting. On one of the first nights I invited Ken to sit in my pod with me to drink a beer and review the day's events, but when we were about to enter together, the military "neighbor" across the boardwalk stopped us. "You can't be in the pod with a man, ma'am. If he comes in, you have to leave the door open." That defeated the purpose of getting into the air conditioning and since beer is contraband we also couldn't drink out in the open. While I have no romantic feelings for Ken, it set my mind to wondering how men and women "hook up" here, as surely some of them do. It looks like the only private places are the pods or the dark corners around the generators.

After my husband's warning, I begin to re-evaluate walking back from the trainings and the guys' tent at night and start asking Ken to walk me back. One night, we spend talking about Islam and Ali tells us many stories of the Prophet Muhammad that especially emphasized the loving and forgiving nature of both Allah and the Prophet. Ali accompanies us on the walk back to my pod and I notice that Ali is now fixated on telling me about hell.

"Do you know about how hell is described in the Koran?" he asks.

"Yes I do," I answer. "We have many of the same concepts in Christianity."

Ali persists in telling all sorts of graphic descriptions of hell from the Koran and the hadiths. "The unbelievers will be cast into the fires and it will burn them forever. The fires will scald their faces and their bodies and they will be covered with burning pitch," he explains. "And when the people in hell are thirsty they will call out for a drink but the drink will scald their insides and make them even thirstier so they call out for it again and again."

Ali is clearly getting worked up and I muse about why. When we get to my pod we are still deep in discussion and it is still so hot so I invite Ken and Ali to come and sit inside where the air conditioning now works. We have collected a few broken chairs so after checking to see that no military neighbors are watching the guys quickly slip inside and sit in a small circle at the end of my bed. I hand out fruit drinks from my refrigerator and some nuts to snack on. Ali keeps talking about hell so I cut in and say, "Ali you really like me, don't you?" smiling. He looks shocked and then I continue, "You're afraid I'm going to hell, no?" I see on his face that I have him nailed.

"Ali," I say as tenderly as I can, "I'm not afraid of hell. I know everything you are saying because it's in the Bible too, these fiery descriptions of hell, but my relationship with God is not like that. Maybe it's because my mother died when I was young, I've known since I was a child that there was something more, someone out there that guided and loved me. My relationship with God is so strong and so filled with love that there is no doubt in my mind about hell. I can't imagine in my worst, most wild imagination the God who walks with me every day and who loves me, throwing me into hell. It's just never going to be that way. But I do appreciate your concern."

Ali is taken aback but doesn't give up. "You have to be a believer, Anne."

"But I am," I say, thinking of when my sister became a fundamentalist Christian and used to call and ask me if I was saved. When I reminded her that we are both baptized and confirmed Catholics she answered, "But do you have Jesus in your heart?" I always wanted to pull her chain and say, "No he's in my *foot*," but I never did. Now I feel the same dynamic at play, but I stay in a loving place.

"Ali, I am a committed Christian. I follow my faith. I am from the people of the Book. You know what the Koran says about the people of the Book." He knows what this means, that Islam recognizes and respects Jews and Christians that seriously follow their faith as co-worshipers of the same God. Then to make him happier I add, "Listen if it makes you happier, Sheik Abdul Azeem and others have even told me that I am a Muslim."

Ali perks up at this and begins peppering me with questions. "Do you believe there is only one God?" he asks.

"Of course I do, that's a basic tenant of Christianity. You know that."

Locked in an energetic dialogue, he asks me, "Do you believe that Muhammad is Allah's prophet?" I have mused on this question a lot and in the end I do think that Muhammad had a real revelation and tried to bring faith to the people. It just seems it got a bit contorted in the way it was played out and there is even evidence in the Koran that Muhammad got confused and hears versed that he later attributed to the devil. But in the main, I think he did hear from an angel and pointed the people of his time away from idol worship and to worship one God, the same God of Abraham and Jacob that Christians and Jews also worship, so I answer him carefully. "Yes, I believe Muhammad is Allah's prophet, just as the others were." Ali jumps up in his chair excitedly. "You *are* a Muslim!" He exclaims, joy erupting from him, and then he qualifies it, "although a *bad* one." I laugh heartily and feel glad to have put his hell fire anxiety over me to rest.

Over the next days we continue to go over the program and discuss the things that motivate terrorists to act. We address these in role-plays and I quickly learn that my Iraqi psychologists and imams are all deeply traumatized themselves. It calls into question if it was the best idea, after all, when we decided that our program implementers should be Iraqi because they know the history, culture and situation on the ground. It seems they also share the same traumas as well, which may be a significant handicap to their performance.

Omar is back in the hot seat again and Wathiq is pretending to be the hardcore detainee.

"Can you tell me how did you get arrested? What happened?" Omar asks Wathiq.

"I was arrested by the Iraqis, Shia like you!" Wathiq spits out.

Omar is not Shia but he has learned not to flinch, not to argue, just to speak gently and carry on. "I'm Sunni," he answers calmly and continues. "What happened when you were in the custody of the Iraqis?"

"They just about killed me," Wathiq says, his voice fading as he re-enters this terrible episode in his memory. I am quite sure it is a real memory, not a made-up one. Omar seems to realize this and hesitates, frightened of it. I coach Omar, "Ask him what they did."

"What did they do to you?" Omar asks.

"They hung me upside down and beat me for hours," he bellows out, "With a wire cord in my genitals." "They beat me until I passed out, and when I came to they beat me some more. I almost died!"

Omar stares at Wathiq, speechless. I wait to see what he will do but he doesn't respond.

"Omar, do you have a response to Wathiq?" I ask.

Omar stares at me in horror. "I don't know what to say," he answers and looks away from Wathiq at me, obviously relieved to disengage from Wathiq.

"What do you feel?" I ask softly.

"Nothing," Omar answers.

"That's not possible, Omar," I say. "He's just told you that he's been hung upside down and beaten in the genitals and almost killed. You must feel something."

"No I don't. It's what they do here. It's normal here," Omar says, looking at me wide-eyed and pleadingly. I feel as if he's begging me to stop but I continue. I understand he is traumatized and unable to respond. He's heard this story before and he's learned to block it out. Now he needs to block Wathiq out as well. I explain to the others that Omar is using post-traumatic avoidance and maybe even dissociating his emotional responses to Wathiq. I ask Omar to try to feel and respond to Wathiq. He cannot. Finally I take over, coaching him.

"My God! How did you survive?" I ask through Omar with a great deal of compassion in my voice.

Wathiq says, "I don't know. The Americans came and when they did the Iraqis cut me down. Then I passed out. I woke up in American custody."

I explain to Omar that he now has an opening. "And the Americans do they beat you this way?" I coach him to ask.

"No, but they tied me in a stress position like this," Wathiq shows his arms tied and hung up behind his back. "They kept me in semi-darkness all day like this and they wouldn't let me use the toilet for hours. They wouldn't untie my hands when I was taken to the toilet and I couldn't wash. I couldn't pray normally and I told them it's against Islam to not let me wash and pray." I am getting angry listening. I know this is a true story. Wathiq has told me part of it before. It happened in Camp Cropper.

"What did they say to that?" I coach.

"They told me to shut up!" Wathiq answers.

"Did they beat you?" I coach Omar to ask.

"No, but once when I was screaming at them about needing to wash and pray properly, that they are acting against Islam, one of the soldiers kicked the door open so hard it slammed me in the face and split my lip open. I still have the scar," he says pointing it out.

I decide to cut the role-play and explain to the group, "Omar has gotten Wathiq into a vulnerable place where he is reliving his experience with the Iraqis and also the Americans. This is going to happen in our groups as well, and it offers a chance now to work through this traumatic experience and begin to address the others traumas that may have come before it. Likely there are many. It also offers an opportunity for Omar to help Wathiq think through and compare his treatment in the hands of the Americans and Iraqis. Of course, 'soft torture' stress positions and 'accidently' beating someone are not right, but even with these injustices, Wathiq is confronted now with seeing that his American captors tried to follow some moral standards, compared to what happened in Iraqi hands.

"If we continue to follow this, we might be able to get Wathiq to move into a discussion where he can begin to talk about what he views as just and unjust actions, what the Koran tells him is allowable and what is not, and why he justifies being signed on to a terrorist ideology. This can begin to move him ideologically, to shake his views a bit. Likely he views his own state under Saddam, and now the Shia, as so unjust to Sunnis that he feels justified in enacting terrorism. And he has his negative views of Americans that may crumble as well. We want to move him to the point where he agrees killing civilians is out of the ballpark and then back him up even further from that point. But we are just at the beginning of finding the traumas that may drive his ideological furor, and we can't let our own fears of the horror of what he's been through be the block to reaching him."

Everyone nods, but I know they cannot let their own defenses down yet. They have lived with horror themselves for far too long and have their limits to trauma as well. Right now, Omar and the rest of the group are not able to respond normally to the traumas that many Iraqis have endured.

"What happens when you hear stories like this?" I ask them. "You all look like you freeze and feel nothing."

One by one, they admit that they just block it out, that they routinely go emotionally numb in the face of any triggers to posttraumatic recall.

We go on to discuss how the Shia militia groups are revenging for so many years of oppression under the Sunni's privileged positions during Saddam's era and the resulting Sunni anger. This jars Omar who is Sunni.

"My family has been targeted four times now," he blurts out. "One family member was killed when the Shia militia injected his veins with sulfuric acid. The next had a ten-inch screw drilled through his skull— that's how we found him. Another had his hands screwed together with the others killed beside him." Omar shakes in terror as he speaks. Together we process that horror and despite the revolting subject matter, I am pleased to see them slowly opening up and facing their own posttraumatic recall.

After our training, I go back to the office to work.

"Don't you think it's a mistake to trust people who wanted to kill us, to work with them?" Susan asks me in a needling voice.

"You mean the trio?" I ask and she nods. "Susan," I answer, "They were studying Islam when we invaded their country. A lot of people were killed and we became the occupiers. From their point of view they signed up to AQ to defend their country and to end the occupation."

"This isn't an occupation," Susan says blithely.

I cannot really believe she just said it, but I stay calm. "Susan, we invaded their country. We are sitting on a U.S. base in a foreign country. Look out the window. There are ten U.S. military armored vehicles parked out there. This is most certainly an occupation."

"But we got rid of Saddam for them. They wanted that and they were happy we did it," she continues. "They were sure celebrating when we pulled down his statue!"

"That's true, most of the people were happy about that. Saddam was a terrible dictator, but Susan, they didn't want us to stay and take control of their country, to set up bases, to put checkpoints all through their cities and towns, and to completely change it's political balance and who controls which resources."

"I don't know about that, but I still say we shouldn't be working with people who wanted to kill us," she concludes as she picks up some files and gets ready to exit the office.

"They were involved in the Internet media and the religious propaganda side of things. They don't have blood on their hands!" I say deciding not to argue any further as she leaves.

Later, the others go earlier to the mess hall for supper, leaving Rick and I who are still crunching on paperwork behind. Rick tells me, "You know I'm just so ready to quit, to pack up my bags and leave." I look up at him and see his exhausted expression as he looks up from the monitor.

"Why, Rick?" I ask him.

"It's just all such a mess around here. You know we had to really fight with the military leadership to be here in Camp Bucca. If General Stone wasn't behind it they wouldn't have given us access to the detainees at all," he explains tiredly.

"I know, Rick, but General Stone is one hundred percent behind us, and Colonel Kato too," I say although I know that both have been concerned about this contractor's performance. "It's hard to work with Jim isn't it?

We all see it, Rick, and it's clear you are the one behind him, propping him up, that you are the hard worker here." Rick is nervous that I state the obvious and doesn't want to answer. "You don't have to say anything Rick, but just keep your chin up. You're doing a great job and without you this program would probably collapse. Don't leave," I tell him. Rick nods and goes back to tapping the keyboard and staring into his screen.

"I still haven't gotten paid." Dr. Tahir announces to me at dinner that night.

Turns out, he hasn't gotten a paycheck for weeks and his personal checks back home are bouncing. "Something is wrong with the payroll." I know he wants my help so I turn to Jim and ask him about it.

Jim rubs his forehead, "Yes, I know. We're working on it. It's been a real mess." I think to myself, *This whole operation is an organizational mess!*

A few days later we are again at lunch, and I am sitting with the trio. Ali is extremely knowledgeable about the Koran and likes to talk about it. I enjoy a good religious chat as well so we get deep into it comparing Christianity to Islam.

"What about the four wives thing?" I ask Ali. "I know a lot of Westerners get crazy over that, but if we are honest with ourselves there are plenty of Western men that have had more than one wife—just in succession versus at the same time—and plenty more have affairs. I'm not sure which is better: multiple wives or divorcing and leaving your wife and children to go on to the next woman or affairs. A healthy marriage with just one wife seems best to me. And if God made the population fifty/fifty then why would he come up with a plan where some men get to hog up all the good women? That pretty much guarantees that guys farther down the food chain are not going to get married."

"No Anne, you are looking at it all wrong," Ali answers quickly shaking his head. "Islam is about solutions. I am sure I'll have more than one wife—I'll probably take three more."

I start to choke on my food, laugh and say, "Come on Ali, that's not fair, that means some other guys go without a woman!"

"You don't understand," he continues calmly with concern in his eyes. "Do you know how many women in Iraq have been widowed and are without a man to provide for and protect them? And women have certain needs too," he hints making his meaning clear. "We have many friends like this and my wife and I have discussed it many times. She is in complete agreement and supports that I will help as many of them as I can."

I want to laugh aloud, but the loving kindness with which he has spoken and the sadness of it strikes me to the core. "Okay, I can accept that," I say. "But what about all these men who are rich and basically get four women to themselves while less well-off men get no one?"

"No young woman would accept to be a second wife just for money," Wathiq says. "Look at us. No one would marry any of us just for that. Why would they, when they can be a first wife to someone younger than us? I had two wives before the war started," Wathiq continues. "I had to travel to Egypt a lot and my wife and I agreed it was better to take a wife there than to be immoral when I travel. I took an Egyptian woman as my second wife and I made a family there as well." I am surprised, but say nothing as Wathiq continues, "It meant I had a wife and children in both places and I lived morally." Then he adds sadness covering his face, "My Egyptian wife divorced me though. When the war broke out she said it was too hard, that if I was never there, she couldn't live that way and wanted to marry someone else. So we agreed to divorce. She has my baby son." After a pause he adds sadly, "I want her to marry me again."

I smile. Life is never as simple as we wish it to be.

Each day we keep training and as we go along more traumas are admitted. I want my team to really understand trauma psychology and to be able to work through their blocked and dissociated emotions so that they can help the detainees move past their own traumas and thereby unlock them from their commitment to violence. On one of the training days I set up a psychodrama asking Abdul Sittar if he can pick one of his experiences in prison that won't be too painful for him to discuss, to help us learn a new technique—psychodrama.

Abdul Sittar agrees. "This is about torture," he says.

Following my lead, Abdul sets up the scene by assigning team members to a role. Abdul Sittar says to Samir, "You are here, hanging from the ceiling upside down." I go and get a chair and ask Samir to stand on it. Abdul Sittar adds a pretend blindfold. Samir complies and closes his eyes.

"You are here just outside the room," Abdul Sittar tells Omar as he takes him near the wall. "You are kneeling and chained here with your hands behind you and so close to the wall that you have to lean your ear against it." He puts Omar in this uncomfortable position and puts a pretend blindfold on him as well. "You hear everything that is going on inside, *and you know that you are next.*"

Abdul Sittar takes Shafik and places him in front of the prisoner (Samir) in a chair and says, "You are the interrogator." I ask if Shafik beats Samir, but Abdul Sittar says no and takes Taha and places him in the scene as well. "You do the beating, whenever [Shafik] tells you to." Abdul Sittar rolls up some paper and places it in Taha's hand as a stick.

I tell Abdul Sittar to instruct everyone to play their roles and give them words to say. He tells Shafik to ask questions, scream "You are lying!" when Samir answers wrongly, and give an order for Taha to beat Samir. He indicates to Taha to beat the prisoner when Shafik tells him to. Omar kneels against the wall blindfolded and listening while Samir screams in pain. Abdul Sittar tells Shafik to tell the prisoner that if he doesn't cooperate they will bring his wife and daughters and undress them in front of the soldiers and even rape them if necessary.

We end the psychodrama with each one describing their emotions within the roleplay and in general to the scene. Samir tells how it feels to be hanging from the ceiling blindfolded and beaten, Shafik how it is to order a beating, Taha to beat another person and Omar how it is to be waiting in horror to be next to enter that room. Everyone feels a lot of fear, horror and sadness.

I ask Abdul Sittar how he feels and he answers peacefully, "It feels good to be understood. I am not alone with this memory anymore."

I notice that Samir is very quiet and avoids looking at Abdul Sittar. He had identified too strongly with Abdul Sittar and cannot handle the traumatic exposure. I ask him if it links to any other traumas in his life.

"We are Shia and during the uprising in 1991 we went to Karbala," Samir tells us. "I was eighteen. There were so many dead bodies in the street that you had to step over them to get anywhere and the stench of them rotting was overwhelming. We searched for my sister's house and when we got there," he pauses to face the memory, rubs his hand over his eyes and continues, "there were four new graves out front. I was sure it was my sister and her family buried there. But later we found her alive. We had to run from Karbala because there were still helicopters flying overhead shooting at anyone who was outside their houses. We ran from them and finally we found a Sunni relative in the military rescue service. He lied for us and told the military that we were Sunni as well." We talk a bit about his memory and Samir adds, "There were so many dead bodies in those times that I puked for a month afterward from the stench of them."

I understand more each day why my psychologists don't show appropriate emotions when they are told traumatic stories—they have had too many traumas themselves and simply dissociate. And it's not just the past. They are living in trauma and are overwhelmed by it. I use each of these instances to try to bring my psychologists back into common humanity, to help them to talk about, and to feel the normal emotions that go with such traumas. I help them understand that nothing is off limits—that *all* their emotions, all their sensory recall and even the horrific experiences themselves are acceptable to feel and discuss. None of it should have happened and none of it is their fault.

"You have to feel your feelings and process your traumas," I tell them. "Otherwise you will shut down when the detainees need your help processing theirs. You can't shut down, you have to be there for them, witness with them, feel with them, and help them to re-access their humanity, so that they can make other choices—nonviolent ones. You must be emotionally and psychologically healthy, then you can fight back in a way that will truly help your country and maybe bring an end to this violence by helping others." I can see in their eyes that they take nurture and courage from me and want to get there.

At lunch one day Dr. Tahir sits by me and tells me, "I have to figure out what to do about my bank account."

"You still haven't gotten paid?" I ask him.

"No, Jim doesn't seem to be able to figure it out," Dr. Tahir signs powerlessly. I ask Dr. Tahir about how his family back home is handling this distress and he opens up about the situation there. "My wife is not speaking to me, and my daughter is furious and she keeps draining the account."

"Why?" I ask.

"It's because last year I decided to take a second wife," Dr. Tahir explains. "I set her up in another city and I didn't tell my wife about it. She found out and she won't speak to me. We haven't been living together since then. It was stupid, I should have told her and gotten her agreement. I guess I just like women," he says scratching his white hair. "My daughter is furious and she keeps emptying the entire account every time I get paid," he explains. "And now with my paycheck being messed up, my daughter is over drafting the account and I can't do anything from here."

"How long has this been going on?" I ask.

"Since I came here," Dr. Tahir says matter-of-factly. "We split up right before I took this job."

I nod, thinking here's another contractor running away from home, family and problems, an injured animal licking his wounds in this conflict zone of Iraq. I wonder how all of these wounded healers will ever be able to turn the extremist detainees from violence. All I can do is my best to train and equip them and then hope for the best.

CHAPTER 67

Problems on the Horizon

About ten days into the training, Ken comes to me and says that Wathiq and Ali want to stay afterwards to talk.

After I dismiss everyone, Wathiq starts out, "Anne, we really appreciate all you are doing and we know you are working from the heart, but we don't think things are working out. We want to go back to Camp Cropper and talk to Colonel Kato.

"What do you mean Wathiq?" I ask. "Are you talking about quitting?" I am horrified at the thought of it.

"Quitting this contractor, yes," he answers. "We don't like Jim and Rick and TRS. We all know that they don't really care about this program. All they care about is money. We are here because we want to change our country. We believed these ideas and we know what it's like to be inside these groups and we want to work with the prisoners, but not like this."

"Okay," I say, quickly calculating what to do. We cannot lose these guys, they are a gold mine in terms of credibility and insider knowledge with the Takfiri detainees. "What do you need? I'll get it for you, just don't give up."

"When we agreed to do this," Ali says, "we spoke about writing our own program, like the one you have made, but that takes time and reference materials and a commitment from the contractor. Colonel Kato promised a whole library of Islamic books. We don't have anything he promised."

I know he's right. The contractors are here to do a job, any job. Jim talks about how proud he'll be if this program actually works but he doesn't really grasp the initiative and he jokes that Islam is Satan's religion. Jim is a juvenile, sexually repressed, recovering alcoholic and two-time divorcee. Rick loves the classified part of the program and playing the "spook" but you could put him on anything classified and he'd be happy. He's also a divorcee and has commented to me that he has no "inner child" because he left him behind years ago making sure he "burned up." They are like the other Americans who have come here for the good salaries and the escape; and most importantly to put the problems of their personal lives on hold.

"Ali, forget about the contractor. You are right about them, but it's not worth focusing on. You cannot believe how many fights I have had with them up to now. But they are the only vehicle we have to do this program. It's too late to find another contractor. If we try to dump this contractor the whole program will go down. We can't let that happen. We all care too much. So forget about them, just tell me what you need. You don't like the Islamic program that the London imams wrote?"

"They put a lot of work into it and we really appreciate it," Ali answers. "But they don't understand the situation here on the ground and some of what they wrote is dangerous for us. It may work in UK but not here. We have an outside invader, lots of Iraqis have been killed, and you can use some of the Islamic verses they have covered to argue *for* jihad here. And it's not only that. I want to teach Islam in the traditional way as I always have, in a group setting with lots of reference materials and teaching them the tenets of the faith with discussion. With some of these Takfiri guys you have to be able to show them in the Islamic reference books what the Companions said, then they will understand and change."

"Okay Ali, I trust you," I say because I know he does know best from the insider point of view about both AQ and the prisons. "If you think that's best, let's talk to Colonel Kato and get you what you need. The only thing that we have to agree on is that these two programs work side by side, that your Islamic teaching and the psychological treatment are moving in tandem."

"Yes, we can work together, of course Anne, but these psychologists are not like you. They don't know what they are doing."

I nod, but tell them about Khapta who will soon be arriving to help. Still, Wathiq holds strong, citing unfair treatment and an unproductive work environment.

"We need to go back to Camp Cropper and talk to Colonel Kato," Ali says. "We can quit for now and then if he gets things straightened out we can return in another program with another contractor."

Wathiq alerts me to other concerns. "There have been threats made by the Shia staff," he admits. "One of them says he waits for the release of the Sunni detainees when they are fully rehabilitated and that the Mahdi army will kill them."

"Who said this?" I ask aghast.

Ali and Wathiq exchange glances. "*Who* said it?" I repeat.

"Madi," Ali answers. "And Taha is also Shia, but he is lying saying he is Sunni when he is not. He changes his prayer to Sunni habits, but he forgets and he reverts naturally to the Shia way of praying. We see him doing this. Why is he lying? We don't feel safe here, Anne, and we don't want the detainees to be deceived and put in danger by them."

I am completely speechless. My mind races thinking what to do. "Okay. I will get to the bottom of this. He can be replaced if necessary. Let me talk to Jim about it."

"We can't work with Madi," Wathiq says.

"Yes, I agree. He'll have to go," I answer.

"But who will take his place?" Ali asks.

"I don't know, maybe I'll have to stay. Let me figure that out. Just tell me now, what do you need to make your program?" I get out a paper and pen.

Ali gives in. "We have our computers and our disks with materials on them, but they don't work well with the sand here. We need external drives. We need a place to work, a desk, and pencils and we need time to write our program."

I write down each thing and together we make a new organizational list of how the groups should be run. I tell them, "Listen guys don't quit. I'll get you what you need. You can start writing tomorrow. Let me talk to Jim in the morning."

We spend another hour talking things through and just as we are gathering up our things to leave the mess hall, Ken, who left to have a smoke, suddenly reappears.

"Fuck!" he exclaims. "We are so fucked. We're locked in here!" It seems the night guard didn't realize we had stayed past our allotted time for training and he has locked us inside the mess hall. The doors are bolted shut as are the front doors and the only exit from the building is out to the yard where the food workers quarters and flush toilets are, surrounded by ten foot high cyclone fencing. We check our phones but none of us has reception to call outside.

"Fuck, we are going to have to sleep in here!" Ken says, kicking a chair. We look at each other and start to laugh.

"Let's go outside and have a look," I say and lead us out to the mess hall courtyard up to the back fence about one hundred yards past the toilets and sleeping quarters of the mess hall staff. "Look your tents are right over this fence," I say pointing out into the darkness. I pull on the gate, locked shut with a chain and padlock, but it does not give.

"Look, it's not that tall," I say. "We can climb it and slip over to the other side. The chain makes a good foothold. Somebody boost me up."

"Climb the fence?!" Ali cries out alarmed. "You forget we were just prisoners. Someone can get confused and we'll get shot!"

We all burst out laughing as we look around.

"Come on, it's not that tall and we can do it fast," I argue. "There's no one here."

Ken already has the idea and he climbs up, swings himself over and jumps to the other side. I'm next. Wathiq and Ali give me a boost and I am soon over as well, just a little less elegantly. Wathiq climbs over, and when Ali is just at the top of the fence, it suddenly occurs to me to take a photo.

"Wait," I call out and grab my camera. "We have to record this moment, the prisoner escaping Camp Bucca!" We all roar with laughter as I snap his picture posed on the top of the fence. I take two pictures and then he swings himself down. We laugh all the way back to the tent where we sit and talk a bit more and then turn in for bed. Ken walks me home along the boardwalks, past the big generators and to the pods. I'm exhausted and fall immediately asleep.

The next day I go to the office and speak with Jim. He is furious with me for agreeing to the trio's demands before talking to him.

"Why *wouldn't* we support them Jim?" I ask. "If we are going to work with the Takfiri hardcore we need them! They are the only ones who have credibility."

Jim throws up his hands in anger and slams one down hard on the table between us. Then he runs his hands through his hair moaning.

"And Jim, you think you can run a deradicalization program with a staff member who is threatening to have the Mahdi Army kill those we release?" I ask him. "It's bad enough the things Dr. Tahir has been saying about the trio. That is not professional and no way to run a team. I've kept silent about him, but what Madi has said is too much. You have to let him go."

"I'm sure he was joking!" Jim protests.

"Some jokes are not funny," I answer.

"We don't have enough psychologists then," Jim argues.

"And you want one that is threatening the detainees lives?" I ask. Jim is silent.

"External drives are a security issue," Rick says looking up from his monitor. "We are not allowed to give them to non-secure staff."

"You've got to be kidding!" I say, again confronted with the bureaucratic style of these two. "They want to write their program! They have computers already. What is a blank external drive going to do to threaten security here?" Rick just shakes his head.

"I'm sure there are solutions. And pencils and paper? Those can't be security risks! And a table to work at? You have them locked in their tent day and night! These are reasonable things they are asking for, guys!"

"There is no mention of desks in their contracts," Jim points out.

Okay this is how it's going to be, I think. "Listen guys, we can't have them quit. Give me the paper, pencils and whatever else you can and I'll figure out the rest. I'm going to tell them to start writing their program and that they don't need to train with us anymore. We don't have time to lose."

"You know I am committed to this program being a success," Jim says as he again throws his hands up in the air. Rick keeps his eyes glued to the monitor. I decide to leave it at that and go off to deliver supplies to the trio. Ken helps me find a large piece of wood and we flip over an unused bed frame to use as a base for the large table we build for the guys to work at in their tent. We help them set up their laptops and lay out their new supplies on it. Ken disappears for a bit and returns with three chairs for their makeshift desk.

"Where did you get these?" I ask.

"From the VIP dining hall," Ken answers laughing. "I took them outside and threw them over the fence we climbed last night. These are General Stone's contribution," Ken laughs—we all do.

After this, we go to the base PX and see if we can buy an external drive. They don't have them, but they sell laptop computers. Wathiq wonders if they should buy one to access their reference disks.

"Listen guys, don't spend your money on a laptop yet. These are things that the contractor should be providing for you. Let me work on getting the external drives for you, just start working with what you have for now." They agree and I see that the trio is back in business.

After another long day of training, we meet again to hang out in the recreation area of the base. I'm surprised the trio are all very good at playing pool—it doesn't fit with my idea of a conservative Salafi imam, but I'm finding that surprises are abundant where they are concerned. I try to take some photos but Wathiq intervenes, "No photos, Anne. In fact, we've been talking about the one you took on the fence and you've got to erase it."

"What? The prison escape photo? Why do you want me to erase it?"

"If anyone sees my face, I can be killed for working in this program," Ali says. "The sheiks we worked for are still in al Qaeda, and they'll hunt me down and my family too. It's too dangerous."

My laughter disappears like frost into the cold air as I listen, but I still can't destroy the photo. "Ali, you know how much I care about you. I can't erase the photo; it's one of the funniest moments of my life seeing you perched up on the fence like an escapee! But you have my word I won't ever do anything with it. You trust me don't you?"

Ali can't refuse and I get to keep the photo although it haunts me a bit having this responsibility.

Later when we sit down Wathiq shows me pictures of his ex-wife and baby son in Egypt, and his wife in Baghdad and their two small children, a boy and a girl. They are all very beautiful.

"My wife called me today from Baghdad," he says. "There was an explosion close to the house, it blew out all the windows and she was crying. It's really hot and the air conditioning is out and I know she's scared. She doesn't have anyone to fix the windows.

"You know we only had three days at home when they let us out of prison," he continues looking at their pictures. "We barely got to talk. Everyone came to see me and I just wanted to hold my daughter non-stop. My wife and her parents don't understand why I came here. Now some of her family thinks I'm working as a spy for the Americans. There wasn't any time and I couldn't explain it to her. I'm afraid they may pressure her to divorce me.

"My daughter clung to me the whole time I was home. I had to peel her off of me when I said goodbye and she couldn't understand why I was leaving when I only just got home." He rubs his forehead and looks pained with guilt.

"Wathiq, your family needs you and you can't do a good job here knowing that your wife is alone and doesn't even understand what you are doing. You have to take a week or two and go home and explain and make sure she's on board and fix the windows and make sure she's safe. Can you take them out of Iraq?" I ask.

"To where?" Wathiq asks. "You know with us there are issues of visas, and it's not easy to travel now."

"How about Jordan?" I ask. "When I leave I'm going to meet Princess Aisha in Amman. She knows about this program and she supports it. Maybe she can help get visas for them."

"No, Jordan is too dangerous. There are too many Iraqis there and some may know us," Wathiq answers.

We discuss Syria, Saudi and so on. "Listen Wathiq," I say. "There are solutions. We just have to find them. It sounds like you all have to get your families out and I'll help you as much as I can. But what you are describing is too much for one person to bear. I don't see how you can function at all. You have to go home and explain things to your wife and then you need to get them out of Baghdad and out of Iraq I think. We'll survive without you. This is important work but you have a family and you have to think about them first. We'll carry on."

"I can't go home," Wathiq says. "We are the trio. We decided we are in this together and we have to do this to save our country. I can't leave without the others."

I argue with him for a bit and see he won't budge. I talk to Ali about it, but he won't encourage Wathiq to go home. They are bonded in a strange way from their prison experience and previous lives together, and I see they are as loyal to each other and to the prison authorities and to the program that won them their freedom as they are to their own families. I decide to respect their bond and just be thankful for their sacrifices in behalf of our program.

"Okay," I say, "But no one's family is going to die on my watch. Please let me help you to get them out of Iraq."

I go to sleep that night furious with the contractors that they don't value the sacrifice and heroism of these three men who are willing to give so much to turn their country around. I think how few of us—General Stone, Colonel Kato, the trio and I—share this vision of changing Iraq by working through the detainees. I realize I am working in a microcosm of Iraq: the Sunni/Shia divide has entered Camp Bucca and infiltrated our contractor's staff as well. We have Dr. Tahir, Taha and the Americans—Jim, Rick and Susan—siding with the Shia and distrusting the very people who are willing to risk their lives and the lives of their loved ones to help us. And Omar, a Sunni, has thrown his hand in with the trio. Ken and I stand in the middle. I'm torn up by watching it play out and I thrash in my bed with frustration thinking about it.

The next morning, I gather Ken and the trio and say, "Let's go to the PX and buy a computer. We have to get this thing on track. This contractor is never going to come through with the external drives. I can pay for it if necessary."

"No," Wathiq says. "I need a new computer. I'll buy it." He shows me his Sony VIAO, another surprise, to see him with the latest small model I would love to have myself. "It's not working," he explains, "Do you think you can ask if there is anyone here who can take a look at it?"

"Yes of course." I answer taking it.

That day General Stone and Colonel Kato arrive back to Camp Bucca and tell me I will have to leave with them in two days if I want to exit the camp by air.

In the meantime, I check with Jim and Rick about getting Wathiq's computer fixed and they say no one can look at it, even though I am sure there are techie guys galore on the base. I understand the limits of crossing lines between contractors and the military but I know most computer guys are pretty generous with their free time if they are convinced the cause is good.

I see Colonel Kato in the mess at lunch and ask him if he can get it fixed.

"Take it back to the U.S. with you and get it fixed and then you can mail it to back to me through the military mail and I'll give it to them," the Colonel answers. I wonder if he realizes that he has just advised me to take an electronic device given to me directly by a former al Qaeda operative through security checkpoints to the U.S. not to mention mailing it back to him via military mail. I imagine entering the airplane security checks answering their questions about any items I may have been asked to carry while having no idea what is on the hard drive of the AQ computer I'm carrying. The bizarre has come to seem second nature at Camp Bucca so I just laugh to myself and say, "Okay, will do."

I continue wrapping up the training but my two weeks are almost finished. Danny, our fourteen year old, is supposed to be flying back to Brussels from his friend's house in Finland and will arrive home soon. I need to make sure that he knows that he has to take a taxi home and that his older sister will be in charge of him for a day until I get there. The only way to use my phone is to stand outside of the FOB in a certain corner to catch a signal, but in the last three days I can't get an international phone signal anywhere with either my Belgian phone nor my Iraqna one. Finally I get through to my husband and ask him to call Danny.

"Anne I can't do it," he says. "It's really tense here. I can't discuss it over the phone but something bad is going to happen today in Baghdad. I'm still packing up and I leave in a few hours. I have to hurry and get to the helicopter to fly out of here!" I keep trying to phone Danny and when I finally reach him, I call Dan back to let him know it's taken care of, but I can't get reach him. I go back to the FOB to check my e-mails and see news that the IZ has had one of the worst mortar attacks yet, with sixty mortars hitting inside the IZ, all right outside the U.S. embassy. Dan's container is there, as well as the walkway known as "death alley" for the many mortar hits it gets.

I feel the icy chill of panic. Dan is exitingIraq today and there's a good chance that he may have been exposed to the mortar fire out on the helo pad. I have a horrible pit in my stomach imagining him surviving two years in Iraq, flying all around the country, only to be killed while leaving on his last day of work. It would be too ironic. I go outside and search for a signal and finally find one, but I cannot reach Dan. I go back inside and ask the FOB commander, an Admiral for help. "I'm sorry to bother you, Admiral but I can't reach my husband, the deputy Ambassador at the U.S. Embassy in Baghdad. There's been a big mortar shower at the embassy and I know he's outside today. I need to call the embassy on the DSN line. Can you help me with that?"

"Sure," he answers.

"Can you give me the embassy number in Baghdad?" I ask. "I don't have it with me. I always call his mobile, but he's not answering now."

I'm completely stupefied to hear they don't have the number to the U.S. Embassy Baghdad.

"You must have a general number to the embassy?" I ask.

"No," his staffersanswer with blank looks, "We never call there."

"How about a directory or an operator who can give us the number?" I persist.

"No, the only directory we have is a military one, and there's no operator," they answer.

"Maybe you can Google it?" one of the staffers suggests.

Google it?! How can I be in a headquarters of one of the best militaries in the world and they don't know how to reach their own Ambassador in country?! I think.

I take the staffer's advice and Google the U.S. Embassy Baghdad and get over six thousand hits. I try to narrow the search but I cannot find anything. Worse, all the stories that come up first are headlines telling about the worst day of mortar fire in the IZ, listing three Americans as critically wounded and thirty Iraqis killed in the attack. I fight panic and keep searching. Finally the Admiral's staff finds a number for the military attaché in the embassy. I call and explain to him who I am and that my husband is the Deputy Ambassador. He puts me through and Damon Wilson, Dan's chief of staff, answers my call.

"Damon!" I call out frantically. "This is Anne! I heard about the mortar attack today. Is Daniel alright?"

"Yes, Anne. His helicopter lifted off about two hours before they hit. He is safely out of range," Damon answers.

"I'm so glad to hear it! I knew he would be outside today on the helo pad and I was sick when I heard about the mortar fire today. And then I couldn't reach him."

"He's fine, Anne," Damon says, but I can hear his voice is choked with emotions. Suddenly I realize he may have friends among the dead and wounded.

"Damon, are you alright? Are you guys okay?" I ask.

"It's pretty bad, we had Americans hit," Damon says his voice still thick with emotion. "I can't discuss it over the phone, but we're okay."

"Damon, I'm so sorry!" I say, ashamed that my focus has been solely the safety of my husband.

"I have to sign off, Anne," Damon says. "It's crazy busy here. But thanks for calling." I want to reach out and hug him through the phone but there's nothing I can do.

After I hang up I return to the outer office to tell the Admiral and his staff that Dan is safe. Susan is standing nearby and snipes from the sidelines, "Well, Anne, I thought you and your husband were against this war. I don't see why you would care if there are Americans wounded in the IZ."

I turn to Susan, stunned. "Susan, I've just spent the last two hours wondering if my husband is killed! Do you mean what you're saying?" She stares back at me coldly, anger blazing in her eyes. "My husband and I may not have been supporters of this war, but all the same my husband served in Iraq for two whole years and I supported him during that time. We have both made huge sacrifices for this effort." I look up at the Admiral and his staff and they looked as dumbfounded as me and embarrassed by her outburst.

Susan turns on her heels and leaves and one of them comes to me and says, "I'm glad he's okay, ma'am. Really I am." After listening to their kind words clearly intended to negate her attack, I walk back to my pod and sit stunned staring at the walls, tears burning in my eyes. I can take everything else, but the hatred inside our team is too much.

After a bit, I walk to the guys' tent and talk with them. "What did you expect?" Ali says. "You know these contractors are not normal."

"Toughen up, Anne," Ken laughs and puffs on his cigarette. "She's just stupid, and the most important thing is that Dan's okay."

After some time Susan emerges from her tent across the way and I get up and walk over to her to see if I can bring some sort of closure to the insult, "Susan," I begin, "I was really blown away by what you said inside the FOB earlier. I know emotions run high here, and I just wanted to check, did you really mean what you said?"

Susan looks me squarely in the eyes while wringing out a shirt she has just washed. As she hangs it to dry on the rope holding her tent steady, she answers coldly, "I meant exactly what I said." Then she turns and goes back inside her tent leaving me speechless again.

The next day at lunch Ali tells me that they still don't have their hard drives and it's time to bow out.

"Colonel Kato is here," I point out. "Let me go and talk to him and make sure we are on the right track. I'm sure he meant it when he promised you reference books and the other things you need."

I go over to Colonel Kato's tableand explain the situation.

"Listen, Anne," Colonel Kato tells me. "As far as I'm concerned you and Ali are in charge on this program. This contractor has been problem after problem, but let's be absolutely clear, you are in charge of the psychological side and he's in charge of the Islamic side."

"Okay, great!" I say relieved that we have Colonel Kato behind us.

"How about the things they need to write their side of the program, Islamic reference books, external drives and so on?" I ask.

"I don't see any problem with that," Colonel Kato tells me.

Elated I go back to the trio and tell them the news. The guys are all really happy and we each return to our respective tasks.

But when the external drives still do not materialize, Wathiq is angry and Jim and Rick do not seem at all willing to support the trio's efforts developing the Islamic program further.

"Don't you have a program already from the London sheiks?" Jim asks.

"Yes," I say, "but it's in English so they can't read it and besides that, these guys know the prisoners and they know what will work and what is dangerous. If they rewrite and run it their way, it will be right for here, I'm sure.

"Listen, when you are assigning detainees to the groups," I say, turning to Rick, "Ali and I want to put together a group of Takfiri that we work together on when I return. Together we think we can crack them."

"I'm not sure the military is going to give them to us," he says. Rickhas been going over who will be admitted to our program and the military is not even sure who is moderate and who is hardcore when they assign prisoners over to our program, so it's looking difficult to know how to form the groups. We are slated to begin in one week so this is a huge problem.

I have only one more day in Camp Bucca before I leave for a month to work on the program from a distance. It's evening and the trio come to talk with me again about everything that is being put in place.

Are you sure you can't stay and help get the program going?" Ali asks. "I don't think it's going to work here without you."

I know he's right but I answer, "I'd like to Ali, but my husband has been working here for two years now and he comes home this week. I have to be there to bring our family back together. It's not right for me to stay here. I already extended my trip so I'm not there when he returns home, and I don't want to hurt him after two years of being gone. I also don't want to hurt my children's feelings. I'm a mother," I explain.

"I'll be in daily contact by e-mail and I will coach the psychologists on everything. And Khapta will be in Iraq in two more weeks and will come here after stopping at Camp Cropper. You are going to love her, Ali. She's a very good psychologist, and she's Muslim. She will supervise."

"I don't think it's going to work with this contractor," Wathiq says. "We can't work with them."

"We need you to stay," Ali says. "What about the replacement for Madi? Jim has let him go finally and not found a replacement. "Who is going to be with me in my group with the hardcore? I need you."

I know he's right. I've seen the psychologists in role-plays and I know they will fail and Khapta won't be coming soon enough. I am wracked with guilt no matter which I choose.

It midnight already. I get my phone and find a signal nearby the port-a-potties. Dan answers.

"Dan I don't think I can come home. I worked so hard on this and it's ready to roll out but I think it will fall apart if I leave. I don't know what to do. I think I need to stay for another month just to get it going." The crackly linekeeps cutting out and I have to call him again and again as I explain.

"Stay for another month?" I hear the shock in his voice. He is silent a minute and then says, "I'm okay with it, but the kids won't be." He has always supported me that way and is emotionally very self-sufficient. He was fine during his two years in Iraq, except for the stress it caused the rest of us. "What about our summer plans and reuniting the family?" he asks.

"I don't know," I say, lost.

"And Jessica's move to Paris? You are not going to be there for that?" The line cuts out and then I cannot get him back on the phone. I have never knowingly made a decision that I thought was bad for my children. I've stressed them by traveling, especially when their father was in Iraq, but I always watched their limits carefully and tried my best to match my need to have a career with their needs to have a stable and nurturing mother beside them. I try repeatedly to call back over the next two hours, but the signal is not strong enough.

I finally go and get my things to wash up and walk down to the latrines. *I can't leave,* I realize as I see the prison brightly lit up in the darkness. *There are twenty thousand men inside the prison and some have been here for four years!* I know that I can make a huge difference about their fates. *I have to stay.* I look in the mirror as I wash my face and begin to cry. The tears fall freely as I splash water again and again on my face. I then hop in the shower and wash my hair and rinse the sand and the long day's stress off my body, the tears still falling. I dress and plod through the rocks back to the corner of my pod "street". It's four a.m. and the sun is already rising. It's beautiful lighting the sky with an orange glow. I dial Dan again and the call finally goes through.

"I've decided," I tell him. "I have to stay." He's good about it so we don't talk much more. "I'll leave as soon as things are stable here. Maybe it won't take a whole month."

"Okay," he says. The signal is bad and the line keeps cutting out so I give up trying to call him back again. There is nothing more to say. I walk back to my pod, go inside, climb into bed and cry myself to sleep.

The alarm goes off in two hours. I'm groggy but I snap to attention and hurry off to the mess hall where I see Jim. "We need to talk," I tell him steering him over to a table.

"Yes, General Stone is leaving at threep.m. so you have to be ready to go," Jim tells me.

"Jim, I'm not going," I say once we are both seated, facing each other. "I'm going to stay."

"What? " Jim asks.

"Jim, the program is going to fall apart. The psychologists you hired are not experienced, Ken doesn't have any real clinical experience with trauma, you say Khapta is needed in Cropper first to work with the juveniles and the trio is about to quit. I have to stay to supervise and help Ali in his group and make sure the program runs," I explain.

"Are you talking about being in the sessions?" Jimasks his voice squeaky with shock.

"Yes, of course," I answer. "Without Madi, I have to stay. There is no one else who can do it."

"You can't be in the sessions!" Jimfires backhis eyes wide and his face panicked. "You're an Ambassador's wife. You think I'm going to take responsibility for putting you in a room with ten detainees!"

"Jim, what do you think I've been doing all this time when I was in the prison interviewing detainees? I'm not afraid."

"I am!" Jim answers. "You can't go in the sessions, Anne! No way! They might find out who you are and try to kill you! Somebody could knife you or strangle you or God knows what and then we'd have a scandal!" Jim takes his napkin and wipes the perspiration forming on his forehead.

"You didn't think I was going to join the sessions a month from now? I plan to bein them. Jim, it's the only way to supervise well." I can't believe how far apart our visions are of this program.

"No you cannot go in the sessions, it's too dangerous," he says, resolute. "And you wanted to fly out of here. In a month I may not have air transport. You have to go today with General Stone."

Softening my voice, and looking into his eyes I ask him, "Jim do you understand what I'm offering you? I don't particularly want to stay. It's been one of the hardest decisions of my life, but I know you need me.

These psychologists aren't equipped. Look at them, they are like young students. And you are going to lose the trio. Ali wants me on his team to take the hardcore. Omar cannot do it without supervision."

Jim is speechless and throws up his hands in anger finally. "No you cannot stay!" he shouts in exasperation. "It isn't the plan. You were scheduled to be out of here after two weeks and that's it! You are leaving today with General Stone and coming back in a month! I not even sure I have a pod for you if you did stay," he continues softening his voice and shaking his head. "You have to go. Just go home, be with your husband and let me figure out how to solve the problems and come back in a month like planned. I'll get Khapta down here earlier if I have to."

"Can you?" I ask, elated at the possibility that there is a solution that does not require me to stay. And I'm beginning to think maybe it's better if I leave. I will be going back with General Stone and he's already invited me to have dinner with him in Cropper. I'll be able to spend the time with him to tell him what the problems are and get the trio what they need to do their part of the program and to get things back into shape from the command down to the contractor. I decide to give in.

"Okay, Jim, I'll go back today," I say with relief flooding over me that I won't be disappointing my husband and children. "But we have to stay in daily e-mail contact and we have to solve the problems with the trio. You have to support them, Jim, and you have to get Khapta down here as soon as she arrives."

"Okay, I promise," he says clearly relieved that I won't be joining the sessions with the detainees in the next week.

Later that day I see Colonel Kato in the FOB foyer. "Can you do me a favor Colonel? Can you go and talk to Jim and Rick and make it clear that you want Ali in charge of the Islamic program working alongside of me running the psychological program? They keep fighting him on taking the lead and we have to support them or they are going to quit on us. And can you tell them to give them the external drives they need and get them the reference books you promised them? I have a list from the trio and I'm going to shop for them in Amman. If I find them we can ask the contractor to get them ordered, right?"

"Yes give them everything they need," Colonel Kato answers without hesitation.

"Can you tell that to Jim and Rick?" I ask. "I think they really need to hear that from you."

"Okay, I'll do it right now," he says turning and marching resolutely toward the contractor's office door. He puts his hand on the knob and then just as suddenly he turns, marches back to me and says, "Come to think of it, it's better if you tell them. Just tell them it's a direct order from Colonel Kato." And as he walks off he adds, "Make sure when you get to Camp Cropper you tell this to Steve, too." I am dumbfounded as he walks out the door. I have little time before I have to leave and go directly to Rick and convey what Colonel Kato just told me.

Rick leans forward and pushes his fingers together, "Colonel Kato said *that*?"

"Yes," I say hoping that we won't have any more conflict.

"Well he's out of his lane," Rick answers.

"His lane?" I ask.

"Yes his lane," Rick says smiling wryly. "We'll see about this."

Only much later do I realize that the military assigns only one person to be the contracting officer and that no one else in the military can give orders to the contractor through any other channel, or "lane". Somehow I have missed "contracting etiquette 101", trespassed totally on Major Thompson's territory as the contracting officer and Rick is now in an impossible position. Major Thompson has also bought into the contractor's fear factor and does not trust the trio as well. As a result he will not be giving permission to give them what they need. A storm is brewing between the trio, the military and contractor but I have seen only the thunderheads, not the lightening yet.

CHAPTER 68

Lightening Strikes

Upon leaving, I fly by helicopter with Raheema to the Basra Air Base, where we board a flight to Baghdad. It's basically a boring ride, but I notice that some people are still wearing their full protective gear. I begin to sleep when suddenly the plane dives and maneuvers right and left, dipping up and down. Everyone is jolted awake and hangs on while we take what I think is heavy turbulence. Minutes later we land in Baghdad International Airport. I am shocked to learn from Raheema that the plane was trying to out-maneuver rifle fire.

"You should have been wearing your flak jacket, Anne," she scolds. "The bullets can penetrate the plane and they were shooting right at us."

Later, General Stone tells me the plane *was* pierced by two bullets. I don't know how to feel, as it's already over, but I'm a bit perturbed that my flak jacket had no plates and no one bothered to tell me to wear it or my helmet.

General Stone has a driver waiting for him and I travel with him to a cozy mess hall. We have a good talk about the problems and needs of the program.

"You think we can really turn them? I need to be sending detainees home and I want to know we are not going to meet them back on the battlefield," he asks.

"Yes," I answer. "As long as we get good supervision for the psychologists and the imams are credible. The Salafi ones are the only ones that the hardcore are going to give the time of day to, so you have to keep the trio on board," I explain.

"The Salafi are the global jihadis, aren't they?" he asks.

I cannot believe we have gone so far on this program and he still doesn't understand these basics.

"No General Stone, Salafis are the conservative Muslims who go back to the fundamentals of the Prophet and his companions. They dress, eat and try to emulate the Prophet's and early companion's lives and they take seriously only the Koran and hadiths attributed to them. Jihadis claim to be Salafi but they are only a small subset. If we have a well-educated moderate Salafi imam talk to them, he can challenge them and show them where they are not following the Koran and the hadiths. This, along with a good psychological program, is what can turn them. If they cannot justify their violence in Islam anymore, and if we address their traumas, grievances and other reasons why they believe violence is the best answer, then we can release them with confidence."

We finish our meal and General Stone stands. "I'll drop you off. We got you a room tonight, no more barracks for you," he says smiling kindly. We part at the hotel with a warm hug and I tell him, "I'll be back in a month; be safe."

The hotel is one of Saddam's converted palaces, the same one that I tried to get myself checked into on my first trip into Camp Cropper. *I got in!* I laugh to myself. My room has two bunks and six twin beds spread about it for ten occupants but no one is here. I choose a bed and lay my things out on it. I take my time in the shower and think about how luxurious a porcelain toilet seems after the horrible port-a-potties in Bucca. Finally I put on my nightie, robe and thongs and walk back to my room. I am just in bed and falling asleep when the door opens.

A petite woman in military fatigues drags a heavy military pack in the door and slides it across the floor. She fumbles about in the dark as I say, "You can turn on the light."

"You sure?" she asks.

"Yes," I say dreamily. "I was just falling asleep, but it's fine."

The soldier flips on the overhead lamp and introduces herself. It turns out she is the head doctor in charge of military mental health in Iraq. I sit up in my bed eager to hear what she has to say. I tell her a bit about myself and that I've been working with NATO conducting a resilience study of military and diplomats to working in the high threat security environment of Iraq.

"I could qualify for that study!" she says. We had mortar here two days ago and we've had them all summer long. I only have four more months to go and I'm outta here. I have to get home to my son!"

I feel like someone has kicked me in the gut as she begins describing in gory details what happened during the latest mortar attack. I know Dan missed the mortar storm by only hours and now I'm talking to someone who was in it. I tell her about my worries that day and we compare notes for about an hour. It's obvious she is in a high arousal state as she continues to animatedly describe her posttraumatic recall long after I stop responding and eventually I fall asleep.

The alarm goes off early and I meet Raheema, who is taking me to the airport. She tells me that I should propose to the head contractors that Jim be replaced.

"We need a new manager," she says, adding, "Do you have any idea how much this contractor is making off of this program? Why don't you offer to run it?" Then she tells me that Colonel Kato is making her life a living hell, that he screams and hollers and throws tantrums anytime she leaves the office and is totally and completely dependent on her being beside him every minute. I wonder if he has regressed to a frightened child state and needs her to mother him. *We are operating a high-level security program in a looney bin!* I think to myself. But I give her a kiss and hug and promise to do my best to try to address all the problems from stateside.

I soon make my way to Amman, where Princess Aisha cancels our meeting, and the next day I start my homeward journey to the U.S. where my family is waiting. I begin to realize I took so much of the trauma I heard and experienced in Iraq onboard and that it is going to race back into my mind until I too work through it all.

The stewardess offers alcohol and I accept everything she brings as I get out my notepad and begin to write. I want to capture all that went on in Iraq while it's still fresh in my mind. As I write, I keep drinking, trying to block out the overwhelming emotions that come with. Finally my hand tires and I fall into an inebriated sleep, glad to shut it all out.

Back in the U.S. , I find that my body has returned home, but my mind has not—especially not at night. The nightmares are overwhelming: the faces, stories, the emotional impressions—all playing themselves out like a movie that I witness firsthand.

In Bucca, I was there for the staff who needed my help. I kept my own emotions at bay and just listened to theirs and witnessed their traumas. I work by opening my boundaries and letting things in. It makes me very good at what I do, but it means I feel what they feel and they sense it in my responses, in the questions I ask, in how I move, and respond to them. But afterwards, it's my turn to process it all and let it painfully pass through me.

Other things eat at me as well. Maybe it's knowing that there is fear, distrust and maybe even hatred in our team and that the Shia members may indeed "out" the trio in a way that will result in their families literally being slaughtered. I've spoken to Princess Aisha about it and she agreed to help with visas but it's more complicated than simply that, and the contractors say it's not their responsibility. It's not, but where is the line one draws when it comes to protecting your staff's children and wives from being murdered? They don't seem to care, but I feel it deeply and it haunts me nightly. Additionally, I feel some kind of posttraumatic survivor's guilt. I'm in safety but the staff I've trained are not.

The nightmares abruptly stop after two weeks, and I feel immense relief to have passed through that psychological torture. I continue to e-mail Steve, Jim and Rick from the contractor's staff about the program, but Rick does not answer any of my posts, Jim doesn't seem to know what to answer and Steve is too far removed from it to give any good feedback. I begin to wonder what has happened after our discussion about Colonel Kato's "direct order" to support the trio and give Ali the lead on delivering the Islamic challenge.

When Sheik Abdul Azeem arrives in Bucca from the UK also to help, I hear from Ken that the divisions become even deeper. To satisfy the organizational chart agreed upon with the military early on, Jim has put Sheik Azeem in the lead position, rather than Ali—despite the fact that Sheik Azeem will not be staying long in Iraq, has failed to produce any useful materials and does not seem to have concrete ideas of how to proceed with the Islamic challenge. I know he has talked a few London extremists out of going on jihad, but I don't think he can be as successful as the trio at actually confronting the Takfiri terrorists active in the prison.

According to Ken, Sheik Abdul Azeem has also become an irritant to Ali and the trio by asking them if they need any advice on Islam, and the team is now further divided. Khapta has also arrived in theater but as she is a Chechen, it takes a long time to process all her papers and she will be delayed in arriving to Camp Bucca. And we have lost another psychologist, as Shafikhas gone to Camp Cropper to work with the juveniles.

When the program starts up, I begin to hear reports from the ground. Omar tells me that the detainees love the guided imageries and beg to repeat the one that takes them on a fantasy flight in which they escape prison and go back home where they can "see, hear, smell and touch" loved ones and their house. It's designed to make leaving prison very tangible and thereby re-instill a desire in emotionally numb prisoners to participate fully. It sounds like it might have worked too well and the detainees are desperate to escape into it.

Shafik writes from Camp Cropper and tells me things are going very well, and when Khapta begins work on the program from Camp Cropper, I feel things are finally coming together.

Ali writes and tells me to hurry back to Camp Bucca because he has some serious Takfiris in his group and that one of them told him that he needs to see the psychologist—he can't handle the things he's done and he is having nightmares. It tells me we designed the program correctly to come at things from both the psychological and religious angles. I try to coach Ali to work with the posttraumatic material but he doesn't have regular access to the e-mail and psychological treatment is not something he's comfortable with so he feels alone, unsupported and demoralized.

The relationship between the contractor and the trio continues to be a major problem. I email Rick, but don't realize he has changed his e-mail address and my requests are never received. Then, Ali writes on behalf of the trio, saying they are totally fed up and are going to quit. I talk them down and then write immediately to Colonel Kato, General Stone and to the head of the contracting firm, still ignorant of the "lanes" that govern contract work with the military.

General Stone responds immediately, of course, and the contractor is furious that I have alerted General Stone and Colonel Kato. The irony of the whole thing becomes even more clear when I learn that General Stone's phone call triggers Steve, the head contractor to fly down to Camp Bucca and talk to the trio, who tell him they are *not* quitting—but they only say this because I talked them into staying calm.

The head contractor, even more angered by this, calls me while I'm in a business lunch and tells me curtly, "We don't need your services anymore." It's like a bolt of lightening out of a clear sky and I am stunned. *I've just been let go from the project I brought from an idea into a well-designed, trained and now about to be fully implemented program. The problems with the trio have been because Jim doesn't know how to manage, Rick has been out of communication, and neither of them understand what drives militant jihadi terrorism or how to address it and therefore do not appreciate their most valuable asset: the three former al Qaeda prisoners who are willing to help them confront the hardest core of all the prisoners. Likewise the military is not clearly communicating what they want from the contractor and giving mixed messages between us, causing this conflict. I have fought long and hard with this contracting staff to birth this program out of nothing and now they have fired me from my own program!*

I fully expect Colonel Kato and General Stone to back me up. They are the ones who asked me to design this program for them. Though they hired me through a contractor that didn't give me any real authority over the program's implementation, I have felt and acted all along that the military was my client and worked closely with both of them.

I communicate with both General Stone and Colonel Kato by e-mail but both are unable to do anything much to address the problems. Colonel Kato writes once fearfully saying he will take care of the trio but as the rules of military to contractor relationships finally become clear for me, I realize that he has seriously violated contractor rules and placed me in an impossible position every time he told me to relay his "direct orders" and straighten out the contractor. When I consult with a lawyer, I learn that I can insist that no one use my written product—which is the entire program—without my approval to transfer copyright to them and receipt of compensation, but I know that will likely mean shutting the whole program down until the military goes through a complicated process of sorting out what has happened. I can't let that happen. It would be killing my own creation. As I try to address the problems with the contractor and get myself briefly reinstated, the pilot program successfully finishes and the contractor is awarded the next contract to carry the full program forward. I know that they will make millions of dollars running a program that I have designed and written for them, but I decline to file a lawsuit, issue a complaint to the contracting office or demand an inquiry of Colonel Kato's behavior that had put me in the middle of such a mess because more than anything else, I want the program to go forward. I risked my life setting it up and I don't want to kill it now.

It's like the fresh air after a thunderstorm when my son points, "It'll be good to have you at home, Mom. Don't fight it." I look into his eyes, hug him close and think, *Maybe, if I let it run without me and hope for the best we will find some success in fighting terrorism.*

CHAPTER 69

Deradicalization - Does it Work?

Aside from getting fired from my own program, I remained intensely curious and hopeful that our deradicalization program in Iraq would
work. Saudi diplomats at the U.S. embassy in New York admitted to me
that success with their programs was minimal, saying that only those in
the initial stages of radicalization were being reached and that they were
having trouble turning the "hardcore". This conclusion was also reported by U.S. researchers and journalists working with the religious education ministry,[293] and it became news when both Saudi and Yemen had
serious failures when severe militants were released after taking part in
their programs and re-emerged as foreign fighters in Iraq (in the case of
Yemen) and active al Qaeda leaders in Yemen and elsewhere (in the case
of Saudi).[294]

The hardcore militant jihadis are likely hard to reach with Islamic
challenge alone because most have seeped themselves in Takfiri ideology, absorbing enough of Islamic scriptures to justify their actions and
rebuff challenges from even well-educated Salafi imams. My addition
of a psychological approach held the possibility of breaking through to
them because they do not have well-honed defenses to their psychological
weaknesses.

In Iraq I did not have continued access to our program to analyze
its results directly, but Ken, Khapta and most of the staff I had trained
remained in place, and the trio were later mollified into returning and
running what was named the Religious Enlightenment Program—their
part of our original design.

The Detainee Rehabilitation Program that I had designed and written with the help of Siraat, Khapta and our team for the military (via the
contractor) was instituted in September of 2007. Well over ten thousand
detainees went through some version of the program. While the original
intent had been for intensive Islamic challenge and psychological group
interventions all day, daily for six weeks, alongside the military's educa-

tional programs in literacy, citizenship and skills training to increase employment prospects after release, the pressures on the U.S. government from the government of Iraq and elsewhere to release detainees rarely made that a real possibility for the majority of detainees. And because it was estimated that nearly eighty percent of the detainees were not ideologically committed to the militant jihadi ideology, most went through a very pared down program. According to Ken, the non-ideologically committed detainees were often released after only going through a four-day program! I had and still have the burning question as I sat by as my program churned out thousands of detainees for release: Did it work? And if not, why not? And if so, what were the elements of success that could enhance a future effort?

For its part, the military tracked recidivism as its main marker of the various programs' success and by that standard there *was* success: there was an extremely low recidivism rate following the release of more than ten thousand detainees. Yet, that does not necessarily mean the program worked, as one can imagine that a once-imprisoned militant would know a lot more after being released to evade a further arrest. And in postwar, still poorly-governed Iraq, released detainees that remained committed to militant jihadi violence could leave the country or lay low and hide, to return to their activities another day.

Moreover, in terms of measuring any success from a program that was not applied uniformly across the entire detainee population, nor well instituted with a well-trained and equipped staff, one must also give a great deal of credit to the greatly changing political situation occurring at the time in Iraq; while Zarkawi, the emir of AQ in Iraq, was eager to kill Shia mainstream Iraqis en masse and often used targeted attacks to stir the sectarian strife, Iraqis were fatigued from sectarian fighting and suffering explosions anywhere, anytime.[295] And those Sunnis who had turned to and embraced al Qaeda and similar ideologies at the start of the U.S. invasion, were already deeply disillusioned with the rampant killings of Iraqi civilians and the conservative interpretation of Islam that al Qaeda was forcing upon their population by 2007. Iraqis, who had previously lived in a secular and much more open society, did not welcome Sharia law, women wearing chadors or the Takfir declarations that justified beheadings, explosions in civilian markets, etc. And much of Baghdad and surrounding territory that had been disputed had also by then been separated by sectarian fighting and even by U.S. installed checkpoints. Likewise, U.S. forces were readying to exit so there was no longer a strong incentive to support insurgency against the foreign forces in Iraq.

So when the U.S. military helped create and fund Sunni Awakening groups to resist al Qaeda in Iraq, whole areas that had been AQ strongholds were changing and AQ operatives no longer found safe harbor. The tribal leaders who joined the Awakening movement as well as many others not active in it, certainly signaled to the newly released detainees that further activity against U.S. forces and the government of Iraq would neither be encouraged or tolerated.

The fact that massive detainee releases were happening at the same time as all these political changes raises the question: Was the rehabilitation program responsible for turning the hearts of those released *or* were the massive changes in the communal and tribal structure of society responsible for keeping them from rejoining AQ and related militant groups? In my mind, the greatly shortened nature of the program and the release of mainly non-ideologically committed detainees makes the latter the most probable conclusion.

When I asked those who remained with the program if they thought it worked and why, they answered differently. Ken pointed out there was far less rioting in the prison, a problem that had plagued Camp Bucca the summer before I arrived, although Cheryl Benard, a researcher at RAND, noted that some of the extremists in Camp Bucca rioted upon learning that the military was instituting an Islamic challenge program.[296] It's unclear to me if the general decrease in rioting occurred with the onset of our program because it was effective or because the prisoners finally understood that taking part in the program was their stepping stone into release.

One area in which the program certainly succeeded was where the military (under General Stone and Colonel Kato) clearly conveyed to the detainees what was required for them for release, including an appearance before the Multi National Forces Reconciliation Committee (MNFRC) board where their incarceration and crimes would be discussed. For detainees who on average spent three hundred and thirty days incarcerated,this sense of having some control and predictability over their futures, rather than being what the Palestinians called "open check" prisoners, was likely heartening. Likewise referring to when the massive releases of detainees occurred Ken noted, "There's also a big psychological effect on the detainees seeing the 'happy bus' pull up, fill up and leave." In my mind these things could lead to a decrease in rioting just as easily as the actual contents of the program.

When detainees appeared before the MNFRC boards the detainees were expected to own up to their crimes and give some display of regret, which Ken felt was, in part, for the military to learn how good their intel was—to check back to the original reports and see that things matched. In that regard, Ken added that the reports were sometimes also missing data that was important for the board to know, so it was important for the military guys to check back with their colleagues to see if the detainees were saying what actually had happened.

At that time the Human Terrain project had also started up, a novel program in which the military began embedding anthropologists, linguistic and cultural experts to help them understand the "human terrain" that they were encountering in the battlefield.[297] These experts would brief the court on the "human terrain" of a detainee's area before he arrived, suggesting whether his crime made sense given what was going on there at the time. For the MNFRC boards, these expert reports were extremely useful and judged a big success according to Ken, who often worked with these teams.

"Honesty was what the MNFRC Boards wanted and they were very willing to forgive and forget if you, as a detainee, cooperated [in giving a full confession] and had good behavior." Ken recalls pointing out to the U.S. military that owning up to one's shortcomings may not be as important for reconciliation in eastern cultures and among Arabs as saving face is. Ken felt it was very difficult for Arabs who live in an honor society where guilt is communal and saving face is paramount, to view admissions of guilt in the same way.

"I remember a young detainee entering our room to get processed before his MNFRC Board. My team went through their well-rehearsed line of questioning, but besides being younger than most of the detainees, he just didn't want to talk. As my team spoke to him he said that Coalition Forces had killed his parents. My team extended their sympathies and probed for more details to correspond with their Human Terrain Data Map, but he shut down. As the detainee left the room, where he would wait for five to ten minutes outside while my team briefed the Board with his SITREP [situation report], I entered the room to help my guys organize their thoughts. They told me what he said and how he was acting. If he was like that with us, chances are he was going to completely shut down in the courtroom. So I took Ammar, one of the interpreters I worked with and went outside to chat with him, to see if I could pick up on anything which could further explain his circumstance in terms of his well-being at the time but also the activities happening in his home town. Combining these two variables would be our brief to the MNFRC Board, assisting them in their decision about release. I began by telling him how sorry I was that his parents had been killed, how distraught he must have felt and how horrible situations like that will bring out the worst in a person, etc. Time was of the essence here, we were essentially holding up the whole process by overshooting our allotted time and the guards were making it known [the courts were waiting for the brief]. The detainee told me how it wasn't fair and how somebody approached him to store weapons at his parents' farm. This, we knew from our human terrain information, was a typical modus operandi for the group operating in the area. They convinced him to take revenge and he did. He also got caught. I told him that this had to be told to the court. That their function was to get his story and that he has to tell it, that it's the right thing to do. He did and the board recommended him for release. Turns out his parents deaths weren't in the MNFRC report . . .This poor kid had never told anyone that his parents and siblings had been killed, he just assumed they knew."

The program set up to culminate in a "confession" and words of regret could also be ethically problematic in terms of coercion because it could lead to panicked confessions when a detainee learned he was about to be turned over to the Iraqis.

"I remember one guy, a red Qaeda guy," Ken recalls. I was processing him on human terrain before his court. He was shitting bricks because he had been told that he'd be handed to the Iraqi's. He said he'd confess to anything (after years of confessing to nothing) so even though he said yes to all counts, it couldn't be trusted because he'd always said no, thinking he'd be released anyway. The Iraqi's don't take to kindly to Sunni extremism and he knew hell was waiting for him. He was handed over to the Iraqi's and worst of all, because he confessed, they got those confessions too . . ."

This was actually something I had worked hard to train our staff to avoid. I didn't want to have our program be a means of eliciting confessions that then were used to turn detainees who could be shown to be guilty over to the Iraqis for convictions. In this case the confession occurred outside our specific program and because the detainee believed it could save him.

A constant issue that plagued the prison staff even before Rohan, Mohammed and I arrived to consult with the military is that the military could not clearly identify who among their prisoners were the militant jihadi ideologues and recruiters and who also was becoming radicalized inside the prison.

Ken wrote, 'In prison they'd radicalize. I always wondered if that's when the leaders would say [to the presumably non-radicalized and easily-released detainees], 'Now go and confess, leave the prison and do X, Y and Z for me outside.' That's a pretty good reason to confess—to get out to do worse shit." Indeed unless the imams and psychologists in our program were spending enough time and clinically good enough to detect who was misrepresenting, we could have no idea when a confession and "rehabilitation" was genuine or faked. My view was if our staff was good it would be possible in the six weeks program to detect most of the time, but far less likely when the staff was so poorly trained and the contact with the detainees was sometimes limited to only four days.

And when massive detainee releases were done in a hurried manner, like when pushed by a public affairs campaign to coincide with Ramadan or Eid, the military would release green guys presumed to be non-radicalized en masse.

"This caused an uproar, especially with the CIA folk and the interrogators," Ken said. "They believed that some of the green guys were actually red [radicalized] but because they had so many to process and such little time and staff, they weren't able to make sure and next thing they knew they were [released] on the happy bus. So what the detainees learned was that all you have to do is say nothing and you'll be let out anyway. Of course, this didn't happen as often as they think."

Another problem that continually plagued our program was that the contractors feared the trio, and even some of the military leaders did not want their involvement,so the contractors relied heavily on Dr. Tahir, the Shia expatriate psychiatrist they'd hired. This was further complicated when Raheema, Colonel Kato's aide, who was also Shia, took exception claiming that I *was* being sectarian when I refused to hire Shia staff— especially Shia clerics—into the program. Of course I was being sectarian! And it was because I knew that AQ operatives in Iraq would never listen to a Shia trying to talk them out of their beliefs. The biggest showdown I had with the contractor on that issue had been when Rick insisted that he would hire a Shia imam as the main cleric for our Islamic challenge program. At that point I asked him, "Don't you realize that the leaders of AQ in Iraq have vowed to kill the Shia?" They backed down but evidently when I was no longer on the scene, they gave in and let Dr. Tahir recruit a majority of Shia including for the Islamic challenge portion of the program.

On a humorous note Ken wrote to me about the ultimate demise of Dr. Tahir from the program and of his last doomed Shia recruit, Dr. Fadl:

> "When I met Dr Fadl he asked me, 'You know who asked me to come here?' and then said, 'George Bush.'
>
> 'George Bush!' I said laughing.
>
> 'Junior, yes. I just came from the White House. They are very busy there, and they need me to clean up this mess.' While I thought, *Who on God's green earth had Dr. Tahir brought onto the program?*
>
> 'I've got to go,' I said. 'Nice meeting you.' I went back to the office and straight into Mark's office and told him. We left it there, not realizing the shit storm that was to follow and went back to work. In two days, I was with Dr. Tahir and we walked into our big tent where everyone slept. All the beds had been moved and many interpreters who were employed as teachers were writing things down on paper in a sort of test scenario. Dr. Fadl was pacing between them all. Abdul Sittar had his arms crossed and was not looking happy. I walked over to him and we huddled in the corner to have a private conversation. 'He's testing the teachers to make them all socials [social workers],' Abdul Sittar informed me.
>
> 'Under whose authority?' I asked. 'And if they become socials, who will be the teachers?' I asked.
>
> 'He's bad Ken, he's a very bad man,' Abdul Sittar said.
>
> I went over to Fadl who said, 'You're in a testing room, don't talk to me now. I am a very busy man.' I couldn't believe

it. And he said it loudly so all the interpreters could see his authority over me. I walked away. I noticed that most if not all those taking this test were Shia—this cat is sectarian!

"So I left and told Mark but he was up to his eyeballs in work and said, 'I'll check the guy out, come back later, just putting out another fire here.' I then went back to the tent. By now the test had finished, and Fadl was declaring who could be socials with a grand speech.

"'Sir Dr. Fadl," I said loudly, 'could I borrow a few minutes of your time. I would love to talk to you. I'm sure I have much to learn from you.' I knew the only way to get him to come with me was to stroke his ego. I think if I had done anything different he may have become violent, although physically he wouldn't have fared well.

'Who approved this?' I asked out of earshot of everyone.

'George did,' he answered.

'George?' I asked. 'Is he in Baghdad?'

'The White House,' he said, patting me on the shoulder. I had my face in my hands, this man was delusional; talking to him was a waste of time. 'I have been selected to clear this mess up.'

'Yes,' I said, 'you told me.' And then came the most wicked thing I have ever heard in all my life.

'We'll begin by hanging all the extremists. This must happen soon because there are lots of them.' I was staring at him. How do you respond when somebody is so delusional and evil?

'Does that not strike you as a logical fallacy?' I asked in vain.

'You can't change these men, you must rid this country of them,' he came back. Then he began about Abdul Sittar. 'He's a very bad man. We should get rid of him too.'

'Why?" I asked. "Is he threatening to hang people?' My concerns completely shifted. This guy was from another planet, that much was clear, but he was in the tent with all the interpreters. Many of them liked him and he was poisoning their minds. I left Fadl there and raised my index finger to the clouds in a 'just hang on there, buddy' movement, and I went back to Mark, who was shocked and very concerned. And angry.

'Mark, you couldn't make this shit up,' I said.

'Ami, send me Fadl's resume,' Mark asked. He printed it out and we went over it. Interpreters were knocking on the door. Some were complaining about the test because they failed, others were asking for their new contract, others wanted to know what was going on. Still others who passed the social wanted to take a clerical test.

'Hang on guys, hang on! We need some time here. I'll come to your tent when we've figured this out. Nothing happens without us approving it,' I told them while Mark was on the phone calling Upsula University in Sweden where apparently Fadl had received his Ph.D. Mark was spelling out his name in numerous different ways and the university had no record of him.

'The guy's a fraud,' Mark said. 'This resume isn't worth the paper it's printed on. This needs to end now.' I went and got him, pushing back all the interpreters with their questions. I walked Dr. Fadl to the office where Mark had arranged witnesses to the conversation.

I was not there but here's what he told me: Mark asked about his Ph.D. and Fadl reeled off all that it entailed. Mark said they had no record of him. A back and forth and then

Fadl said, 'I'm an Arab. I can lie. So what!' His DOD badge was taken off him and he was detained in a tent with a soldier. Mark was pretty shocked. The man wasn't just a fraud; he was insane. But Dr. Fadl wasn't stupid. He left the tent that he was put in and the soldier tried to stop him. 'Touch me and you'll be in big trouble with George.' The soldier didn't know what to do, so he came to the office and told us. A team of soldiers went and got him and remained in the tent until he was promptly taken away—planned for the following evening.

That night as Mark told me about his conversation with Fadl over a cigar we were really wondering who hired this guy. 'Seriously Mark,' I said, 'we need to find out how he got here, who vetted him. He's not just bad, he's pretty fucking dangerous. Do you think we could detain him in the TIF [prison]? He certainly fits the bill.'

'Nope,' Mark said. 'He's a Swedish citizen and hasn't committed a crime. Not yet anyway...' The next day we continued as usual. I had a meeting with Dr. Tahir and his team about the reports. Ami and Mark were in the office. Suddenly, for no reason at all, Dr. Tahir got up and shouted, 'I'm sick of this. I'm not a translator, I'm a SME [subject matter expert]. I shouldn't be made to do this.'

'Well, Dr. Tahir, Feras is here to translate for me. Aren't you Feras?' I said looking wide-eyed at Feras.

'Yeah, but Dr. Tahir isn't giving me a chance. But okay, I'll do the translations; that's what I'm here for. It's easy.' Feras said as he lounged in a chair.

And so I began again and Feras began to translate. 'That's it!' Ali shouted, 'I quit. I hate it here. I hate everything about this place. I have no respect. I QUIT! I QUIT! I QUIT!' and he stormed out.

> The plan was that Dr. Fadl and Dr. Tahir were to fly out from Bucca to Kuwait and then back to London. But in Kuwait, they hopped on another flight to Baghdad where apparently they argued their case with management there. I don't know what happened, but for sure it must have been amusing."

In February 2009, I go to Amman, Jordan to interview among the Iraqi diaspora and met some former detainees who had gone through the program. One of these is Tawfik[1], a Sunni emir of a large territory near Baghdad who had been imprisoned after an explosion killing American forces. He invites me into the diwan area of his home. Tawfik claims that he was accused but not guilty of planning, aiding and harboring terrorists who attacked U.S. forces and had been imprisoned in Abu Ghraib, Bucca and Cropper prisons where he claimed to have been mistreated.

He tells me, "Once I talked back to the guards and they put me in one of those cement boxes that you use for shelter from the mortars. They put bars on the sides and put me in there for two days. You can see I am tall and I couldn't stand up."

Upon checking in to the prison, Tawkik says they were told to undress and put their hands against the wall. "So we took off our robes and did so," he says. "But then with female U.S. soldiers present, we were told to take *all* our clothes off—our underwear also. I refused until this big black soldier came and threatened me so I took my underwear off too and put my hands against the wall. Then they told us to spread our legs and they began to photograph us! And they photographed our private parts while laughing at us. You must understand for us to get naked in front of each other is not acceptable. If this happened in my area I could have people killed for this humiliation!"

"Was the intake procedure perhaps a medical check to verify any wounds and your physical condition upon admission to the prison?" I ask.

He shot back, "So they had to photograph us naked in front of female soldiers and laugh at us while they were doing it? Tell me what medical procedure that serves?"

But the worst was when Tawfik told me with sarcasm dripping from his lips, "I went through your rehabilitation program; I can tell you all about it! The quaking imams were too afraid to enter our cell so they stood in front of the cyclone fencing and shouted passages to us that were supposed

1 A pseudonym

to talk us out of extremist views while we spat at them and insulted them, saying, 'What the hell do you know?' Finally they would beg us, 'We both have to get this done or you don't get out. You know we have to finish these lessons so please just go along,' and then we would be quiet and let them finish."

"The imams didn't sit with and actually talk with you?" I ask, shocked.

"No they were too afraid of us!" Tawfik answers."They didn't change any of our minds if we were extremists at the time!"

"Were you evaluated by a psychologist or even talked to one?" I ask, trying to grasp at any good part of our program.

"Listen, Dr. Anne," the emir says, "I can see you are a sincere person and I'm sure the program you designed was good, but I can tell you from my own experience that if the program was intended to change anyone's mind, the way it was carried out and the people who did it were a complete joke!"

The emir then tells me his family was scammed during his three years of imprisonment by an American forces-paid interpreter in Camp Bucca who told the emir's family that he could arrange his early release if they met him at the airport with cash. Tawfik's son, who is also present, confirms that the family brought and delivered an envelope of cash during an elaborate scheme in which they were told that Tawfik was about to emerge out of an armored jeep, but after the interpreter's man received the cash and drove away, the prisoners who emerged did not have Tawfik among them.

"How many families do you think this interpreter scammed?" Tawfik asks me. "Now you see how corrupt your whole prison system was?"

While I don't know if the emir was lying I don't think he had any reason to misrepresent the rehabilitation program as he experienced it and I think he was genuine about the scam as well because he gave me detailed information to report back to the military in order the catch the interpreter-turned-scammer, which I attempted to do after the meeting.

My greatest shock however came from the aftermath of the trio's involvement. Unfortunately someone somehow learned of their involvement and when the program disbanded and the trio returned to their homes in Baghdad, Mahmud was targeted and killed by al Qaeda. Wathiq and Ali found their greatest troubles coming from the Shia-dominated government of Iraq, who did not easily forgive them for their former AQ activities, despite the fact that they had risked their lives working to fight extremism in Iraq in our prisons for the past year. Both were arrested and treated harshly in Iraqi prison during which time Ali's wife collapsed with a stress-induced illness. Ali was released but Wathiq remains in Iraqi prison to this day. When I asked Ali repeatedly what we could do to help him, he didn't answer. I assume he either believed it was hopeless or could not risk being involved, but it troubles me still to know that Wathiq is still in Iraqi prison.

When I wrote and asked Ali his memories of the program and if he thought it worked he wrote back:

> Hi habibi, I read your message and there were good and bad memories flashing in my mind...things that I laughed about and things I felt really sorry about . . . but that is life as we know it. As for Wathiq, I am sorry to tell you that he went to jail—and for a silly mistake too. He was about to be released because he was not guilty, but he changed his statements in front of the judge to save one of his friends, and the judge was pissed off for that. They were both incarcerated for the rest of their lives. As for Sheikh Mahmud, I still cannot believe he is gone...as I write these words my heart is bleeding for them. My wife is better than before. She is completely depending on natural sources of foods—no junk foods, no cans, nothing with preservatives as told by the doctor . . .but this is only slowing her disease.

> As for the program, it was successful to an extent (theoretically), but we expected some mistakes when is comes to practice and were able to fix the wrong things. But alas, the new army forces did not understand the full idea. If [General] Stone, [Colonel] Kato and [Major] Thompson were in the program all the time, I think it would achieve its goal because they trusted us [the trio] and we were doing the job as our religion teaches us. But the new army forces could not grasp the core idea of the program, which was turning the extremists into moderates, and many of them could not deal with it professionally.

> I agree with you that the program failed, but it was not because the program was wrong. Firstly, half of the program was depending on psychology and you were gone. With all the lame teachers we had, I still heard good stories from the

detainees, and they loved this side of the program, so imagine if you were there!!!

Secondly, the program was designed for Sunni detainees only, so why where there Shia teachers? I would understand if they were good teachers, but they were good in everything except Islamic teaching; and it was all because the people who were recruiting (Sheikh Muhammed and Shafik) were Shia. I swear to you, Anne, that some of them were grocers and barbers. I submitted a report to the contractor to replace the bad teachers after we conducted an easy Islamic exam in which more than half of them failed, and their response was that we better keep them and send them to Bucca instead of the long process of recruiting new good ones!

Thirdly, the false promises we made to the juveniles. The new Army forces told us that the juvies would be released as soon as they finish, but that was not true, and we lost the confidence and faith that we had gained though the hard process of teaching.

Fourth, many of the Sunni teachers were associated with the Iraqi Islamic party, and they were saying that their Islamic party conducts this program. As you know well, the Islamic party is called the coward party, the surrender party or even the infidels party amongst the extremists. I trust you can guess how the extremists treated these teachers!!

This is my view about the program, but still, there are individual successes here and there. I will give you one example. A few weeks ago, I was in my job and someone called me Sheikh Ali thrice. I was astonished to see one of the students I taught in my special program (Lion Spirit) and he held me tight and was glad to see me. He was an extremist and knew many fanatics, but he thanked me because he saw things he never knew before in the program.

Stay safe,

Ali

Indeed Ali's list was probably at the heart of things. My personal view after working on the program and hearing limited views of how it ultimately was carried out is that the claims of success measured in terms of recidivism were far more a result of the changing political situation in Iraq than our program. All the same, the program did touch thousands of lives and when it touched those extremists who were released it sounds like Sheik Ali, Ken and others saw real evidence of a change of heart in some of the detainees.

As I finished this book I crossed paths with General Stone again in the Fall of 2012 at a small meeting held at the U.S. State Department. He gave a presentation on work he had helped lead, following our efforts in Iraq, with the United Nations and the Department's Global Counter-terrorism Forum (a group of thirty countries including many with Muslim populations) and outlined best practices for rehabilitation and reintegration of violent extremist offenders. Recognizing that prisons can be incubators for violent extremist ideology—or institutions for reform, the group agreed that psychologists are necessary in rehabilitation efforts to address "the social context and psychological make-up that made the individual vulnerable to militant ideology and the motivational factors that contributed to his or her decision to engage in terrorist activity." Likewise they recognized that former violent extremists and charismatic members of the community are also useful in these efforts. Both of these were things I had fought hard to include in our program in Iraq.

As General Stone harked back to the outcomes of our efforts in Iraq, which he felt were very positive, he emphasized that the psychological piece was extremely important in getting a change of heart among the extremist detainees, as was using the former Al Qaeda cadres in our program to challenge the militant jihadi ideology, saying that Sheik Ali and the others had tremendous credibility in reaching those already deeply engaged. Although disturbingly, the General recalled that more than a small number of deeply engaged extremists—those who had blood on their hands—committed suicide when convinced that what they had done was indeed not Islamic or in the "path of Allah". While he joked that the suicide of a dedicated extremist was perhaps not a bad thing, he acknowledged that it was, of course, not a good outcome for a rehabilitation program. For me this underlined my argument that we cannot simply expect Islamic challenge to be enough in this type of work. When a person has adopted a virulent ideology, he has done so because it meets inner needs and if he then becomes convinced that it's not correct, he needs something new to replace it—a new way of living—or else he's lost and may not be able to find his way out of the movement, even choosing to suicide in despair. But when the inner workings of the individual and his needs that were met by engaging in terrorism are understood and addressed properly, then we can truly work not to just disengage, but also to help him deradicalize as well.

John Horgan and others have argued that deradicalization is not a realistic goal in most cases—that disengagement is.[298] Certainly it's true that disengagement rather than deradicalization is the more likely outcome when no intervention takes place and natural forces are at work. Indeed many terrorists spontaneously disengage from terrorism for many reasons: burnout, fear of arrest, disenchantment, competing desires and responsibilities, age, disinterest, etc., but many of these may remain ideologically committed. They do not relinquish their extremist views and may continue to harbor beliefs that in certain circumstances terrorism is absolutely morally justified.

But the fact that disengagement is the more normal natural outcome than deradicalization does not mean that, if one actually intervenes and is armed with clinical skills and Islamic knowledge, the trajectory into terrorism as well as the pathways out of it that exist on a continuum cannot be manipulated. There are many roles along the terrorist trajectory that an individual may first take and then transition into others as he goes deeper into it. I remain a firm believer that militant jihadi terrorists can also be worked backwards through that trajectory as well. And that can happen on the streets of Belgium with someone like Hamid who pulls street kids out of the same movement he once served, in London with Suliayman working in a community center, or in the prisons in a war-torn country. The success stories there and those that occurred among the hardcore in Iraq teaches us that if we equip ourselves psychologically and Islamically to be able to engage terrorists on a human level and work with them as real individuals with real pain within the socio, political, cultural, and psychological contexts of their lives, we can bring about deep and lasting change.[299]

CHAPTER 70

Sodomy and Terrorism

In October 2007, I'm back in Casablanca for a NATO Advanced Research Workshop entitled "Identity Loyalty and Security". I have kept up with Abdul, my translator from the last trip, and he's collected survey research data for me in Morocco on civilian psychological resilience to terrorism and is ready to go out for more interviews.

As Abdul and I cross Casablanca back to the Sidi Moumen slum, I recall the correspondence I had earlier with psychoanalyst Lloyd deMause about the origins of terorrism. Lloyd claims that all terrorists are reenacting childhood abuse and asserted that Arabs in particular have a history of sodomizing their young boys, leading to a perfect staging ground for young men to psychologically split off the "bad" victim self, project that bad onto others and then destroy it in acts of terrorism.

Lloyd supports his argument with articles from the seventies but they described how older boys and men who were precluded from having sexual relations with women in strict Arab and Muslim societies turned to younger boys for sex. Reading the articles I felt disgusted and sad for the victims and wondered about sexually repressive societies that often end up with strange ventings of the male sexual urge. Certainly I had seen cases of incest among fundamentalist Christians in the U.S. who wouldn't dare have extramarital affairs but did turn to their daughters for sexual gratification. Yet when I considered sodomy among Muslim populations who germinate terrorists, I still do not feel convinced that the victims of sodomy would be anymore likely to become terrorists than the men and boys that preyed upon them, but as I wrote previously, while in Palestine I did start asking more questions and now that I am in Morocco with Abdul it, occurs to me to ask him as well.

"Is sodomy enacted upon young boys prevalent in Morocco?" I ask.

"I don't think it's widespread here," Abdul says, "In the Gulf states, yes, but not here."

I drop it and we return to walk around the slums where poverty and despair is enough to drive anyone to want an escape at high personal costs. Though, this time Abdul and I don't find any extremists or those that know them so after some more general interviews in the slum we return to the hotel just as the conference supper is about to begin. I ask Mokhtar, one of the conference cohosts, if I can pay for Abdul to be invited as well and he agrees so we take our places at a table that has huge windows open along the seaside. Before dinner Abdul and I go to stand by the window looking out and listening as the waves of the Atlantic are crashing on the cliffs below. Abdul suddenly takes fright and backs away from the window.

"Are you afraid of heights?" I ask.

"No, of the sea," he answers.

"Come, and stand here with me, I'll hold your hand," I tell him, activating my psychologist self. He obeys and I hold his hand as we look at the waves together. "Why do they frighten you?"

"[When I was a small boy] a fisherman found me already drowned and he took my body to the shore," Abdul says. "Somehow he got me to breathe again so I was saved." He drops my hand and backs away from the window, so close to the traumatic memory that no amount of coaxing will bring him back to the window. I call him back, but he says, "No, I'm afraid I'll fall in and drown again."

"I won't let you fall in," I say, reminding him that he is here now with me and not small a small boy walking into the waves, misunderstanding how far he can go before being swept away. He's buying it to an extent but prefers to be seated. But even when we sit at the table I can sense that the open window disturbs Abdul – he's still afraid and tells me he feels vertigo. We talk quietly about it for a while and I hold his hand firmly under the table – as a continued sign of support and to calm him.

At the dinner our colleagues get into a lively conversation, but Abdul is already triggered into a posttraumatic recall and does not participate. I turn to him and ask what is going on inside.

"Some thing very bad happened to me," Abdul answers quietly as I still hold his hand tightly. "I've never told anyone about it."

"You can tell me," I answer quietly.

"No it's too horrible to put into words," he answers, trembling.

"Someone hurt you?" I ask. He nods and I can see he is regressed by age, caught up in his memory somewhere. "You were a child?"

"Yes, ten years old," he answers. "What happened?" I ask. "It was a friend of my father's," Abdul says getting more terrified.

I squeeze his hand. "He hurt you?"

"Yes, he sodomized me," Abdul answers and then he panics. "I should have never told you that! I've never told anyone."

I spend the rest of the dinner putting in small quips to the conversation when called upon, but I am otherwise locked on to Abdul, trying to convince him that of course he kept it a secret because rapists generally threaten their victims not to tell, but that now that he's an adult it's time to face it. As we talk I keep thinking to myself, *Geez was Lloyd right? Is this what happens to young boys here?* But when I get more time to reflect I realize that Abdul's story could just as well have been told to me in the U.S., or anywhere, and Abdul has not become a terrorist—far from it. Maybe it happens more here, but this one case can't confirm or disconfirm that.

Abdul and I keep talking while he reveals more details to me, his face a picture of complete and utter shock, and I try to provide emergency "therapy". As the evening event draws to a close Abdul feels obliged to leave, and though the conference absorbs my time over the next few days, I tell Abdul that I won't leave him alone with this horrible memory and I

don't. As soon as I get to the Internet I write him:

> Dearest Abdul, I don't know when you will read this but I just wanted to tell you I am very sad and sorry for your pain that you shared tonight. I'm glad you are not alone with such a sad thing anymore. I will be happy to help you as I can. If you want to write and tell me what happened I think it will be good for you, but you should do it slowly and not push yourself. It was a very big step to trust and to tell it at all. If we were in another setting, I would have asked you more but I didn't want you to have a bad reaction in front of other people. I could see the pain of it on your face and, I'm sure, in your body. Just remember many people have experienced such things as children, and it's always horrible and unfair and terrifying, but you can move beyond it. God always gives us what we need when we call to him. I will come back to Casa for sure so we can talk in person too, but please when you are ready tell me what happened in small pieces. Don' t try to write the whole story at once because

it will cause you to relive it—just like the drowning —and it will be very painful emotionally and physically upsetting. It's better to work with it in very small pieces until you tell the whole story bit by bit. That way you protect yourself as you heal. Try to see yourself also as the caring young man you have become and extend that care to the younger you, who holds this memory. If you can hold yourself and remind your younger self that all is okay, it's in the past, it was a terrible moment but it is really over, you can speak about it, remember it and heal all the things that it did to you, your mind and your soul.

Take care, my friend. I pray that Allah is watching over you every minute and sending angels to protect you and comfort you.

As is often the case with trauma survivors, they open up momentarily to share a trauma, and then shut down again. It isn't until I'm back in Belgium that Abdul writes back:

Dear Anne,

Thank you so much for your willingness to help, but I do not think I want to go through that again. It spoilt my night. It always ruins my time whenever I look at this "scar" in the mirror. It [the memory] keeps recurring during daytime, or as nightmares although it happened to me a long time ago. But it is OK now. I have developed this ability, which makes it possible for me to go to this world where I would be just watching that person far-off. It works for me but I feel sad for the person though. Please do not press me into telling more. I just can't and I am too much ashamed of myself. See, I did not plan at all to tell you but when you took me to that window and when you kept patting on my back and treated me as if I was your real son, and when you said I was like your kid sitting next to you, I felt like crying and I wanted to hug you and bury my face and feel safe. I wanted to tell you all about it because I can't tell my own Mom. I hope I'm not being stupid. I hope you will understand; you are a mother yourself. It was then when I could not help telling you. I am not sure I will be able to look at you in the eye as I used to do with you knowing that. I wish I could unsay what I said.

I brought it all on myself. But I was too young to realize that. Besides I was no Lolita or a nymphet for that to happen to me. Not that I'm not saying it should happen to girls, but I must have looked like a girl. I should have gone on a diet, and Dad shouldn't have left me there alone. OK, I also told you because you are foreign to my culture and you are not going to stigmatize me.

Last time I told you that I have problems remembering stuff, you said it could be lack of sleep; maybe you are right after all, bearing in mind all those nightmares and the countless, sleepless nights. But I also have problems with concentration. I can't have a conversation for more than five minutes without wandering away. Perhaps you have noticed that, although I tried hard to hide it. And when in a classroom, I am absent-minded almost all the time to the extent that I always have to copy the notes of my classmates.

My two brothers are happy that I am away from home, because finally they can breathe freely. They are so tired of my policing them. Again I really do hate myself for that. It's not fair; they should have a normal life. When an adult male is near them, I will be listening to every word he says, watching every touch, or just looking for any suspicious look. Yesterday I started at the noise of a bike and I thought my sister was screaming for help. My sister has three kids. I made it my duty to watch over them. When I am around, I cannot trust them to their father, let alone a stranger. I can't let my sister ask someone else to babysit. I always step forward no matter how busy or tired I am. This is so nerve-wracking and the load is so heavy.. . .I have a strong feeling that I am trying to help all those "defenseless, vulnerable" people around me (women and kids) because I get the impression that they are the ones who were abused, and not me, and I want to make up for my mistake because I was not there for them when it happened to them. I know this is absurd and not true but that's how I feel, or rather how I want to feel. Whatever the reason is, I just want to have a normal life like the rest. I want to take care of my future as well. I want to let go and have a life.

I only have one male friend, or at least I want to make myself think so to feel normal. To this day, I only deal with adult males as an obligation. I am not worrying about my sexuality. I am a straight, healthy, young guy, but I do not think my attitude towards men is normal. . . . I have this fantasy: I dream of taking all the kids and women to this island where men do not exist (do not laugh).

It is needless to say how grateful I am to you already. I know I can't pay you back no matter what I do, but do help me out with whatever advice you see helpful.

God bless you,

Abdul

Abdul and I continue our correspondence for a few emails, in which I guide him through. Abdul goes through periods of embracing my help but then goes silent for about a year. When he does write again, he resumes with simple social letters to catch up, so I do not mention the abuse again, and I'm so happy when I send him our family Christmas card, with my first grandchild in my arms, and finally hear good news from:

Hi Anne,

I wish you every success for the NEW HAPPY YEAR 2012. Wow, you look gorgeous as always! Guess what? I have a family of my own now. I'd dated this great woman for a year and last July we decided to get married. I've never been happier in my life. I'm blessed. You know what? In 9 months, I'm going to be a daddy. The other day we had this pregnancy test and it was positive!!! This is unreal! We are seeing a gynecologist this afternoon. That'll be our first step towards a thousand miles journey. I'm so joyful and I just want to share the joy with you. I hope my child will be as beautiful as the one you're holding between your arms.

I look forward to 2012 and I wish you joy and happiness.

All the best,

Abdul

Of course I wrote back to congratulate him and then when writing this chapter I wrote him again to ask permission to tell his story. Abdul wrote back telling me it's a daughter he is happily awaiting and agreed to sharing his story,[300] saying,

"I'm happy that I managed to put behind me the past although it still haunts me sometimes through nightmares. But my wife is always next to me, and we kind of help each other when the past is triggered. My wife also suffered a lot. She was forced to leave school at the age of sixteen and marry a man three times her age. Her parents were not swayed by her two suicide attempts because for them the "best" possible thing that could happen to a woman is marriage. So we share a dark past and we kind of turn to each other for solace. That has helped a lot."

I don't think Abdul ever worked through entirely what happened to him, hence the nightmares and I expect he's probably a very overprotective husband and father. But he's the furthest thing from a terrorist and his wife is also not a terrorist, although many would label a forced marriage at sixteen as abuse. So while I'm certain that Lloyd's theory that child abuse underlies the move into violence holds up for some, terrorism is also highly contextual and relies on more than just individual vulnerabilities. The lethal mix of other necessary factors—exposure to a violet ideology that justifies terrorism, a group that can equip the terrorist and social support for getting on the terrorist trajectory—must also be active to some extent. Ultimately, each person has their own individual threshold for what will drive them into terrorism.

CONCLUSION

Talking to Terrorists reflects ten years of field study: chasing down, spending time with and finding ways to interview terrorists, their family members, close associates, friends and even their hostages, who spent days with suicide terrorists in activated states. During these ten years I conducted more than four hundred interviews in many parts of the world trying to learn about their motivations for committing terrorist acts.

What I learned above all else is that no one is born a terrorist. Something has got to put them on the terrorist trajectory, and if we are clever in our approaches to dealing with terrorists, we can also take them back off of it. As I learned by advising the Home Office in the UK, interviewing and consulting with many of those doing interventions there and elsewhere, and designing the world's largest program to "deradicalize" and rehabilitate over 20,000 detainees held by the U.S. forces in Iraq, it *is possible* to move terrorists back off the terrorist trajectory. Certainly not *all* terrorists will deradicalize; some will only disengage and some will never do either. And for that latter group we need military and police interventions. But for the former we need understanding of the reasons and means by which individuals become terrorists. And comprehending that the lethal cocktail of terrorism consists of the interaction of four things: a terrorist group, vulnerable individuals, social support and a terrorist ideology, makes it easier to come to solutions for how to prevent engagement and disengagement in terrorism. As long as groups struggle politically, those who turn to terrorism to try to violently force their solutions will likely always exist; terrorism as a tactic is just too enticing for those who judge violence as the most useful way to press toward their political goals. So, we need to become savvy enough to engage those who might move to endorse terrorism to become and stay engaged in the normal political process. And in some cases that requires changes on our part: cleaning up corruption, addressing real and perceived grievances, or sharing territory, resources and power in equitable ways with groups who may feel or actually are disenfranchised.

The ideologies that terrorist groups use to convince their support bases and adherents that attacking civilians is appropriate change over time. Currently (and as written about in Rapoport's theory of the four waves of terrorism), religion has become a central theme in terrorism, used to both justify terrorists acts and to establish a basis for the organizing principles of bringing in a new world order in support of that religion.[301] The "martyrdom" ideology, currently used by al Qaeda, militant jihadis, the Chechens and many of the Palestinian terrorist groups written about in this book,is currently in vogue among many groups, taking advantage of individual vulnerabilities and marrying them to a distorted version of Islam that propels them into becoming human bombs. Eventually this ideology will be discredited, and others will likely rise to replace it. And of course we should do everything we can to speed this process, but we should not delude ourselves into thinking that something new will not eventually rise in its place. Just as crime is a fact of life, there is probably no end to terrorism,just good multi-level and well-thought interventions that contain and reduce it.

At present, militant jihadi groups convince their adherents to become "cosmic warriors" (as Mark Juergensmeyer coined the term),[302] fighting a demonized enemy according to what the recruit comes to believe are the dictates of God. And in the cosmic struggle in defense of Islam, Muslims and Islamic lands extreme measures are justified, including suicide bombers that target civilians. But as we learned in Iraq, where terrorists groups used beheadings, bombed public places and targeted other Muslim civilians including women and children, and as we learned in Beslan from the deadly mass hostage-taking of children, when terrorists go too far they offend and begin to lose their support base of funding, social support and future recruits. They also lose their legitimacy in terms of being able to convince their cadres to carry out terrorist operations. So terrorist groups that want to survive have to limit themselves to some extent. On the other hand when we leave a heavy military footprint, when people live under occupation and fear of threat, and when victimhood can legitimately be claimed, terrorists can advance their arguments and gather and motivate their cadres more easily.

As I went deep into the lives of terrorists, I learned that context is all-important. Terrorist groups recruit individuals to their ranks by appealing to their inner needs and vulnerabilities,which are then exploited to move them along the terrorist trajectory. Needs and vulnerabilities are defined primarily by the psycho-social, cultural, organizational and political context in which these individuals live, and so, we must understand and address context to understand the birth of a terrorist and to contribute to his disengagement from terrorism.

The individual's motivations for terrorism that I found tend to be delineated between active conflict zones (where trauma, loss and a desire for revenge are more active) and non-conflict zones (where social marginalization, alienation, secondary trauma, sensitivity to the suffering of others, a desire to prove one's manhood, to belong, to protect others, to have an adventure or to be a hero are more prevalent). Humiliation and frustrated aspirations are motivators crossing both areas, and neither group of motivations are totally delineated. For instance, recruiters working in non-conflict zones bring the violence, traumas and bereavement occurring inside conflict zones back into the non-conflict zones via graphic images and video feed on the Internet. And when sacred values are trampled upon in either area (as with the cartoon depictions of the Prophet Muhammad, the desecration of the Koran, etc.) these things can incite individuals to embrace terrorism. Pockets of extreme violence may also exist within non-conflict zones, such as inner cities where gangs are rife or even within a violent family context. We also found that experiences of violence opened the doors for the belief that engaging in violence could bring solutions. Likewise, when we found religious fanaticism, it was often linked to cumulative traumatic experiences that piled up and pushed the individual into embracing a virulent terrorist ideology.

The terrorists that I studied were not insane killers. Instead they were rational actors considering their choices within the context of their religious beliefs.[303] But many—especially inside conflict zones—while not insane, were certainly psychologically disturbed, especially by psychological trauma and bereavement.

Indeed, we found that the "martyrdom ideology" takes advantage of the dissociative mindset that results from PTSD, deepening it as it takes the person into a commitment to give up his own life. This calms him as he exits from traumatic flashbacks, constant bodily hyperarousal and emotional pain to pass into what he believes will be an instant entrance to paradise. It offers those who long to reunite with loved ones who were killed the perceived ability to do so, and suggests that "martyring" oneself to exit from life is honorable versus a forbidden act. Terrorism that uses this ideology does apply psychological first aid for trauma victims, sadly though offering only a short-term fix, as it results in the death of those who take it on.

As we developed our research method of conducting psychological autopsies of those who had volunteered to go as suicide bombers, I found that one of the best indicators of willingness to die, especially in conflict zones, was the depth of emotional pain, or "psychache" as suicidologist Edwin Shneidman[304] would term it. Many are also given the assurance that their children, parents and extended family members will be respected, provided for by their cadres after their deaths, and also granted entry into paradise. When psychache is present and suiciding on behalf of the group while targeting others is both venerated and encouraged by the surrounding social group, those in deep emotional pain can readily endorse terrorism.

While sexuality is a central part of life for all people, I did not find the promise of seventy-two virgins in the afterlife to be much of a motivating factor for militant jihadis, acting perhaps only as a comfort but not the primary motive for "martyrdom". Instead, anger at the targeted group and desire for revenge were much more powerful motivators. Certainly sexual frustration can exacerbate an already difficult life, and the sexual assault of minors, especially boys in cultures where girls are off limits but turning to boys is allowed, may be a traumatic or humiliating ingredient that moves some young men along the terrorist trajectory although I also found cases where that was *not* the case. Coercion can also be used to push a male or female cadre who wants to hide homosexuality or an illicit relationship forward to death, though I did not often find that a factor. Chillingly among those I interviewed, it appeared that most were willing participants.

Fugitives and prisoners who were tortured or harshly treated and then volunteer for suicide missions also make it clear that if we want to turn the tide on populations who embrace these methods, we may have to consider offering amnesties and remember that getting caught is deemed far worse than exploding oneself.

Terrorist instigators, ideology and charismatic leaders are also important ingredients of the terrorist mix. I found repeatedly that dramatically-presented video and audio clips of traumatic images paired with Islamic verses and songs can incite a religious fury and sense of duty to fight for the downtrodden, especially if the victims are portrayed as "fictive kin". Such materials cleverly manipulate believers into accepting the martyrdom ideology and the terrorist group's claims of victimhood. The power of relationships, also utilized in these videos, to move one along the terrorist trajectory should never be underestimated. Counter-terrorism expert Marc Sageman claims that the "gang of guys" is a powerful motivating factor,[305] and I would also add the power of other relationships: the mentor and charismatic leader as father figure, the "ummah" and "brothers" as replacement family members, the alluring girl who will accept only a "jihadi" husband, the fiery instigator who fills the recruit with a longing for justice and belief that terrorism can achieve—these are also highly important in the terrorist mix, especially for those who have suffered traumatic bereavement and have lost important family members in their lives.

While I studied groups who make use of the "martyrdom" ideology by twisting Islam and its teachings to take advantage of those who willingly trade in their suffering lives for the belief of entry into a better world, I can emphatically state that Islam itself is not the problem. All religions can be twisted to promote fanaticism and groups that make distorted religious claims can convince their cadres that they are becoming "cosmic warriors" engaged in a battle ordained by God on behalf of religion and as such, extreme means are justified. While we currently see a spate of religiously-motivated militant jihadi terrorists, a distorted version of Islam is not alone in doing so. In the nineties I served as an expert witness in a legal case in which a woman was incited to abortion clinic violence by being given the "Army of God" manual, a book that invoked Christian scriptures and claimed the souls of dead fetuses were calling out for warriors to rise and strike abortion clinics.[306] In 1995 Jewish fundamentalists believing they must save their vision of a religious Israel assassinated Prime Minister Rabin, and in 1994 settler Baruch Goldstein went to a mosque in Hebron and opened fire on worshipping Muslims (as discussed in Chapter Thirty-Three).

Although terrorists tend to be predominantly men, females are also among their ranks and I went to lengths to capture some of them in my interviews as well. I found that while female in the groups I studied rarely enter the leadership ranks nor have any great decision making powers, they perform various roles from translator, instigator, fund raiser, money and message courier, to bearers of death as suicide bombers. And females in conflict zones often volunteer for suicide missions more than the men because fighting roles are blocked. Contrary to some claims, I did not find that women joined the ranks of terrorist cadres to fight for equality but instead found their motivations to match those of their male counterparts with whom they plotted. Female terrorists, I also found, have a special fascination among the public, and they thereby capture media attention and horrify in a special way, something terrorists aim for. Women are also more easily able to trick and pass security due to respect for female modesty and the fact that few of us like to admit to the potential violence of women.

Terrorism is a complex phenomenon and while I did find patterns in terrorist behaviors, no two terrorists are alike. While the ideology a group uses to convince its members to enact political violence may be the same across regions, the individual motivations for joining may differ quite a lot from within conflict zones to outside of them–so context is important. Groups also compete for and recruit members differently according to the socio-political-religious context, and social support for terrorism also varies considerably according to the region. But no matter where and how terrorism arises, we as Americans are targets.

This book concentrates on interviews outside of the country, yet its content is also relevant to the militant jihadis who have been active inside the U.S. as their methods of recruitment, motivations, terrorist trajectories and ideologies are the same. Often over the years as I presented my find-ings at conferences, I was asked why we don't yet in the U.S. see suicide terrorism, as we too have a Muslim minority like Europe (estimated in the U.S. between two and seven million, with only a tiny fraction of that number radicalized). At the time I was being asked, I pointed out that our Muslim immigrant populations are much more resistant to the militant jihadi ideology because they for the most part arrived in the U.S. with good educations and significant means and they are not blocked from advanc-ing, but rather thrive here following the "American dream". Their counter-parts in Europe, however, are more vulnerable to the militant jihadi groups and ideology because many arrived poor and illiterate, were recruited to manual labor jobs and often find themselves rejected from easily entering mainstream society, leaving them—and especially their children born in Europe—alienated, marginalized, angry and open to fighting against the society they live under.

At the time I pointed to the Somali population in Minneapolis/St Paul and predicted that if we did see U.S. Muslims take on the militant jihadi ideology, it would be from such population bases: recently immigrated, refugee status, still connected to an conflict zone where militant jihadis are active,and marginalized and disenfranchised as new immigrants in the U.S. (in the Somali case unfortunately due in part to race). I was right. In the last decade we have seen over forty Americans (many from the Minnesota diaspora community) leave the U.S. to volunteer in Somalia as mujahedeen and for suicide missions.[307] One of them, American-born Omar Hammami (aka Abu Mansoor Al-Amriki) became one of Al Shabaab's foreign-born leaders, gaining notoriety for rapping about "jihad" in English and credited with drawing hundreds of foreign fighters to Somalia.[308] While al Shabaab has now affiliated with al Qaeda and made clear that the U.S. is one of its targets we have thankfully had none of their recruits activate for missions inside the U.S.

We have also now seen inside the U.S. what is referred to as active shooters–terrorists who take guns or assault weapons into crowded places with the intent to kill as many as possible before ultimately being shot to death. One of these, Nidal Hasan, a U.S. military psychiatrist, entered his military base to do just that. Interestingly Hasan, a Muslim of second-generation Palestinian heritage, was likely acutely aware of and exposed on an emotional level to what occurred in the second Palestinian Intifada, including the "martyrdom" ideology and glorification of those who "martyred" themselves for their cause. Disturbed by the idea that the U.S. military was fighting in Islamic lands with Muslim people (Afghanistan and Iraq) and soon to be deployed himself, Hasan began to pose some of his questions to American-born cleric and terrorist instigator Anwar al Awlaki (Awlaki then resided in Yemen and had also corresponded with the Minnesota group that recruited for al-Shabaab and with three of the September 11th bombers. Awlaki has since been killed by a U.S. drone attack). Once sufficiently radicalized, Nidal Hassan felt justified to take his weapon and go and kill as many of his military coworkers as possible before potentially being shot dead himself.[309]

Similarly, we have seen foreign-born individuals, some naturalized citizens, living inside the U.S. radicalized to plot attacks here–often against military bases and personnel but also against the general population. Faisal Shahzad was one of these. A first generation naturalized U.S. citizen from Pakistan, Shahzad claimed he took inspiration from Pakistani extremists to attempt to explode a car packed with explosives that he parked on New York's Times Square in May of 2010. Like Nidal Hasan, Shahzad followed the teachings of Anwar al Awlaki (over the Internet) and was radicalized in part by his anger over the U.S. policy of using drone strikes in Pakistan, a U.S. policy that has been successful in decapitating many terrorist leaders hiding in Pakistan, although simultaneously and indiscriminately targeting young men of military age and even women and children who happened to be in the target area.[310]

Radicalization and recruitment to extremist groups in prison happens here as well and is also a concern to authorities although at present less so among militant jihadi groups.[311] And homegrown terrorists in the U.S. may also radicalize as they interact with extremist clerics and instigators and their materials over the Internet. Digital publications,including the al Qaeda-sponsored "Inspire" magazine that urges readers to take up a "defensive jihad" against the U.S. from inside its borders,have become a serious concern. Samir Khan,its publicist and an American citizen of Pakistani origin,penned articles (up to his death by U.S. drone strike) that instructed readers how to make bombs and use other self-generated measures to target and kill American military and diplomatic personnel here in the homeland.[312] Similarly, Adam Gadahn, is another American-born instigator who functions as a spokesman for al Qaeda, pointing to the victimhood of the Muslim "ummah" and speaking over the Internet in perfect American English about the"collateral damage" of U.S. attacks as well as outright military misdeeds and extorts American Muslims to rise up and attack their country from within.[313]

The numbers of militant jihadis arising from the Muslim population here is extremely small by proportion and should not be overdramatized, as there are also "white" supremist terrorists who pose, as much, if not a greater threat. Yet any one terrorist who manages to carry out a lethal attack can kill many. Of the militant jihadis who have been involved in domestic terrorism plots, the majority here have been male,are both immigrants and native-born, and range in age from eighteen to seventy years old. The common theme among them has been exposure to a terrorist group, either an actual recruiter or via the Internet, creating within them a fanaticism that motivated them into plotting potentially lethal acts of terrorism. When one examines their individual vulnerabilities and motivations for taking this ideology on, identification with Muslim victims, social marginalization, alienation, desire to belong and be a hero, fury over the violation of sacred values, and secondary traumatization are present. Thankfully the level of social support for militant jihadi terrorism at present in the U.S. is small to nonexistent but the fact that al Qaeda now aims Internet recruiting to our population is of concern.

Of the militant jihadi homegrown terrorists that self-radicalize over the Internet,we have also seen many young Muslim men–converts, reverts and mainstream Muslims, legal and illegal immigrants as well as citizens— caught and even entrapped by FBI and security forces "sting" operations. There are certainly concerns about security forces posing as al Qaeda and taking aspiring terrorists along with them into deepening their commitment to the militant jihad. However, it is also horrifying to see Moroccan-born illegal immigrant Amine el Khalifi of the Washington D.C. metro area so ready to volunteer himself to the cause that he arrived on Capitol Hill wearing a suicide vest and carrying an automatic weapon with intent to use them against us.[314] It's troubling to realize that there are persons who live among us who are vulnerable to charismatic and convincing leaders (whether real or posing as real)who can using the militant jihadi ideology to move them so far along the terrorist trajectory to carry out terrorist acts against us here in the homeland.

As we recognize that Americans at home and abroad are not immune to terrorism and that we can and probably will see more of it on our home soil, we need to do what we can to understand and stop it. We must be more clever and through surveillance, policing and social policies catch plotters before they act and where possible create social policies that both prevent individuals from being vulnerable to such ideologies and from moving to action.

From what I learned, I know that is possible. In all cases, it requires addressing their contexts. If they are feeling marginalized, disenfranchised, hopeless, sensitive to the pain of others, and identify with that pain and feel pain themselves, we may have to address what hurts to make them more resistant to terrorist groups and ideologies. This may mean coming to political stances where we do not support corrupt regimes or dictators and reducing our military footprint—making sure military misdeeds do not occur and when they do are swiftly and publicly addressed. It may also require carefully-crafted social programs and bringing these programs to where they are needed: the street, prisons, community centers, troubled neighborhoods, the Internet, etc. Likewise we need to catch and block the recruiters—those working in person in troubled communities, targeting troubled individuals, working in prisons and over the Internet and that also requires good surveillance and policing as well as clever psychological prevention and countering methods.

We also need to discredit their ideologies and their actions. Some of that they do themselves when they go too far, but we can also be far more creative in creating Internet and other materials that challenge their messages of hate and death. And we need to understand that fight is not just a battle of Islamic challenge—attacking the distorted view of Islam— but is also an emotional one. They are adept at using emotionally evocative images of victimhood and pairing it with scriptures and admonitions to action. Their propaganda materials are excellent examples of emotionally-based manipulations that use secondary trauma, identification with the victims and a sense of "fictive kin" to take potential recruits beyond what is truly scripturally-based and beyond common views of objective reality and into their first premise of victimhood upon which they build an entire ideology justifying terrorist violence. We need to get as clever as they are in creating materials that effect emotions in the same manner but do so to endorse nonviolent solutions and to debunk their emotionally-based manipulations. We can win the fight against militant jihadi terrorism but to do so we need insight to understand where, when, why and how the terrorist's trajectory can and does begin and about the opportunities we have to change this course and save the lives of both the terrorist and the victim.

I hope that my in-depth interviews and research of ten years of talking to terrorists presented in this book and additional material that I maintain on my website (www.AnneSpeckhard.com) will begin to provide us some answers in constructing our solutions.

ACKNOWLEDGEMENTS

This book represents ten years of research and countless helpers along the way. In every foreign country I worked in, I had multiple guides who translated and helped me to locate the right people to interview, who in turn led me further inward along a pathway of contacts deeper and closer to the topic of study. I cannot name them all, but to all of them I am forever grateful for the time and care they spent to further this project.

In Russian speaking countries my Russian was good enough to understand what I was being told, but I needed help finding the subjects, to explain culturally related references and to finesse my English questions into sympathetic and sensitive versions in Russian. The hostages project began out of friendship with Dr. Nadezhda Tarabrina—or Nadya to me—with whom I worked in Moscow, and led to work in Minsk with Natasha Mufel and in Beslan with Madina, "Uncle Volodoya" and Zarina Kadieva. Thanks to all of you for your courageous work listening to harrowing stories from hostages who survived, when so many others did not.

In Chechnya my collaborator and esteemed colleague, Dr. Khapta Akhmedova, made all of the interviews in the refugee camps in Ingushetia and inside Chechnya that we then pored over, analyzed and wrote up together. When she sent her sister Seda Akhmedova to come live with us for a year, I made a dear friend and learned even more about the situation and motivations of extremists there. Thank you to both Khapta and Seda, who both I am sure are continuing to do great work in this world!

In Morocco, many thanks to Professor Mokhtar Benabdallaoui and his wife Sadjida for generously hosting me in their home in Casablanca, taking me to Rabat and Marrakesh, providing me with loads of cultural and language lessons and helping me set up interviews. A student I refer to by the pseudonym Abdul went twice with me deep into the Sidi Moumen slums as well as shared his own story with me, and another, Makda, helped orient me in my first days.

In Belgium I worked with three young guides who did their best to introduce me to subjects close to or involved in extremism. My thanks to Najim Gharbi in Antwerp, and Michael Harrouk and Samir in Brussels. Thanks also to Georges Chebib, Hamid and Jenny Sebaly, Ghassan Schbley, Jean-Marc El Arid, along with many others from the Lebanese and Arab diaspora in Brussels who often met with me after I returned from interviews with radicalized European second generation Muslims in Belgium, France, the Netherlands and the UK. They listened to what I had learned and argued the other side, thereby creating a very helpful balance.

Abdul Latif and Majid Tramboo of the Kashmir Center in Belgium also introduced me to many Kashmiris who had been involved in their insurgency and with terrorism, and Abdul Latif shared with me his own story of transition from militant to prisoner to activist and journalist, which unfortunately I was not able to include here.

In the UK, I thank the many guides and helpers who made introductions and provided background help for me, including but not limited to: Paul Addae, Abdur Rahmaan Anderson, Alyas Karmani, Asim Hafez, Musa Admani, Clive Stafford Smith, Nasreen Suleaman, Mohammed Abbasi, Robert Lambert, Yusef Chambers, Sulaiyman and many others.

And I will always remain deeply grateful to Tony Heal of the UK Home Office and Noel Warr of the London Metropolitan Police, who allowed the Siraat team to come to our rescue in Iraq when we needed Islamic challenge materials to be developed quickly. I learned an immense amount from these imams working in Scotland Yard and the UK prison system and will always remain in their debt for helping us so extensively in preparing the highest quality professional materials for the Islamic challenge portion of our detainee rehabilitation program.

In Iraq, Dr. Khapta Akhmedova came to help and stayed on in Iraq when I was not able to, helping to take the program from the first stages to full fruition. Ken Reidy, Sheiks Musa Admani and Abdul Sittar and so many others helped as well.

From Iraq, Sheiks Ali, Wathiq and Mahmoud remain forever in my heart. Their courage and dedication to their faith—changing and correcting their own course when they felt they had been mistaken—and then being willing to risk everything to help change others leaves a lasting imprint to this day. How can I ever forget Sheik Mahmoud who lost his life for this work? Thank you all, from the depths of my heart!

In Jordan, I enjoyed the tremendous support and hospitality of psychologist Dr. Tayseer Shawash and his wife, Nancy. Tayseer, you listened so kindly every time I came out of Iraq exhausted and were so perceptive to what I needed to hear and do next. I also thank HRM Princess Aisha Bint Al Hussein who generously offered her assistance during that challenging time. And thanks to Iraqi, Hala Sarraf who gave her time to helping to locate and translate for interviews with diaspora Iraqis—some a bit fiery—living in Jordan at the time.

In Gaza, Mohammed (the Gazan) guided, translated, hosted us and then told his own story for years leaving a lasting impression of life in Gaza. In the West Bank, Jamilah, Yousef, Omar and Alla located subjects and traveled with me, sometimes endangering their own lives for the project. Thank you for all you showed me of how Palestinians live, think, feel, laugh, and cry and how so many try to thrive under very difficult circumstances.

And of course in Palestine, I will never forget traveling with my beloved students, Ken Reidy and Al (who wants to be known by a pseudonym), who were by my side throughout Palestine and gave me the courage to ever step foot into a terrorist's home. Thanks guys for all we learned together and for all the laughs and good times!

In France, psychologist Dr. Latefa Belarouci ventured with me deep into the slums of Paris. In Lebanon, with the help of my good friend Georges Chebib and his father I interviewed a high-ranking member of Hezbollah to start a study there and stayed in the Chebib family home.

And thanks to all of the persons presented in this book, whether making choices for good or for evil, for being willing to sit with me, honoring my safety, and for opening up and trying to explain yourselves, your family members, friends, loved ones, community members and your experiences. Thank you for sharing your thoughts and feelings and inner lives. While I could not include all of my interviews in this book I do include many more on my website (www.AnneSpeckhard.com).

Once I turned from interviewing to writing, my thanks goes to my agent, Rebecca Friedman, for believing in me and encouraging me every step of the way along with Cara Hoffman who helped me to edit some of the first chapters before writing success overtook her editing career!

And I give my utmost gratitude to Jayne Carapezzi Pillemer, my editor who spent countless hours going over every word, helping me to tell these stories in ways that captivate and get my ideas across. Jayne quipped once that this book will be like our baby that– we "birthed" together. So true – she was a wonderful and lovely midwife to a creative process! Thank you Jayne for all your helpful insights, reflections, edits and suggestions in putting this book together.

Thanks also to Gerry Chiarutini for reading and commenting on the first draft of the book. Thank you to Dr. Reuven Paz for also reading the book ahead of time and the lovely foreword. And to Nikki Hensley for the book layout and e-pub design. And thanks to my daughter Jessica Speckhard, the artist, for the cover design!

And speaking of children, thanks to mine for putting up with and encouraging me when I went on research trips, chased terrorists and then returned home to write about them. There were some nights when I was so glued to the computer screen that I forgot to make them dinner until late! The question, "Mom, are you still planning to make dinner?" was probably a question asked too often in my home during the Belgian years. They joke about being both proud and traumatized by my work. I hope the proud always outshines the fear.

And thanks to my husband for always encouraging me to follow my heart, pursue my dreams and not worry about whether it makes any income or not. His line always was, "One of us has to be working on making this world a better place." I'm sure he's made his own dent for bettering our world, probably much deeper than I, when he served as a diplomat and now as he continues to serve in the private sector. And thank you, Daniel, for taking us overseas and starting all our "global" adventures—introducing me to a much larger world! Thanks also to the U.S. Department of Defense who funded some of my academic research as well as some of my work representing the U.S. serving on Research Task Groups for NATO.

In addition to my research collaborators to whom I am immensely thankful, many other colleagues blazed the trail ahead giving me the courage while others helped form my opinions, and I owe a great debt for their ideas. Many spent long hours discussing these issues with me—sometimes in academic conferences, other times at home over a meal or out somewhere over dinner or with drinks in hand; others had been out in the field as well and compared notes with me, some served alongside me on NATO Research Task Forces meeting all over the world, and many, many became dear friends along the voyage. I am thankful to all of them (listed here in alphabetical order and I hope I did not miss any!): Paul Addae, Dr. Yonah Alexander, Dr. Maria Alvanou, Dr. Rogelio Alonso, Abdur Rahmaan

Anderson, Nichole Argo, Dr. Scott Atran, Ambassador Daniel Benjamin, Peter Bergen, Dr. Mia Bloom, Laila Bokhari, Dr. Bruce Bongar, Dr. Christopher Boucek, Dr. Jarret Brachman, Dr. Karla Cunningham, Dr. Martha Crenshaw, Lloyd deMause, Dr. Adam Dolnik, Dr. John Esposito, Laurie Fenstermacher, Andrew Garner, Dr. Boaz Ganor, General John Gardner, Rohan Gunaratna, Dr. Mohammed Hafez, Dr. Hassan Hanafi, Nasra Hassan, Dr. Bruce Hoffman, Michael Hopmeier, Dr. John Horgan, HRM Princess Aisha Bint Al Hussein, Dr. Brian Jenkins, Dr. Berto Jongman, Dr. Mark Juergensmeyer, Dr. Valery Krasnov, Dr. Arie Kruglanski, Dr. Robert Leiken, Dr. Brynjar Lia, Dr. David Mandel, Dr. Montgomery Mcfate, Dr. Ariel Merari, Dr. Assaf Moghadam, Dr. Ces Moore, Dr. Robert Lambert, Dr. Walter Laqueur, Dr. Peter Neumann, Dr. Robert Pape, Dr. Reuven Paz, Dr. Ami Pedazhur, Dr. Jerrold Post, Peter Probst, Farhana Qazi, Dr. David Rapoport, Dr. Fernando Reinares, Dr. Olivier Roy, Dr. Marc Sageman, Dr. Eyad Sarraj, Ghassan Schbley, Dr. Alex Schmid, Dr. Michael Taarnby, Yoram Schweitzer, Deborah Scroggins, Dr. Tayseer Shawash, Dr. Andrew Silke, Dr. Steve Simon, Dr. Joshua Sinai, Dr. Stephen Sloan, Bernard Snoek, Dr. Jessica Stern, General Douglas Stone, Dr. Thalia Tzanetti, Dr. Jeff Victoroff, Dr. Leonard Weinberg, Dr. Quintan Wictorowitz, Dr. Paul Wilkinson and Dr. Philip Zimbardo. Thank you for sharing your experiences, thoughts, opinions, encouragement, good times and friendship with me!

ABOUT THE AUTHOR

Anne Speckhard, Ph.D. is an Adjunct Associate Professor of Psychiatry at Georgetown University Medical School. Dr. Speckhard has been working in the field of posttraumatic stress disorder (PTSD) since the 1980's and has extensive experience working in Europe, the Middle East and the former Soviet Union. She was the chair of the *NATO Human Factors & Medicine Research and Technology Experts Group (HFM-140/RTG) on the Psychosocial, Cultural and Organizational Aspects of Terrorism,* served as the co-chair of the *NATO-Russia Human Factors & Medicine Research Task Group on Social Sciences Support to Military Personnel Engaged in Counter-Insurgency and Counter-Terrorism Operations* and served on the *NATO Human Factors & Medicine Research Task Group Moral Dilemmas and Military Mental Health Outcomes.* She is a member of the United Nations Roster of Experts for the Terrorism Prevention Branch Office on Drugs and Crime and was previously awarded a Public Health Service Fellowship in the United States Department of Health & Human Services where she served as a Research Fellow. She has provided expert consultation to numerous European governments as well as the U.S. Department of Defense regarding programs for prevention and rehabilitation of individuals committed to political violence and militant jihad. In 2006-2007 she worked with the U.S. Department of Defense to design and pilot test the Detainee Rehabilitation Program in Iraq. In 2002, she interviewed hostages taken in the Moscow theater about their psychological responses and observations of the suicidal terrorists and did the same in 2005 with surviving hostages from the Beslan school take-over. Since 2002, she has collected more than four hundred research interviews of family members, friends, close associates and hostages of terrorists and militant jihadi extremists in Palestine, Israel, Iraq, Lebanon, Morocco, Russia, Chechnya, Belarus, Netherlands, United Kingdom, Belgium and France. Dr. Speckhard is the director of the *Holocaust Survivors Oral Histories Project – Belarus*, a project constructing the history of the Minsk Ghetto and Holocaust in Belarus through oral histories and archival research. She also researched traumatic stress issues in survivors of the Chernobyl disaster and has written about stress responses to toxic disasters. Dr. Speckhard worked with American expatriates after 9-11 (at SHAPE, NATO, the U.S. Embassy to Belgium and Mission to the EU) and conducted research on acute stress responses to terrorism in this population. She also studies psychological resilience to terrorism. Dr. Speckhard co-directed the *NATO Advanced Research Workshops - Ideologies of Terrorism: Understanding and Predicting the Social, Psychological and Political Underpinnings of Terrorism and Understanding and Addressing the Root Causes of Radicalization among Groups with an Immigrant Heritage in Europe* and served on the *NATO/Russia Counter-Terrorism Advisory Group.* Dr. Speckhard consults to governments and lectures to security experts worldwide.

Website: www.AnneSpeckhard.com

Glossary

Abaya – a floor-length, loose-fitting, long-sleeve, robe-like dress worn by women

Active shooter – an armed person who uses deadly force (usually a gun) to kill others with the intention to keep killing until he himself is killed

Administrative detention/open check prisoner – arrest and detention without trial for security purposes. Without a trial there is also no sentence, so the prisoner does not know how long he will be held.

al Aqsa Martyrs Brigade – a Fatah linked coalition of militias that formed to resist the IDF in the West Bank and Gaza and then transitioned during the second Intifida into a terrorist organization targeting civilians with suicide operations within Israel.

al Aqsa Mosque – is the third holiest site in Sunni Islam, a mosque built upon the Temple Mount, the place where the Jewish temple once stood and the holiest site in Judaism.

al Shabaab – a Somali-based terrorist organization currently linked to Al Qaeda

al Qaeda – a global terrorist organization led by Osama bin Ladin from 1989-2011

Allah – "God" in Arabic

Allahu Akbar – an Arabic expression translating to "God is Great"

Arab Israeli – non-Jewish Israeli citizens of Arabic (usually Palestinian) cultural or linguistic heritage who usually identify themselves as Arab or Palestinian by nationality but Israeli by citizenship. Approximately twenty percent of Israel's population is Arab Israeli, and many of these have family ties in the West Bank and Gaza.

Army of Islam – terrorist group in the Gaza Strip responsible for the kidnapping of Alan Johnston

Dissociation – a psychological symptom following deep traumatization, the essential feature of which is a disruption in the usually integrated functions of consciousness, memory, identity or perception. Can include the unconscious erection of a barrier, walling off negative emotions and memories of a traumatic event.

Eid al-Fitr or Eid – the Muslim holiday marking the end of the Islamic holy month of Ramadan

Eid al Ahda – the Muslim holiday known as the Greater Eid or the Festival of Sacrifice commemorating Abraham's willingness to sacrifice his son Ismael in an act of obedience to Allah, before Allah intervened to provide a sheep to sacrifice in his place.

Emir – a prince, high-ranking sheikh or commander

(Violent) Extremism – behavior that justifies, instigates, glorifies and engages in violence, including criminal activity, terrorism, hate crimes, etc. to change the existing political order.

Ezzedeen Al-Qassam Brigades – the militant arm of Hamas

Fatah – a Palestinian nationalistic political party, the largest faction of the PLO founded in part by Yasser Arafat

Fatah Tanzim – a militant wing of Fatah, established in 1995

Federal soldier – a soldier from the Russian federation

Fictive kin – relational ties not based on either blood or marriage

Flashback – an unbidden intrusion of a traumatic memory or fragment of it, which can include a vivid full sensory reliving of the memory in total or in parts made up of sensory images, sounds, smells, tactile sensations or emotions. Flash-backs may cause a person to lose touch with reality and reenact the event for a period of seconds, hours or longer.

Foreshortened future – belief that one's life will be cut short, one will not live long enough to be married, have children, etc.

Freedom fighter – one who engages in armed or nonviolent resistance to oppose an enemy invader or occupier, or an oppressive or illegitimate government.

FSB – security organ of the Russian Federation, formerly known as the KGB

Hadith –tradition based on reports of the sayings and life of the Prophet Muhammad and his companions.

Hamas – the Palestinian Islamist political party founded in 1987 that currently governs the Gaza Strip. Designated in 1993 by the U.S. as a terrorist organization.

Hidjab – Islamic headscarf

Hyperarousal (traumatic) – bodily arousal after a trauma causing difficulty concentrating, irritability or outbursts of anger, hypervigilance, sweaty palms, racing heart or difficulty falling or staying asleep

Inshallah – God willing

Intifada - uprising

Israel Defense Forces (IDF) – the military of Israel

ista shaheed – in Islam, the act of martyrdom or seeking martyrdom

(Militant) Jihad– those who follow a distorted version of Islam in which terrorism is glorified and the proponents believe that to die in armed struggle or as a suicide operative will make them an Islamic martyr. Often these groups and individuals also believe in the practice of naming other Muslims "Takfir" and in the global struggle to restore the Islamic caliphate.

Kaaba – a black cubical structure in Mecca, the holiest site in Islam, the direction to which Muslims face in prayer

Keffiyeh – traditional Arab headdress for males made from a square woven cotton scarf

Koran/quran – the holy book of Islam meaning literally the recitation, considered the verbatim word of God as revealed by the angel Gabriel to the Prophet Muhammad.

Marhaba – "welcome" in Arabic

Molotov cocktail – an incendiary device, often made from a bottle filled with a flammable liquid and a wick made of cloth stuffed inside the bottle's neck

Mossad –Israel's Institute for Intelligence and Special Operations responsible for intelligence collection, covert operations and counter-terrorism.

Mujahedeen – Islamic warriors on jihad

Mukataa – the offices and administrative center of the Palestinian National Authority

Muslim Brotherhood – the Society of the Muslim Brothers founded in Egypt in 1928 as a pan-Islamic Islamist political and social movement making up the largest political opposition in many Arab states today and having an estimated two million members worldwide today.

Obituary – a gathering and funeral celebration, in these pages always for a "martyr"

Palestinian (National) Authority (PA) - the interim administrative organization formed in 1994 after the Oslo Accords to govern parts of the West Bank and Gaza. Later renamed the Palestinian National Authority (PNA).

Palestinian Islamic Jihad (PIJ) – an Islamic Palestinian nationalist organization that opposes the existence of Israel. Designated by the U.S. as a terrorist organization.

Palestinian Liberation Authority (PLO) – a political and paramilitary organization formed in 1964 and recognized by the United Nations and many states as the sole legitimate representative of the Palestinian people. Prior to 1991, the U.S. and Israel considered the PLO as a terrorist organization.

Popular Front for the Liberation of Palestine (PFLP) - a Palestinian Marxist-Leninist organization found in 1967 and the second largest political party of the PLO.

Posttraumatic stress disorder (PTSD) – a severe anxiety disorder lasting for longer than one month after the experience of a traumatic event, including traumatic intrusions (flashbacks, nightmares, etc.), avoidance and bodily hyperarousal that cause significant difficulties in functioning normally.

Psychache – overwhelming psychic pain

Psychological autopsy – the procedure of investigating a person's death by reconstructing their thoughts, actions, feelings and events that lead to their death from records and information gathered from friends, close acquaintances and family members..

Radicalization – the process by which an individual increasingly adopts extreme political, social, ideological or religious ideals that reject the existing order.

Ramadan – the ninth month of the Islamic calendar observed with fasting from sunrise to sundown

Red Crescent – the Islamic Red Cross

Saladin Riskalin Martyrs Brigade – a small force of suicide attackers organized and dispatched by Chechen separatist commander Shamil Basayev and after his death reactivated by the Causasus Emirate. Designated in 2003 by the U.S. as a terrorist organization.

Salaam Aleikum - Wa-Aleikum Salaam – Arabic greeting of peace meaning, "Peace bBe unto you and the answer of upon you be peace".

Secondary traumatization – psychological traumatization occurring vicariously through empathetic engagement with a victim of trauma

Shabak – acryonym for the Shin Bet or Israel's internal security service

Shahada – the Islamic declaration of belief in the oneness of God and the acceptance of

Shaheed/shaheeda - Arabic term used to refer to Islamic martyrs, those who die for the sake of Allah or in defending Islamic lands, or as defined by the Koran and hadiths as ways in which martyrdom may be obtained. Often applied by Arabic speakers to suicide bombers, although ista-shaheed is also used for self-martyrdom. Female version is shaheeda.

Sharia – body of Islamic law governing both the private and public spheres

Shia – the minority branch of Islam that follows Ali, Prophet Muhammad's son-in-law as the rightful successor to Muhammad and considers Ali as the first imam.

Spetsnaz – Russian Special Forces

Suicide bomber – an individual carrying a bomb or driving a vehicle filled with explosives to a target or who otherwise attempts to detonate an explosive device with the aim of dying to kill.

Sufism – a mystical sect of Islam

Sunni – the largest and majority sect of Islam

Takfir – the practice of one Muslim declaring another as an unbeliever, and in the case of extremists, is followed by the belief that it is acceptable to execute the declared unbeliever.

Terrorism - non-state actors organized in some kind of chain of command or conspiratorial cell structure, who systematically use violence and the threat of violence against civilians, noncombatant targets and property (including iconic targets) often in a campaign of attacks with the intent to intimidate, coerce, induce fear and thereby sway public opinion and government policy to advance their political/ideological goals. Terrorist acts are not aimed only at the actual victims but makes use of the media to spread fear, psychological repercussions and amplify their message far beyond the actual target. Some terrorist groups attack both civilians and government/military targets, blurring the lines between insurgent and revolutionary behavior and terrorism.

Thobe – an ankle length traditional Islamic robe, usually with long sleeves worn by men

Wahhabi/Wahhabist - a non-indigenous form of Islam originating in the Arabian Penisula in the 18th century from a reformist movement begun by Mohamed ibn Abd al Wahhab (1703-1791), intended to return Islam to its original purity. Wahhab condemned idolatry in all forms, as well as anything that could possibly be interpreted as an intermediary to God, and ordered the destruction of sacred tombs, shrines, etc. and not only allowed, but also called for, waging war on fellow Muslims who had reverted back to a state of jahiliyyah (the state of barbarism and ignorance that prevailed in the Arabian peninsula prior to Muhammad's revelations). While the label Wahhabism denotes a totally other and neutral meaning in the Gulf States and elsewhere in the world where it is practiced peacefully, it should be understood that in Russia, Chechnya, the Caucuses, and the other former Soviet Union republics, this label denotes an ultra militant form of Islam and refers to militant religious groups that promote jihad and terrorism—so much so that in Russian the word "wahhabist" has become synonymous with terrorist.

Zionism – a Jewish nationalist movement supporting a Jewish nation state in the land of Israel.

ENDNOTES

[1] In 1999, at the request of the local Jewish population in Minsk, Belarus, I established the Holocaust Oral History Project – Belarus in which all of the remaining survivors (n=65) of the Holocaust still living in Minsk and able to give a history were interviewed. One of these histories, – that of Leeza Stein ultimately became a screenplay entitled "Beyond the Pale". More information on the project is available at http://www.annespeckhard.com/Anne_Speckhard/Holocaust_Oral_History_Project_-Belarus.html

[2] Hoffman, B. (1998). *Inside terrorism*. New York: Columbia University Press.

[3] Throughout this book, I have consciously chosen to use the words militant jihad and militant jihadi to refer to those militants and terrorists who follow a distorted version of Islam (that some would even argue is not Islam), in which terrorism, or attacks on civilians for the purpose of advancing political goals, is glorified and the proponents of such believe that to die for the terrorist cause is to die as an Islamic martyr. Often these groups and individuals also believe in the practice of naming other Muslims as Takfir, or as apostates and outside of the faith, and then justify killing them as well. Some adherents also believe they are in a cosmic struggle to restore the Islamic caliphate. While many terrorist groups are nationalistic in their political goals, many of these have \ adopted aspects of this global ideology, which I refer to as a "militant jihadi" ideology throughout the book. I chose these words carefully, consciously leaving out any use of the word Islam, although I did retain the word "jihad" because they themselves believe that they are mujahedeen, or great cosmic warriors, fighting jihad. In using these words, I mean no disrespect for Islam nor for the billions of peaceful Muslims around the world following their faith and struggling for the "greater jihad" (i.e. overcoming one's base desires to arrive at wise and Godly living).

[4] Juergensmeyer, M. (2000). *Terror in the Mind of God: The Global Rise of Religion Violence*. Berkeley and Los Angeles: University of California Press.

[5] Post, J. (2005). When hatred is bred in the bone: Psycho-cultural foundations of contemporary terrorism. *Political Psychology*, 26(4).

[6] Edwin Shneidman (1993) Suicide as psychache: A clinical approach to self-destructive behavior. Jason Aronson Rowman & Littlefield Publishers, Inc. Northvale, NJ. p. 258

[7] Comparing notes with Gerry Chiaruttini, a good friend a bit older than me who was educated by the Jesuits, we both recall in our youth being taught by Catholic nuns and priests that to die for God and faith ensured entry to heaven, whereas having a "mortal sin" on one's conscience might end in one's eternal damnation, thus salvation was not sure. Becoming a Catholic "martyr" was held up as desirable and the highest honor. Later then hearing similar stories from Islamic would be "martyrs" who also were not certain that they would avoid their terrifying version of hell and damnation, I was not surprised to see how attracted they were to "martyrdom", seeing it as a guaranteed path to paradise. Of course a huge difference is that in the distorted militant jihadi

view of Islam in which believers are equipped for suicide missions; it is not just dying for Islam that wins one the rewards of "martyrdom" but taking one's own life while killing others–a sad distortion of religion indeed.

[8] For more on these subjects see: Moghadam, A. (2008). *The globalization of martyrdom: Al Qaeda, salafi jihad, and the diffusion of suicide attacks* Baltimore: John Hopkins University Press; Pedahzur, A. (2006). *Root causes of suicide terrorism: The globalization of martyrdom.* New York: Routledge; Speckhard, A. (2006). Sacred terror: Insights into the psychology of religiously motivated terrorism. In C. Timmerman, D. Hutsebaut, S. Mells, W. Nonneman & W. V. Herck (Eds.), *Faith-based radicalism: Christianity, Islam and Judaism between constructive activism and destructive fanaticism.* Antwerp: UCSIA also accessible on my website www.AnneSpeckhard.com and Stern, J. (2003). *Terror in the Name of God: Why Religious Militants Kill.* New York: Harper-Collins.

[9] It should be noted that Arabic names in particular often sound similar. When pseudonyms are used they should not be confused for other real people of the same or similar names.

[10] There are several hundred definitions of terrorism, and scholars struggle to come to a consensus. My use of the word refers to non-state actors organized in some kind of chain of command or conspiratorial cell structure, who systematically use violence and the threat of violence against civilians, noncombatant targets and property (including iconic targets) often in a campaign of attacks with the intent to intimidate, coerce, induce fear and to thereby sway public opinion and government policy to advance their political/ideological goals. Terrorist acts are not aimed only at the actual victims but make use of the media to spread fear, psychological repercussions and amplify their message far beyond the actual target. Some terrorist groups attack both civilians and government/military targets, blurring the lines between insurgent and revolutionary behavior and terrorism.

[11] It should be noted that Arabic names in particular often sound similar. When pseudonyms are used they should not be confused for other real people of the same or similar names.

[12] These wars followed the disintegration of the Soviet Union when Moscow peacefully granted independence to the former republics of Ukraine, Belarus, Azerbaijan, Kazakhstan, and Uzbekistan, among others, but not to Chechnya, which was rich with oil and a territory *inside* Russia rather than a former republic. For more on this subject see: Speckhard, A., & Akhmedova, K. (2006). The New Chechen Jihad: Militant Wahhabism as a Radical Movement and a Source of Suicide Terrorism in Post-War Chechen Society. *Democracy and Security*, 2(1), 103-155.

[13] The move to suicide terrorism or "martyrdom missions," as the Chechen terrorists would call them, was a simple transition bound up in the political disappointment of the unwillingness of western democracies to cross Russia and support the rebels in their fight for independence. Unsupported, the Chechens turned to those who would assist them: their "Muslim brothers" in the

Middle East. And at that time the Arabs and Muslims who had gathered from countries all over the world for the "jihad" or holy war against the former Soviet Union in Afghanistan were still euphoric over their victory and keen to repeat and spread their success. Many were in search of a new cause, and jumped at the opportunity to help their Muslim brothers in Chechnya. Thus the independence movement in Chechnya began to transition from purely secular in 1998 into one heavily influenced by the militant jihadist ideology. A strong influx of money, training, and leadership from the Middle East transformed the movement, and the leaders of the Chechen rebels turned from guerilla warfare to terrorism, with suicide terrorism as their centerpiece. For a thorough discussion on this see: Speckhard, A., & Akhmedova, K. (2006). The New Chechen Jihad: Militant Wahhabism as a Radical Movement and a Source of Suicide Terrorism in Post-War Chechen Society. Democracy and Security, 2(1), 103-155.

[14] For more on this see: Speckhard, Anne & Akhmedova, Khapta (2006) "The New Chechen Jihad: Militant Wahhabism as a Radical Movement and a Source of Suicide Terrorism in Post-War Chechen Society" Democracy & Security 2:1-53, 2006.

[15] The main difference between the Chechens affiliated with the militant jihadi ideology and their "Muslim brothers" who support al Qaeda is that the Chechens are focused locally on winning independence—their "jihad" was and remains against the Russians only. The foreign fighters and those that poured funds into Chechnya from Arab nations and Europe however are more globally minded and more closely affiliated to the global militant jihadi ideology of al Qaeda and other affiliated groups.

[16] For the published research results of these studies see: Speckhard, A., & Akhmedova, K. (2005). Mechanisms of Generating Suicide Terrorism: Trauma and Bereavement as Psychological Vulnerabilities in Human Security - The Chechen Case. In J. Donnelly, Anna Kovacova, Joy Osofsky, Howard Osofsky, Caroline Paskell & J. Salem-Pickartz (Eds.), *Developing Strategies to Deal with Trauma in Children - A Means of Ensuring Conflict Prevention, Security and Social Stability. Case Study: 12–15-Year-Olds in Serbia* (Vol. 1, pp. 59-64). Brussels: NATO Security Through Science Series E Human and Societal Dynamics, IOS Press.; Speckhard, A., & Ahkmedova, K. (2006). The Making of a Martyr: Chechen Suicide Terrorism. *Journal of Studies in Conflict and Terrorism*, 29(5), 429-492.; Speckhard, A., & Akhmedova, K. (2006). Black Widows: The Chechen Female Suicide Terrorists. In Y. Schweitzer (Ed.), *Female Suicide Terrorists*. Tel Aviv: Jaffe Center Publication.; Speckhard, A., & Akhmedova, K. (2007). Black Widows and Beyond: Understanding the Motivations and Life Trajectories of Chechen Female Terrorists. In C. Ness (Ed.), *Women Terrorists and Militants: Agency, Utility and Organization* Taylor and Francis.; Speckhard, A. (2004). Soldiers for God: A Study of the Suicide Terrorists in the Moscow Hostage Taking Siege. In O. McTernan (Ed.), *The Roots of Terrorism: Contemporary Trends and Traditional Analysis.* Brussels: NATO Science Series.; Speckhard, A., Tarab-

rina, N., Krasnov, V., & Mufel, N. (2005). Stockholm Effects and Psychological Responses to Captivity in Hostages Held by Suicidal Terrorists. *Traumatology*, 11(2).And Speckhard, A., Tarabrina, N., Krasnov, V., & Mufel, N. (2005). Posttraumatic and acute stress responses in hostages held by suicidal terrorists in the takeover of a Moscow theater Traumatology, 11(1), 3-21.

[17] KGB is the acronym for the national security agency of the Former Soviet Union. The KGB was responsible for internal security, intelligence, and functioned as the secret police active from 1954 until 1991.

[18] Berezovsky is a London oligarch who was in a rivalry with Putin at the time.

[19] Wahhabism is a non-indigenous form of Islam originating in the Arabian Peninsula in the 18th century from a reformist movement begun by Mohamed ibn Abd al Wahhab (1703-1791) to return Islam to its original purity. Wahhab based his ideas on a strict interpretation of the Quran, and his movement had as its central tenant the oneness of God. He condemned idolatry in all forms as well as anything that could possibly be interpreted as an intermediary to God, ordering the destruction of sacred tombs, shrines, etc. He also not only allowed, but also called for waging war on fellow Muslims who had reverted back to a state of jahiliyyah –, or the state of barbarism and ignorance that prevailed in the Arabian peninsula prior to Mohamed's revelations. Wahhabism as a belief system, although not in itself necessarily militant, is the subset of Islam that has been used to inform the terrorist ideology, which is at the basis of the current worldwide militant jihad. For a discussion of this history see: Sageman, M. (2004). *Understanding Terror Networks*: University of Pennsylvannia Press.Pgs. 8, 58 and Esposito, J. (2002). *Unholy war: Terror in the name of Islam* New York: Oxford Univerisity Press. Pgs. 446-49 and 114-116 for a discussion of how Muhammad ibn Abd al Wahhab built upon the ideas of Ibn Taymiyya, whose fatwa allowing jihad against the warring Mongols (who claimed to be Muslims) opened the door for warfare against unIslamic or unbelieving Muslims. For a further discussion of how Wahhabism was imported into the Chechen rebel movement transitioning it into a "jihad" see:Speckhard, Anne & Akhmedova, Khapta (2006) "The New Chechen Jihad: Militant Wahhabism as a Radical Movement and a Source of Suicide Terrorism in Post-War Chechen Society" Democracy & Security 2:1-53, 2006.

[20] During the fall of the Soviet Union, Muslims the world over were eager to support the resurgence of Islam throughout the region, and as a result money from richer countries poured into the former Soviet republics to support the rebuilding of mosques, schools and other forms of Islamic expression. The same took place in Chechnya. However, with the move by Moscow in 1994 to crush the Chechen independence movement and the subsequent war (1994-1996), this influx of foreign money took an ill-fated turn. As the Russian forces invaded, the militant jihadists (who had just won their war with the Soviet Union in Afghanistan) turned their concern to other conflict zones involving Muslims. The plight of the Chechens during the war and the numerous human rights abuses that occurred at the hands of the Russians were

well publicized; hence Chechnya became identified by these jihadi groups as one of the most important new battlegrounds. Money, which had already been pouring in from foreign countries to rebuild Islamic institutions, now became much more tightly focused on the perceived oppression of the Chechens who were caught up in armed conflict to win their independence; and the militant form of Wahhabism, which had sustained the Afghan jihadists, began its journey into Chechnya. It was carried in by many means, including via foreign fighters with Afghan war experience who appeared in Chechnya to aid in what they saw as the "jihad" against Russia. The most notable of these was Saudi-born Khattab who came to Chechnya in 1995.

[21] This widely distributed book was introduced between the two wars of independence by Arabs who entered Chechnya to support the rebel movement. It was entitled "There is Only One God", and it contested many of the indigenous Chechen Sufi-based Islamic practices such as tombs honoring Islamic saints and argued that that the Wahhabi way was the only true practice of Islam. The book was widely available before the second Chechen war of independence but became a contraband item during and afterward.

[22] Chechnya Advocacy Network June 10, 2012 Refugees and Diaspora http://www.chechnyaadvocacy.org/refugees.html

[23] For the full report of this thought experiment see: Speckhard, A. (2012). Taking on the persona of a suicide bomber: A thought experiment. *Perspectives on Terrorism*, 6(2). Retrieved from http://www.terrorismanalysts.com/pt/index.php/pot/article/view/speckhard-taking-on-the-persona

[24] For more on this see: Speckhard, A., & Akhmedova, K. (2006). Black Widows: The Chechen Female Suicide Terrorists. In Y. Schweitzer (Ed.), *Female Suicide Terrorists*. Tel Aviv: Jaffe Center Publication.andSpeckhard, A., & Akhmedova, K. (2007). Black Widows and Beyond: Understanding the Motivations and Life Trajectories of Chechen Female Terrorists. In C. Ness (Ed.), *Women Terrorists and Militants*: *Agency, Utility and Organization* Taylor and Francis.

[25] This thought experiement in some ways echoed an earlier one conducted by Stanford Professor Philip Zimbardo in which he brought young male volunteers into a two-week long role play in which they took on the roles of prisoners and prison guards. Dr. Zimbardo had to curtail his experiement before its conclusion due to its disastorous results:the role playing guards became sadistic and the pretend prisoners began to become depressed and show signs of such extreme stress. We, of course, were aware of his experiement and how easily subjects can fall into roles suggested for them, so we also took great care in screening and were careful not to harm our participants. For more on Zimbardo's experiment see: The Stanford Prison Experiment at http://www.prisonexp.org

[26] Also referred to in clinical and other helper settings by Charles Figley as compassion fatigue. See "Compassion fatigue as secondary traumatic stress disorder: An overview. Compassion fatigue: Coping with secondary traumatic stress disorder in those who treat the traumatized. Figley, Charles R. Figley, Charles

R. (Ed). (1995). *Compassion fatigue: Coping with secondary traumatic stress disorder in those who treat the traumatized.* Brunner/Mazel psychological stress series, No. 23. (pp. 1-20). Philadelphia, PA, US: Brunner/Mazel.

[27]For further discussion on this see: Maeseele, P. V., G; Stevens, I. & Speckhard, A. (2008). Psycho-social resilience in the face of a mediated terrorist threat. *Media War & Conflict*, 1(1), 50-69. Retrieved from http://www.coe.int/t/dg4/majorhazards/ressources/virtuallibrary/materials/belgium/media,war,conflict.pdf Pg 52. [28]Argo, N. (2006) Personal communication.

[29]Hass, A. (2004, March 3). When Death is Normal. *Haretz.*

[30]Atran, S. (2003).Genesis of Suicide Terrorism. *Science*, 299(5612), 1534 - 1539.

[31]See: Speckhard, A., & Ahkmedova, K. (2006). The Making of a Martyr: Chechen Suicide Terrorism. *Journal of Studies in Conflict and Terrorism*, 29(5), 429-492.

[32]Bruce Bongar personal communication as well as Bongar, Bruce (2004) Suicide Terrorism. Paper presented for Suicide Terrorism: Strategic Importance and Counterstrategies, NATO Advanced Research Workshop.

[34]For the scientific report of this study see: Speckhard, A. (2012). Taking on the persona of a suicide bomber: A thought experiment. Perspectives on Terrorism, 6(2). Retrieved from http://www.terrorismanalysts.com/pt/index.php/pot/article/view/speckhard-taking-on-the-persona. pp 51-73.

[33]Israel Ministry of Foreign Affairs (November 9, 2004) PFLP terrorists behind Tel Aviv suicide bombing arrested. http://www.mfa.gov.il/MFA/Terrorism-+Obstacle+to+Peace/Terrorism+and+Islamic+Fundamentalism-/PFLP+terrorists+behind+Tel+Aviv+suicide+bombing+arrested+9-Nov-2004.htm?DisplayMode=print Accessed June 12, 2012.

[35]Disgusted hearing this, I want to question him more to verify the Israeli soldiers' treatment of him and ensure he isn't exaggerating, but I know it is unwise to interrupt his flow. I decide to wait and see if I hear this again from other subjects who were also arrested—unfortunately, I later do hear the same repeatedly.

[36]Mustafa never tells us the prison he was held in, but the most frequently used prisons by the Israelis inside Israel for interrogation are al Jalameh, al Mlabbes, Asqalan, and al Muskubieh, which are all run by the Shabak, and the Israeli General Security Agency similar to our FBI. There are also Israeli military detention centers inside the West Bank where Palestinians are held under military control, and though prisoners are not supposed to be held for more than eight days, they are often interrogated with the Shabak present and detained for much longer.

[37]Edwin Shneidman (1993) Suicide as psychache: A clinical approach to self-destructive behavior. Jason Aronson Rowman & Littlefield Publishers, Inc. Northvale, NJ

[38]Only one Palestinian mother is known for urging her son to go as a suicide bomber.

[39] The organization of Palestinian boy and young men into political factions in the same way boys in other cultures support sports teams is a reflection made by Israeli counter-terrorism expert Ariel Merari.

[40] Bloom, M. (2005). *Dying to Kill: The Allure of Suicide Terror*: Columbia University Press.

[41] Shikaki, K. (2006). Willing to Compromise: Palestinian Public Opinion and the Peace Process. *Special Report No. 158*, 1-16 United States Institute of Peace.

[42] (FIDH), Fédération Internationale des ligues des Droits de l'Homme. "Palestinian Prisoners in Israel: The Inhuman Conditions Being Suffered by Political Prisoners." (July 13, 2003), http://www.fidh.org/Palestinian-Prisoners-in-Israel.

[43] International, Defence for Children. "Palestinian Prisoners Day 2009: Highest Number of Children Currently in Detention since 2000." (April 18, 2009), http://www.dci-pal.org/english/display.cfm?DocId=1126& CategoryId=1.

[44] As I was listening and did not want to interrupt the flow when she mentioned this place, I later forgot to ask and failed to confirm its spelling.

[45] Kalman, Matthew. "The Woman in the Way of Palestinian Prisoner Deal." *Time* (December 30, 2009), http://www.time.com/time/world/article/0,8599,1950487,00.html.

[46] B'tselem. (January 1, 2011). Administrative detention. *B'Tselem - The Israeli Information Center for Human Rights in the Occupied Territories*. Retrieved from http://www.btselem.org/administrative_detention.

[47] B'tselem. (January 1, 2011). Administrative detention. B'Tselem - The Israeli Information Center for Human Rights in the Occupied Territories. Retrieved from http://www.btselem.org/administrative_detention.

[48] Eyadat, F. (October 16, 2008). Two Palestinian girls detained in Israel without trial for months. Haaretz. Retrieved from http://www.haaretz.com/print-edition/news/two-palestinian-girls-detained-in-israel-without-trial-for-months-1.255577

[49] According to sources, the $25,000 payout was rarely, if ever, the full amount that reached a "martyr's" family. Instead a "public check" went to the family but in reality that check was delivered through Palestinian organizations that took a substantial cut and then the money that was left over was given either in kind to rebuild a destroyed house or in an actual payout usually equal to or less than five thousand dollars. For more on this see: BBC News. (March 13, 2003). Palestinians get Saddam funds. Retrieved from http://news.bbc.co.uk/2/hi/middle_east/2846365.stm

[50] Indeed within less than two years of him telling us this, in January of 2006, the Palestinians were allowed to hold elections and Fatah, the PA ruling party, was swept out of office by the resounding victory of Hamas. While it surprised the world, most analysts concluded that Hamas victory occured in response to Palestinians anger over corruption within the PA and a desire for a more honest political party versus any desire to embrace the radical Islamist position or violence against Israel that Hamas also puts forward.

[51] See: Hafez, M. (2006). *Manufacturing Human Bombs: The Making of Palestinian Suicide Bombers*. Washington, D.C.: United States Institute of Peace Press Books. And Hafez, M. M. (2007).*Suicide Bombers in Iraq: The Strategy and Ideology of Martyrdom*. Washington, D.C.: United States Institute of Peace Press.

[52] The green line refers to the demarcation lines set out in the 1949 Armistice Agreements between Israel and its neighbors (Egypt, Jordan, Lebanon and Syria) after the 1948 Arab-Israeli War, lines that were drawn in green ink on the map while the talks were going on. It also refers to the temporary borders between Israel and the territories captured in the Six-Day War, including the West Bank, Gaza Strip, Golan Heights and Sinai Peninsula (the latter has since been returned to Egypt). The green line basically differentiates between those areas that are administered as part of the State of Israel, and the areas outside it, which are administered by the Israeli military or the Palestinian National Authority.

[53] Right of return is the Palestinian demand for Palestinians who were kicked out or fled Israel to be allowed to return to resettle in Palestine when it achieves statehood. Some estimates of the current number of first-generation Palestinian refugees and their descendants is over four million.

[54] Sarraj, E. (April 8, 2002). Why we blow ourselves up. *Time*. Retrieved from http://www.time.com/time/magazine/article/0,9171,1002161,00.html.

[55] Merari, A. (2003). Suicide Terrorism - unpublished manuscript.

[56] Peace Now reports in 2007 that "For many years the state of Israel has been seizing thousands of dunams of private Palestinian land in order to construct settlements. The claim by the State and settlers that the settlements have been constructed on state land is misleading and false." They also state that "130 West Bank settlements were constructed either entirely or partially on private Palestinian land," and "that approximately fifty-one thousand dunams of the land used by the settlements is actually private Palestinian land" and that this "accounts for thirty-two percent of land used for settlements." They also state, "Construction of settlements on private Palestinian land is illegal according to Israel's Supreme Court ruling, (i.e. the Elon More precedent of 1979), and thus cannot be authorized." Lastly they claim that these facts have "been hidden by Israel for years" in order to maintain positive international relations. See: Etkes, D., & Ofran, H. (March 14, 2007). Settlement are built on private Palestinian land. Retrieved from http://peacenow.org.il/eng/content/settlement-are-built-private-palestinian-land

[57] Applied Research Institute Jerusalem. (October 24, 2000). Jid Oneim settlers attack Beit Foreek villagers in Nablus. Retrieved from http://www.poica.org/editor/case_studies/view.php?recordID=107

[58] Marcus, I., & Nan Jacques Zilderdik. (March 13, 2011). PA tv glorified terrorist who killed three in Itamar in 2002. Palestinian Media Watch. Retrieved from http://www.palwatch.org/main.aspx?fi=157& doc_id=4794

[59] Gedalyahu, T. B. (March 12, 2011). Victims identified as family of Rabbi Fogel of Yeshiva Itamar. *Israel National News*. Retrieved from http://www.israelnationalnews.com/News/News.aspx/142842#.TsVyBWC3lQg

[60] Sherwood, H. (March 14, 2011). Israelis and Palestinians in shock after Fogel family massacre. *The Guardian*. Retrieved from http://www.guardian.co.uk/world/2011/mar/14/fogel-family-massacre-israelis-palestinians

[61] Some news reports differ from this account stating that Yousef (armed with an AK-47 assault rifle) positioned himself near one of Itamar's gates and waited for a patrol vehicle from the settlement's security squad to drive past, at which time he shot Shlomo Miller, the settlement's security coordinator. Miller's fellow guards rushed to the scene after hearing the volley of shots and shot Yousef to death. Yousef killed only Shlomo Miller. Yousef is also identified as being employed by the PA as a member of the Palestinian security forces See: King, L. (August 14, 2004). W. Bank settler slain in ambush. *Los Angeles Times/World*. Retrieved from http://articles.latimes.com/2004/aug/14/world/fg-mideast14.

[62] Alheisi, R. (April 4, 2010). Waiting To Return Home: Palestinian Martyrs in Israeli "Cemeteries of Numbers" and Morgues. *My Palestine*. Retrieved from http://avoicefrompalestine.wordpress.com/2010/04/17/waiting-to-return-home-palestinian-martyrs-in-israeli-"cemeteries-of-numbers"-and-morgues/

[63] Cain, K., Postlewait, H., & Thomson, A. (2004). Emergency Sex and Other Desperate Measures: A True Story From Hell On Earth. New York: Miramax.

[64] Israeli Ministry of Foreign Affairs Website. (April 2, 2002). Yasser Arafat's "ta'a" Compound in Ramallah - A Center for Controlling and Supporting Terrorism. Retrieved from http://www.mfa.gov.il/MFA/Government/Communiques/2002/Yasser+Arafat-s+ta-a+Compound+in+Ramallah+-+A.htm

[65] The Telegraph. (May 1, 2002). Arafat siege to end as handover agreed. Retrieved from http://www.telegraph.co.uk/news/1392784/Arafat-siege-to-end-as-handover-agreed.html

[66] CNN. (September 30, 2002). Israel leaves Arafat compound. Retrieved from http://europe.cnn.com/2002/WORLD/meast/09/29/mideast/index.html

[67] A Hadith is a tradition or saying attributed from his companions to the Prophet Muhammad.

[68] Lloyd deMause personal communication in 2004. For his complete argument see his chapter on the Childhood Origins of Terrorism in deMause, L. (2002). *The emotional life of nations*: Other Press.

[69] As reported by B' Tselem, an Israeli human rights organization, between 2000 and the end of 2005, Israeli security forces assassinated 203 Palestinian terrorists, killing an additional 114 people in the process. The targets were mostly members of Hamas, Palestinian Islamic Jihad, and the al Aqsa Martyrs Brigade and in 2004 Israel began targeting Hamas political leadership as well. One mathematical analysis of Israel's targeted assassination campaign demonstrates that targeted killing did not result in Israel achieving its stated strategic desired end state of reducing numbers of Palestinian attacks although it may have decimated the ranks of terrorist leaders. See:

Boyden, A. W., Menard, P. P., & Ramirez, R. (December 2009). Making the case: What is the problem with targeted killing? Retrieved from http://www.dtic.mil/cgi-bin/GetTRDoc?AD=ADA514257. Another analysis reported that targeted assassinations had no positive impact on the rates of Palestinian violence - see: Hafez, M. M., & Hatfield, J. M. (September 22, 2006). Do targeted assassinations work? A multivariate analysis of Israel's controversial tactic during Al-Aqsa uprising. *Conflict & Terrorism*, 29(4). For more discussion on this topic see: Byman, D. (March/April 2006). Do targeted killings work? 85(2). Retrieved from http://www12.georgetown.edu/sfs/cpass/Articles/BymanTargetedKillings.pdf and Eisenstadt, M. (August 2001). Pre-emptive targeted killings as counter-terrorism tool: An assessment of Israel's approach. *Peacewatch*; August 28, 2001.

[70] For a more complete discussion of this whole topic see: Speckhard, A. (2010). Research challenges involved in field research and interviews regarding the militant jihad, extremism and suicide terrorism. *Democracy and Security*, 199-222.

[71] For more on Muna see: Kalman, M. (December 30, 2009). The woman in the way of Palestinian prisoner deal. *Time* Retrieved from http://www.time.com/time/world/article/0,8599,1950487,00.html and Tarnopolsky, N. (October 20, 2011). Palestinian terrorists released by Israel unexpectedly shows up in Turkey. *Global Post*. Retrieved from http://www.globalpost.com/dispatches/globalpost-blogs/the-casbah/palestinian-terrorist-released-israel-unexpectedly-shows-turk

[72] Berko, A. (2007). *The path to paradise: The inner world of suicide bombers and their dispatchers*. Westport, Connecticut: Praeger Security International.

[73] Yoram Schweitzer provided the information about the Israeli version of the explosion in a personal communication. Yoram Schweitzer (2005, personal communication)..

[74] At the time Barbara Victor's book was just in circulation and she was claiming that Palestinian women were motivated to join the ranks of men as suicide bombers in part to achieve equality. See: Victor, B. (2003). *Army of Roses: Inside the world of Palestinian women suicide bombers*. London: Robinson. In my opinion, Victor's analysis is off the mark, and I found in my interviews thatmany of her informants were not happy with her either. For a more accurate and contextual analysis of how female terrorists activate and why, I would recommend Clara Beyler, Mia Bloom, Karla Cunningham, Deborah Scroggins, Cindy Ness, Yoram Schweitzer and Farhana Ali (now Qazi) who have all written sensitive pieces on female suicide terrorists as well as my own work on the topic: Beyler, C. (February 12, 2003). Messengers of death - Female suicide bombers.*International Institute for Counter-Terrorism*. Retrieved from http://ict.org.il/apage/printv/10728.php.; Bloom, M. (2011).; *Women and terrorism: Bombshell*. Philadelphia: University of Pennsylvannia Press. Cunningham, C. (2007). Countering Female Terrorism. *Conflict & Terrorism*, 30(2), 113-129.; Ness, C. (Ed.). (2008). *Female Terrorism and Militancy: Agency, Utility and Organization* Taylor and Francis. Routledge.; Scroggins,

D. (2012). Wanted women: Faith, lies and the war on terror: the lives of Ayaan Hirsi Ali and Aafia Siddiqui. New York: Harper Collins.; Schweitzer, Y. (Ed.). (2006). *Female Suicide Bombers: Dying for Equality?* : The Jaffee Center for Strategic Studies and (Qazi) Ali, F. (2005). Muslim female fighters: an emerging trend. *Terrorism Monitor*, 3(21); Speckhard, A. (2008). The Emergence of Female Suicide Terrorists.Studies in Conflict and Terrorism 31, 1-29. Speckhard, A. (2009). Female suicide bombers in Iraq. *Democracy and Security*, 5(1), 19-50.; Speckhard, A., & Akhmedova, K. (2006). Black Widows: The Chechen Female Suicide Terrorists. In Y. Schweitzer (Ed.), Female Suicide Terrorists. Tel Aviv: Jaffe Center Publication.andSpeckhard, A., & Akhmedova, K. (2008). Black Widows and Beyond: Understanding the Motivations and Life Trajectories of Chechen Female Terrorists. In C. Ness (Ed.), *Female Terrorism and Militancy: Agency, Utility and Organization: Agency, Utility and Organization* Routledge.

[75] Berko, A. (2007). *The path to paradise: The inner world of suicide bombers and their dispatchers*. Westport, Connecticut: Praeger Security International. Page 78.

[76] Berko, A. (2007). *The path to paradise: The inner world of suicide bombers and their dispatchers*. Westport, Connecticut: Praeger Security International. Pp. 115, 121

[77] Berko, A. (2007). *The path to paradise: The inner world of suicide bombers and their dispatchers*. Westport, Connecticut: Praeger Security International. Page 118.

[78] Vered Levy-Barzilai. (June 2002). Media Echoes: Interview with a suicide bomber. *Haaretz*. Retrieved from http://www.therazor.org/oldroot/Summer02/sbombinterview.htm

[79] Berko, A. (2007). *The path to paradise: The inner world of suicide bombers and their dispatchers*. Westport, Connecticut: Praeger Security International. Page 117.

[80] According to Yoram Schweitzer (2005, personal communication) he learned in his interviews that Arin was to detonate minutes after the boy, thus causing maximum carnage as civilian helpers and the rescue workers gathered at the site of the first explosion. Arin confirmed this in an interview she gave to Defense Minister Benjamin Ben-Eliezer in prison explaining that she and the boy were positioned in such a way that when everyone ran from his explosion she would be standing by to wait a few minutes until a panicked crowd formed around her to detonate. See: Vered Levy-Barzilai. (June 2002). Media Echoes: Interview with a suicide bomber. *Haaretz*. Retrieved from http://www.therazor.org/oldroot/Summer02/sbombinterview.htm

[81] Berko, A. (2007). *The path to paradise: The inner world of suicide bombers and their dispatchers*. Westport, Connecticut: Praeger Security International. Page 117.

[82] See: Hass, A. (2004, March 3). When Death is Normal. *Haretz*. and Speckhard, A. (2012). Taking on the persona of a suicide bomber: A thought experiment. *Perspectives on Terrorism*, 6(2), 51-73. Retrieved from http://www.terroris-

manalysts.com/pt/index.php/pot/article/view/speckhard-taking-on-the-persona

[83] Berko, A. (2007). *The path to paradise: The inner world of suicide bombers and their dispatchers*. Westport, Connecticut: Praeger Security International. Page 119.

[84] Berko, A. (2007). *The path to paradise: The inner world of suicide bombers and their dispatchers*. Westport, Connecticut: Praeger Security International. Page 117.

[85] Wafa Idris, the first successful female Palestinian suicide bomber, exploded herself on January 27th, 2002, whereas the battle of Jenin (a part of the IDF's Operation Defensive Shield), which Omaia refers to as the big operation, took place April 1-11, 2002. The IDF had entered the camp a month previously as well, likely the operation she refers to as the smaller operation. Omaia recalls that she volunteered two weeks prior to the IDF incursions, so she likely volunteered herself in February, 2002 just after Wafa exploded herself, although her comments make it sound otherwise—that she volunteered *before* Wafa had exploded herself.So, if Omaia had gone immediately on her mission she might have become the first Palestinian female bomber. Given that Wafa exploded herself at the end of January, it's possible. We, however, failed to clarify on this point. Omaia, however, went operational well after Wafa, as she was vetted for two weeks after volunteering, made her video and then waited for another three months to go on her mission due to the delays caused by the IDF invasions.

[86] If I ever feel nervous about an attack, I remind myself as the bouncer checks my bag upon entering, that it was the security guard (Avi Tabib) in that incident, who saved everyone else in the 2003 attack by preventing suicide bomber, Asif Mohammed Hanif, from entering the bar. Instead, Hanif blew himself up at the entrance killing the security guard (Avi Tabib) instantly. Omar Khan Sharif, the second in the pair who tried to bomb Mike's Place, ran off when he wasn't able to detonate his belt for the secondary explosion. His body eventually washed up in the sea nearby, cause of death unknown. For more on this attack see: Khazzoom, L. (August 29, 2003). Tel Aviv bar and bomb target slowly getting its groove back. *jweekly.com*. Retrieved from http://www.jweekly.com/article/full/20444/tel-aviv-bar-and-bomb-target-slowly-getting-its-groove-back/ And for profiles on the bombers see: Global Jihad. (May 18, 2007).; Asif Mohammed Hanif. Retrieved from http://www.globaljihad.net/view_page.asp?id=204 and Global Jihad. (May 18, 2007). And Omar Khan Sharif. Retrieved from http://www.globaljihad.net/view_page.asp?id=205

[87] Wadie Haddad was the deputy of George Habash who founded the PFLP in 1967 after the Six-Day War.

[88] BBC News. (September 12, 1970). 1970: Hijacked jets destroyed by guerrillas. Retrieved from http://news.bbc.co.uk/onthisday/hi/dates/stories/september/12/newsid_2514000/2514929.stm

89 See: Council on Foreign Relations. (October 31, 2005). PFLP, DFLP, PFLP-GC, Palestinian leftists. Retrieved from http://www.cfr.org/israel/pflp-dflp-pflp-gc-palestinian-leftists/p9128

90 Council on Foreign Relations. (October 31, 2005). PFLP, DFLP, PFLP-GC, Palestinian leftists. Retrieved from http://www.cfr.org/israel/pflp-dflp-pflp-gc-palestinian-leftists/p9128

91 For more on this event see: BBC News. (September 12, 1970). 1970: Hijacked jets destroyed by guerrillas. Retrieved from http://news.bbc.co.uk/onthisday/hi/dates/stories/september/12/newsid_2514000/2514929.stm; PBS. (February 14, 2006). The American hijacker: The hijacking. Retrieved from http://www.pbs.org/wgbh/amex/hijacked/sfeature/sf_american_04.html

92 Years later, Leila Khalid transitioned into politics and served in 2009 as a member of the Palestinian National Council. Carlos the Jackal was captured and is currently serving a life sentence in France.

93 Ahmed is referring to when U.S. pressure on Sudan culminated in the Sudanese government's surrender of Carlos. At the same time, Ahmed tells us that Abdullah Ocalan, who was hiding with the help of Greek diplomats in Nairobi, was also given over to the Turks by the Kenyans, with Ahmed complaining "This is not the first time Kenya gave up people. In 1978 they gave four of our PFLP [militants] to the authorities and in 1980 also." Ocalan was the Kurdish founder of the Revolutionary organization called Kurdistan Workers' Party (PKK), founded in 1978, that carried out many terrorist attacks against the Turkish government including suicide bombings

94 At this point in the interview, Ahmed goes on for about an hour talking politics. He gave his opinion on the Chechen struggle included the following statements, "In Chechnya, the revolution was not for the benefit of [ordinary] Chechens. Their condition was not so bad. Bands of Chechen [militants] controlled the economy. The U.S. planned to make Russia weak and the U.S. made the war in Chechnya." Ahmed is correct that many of the Chechen rebels had been in the illegal smuggling trade and formed part of the basis for the armed struggle in Chechnya—but the Chechen struggle for independence was not a U.S.-backed revolution by any means. Indeed, the lack of western support to the Chechen rebels may have been part of what drove them ultimately into the arms of Middle Eastern militant jihadi ideologues and the use of "martyrdom" missions. And while the Chechen people supported independence from the former USSR and Russia during the first war, only the rebels continued the struggle. Their struggle, however, transitioned foreign fighters, ideology and funds from the Middle East entered into Chechnya to shore up what became their "jihad". For a much more in-depth discussion of the Chechen situation see: Speckhard, Anne & Akhmedova, Khapta (2006) The New Chechen Jihad: Militant Wahhabism as a Radical Movement and a Source of Suicide Terrorism in Post-War Chechen Society Democracy and Security 2(1) pg. 1-53.; Anne Speckhard & Khapta Ahkmedova (2006) The Making of a Martyr: Chechen Suicide Terrorism, Journal of Studies in Conflict and Terrorism Volume 29, Issue 5.; Speckhard, A., & Akhmedova,

K. (2008). Black Widows and Beyond: Understanding the Motivations and Life Trajectories of Chechen Female Terrorists. In C. Ness (Ed.), *Female Terrorism and Militancy: Agency, Utility and Organization: Agency, Utility and Organization* Routledge.;Akhmedova, K., & Speckhard, A. (2006). A multi-causal analysis of the genesis of suicide terrorism: The Chechen case. In J. Victoroff (Ed.), *Social and psychological factors in the genesis of terrorism* (pp. 324-354): IOS Press. "It's the same in the Bosnia/Kosovar case," Ahmed also told us. "The U.S. and Europeans were not involved [in saving the Bosnians and Kosovars]; they wanted to destroy the Serbian system because it wasn't going to their benefit." He continued on about Ceauşescu, Romania and American interests and about the Cold War struggle between communist and capitalist forces. In some cases he was very well informed, in others he seemed to have absorbed pure communist propaganda.

[95] David C. Rapoport.(Spring/Summer 2002).The four waves of rebel terror and September 11. *Anthropoetics*, 8(1). Retrieved from http://www.anthropoetics.ucla.edu/ap0801/terror.htm

[96] Bloom, M. (2005). *Dying to Kill: The Allure of Suicide Terror*: Columbia University Press.

[97] Greenberg, J., & Neilan, T. (June 3, 2002). Palestinian court orders release of top militant wanted by Israel. *New York Times*. Retrieved from http://www.nytimes.com/2002/06/03/international/04CND-ISRA.html

[98] Indeed Yasser Arafat is among these Nobel Prize winners for his role in negotiating the Oslo Accords. For the Bloom quote see Bloom, M. (2011). *Women and terrorism: Bombshell*. Philadelphia: University of Pennsylvania Press. Page 18.

[99] Greenberg, J., & Neilan, T. (June 3, 2002). Palestinian court orders release of top militant wanted by Israel. *New York Times*. Retrieved from http://www.nytimes.com/2002/06/03/international/04CND-ISRA.html

[100] CNN World. (October 17, 2011). Rechavam Zeevi: A controversial figure. Retrieved from http://articles.cnn.com/2001-10-17/world/israel.zeevi.profile_1_palestinians-israeli-army-parliament?_

[101] BBC News. (December 4, 2007). Israeli minister's killer jailed. Retrieved from http://news.bbc.co.uk/2/hi/middle_east/7125686.stm

[102] Hass, A. (April 4, 2007). The Holocaust as political asset. *Haaretz*. Retrieved from http://www.haaretz.com/print-edition/opinion/the-holocaust-as-political-asset-1.218447

[103] Koppel, T. (Writer). (2005). Reign of Terror, *Nightline*: ABC News.

[104] Israel Ministry of Foreign Affairs. (March 14, 2006). IDF operation in Jericho to arrest murderers of Israeli minister Ze'evi. Retrieved from http://www.mfa.gov.il/MFA/Government/Communiques/2006/IDF+operation+in+Jericho+to+arrest+murderers+of+Israeli+minister+Zeevi+14-Mar-2006.htm

[105] Erlanger, S., & Myre, G. (March 15, 2006). Israelis seize six in raid on prison in the West Bank. *The New York Times*. Retrieved from http://www.nytimes.com/2006/03/15/international/middleeast/15mideast.html

[106] Edelman, O. (March 12, 2007). Rehavam Ze'evi assassin jailed for two life terms plus 100 years. *Haaretz*. Retrieved from http://www.haaretz.com/news/rehavam-ze-evi-assassin-jailed-for-two-life-terms-plus-100-years-1.234461

[107] Weiss, E. (December 25, 2008). Israel sentences PFLP leader to 30 years in prison. *Ynetnews*. Retrieved from http://www.ynetnews.com/articles/0,7340,L-3644555,00.html

[108] Weiss, E. (December 25, 2008). Israel sentences PFLP leader to 30 years in prison. *Ynetnews*. Retrieved from http://www.ynetnews.com/articles/0,7340,L-3644555,00.html

[109] Israel Ministry of Foreign Affairs. (July 2, 2002). Suicide bombers from Jenin Available from http://www.mfa.gov.il/MFA/MFAArchive/2000_2009/2002/7/Suicide%20Bombers%20from%20Jenin

[110] UNRWA. Jenin Refugee Camp. Retrieved from http://www.unrwa.org/etemplate.php?id=118

[111] According to the Council on Foreign Relations, the al Aqsa Martyrs Brigade is described as a decentralized network of West Bank militias affiliated with former Palestinian leader Yasser Arafat's Fatah faction. They emerged at the start of the second Intifada in response to Ariel Sharon and his one thousand armed guards marching up to and entering the al Aqsa mosque in east Jerusalem. The Brigades initially targeted only Israeli soldiers and settlers in the West Bank and Gaza Strip using shootings to do so. However, in early 2002 when the Palestinian death toll from the second Intifada was nearing one thousand, they joined Hamas and Palestinian Islamic Jihad in carrying out a string of terrorist attacks, mostly suicide operations, against civilians inside Israel. The U.S. State Department designated the al Aqsa Martyrs Brigade as a foreign terrorist organization in 2002 and describe them as consisting of localized, autonomous units that mostly act independently of each other, united under a common alliance to Fatah. Fatah leaders claim there is no supervisor-subordinate role between Fatah and al Aqsa, and that they have never been able to exercise effective control of the martyrs' brigades. See: Fletcher, H. (April 2, 2008). Al Aqsa Martyrs Brigade. *The Council on Foreign Relations*. Retrieved from http://www.cfr.org/israel/al-aqsa-martyrs-brigade/p9127

[112] Toomey, C. (June 11, 2006). Discussing the politics of murder. *The Sunday Times*. Retrieved from http://www.christinetoomey.com/content/?p=110

[113] Toomey, C. (June 11, 2006). Discussing the politics of murder. *The Sunday Times*. Retrieved from http://www.christinetoomey.com/content/?p=110

[114] A Molotov cocktail is an improvised incendiary device—a homemade bomb. It is made from a breakable bottle containing a flammable substance such as gasoline with a cloth wick usually soaked in alcohol or kerosene held in place by the bottle's stopper. When ready to use, the militant lights the wick and throws the bottle at a target where it smashes and causes a fireball followed by a raging fire.

[115] Issacharoff, A., Benn, A., & Harel, A. (July 15, 2007). Fatah men, including Zubeidi, turn in their guns in amnesty deal. *Haaretz*. Retrieved from http://

www.haaretz.com/news/fatah-men-including-zbeidi-turn-in-their-guns-in-amnesty-deal-1.225526

[116] ProCon.org. (June 18, 2008). Where is Hebron, and what is its religious significance to Jews and Muslims? Retrieved from http://israelipalestinian.procon.org/view.answers.php?questionID=987

[117] Historically Hebron had a significant Jewish population but after Arab riots in 1929 most Jews left and did not return until after the 1967 Arab-Israeli War when the Israeli occupation occurred and then numerous Jewish settlements were established outside Hebron that continue to proliferate today

[118] Twenty-six miles is approximately forty-two kilometers.

[119] The Hamas position of decimating Israel may have changed in July 2009 when Khaled Meshal, Hamas's Damascus-based political bureau chief, said the organization was willing to cooperate with a resolution to the Arab-Israeli conflict which included a Palestinian state based on 1967 borders, provided that Palestinian refugees hold the right to return to Israel and that East Jerusalem be the new nation's capital. See: Bronner, E. (April 22, 2008). Carter says Hamas and Syria are open to peace. *The New York Times*. Retrieved from http://www.nytimes.com/2008/04/22/world/middleeast/22mideast.html?_r=1

[120] This interview occurs in 2005, a year before the Hamas victory, and is at a time when many West Bank Palestinians are becoming disillusioned with Fatah and the PLO, feeling that corruption is widespread and that Hamas leaders, at least, are not corrupt because their religious beliefs forbid it. Especially during the second Intifada that is at this time on it's fifth year, Palestinians feel angered over the frequent Israeli incursions into the West Bank and the 24-hour curfews. And many are forced to turn to Hamas to keep the food supplies open and the social programs running, services for which the PA has let them down. It's clear from his opening remarks that Ziad shares many of these sentiments. Yet Hamas is also the organization that claimed his son for a suicide mission. For background on Hamas see: Council on Foreign Relations. (October 20, 2011). Hamas. *Backgrounder*. Retrieved from http://www.cfr.org/israel/hamas/p8968and for further remarks about Hamas influence in Hebron during that time period seeSmith, J. (June 24, 2003). The Palestinian football martyrs.The Free Library. Retrieved from http://www.thefreelibrary.com/SUICIDE+UNITED%3B+Thaer's+brother+was+one+of+nine+players+from+the+same...-a0104059976

[121] The PLO Negotiations Affairs Department claims the following: "Since the military occupation began in 1967, more than 24 homes have been demolished in the old city of Hebron to make way for these illegal colonies," that "an additional 14 homes have been illegally confiscated by Israel since January 2002" and that "more than 100 homes (inhabited by approximately 500 people) have been abandoned by their Palestinian owners due to extreme harassment by Israeli settlers and the Israeli army and 1,500 Palestinian shops, situated in the heart of the old city, have been closed down by the Israeli army". See: The PLO Negotiations Affairs Department. (December 2002). Fact sheets and

frequently asked questions. Retrieved from http://www.robat.scl.net/content/NAD/faqs/fact_sheets/hebron.php#footer20

[122] Dov Dribin's son for instance, was perhaps the worst: accused of killing two Palestinian shepherds, one in 1991 and another in 1993, Dov Dribin also ran over a Palestinian with his tractor and beat him with a club in 1998, and was himself killed in an altercation (perhaps by friendly fire) between settlers and the Palestinian shepherd, whose dog he had shot. See: Meehan, M. (May June 1998). Shooting of infamous Kiryat-Arba-born "cowboy"by Jewish settler stirs tension in Hebron hills *Washington Report on Middleeastern Affairs report from the Jerusalem Journal*, 10,94. Retrieved from http://www.wrmea.com/component/content/article/194-1998-may-june/2952-shooting-of-infamous-kiryat-arba-born-qcowboyq-by-jewish-settler-stirs-tension-in-hebron-hills-.html

[123] B'Tselem, an Israeli human rights organization reported that with the outbreak of the second Intifada in 2000 and the tight closure on the West Bank and Gaza, the hundred and ten thousand Palestinians who worked in Israel (one fourth of the Palestinian workforce) found it difficult, if not impossible, to continue working in Israel. This caused dire hardship for them and for the large numbers dependent on them. Unemployment soared and by 2007, less than one tenth of the Palestinian workforce (68,000 Palestinians) worked in Israel and in the Jewish settlements in the West Bank, often at below poverty wages and some also in abusive circumstances. B'Tselem reports: "The tight closure on the West Bank and the Gaza Strip in recent years has taken the bread off the tables of thousands of Palestinian workers. Just prior to the outbreak of the second intifada, 110,000 Palestinians worked in Israel, some one-fourth of the Palestinian workforce, and the unemployment rate stood at ten percent. When the intifada began, the unemployment rate in the Occupied Territories jumped and has remained high ever since. By way of illustration, in the first quarter of 2007, some 68,000 Palestinians, less than one-tenth of the Palestinian workforce, worked in Israel and in the Jewish settlements in the West Bank. More than twenty percent of Palestinian jobseekers were unemployed. The Palestinians who had jobs were not guaranteed a suitable living, given the low wages in the Occupied Territories and the large number of persons dependent on the workers. More than one-half of the employees in the Occupied Territories earned a monthly wage that left them and their dependants under the poverty line." See: B'tselem. (January 1, 2011). Workers from the occupied territories. *B'Tselem - The Israeli Information Center for Human Rights in the Occupied Territories*. Retrieved from http://www.btselem.org/workers

[124] Fadi's Jihad Mosque soccer team was affiliated with the A-Rabat Mosque in the Abu Katila neighborhood of Hebron according to Haaretz see: Regular, A. (May 30, 2003). Hebron's playing—and plotting—field. *Haaretz*. Retrieved from http://www.haaretz.com/print-edition/news/hebron-s-playing-and-plotting-field-1.89861

[125] Newsweek. (July 7, 2003). The Jihad soccer club. Retrieved from http://www.newsweek.com/2003/07/06/the-jihad-soccer-club.html

[126] Newsweek. (July 7, 2003). The Jihad soccer club. Retrieved from http://www.newsweek.com/2003/07/06/the-jihad-soccer-club.html

[127] Haaretz. (November 15, 2007). French court examines footage of Mohammad al-Dura's death. Retrieved from http://www.haaretz.com/news/french-court-examines-footage-of-mohammad-al-dura-s-death-1.233240

[128] For further discussion on this see: Akerman, P. (May 29, 2008). Mohammed al-Durra footage may have been a hoax. *News.com.au.* Retrieved from http://www.news.com.au/top-stories/historic-image-may-have-been-a-hoax/story-e6frfkp9-1111116475725The Jerusalem Post. (May 29, 2008) and Myth & Muhammad al-Dura. Retrieved from http://web.archive.org/web/20080531174606/http://www.jpost.com/servlet/Satellite?pagename=JPost/JPArticle/ShowFull& cid=1212041429387

[129] Despite there being some questions in the story, pictures of Mohammad Durrah huddling in his father's arms have become iconic among Palestinians. His death is an extremely emotional event burned into the collective consciousness of Palestinians and Arabs worldwide and has been used as a rallying call to incite many to violence.

[130] Abdullah Kawasmeh the 43-year-old leader of the Ezzedeen al Qassam Brigades in Hebron working under the general Hamas area leadership of Ahmed Bader allegedly recruited and dispatched Fadi and a half-dozen other young men in the neighborhood from the Jihad Mosque and elsewhere into suicide missions. See Regular, A. (May 30, 2003). Hebron's playing, and plotting, field. *Haaretz*. Retrieved from http://www.haaretz.com/print-edition/news/hebron-s-playing-and-plotting-field-1.89861

[131] Newsweek. (July 7, 2003). The Jihad soccer club. Retrieved from http://www.newsweek.com/2003/07/06/the-jihad-soccer-club.html

[132] Newsweek. (July 7, 2003). The Jihad soccer club. Retrieved from http://www.newsweek.com/2003/07/06/the-jihad-soccer-club.html

[133] Newsweek. (July 7, 2003). The Jihad soccer club. Retrieved from http://www.newsweek.com/2003/07/06/the-jihad-soccer-club.html

[134] Ezzedeen AL-Qassam Brigades Information Office Website. (March 8, 2003). Fadi Zeyad El-Fakhouri. Retrieved from http://www.qassam.ps/martyr-35-Fadi_Zeyad_El_Fakhouri.html

[135] Ezzedeen al Qassam Brigades Information Office. (March 8, 2003). Fadi Zeyad El-Fakhouri. *Al Qassam Website.* Retrieved from http://www.qassam.ps/martyr-35-Fadi_Zeyad_El_Fakhouri.html

[136] Muslims are called by duty to pray five times a day at prescribed hours. Devout Muslims usually keep the prayer schedule, although some will skip the predawn prayer if they are too tired to rise. Fadi, according to his father, was obviously very devout, praying through the nights.

[137] Newsweek. (July 7, 2003). The Jihad soccer club. Retrieved from http://www.newsweek.com/2003/07/06/the-jihad-soccer-club.html

[138] Newsweek. (July 7, 2003). The Jihad soccer club. Retrieved from http://www. newsweek.com/2003/07/06/the-jihad-soccer-club.html

[139] Newsweek. (July 7, 2003). The Jihad soccer club. Retrieved from http://www. newsweek.com/2003/07/06/the-jihad-soccer-club.html

[140] Gilmore, I. (June 8, 2003). Mosque football team was terrorists' cover. *The Telegraph*. Retrieved from http://www.telegraph.co.uk/news/worldnews/ middleeast/israel/1432360/Mosque-football-team-was-terrorists-cover.html

[141] Fadi's Jihad Mosque soccer team was affiliated with the A-Rabat Mosque in the Abu Katila neighborhood of Hebron according to Haaretz see: Regular, A. (May 30, 2003). Hebron's playing, and plotting, field. *Haaretz*. Retrieved from http://www.haaretz.com/print-edition/news/hebron-s-playing-and-plotting-field-1.89861

[142] The Ezzedeen al Qassam Brigades' Information Office website also contends the losses were greater than reported by Israel, "Settler and occupation Internet sources clearly indicated great losses among the guards and settlers. But the official military spokesman claimed that there were no injured after a gun battle of more than an hour and a detonated explosive belt in a crowd of settlers! Fadi's and Hazem's operation was a painful response to the claim that the Palestinian resistance in the West Bank was broken. And it was another harsh reminder to settlers that they'll never be safe on the land they stole. And it was yet another security failure for the occupation army." Ezzedeen al Qassam Brigades Information Office. (March 8, 2003). Fadi Zeyad El-Fakhouri. *Al Qassam Website*. Retrieved from http://www.qassam.ps/ martyr-35-Fadi_Zeyad_El_Fakhouri.html

[143] Gilmore, I. (June 8, 2003). Mosque football team was terrorists' cover. *The Telegraph*. Retrieved from http://www.telegraph.co.uk/news/worldnews/ middleeast/israel/1432360/Mosque-football-team-was-terrorists-cover.html

[144] According to Islamic beliefs martyrs go straight to paradise. And once there they also elect seventy family members who at their death bypass the judgment day that an ordinary Muslim faces when he dies. Thus, Ziad is expecting that Fadi is already in paradise and that after death he is sure to join him as well. Fadi, according to Islamic beliefs, will also receive the many honors that a martyr receives in paradise: seventy-two virgins will serve him in his exalted position where he lives in a place of great beauty and joy

[145] In Palestinian obituaries, the casket that is paraded through town is sometimes empty in the case of suicide bombers because it is the practice of the Israeli government to withhold the partially blown up corpse from the family who are then unable to perform proper Islamic burial and funeral rites for their deceased child. For a discussion of Israel's policy of keeping the bodies of enemy combatants, denying their families the ability to give them a religious burial, an action that violates the Geneva Convention see: Kate. (July 5, 2011). Israel's secret cemetery of Palestinian combatants. *Mondoweiss*. Retrieved from http://mondoweiss.net/2011/07/israels-secret-cemetery-of-palestinian-combatants.html Alheisi, R. (April 4, 2010). Waiting To Return Home: Palestinian Martyrs in Israeli "Cemeteries of Numbers" and Morgues. *My Pales-*

tine. Retrieved from http://avoicefrompalestine.wordpress.com/2010/04/17/ waiting-to-return-home-palestinian-martyrs-in-israeli-"cemeteries-of-numbers"-and-morgues/ In Fadi's case, (perhaps) because his action occurred inside the West Bank, his father was able to recover his body.

[146] Allowing Ziad to reexperience it and tell me about the traumatic death of his son in this way with few to no interruptions, questions, or challenges from my side, was likely therapeutic for him as I provided a safe environment and relationship to "hold" his emotions as he rehashed through this unbearably painful chapter in his life again. It gave him a chance to work through some things he normally would avoid and couldn't bear to return to without someone listening and not turning away from the horror, grief and troubling aspects of all he had to tell. Often I felt this was something I could give back in return to interviewees in exchange for their honest sharing of difficult emotional experiences.

[147] Ziad is referring to the hundreds of collaborators that Israeli security forces blackmail and pay to give them information about militants.

[148] Indeed regular suicide has strong parallels. A strong warning sign of an extremely serious potential suicide is when a person who has been deeply depressed suddenly disengages from life—gives away possessions, stops going to work or school—and also suddenly seems on top of the world, even euphoric. The decision to suicide can bring tremendous relief from the burden of dealing with psychic overload, the overwhelming pain that usually drives a suicide. And once one has definitely decided to suicide and moves into a dissociative mode, he may be very hard to stop. In Fadi's case, it seems he had seen too much and step by step been radicalized into making this decision. His father may be right that he would not have been able to prevent Fadi from enacting his "martyrdom" wish once he was fully engaged.

[149] Myre, G. (June 22, 2003). After cease-fire talks stall, Israelis kill a Hamas leader. *The New York Times*. Retrieved from http://www.nytimes.com/2003/06/22/world/after-cease-fire-talks-stall-israelis-kill-a-hamas-leader.html

[150] Regular, A. (May 30, 2003). Hebron's playing—and plotting—field. *Haaretz*.

[151] Ian Lustick who studied this case reports that Baruch Goldstein carried out his massacre on the Jewish holy day of Purim to interrupt the Israeli-Palestinian peace process. On Purim, devout Jews read and sometimes even reenact the story of Esther in which she saves the Jews from a massacre that gets turned around so that the enemies of the Jews are killed. In his 1988 treatise, Ian Lustick states that Goldstein was in his own way reenacting that part of the story of Esther. Likewise he reports that Goldstein was a fundamentalist Jew who was not deranged but rather a rational actor following his belief system and quotes Goldstein widow who also said that her husband fully intended his act to disrupt the Israeli-Palestinian peace process. Lustick, I. (1994). Preface, For the land and the Lord (2nd ed.). New York: Council on Foreign Relations

[152] BBC News. (February 25, 1994). Jewish settler kills thirty at holy site. Retrieved from http://news.bbc.co.uk/onthisday/hi/dates/stories/february/25/newsid_4167000/4167929.stm

[153] BBC News. (February 25, 1994). Jewish settler kills thirty at holy site. Retrieved from http://news.bbc.co.uk/onthisday/hi/dates/stories/february/25/newsid_4167000/4167929.stm

[154] Middle East Journal, *Chronology*, vol 48, no 3 (Summer 1994) p. 511 ff.

[155] BBC News. (February 25, 1994). Jewish settler kills thirty at holy site. Retrieved from http://news.bbc.co.uk/onthisday/hi/dates/stories/february/25/newsid_4167000/4167929.stm

[156] BBC News. (February 25, 1994). Jewish settler kills thirty at holy site. Retrieved from http://news.bbc.co.uk/onthisday/hi/dates/stories/february/25/newsid_4167000/4167929.stm

[157] According to news and other sources at least ten thousand people have visited the shrine. On the sixth anniversary of the massacre in March 2000, bawdy shrine-goers dressed up in a bizarre reenactment of Goldstein's Purim crime as they waved semi automatic rifles in the air, prayed, danced and sang around his tomb, stating that they were paying tribute to Goldstein who they claimed had been *murdered* by the Arabs! If one searchs for Goldstein's motivations for terrorism it seems that before his act Goldstein served as the Kirayat Arba settlement's main emergency doctor and often treated victims of the violent clashes between Israelis and Palestinians. He became increasingly militant as he witnessed violence and over time he began to intensely hate Palestinians and eventually refused to treat them, some claiming that he would even refuse to treat Israeli Arabs serving in the Israeli military. Goldstein like many other Israeli settlers was a U.S.-born Jew who had immigrated to Israel with what appears to be a cowboy mentality of conquering the natives. He was a member of the Jewish Defense League, a violent organization established by American Rabbi Meir Kahane, and he belonged to the Kach far-right political party in Israel that was barred in 1988 from entering the Knesset (Israeli parliament) on grounds that it incited racism. Today (after Goldstein's death) the Kach party is considered a terrorist organization by the EU, Israel and the U.S. In bringing up Goldstein's despicable crime, Ziad wants us to understand that if Goldstein was at all representative of the settlers of Kirayat Arba, or the neighbors that Fadi had attacked in his suicide mission. Goldstein is not the first American behind a terror attack against Palestinians in Israeli-held areas. In 1982, Alan Goodman staged a shooting spree outside the holy al Aqsa mosque in Jerusalem, killing two people. In these two acts we see what looks to be an unremitting cycle of hatred, violence and revenge. See: BBC News. (March 21, 2000). Graveside party celebrates Hebron massacre. Retrieved from http://news.bbc.co.uk/2/hi/middle_east/685792.stm; BBC News. (February 25, 1994).; Jewish settler kills thirty at holy site. Retrieved from http://news.bbc.co.uk/onthisday/hi/dates/stories/february/25/newsid_4167000/4167929.stm; and US Department of State Office of the Coordinator for Counter-terrorism. (April, 2005). Country reports on terrorism 2004. Retrieved from http://www.state.gov/documents/organization/45313.pdf

[158] Newsweek. (July 7, 2003). The Jihad soccer club. Retrieved from http://www.newsweek.com/2003/07/06/the-jihad-soccer-club.html

[159] Israel Ministry of Foreign Affairs. (January 30, 2003). The Role of Palestinian Women in Suicide Terrorism. Retrieved from http://www.mfa.gov.il/MFA/MFAArchive/2000_2009/2003/1/The%20Role%20of%20Palestinian%20Women%20in%20Suicide%20Terrorism

[160] Interview by Yoram Schweitzer with Nasser Shawish of Fatah on January 19, 2005, Reported in Schweitzer, Y. (Ed.). (2006). *Female Suicide Bombers: Dying for Equality?* : The Jaffee Center for Strategic Studies. Pp. 28-29.

[161] Interview by Yoram Schweitzer with Nasser Shawish of Fatah on January 19, 2005, Reported in Schweitzer, Y. (Ed.). (2006). *Female Suicide Bombers: Dying for Equality?* : The Jaffee Center for Strategic Studies. Pp. 28-29.

[162] Abu Hanoud was, according to Israeli officials, the Hamas operative responsible for the Sbarrao pizza restaurant and Dolphinarium suicide bombings, two of the most lethal attacks inside Israel. He was on Israel's most wanted list. He and two other Hamas operatives, Mahmoun Rashid Hashaika and his brother Ahmed, were killed near the village of Kfar Farah, close to the West Bank city of Nablus when Israeli helicopter fired missiles on the taxi in which they were riding. 20,000 Palestinians attended the funeral procession and tens of thousands more demonstrated in Gaza. Mourners chanted, "Sharon, wait, revenge is coming soon," and the Hamas leader in Nablus, Teissir Imran, told the crowd, "Sharon opened the door to hell, for himself and his people." Later Hamas, in a published declaration, threatened that "revenge will be ours soon, powerfully and in Tel Aviv." A senior Hamas official in Gaza, Abdel Aziz Rantissi said, "Experience shows that the organization has always responded to Israel's crimes and always strikes back. God willing, there will be a painful response against the enemy." For more details see: Israeliinsider. (November 24, 2001). Hamas vows revenge after IDF eliminates "most wanted" Abu Hanoud. Retrieved from http://www.israelinsider.com/channels/security/articles/sec_0145.htm

[163] Schweitzer, Y. (Ed.). (2006). *Female Suicide Bombers:Dying for Equality?* : The Jaffee Center for Strategic Studies

[164] Yoram Schweitzer personal communication 2006 regarding his in prison interview of Nasser Shawesh January 19, 2005.

[165] Yoram Schweitzer personal communication 2007 regarding his in prison interview of Nasser Shawesh January 19, 2005.

[166] By some definitions of terrorism it could even be argued that Darine's individual act was not one of terrorism but of resistance because, although a terrorist group (Al Aqsa Martyrs Brigade) equipped and sent her, her act did not target civilians but was rather aimed at the *military* arming a checkpoint. This is a thorny point -the difference between a terrorist and a legitimate resistance or freedom fighter – and is often argued by those dealing with terrorism. In many definitions intentionally targeting civilians is seen as a distinguishing difference. In this case the Al Aqsa Martyrs Brigade routinely targeted civilians, whereas Darine's specific act did not.

[167] The mosque is built over the ruins of the historical Jewish temple and overlooks the Western praying wall. In that fight Palestinian youth hurled stones from

overhead to the Jewish worshippers at the Wall. Israeli police retaliated by using stun guns on worshippers above in the mosque compound.

[168] This was considered the worst Palestinian atrocity in Israel during eighteen months of fighting.

[169] Leila Khaled was born in 1944 and was involved in several hijackings in behalf of the PFLP. The one that Ken refers to where Khaled is sometimes said to have stuffed hand grenades into her bra occurred in 1970. It was foiled by Israeli air marshals who, when Khaled and her co-conspirator took pistols out to hijack the plane, killed him and overpowered her. The plane was landed in England, and she was taken into custody there and later released as part of a prisoner exchange. For her own record of these events see: Guardian, T. (January 25, 2001). 'I made the ring from a bullet and the pin of a hand grenade'. Retrieved from http://www.guardian.co.uk/world/2001/jan/26/israel

[170] Hammer, J. (April 15, 2002). How two lives met in death. *Newsweek*. Retrieved from http://www.robincmiller.com/articles/a15.htm

[171] Israel Ministry of Foreign Affairs. (January 30, 2003). The Role of Palestinian Women in Suicide Terrorism. Retrieved from http://www.mfa.gov.il/MFA/MFAArchive/2000_2009/2003/1/The%20Role%20of%20Palestinian%20Women%20in%20Suicide%20Terrorism

[172] Bennet, J. (June 13, 2002). In suicide bombings, the taxi man got away. *The New York Times*. Retrieved from http://www.nytimes.com/2002/06/13/world/mideast-turmoil-violence-in-suicide-bombings-the-taxi-man-got-away.html

[173] See Victor, B. (2003). *Army of Roses: Inside the world of Palestinian women suicide bombers*. London: Robinson. Pages 214-215 and Bennet, J. (June 13, 2002).;Mideast Turmoil: Violence; in suicide bombings, the taxi man got away. *The New York Times*. Retrieved from http://www.nytimes.com/2002/06/13/world/mideast-turmoil-violence-in-suicide-bombings-the-taxi-man-got-away.html

[174] Bennet, J. (June 13, 2002). Mideast Turmoil: Violence; in suicide bombings, the taxi man got away. *The New York Times*. Retrieved from http://www.nytimes.com/2002/06/13/world/mideast-turmoil-violence-in-suicide-bombings-the-taxi-man-got-away.html

[175] Victor, B. (2003). *Army of Roses: Inside the world of Palestinian women suicide bombers*. London: Robinson. Pages 217.

[176] Victor, B. (2003). *Army of Roses: Inside the world of Palestinian women suicide bombers*. London: Robinson. Pages 216.

[177] Victor, B. (2003). *Army of Roses: Inside the world of Palestinian women suicide bombers*. London: Robinson. Pages 226.

[178] Israel Ministry of Foreign Affairs. (January 30, 2003). The Role of Palestinian Women in Suicide Terrorism. Retrieved from http://www.mfa.gov.il/MFA/MFAArchive/2000_2009/2003/1/The%20Role%20of%20Palestinian%20Women%20in%20Suicide%20Terrorism

[179] Israel Ministry of Foreign Affairs. (January 30, 2003). The Role of Palestinian Women in Suicide Terrorism. Retrieved from http://www.mfa.gov.il/MFA/

MFA Archive/2000_2009/2003/1/The%20Role%20of%20Palestinian%20
Women%20in%20Suicide%20Terrorism

[180] Victor, B. (2003). Army of Roses: *Inside the world of Palestinian women suicide bombers*. London: Robinson.

[181] Hammer, J. (April 15, 2002). How two lives met in death. *Newsweek*. Retrieved from http://www.robincmiller.com/articles/a15.htm

[182] Leung, R. (2003). The Bomber Next Door: 60 Minutes II What Makes A Female Suicide Bomber Tick? Retrieved from http://www.cbsnews.com/stories/2003/05/23/60II/main555401.shtml

[183] Leung, R. (2003). The Bomber Next Door: 60 Minutes II What Makes A Female Suicide Bomber Tick? Retrieved from http://www.cbsnews.com/stories/2003/05/23/60II/main555401.shtml

[184] The Israeli government practice is to withhold the partially blown up corpses of suicide bombers preventing the family from performing proper Islamic burial and funeral rites for their deceased child. For more on this issue see: Kate. (July 5, 2011). Israel's secret cemetery of Palestinian combatants. *Mondoweiss*. Retrieved from http://mondoweiss.net/2011/07/israels-secret-cemetery-of-palestinian-combatants.html and Alheisi, R. (April 4, 2010). Waiting To Return Home: Palestinian Martyrs in Israeli "Cemeteries of Numbers" and Morgues. *My Palestine*. Retrieved from http://avoicefrompalestine.wordpress.com/2010/04/17/waiting-to-return-home-palestinian-martyrs-in-israeli-"cemeteries-of-numbers"-and-morgues/

[185] Victor, B. (2003). *Army of Roses: Inside the world of Palestinian women suicide bombers*. London: Robinson. Pages 206, 220-221

[186] Usher, G. (March 29, 2002). At 18, bomber became martyr and murderer. *The Guardian*. Retrieved from http://www.guardian.co.uk/world/2002/mar/30/israel3

[187] Israel Ministry of Foreign Affairs. (January 30, 2003). The Role of Palestinian Women in Suicide Terrorism. Retrieved from http://www.mfa.gov.il/MFA/MFA Archive/2000_2009/2003/1/The%20Role%20of%20Palestinian%20Women%20in%20Suicide%20Terrorism

[188] There is no question that Wafa carried a bomb into Jerusalem, and it appears that she volunteered herself into an operation; however, it is unclear if her sending group intended for her to detonate herself. Her brother Khalid reports that Wafa did make a last testament or video as is customary, and the Israel Foreign Ministry reports the same. This was taken by some as an indication that she was never intended to be a suicide bomber, but only to plant her bomb and detonate it from afar. However it could also mean that there wasn't time to make the video and last testament, as readying a woman for a suicide operation run by male operatives requires special precautions. Wafa for instance would likely not want a male to dress her or strap on her suicide vest—issues that could have caused more complicated preparations. Also because the sending organization was not sure how her operation would be accepted in Palestinian society - if she was intended as the first Palestinian suicide bomber – they may have decided not to make one. A witness who saw Wafa in the

store said that Wafa got caught in the doorway and some felt it was the cause that detonated her bomb. When Yoram Schweitzer interviewed Palestinian Fatah and Hamas operatives in prison, he reported that they felt that Wafa was meant to be a bomber, but not all agreed. She could have accidentally become one out of panic or confusion if she pushed the wrong button (she had two), or the doorway somehow detonated her device. Or it may be that in a consummate act of feminism, she alone decided to take it the whole way: once she had been equipped by the group with a bomb and a detonator, she decided to explode herself as the first Palestinian female suicide bomber. If this was the case one should not mistake her taking the act in her own hands as feminist motivations for going as a bomber as she had many other more pressing trauma and revenge motivations. And it may also be she was intentionally sent to be the first female Palestinian bomber. The fact that she told friends she was going to Jerusalem and not returning seems that she was intending to die. The Israeli authorities, after investigating the case, decided she was intended to be a suicide bomber. See: Israel Ministry of Foreign Affairs. (January 30, 2003). The Role of Palestinian Women in Suicide Terrorism. Retrieved from http://www.mfa.gov.il/MFA/MFAArchive/2000_2009/2003/1/The%20Role%20of%20Palestinian%20Women%20in%20Suicide%20Terrorism

[189] This seems to be a mistake in translation, or in my getting the number wrong as it was translated to me, or perhaps Khalid is speaking about the larger surrounding area as the al Am'ari Camp had a population of 5,719 inhabitants in mid-year 2006 according to the Palestinian Central Bureau of Statistics (http://www.pcbs.gov.ps/Portals/_pcbs/populati/pop07.aspx) and according to UNWRA the al Am'ari camp has 10,377 registered refugees.

[190] Victor, B. (2003). *Army of Roses: Inside the world of Palestinian women suicide bombers*. London: Robinson.

[191] Victor, B. (2003). *Army of Roses: Inside the world of Palestinian women suicide bombers*. London: Robinson.

[192] Victor, B. (2003). *Army of Roses: Inside the world of Palestinian women suicide bombers*. London: Robinson.

[193] See for instance: Israel Ministry of Foreign Affairs. (February 12, 2003). Blackmailing Young Women into Suicide Terrorism. Retrieved from http://www.mfa.gov.il/MFA/Government/Communiques/2003/Blackmailing%20Young%20Women%20into%20Suicide%20Terrorism%20 in which the Israeli government claims that women were impregnated and even raped by Tanzim operatives in order to coerce them into suicide terrorism. This seems highly unlikely given the numbers of women who according to senders volunteered themselves to go, although the Israelis claim this information came out in interrogations. Yoram Schweitzer told the author on many occasions from 2004-2006 that he never found evidence from Fatah or Hamas operatives that he was interviewing in prison, nor from the imprisoned female bombers he

interviewed that they had been blackmailed or coerced into their missions. He felt that their emotional traumas were exploited, and they were often dispatched to their missions by senders who were more than willing to accept offers from women who had just suffered a traumatic loss or were otherwise upset enough to volunteer themselves. However in the case of Reem Riyashi, he did hear from Hamas operatives that there was some question of whether she was sent under strange circumstance involving her having been compromised by a Hamas lover, but that was the exception.

[194] See: Alheisi, R. (April 4, 2010). Waiting To Return Home: Palestinian Martyrs in Israeli "Cemeteries of Numbers" and Morgues. *My Palestine*. Retrieved from http://avoicefrompalestine.wordpress.com/2010/04/17/waiting-to-return-home-palestinian-martyrs-in-israeli-"cemeteries-of-numbers"-and-morgues/

[195] Bennet, J. (July 28, 2002). Stalemate in Mideast After Deadly Bombing. *The New York Times*. Retrieved from http://www.nytimes.com/2002/07/28/world/stalemate-in-mideast-after-deadly-bombing.html?ref=salahshehada

[196] BBC News. (July 4, 2007). BBC's Alan Johnston is released. *BBC News* Retrieved from http://news.bbc.co.uk/2/hi/6267928.stm

[197] McElroy, D. (April 15, 2011). Italian activist killed in Gaza: the Alan Johnston kidnapping. *The Telegraph*. Retrieved from http://www.telegraph.co.uk/news/worldnews/middleeast/palestinianauthority/8453318/Italian-activist-killed-in-Gaza-the-Alan-Johnston-kidnapping.html

[198] See Cabbage, M. (July 7, 2002). Desperation turns Gaza into cradle of Palestinian radicals. *Orlando Sentinel*. Retrieved from http://articles.orlandosentinel.com/2002-07-07/news/0207070328_1_gaza-strip-jabalya-refugee-camp-gaza-population

[199] See Cabbage, M. (July 7, 2002). Desperation turns Gaza into cradle of Palestinian radicals. *Orlando Sentinel*. Retrieved from http://articles.orlandosentinel.com/2002-07-07/news/0207070328_1_gaza-strip-jabalya-refugee-camp-gaza-population

[200] See Cabbage, M. (July 7, 2002). Desperation turns Gaza into cradle of Palestinian radicals. *Orlando Sentinel*. Retrieved from http://articles.orlandosentinel.com/2002-07-07/news/0207070328_1_gaza-strip-jabalya-refugee-camp-gaza-population

[201] Projected Mid-Year Population for Gaza Governorate by Locality 2004-2006 Palestinian Central Bureau of Statistics

[202] Palestinian Media Watch. (December 5, 2002). Suicide terror & shahada: Success of shahada promotion. Retrieved September 29, 2011, from http://palwatch.org/main.aspx?fi=479

[203] Palestinian Media Watch. (December 5, 2002). Suicide terror & shahada: Success of shahada promotion. Retrieved September 29, 2011, from http://palwatch.org/main.aspx?fi=479

[204] See Cabbage, M. (July 7, 2002). Desperation turns Gaza into cradle of Palestinian radicals. *Orlando Sentinel*. Retrieved from http://articles.orlandosentinel.

com/2002-07-07/news/0207070328_1_gaza-strip-jabalya-refugee-camp-gaza-population

[205] For an interesting analysis of grafitti from a foreign couple living in Gaza for over six years who wrote a book about the graffiti of the Second Intifada along with their reflections of all they saw and learned speaking with members of Hamas in Gaza see: Oliver, A. M., & Steinberg, P. F. (2005). *Road to martyr's square: A journey into the world of the suicide bomber.* New York: Oxford University Press.I learn about.

[206] Some of these homes razed posed a threat, in that smuggling tunnels existed beneath them, but Human Rights Watch claimed that others did not pose any specific threat but were razed nonetheless, in violation of international law in order for the Israelis to create their border buffer zone. See: Human Rights Watch. (October, 2004). Razing Rafah: Mass home demolitions in the Gaza Strip. Retrieved from http://www.israeloccupation.info/files/Razing%20 Rafah.pdf

[207] A journalist reports that the Israeli Gaza divisional commander, Brigadier-General Gadi Shamni, described the attack as a cynical abuse of his soldiers' attempts to treat women with dignity. He said, "We're doing our best to be humanitarian, to consider the problems associated with searching women. She said she had a medical problem, that's why the soldiers let her in, to check her in private because she is a woman. That's a very cruel, cynical use of the humanitarian considerations of our soldiers." See: McGreal, C. (January 14, 2004). Human-bomb mother kills four Israelis at Gaza checkpoint. *The Guardian.* Retrieved from http://www.guardian.co.uk/world/2004/ jan/15/israel in

[208] McGreal, C. (January 14, 2004). Human-bomb mother kills four Israelis at Gaza checkpoint. *The Guardian.* Retrieved from http://www.guardian.co.uk/ world/2004/jan/15/israel

[209] McGreal, C. (January 14, 2004). Human-bomb mother kills four Israelis at Gaza checkpoint. *The Guardian.* Retrieved from http://www.guardian.co.uk/ world/2004/jan/15/israel

[210] McGreal, C. (January 14, 2004). Human-bomb mother kills four Israelis at Gaza checkpoint. *The Guardian.* Retrieved from http://www.guardian.co.uk/ world/2004/jan/15/israel

[211] McGreal, C. (January 14, 2004). Human-bomb mother kills four Israelis at Gaza checkpoint. *The Guardian.* Retrieved from http://www.guardian.co.uk/ world/2004/jan/15/israel

[212] McGreal, C. (January 14, 2004). Human-bomb mother kills four Israelis at Gaza checkpoint. *The Guardian.* Retrieved from http://www.guardian.co.uk/ world/2004/jan/15/israel

[213] Mcgirk, T. (May 3, 2007). Palestinian moms becoming martyrs. Retrieved from http://www.time.com/time/magazine/article/0,9171,1617542,00.html

[214] Schweitzer, Yoram (2007) Personal Communication.

[215] See: Mcgirk, T. (May 3, 2007). Palestinian moms becoming martyrs. Retrieved from http://www.time.com/time/magazine/article/0,9171,1617542,00.html

and Kalman, M. (March, 2007). Horrific video of a child sending her suicide bomber mother to her death. Retrieved from http://www.dailymail.co.uk/news/article-444058/Horrific-video-child-sending-suicide-bomber-mother-death.html

[216] Kalman, M. (March, 2007). Horrific video of a child sending her suicide bomber mother to her death. Retrieved from http://www.dailymail.co.uk/news/article-444058/Horrific-video-child-sending-suicide-bomber-mother-death.html

[217] See: Catholic Friends of Israel. (April 21, 2009). Pope Benedict's 2006 Regensburg Address - a refresher course. Retrieved from http://catholicfriendsofisrael.blogspot.com/2009/04/pope-benedicts-2006-regensburg-address.html

[218] Palestinians like many Arabs believe in keeping land and assets in the family and allow first cousins to marry, a practice that can result in genetic abnormalities.

[219] They were big burly bearded guys but their appearance is no reason to have suspected them, as they could just have well been dedicated Muslim doctors. I had nothing but a gut feeling to think that these doctors were involved with militants. It was common at that time that many, if not most, Palestinians supported militants. I had been introduced to them and assured that they would help me find willing subjects for my research through an American who someone else introduced me to. She had lived and worked in Hebron, but later I found out her reputation was dodgy – she had an affair with a local Palestinian and they had planned to marry. However it worked out differently: he followed his family's directive and married a local woman instead and she left Hebron distraught after learning that he had. I only learned this much later after the trip.

[220] Rachel Corrie was a young American activist who was killed as she stood in front of an Israeli bulldozer in Gaza protesting home demolitions. She was mowed down by an Israeli bulldozer whose driver later claimed not to have seen her. There was considerable outcry over the incident.

[221] UNRWA. Jenin Refugee Camp. Retrieved from http://www.unrwa.org/etemplate.php?id=118

[222] The Israelis called it Operation Defensive Shield, when they entered in 2002 the major cities of the West Bank, including Jenin, to arrest and clear out the terrorist groups who were sending a suicide bomber per week into Israel.

[223] See: deMause, L. (2002). The childhood origins of terrorism *The emotional life of nations*: Other Press.

[224] Pini is referring to the American Israel Public Affairs Committee (AIPAC) espionage scandal in 2004-2005, during which news leaked about the FBI having US citizen Lawrence Franklin under surveillance as a spy for the Israelis while working as a policy analyst in the Pentagon. According to FBI surveillance tapes, Franklin relayed top-secret information regarding United States policy towards Iran to Israel through officials at AIPAC. While Israel and AIPAC both vociferously denied the charges, Franklin pled guilty to several espionage-related charges and was sentenced in January 2006 to nearly thir-

teen years of prison, later reduced to ten months house arrest. Two former AIPAC employees were also indicted, but the case was dismissed. The case was heatedly in the news at the time Pini is speaking to me. See: Markon, J. (September 30, 2005). Guilty plea planned in secrets case. *The Washington Post.* Retrieved from http://www.washingtonpost.com/wp-dyn/content/article/2005/09/29/AR2005092901267.html

[225] Johnston, D., & Rutenberg, J. (June 13, 2006). Rove won't face indictment in CIA leak case. *New York Times.* Retrieved from http://www.nytimes.com/2006/06/13/washington/13cnd-leak.html?_r=1& oref=slogin

[226] Sami is referring to Rachel Corey who was killed in Gaza in a human rights protest against the razing of an area of homes and buildings in the city of Rafah.

[227] In 2012 when I asked Paul for the truth, he told me that he was not trying to recruit me into the CIA and actually thought I was probably *already* working undercover—he still sometimes thinks that. And he assured me that the Israelis had not taken his passport but had assisted him in getting it back from the taxi we had taken from Taba in which he had lost it. As that was unlikely true I challenged him on that, but he insisted, with a strange look crossing his face.

[228] Sidi Moumen near to upscale Casablanca's downtown neighborhood includes the shantytown area of Casablanca where three hundred thousand mostly illiterate and unemployed residents live.

[229] A Caged Prisoners report details testimony of French, UK and others of Moroccan heritage who claim to have been victims of U.S. rendition to and torture in Moroccan prisons. The report states, "It is now established that Morocco played a central role in the worldwide network of secret prisons developed by the CIA after the 9/11 attacks. As early as 2002, Morocco can credibly be said to have become a torture centre used by the US in their War on Terror." See: Mafille, A. (May 24, 2012). Cabablanca bombings, the day after. Retrieved from http://www.cageprisoners.com/our-work/opinion-editorial/item/4248-casablanca-bombings-the-day-after

[230] The Beslan terrorists took over one thousand hostages—seven hundred seventy-seven of them children. The three-day siege ended when Russian forces stormed the building using military tanks, incendiary rockets and other heavy weapons. Three hundred thirty-three hostages were killed in the shoot-out that ensued, including one hundred and eighty-six children, and hundreds more were injured. For an excellent analysis of the siege see Dolnik, A. (2007). *Negotiating the Impossible? The Beslan Hostage Crisis.* London: Royal United Services Institute.

[231] Evidently this along with hiding guns beneath the floorboards inside the school had been prearranged by the terrorists with some supposed paid collaborator.

[232] There remains considerable controversy over this although in Aslan's subsequent chapter he states that he personally overheard the female bombers arguing and expressing their upset over being involved in taking children hostages

[233] Vadeem is referring to that at the time of making their demands, the Beslan hostage-takers named a group of four senior officials as negotiators that they

wished to work through, including North Ossetia's President, Alexander Dzasokhov. Dzasokhov, who was in Beslan at the time of the siege, claims he wanted to go to the school, but was stopped stating that "a very high-ranking general from the Russian Interior Ministry told him, 'I have received orders to arrest you if you try to go.'" As a result Dzasokhov did not appear at the school advocating for the hostages. For more on this see: McAllister, J. F. O. (September 12, 2004). Communication breakdown. *Time*. Retrieved from http://www.time.com/time/magazine/article/0,9171,695816,00.html

[234] She refers to Ruslan Aushev, the ex-President of Ingushetia

[235] Vladimir Khodov, the only Ossetian among the hostage-takers, was from nearby Elkhotovo where he was wanted for detonating a bomb in the market-place. He referred to himself as Abdullah and kept his identity hidden during the siege and only at the end spoke in Ossetian to fool the hostages into thinking that he was a rescuer, while he actually led them further into the school to their demise. For more on the identities of the hostage takers see: Martinfrost website. Beslan school hostage crisis.fromhttp://www.martinfrost.ws/html-files/beslan_siege.html#Identities_of_those_responsible

[236] The terrorist here is referring to Ahmed Kadyrov, the Russian supported leader of Chechnya who the rebels despised and who they had assassinated in May of 2004.

[237] This echoes Bedouin traditions of raiding and taking beautiful women as concubines and wives.

[238] Larisa also noted that he told her he had used the pseudonym Basengor in a previous operation.

[239] Larisa may have been asking him in a pointed way how could the North Osse-tians be held responsible for when most of the news out of Chechnya was being censored by the Russians during these years

[240] For a discussion of the actual negotiations see: Dolnik, A. (2007). *Negotiating the Impossible? The Beslan Hostage Crisis*. London: Royal United Services Institute

[241] MosNews. (October 19, 2004). Drugs used by Beslan terrorists puzzle Russian experts. Retrieved from http://rense.com/general58/drugsusedbybeslan.htm

[242] This is a bit of a slur as in the former Soviet Union being an orphan is often considered an undesirable trait making someone less marriageable because the orphan may carry a defect could be transmitted to their offspring. This is believed so because the women who give up their children to orphanages are often alcoholic or drug addicted, from the Roma people (who are not held in high esteem), or may have left the child because of some genetic defect – all unfavorable traits that are unknown and may be passed into the next generation.

[243] As mentioned previously Vladimir Khodov was the only Ossetian among the hostage-takers.

[244] The mayor of Moscow.

[245] Nalchik is the capital of the Russian republic of Karbardino-Bulkaria

[246] A raid by an estimated two hundred armed militants on nine targets including the Nalchik airport, the Interior Ministry, several police stations and FSB headquarters occurred on the morning of October 13th, 2005 (a little more than one month after we left) in Nalchik in the Kabardino-Balkar Republic of Southern Russia. The gunmen captured some of the buildings with hostages inside and gunfights continued on into the following day with more than one hundred people killed and many others wounded during the ensuing shoot-out that continued into the following day. Shamil Basayev claimed responsibility for the attacks against the government centers in Nalchik, stating that forty-one of their militants had died in the attack as "martyrs". Later that number turned out to be much higher at ninety-two. Likewise the Ingush Jamaat who carried out the actual assaults were said to have been part of the "Caucasian Front", a newly formed militant group inspired by the Chechen rebels that formed to make an armed struggle against what they claim are repressive FSB and police brutality in the Muslim predominated territories of the area. See Basayev's announcement on the KavKaz website Basayev, S. (October 17, 2005). Nalchik attacked by 217 Mujahideen. *KavKaz Center Website*. Retrieved from http://www.kavkazcenter.com/eng/content/2005/10/17/4156. shtml;Associated Press. (October 14, 2005). Russia says rebel assault over; toll tops 100. *NBC News*. Retrieved from http://www.msnbc.msn.com/id/9681595/#.UEGbQEK_BcR and Fuller, L. (October 12, 2008). Three years after Nalchik, North Caucasus resistance remains potent, deadly force. *Radio Free Europe*. Retrieved from http://www.rferl.org/content/Three_Years_After_Nalchik_North_Caucasus_Resistance_Remains_Potent_Deadly_Force/1329090.html

[247] For more on the identities of those involved see: Martinfrost website. Beslan school hostage crisis.fromhttp://www.martinfrost.ws/htmlfiles/beslan_siege. html#Identities_of_those_responsible

[248] As Putin consolidated his power he began organizing what became known as his "vertical" in which he appointed government officials who were beholden to and answered to him negating much of the democratic reforms that had been in the making.

[249] Speckhard, A., & Akhmedova, K. (2006). The New Chechen Jihad: Militant Wahhabism as a Radical Movement and a Source of Suicide Terrorism in Post-War Chechen Society. *Democracy and Security*, 2(1), 103-155.

[250] Miller, J. (2005, Feb 3, 2005). Another Beslan? It's a byword for horror: Russia's 9/11. *Channel 4 News*, from http://www.channel4.com/news/2005/02/week_1/03_basayev.html

[251] In the past before the Dubrovka Theater hostage-taking, the organizer of this and the Moscow event, rebel leader, Shamil Basayev had arranged a mass-hostage taking in Budynovsk, where he did negotiate for his fighters to gain safe passage. But in that case the Chechen fighters had been trapped by the Russian military and were likely to be decimated so they resorted to taking hostages in Budynovsk as a means of escape.
Here in Beslan, the scenario is completely different.

[252] Nightline, A. (July 29, 2005). Chechen guerilla leader calls Russians "terrorists". Retrieved from http://abcnews.go.com/Nightline/International/story?id=990187& page=1#.T5mRi5i_BoE

[253] Speckhard, A. (2006). The New Global Jihad, 9-11 and the Use of Weapons of Mass Destruction: Changes in Mindset and Modus Operandi. *Democracy and Security*, 2(2), 287 - 298

[254] BBC News. (September 17, 2004). Excerpts: Basayev claims Beslan. Retrieved from http://news.bbc.co.uk/2/hi/3665136.stm

[255] An investigative website identifies at least six Ingush among the hostage-takers: Magomed Yevloyev - nicknamed Magas, Ingush national also involved in the Basayev's attack on Nazran (leader); Ali Taziyev - Ingush ex-policeman, debate rages whether an alias/stolen identity of Khochubarov or Yevloyev; Adam Kushtov - 17-year-old Ingush who fled the 1992 ethnic cleansing in North Ossetia to Ingushetia; Issa Torshkhoev - 26-year-old Ingush native of Malgobek where he was unable to find work. Five of his friends were killed in March 2004 after his house was raided by Russian police. Had a prior conviction for robbery; Abdul Azeem Tsechoyev - 35-year-old Ingush native of Sagopshi, owned the GAZ-66 that drove the hostage-takers to the school and Bei-Alla Tsechoyev - 31-year-old brother of above, also spelled Bay. Had a prior conviction for possessing illegal firearms. Martinfrost website. Beslan school hostage crisis.fromhttp://www.martinfrost.ws/htmlfiles/beslan_siege.html#Identities_of_those_responsible

[256] According to Khapta, the authorities at first declared that Belita Nogaeva carried out the suicidal terror act near the subway station Rijskaya in Moscow, but in April 2005 the Office of Public Prosecutor has declared that she participated in the school takeover in Beslan.

[257] Maryam Taburova was one of two women who participated in the school takeover in Beslan on September 2004. This was confirmed officially in April 2005.

[258] Nabil is referring to the terror act carried out by two Tunisians carrying forged Belgian passports who had killed Afghan General Massoud by exploding the camera that was placed in front of him during the interview he had agreed to give the pair. The attack had allegedly been planned by Tarek Maaroufi, a Tunisian-born Belgian citizen and one of the leading al Qaeda agents in Europe, as a gift to Osama bin Laden just before 9-11, eliminating his potential threat in Afghanistan. See: Belien, P. (November 30, 2005). Belgian export: suicide bombers. *The Brussels Journal*. Retrieved from http://www.brusselsjournal.com/node/530.

[259] Vlaams Belang (translated as Flemish Interest) is a Belgian far right political party that advocates for an independent Flanders (the Flemish speaking part of Belgium) and strict limits on immigration including requiring immigrants to adopt Flemish culture and language. The Vlaams Belang party was born out of the controversial Vlaams Blok party that in 2004 was condemned in court for racism. One of its slogans was roughly translated "Adapt or get out!"

[260] BBC News. (December 2, 2005). Journey of Belgian female bomber. Retrieved from http://news.bbc.co.uk/2/hi/europe/4491334.stm

[261] BBC News. (December 2, 2005). Journey of Belgian female bomber. Retrieved from http://news.bbc.co.uk/2/hi/europe/4491334.stm

[262] Smith, N. (December 4, 2005). Making of Muriel the suicide bomber. *Sunday Times Review*. Retrieved from http://www.rickross.com/reference/islamic/islamic69.html

[263] Smith, N. (December 4, 2005). Making of Muriel the suicide bomber. *Sunday Times Review*. Retrieved from http://www.rickross.com/reference/islamic/islamic69.html

[264] Smith, N. (December 4, 2005). Making of Muriel the suicide bomber. *Sunday Times Review*. Retrieved from http://www.rickross.com/reference/islamic/islamic69.html

[265] Smith, N. (December 4, 2005). Making of Muriel the suicide bomber. *Sunday Times Review*. Retrieved from http://www.rickross.com/reference/islamic/islamic69.html

[266] In her quest for a new and redeemed identity, Muriel first renamed herself with the Islamic name Myriam, cleaned up from her drug habits and began on the Salafi path before stepping into Takfiri beliefs and embracing the al Qaeda ideology. A guilt-ridden woman would certainly resonate with the promise of being absolved of her drug using past and deep self-condemnation over surviving when her brother did not and gaining instant access to paradise upon completing her suicide act.

[267] Smith, N. (December 4, 2005). Making of Muriel the suicide bomber. *Sunday Times Review*. Retrieved from http://www.rickross.com/reference/islamic/islamic69.html

[268] Smith, N. (December 4, 2005). Making of Muriel the suicide bomber. *Sunday Times Review*. Retrieved from http://www.rickross.com/reference/islamic/islamic69.html

[269] Randall, C. (March 27, 2012). Focus moves to France's home-grown extremists. The National. Retrieved from http://www.thenational.ae/news/world/europe/focus-moves-to-frances-home-grown-extremists

[270] See: Mir, A. (March 30, 2012). Pakistan turning into a haven for Al Qaeda's white jehadis. *Rediffnews*. Retrieved from http://www.rediff.com/news/slide-show/slide-show-1-pakistan-turning-into-a-haven-for-al-qaedas-white-jehadis/20120330.htm
andNelson, D. (September 25, 2009). Pakistan discovers 'village' of white German al-Qaeda insurgents. *The Telegraph*. Retrieved from http://www.telegraph.co.uk/news/worldnews/asia/pakistan/6226935/Pakistan-discovers-village-of-white-German-al-Qaeda-insurgents.html

[271] Genuine Salafi adherents argue that militant jihadis who claim to be Salafi do not in fact share their beliefs. See: Siraat. (November, 2011). Why the Salafis are not a terror problem. In A. Speckhard (Eds.), Psychosocial, organizational and cultural aspects of terrorism Available from http://ftp.rta.nato.int/public//

PubFullText/RTO/TR/RTO-TR-HFM-140///TR-HFM-140-09.pdf and for a simple explanation on this topic see

Scroggins, D. (2012). *Wanted women: Faith, lies and the war on terror: the lives of Ayaan Hirsi Ali and Aafia Siddiqui*. New York: Harper Collins.

[272] Kafir means rejecter in Arabic and refers to a person who does not recognize Allah, the Prophet Muhammad or who hides, denies, or covers the truth. It is used to refer to an unbeliever, apostate or infidel.

[273] Sageman, M. (2004). *Understanding Terror Networks*: University of Pennsylvannia Press.

[274] The Jamestown Foundation. (January 24, 2008). Chechnya's exodus to Europe. *North Caucasus Weekly*, 9(3),

[275] The Jamestown Foundation. (January 24, 2008). Chechnya's exodus to Europe. *North Caucasus Weekly*, 9(3),

[276] Deutsche Presse Agentur. (June 25, 2003). Belgium "to grant Chechen refugees political asylum". Retrieved from http://reliefweb.int/report/russian-federation/belgium-grant-chechen-refugees-political-asylum

[277] For more on Al Qaeda and its leadership see: Benjamin, D., & Simon, S. (2002). *The age of sacred terror*. New York: Random House; Bergen, P. (2006). *The Osama bin Laden I know*. New York: Simon & Schuster.;Gunaratna, R. (2003). *Inside Al-Qaeda: Global Network of Terror:* Berkley Trade.;Schmid, A. (2011). The Routledge handbook of terrorism research. New York: Routledge.; Schweitzer, Y., & Shay, S. (2003). *The Globalization of Terror: The Challenge of Al - Qaida and the Response of the International Community:* Transaction; Sinai, J. (2012). Terrorism bookshelf: Top 150 books on terrorism and counter-terrorism. *Perspectives on Terrorism*, 6(2). Retrieved from http://www.terrorismanalysts.com/pt/index.php/pot/article/view/sinai-terrorism-bookshelf/381 For an analysis of the writings of al Suri see Lia, B. (November, 2011). Explaining Al Qaeda's continuing appeal. In A. Speckhard (Eds.), NATO Human Factors & Medicine Research & Technology Organization Research Task Group 140 Final Report on Psychosocial, Organizational and Cultural Aspects of Terrorism Available from http://ftp.rta.nato.int/public//PubFullText/RTO/TR/RTO-TR-HFM-140///TR-HFM-140-05.pdf and Paz, R. (2011). Reading their Lips: The Credibility of Militant Jihadi Websites as "Soft Power" in the War of the Minds. In A. C. Speckhard (Eds.), RTO Technical Report (Vol. Psychosocial, Organizational and Cultural Aspects of Terrorism, Available from http://ftp.rta.nato.int/public//PubFullText/RTO/TR/RTO-TR-HFM-140///TR-HFM-140-06.pdf

[278] For a very in-depth analysis of the militant jihad in the UK see: Wiktorowicz, Q. (July 28, 2005). *Radical Islam rising: Muslim extremism in the West*: Rowman & Littlefield Publishers.

[279] Robert Winnett, Christopher Hope, Swinford, S., & Watt, H. (April 25, 2011). WikiLeaks: Guantánamo Bay terrorists radicalised in London to attack Western targets. *The Telegraph*. Retrieved from http://www.telegraph.co.uk/news/worldnews/wikileaks/8472784/WikiLeaks-Guantanamo-Bay-terrorists-radicalised-in-London-to-attack-Western-targets.html

[280] Hope, C. (May 21, 2012). Extremist preachers now radicalising young Muslims in private homes, says senior Government security adviser. *The Telegraph*. Retrieved from http://www.telegraph.co.uk/news/uknews/terrorism-in-the-uk/9071604/Extremist-preachers-now-radicalising-young-Muslims-in-private-homes-says-senior-Government-security-adviser.html

[281] See: Mandel, D. R. (November 2011). The role of instigators in radicalization to violent extremism. In A. Speckhard (Eds.), NATO Human Factors & Medicine Research & Technology Organization Research Task Group 140 Final Report on Psychosocial, Organizational and Cultural Aspects of Terrorism Available from http://ftp.rta.nato.int/public//PubFullText/RTO/TR/RTO-TR-HFM-140///TR-HFM-140-02.pdf and Mandel, D. R. (2002). and Evil and the instigation of collective violence. *Analyses of social issues and public policy*, 101-108. Retrieved from http://individual.utoronto.ca/mandel/asap02.pdf

[282] Hope, C. (May 21, 2012). Extremist preachers now radicalising young Muslims in private homes, says senior Government security adviser. *The Telegraph*. Retrieved from http://www.telegraph.co.uk/news/uknews/terrorism-in-the-uk/9071604/Extremist-preachers-now-radicalising-young-Muslims-in-private-homes-says-senior-Government-security-adviser.html

[283] MEMRI. (July 24, 2003). Al-Qaradhawi Speaks On The Legitimacy Of Martyrdom Operations - Source: Al-Sharq Al-Awsat.

[284] MEMRI. (October 1, 2003). The new Egyptian mufti - Dr. Sheikh 'Ali Gum'a: Opinions about jihad, supporting suicide bombings and forbidding Muslims in the U.S. military from fighting other Muslims. *Special Dispatch Series, 580*. Retrieved from http://www.memri.org/report/en/print961.htm

[285] For further discussion on European radicalization see Leiken, R. (2011). *Europe's angry Muslims: The revolt of the second generation*. New York: Oxford University Press and Pick, T. M., Speckhard, A., & Jacuch, B. (Eds.). (2009). *Home-Grown Terrorism: Understanding and Addressing the Root Causes of Radicalisation among Groups with an Immigrant Heritage in Europe* Amsterdam: IOS Press BV.

[286] Richard Colvin Reid was a third generation immigrant (on his father's side) – born to a white British mother and British second generation immigrant Jamaican father. As a young man, Reid was in and out of prison for petty crimes until he converted to Islam on his last incarceration. Then upon his release, Reid attended the Finsbury Mosque, led at the time by the fiery extremist al Masri and began his journey into extremism. Reid traveled to Pakistan during this time period where he is believed to have been further radicalized and where he apparently volunteered for a suicide mission and taught to make a shoe bomb. He currently serves a prison sentence in the US. For more on this story see: Gibson, H. (January 21, 2002). Looking for trouble. *Time*. Retrieved from http://www.time.com/time/world/article/0,8599,193661,00.html; Elliot, M. (February 16, 2002). The Shoe Bomber's World. *Time*. Retrieved from http://www.time.com/time/printout/0,8816,203478,00.html and Mueller, J. (June, 2012). Terrorism since 9/11: The American cases. Retrieved from http://psweb.sbs.ohio-state.edu/faculty/jmueller/SINCE.pdf

[287] Indeed in June 2007, Bilal Abdulla, a UK-born Iraqi doctor raised primarily in Baghdad, crash-bombed his burning jeep into the Glasgow airport and had situated lethal car bombs to explode near crowded London nightspots. Before his trial, Abdulla said his terror acts were in response to the 1991 Gulf War and the 2003 US coalition-led invasion of Iraq. He explained, "I wanted the public to taste what is going on, for them to have a taste of what the decisions of their democratically elected murderers did to my people." See: Stringer, D. (December 16, 2008). Iraqi terrorist doctor convicted in England. *Huffington Post*. Retrieved from http://www.huffingtonpost.com/2008/12/16/iraqi-terrorist-doctor-co_n_151434.html

[288] Weaver, M. A. (June 8, 2006). The short, violent life of Abu Musab al-Zarqawi. *The Atlantic*. Retrieved from http://www.theatlantic.com/magazine/archive/2006/07/the-short-violent-life-of-abu-musab-al-zarqawi/304983/2/

[289] JAM is the acrynoym for the the Jaish al Mahdi or Mahdi Army, an Iraqi paramilitary force created by Iraqi Shia cleric Muqtada al Sadr in June of 2003.

[290] Marcos Arvelo personal communication November 2005.

[291] I remain grateful to Noel Warr of the London Metropolitan Police who released the imams working in Siraat from their normal prison-related duties working on their rehabilitation and deradicalization efforts to aid ours in Iraq and of course to AbdurRahmaan Anderson and the staff of the Siraat team who once overcoming their hesitation about adding the Americans enthusiastically poured their knowledge writing the highly thoughtful Islamic challenge portion of our detainee rehabilitation program.

[292] Founded in 1928 in Egypt by the Egyptian Islamic scholar Hassan al Banna, the Muslim Brotherhood currently has an estimated two million members and functions as one of the largest opposition factions in many Arab states. The MB has been suppressed both in Egypt and in Syria over the years. The Palestinian faction, Hamas, was directly criticized by al Qaeda in 2005 when it participated in elections, with AQ leaders arguing that the powers to be would never allow a Hamas-led Palestinian government—which to some extent did occur when Hamas won its landslide victory. The Muslim Brotherhood slogan "Islam is the solution" supports its stated goal of using the Koran and Sunnah as the sole reference point for ordering familial, community and state life.

[293] See: Boucek, C. (August 16, 2007). Extremist Reeducation and Rehabilitation in Saudi Arabia *Terrorism Monitor*, 5 (16). and Boucek, C. (2008). The Sakinah Campaign and Internet Counter-Radicalization in Saudi Arabia *CTC Sentinel* 1(9). Retrieved from <http://carnegieendowment.org/publications/index.cfm?fa=view& id=20423& prog=zgp& proj=zme>

[294] For a detailed analysis on this see: Brooks, M., & Miller, D. (2009). Inside the detention camps: A new campaign in Iraq. *1rst Quarter*(52). Retrieved from http://www.dtic.mil/dtic/tr/fulltext/u2/a501229.pdf

[295] Interestingly in 2012 with the release of captured letters from Osama bin Ladin, we learn that bin Ladin also was not pleased with Zarkawi's emphasis on targeting the Shia in Iraq.

[296] Cheryl Benard, O'Connell, E., Cathyrn Quantic Thurston, Villamizar, A., Loredo, E. N., Sullivan, T., et al. (June 7, 2011). The battle behind the wire: U.S. prisoner and detainee operations from World war II to Iraq.

[297] The Human Terrain System Project is an Army led initative to provide and attach sociocultural teams to military commanders and staffs deployed in Afghanistan and Iraq. The purpose of these teams is to "support operational decision-making, enhance operational effectiveness, and preserve and shared sociocultural institutional knowledge". The teams are embedded with the troops, "have an operationally focused sociocultural capability, and conduct operationally relevant, sociocultural research and analysis and develop and maintain a sociocultural knowledge base for the U.S. military troops". See: U.S. Army. The Human Terrain System. Retrieved from http://humanterrain-system.army.mil/Default.aspx

[298] Horgan, J. (2008). Deradicalization or Disengagement? A Process in Need of Clarity and a Counter-terrorism Initiative in Need of Evaluation *Perspectives on Terrorism*, II(4).

[299] For further discussion on existing deradicalization programs see: Cheryl Benard, O'Connell, E., Cathyrn Quantic Thurston, Villamizar, A., Loredo, E. N., Sullivan, T., et al. (June 7, 2011). The battle behind the wire: U.S. prisoner and detainee operations from World war II to Iraq.; Boucek, C. (August 16, 2007). Extremist Reeducation and Rehabilitation in Saudi Arabia *Terrorism Monitor*, 5 (16).; Boucek, C. (2008). The Sakinah Campaign and Internet Counter-Radicalization in Saudi Arabia CTC Sentinel 1(9). Retrieved from <http://carnegieendowment.org/publications/index.cfm?fa=view& id=20423& prog=zgp& proj=zme>; Horgan, J. (2009). *Leaving Terrorism Behind: Individual and Collective Disengagement.* New York: Routledge.; Rabasa, A., Pettyjohn, S. L., Ghez, J. J., & Boucek, C. (2010). Deradicalizing Islamist Extremists. Retrieved from http://www.rand.org/content/dam/rand/pubs/monographs/2010/RAND_MG1053.pdf and Horgan, J. (2009). *Leaving Terrorism Behind: Individual and Collective Disengagement*. New York: Routledge.

[300] I'm happy to report that just prior to putting this book to press Abdul wrote to announce the birth of his healthy and beautiful baby daughter!

[301] David C. Rapoport.(Spring/Summer 2002).The four waves of rebel terror and September 11. *Anthropoetics*, 8(1). Retrieved from http://www.anthropoetics. ucla.edu/ap0801/terror.htm

[302] Juergensmeyer, M. (2000). *Terror in the Mind of God: The Global Rise of Religion Violence*. Berkeley and Los Angeles: University of California Press.

[303] For more on the rational mind argument when considering religious, especially militant jihadi actors looked at within the context of their own religious beliefs see: Wiktorowicz, Q. (2005). *Radical Islam rising: Muslim extremism in the West:* Rowman & Littlefield Publishers.

[304] Shneidman, E. S. (1996). *The Suicidal Mind*: Oxford University Press.

[305] Sageman, M. (2004). *Understanding Terror Networks*: University of Pennsylvannia Press.

[306] The Army of God is a U.S. based group that uses Christian scriptures to advocate for terrorist attacks including against abortion providers including bombing abortion clinics, destroying property and assassinating abortion providers. While I was given a copy of the Army of God manual for use in the lawsuit I have never seen it publically available. The Army of God website is at http://www.armyofgod.com

[307] Straziuso, J., Forliti, A., & Watson, J. (January 14, 2012). Al Shabaab's American recruits in Somalia. *Huffington Post*. Retrieved from http://www.huffingtonpost.com/2012/01/14/americans-al-shabaab_n_1206279.html

[308] Elliott, A. (January 27, 2010). The jihadist next door. *The New York Times*. Retrieved from http://www.nytimes.com/2010/01/31/magazine/31Jihadist-t.html?pagewanted=all

[309] See: BBC News. (November 12, 2009). Profile: Major Nidal Malik Hasan. Retrieved from http://news.bbc.co.uk/2/hi/8345944.stm and Huffington Post. (September 6, 2012). Imam Al Awlaki says he did not pressure accused Fort Hood gunman Nidal Hasan. Retrieved from http://www.huffingtonpost.com/2009/11/16/imam-al-awlaki-says-he-di_n_358748.html

[310] Eposito, R., Vlasto, C., & Cuomo, C. (May 6, 2010). Sources: Shahzad had contact with Awlaki, Taliban chief, and Mumbai massacre mastermind. *ABC News*. Retrieved from http://abcnews.go.com/Blotter/faisal-shahzad-contact-awlaki-taliban-mumbai-massacre-mastermind/story?id=10575061#.UEkjPEK_BcQ

[311] Cratty, C. (June 15, 2011). Lawmakers disagree on prisons' role in Islamic radicalization. *CNN*. Retrieved from http://articles.cnn.com/2011-06-15/politics/house.radicalization.hearing_1_radicalization-prison-terror-groups?_s=PM:POLITICS

[312] Brown, R., & Severson, K. (September 30,2011). 2nd American in strike waged Qaeda media war. *The New York Times*. Retrieved from http://www.nytimes.com/2011/10/01/world/middleeast/samir-khan-killed-by-drone-spun-out-of-the-american-middle-class.html?_r=0

[313] Huffington Post. (August 3, 2011). Adam Gadahn urges U.S. Muslims to start killing Americans. Retrieved from http://www.huffingtonpost.com/2011/06/03/adam-gadahn-urges-muslims-kill-americans_n_871190.html

[314] Horwitz, S., Wan, W., & Wilber, D. Q. (February 17, 2012). Federal agents arrest Amine El Khalifi; he allegedly planned- to bomb Capitol. *The Washington Post*. Retrieved from http://www.washingtonpost.com/world/national-security/federal-agents-arrest-man-who-allegedly-planned-suicide-bombing-on-us-capitol/2012/02/17/gIQAtYZ7JR_print.html

[315] Rohan later tells me that at that time both in Washington D.C. and Baghdad, there was opposition to launching a rehabilitation program in Iraq and that he was arguing for it to come into being. While Rohan and Ustaz Mohammed did not return to write the program with me, Rohan did return at a later date, at the invitation of General David Quantock, with Ami Angell to review the program and help lay the plans to transfer the program to the Iraqis in 2010.

BIBLIOGRAPHY

Alheisi, R. (April 4, 2010). Waiting To Return Home: Palestinian Martyrs in Israeli "Cemeteries of Numbers" and Morgues. *My Palestine.* Retrieved from http://avoicefrompalestine.wordpress.com/2010/04/17/waiting-to-return-home-palestinian-martyrs-in-israeli-"cemeteries-of-numbers"-and-morgues/

Ali, F. (2005). Muslim female fighters: an emerging trend. *Terrorism Monitor,* 3(21).

Akerman, P. (May 29, 2008). Mohammed al-Durra footage may have been a hoax. *News.com.au.* Retrieved from http://www.news.com.au/top-stories/historic-image-may-have-been-a-hoax/story-e6frfkp9-1111116475725

Akhmedova, K., & Speckhard, A. (2006). A multi-causal analysis of the genesis of suicide terrorism: The Chechen case. In J. Victoroff (Ed.), *Social and psychological factors in the genesis of terrorism* (pp. 324-354): IOS Press.

Applied Research Institute Jerusalem. (October 24, 2000). JidOneim settlers attack BeitForeek villagers in Nablus. Retrieved from http://www.poica.org/editor/case_studies/view.php?recordID=107

Atran, S. (2003).Genesis of Suicide Terrorism. *Science,* 299(5612), 1534 - 1539

Associated Press. (October 14, 2005). Russia says rebel assault over; toll tops 100. *NBC News.* Retrieved from http://www.msnbc.msn.com/id/9681595/#.UEGbQEK_BcR

Basayev, S. (October 17, 2005). Nalchik attacked by 217 Mujahideen. *KavKaz Center Website.* Retrieved from http://www.kavkazcenter.com/eng/content/2005/10/17/4156.shtml;

BBC News. (September 12, 1970). 1970: Hijacked jets destroyed by guerrillas. Retrieved from http://news.bbc.co.uk/onthisday/hi/dates/stories/september/12/newsid_2514000/2514929.stm

BBC News. (February 25, 1994). Jewish settler kills thirty at holy site. Retrieved from http://news.bbc.co.uk/onthisday/hi/dates/stories/february/25/newsid_4167000/4167929.stm

BBC News. (March 21, 2000). Graveside party celebrates Hebron massacre. Retrieved from http://news.bbc.co.uk/2/hi/middle_east/685792.stm

BBC News. (March 13, 2003). Palestinians get Saddam funds. Retrieved from http://news.bbc.co.uk/2/hi/middle_east/2846365.stm

BBC News. (September 17, 2004). Excerpts: Basayev claims Beslan. Retrieved from http://news.bbc.co.uk/2/hi/3665136.stm

BBC News. (December 2, 2005). Journey of Belgian female bomber. Retrieved from http://news.bbc.co.uk/2/hi/europe/4491334.stm

BBC News. (July 4, 2007). BBC's Alan Johnston is released. *BBC News* Retrieved from http://news.bbc.co.uk/2/hi/6267928.stm

BBC News. (December 4, 2007). Israeli minister's killer jailed. Retrieved from http://news.bbc.co.uk/2/hi/middle_east/7125686.stm

BBC News. (November 12, 2009). Profile: Major Nidal Malik Hasan. Retrieved from http://news.bbc.co.uk/2/hi/8345944.stm

Belien, P. (November 30, 2005). Belgian export: suicide bombers. *The Brussels Journal*. Retrieved from http://www.brusselsjournal.com/node/530

Cheryl Benard, O'Connell, E., Cathyrn Quantic Thurston, Villamizar, A., Loredo, E. N., Sullivan, T., et al. (June 7, 2011). The battle behind the wire: U.S. prisoner and detainee operations from World war II to Iraq

Bennet, J. (June 13, 2002). In suicide bombings, the taxi man got away. *The New York Times*. Retrieved from http://www.nytimes.com/2002/06/13/world/mideast-turmoil-violence-in-suicide-bombings-the-taxi-man-got-away.html

Bennet, J. (June 13, 2002). Mideast Turmoil:Violence; in suicide bombings, the taxi man got away. *The New York Times*. Retrieved from http://www.nytimes.com/2002/06/13/world/mideast-turmoil-violence-in-suicide-bombings-the-taxi-man-got-away.html

Bennet, J. (July 28, 2002). Stalemate in Mideast After Deadly Bombing. *The New York Times*. Retrieved from http://www.nytimes.com/2002/07/28/world/stalemate-in-mideast-after-deadly-bombing.html?ref=salahshehada

Benjamin, D., & Simon, S. (2002). *The age of sacred terror*. New York: Random House.

Bergen, P. (2006). *The Osama bin Laden I know*. New York: Simon & Schuster.

Berko, A. (2007). *The path to paradise: The inner world of suicide bombers and their dispatchers*. Westport, Connecticut: Praeger Security International.

Beyler, C. (February 12, 2003). Messengers of death - Female suicide bombers. *International Institute for Counter-Terrorism*. Retrieved from http://ict.org.il/apage/printv/10728.php.

Bloom, M. (2005). *Dying to Kill: The Allure of Suicide Terror*: Columbia University Press

Bloom, M. (2011). *Women and terrorism: Bombshell*. Philadelphia: University of Pennsylvannia Press.

Bongar, Bruce (2004) Suicide Terrorism. Paper presented for Suicide Terrorism: Strategic Importance and Counterstrategies, NATO Advanced Research Workshop.

Boyden, A. W., Menard, P. P., & Ramirez, R. (December 2009). Making the case: What is the problem with targeted killing? Retrieved from http://www.dtic.mil/cgi-bin/GetTRDoc?AD=ADA514257

Boucek, C. (August 16, 2007). Extremist Reeducation and Rehabilitation in Saudi Arabia *Terrorism Monitor*, 5 (16).

Boucek, C. (2008). The Sakinah Campaign and Internet Counter-Radicalization in Saudi Arabia *CTC Sentinel* 1(9). Retrieved from <http://carnegieendowment.org/publications/index.cfm?fa=view& id=20423& prog=zgp& proj=zme>

Bronner, E. (April 22, 2008). Carter says Hamas and Syria are open to peace. *The New York Times*. Retrieved from http://www.nytimes.com/2008/04/22/world/middleeast/22mideast.html?_r=1

Brooks, M., & Miller, D. (2009). Inside the detention camps: A new campaign in Iraq. *1rst Quarter*(52). Retrieved from http://www.dtic.mil/dtic/tr/fulltext/u2/a501229.pdf

Brown, R., & Severson, K. (September 30,2011). 2nd American in strike waged Qaeda media war. *The New York Times.* Retrieved from http://www.nytimes. com/2011/10/01/world/middleeast/samir-khan-killed-by-drone-spun-out-of-the-american-middle-class.html?_r=0

B'tselem. (January 1, 2011). Administrative detention. *B'Tselem - The Israeli Information Center for Human Rights in the Occupied Territories.* Retrieved from http://www.btselem.org/administrative_detention

B'tselem. (January 1, 2011). Workers from the occupied territories. *B'Tselem - The Israeli Information Center for Human Rights in the Occupied Territories.* Retrieved from http://www.btselem.org/workers

Byman, D. (March/April 2006). Do targeted killings work? 85(2). Retrieved from http://www12.georgetown.edu/sfs/cpass/Articles/BymanTargetedKillings. pdf.

Cabbage, M. (July 7, 2002). Desperation turns Gaza into cradle of Palestinian radicals. *Orlando Sentinel.* Retrieved from http://articles.orlandosentinel. com/2002-07-07/news/0207070328_1_gaza-strip-jabalya-refugee-camp-gaza-population

Cain, K., Postlewait, H., & Thomson, A. (2004). *Emergency Sex and Other Desperate Measures: A True Story From Hell On Earth.* New York: Miramax.

Catholic Friends of Israel. (April 21, 2009). Pope Benedict's 2006 Regensburg Address - a refresher course. Retrieved from http://catholicfriendsofisrael. blogspot.com/2009/04/pope-benedicts-2006-regensburg-address.html

Chechnya Advocacy Network. (June 10, 2012). Refugees and Diaspora http:// www.chechnyaadvocacy.org/refugees.html

CNN. (September 30, 2002). Israel leaves Arafat compound. Retrieved from http://europe.cnn.com/2002/WORLD/meast/09/29/mideast/index.html

CNN World. (October 17, 2011). RechavamZeevi: A controversial figure. Retrieved from http://articles.cnn.com/2001-10-17/world/israel.zeevi. profile_1_palestinians-israeli-army-parliament?_

Council on Foreign Relations. (October 31, 2005). PFLP, DFLP, PFLP-GC, Palestinian leftists. Retrieved from http://www.cfr.org/israel/pflp-dflp-pflp-gc-palestinian-leftists/p9128

Council on Foreign Relations. (October 20, 2011). Hamas. *Backgrounder.* Retrieved from http://www.cfr.org/israel/hamas/p8968

Cratty, C. (June 15, 2011). Lawmakers disagree on prisons' role in Islamic radi-calization. *CNN.* Retrieved from http://articles.cnn.com/2011-06-15/poli-tics/house.radicalization.hearing_1_radicalization-prison-terror-groups?_ s=PM:POLITICS

Cunningham, C. (2007). Countering Female Terrorism. *Conflict & Terrorism,* 30(2), 113-129.

deMause, L. (2002). *The emotional life of nations*: Other Press.

Dolnik, A. (2007). *Negotiating the Impossible? The Beslan Hostage Crisis. London*: Royal United Services Institute.

Deutsche PresseAgentur. (June 25, 2003). Belgium "to grant Chechen refugees political asylum". Retrieved from http://reliefweb.int/report/russian-federation/belgium-grant-chechen-refugees-political-asylum

Edelman, O. (March 12, 2007). RehavamZe'evi assassin jailed for two life terms plus 100 years. *Haaretz*. Retrieved from http://www.haaretz.com/news/rehavam-ze-evi-assassin-jailed-for-two-life-terms-plus-100-years-1.234461

Eisenstadt, M. (August 2001). Pre-emptive targeted killings as counter-terrorism tool: An assessment of Israel's approach. *Peacewatch*; August 28, 2001.

Elliot, M. (February 16, 2002). The Shoe Bomber's World. *Time*. Retrieved from http://www.time.com/time/printout/0,8816,203478,00.html and Mueller, J. (June, 2012). Terrorism since 9/11: The American cases. Retrieved from http://psweb.sbs.ohio-state.edu/faculty/jmueller/SINCE.pdf

Elliott, A. (January 27, 2010). The jihadist next door. *The New York Times*. Retrieved from http://www.nytimes.com/2010/01/31/magazine/31Jihadist-t.html?pagewanted=all

Erlanger, S., & Myre, G. (March 15, 2006). Israelis seize six in raid on prison in the West Bank. *The New York Times*. Retrieved from http://www.nytimes.com/2006/03/15/international/middleeast/15mideast.html

Esposito, J. (2002). *Unholy war: Terror in the name of Islam* New York: Oxford Universiity Press.Pgs. 446-49 and 114-116.

Eposito, R., Vlasto, C., & Cuomo, C. (May 6, 2010). Sources: Shahzad had contact with Awlaki, Taliban chief, and Mumbai massacre mastermind. *ABC News*. Retrieved from http://abcnews.go.com/Blotter/faisal-shahzad-contact-awlaki-taliban-mumbai-massacre-mastermind/story?id=10575061#.UEkj-PEK_BcQ

Etkes, D., & Ofran, H. (March 14, 2007). Settlement are built on private Palestinian land. Retrieved from http://peacenow.org.il/eng/content/settlement-are-built-private-palestinian-land.

Eyadat, F. (October 16, 2008). Two Palestinian girls detained in Israel without trial for months. *Haaretz*. Retrieved from http://www.haaretz.com/print-edition/news/two-palestinian-girls-detained-in-israel-without-trial-for-months-1.255577

Ezzedeen al Qassam Brigades Information Office. (March 8, 2003). FadiZeyad El-Fakhouri. *Al Qassam Website.* Retrieved from http://www.qassam.ps/martyr-35-Fadi_Zeyad_El_Fakhouri.html

FédérationInternationale des ligues des Droits de l'Homme. "Palestinian Prisoners in Israel: The Inhuman Conditions Being Suffered by Political Prisoners." (July 13, 2003), http://www.fidh.org/Palestinian-Prisoners-in-Israel.

Fletcher, H. (April 2, 2008). Al Aqsa Martyrs Brigade. *The Council on Foreign Relations*. Retrieved from http://www.cfr.org/israel/al-aqsa-martyrs-brigade/p9127

Figley, C. (1995). Compassion fatigue as secondary traumatic stress disorder: An overview. *Compassion fatigue: Coping with secondary traumatic stress disorder in those who treat the traumatized*. Figley, Charles R. Figley, Charles R. (Ed). (1995). Compassion fatigue: Coping with secondary traumatic stress disorder in those who treat the traumatized. Brunner/Mazel psychological stress series, No. 23. (pp. 1-20). Philadelphia, PA, US: Brunner/Mazel.

Fuller, L. (October 12, 2008). Three years after Nalchik, North Caucasus resistance remains potent, deadly force. *Radio Free Europe.* Retrieved from http://www.rferl.org/content/Three_Years_After_Nalchik_North_Caucasus_Resistance_Remains_Potent_Deadly_Force/1329090.html

Gedalyahu, T. B. (March 12, 2011). Victims identified as family of Rabbi Fogel of Yeshiva Itamar. *Israel National News.* Retrieved from http://www.israelnationalnews.com/News/News.aspx/142842#.TsVyBWC3lQg

Gibson, H. (January 21, 2002). Looking for trouble. *Time.* Retrieved from http://www.time.com/time/world/article/0,8599,193661,00.html

Gilmore, I. (June 8, 2003). Mosque football team was terrorists' cover. *The Telegraph.* Retrieved from http://www.telegraph.co.uk/news/worldnews/middleeast/israel/1432360/Mosque-football-team-was-terrorists-cover.html

Global Jihad. (May 18, 2007).Asif Mohammed Hanif. Retrieved from http://www.globaljihad.net/view_page.asp?id=204

Global Jihad. (May 18, 2007). Omar Khan Sharif. Retrieved from http://www.globaljihad.net/view_page.asp?id=205

Greenberg, J., & Neilan, T. (June 3, 2002). Palestinian court orders release of top militant wanted by Israel.*New York Times.* Retrieved from http://www.nytimes.com/2002/06/03/international/04CND-ISRA.html

Guardian, T. (January 25, 2001). 'I made the ring from a bullet and the pin of a hand grenade'. Retrieved from http://www.guardian.co.uk/world/2001/jan/26/israel

Gunaratna, R. (2003). *Inside Al-Qaeda: Global Network of Terror*: Berkley Trade.;

Haaretz. (November 15, 2007). French court examines footage of Mohammad al-Dura's death. Retrieved from http://www.haaretz.com/news/french-court-examines-footage-of-mohammad-al-dura-s-death-1.233240

Hafez, M. (2006). *Manufacturing Human Bombs: The Making of Palestinian Suicide Bombers.* Washington, D.C.: United States Institute of Peace Press Books.

Hafez, M. M., & Hatfield, J. M. (September 22, 2006). Do targeted assassinations work? A multivariate analysis of Israel's controversial tactic during Al-Aqsa uprising. *Conflict & Terrorism*, 29(4).

Hafez, M. M. (2007). *Suicide Bombers in Iraq: The Strategy and Ideology of Martyrdom.* Washington, D.C.: United States Institute of Peace Press.

Hammer, J. (April 15, 2002). How two lives met in death. *Newsweek.* Retrieved from http://www.robincmiller.com/articles/a15.htm

Hass, A. (2004, March 3). When Death is Normal. *Haaretz.*

Hass, A. (April 4, 2007). The Holocaust as political asset. *Haaretz.* Retrieved from http://www.haaretz.com/print-edition/opinion/the-holocaust-as-political-asset-1.218447

Hassan, N. (November 19, 2001). Letter from Gaza: Talking to the "human bombs". *The New Yorker.* Retrieved from http://www.newyorker.com/archive/2001/11/19/011119fa_FACT1?currentPage=all

Hoffman, B. (1998). *Inside terrorism*. New York: Columbia University Press.

Hope, C. (May 21, 2012). Extremist preachers now radicalising young Muslims in private homes, says senior Government security adviser. *The Telegraph*. Retrieved from http://www.telegraph.co.uk/news/uknews/terrorism-in-the-uk/9071604/Extremist-preachers-now-radicalising-young-Muslims-in-private-homes-says-senior-Government-security-adviser.html

Horgan, J. (2008). Deradicalization or Disengagement? A Process in Need of Clarity and a Counter-terrorism Initiative in Need of Evaluation *Perspectives on Terrorism, II*(4).

Horgan, J. (2009). *Leaving Terrorism Behind: Individual and Collective Disengagement*. New York: Routledge.

Horwitz, S., Wan, W., & Wilber, D. Q. (February 17, 2012). Federal agents arrest Amine El Khalifi; he allegedly planned to bomb Capitol. *The Washington Post*. Retrieved from http://www.washingtonpost.com/world/national-security/federal-agents-arrest-man-who-allegedly-planned-suicide-bombing-on-us-capitol/2012/02/17/gIQAtYZ7JR_print.html

Huffington Post. (August 3, 2011). Adam Gadahn urges U.S. Muslims to start killing Americans. Retrieved from http://www.huffingtonpost.com/2011/06/03/adam-gadahn-urges-muslims-kill-americans_n_871190.html

Huffington Post. (September 6, 2012). Imam Al Awlaki says he did not pressure accused Fort Hood gunman NidalHasan. Retrieved from http://www.huffingtonpost.com/2009/11/16/imam-al-awlaki-says-he-di_n_358748.html

Human Rights Watch. (October, 2004). Razing Rafah: Mass home demolitions in the Gaza Strip. Retrieved from http://www.israelsoccupation.info/files/Razing%20Rafah.pdf

Israeliinsider. (November 24, 2001). Hamas vows revenge after IDF eliminates "most wanted" Abu Hanoud. Retrieved from http://www.israelinsider.com/channels/security/articles/sec_0145.htm

Israeli Ministry of Foreign Affairs Website. (April 2, 2002). Yasser Arafat's "ta'a" Compound in Ramallah - A Center for Controlling and Supporting Terrorism. Retrieved from http://www.mfa.gov.il/MFA/Government/Communiques/2002/Yasser+Arafat-s+ta-a+Compound+in+Ramallah+-+A.htm

Israel Ministry of Foreign Affairs. (July 2, 2002). Suicide bombers from Jenin Available from http://www.mfa.gov.il/MFA/MFAArchive/2000_2009/2002/7/Suicide%20Bombers%20from%20Jenin

Israel Ministry of Foreign Affairs. (January 30, 2003). The Role of Palestinian Women in Suicide Terrorism. Retrieved from http://www.mfa.gov.il/MFA/MFAArchive/2000_2009/2003/1/The%20Role%20of%20Palestinian%20Women%20in%20Suicide%20Terrorism

Israel Ministry of Foreign Affairs. (January 30, 2003). The Role of Palestinian Women in Suicide Terrorism. Retrieved from http://www.mfa.gov.il/MFA/MFAArchive/2000_2009/2003/1/The%20Role%20of%20Palestinian%20Women%20in%20Suicide%20Terrorism

Israel Ministry of Foreign Affairs. (February 12, 2003). Blackmailing Young Women into Suicide Terrorism. Retrieved from http://www.mfa.gov.il/MFA/

Government/Communiques/2003/Blackmailing%20Young%20Women%20
into%20Suicide%20Terrorism%20

Israel Ministry of Foreign Affairs (November 9, 2004) PFLP terrorists behind Tel Aviv suicide bombing arrested.http://www.mfa.gov.il/MFA/Terrorism-+Obstacle+to+Peace/Terrorism+and+Islamic+Fundamentalism-/PFLP+terrorists+behind+Tel+Aviv+suicide+bombing+arrested+9-Nov-2004.htm?DisplayMode=print Accessed June 12, 2012.

Israel Ministry of Foreign Affairs. (March 14, 2006). IDF operation in Jericho to arrest murderers of Israeli minister Ze'evi. Retrieved from http://www.mfa.gov.il/MFA/Government/Communiques/2006/IDF+operation+in+Jericho+to+arrest+murderers+of+Israeli+minister+Zeevi+14-Mar-2006.htm

Issacharoff, A., Benn, A., & Harel, A. (July 15, 2007). Fatah men, including Zubeidi, turn in their guns in amnesty deal. *Haaretz*. Retrieved from http://www.haaretz.com/news/fatah-men-including-zbeidi-turn-in-their-guns-in-amnesty-deal-1.225526

International, Defence for Children. "Palestinian Prisoners Day 2009: Highest Number of Children Currently in Detention since 2000." (April 18, 2009), http://www.dci-pal.org/english/display.cfm?DocId=1126& CategoryId=1.

The Jamestown Foundation. (January 24, 2008). Chechnya's exodus to Europe. *North Caucasus Weekly*, 9(3),

The Jerusalem Post. (May 29, 2008) Myth & Muhammad al-Dura. Retrieved from http://web.archive.org/web/20080531174606/http://www.jpost.com/servlet/Satellite?pagename=JPost/JPArticle/ShowFull& cid=1212041429387

Johnston, D., & Rutenberg, J. (June 13, 2006). Rove won't face indictment in CIA leak case. *New York Times.* Retrieved from http://www.nytimes.com/2006/06/13/washington/13cnd-leak.html?_r=1& oref=slogin

Juergensmeyer, M. (2000). *Terror in the Mind of God: The Global Rise of Religion Violence.* Berkeley and Los Angeles: University of California Press.

Kalman, M. (March, 2007). Horrific video of a child sending her suicide bomber mother to her death. Retrieved from http://www.dailymail.co.uk/news/article-444058/Horrific-video-child-sending-suicide-bomber-mother-death.html

Kalman, M. (December 30, 2009). The woman in the way of Palestinian prisoner deal. *Time* Retrieved from http://www.time.com/time/world/article/0,8599,1950487,00.html

Kate. (July 5, 2011). Israel's secret cemetery of Palestinian combatants. *Mondoweiss*. Retrieved from http://mondoweiss.net/2011/07/israels-secret-cemetery-of-palestinian-combatants.html

King, L. (August 14, 2004). W. Bank settler slain in ambush. *Los Angeles Times/World.* Retrieved from http://articles.latimes.com/2004/aug/14/world/fg-mideast14

Khazzoom, L. (August 29, 2003). Tel Aviv bar and bomb target slowly getting its groove back. *jweekly.com*. Retrieved from http://www.jweekly.com/article/full/20444/tel-aviv-bar-and-bomb-target-slowly-getting-its-groove-back/

Koppel, T. (Writer). (2005). Reign of Terror, *Nightline*: ABC News.

Leiken, R. (2011). *Europe's angry Muslims: The revolt of the second generation.* New York: Oxford University Press

Leung, R. (2003). The Bomber Next Door: 60 Minutes II What Makes A Female Suicide Bomber Tick? Retrieved from http://www.cbsnews.com/stories/2003/05/23/60II/main555401.shtml

Lia, B. (November, 2011). Explaining Al Qaeda's continuing appeal. In A. Speckhard (Eds.), NATO Human Factors & Medicine Research & Technology Organization Research Task Group 140 Final Report on Psychosocial, Organizational and Cultural Aspects of Terrorism Available from http://ftp.rta.nato.int/public//PubFullText/RTO/TR/RTO-TR-HFM-140///TR-HFM-140-05.pdf

Lustick, I. (1994). Preface, For the land and the Lord (2nd ed.). New York: Council on Foreign Relations.

Maeseele, P. V., G; Stevens,I. & Speckhard, A. (2008). Psycho-social resilience in the face of a mediated terrorist threat. *Media War & Conflict*, 1(1), 50-69. Retrieved from http://www.coe.int/t/dg4/majorhazards/ressources/virtuallibrary/materials/belgium/media,war,conflict.pdfPg 52.

Mafille, A. (May 24, 2012). Cabablanca bombings, the day after. Retrieved from http://www.cageprisoners.com/our-work/opinion-editorial/item/4248-casablanca-bombings-the-day-after

Mandel, D. R. (2002).and Evil and the instigation of collective violence. Analyses of social issues and public policy, 101-108. Retrieved from http://individual.utoronto.ca/mandel/asap02.pdf

Mandel, D. R. (November 2011).The role of instigators in radicalization to violent extremism. In A. Speckhard (Eds.), NATO Human Factors & Medicine Research & Technology Organization Research Task Group 140 Final Report on Psychosocial, Organizational and Cultural Aspects of Terrorism Available from http://ftp.rta.nato.int/public//PubFullText/RTO/TR/RTO-TR-HFM-140///TR-HFM-140-02.pdf

Marcus, I., & Nan Jacques Zilderdik. (March 13, 2011). PA tv glorified terrorist who killed three in Itamar in 2002. *Palestinian Media Watch.* Retrieved from http://www.palwatch.org/main.aspx?fi=157& doc_id=4794

Markon, J. (September 30, 2005). Guilty plea planned in secrets case. *The Washington Post.* Retrieved from http://www.washingtonpost.com/wp-dyn/content/article/2005/09/29/AR2005092901267.html

Martinfrost website. Beslan school hostage crisis.fromhttp://www.martinfrost.ws/htmlfiles/beslan_siege.html#Identities_of_those_responsible

McAllister, J. F. O. (September 12, 2004). Communication breakdown. *Time.* Retrieved from http://www.time.com/time/magazine/article/0,9171,695816,00.html

McElroy, D. (April 15, 2011). Italian activist killed in Gaza: the Alan Johnston kidnapping. *The Telegraph.* Retrieved from http://www.telegraph.co.uk/news/worldnews/middleeast/palestinianauthority/8453318/Italian-activist-killed-in-Gaza-the-Alan-Johnston-kidnapping.html

Mcgirk, T. (May 3, 2007). Palestinian moms becoming martyrs. Retrieved from http://www.time.com/time/magazine/article/0,9171,1617542,00.html

McGreal, C. (January 14, 2004). Human-bomb mother kills four Israelis at Gaza checkpoint. *The Guardian*. Retrieved from http://www.guardian.co.uk/world/2004/jan/15/israel in

Meehan, M. (May June 1998). Shooting of infamous Kiryat-Arba-born "cowboy" by Jewish settler stirs tension in Hebron hills *Washington Report on Middleeastern Affairs report from the Jerusalem Journal*, 10,94. Retrieved from http://www.wrmea.com/component/content/article/194-1998-may-june/2952-shooting-of-infamous-kiryat-arba-born-qcowboyq-by-jewish-settler-stirs-tension-in-hebron-hills-.html

MEMRI. (July 24, 2003). Al-Qaradhawi Speaks On The Legitimacy Of Martyrdom Operations - Source: Al-Sharq Al-Awsat.

MEMRI. (October 1, 2003). The new Egyptian mufti - Dr. Sheikh 'Ali Gum'a: Opinions about jihad, supporting suicide bombings and forbidding Muslims in the U.S. military from fighting other Muslims. *Special Dispatch Series, 580*. Retrieved from http://www.memri.org/report/en/print961.htm

Merari, A. (2003). Suicide Terrorism - unpublished manuscript.

Middle East Journal, *Chronology*, vol 48, no 3 (Summer 1994) p. 511 ff.

Miller, J. (2005, Feb 3, 2005). Another Beslan? It's a byword for horror: Russia's 9/11. *Channel 4 News*, from http://www.channel4.com/news/2005/02/week_1/03_basayev.html

Mir, A. (March 30, 2012).Pakistan turning into a haven for Al Qaeda's white jehadis. *Rediffnews*. Retrieved from http://www.rediff.com/news/slide-show/slide-show-1-pakistan-turning-into-a-haven-for-al-qaedas-white-jehadis/20120330.htm

Moghadam, A. (2008). T*he globalization of martyrdom: Al Qaeda, salafi jihad, and the diffusion of suicide attacks* Baltimore: John Hopkins University Press.

MosNews. (October 19, 2004). Drugs used by Beslan terrorists puzzle Russian experts. Retrieved from http://rense.com/general58/drugsusedbybeslan.htm

Myre, G. (June 22, 2003). After cease-fire talks stall, Israelis kill a Hamas leader. *The New York Times*. Retrieved from http://www.nytimes.com/2003/06/22/world/after-cease-fire-talks-stall-israelis-kill-a-hamas-leader.html

Nelson, D. (September 25, 2009). Pakistan discovers 'village' of white German al-Qaeda insurgents. *The Telegraph*. Retrieved from http://www.telegraph.co.uk/news/worldnews/asia/pakistan/6226935/Pakistan-discovers-village-of-white-German-al-Qaeda-insurgents.html

Ness, C. (Ed.). (2008). *Female Terrorism and Militancy: Agency, Utility and Organization Taylor and Francis*.Routledge.

Newsweek. (July 7, 2003). The Jihad soccer club. Retrieved from http://www.newsweek.com/2003/07/06/the-jihad-soccer-club.html

Nightline, A. (July 29, 2005). Chechen guerilla leader calls Russians "terrorists". Retrieved from http://abcnews.go.com/Nightline/International/story?id=990187& page=1#.T5mRi5i_BoE

Oliver, A. M., & Steinberg, P. F. (2005). *Road to martyr's square: A journey into the world of the suicide bomber*. New York: Oxford University Press.

Palestinian Media Watch. (December 5, 2002). Suicide terror & shahada: Success of shahada promotion. Retrieved September 29, 2011, from http://palwatch. org/main.aspx?fi=479

Paz, R. (2011). Reading their Lips: The Credibility of Militant Jihadi Websites as "Soft Power" in the War of the Minds. In A. C. Speckhard (Eds.), RTO Technical Report (Vol. Psychosocial, Organizational and Cultural Aspects of Terrorism, Available from http://ftp.rta.nato.int/public//PubFullText/RTO/ TR/RTO-TR-HFM-140///TR-HFM-140-06.pdf

Pedahzur, A. (2006). *Root causes of suicide terrorism: The globalization of martyrdom*. New York: Routledge.

Pick, T. M., Speckhard, A., & Jacuch, B. (Eds.). (2009). *Home-Grown Terrorism: Understanding and Addressing the Root Causes of Radicalisation among Groups with an Immigrant Heritage in Europe* Amsterdam: IOS Press BV.

PLO Negotiations Affairs Department. (December 2002). Fact sheets and frequently asked questions. Retrieved from http://www.robat.scl.net/content/ NAD/faqs/fact_sheets/hebron.php#footer20

Post, J. (2005). When hatred is bred in the bone: Psycho-cultural foundations of contemporary terrorism. *Political Psychology*, 26(4).

ProCon.org. (June 18, 2008). Where is Hebron, and what is its religious significance to Jews and Muslims? Retrieved from http://israelipalestinian.procon. org/view.answers.php?questionID=987

Rabasa, A., Pettyjohn, S. L., Ghez, J. J., & Boucek, C. (2010). Deradicalizing Islamist Extremists. Retrieved from http://www.rand.org/content/dam/rand/ pubs/monographs/2010/RAND_MG1053.pdf and

Randall, C. (March 27, 2012). Focus moves to France's home-grown extremists. *The National*. Retrieved from http://www.thenational.ae/news/world/europe/ focus-moves-to-frances-home-grown-extremists

Rapoport, D.C. (Spring/Summer 2002). The four waves of rebel terror and September 11. *Anthropoetics*, 8(1). Retrieved from http://www.anthropoetics. ucla.edu/ap0801/terror.htm

Regular, A. (May 30, 2003). Hebron's playing—and plotting—field. *Haaretz*. Retrieved from http://www.haaretz.com/print-edition/news/hebron-s-play- ing-and-plotting-field-1.89861

Sageman, M. (2004). *Understanding Terror Networks*: University of Pennsylvan- nia Press.Pgs. 8, 58.

Sarraj, E. (April 8, 2002). Why we blow ourselves up. *Time*. Retrieved from http:// www.time.com/time/magazine/article/0,9171,1002161,00.html

Schmid, A. (2011). *The Routledge handbook of terrorism research*. New York: Routledge.;

Schweitzer, Y., & Shay, S. (2003). *The Globalization of Terror: The Challenge of Al - Qaida and the Response of the International Community*: Transaction;

Schweitzer, Y. (Ed.). (2006). *Female Suicide Bombers: Dying for Equality?* : The Jaffee Center for Strategic Studies

Scroggins, D. (2012). *Wanted women: Faith, lies and the war on terror: the lives of AyaanHirsi Ali and AafiaSiddiqui*. New York: Harper Collins.

Sherwood, H. (March 14, 2011). Israelis and Palestinians in shock after Fogel family massacre. *The Guardian*. Retrieved from http://www.guardian.co.uk/world/2011/mar/14/fogel-family-massacre-israelis-palestinians

Shikaki, K. (2006). Willing to Compromise: Palestinian Public Opinion and the Peace Process. *Special Report No. 158*, 1-16 United States Institute of Peace.

Shneidman, E. (1993) Suicide as psychache: A clinical approach to self-destructive

behavior. Jason Aronson Rowman& Littlefield Publishers, Inc. Northvale, NJ. p. 258.

Sinai, J. (2012). Terrorism bookshelf: Top 150 books on terrorism and counterterrorism. *Perspectives on Terrorism, 6*(2). Retrieved from http://www.terrorismanalysts.com/pt/index.php/pot/article/view/sinai-terrorism-bookshelf/381

Siraat. (November, 2011). Why the Salafis are not a terror problem. In A. Speckhard (Eds.), Psychosocial, organizational and cultural aspects of terrorism Available from http://ftp.rta.nato.int/public//PubFullText/RTO/TR/RTO-TR-HFM-140///TR-HFM-140-09.pdf

Smith, J. (June 24, 2003). The Palestinian football martyrs.The Free Library. Retrieved from http://www.thefreelibrary.com/SUICIDE+UNITED%3B+Thaer's+brother+was+one+of+nine+players+from+the+same...-a0104059976

Smith, N. (December 4, 2005). Making of Muriel the suicide bomber. *Sunday Times Review*. Retrieved from http://www.rickross.com/reference/islamic/islamic69.html

Speckhard, A. (2004). Soldiers for God: A Study of the Suicide Terrorists in the Moscow Hostage Taking Siege. In O. McTernan (Ed.), *The Roots of Terrorism: Contemporary Trends and Traditional Analysis*. Brussels: NATO Science Series.

Speckhard, A. (2006). Sacred terror: Insights into the psychology of religiously motivated terrorism. In C. Timmerman, D. Hutsebaut, S. Mells, W. Nonneman& W. V. Herck (Eds.), *Faith-based radicalism: Christianity, Islam and Judaism between constructive activism and destructive fanaticism*. Antwerp: UCSIA also accessible on my website www.AnneSpeckhard.com

Speckhard, A. (2006). The New Global Jihad, 9-11 and the Use of Weapons of Mass Destruction: Changes in Mindset and Modus Operandi. *Democracy and Security*, 2(2), 287 - 298

Speckhard, A. (2008). The Emergence of Female Suicide Terrorists.*Studies in Conflict and Terrorism* 31, 1-29.

Speckhard, A. (2009). Female suicide bombers in Iraq. *Democracy and Security*, 5(1), 19-50.

Speckhard, A. (2010). Research challenges involved in field research and interviews regarding the militant jihad, extremism and suicide terrorism. *Democracy and Security*, 199-222.

Speckhard, A. (2012). Taking on the persona of a suicide bomber: A thought experiment. *Perspectives on Terrorism*, 6(2). Retrieved from http://www. terrorismanalysts.com/pt/index.php/pot/article/view/speckhard-taking-on-the-persona.pp 51-73.

Speckhard, A., & Akhmedova, K. (2005). Mechanisms of Generating Suicide Terrorism: Trauma and Bereavement as Psychological Vulnerabilities in Human Security - The Chechen Case. In J. Donnelly, Anna Kovacova, Joy Osofsky, Howard Osofsky, Caroline Paskell& J. Salem-Pickartz (Eds.), *Developing Strategies to Deal with Trauma in Children - A Means of Ensuring Conflict Prevention, Security and Social Stability. Case Study: 12–15-Year-Olds in Serbia* (Vol. 1, pp. 59-64). Brussels: NATO Security Through Science Series E Human and Societal Dynamics, IOS Press.

Speckhard, A., & Akhmedova, K. (2006). *Black Widows: The Chechen Female Suicide Terrorists.* In Y. Schweitzer (Ed.), Female Suicide Terrorists. Tel Aviv: Jaffe Center Publication.

Speckhard, A., & Ahkmedova, K. (2006). The Making of a Martyr: Chechen Suicide Terrorism. *Journal of Studies in Conflict and Terrorism*, 29(5), 429-492.

Speckhard, A., & Akhmedova, K. (2006). The New Chechen Jihad: Militant Wahhabism as a Radical Movement and a Source of Suicide Terrorism in Post-War Chechen Society. *Democracy and Security*, 2(1), 103-155.

Speckhard, A., & Akhmedova, K. (2006). Black Widows: The Chechen Female Suicide Terrorists. In Y. Schweitzer (Ed.), *Female Suicide Terrorists.* Tel Aviv: Jaffe Center Publication.

Speckhard, A., & Akhmedova, K. (2007). Black Widows and Beyond: Understanding the Motivations and Life Trajectories of Chechen Female Terrorists. In C. Ness (Ed.), *Women Terrorists and Militants: Agency, Utility and Organization* Taylor and Francis.

Speckhard, A., Tarabrina, N., Krasnov, V., & Mufel, N. (2005). Posttraumatic and acute stress responses in hostages held by suicidal terrorists in the takeover of a Moscow theater *Traumatology*, 11(1), 3-21.

Speckhard, A., Tarabrina, N., Krasnov, V., & Mufel, N. (2005). Stockholm Effects and Psychological Responses to Captivity in Hostages Held by Suicidal Terrorists. *Traumatology*, 11(2).

Straziuso, J., Forliti, A., & Watson, J. (January 14, 2012). Al Shabaab's American recruits in Somalia. *Huffington Post*. Retrieved from http://www.huffingtonpost.com/2012/01/14/americans-al-shabaab_n_1206279.html

Stern, J. (2003). *Terror in the Name of God: Why Religious Militants Kill.* New York: Harper-Collins.

Stringer, D. (December 16, 2008). Iraqi terrorist doctor convicted in England. *Huffington Post*. Retrieved from http://www.huffingtonpost.com/2008/12/16/iraqi-terrorist-doctor-co_n_151434.html

Tarnopolsky, N. (October 20, 2011). Palestinian terrorists released by Israel unexpectedly shows up in Turkey. *Global Post*. Retrieved from http://www.

globalpost.com/dispatches/globalpost-blogs/the-casbah/palestinian-terrorist-released-israel-unexpectedly-shows-turk

The Telegraph. (May 1, 2002). Arafat siege to end as handover agreed. Retrieved from http://www.telegraph.co.uk/news/1392784/Arafat-siege-to-end-as-handover-agreed.html

Toomey, C. (June 11, 2006). Discussing the politics of murder. *The Sunday Times*. Retrieved from http://www.christinetoomey.com/content/?p=110

UNRWA. Jenin Refugee Camp. Retrieved from http://www.unrwa.org/etemplate.php?id=118

U.S. Army. The Human Terrain System. Retrieved from http://humanterrainsystem.army.mil/Default.aspx

U.S. Department of State Office of the Coordinator for Counter-terrorism. (April, 2005). Country reports on terrorism 2004. Retrieved from http://www.state.gov/documents/organization/45313.pdf

Usher, G. (March 29, 2002). At 18, bomber became martyr and murderer. *The Guardian*. Retrieved from http://www.guardian.co.uk/world/2002/mar/30/israel3

Vered Levy-Barzilai. (June 2002). Media Echoes: Interview with a suicide bomber. *Haaretz*. Retrieved from http://www.therazor.org/oldroot/Summer02/sbombinterview.htm

Victor, B. (2003). *Army of Roses: Inside the world of Palestinian women suicide bombers*. London: Robinson.

Weaver, M. A. (June 8, 2006).The short, violent life of Abu Musab al-Zarqawi. *The Atlantic*. Retrieved from http://www.theatlantic.com/magazine/archive/2006/07/the-short-violent-life-of-abu-musab-al-zarqawi/304983/2/

Weiss, E. (December 25, 2008). Israel sentences PFLP leader to 30 years in prison. *Ynetnews*. Retrieved from http://www.ynetnews.com/articles/0,7340,L-3644555,00.html

Robert Winnett, Christopher Hope, Swinford, S., & Watt, H. (April 25, 2011). WikiLeaks: Guantánamo Bay terrorists radicalised in London to attack Western targets. *The Telegraph*. Retrieved from http://www.telegraph.co.uk/news/worldnews/wikileaks/8472784/WikiLeaks-Guantanamo-Bay-terrorists-radicalised-in-London-to-attack-Western-targets.html

Wiktorowicz, Q. (2005). *Radical Islam rising: Muslim extremism in the West*: Rowman& Littlefield Publishers.

Zimbardo, P. The Stanford Prison Experiment at http://www.prisonexp.org

SUICIDE+UNITED%3B+Thaer's+brother+was+one+of+nine+players+from+the+same...-a0104059976

Index

CPSIA information can be obtained at www.ICGtesting.com
Printed in the USA
BVOW01s1552100816

458167BV00006B/229/P